D1806342

Sporting Magazine, Volume 32

Published by John Wheble, Warwick Square London.
1808.

Twelfth of the Improv'd Work

THE
Sporting Magazine
OR
MONTHLY CALENDAR,
OF THE
TRANSACTIONS OF
THE TURF, THE CHASE,

And every other Diversion

Interesting to the

Man of Pleasure, Enterprize & Spirit.

VOL. 32.

London:
Printed for J. Wheble, 18, Warwick Square.
1808

AW

THE
SPORTING MAGAZINE;
OR,
MONTHLY CALENDAR
OF THE
TRANSACTIONS
OF
THE TURF, THE CHASE,
And every other Diversion interesting to
THE MAN OF PLEASURE, ENTERPRISE, AND SPIRIT.

APRIL, 1808.

CONTAINING

Richard, late Earl Grosvenor.... *Page* 3
Game Licenses.................... 3
Bettings at Tattersall's.......... 4
Hunting Season Concluded 5
 Northern Coursing................ 6
Disputes between Gentlemen, on Points
 of Honour, &c. &c............. 7
 Intended Duel Prevented.......... 7
 The King *v.* Faden.............. 7
Sporting Anecdotes of Colonel John
 Mordaunt 9
Remarks on the Trespass Causes tried
 at the Horsham Assizes 13
The World, a new Comedy 14
Bonifacio and Bridgetina—a Dramatic
 Satire 16
Trial for a Murder in a Duel......17
The Two Barons, Duben and Wrede..21
Alphabetical List of Stallions to Cover
 in 1808 22
Successful Treatment of Blindness in
 a Mare 24
Gaming—Mazzinghi *v.* Stephenson..26
A German Winter Amusement........26
Winners of the Derby and Oaks' Stakes 27
Remarkable Inscription 28
The Amusements of Paris described..29
 Old Women and Girls 29
 A Flea Drawing an Elephant......30
 Two Fleas fighting a Duel.......30
 Mechanical Horses..............31

Boxing, between Belcher and Dog-
 herty ....*Page* 33
The Philosophical Gamester 37
Pedigree and Performances of Ditto ..37
FEAST OF WIT 39
 The Ghost...................40
 The Puff Military 41
 Clerical Arithmetic...........42
 The Constable Hoaxed 42
Caractacus, a new Pantomime......43
Eleanor......................43
SPORTING INTELLIGENCE 44
 Norbrook Races 44
 Malton Fair..................45
 Boxing 45
 Pigeon Shooting..............45
 Rowing Match against Time 46
 Lesson to Poachers and Buyers of
 Game.......................46
 Extraordinary Walking 47
 Burton-Hunt Races............48
 Death of an old Sportsman 49
 Method of discovering Canine Mad-
 ness 50

POETRY.

Epilogue to the Comedy of the World 51
Song sung by Mr. Munden 52
Bull-baiting...................52

RACING CALENDAR 1

*Embellished with—I, An elegant Engraving of Richard, late Earl Grosvenor.
II, Portrait of Eleanor, bred by Sir Charles Bunbury.*

LONDON:
PRINTED FOR THE PROPRIETORS,
By J. Pittman, Warwick Square;
AND SOLD BY J. WHEBLE, 18, WARWICK-SQUARE; C. CHAPPLE, 66, PALL-MALL;
J. BOOTH, DUKE-STREET, PORTLAND-PLACE; JOHN HILTON, NEWMARKET;
AND BY ALL THE BOOKSELLERS IN TOWN AND COUNTRY.

TO CORRESPONDENTS.

THE Article on "The Harmonious Change of Ringing Contested," has been received, but must stand over until next month, when it shall certainly appear.

An account of the Irish Stallions will be given in our next Number.

ERRATUM.

General Whitelocke's Father was JOHN *Whitelocke, Esq, not* BULSTRODE, *as in our last Magazine.*

Gentlemen disposed to favour the Publisher of this Magazine with Original Paintings of Sporting Subjects, are assured that the utmost care shall be taken of them, and of their being safely returned. The Engravings thus taken, will be executed by the most approved Artists, and in the first style of excellence.

Sir Josh.ª Reynolds pinx.ᵗ   H.R.Cook sculp.ᵗ

RICHARD, late EARL GROSVENOR.

Published May 1.ˢᵗ 1806. by J. Wheble, Warwick Square.

THE
SPORTING MAGAZINE;
FOR APRIL, 1808.

RICHARD,
LATE EARL GROSVENOR.

An Engraving by H. R. Cook, from an Original Painting by Sir Joshua Reynolds.

" THE late Earl Grosvenor," if the Engraver had so thought proper, might as well have been called " Richard the first Earl Grosvenor," as the progressive honours of the peerage were wholly conferred on him. His Lordship's father was Sir Robert Grosvenor, of Eaton, in the County Palatine of Chester, Bart. born May 7, 1695, and had two sons and four daughters; the eldest of the two sons, Sir Richard Grosvenor, Bart. the subject of our present copper-plate, was born June 18, 1731; created Baron Grosvenor, of Eaton, in the County Palatine of Chester, April 8, 1761; Viscount Belgrave and Earl Grosvenor, July 5, 1784.—His Lordship died in 1802, and was succeeded by his only son Robert, now Earl Grosvenor. Wishing to extend our biography no further than to what relates to sporting, we shall only refer our readers to the SPORTING MAGAZINE for the months of January and February last, in which will be found a short account of his Lordship's high character on the turf, and, with it what has cost a valuable correspondent many tedious hours, accurately to compile and arrange, A LIST OF HIS LORDSHIP'S STUD.

GAME LICENCES.

IN the House of Commons on the 2d instant, the Chancellor of the Exchequer gave notice, of his intention to have the game certificate duty collected with the assessed taxes, and that woodcocks, snipes, &c. would, as far as related to the licence, be considered as game.

On the report of the committee being brought up on a subsequent day, the Chancellor of the Exchequer said, it was not only his wish that shooting woodcocks and snipes, but likewise rabbits, out of warrens, should be subject to the game laws. Mr. Calcraft asked if sparrows and blackbirds were to come under the act, or whether persons were permitted to shoot at all, without paying for a licence? As the money for the licences is to be collected with the assessed taxes, an additional 10 per cent will of course be added to the former duty. Some little discussion has taken place on the subject in

A 2   Parliament;

Parliament; and the public prints have not been sparing in animadversion thereon—as witness the following:—

TO THE PRINTER.

Sir—The extension of the Game Laws to Snipes and Woodcocks, considered as a measure of Finance, is by no means of material importance; but, upon reflexion, it will be found to extend the sphere of those laws, already tyrannical, vexatious, and oppressive in the extreme; and it can be considered in no other view than as a further stride upon our natural privileges, and a curtailment, by the hand of power, of the small remains of rural amusement left amongst us.

That any animal, or bird, *terræ naturæ*, should be reserved solely for the great, luxurious, and powerful, is contrary to my ideas of equity and justice; and though the Game Laws originated at an early period, were enforced by the sword and mandates of the conqueror, and sanctioned by the acts of succeeding obsequious Legislators, it cannot be inferred from hence that they are just, equitable, and worthy to be extended by an enlightened Legislature. Such a measure can only be viewed with disgust and detestation by every liberal mind: a penalty may, at some more remote period, attach to shooting a moor-hen, or the sparrow; and the badger, the fox, and the weasel, may have their rotation on the proscribed list for curtailing the recreation of Englishmen.

Our continental neighbours, we are constantly told, are in the most disgraceful vassalage; this I believe; but the revolution banished Game Laws from their code, and we have not heard they are revived by Napoleon, who probably has been too much taken up in the pursuit of Royal Game, to attend to hares and partridges; the former are now somewhat diminished; and an importation of Royal Tigers from Bengal, for his amusement, may, very likely, soon claim his attention; how far snipes and woodcocks will be advanced in his system, time can only determine.

For my own part, I am no sportsman; but I must confess when I see every proposition of Ministers, however encroaching, acceded to, I am at a loss to conceive where it will end; privation of money, of amusement, and of every thing valuable among us, to feed army agents, government contractors, and loan jobbers; whilst reversions, to support the dignified splendour of Noble Lords and Princes, graced with every *public*, *social*, and *domestic* virtue, constitute the basis of the prosperity of Britain; and certainly, if the luxury of these men prove the happiness of a state, Britain must be envied; but true it is, the Romans were luxurious, and their Governors rapacious and oppressive, in the reign of Nero; and those evils, combined with profligate soldiers, who, we are told, are our best defenders, proved the ruin of that extensive Empire.

CRITO.

April 12, 1808.

BETTINGS FOR THE DERBY AND OAKS', &c.

THE following is a statement of the bettings at Tattersall's, the 25th instant:—

FOR THE DERBY.

9 to 2 agst Rubens
6 to 1 agst Chester
6 to

26 to 1 agst Trafalgar
9 to 1 agst Lord Stawell's colt,
  out of David's dam
8 and 9 to 1 agst Mr. Ladbroke's
  Tristram
11 and 12 to 1 agst Clinker
100 to 7 agst Colonel Childers's
  colt
100 to 7 agst Weaver
100 to 7 agst Vandyke
8½ to 1 agst a sealed up horse,
  the seal to be opened on
  Monday before the race.
And 1000 to 1 agst a sealed up one,
  barring all the favourites;
  the seal to be opened the
  3d of May.
Bets to a large amount offered,
that Buckle, Chifney, or Arnold,
rides the winner.

OAKS' STAKES.

7 to 1 agst the Duke of Grafton's
  Hornby-Lass filly
7 to 1 agst all Lord Egremont's
  fillies
8 to 1 agst Sir Charles Bunbury's
8 to 1 agst Mr Goodisson's
10 to 1 agst Gooseander
10 to 1 agst Anna
10 to 1 agst the Alexina filly.

CLARET STAKES.

6 to 4 agst Giles Scroggins
7 to 4 agst Eaton
4 and 5 to 1 against any other.

HUNTING SEASON CON-
CLUDED.

LORD Derby's Stag-hounds are,
we understand, gone back from
the Oaks to Lancashire : they have
had many good runs during the
season, and his Lordship not unfrequently one of the field.

The King's Hounds, though in
equally good condition, have not
been quite so celebrated, or so well
attended, as when his Majesty
joined in the chase. The Marquis
Cornwallis, in his official capacity,
and the Duke of Cumberland, have
been partakers in several long and
severe runs lately, and when but
few horsemen were to be seen,
at the taking of the deer.

The Duke of Rutland's hounds
have shewn more sport this year
than any other. His Grace keeps
three packs : they are hunted by
Shaw, who is supposed to be the
first huntsman in the kingdom ;
and seldom have a run of less than
an hour and a half, or two hours.
The beginning of this month, they
found at Stonesby Gorse, and, after
a most severe run of three hours
and a half over the best part of Leicestershire, killed their fox.—The
field consisted of at least three hundred people, of whom only three
were in ; viz. Mr. Cholmley, Mr.
Manners, and Mr. Wardell.

The inhabitants of Granby-Street,
Leicester, were, on Saturday the
9th, agreeably surprised with the
termination of a Fox-chase. The
Quorn Hounds about two o'clock
found a fox at Stewart's Hay, from
whence he broke in gallant style
for Martinshaw, Enderby, Ayle-
stone Gorse, and ultimately came
over the South fields, crossed the
Dew walk, and after a run of three
hours, (the last 7 miles without
a check) took refuge under a shed
in the woodyard of Mr. Harrison,
with the hounds close at his brush ;
Mr. Ashton Smith, *as usual* at the
tail of his hounds, succeeded after
much trouble in dragging Reynard
from his hiding place, and after
pocketing his brush, gave him up
to his pursuers. Being the only
red coat present, he took charge of
the pack, and so ably headed them,
               to

to kennel, as he had gallantly followed them during the chase.

Of the North Country Hounds, we find the following recorded in the York Herald, of the 23d inst. by way of a winding up for the season.—The Fox Hounds of Lord Darlington, in the best country in England, have much distinguished themselves. Their fire and spirit in drawing a cover, seem acknowledged as pre-eminent.

The hunting of the Confederate Hounds of Mr. Watt and Sir M. Masterman Sykes, is alike the subject of praise. No Hounds kill so constantly, or afford the Rider so many opportunities of distinguishing himself: their country is not so favourable as that of Lord Darlington.

Mr. L. Fox's Hounds are very good, and deservedly well reported by every Sportsman that has followed them; and his kind attention in often throwing off in the neighbourhood of York, has given much satisfaction to the resident gentlemen.

Mr. Osbaldeston's Hare Hounds, (hunted by himself,) have afforded uncommon sport.

And Colonel Thornton's Lap-Dog Beagles, during the latter end of the Scarborough season, produced much amusement in that neighbourhood.

The Easingwold Hounds have in their country been well followed, and the York Subscription Hounds have, under the care and conduct of their old and steady master, John Yeoman the Huntsman, given much dashing sport to the gentlemen of York and the neighbourhood.

Amongst the most distinguished riders which have come to our knowledge through the season will be found—

In Lord Darlington's Hunt,—Sir T. Pilkington, Sir F. Boynton, Sir E. Smith, Messrs. Hawke, Mellish, Treacher, Frankland, Parker, Wentworth, Wainman, Bell, Livesy, Stourton, Silvertop, A. Hawksworth, Shepherd, Scott, Armstrong, Waring, Batty, Oliver, &c. &c.—and Lord Darlington, who is always with his Hounds, and for whom no day is ever too long.

In the Confederate Hunt,— a number of the above gentlemen; also Messrs. W. Legard, Sykes, Best, Osbaldeston, Lascelles, Hill, Sconswar, Scatchard, Foord, &c. &c.—and a number of those gentlemen farmers who "dashed" through the ditches of half the country, in order to prepare themselves for the last Farmer's Stakes at Malton.

In Mr. Fox's Hunt, —also a number of the above distinguished riders; likewise Messrs. Jadis, Sotheron, Clough, Gascoigne, &c. &c.

NORTHERN COURSING.

This diversion, through the whole winter, has been much impeded, particularly on the Wolds, by unceasing snow-storms, from the beginning of November. Judging from the Malton Meeting, the blood of Snowball seems to hold its former pre-eminence. The real Derbyshire breed, derived from Mr. Mundy, if it does not absolutely hold the first place, unquestionably possesses the second; and are the only greyhounds, bred in an inclosed country, who have been able to stand the severe test of a perfectly open one, and courses of three or four miles continuance.

DISPUTES

DISPUTES
BETWEEN GENTLEMEN,

On Points of Honour, &c. &c. &c.

WE lament the want of room for an article, intended to appear under this head; viz. remarks on the trial of the cause between General Gwynne and Colonel Watson—*see page* 297, *last month.*—This article shall appear in our next Magazine.

INTENDED DUELS PREVENTED.

EARL Fitzwilliam and Major Bower were about to fight a duel on Doncaster Race Course, this month, in consequence of an assertion of the Major's at the last Malton Election, that his Lordship had *trafficked* (*i. e.* sold) a seat for the Borough of Malton. On explanation it proved to be unfounded, and was so acknowledged by Major Bower.

Some harsh language having passed in the streets of Portsmouth, between Captain Manby, of his Majesty's ship Thalia, and Captain G——, of the Royal Marines, they met on South-Sea Common lately; but while settling the distance, the Hon. Captain Boyle came with an order from Admiral Montagu, to put Captain Manby under arrest—since which, Captain Manby sent the following *dictatorial* letter to the Printer of a Newspaper that had mentioned the misunderstanding in his publication :—

His Majesty's Ship Thalia, Portsmouth, April 16, 1808.

SIR—A gross statement having appeared in your paper of yesterday's date, respecting a conversation which you represent to have passed between a Captain G. of the Royal Marines and myself, and

that he, Captain G. should say—I was a liar—I call on you to contradict this assertion, as it did not allude to me. The term was used in the conversation, as having been made to a third person, an Officer of high rank, whose name I am not at liberty now to mention. The whole circumstance is of such a nature, I did not expect remarks to be made on it in a public paper, and desire no further observations may appear, as the whole proceedings must be laid before the public.—I am, Sir, your humble servant, THOMAS MANBY.

P. S. The statement of the above circumstance has been laid before the Admiralty, by me,

GEO. MONTAGU, Admiral.

THE KING v. FADEN.

WE shall not close our observations under this head, without adverting to the trial of John Faden, Adjutant of Marines, as inserted in our Magazine for last month, page 313. The charge against the prisoner was for an assault, and committing a rape, on Elizabeth Stapleford, in the Marine Barracks, at Portsmouth, and of which he was acquitted.

That the conduct of the Jury, in pronouncing the prisoner *Not Guilty*, was very proper, no one will deny; but we are not inclined to think so favourably of Mr. Faden, who availed himself of the power to commit an outrage, and had not afterwards the humanity to qualify it with the common feelings of a man.

This poor girl, though not abused in the way which the law requires to constitute the crime charged, is by this hero of Marines, this despoiler of female innocence, first ruined by partial violence, and afterwards

terwards abandoned to disgrace and infamy. Thus exposed, with the loss of character, she is urged by agonising torture and resentment to seek for justice : more happy, however, may she now feel herself that she has failed in her purpose. The man that has wronged her lives—and he lives in the opinion of the world less favoured than his unfortunate victim.

The arguments and sophistry of the Counsel for the prisoner, and the reasoning of Serjeant Marshall, who sat as Judge on the trial, are scarcely deserving of notice. Burroughs, the prisoner's Counsel, would insinuate, that a woman could not be virtuous who expressed her love of a man ; and Marshall talked of two sorts of honour in the world—we know but of one. He likewise observed, that the prosecutrix should have considered the *difference of situation* between her and the prisoner— Mighty difference, truly, between the *exalted character* of an Adjutant of Marines, whose warrant or commission costs nothing, and a virtuous young woman, decently brought up, and perhaps of as good a family as that of Mr. Faden!— Suppose any one had treated a sister of Faden's (if he has one) in the way that Faden treated the unfortunate girl, Miss Stapleford— what would have been the feelings he would have indulged on such an occasion ?

QUI-TAM ATTORNEY.

The King v. Rushworth.

THE defendant having been reported in contempt by the Master, for giving evasive answers to certain interrogatories put to him, was brought up for judgment.—It appeared that he had been in the habit of bringing *qui-tam* actions upon the game laws, in the names of two of his labourers,' and while they appeared upon the records of the Court, he was himself the substantial plaintiff, and took all the benefits of costs, &c. to himself ; but when the adverse party obtained a verdict, he had only a beggar to look to for the expence he had been wantonly put to.—The Attorney General, Mr. Topham, and Mr Scarlet, addressed the Court in mitigation.

Mr. Garrow spoke in support of the prosecution.—He said the defendant was a wholesale dealer in *qui-tam* actions, and used the names of beggars to harrass and perplex his neighbours. A greater scourge, he said could not exist in society ; and he thought the defendant's conduct merited their Lordships' severest animadversion. If, on the contrary, he was suffered to go unpunished, it would be encouraging a *breed* of Attornies, whose only end was to harrass and oppress the King's subjects.

The Court observed, that the defendant's conduct was extremely disgraceful, and it might be fit that he should no longer continue on the rolls of that Court ; but as there was no specific charge urged against him, which by indictment he could have been found guilty upon, it would be mercy to give him an opportunity of redeeming his character ; the opinion of the Court therefore, was, that he should be suspended for twelve months from practising, and if he did not then conduct himself more honourably, it would be a question with the Court, whether or not its Rolls should not be relieved altogether from his name.

SPORTING ANECDOTES
OF
THE LATE COL. J. MORDAUNT,
Of the Honourable East-India Company's Madras Establishment.

HE was a natural son of the late Earl of Peterborough, and, together with an elder brother by the same mother, was at an early age put out to nurse. Harry, the eldest, was a pining, spiritless starving; while John, the subject of this memoir, was active, lively, and of an uncommonly fine form. He was more of the Apollo Belvidere, though more rigid in muscle, than any other person I ever saw.

John was too wild to learn much; his whole time was devoted to truancy; and, as he often said, "one half of his days were spent in being flogged for the other half." Hence he was in no danger of a professorship, if we except those arts in which the celebrated Breslaw, Jones, &c. took their degrees! In such, John was completely at home, and they were certainly of some use to him, as will be hereafter seen.

When John was taken from school, he was about as learned as when he first was sent there; however, when this was ascertained, and a quarrel was commenced on the occasion, he very handsomely stept forth to exculpate his master; whose attention he declared to be unparalleled, and, slipping off his clothes, exhibited the earnestness of the good man's endeavours; humorously observing, that "as nothing could be got into his brains, his master had done his best to impress his instructions on the opposite seat of learning."

At the time that John was to pass muster before the India directors he was out of the way, and it

was nearly too late, when he was found at marbles in Dean's yard. No time was lost in coaching him up to Leadenhall-street, where, being bent more on his pastime than on the grave questions put by his examiners, he was near being rejected as an idiot; when one of the quorum, who knew the youth's trim well, and who probably wished to see John appointed, asked him if he understood cribbage? John's soul was instantly roused, his eyes glistened, and regardless of every matter relative to his appointment, he pulled out a pack of cards, so greasy as scarcely to be distinguished, and offered "to play the gentleman *for any sum he chose!*"

The youth now felt himself at home, and speedily convinced them that, however ignorant he might be of the classics, he was a match for any of them at cards! He was passed, and dispatched to Portsmouth, where he was to embark in an India ship ready to sail with the first fair wind; but as that was not to be had for some days, the person who had charge of him put him on board, and returned to town.

John's gaiety of disposition soon made him the fiddle of the crew; all on board loved him. He was elegant in his make, graceful in his movements, (though he never could be made to walk a minuet by his dancing-master,) of a very animated countenance, strongly marked with good nature, spirit, and dignity; his features were regular and handsome, his eyes keen and commanding, and, on the whole, we may say he was such as is rarely seen!

He could not bear to mope about the ship, whilst waiting for a wind, but frequently lent a pull in the boats, which occasionally were sent for provisions, &c.

B   One

One day, however, John strayed into the town, and got into company with some girls, who soon eased him, not only of his money, but of his buckles, handkerchief, and every thing that could possibly be dispensed with. At this unlucky moment, the wind being fair, the signal was made for sailing, and the boat's crew were compelled, after a short but active search, to put off, with heavy hearts, thinking they had seen the last of their favourite.

John came down to the beach too late! The boat was just arriving at the ship, which was lying to for her, and sailed immediately from the Motherbank. What was to be done? He had no money, and not a soul would put off on such a trip without being previously well paid! The matter was to all appearance come to the worst, when seeing two watermen at cards in the stern sheets of a boat, he was led by an irresistible impulse to see how matters went on!

The owner of the boat was losing his money at all-fours, when John requested that he might play a hand or two for him; offering to abide himself by any loss during his own play. The man agreed, and John not only won back the losings, but eased his opponent of all his money. The waterman was asked to take him on board, but no promise of money could tempt him ; " it was too far," and, " mayhap might never get a penny by it," " had been sarved so before," and all the host of objections, common among interested persons, were raised ! At length the waterman, taking hold of John's button, drew him aside from the many who were there laughing at his misfortune, and said he had observed, that in dealing there seemed to be something uncommon; besides that,

" he had turned up *Jack* plaguy often;" " now, young'ne, I've a notion that didn't come by nature, and if so be you'll shew me how to do it, I will take you aboard at all risks."

The bargain was struck ; the man being instructed how to turn up *Jack*, with the aid of three of his friends sailed and rowed with such effect as to get within notice of the vessel before dark. The sails were backed, and John facetiously observed as he quitted the boat, " Now, my honest friend, you have turned up *Jack* in earnest," meaning that the waterman had fairly fulfilled his promise, by putting him (John Mordaunt) on board.

On his arrival at Madras, John was received with open arms by all his countrymen; but General Sir John Clavering, who was then commander-in-chief in India, and who was, accordingly, second in council at Calcutta, having promised to provide for him, John went on to Bengal, where he was appointed an honorary aid-du-camp to that officer, still retaining his rank on the Madras establishment, where he was afterwards subjected to much ill-will and obloquy !

He was soon found deficient even in writing a common letter; and it is really surprising, that, under the consciousness of being so very deficient in this branch, and in a circle so eminent for superior education, Mordaunt should have taken no pains to improve himself. He surpassed in almost every thing he undertook, yet, seemingly, more by intuition than by any study or effort to excel. This ignorance in writing was the more remarkable, as he generally conversed with perfect propriety; often indeed with elegance of diction, and with a precise appropriation of his words to the

the particular occasion. He spoke the Hindoo language fluently, and was a tolerable Persian scholar; yet he could not write two lines of English correctly. I once had occasion to borrow a horse from him for a day or two: he sent the animal to me with the following note:

"You may kip the hos as long as you lick."

This excellence of temper, under all the jokes to which this unhappy deficiency subjected him, was wonderful. He knew his failing, and allowed it to stand as a butt for the amusement of his friends; but was highly offended at the attempt of any one, whom he did not feel a partiality for, to excite a laugh at his expence; and, more than once, in my hearing, has astonished persons of that description into the most complete humility. Once, in particular, a very worthy young man of the name of James P——, who was rather of the more silly order of beings, thinking he could take the liberty of playing with, or rather upon him, in a large company called to Mordaunt, desiring him to say what was the Latin for a goose? The answer was briefly, "I don't know the *Latin* for it, but the *English* for it is *James P——*."

It should have been premised, that the foregoing question was put to Mordaunt, in consequence of his having, in a note sent to a person who had offended him, required "an immediate *anser* by the bearer." The gentleman addressed, wishing to terminate the matter amicably, construed the word literally, and sent a *goose* by the bearer; stating also, that he would partake of it the next day. This, to a man of Mordaunt's kidney, was the high road to reconciliation; though to nine persons in ten, and

especially to those labouring under such a desperate deficiency in point of orthography, it would have appeared highly insulting!

It may readily be supposed, that Mordaunt was more ornamental than useful in General Clavering's office; however, the latter could not help esteeming him, and had he lived, would probably have effected Mordaunt's removal from the Madras to the Bengal army.— The Madras officers never failed to notice, sometimes, indeed, in rather harsh terms, the injustice of an officer being on their rolls, who never joined his regiment for nearly twenty years, and whose whole time was passed in the lap of dissipation.

Being on a party of pleasure to the northward, and near to Lucknow, the capital of Oude, and the residence of the late Nabob Vizier, Asoph ul Doulah, Mordaunt, of course, had the curiosity to see both the prince and his court. The free open temper of Asoph pleased Mordaunt, whose figure and manner made a great impression on his illustrious host. The latter was fond of hunting and shooting; to cock-fighting, indeed, he was so partial, that he has even neglected due attendance to business of importance with the several residents, while engaged in a main with his "dear friend Mordaunt," who was completely skilled in that branch of barbarity.

Though I cannot say it ever appeared to me as a very faithful resemblance, yet there is sufficient of character, and some other good points, in the portrait intended to represent Mordaunt, in the celebrated picture of the cock-pit, executed by Zoffani, while at the Nabob's court, to give some idea of the manly, dignified, and elegant

person

person of the subject of this memoir. He is therein represented as in the act of handing a cock, on which he bets highly, in opposition to a bird of his Highness the Nabob, who is pourtrayed, in a loose undress, on the opposite side of the pit.

The figures, however, possess some merit, from the insight they give into the open, independent, yet unassuming, air of Mordaunt, and the familiar manner in which the Nabob stooped to join in diversion with him, and, indeed, with every European gentleman who wished to partake of such amusements as characterised that weak, idle, and contemptible prince.

Mordaunt became such a favourite, that he was retained by the Vizier at his court, in capacity of aid-du-camp, though he never attended but according to his own fancy, and then, generally, either to shoot or to gamble with him. The various applications and sarcasms directed against Mordaunt, as an absentee from his corps for so many years, and at the distance of full two thousand miles, were alike disregarded by himself and by the supreme government, of which all the individuals were personally attached to him.

Mordaunt was in the receipt of a handsome salary, and possessed many distinguished privileges under the patronage of the Vizier, who often used to refer Europeans to him on occasions requiring his advice; though now and then he used to have recourse to the same excuse when he did not wish to comply. On every such occasion Mordaunt was friendly; for instance—

Mr. Zoffani, in a humorous moment, had painted the Nabob at full length, but in high caricature.

The picture being at Colonel Martine's, where old Zoffani resided, and the Colonel's house being frequented by immense numbers of the natives, especially of those who, when the Nabob wanted money, took his jewels to the Colonel's to be pledged, it was not long before the prince was informed of the joke. In the first moments of irritation, he was disposed to make the painter a head shorter, and to dismiss the Colonel, who was his chief engineer, and had the charge of his arsenal; but, as nothing could be done without his "dear friend Mordaunt," a message was dispatched, requiring his immediate attendance, on "matters of the utmost importance." This being a very stale mode of summoning Mordaunt, who would attend, or rather visit, only when it pleased himself, would have probably been disregarded, had not the messenger stated that the Nabob was incensed against Martine and Zoffani.

Mordaunt found the Nabob foaming with rage, and about to proceed with a host of rabble attendants to the Colonel's : however, he got the story out of the Nabob as well as he could, and argued him into a state of calmness, sufficient to let his purpose be suspended until the next day. So soon as it could be done with safety, Mordaunt retired; and, as privately as possible, sent a note to Zoffani, with intelligence of the intended visit.

No time was lost, and the laughable caricature was in a few hours changed, by the magic pencil of Zoffani, into a superb portrait, highly ornamented, and so inimitably resemblant of the Vizier, that it has been preferred to all which have been taken at sittings. The Vizier did not fail to come, his mind fond full of anxiety for the honour of his dignified person, attended by Mordaunt, whose feelings for his friend's fate were speedily dissipated, when, on entering the portrait-chamber, the picture in question shone forth so superbly, as to astonish the Vizier, and to sully even the splendour which his whole equipage displayed on the occasion.

Asoph was delighted, hurried the picture home, gave Zoffani ten thousand rupees for it, and ordered the person who had informed him of the *supposed* caricature, to have his nose and ears cut off.— Mordaunt, however, was equally successful in obtaining the poor fellow's pardon; and as the Nabob would not detain him as a servant, very generously made him one of his own pensioners.

At another time, the *hajam*, or barber, who cut his Excellency's hair, happened to draw blood, by going a little into the quick. This is considered as an offence of the highest atrocity; because crowned heads, throughout India, become degraded, if one drop of their blood be spilt by a barber; over whom a drawn sword is always held while performing his duty, to remind him of his fate in case of the slightest incision.

The Nabob, actuated by the common prejudice above described, had ordered the barber to be baked to death in an oven, when Mordaunt applied for his pardon.—He could only obtain it conditionally; and, to be sure, the condition was both ludicrous and whimsical. Balloons were just invented when this happened; and Colonel Martine, being very ingenious, had made one which had taken up a considerable weight for short distances.

The Nabob changed suddenly from great wrath to a sudden laugh, which continued so long as to alarm Mordaunt; whose pleasure was extreme when he heard, that, instead of being *baked*, the barber was to mount in the balloon, and to *brush* through the air, according as chance might direct him.

It was accordingly so settled; the balloon being sent off from his Highness's fore-court, the barber was carried, more dead than alive, at a prodigious rate, to Poliergurge, distant about five miles from the city of Lucknow.

To be continued.

REMARKS
ON THE
TRESPASS CAUSES TRIED AT THE HORSHAM ASSIZES.

In a Letter to the Printers of the Lewes and Brighthelmstone Journal.

GENTLEMEN,   March 26, 1800.

MY name, which you will herewith receive, I trust will be sufficient authority for the insertion of the following plain statement of facts in your next Journal, on the subject of the trespass causes brought before the Court at the late Assizes at Horsham *(given in our last Number, page 278).*

Had evidence been called in defence of the actions, the following facts would have come out, and probably have given to the business a termination different from that which the defendant experienced; and which can be attributed only to the sudden and severe illness of Colonel Hawker, which prevented his attendance at the Assizes.

A notice of trespass was served on certain Officers of the 14th Lt. Dragoons, and also on H. Bradley, their huntsman, on the 9th of November,

14

vember, 1807, after which no trespass was committed until the 12th of January, 1808, and the circumstances of that trespass were as under :—

Mr. Harben, who is the occupier of nearly 1000 acres of land, and the proprietor of two manors, one of them extensive, and who also lets to Mr. T. Woodhams, and Mr. Hardwick, of Alfriston, upwards of 1300 acres of land, invited a gentleman of the Weald of Sussex to bring his hounds, and have a day's sport over his estate, to partake of which the Officers of the 14th Light Dragoons, with a PART of their hounds, were also invited.

Mr. Martin, of Firle, to whose hounds Mr. Harben is a subscriber, agreed, ON THAT DAY, to hunt near Beddingham, that he might not interfere with the amusement of Mr. H. and his friends. A hare was found by Mr. Martin's hounds, which led them a long chase, and at length ran into the other two packs, that were searching for a hare; the dogs of course all joined in the hunt; and Mr. Martin expressed a wish that they might not be separated until the hare was killed, which was agreed upon; but unluckily the hare crossed the water near Alfriston, and pursued her course through the grounds of Mr. Hitchens and Mr. Woodhams. The Officers, who had notices served on them on the 9th of November, as before stated, DID NOT follow their hounds, but merely sent their huntsman to fetch them back, as soon as the hare should be killed, and for this offence Mr. Hitchens and Mr. Woodhams recovered forty shillings damages on each action.

The Officers in question had invariably declared, that they would not sport on the lands of any gentleman in defiance; and in proof of this assertion, and of their obedience to the laws, no stronger evidence can be adduced, than their extreme forbearance, in not following their hounds under the circumstances before mentioned, and of no trespass being alledged between the 9th of November, 1807, and the 12th of January last, when Bradley, instead of committing a wanton trespass, followed his dogs from necessity, in order to bring them back, in safety, at the conclusion of the chase.

It may be further stated, that these Military Gentlemen had leave to hunt from the Earl of Chichester, the late Lord Gage, T. H. Harben, Esq. John Beau, Esq. Mr. Farncomb, of Bishopstone, and other Gentlemen.

The action brought by Mr. W. Hardwick, it is expected will be submitted to a future decision.

DRURY-LANE THEATRE,
MARCH 1.

THE WORLD—A NEW COMEDY,

WAS last night performed at this Theatre. It is ascribed to Mr. Kenny, and the following are the persons of the Drama:—

Cheviot	Mr. Elliston.
Echo	Mr. Bannister.
Withers	Mr. Wroughton.
Index	Mr. Matthews.
Subtle	Mr. Wewitzer.
Social	Mr. Purser.
Loiter	Mr. De Camp.
Dauntless	Mr. Palmer.
Author	Mr. Russell.
Margin	Mr. Maddocks.
Lady Bloomfield	Mrs. Jordan.
Mrs. Barclay	Mrs. Powell.
Eleanor Barclay	Miss Boyce.

THE

THE FABLE.

The story turns principally on the characters of Cheviot and Echo. The latter has been long kept out of the world by the partiality of parents, and at length arrives in town, in order to commence man of business, and pay his addresses to Lady Bloomfield, a young and fashionable widow, whose father, a rich merchant, had been indebted to the father of Echo for his prosperity. Young Echo, with the best natural disposition, is led to imitate every blockhead, and fall into every absurdity, in order to make a figure, and keep well with the world. With this view he has been induced to abandon Eleanor Barclay, an amiable girl, of a poor family, to whom he had been attached in the country, and whom he deserts in a state of adversity. Cheviot is a foundling, a dependent from his infancy on a Mr. Davenant, a man of fortune, in Northumberland, who has placed him, to be initiated in trade, with Subtle, a gambling and speculating merchant. The high spirit of Cheviot revolts from the practices of his preceptor, and he therefore leaves him, and becomes author, rather than resort to his protector for further assistance; Davenant having never admitted him to his presence, he disdains complaining to him, or continue to be treated as a mere object of charity. He is discovered in London by Withers, who had been his occasional visitor in the country, and being taxed by him with the restlessness of his disposition, enters into a vindication of his feelings, in which he throws some reproach on the parents who thus deserted him in a state of dependence, so repugnant to his feelings. A variety of incidents, which it is not our province to enumerate, occur, in which Cheviot engages the affections of Lady Bloomfield, and discovers Mrs. Barclay and Eleanor, whom Echo had deserted, prisoners in the King's Bench. Their rivalship, as admirers of Lady Bloomfield, brings them into contention; and Cheviot, by a strong and planned attack on the feelings of Echo, rouses him to assert an independence of sentiment, and follow the laudable impulse of his heart; in consequence of which he shakes off his unfeeling and worthless companions and advisers, and is restored to his Eleanor. Cheviot is ultimately discovered to be the son of Davenant, who, under the name of Withers, had visited him as a stranger, and who, principally to avoid the odium of the world, as he was the offspring of an illicit attachment, had never avowed him but as an object of charity. Mrs. Barclay is found to be his mother, who, since she had been seduced by Davenant, had become the wife of another. The parties all meet, and become reconciled, in the house, and through the benevolent mediation of Lady Bloomfield, to whom Cheviot, though his pride and poverty had before induced him studiously to conceal his passion, is now encouraged to avow it; and the offending parties acknowledge the evils of sacrificing their peace of mind, and the honourable dictates of conscience, to the opinion of a misjudging world.——Some other characters, and especially that of Index, (a bustling good-humoured old bachelor, who knows every thing, and every body,) are active in the business of the piece, though not intimately connected with its main purpose.

The above sketch of the fable will afford a pretty correct idea of the business of this piece, which experienced a very favourable reception

ception from one of the most crowded audiences we have seen this season. The dialogue is spirited and well written, and calculated in many parts to produce a strong impression, but at the same time it is often too much laboured and unnecessarily protracted. The characters are in general well drawn, that of Cheviot is the most prominent. The sentiments of independence and generosity which he utters are naturally introduced, and happily expressed; those common places, which often disgust in dialogue of the sententious kind, being in general successfully avoided. The character of Echo is the next in importance, and both these parts were excellently sustained by Elliston and Bannister. Some of the scenes evince a considerable knowledge of stage effect. There is one extremely diverting, where Echo repeats aloud the speech with which he intends to address Lady Bloomfield, while she, unknown to him, has entered the room, and is close at his back. There is also another very good scene in a bookseller's shop, but which it would not be easy for us to describe within the compass to which we must confine this article. One of the most striking defects of the piece is the improbability of the circumstances of the plot, which neither the skill of the author nor the fascination of the acting can disguise. There is also something very indelicate, if not immoral, in the foundation of the story. It has, however, been well contrived, that this should be kept out of sight as long as possible, and it is only in the last scene that the mind of the spectator is awakened to it.—Mrs. Jordan, Mrs. Powell, and Miss Boyce, gave full effect to their respective parts, and all the other characters were remarkably

well sustained. Upon the whole, this play possesses a considerable share of merit, and its announcement for repetition was received with universal applause. The prologue was spoken by De Camp, and the epilogue by Elliston. The latter is distinguished by some very happy allusions to the title of the play, which were greatly applauded.

BONIFACIO AND BRIDGETINA.

COVENT-GARDEN, MARCH 1.

A Satire on the Melo-dramatic mania of the present day, entitled as above, was produced at this Theatre last evening. The idea of this burlesque is taken from the French of Mons. Martainville; and a comic conversation, supposed to pass in the box-lobby between the Author, Box Book-keeper, and one of the audience, is introduced, by way of prelude, to inform the public what species of farce they are to expect—from this we easily anticipate a travesty after the manner of *Tom Thumb the Great*, or *Chrononhotonthologos*. The piece then commences with a beautiful view of a castle, forest, and hermitage, where Sir Hildebrand, in mock heroics, informs his confidante, Nicholas, that a sorcerer has robbed him of his daughter, his nephew, and his castle. The recovery of these, and the subjugation of the tyrant wizard, form the groundwork of the succeeding scenes, in which are presented every species of pageantry and splendor usually exhibited in pieces of a more serious nature, interspersed with robbers, enlivened with caves and spectres, and finishing with a combat and con-

conflagration. The music accompanying the action is in the same burlesque style, as are also the words of the songs. Messrs. Simmons, Farley, and Blanchard, are the heroes; Mrs. Gibbs and Mrs. Liston the heroines; whose tragicomic adventures diversify the piece. The prelude and the first act were very well received; but some disapprobation was expressed during the second act; it was however given out for repetition. It is, upon the whole, very diverting, and the music and scenery are extremely beautiful. The house was quite full.

MURDER IN A DUEL.

WEXFORD ASSIZES, MARCH 28.

The King v. Alcock and Derenzy.

THIS morning, shortly after eleven o'clock, the Court sat, and William Congreve Alcock, and Henry Derenzy, were put to the bar; the former indicted for the Wilful Murder of John Colclough, Esq. and the latter for aiding and assisting in the committal of the said murder.

Sir Jonah Barrington, as Counsel for the Crown, stated the case. He began by suggesting the absolute necessity there was for bringing forward a prosecution in the present instance; it was, he said, most material for the satisfaction of the friends of him who had fallen, as well as for the friends of him who survived; the present case was not that of a fair duel, in consequence of a previous quarrel; quite the reverse—it was one party in the country taking away the life of a man who was beloved by an opposite party, merely for the pur-

pose of preventing the ascendancy of that party in the country. The private enquiries of Mr. Colclough's friends convinced them that they would be deeply culpable if they did not prosecute; they were convinced that Mr. Colclough was the man insulted, and that the duel arose, not in consequence of injured honour, but from a pre-determination to carry the arbitrary views of a party into effect, at the risk of the life of one or both of the combatants.

The duel did not arise in consequence of any thing that passed in a moment of irritation, but from a very distant and stale cause; and in laying before them the circumstances, he should have occasion to draw their attention to a very remote period indeed. He then went into a statement of the different contested elections which had been within these few years in the county of Wexford. A party had grown up in the county; it had taken root there; and, like a great tree, extended its branches so completely as to cast a shadow over the entire county. Mr. Colclough, on whose character he pronounced a just eulogium, had come forward to free his native county from the bondage in which it was held; he put the axe to the branches of this great tree, and lopped them off; he put the axe to the root, but it stopped short, for when it was found that his success on the election was certain, his ruin was determined, and upon the part of the prisoner Alcock it was avowed. For this reason, and for this alone, Mr. Colclough lost his life, and it was reserved for the said county of Wexford to hold up to the United Kingdom the melancholy spectacle of their Representative being called to the bar for the murder of his fellow-

C

low-candidate, while in the act of receiving the suffrages of his fellows.

Sir Jonah Barrington then went into a statement of the facts of the case, which were to be afterwards proved. A gentleman of the name of Pierce Newton King had, he said, on the first day of the election, declared in the presence of Mr. Alcock, and being, at the time, one of his Committee, that if any man should receive the vote of the tenant of a gentleman, who did not espouse the cause of the candidate so receiving the vote, it was to be made with that candidate a personal matter, and he was to be personally liable: this principle, he said, was avowed and acted on; for when the tenants of Mrs. Chumly determined to assert their independence, and to vote for Mr. Colclough, contrary to the direction of Mrs. Chumly, Mr. Colclough was then called to the ground, and there forfeited his life because he would not give up the votes which had been so voluntarily given to him. Sir Jonah then went into a statement of many other facts, which we forbear to mention, as they afterwards appear in evidence.

William H. Carroll was then called. Witness remembers the late election for the county of Wexford. Mr. Alcock, Mr. Colclough, Colonel Ram, and Mr. Sheridan, were the candidates. Witness was agent for Mr. Colclough; was present when a duel was fought between him and Mr. Alcock, in which Mr. Colclough fell; a Mr. Perceval was second to Alcock, and Mr. H. Colclough to the deceased. Mr. Alcock wore spectacles; they appeared to be brown mounted. Heard Mr. H. Colclough strongly remonstrate against his wearing them. The first remonstrance was

in Arkandrage House, while preparing the pistols, and was addressed to Mr. Perceval, Mr. King, and Mr. Derenzy. Mr. Perceval stated, that for his part he had no objection to the spectacles being taken off, but could not answer for it, and would consult Mr. Alcock. Mr. King said, he did not believe Mr. Alcock would take off his spectacles, and pledged his honour it was his decided belief Mr. Alcock could not see four yards.— Previous to this it had been agreed, that there should be no spectacles worn. After some further conversation, Mr. Henry Colclough put a stop to the discourse, by saying, that Mr. Alcock should not wear spectacles, as, on a former occasion with Sir John Newport, he had not worn them.

While the pistols were loading, the prisoner Derenzy was busy scraping the balls. The application to take off the spectacles was again made, after the ground was measured, loud enough for Mr. Alcock to hear it, but I did not hear any words immediately addressed to Mr. Alcock.

After the ground was measured, Mr. Perceval came up to Mr. H. Colclough, and told him he believed Mr. Alcock would not take off his glasses. Mr. Henry Colclough lamented it very much, and said aloud, "If you do not take off the spectacles, I withdraw the pledge I have given that there shall be no prosecution; so that if any thing unpleasant occurs, Mr. Alcock must stand the prosecution." Mr. Alcock heard this, but took no notice of it, except by bowing.— Mr. Perceval and Mr. Derenzy placed Mr. Alcock, and Mr. Henry Colclough alone placed Mr. Colclough on the ground.— Mr. Perceval gave Mr. Alcock his pistol,

pistol, and Mr. H. Colclough gave Mr. Colclough his. They were to fire after the words—" one, two," —and at " two" they were to fire.—Before the pistols were given, Mr. Derenzy not approving of the manner in which Mr. Alcock stood, made him alter his position; this was after the ground was measured. He put his side more to Mr. Colclough, and shook him by the arm. After the pistols had been given to the parties, a conversation took place who should give the signal, which ended in Mr. Colclough tossing up a dollar, and Mr. H. Colclough having won the toss, it was agreed that he should give the signal. The prisoner, Derenzy, during this conversation, was standing near Alcock, but after it was arranged, he fell back among Alcock's friends. About two minutes after, the word was given; when one was pronounced, they raised their arms, and when two, they fired. Mr. C. received the ball immediately under his right arm; he fell instantly on his back, and expired. About four hours before the duel took place, witness heard Mr. Bagnal assert to Mr. Alcock, that Mr. Colclough did not interfere with Mrs. Chumly's tenants, and if any one was to blame, it was he, Mr. Bagnal, and desiring Mr. Alcock to attach the quarrel on him. Mr. Colclough was near-sighted. He wore a glass, but witness never observed him wearing spectacles.

This witness, on his cross-examination, stated, that if the circumstance of the spectacles, with respect to which he did not wish to give an opinion, was unconnected, he thought it was a fair duel.

Mr. Bagnal Colclough was then called. He stated, that on the first day of the election he was present on the hustings, when Mr. Pierce Newton King, who was Mr. Alcock's particular friend, stated, that if any one should, during that election, dare to interfere with his tenants, or separate the interest of the landlords and tenants, he would call him personally to account for his ungentlemanlike conduct.—Witness also remembered the 30th of May, the day on which the fatal business happened; he saw Mr. Alcock that day in the Court-house, and having heard that some altercation had taken place about the tenants of Mrs. Chumly voting for Mr. Colclough, he had a conversation with Mr. Alcock on the subject, during which he pledged him his honour, that Mr. Colclough had not in the slightest degree interfered; he (the witness,) was the person, and he was ready to answer for it in five minutes. When this conversation took place, Mr. Alcock, had light-coloured spectacles on silver mounted; he also wore a brown coat, with brass buttons, a light-coloured waistcoat, and a white neckcloth. Afterwards, on the ground, Mr. Alcock wore spectacles, but they were not mounted in the same manner as those he wore when he spoke to him in the Court-house; the spectacles he wore on the ground were dark mounted, and he had then on him a black waistcoat and breeches, and a black neckcloth.

Mr. Edward Carr deposed, that on the morning of the day on which Mr. Colclough was shot, some of the tenants of Mrs. Chumly came into his booth on Mr. Colclough's tally. Shortly after, Mr. Alcock and Mr. Roper White came in, being, as he believed, sent for on the occasion, and Mr. M'Cord, a friend of the deceased, who was then at the time in their presence, asked the

the tenants, if Mrs. Chumly were present, whom they would vote for? their answer was, they would vote for Mr. Colclough.

Mr. Charles Elgee was agent for Mr. Colclough; he was stationed in the tally-room of the Barony of Bantry; nineteen of the tenants of Mrs. Chumly came there on the morning of the day Mr. Colclough was killed, and offered themselves as his voters. The witness asked whether they came there with their own free will, or whether they were tampered with? They said they came with their own free will; in consequence of which he put them on the tally; afterwards in the street, he heard Mr. Alcock accuse Mr. Colclough of behaving in an unhandsome manner with the tenants, in bringing them over to his side. Mr. Colclough answered, " On my honour, I did not interfere with any gentleman's tenants, and those in particular." Mr. Alcock replied, " Either you or your agents did, and by G—d I will make it personal with you in half an hour, if they are not given up."

Mr. Dudley Colclough stated, that having heard of the quarrel, he endeavoured to reconcile matters, and for that purpose he went up to Mr. Alcock, who was in the Court-house Hall with Colonel Piggot; but Colonel Piggot, taking Mr. Alcock away, said, " Come, come, there is no use in this, the business is fixed."

Mr. Joshua Sutton was at Lady Colclough's house, when Mr. Perceval came there to know whether Mr. Colclough would give up the tenants? and the answer was, that Mr. Colclough did not interfere, but would not give up the freeholders who would vote for him. On his cross-examination, he admitted

that Mr. Perceval, accompanied by Lord Valentia, came to Lady Colclough's, for the purpose of postponing the duel until after the election, but did not believe they came from Mr. Alcock.

Dr. Baxwell proved that the spectacles Mr. Alcock wore at the time of the duel were different from those he wore at any other time.

The case being here closed on the part of the Crown, Lord Valentia was sworn on the part of the prisoners. His lordship stated, that he was deputed by Mr. Alcock's committee to carry a message to Mr. Colclough, in which message, Mr. Alcock being called in, acquiesced. The purport of the message was, that they considered Mr. Alcock as the representative of the party; that they would wish therefore that the business should be postponed until after the election, and that if any loss of character resulted to Mr. Alcock, from withdrawing the challenge, they would take it on themselves. The answer given to his Lordship by Mr. Colclough's friends was, that since Mr. Alcock had committed himself so far, he must meet Mr. Colclough in half an hour.—Lord Valentia also stated, that he was on the ground when the duel took place, previous to which he met Mr. Bagnal Colclough, and having entered into conversation with him, Mr. M'Cord came up, and took Mr. Bagnal Colclough away, saying, you must not speak to Lord Valentia, lest any conciliation should take place.

Lord Valentia then underwent a long cross-examination by Sir Jonah Barrington, but nothing material came out.

Mr. William Perceval, the second of Mr. Alcock, stated, that he went three times to Mr. Colclough's, in order to see him, and have the business

business settled, but could not be allowed to see him by his friends. The proposal he had to make was, that Mr. Alcock did not want both the voices of Mrs. Chumly's tenants, but was willing they should poll for Mr. C. and Mr. A. When the witness mentioned this proposal, Mr. M'Cord said, " We must have all or none—Mr. Colclough's carriage is at the door, and they must go out."—Time and place were then fixed, and it was agreed that only three friends on each side should accompany them. Lord Valentia, Mr. Derenzy, and Mr. King, were the three that the witness took with him; several hundreds were however on the ground.

Mr. Gilbert Austin proved, that the effect of the glasses which Mr. Alcock wore on that day, on a defective eye, was, that the object is made clearer, but more defined, and that it is diminished in size and light. He did not think it rendered the hitting a distant object more secure.

Mr. Pierce King was then produced, and identified the glasses, as being the same worn by Mr. Alcock at the time of the duel. This he did by a small flaw on one of them, which he had taken particular notice of.

The evidence on the part of the prisoner was here closed, and Baron Smith commenced his charge. He stated to the jury what the line was, namely, that if, in a premeditated duel, the life of a man was lost, the survivor was guilty of murder.

The jury retired, and in about three minutes returned a verdict of *Not Guilty*, as to both.

The Court was instantly in an uproar. During the whole of the day it was crowded to an excess. The trial was not over until half past nine o'clock.

THE TWO BARONS, DUBEN AND WREDE.—A DUEL.

ON the 12th of February, a very remarkable duel was fought near the Austrian fortress of Brannau, with a publicity and solemnity we believe altogether unexampled in modern times, and which assimilates this combat to the legal and judicial duels of the feudal ages. The parties were, Baron Von Duben, formerly Swedish Minister at Vienna, and Baron Von Wrede, a General in the Bavarian service; and the occasion of it, as far as we recollect in general, was this: Some dispatches, which had been sent from Vienna to Stockholm, by the Swedish Minister, were intercepted by the French, and made public. In these, Baron Duben had reflected very severely upon the conduct of the Bavarian troops in the campaign of 1805, accusing them of surpassing even the French in acts of pillage and cruelty. This was resented as a calumny on the Bavarian military. General Wrede, as the principal officer, immediately challenged Baron Duben, with an intimation, that if he himself should fall, the Baron would be called out by the next in rank, and so on, till he was killed. The parties could not come together immediately; the respective Sovereigns both forbade their fighting; but the Swede ventured in a case of this kind to disobey, and travelled into the South of Germany to meet his enemy. But here he found that the Bavarian General had been more obedient to his master, and had, on command, neglected to attend his appointment. On this, the Minister posted the General as a coward in the public prints of Germany, about a year since; and the general opinion was of course

course in his favour. We find from the late French papers, that the duel was fought on the 12th of Feb. near Brannau, " *in the presence of a great number of the inhabitants.*" Baron Duben came from Vienna on purpose, and had been already a week there; General Wrede arrived the day before. The parties met in the village on the Bavarian side of the Inn; and after the seconds, (the English Colonel Burcke, and Count Von Rechberg) had made the arrangements, they entered the lists, *which were beset by Bavarian military,* and placed themselves at a distance of fifteen paces. Baron Duben fired, and the ball passed the right ear of his adversary. Gen. Wrede's first pistol missed fire. The Baron's second fire was equally ineffectual, the ball passing the General's breast. The General's next pistol flashed in the pan. Enraged at this repeated mischance, he drew his sword, and advanced towards the Baron; but the seconds rushed forward, and declared that the combatants had acted like men of honour, and that nothing further could or should be done. They then departed from each other in a state of perfect reconciliation.

ALPHABETICAL LIST
OF
STALLIONS TO COVER IN 1808.

Continued from our last Volume, page 304.

DRIVER, at Mr. W. Lee's, Leckonfield Parks, near Beverley, Yorkshire, at 2gs. and 2s. 6d.—By Trentham; dam, Coquette, by Mr. Compton's Barb.

HONEYCOMB, at Ferrybridge, at 5gs.—By Drone; dam, Miss West, by Match'em, Regulus, Crab, Childers, Basto, &c.

REMEMBRANCER, at Streatlam-Castle, near Barnard-Castle, Yorkshire, at 8gs. and 10s. 6d.—By Pipator; dam, Queen Mab, by Eclipse, out of the Old Tartar Mare.

SANCHO, at Hodsack Priory, near Blyth, Nottinghamshire, at 10gs. and 10s. 6d.——By Don Quixotte; dam, (own sister to Maid-of-all-Work) by Highflyer, out of a sister to Tandem, by Syphon.

SCAPEFIRE, at Skelton, near York, at one guinea and 2s. 6d.—By Stride; dam, Nanberry, by Ruler, Le Sang, Sampson, Old Crab.

SHUTFLE, at the same place as Hambletonian, at 10gs. and 10s. 6d.—By Young Marsk; dam by the Vauxhall-Snap; grandam, Hip, by King Herod, out of a sister to Mirza, by the Godolphin Arabian.

SIR CHARLES, at Ainderby-Steeple, near Northallerton, Yorkshire, at 5gs. and 5s.—By the Arabian Selim; dam, Lavina, by King Fergus, Snap, out of Pyrrha, by Match'em.

SIR HARRY DIMSDALE, at Old Durham, at 10gs. and 10s. 6d.—By Sir Peter Teazle, out of Contessina, by Young Marsk.

SIR OLIVER, at Altrincham, Cheshire, at 5gs. and 10s. 6d.—Own brother to Fyldener, by Sir Peter Teazle, out of Fanny, by Diomed.

SIR SOLOMON, at Rufford, Nottinghamshire, at 10gs. and 10s. 6d.—By Sir Peter Teazle; dam, Matron, by Florizel, out of Maiden, by Match'em.

SIR ULIC M'KILLIGUT, at Hedgeford, near Rugeley, Staffordshire, at 3gs. and 5s.—By Whiskey, out of Amelia, by Highflyer.

SORCERER,

SORCERER, at Great Barton, near Bury St. Edmund's, at 15gs. and 10s. 6d.—By Trumpator, out of Young Giantess, the dam of Eleanor, Julia, Lydia, &c.

STAMFORD, at Cantley, three miles from Doncaster, at 10gs. and 10s. 6d.—By Sir Peter Teazle; dam, Horatia, by Eclipse, out of Countess, the dam of Delpini, &c.

STAVELEY, at Blyth, Nottinghamshire, at 5gs. and 5s.—By Shuttle; dam by Drone; grandam, (Trimbush's dam) by Match'em.

STRIDE, at Snape Hall, near Bedale, Yorkshire, at 7gs. and 5s. ——By Phenomenon; dam by Goldfinder, out of Lovely, by Babram.

TEDDY THE GRINDER, at Mr. Durand's Warren, Epsom Downs, at 5gs. and 10s. 6d.—By Asparagus; dam, Stargazer, by Highflyer, out of Miss West, by Match'em.

TIMOTHY, at Moor Town, near Leeds, Yorkshire, at 5gs. and 5s.—By Delpini, out of Cora, by Match'em.

TOTTERIDGE, at Totteridge, near Barnet, Herts, at 5gs. and 10s. 6d.—By Dungannon, out of Marcella, the grandam of Pavilion, &c.

TRAFALGAR, (late Lord Darlington's) at the same place as Sancho, at 3gs. and 5s.—By Sir Peter Teazle, out of Æthe, by Young Marsk.

TRAVELLER, at Castle Howard, Yorkshire, at 3gs. and 5s.—By Highflyer, out of a sister to Proserpine, by Henricus.

TRUMPATOR, at Newmarket, (twenty mares) at 20gs. and one guinea each.—By Conductor, out of Brunette, by Squirrel.

WALTON, at Newmarket, at 10gs. and 10s. 6d.—Own brother to Ditto, by Sir Peter Teazle; dam by Dungannon, grandam by Prophet, out of Virago, (Saltram's dam) by Snap.

WARRIOR, at Lytham, near Preston, Lancashire, at 5gs. and 10s. 6d.—By Sir Peter Teazle; dam by Young Marsk, Match'em.

WAXY, at Newmarket, at 10gs. and 10s. 6d.—By Pot8o's; dam, Maria, by King Herod, out of Lisette, by Snap.

WHISKEY, at the same place as Sorcerer, at 10gs. and 10s. 6d.—By Saltram, out of Calash, by King Herod.

WINDLE, at Garswood, near Warrington, Lancashire, at 5gs. and 10s. 6d.—Own brother to Ashton, by Beningbrough, out of Mary-Ann, by Sir Peter Teazle, Young Marsk, Match'em.

WIRRAL, at Hooton, Cheshire, at 2gs. and 5s.—By Young Woodpecker, dam by Highflyer, out of Popinjay's dam.

WOLDSMAN, at Shipton, near York, at 3gs. and 5s.—By Sir Peter Teazle; dam, Young Rachel, by Volunteer, out of Rachel, by Highflyer.

YOUNG ALEXANDER, at Mr. Thomas Gamon's, Almere, near Churton, Derbyshire, at 2gs.—By Alexander, dam by Marquis, Black Jack, &c.

YOUNG ECLIPSE, at Bagshot Park, and at Mr. Haynes's Stables, in Riding-House-Lane, Cavendish-Square, London, at 2gs. and 5s.—By Young Eclipse, out of Augusta, by Old Eclipse.

YOUNG SELIM, at the same place as Sir Charles, at 5gs. and 5s. —By the Arabian Selim, out of Enterprise, by Young Marsk.

YOUNG WOODPECKER, at Jervaux-Abbey, near Middleham, Yorkshire, at 5gs.—Own brother to Chanticleer, by Woodpecker; dam

dam by Eclipse, out of Rosebud, by Snap.

ZACHARIAH, at Mr. Davis's Farm, at Murton, near York, at 5gs. and 5s.—Own brother to Beningbrough.

For the Sporting Magazine.

SUCCESSFUL TREATMENT OF BLINDNESS IN A MARE.

THE following remarkable and perfect cure of total blindness, is extracted from vol. ii. pa. 499, of Mr. Lawrence's Philosophical and Practical Treatise on Horses.—Blindness is a misfortune to which horses are peculiarly liable; and as it has, with much reason, been supposed, that with proper treatment and assiduity the sight of many which become blind might be preserved, the giving as extensive publicity as possible to the following case may have beneficial effects, both with respect to a rational method of treatment, and to the avoidance of those cruel and absurd pretended remedies often recommended by the ignorant.—For the portrait of the mare, we refer our readers to vol. xxiv. p. 116.

" In 1781, my favourite brown mare had a weeping in one of her eyes, with swelling of the lids; it passed off after a while, unattended to; a short time after, the other eye was affected in the same manner. Eye-water was used, and bleeding, and the mare being wanted for a particular occasion, was physicked. The disease remitted and exacerbated alternately for a month or two, until at length it became very serious; one eye was exceedingly swollen, and opened with great difficulty, discharging d scalding serum which almost brought off the hair; the coats of the other were thickened, and looked very dull.

" By and by, the ball of the one was inflamed to the highest possible degree, and the other, although not so much inflamed, seemed to admit little or no light. There appeared a white speck upon the pupil, and several ignorant fellows who saw the mare were exceedingly desirous of having, I know not what, escharotic powders blown into the eyes, with a view of scouring off what they supposed to be films upon the external coats, not being aware that the disease was purely internal; and it is shocking to reflect upon the useless tortures the poor animal would have endured in such hands. Repellents either increased the inflammation, or had no effect at all. Nitre was given. A dose of physic checked the inflammation, but total blindness shortly followed. By the advice of my surgeon, I applied to Snape, the King's farrier, who pronounced the mare incurable. I then sent her to Layton, a very eminent farrier, at Walham Green, with my particular request that he would undertake the case, which he declined, as hopeless.

" Thus left to my own efforts, and my affections deeply interested, I was determined no exertions of either thought or care should be wanted; and luckily I was seconded by a skilful groom, a son of old Mendham, well known as a humble stable attendant at Newmarket.—It must be premised, that the mare had had a slight fit of the staggers about a year before, which had been neglected, but her eyes were of most perfect conformation, and in their natural state as clear and diaphanous as a polished mirror. After turning over all my veterinary oracles, otacles, I formed my plan, and having previously obtained the approbation of a regular medical friend, I began my operations.

" I judged that the humours were condensed, and that topical applications were indicated to render them fluid, and fit for absorption and circulation; and that a number of drains, or issues, were immediately necessary, for the purposes of evacuation and revulsion. I supposed, right or wrong, that peculiar benefit would be derived from the proximity of the issues to the parts affected, on which particular I should, at this day, be thankful for information.

" A soft leather half-hood, with holes for the ears and eyes, was made, intended to cover and secure poultices. Five rowels were cut; one in each cheek under the ear, under the throat, in the chest, and the belly. The eyes were poulticed with hot bran, and laid, *aqua vegeto* occasionally added, a number of times during the day, and very early in the morning, poultices continually remaining upon the head : this course was sedulously observed during a month or six weeks, all which time the rowells, or most of them, were running, an opening diet and a little salts, with walking exercise. After a week, the inflammation gradually subsided, but there were no signs of returning sight until the end of a month or five weeks, when we were indulged with hope one day, and driven to despair the next ; in short, the jokers were busy, but I was determined to persevere.

" We were soon after agreeably surprised with considerable amendment in one eye, and in a week or two more, the mare could endure the light with both, and saw very clearly ; there still, however, continued a blue cloudiness, which was not dispersed until some months afterwards. The poultices were discontinued ; but the eyes were strictly guarded from the light by the hood before mentioned, the eye-holes being filled with soft leather ; nor did I expose the eyes to the light for nearly two months after the return of sight, riding the mare blinded. After the poultices, *aqua vegeto* was used twice a day, salts, and a short course of cinnabar in cordial balls. I highly enjoyed the first little journey I made without the blinds, the animal stopping a great number of times upon the road, to examine different objects, with as much curiosity as if she had entered upon a new world. Her eyes remained perfect until her death, which happened six years afterwards, from an apoplectic fit as was supposed, she being seen well in the field at night, and found dead in the morning. I tried the above method with two horses afterwards, but by no means with corresponding success ; which, indeed, I did not expect, their eyes being naturally small, and of defective form.

" The conclusions to be drawn from this case are, that the grand dependence for cure is upon the timely insertion of a sufficient number of rowels, and upon keeping the eyes strictly from exposure to the light ; that repellants are not always successful, but I presume more particularly indicated in weakness and dilatation of the vessels ; and that purgatives may be injurious."

Mr. Lawrence afterwards repeats his cautions against the common practice of blowing powdered glass, or other corrosive articles, into the eyes of horses, or of using ointments and washes of the same nature, in the case of specks supposed to be situate upon the external coat ; observing, page 505, " that before their use be hazarded, it should be well ascertained that the defect intended to be removed be really situate upon the outer coat of the eye ; since such remedies can have no possible effect upon the internal parts, and may inflame, irritate, and torture, to no manner of purpose."

GAMING.

Mazzinghi v. Stephenson.

THIS was an action for a bond debt of 73*l*. The execution of the bond was proved by Mr. Harwood. The defence was, that this was a gaming debt, the money had been lost at " Faro," in the house No. 40, Pall-Mall, then occupied by the plaintiff, who had had an employment in the Alien Office, but was said to have been obliged to quit the country for some political correspondence not strictly correct.

Chief Justice Mansfield, however, was of opinion, that the defence was not so clearly made out as to invalidate a bond, though there could be little doubt as to the fact in the private judgment of any person. The evidence was deficient, he observed, in two respects ; 1st, as to the precise bond in question being for any gaming debt at all; and next as to the debt being contracted at the particular game called " Faro," which formed part of the defendant's plea. There was a question, whether the proof of the particular game was essential, as it was stated, in the plea. In his opinion, the plaintiff was entitled to recover, the defendant not having made good his plea. My Lord Mansfield had repeatedly said, that in cases of this kind, you should " *hit the bird in the eye.*" It was contended on the part of the defendant, that the name of the game was merely circumstantial and illustrative, and not essential. The Judge, on the other hand, thought it was part of the issue.

Verdict for the plaintiff.

A GERMAN WINTER AMUSEMENT.

TRAINEAU parties may be reckoned among the amusements of Germany. These can take place in the time of frost only, and when there is a considerable quantity of snow upon the ground.

A traineau is a machine in the shape of a horse, lion, swan, or in that of a griffin, unicorn, or in some other fanciful form, without wheels, but made below like a sledge, for the convenience of sliding over the snow. Some are gilded and otherwise ornamented, according to the whim of the proprietor. A pole stands up from one side, to which an ensign or a flag is fastened, which waves over the head of those placed in the machine. The lady, wrapped in fur, sits before, and the gentleman stands behind on a board made for that purpose.

The whole is drawn by two horses, which are either conducted by a postilion, or driven by the gentleman. The horses are gaudily ornamented, and have bells hanging from the trappings which cover them.

The party consists generally of many traineaus, each attended by
two

two or three servants on horseback with flambeaux.—This amusement is taken when it begins to grow dark : one traineau takes the lead, the rest follow at a convenient distance in a line, and drive for two or three hours through the principal streets and squares of the town. The horses go at a brisk rate; the motion of the traineau is easy and agreeable; and the bells, ensigns, and torches, make a very gay and showy appearance.

WINNERS OF THE DERBY AND OAKS' STAKES.

THE following is a complete List of the Winners of the Oaks' Stakes at Epsom since their first commencement :—

Owners.	Winners.	Sires.	Years.
Lord Derby's	Bridget	King Herod	1779
Mr. Douglas's	Tetotum	Match'em	1780
Lord Grosvenor's	Faith	King Herod	1781
Lord Grosvenor's	Ceres	Sweetwilliam	1782
Lord Grosvenor's	Maid of the Oaks	King Herod	1783
Mr. Burlton's	Stella	Plunder	1784
Lord Clermont's	Trifle	Justice	1785
Sir F. Standish's	Yellow Filly	Tandem	1786
Mr. Vernon's	Annette	Eclipse	1787
Lord Egremont's	Nightshade	Pot80's	1788
Lord Egremont's	Tag	Trentham	1789
Duke of Bedford's	Hippolyta	Mercury	1790
Duke of Bedford's	Portia	Volunteer	1791
Lord Clermont's	Volante	Highflyer	1792
Duke of Bedford's	Celia	Volunteer	1793
Lord Derby's	Hermione	Sir Peter Teazle	1794
Lord Egremont's	Platina	Mercury	1795
Sir F. Standish's	Parisot	Sir Peter Teazle	1796
Lord Grosvenor's	Nikè	Alexander	1797
Mr. Durand's	Bellissima	Phenomenon	1798
Lord Grosvenor's	Bellina	Rockingham	1799
Lord Egremont's	Ephemera	Woodpecker	1800
Sir C. Bunbury's	Eleanor *	Whiskey	1801
Mr. Wastell's	Scotia	Delpini	1802
Sir T. Gascoigne's	Theophania	Delpini	1803
Duke of Grafton's	Pelisse	Whiskey	1804
Lord Grosvenor's	Meteora	Meteor	1805
Hon. B. Craven's	Bronze	Buzzard	1806
General Grosvenor's	Briseïs	Beningbrough	1807

* Eleanor won the Derby Stakes the day before.

THE following is a complete List of the Winners of the Derby Stakes at Epsom, since their first commencement :—

Owners.	Winners.	Sires.	Years.
Sir C. Bunbury's	Diomed	Florizel	1780
Mr. O'Kelly's	Young Eclipse	Eclipse	1781
Lord Egremont's	Assassin	Sweetbriar	1782
Mr. Parker's	Saltram	Eclipse	1783
Mr. O'Kelly's	Serjeant	Eclipse	1784
Lord Clermont's	Aimwell	Marc Antony	1785
Mr. Panton's	Noble	Highflyer	1786
Lord Derby's	Sir Peter Teazle	Highflyer	1787
His R. H. the P. of Wales's	Sir Thomas	Pontac	1788
Duke of Bedford's	Skyscraper	Highflyer	1789
Lord Grosvenor's	Rhadamanthus	Justice	1790
Duke of Bedford's	Eager	Florizel	1791
Lord Grosvenor's	John Bull	Fortitude	1792
Sir F. Poole's	Waxy	Pot8o's	1793
Lord Grosvenor's	Dædalus	Justice	1794
Sir F. Standish's	Spread Eagle	Volunteer	1795
Sir F. Standish's	Didelot	Trumpator	1796
Duke of Bedford's	Br. Colt, out of Celia's dam	Fidget	1797
Mr. Cookson's	Sir Harry	Sir Peter Teazle	1798
Sir F. Standish's	Archduke	Sir Peter Teazle	1799
Mr. Wilson's	Champion	Pot8o's	1800
Sir C. Bunbury's	Eleanor *	Whiskey	1801
Duke of Grafton's	Tyrant	Pot8o's	1802
Sir H. Williamson's	Ditto	Sir Peter Teazle	1803
Lord Egremont's	Hannibal	Driver	1804
Lord Egremont's	Cardinal Beaufort	Gohanna	1805
Lord Foley's	Paris	Sir Peter Teazle	1806
Lord Egremont's	Election	Gohanna	1807

* Eleanor won the Oaks' Stakes the next day.

REMARKABLE INSCRIPTION

ON A MONUMENT LATELY ERECTED IN HORSLEY-DOWN CHURCH, IN CUMBERLAND.

HERE lie the bodies
Of THOMAS BOND and MARY his wife.
She was Temperate, Chaste, and Charitable ;
BUT
She was Proud, Peevish, and Passionate.
She was an affectionate Wife, and a tender Mother ;
BUT
Her Husband and Child, whom she loved,
Seldom saw her countenance without a disgusting frown,
Whilst

Whilst she received Visitors, whom she despised, with an endearing
smile.
Her behaviour was discreet towards strangers,
BUT
Imprudent in her Family.
Abroad, her conduct was influenced by good breeding,
BUT
At home, by Ill-temper.
She was a professed enemy to Flattery,
And was seldom known to praise or commend;
BUT
The talents in which she principally excelled,
Were difference of opinion, and discovering flaws and imperfections.
She was an admirable economist,
And, without prodigality,
Dispensed plenty to every person in her Family;
BUT
Would sacrifice their eyes to a Farthing Candle.
She sometimes made her Husband happy with her good qualities;
BUT
Much more frequently miserable, with her many Failings;
Insomuch that in thirty years cohabitation he often lamented that,
maugre all her Virtues,
He had not, in the whole, enjoyed two years of Matrimonial Comfort.
AT LENGTH,
Finding that she had lost the affections of her Husband,
As well as the regard of her Neighbours,
Family disputes having been divulged by Servants,
She died of Vexation, July 20, 1768,
Aged 48 years.
Her worn-out Husband survived her four months and two days,
And departed this Life, Nov. 28, 1768,
In the 54th Year of his Age.

William Bond, brother to the deceased, erected this Stone,
As a *Weekly Monitor* to the surviving Wives of this Parish,
That they may avoid the infamy
Of having their Memories handed down to Posterity
With a *patch-work* Character.

THE AMUSEMENTS OF PARIS DESCRIBED.

Continued from page 289 of our last Number.

OLD WOMEN AND GIRLS.

ATTEND to that girl crying till she is hoarse, " Fifty tooth-picks for two sous, *cinquante cure-dents pour deux sous!*" She sells but little of her goods; she is ugly, nobody will buy; and yet she lives. I prefer those cunning wits, whose industry speculates upon that inexhaustible fund, the curiosity of mankind.

mankind. Here stands an old-woman, who reads, with a harsh voice, from a printed sheet of blotting paper, what has happened in the last sitting of the council of state. She hardly closes her mouth before her more aged neighbour opens her faded lips, pours forth a torrent of printed eloquence against the perfidy of the English; pointing, at the same time, to a wooden cut which decorates her hand-bill, and in which his Britannic majesty is very ill-treated. The droll delivery of the two old women is heard gratis, and their hand-bills cost only one sous.

Let us quit these haggard figures for your pretty round-faced wench, who has set up a table, on which stands about half a dozen of tin or plated candlesticks. She holds a woollen rag in her hand, which she dips into a red powder, and, while she rubs the candlesticks quite bright, she extols, in a mellifluous tone, and with dimples in her cheeks, the admirable qualities of her powder. She asks the bystanders for thimbles or shoe-buckles, gives them back as bright as new, and even promises to cure pimples in the face with her powder; but no one offers his face for this experiment. A merry soldier goes by, shews her a scar on his cheek, and laughing, asks whether she can remove that too? She answers, yes; and promises, for this purpose, to pay him a visit in the evening. I could wager that this girl has invented a powder which yields more profit, and costs less, than the golden powder of the famous alchymists.

A FLEA DRAWING AN ELEPHANT.

But what is that sailor doing with his microscope? where did he get this dirty instrument, patched together with wire? what does he shew through it? Nothing more or less than a flea: for this he gets one sous. Only see his neighbour, about one hundred yards farther, knows likewise how to turn trifles to the best account. The cunning dog found means to get a few sheets of the paper which painters use to draw transparencies, and now shews for one sous to the wondering crowd, how pictures can be copied with the utmost expedition.

Let us enter this booth, where the inscription announces a wonder. He who will not believe, let him come and see! What pray?— A flea drawing an elephant; a flea conducting a carriage with six horses carrying ladies and gentlemen; a flea on whose foot a metal ball has been fastened with a golden chain, with which he merrily leaps to and fro. All this is not fiction. A man has really taken the vast trouble to make the elephant, carriage, chains, &c. of gold so very small, and to fasten them to the flea.

TWO FLIES FIGHTING A DUEL.

But still more ludicrous and more inventive is the artist's producing two flies fighting a duel with the small sword. It is thus contrived: two flies are fastened to two needles, placed perpendicularly behind their wings, so that they keep their six legs stretched out before them. They are fixed very nearly facing each other, and a little ball of cork is then given to each of them, in which is fastened a small straw. As soon as this ball touches their feet, they endeavour to seize it to hold themselves by: on this touch the ball keeps moving backwards and forwards, and consequently the straw turns against the enemy.— Each party moving in the same manner,

manner, the two straws often clash together like two swords; and this constitutes the duel of the flies.

MECHANICAL HORSES.

Close by this fencing and hopping-room, we are invited to undertake a little journey of several hundred leagues, on mechanical horses, with the great promise, that this great distance shall be travelled in a time incredibly short. Well; we laugh sarcastically, and yet enter. No sooner is the dirty curtain raised, than we are convinced, at the first look, that we see nothing before us but a kind of caroussel, remarkable only for its requiring no person to turn it; as the rider, by tightly pulling the bridle, sets the centre wheel in motion, and consequently turns himself with great velocity.

This fun costs only four sous. But that you may not throw away your money, I warn you against yonder bald-pated fellow, who has put up a large tube of paste-board, directed towards the sky, and civilly asks every body to look up. On this occasion he makes a long speech, which the crowd think very learned, about different vapours and their properties; assuring them that the glasses in his tube are so finely polished, that the vapours before it are concentrated into various extraordinary forms. It cannot be done in all weathers, but this particularly is a day to exhibit every thing in the most charming manner. I confess to you, my dear friend, that old bald-pate lately spoke so well and so ingeniously, that I suffered myself to be tempted to step before his tube. He then pulled a thread, unperceived, and a centaur passed between my eye and the ordinary window-glass, which he probably cut out of some book of

prints, such as are usually manufactured at Nuremberg. I suddenly withdrew my head quite ashamed, and sneaked away to make room for another.

But why should I be ashamed, thought I, as I retired; this daily happens in my own country, where great poets and philosophers, with much bawling, hold their tubes before our eyes, promising us, God knows what wonders. We are good-natured; we look into them, and what do we behold? Some little monster of the puppet-fair.

BLIND MEN AND DOGS.

This day, my sweet friend, we pursue our excursion in dry weather. The objects will not always be of the same merry cast as before, and I will not answer for it that a tear may not now and then steal into your eye. Just by, we meet with a blind man singing his song in simple and affecting accents. Beside him lies a faithful guide, the shaggy dog, sometimes shaking his bell. Not far from him sits another blind man, who probably cannot sing: instead of singing, a kind of stage stands before him, on which several bells of various tones are suspended, which he puts in motion with threads. He does not beg aloud; but only puts his hand now and then into his hat, to try whether he can grasp the charitable token of some passing benefactor. He generally draws his hand back empty.

We do not go far, without encountering a third poor wretch bereft of the most valuable of the senses. He has an old harpischord placed before him on the Boulevards, and is thumping a sonata with all his might. Numbers of people stop to hear his performance; but the pewter cup, fastened in front

front of his instrument, seldom resounds with the boon of pity.

We scarcely leave him, when we meet a fourth blind man endeavouring to touch the heart by means of a fiddle out of tune. He plays it walking: his dog fastened by a little chain to a button of his waistcoat, goes cautiously before him. However, I once witnessed how this poor skeleton of a dog was irresistibly tempted, by a bone which had been thrown away, to run into a corner, where his unsuspecting master was on the point of dashing against the wall all his wealth—his head and his violin. But among the many blind men who are to be met with in the streets of Paris, singing, playing, or ringing, none gather a more inquisitive crowd round them, than two men who play at piquet the live-long day ; not to lose, but to win money : who, with the most wonderful discrimination, feel and name the cards, contrive to interest every one who has the least idea of the game for some minutes, and when they retire at night, are always both winners.

But let us leave these blind people, the sight of whom only dejects those possessed of vision ; though the Parisians, steeled by custom, for the most part pass them with indifference. I often saw elderly women, especially in the evening, who, to judge from their baskets, were cookmaids, and who, by giving alms to the poor blind, no doubt, hoped to stifle the reproaches of their consciences for taking too large a market-penny.

MUSICIANS.

Let us rather direct our steps to yon musical artist, who by the dexterity he has acquired really deserves admiration. He alone plays a whole symphony *(concertante)* upon five instruments at once. With one hand he grasps and holds a double flageolet, whose mouthpieces he constantly moves to and fro on his lips ; sometimes, too, he plays both at the same time: with the other he fingers the harp very dexterously : with one foot he beats a tabor, and with the toes of the other he rattles the castanet. It sounds very well, you hear ; and the poor devil fags as hard as Mademoiselle Maillard in the great opera, dearly earning his few sous.

Don't let us pass yon harper without dropping a trifle into his plate. His execution certainly is not the most pleasing; but the poor young girl who stands by him with her eyes fixed on the ground, singing, constantly singing, is entitled to our mite, because her downcast looks seem to say : " I know very well I sing badly, but my father wants bread !" The two children, who sing a duet on the bridge, do quite the reverse. The song is intended to move the heart, and would produce that effect if the children did not squall so thoughtlessly, and look about in such an impudent manner. Their look and notes only raise the idea that they will one day become two worthless creatures.

MOVING MENDICANTS.

A group of children to whom I shall not lead you, for fear of giving you too much pain, is much more likely to excite pity. In the Rue Vivienne I have seen, for more than three weeks, yet always in the evening when it was dark, three wretched children lying in the mud. The eldest, a boy of about ten years, sat reclined against the wall, holding on his lap another wrapped in rags, three years old at farthest, and usually moaning. By his side sat or lay a third symbol of misery, about

about five years old. These children did not beg; but had the end of a tallow candle placed before them, near which, upon a rag, lay a paper with the following simple and moving inscription : "We have neither father nor mother." Few of the passengers remained unmoved, and the street being much frequented, they always obtained a rich harvest. With pleasure I remarked that the soldiers in particular gave, and gave the most. One night I found one of those people deeply affected. He wore large black whiskers, which, in wild constrast with the emotion of the muscles of his face, lighted by the glimmer of the candle, threw their shade upon a tear. He surveyed the group for some minutes in silence; the poor little wretch was just whining dolefully, because it was cold. The soldier briskly put his hand in his pocket, gave to the elder boy two pieces of silver coin (I believe two twelve-sous pieces), on condition of his carrying the child home immediately, and warming it. He repeated this condition three or four times, and made the boy as often promise to perform it. He then retired. As he turned round I accosted him.—" You certainly are a father," said I. " Oui, monsieur," answered he, rather roughly, and hastened away. I stopped some time to see whether the boy would keep his promise, and take the children home ; but he did not. That the police should have suffered such a scene for so many weeks, does not please me. It seems almost impossible that the poor children should remain in health all the winter.

In Paris, beggars seldom or never ask charity. You only hear at times, Monsieur, je meurs de faim (sir, I am starving), whispered behind you.

Every pauper endeavours to establish a kind of just claim to what is given him. One runs with a broom in his hand, when he sees a person crossing a dirty part of the street, and quickly sweeps away the mud; another profits of a shower, which fills the middle of the street with water, lays a plank across, and in a friendly manner helps you over. He judges who can afford to give him something by their clothes : all that he supposes to be poor he suffers to pass gratis : and if a handsome girl appear, he escorts her with the utmost gallantry.

To be continued.

BOXING.

ON Tuesday, the 5th, the long-intended matches between Dutch Sam and William Cropley, Tom Belcher and Dogherty, were to have taken place at Moulsey Hurst ; a vast concourse of all descriptions arrived on the spot by the usual channels of conveyance, and by eleven o'clock a rope ring was formed, and the combatants were every moment expected to make their appearance.

The first match to be decided was that between Dutch Sam and Cropley, and their respective friends were sporting their bets freely. Mendoza was to have been second to Dutch Sam, and Harry Lee to Cropley. At this critical moment, when the spectators flattered themselves that they were on the point of reaping the reward of all their fatigue, a party of Bow-street Officers arrived, with a special warrant from the Magistrates, against Dutch Sam and Tom Belcher. These two heroes were accordingly apprised of the measure, and immediately

E diately

diately bound over to keep the peace within the four immediately surrounding counties. Jackson, one of the umpires, was the first to announce this woeful disappointment, and the melancholy news soon flew through the crowd.

In vain did some of the noble amateurs offer the combatants a full indemnification for the consequences—they feared the iron hand of justice too much to brave its terrors ; they declined the offer, and the mob left the ground. The town of Little Hampton, however, was soon filled by the returning crowd, and the overflow spread itself into Twickenham.

The day, however, did not pass without some sport. Two battles took place—one was between two coal-heavers, of no note or science. The other was between Jemmy from Town and the Gipsey. They fought twenty-five rounds, at the conclusion of which victory was declared in favour of Jemmy.— There was not the least interest in these fights. None of the amateurs considered them worth their notice or attention, and they were given merely to amuse the refuse of the meeting, who were determined not to separate without some fun.

Among the most dashing amateurs on the ground were, the Earl of J. in a barouche and four ; the Hon. B. C. in a barouche and four ; Earl C. on horseback, &c. &c.

We were also informed, that previous to the departure of Belcher and Dockarty from Hampton, the chaises which held the pugilists and their friends met, when Dockarty accused Belcher of timidity in not facing him, whose liberty was as dear as that of any other man, and he would fight him on that spot. Belcher jumped out of the chaise,

and began to strip, and Dockarty did the same, and observed, that he would fight even for a dram.

These appearances, however, ended in another disappointment, for however willing Belcher might have been to fight, Mendoza and his companions, in a *safe match,* prevented him, and the chaise was driven off, amidst more disapprobation than had been ever witnessed before.

It was appropriately observed, by a gentleman amateur, to the nobility and gentry present, that the pugilists of the day, who could make from *fifty* to *one hundred pounds* by sparring every other month, would not condescend to fight for subscription purses, if they even supposed they had a chance of being beaten.

But the disappointment of the pugilists at Moulsey Hurst was not of long duration. On Thursday, the 14th instant, the match that was fixed for the first place was positively decided on a summit, half a mile from the Rubbing-house on Epsom Downs. It would be superfluous to give any description of the perfections of Belcher in the art of boxing, his recent combats having made him universally known as a professor inferior in science, and what is technically termed *pluck*, to no one. With respect to Dogherty, his combats, although very frequent, have been with novices, and consequently he could not have acquired much fame; but his last combat with young Crib, three months since, gave proofs of improvement, and his present adversary was the nearest professor with whom he could contend, to stamp his fame with another victory. His friends had entertained sanguine hopes of his success,

success, considering Belcher as a man not likely to administer to him as much beating as he should be capable of *carrying away*, or able to *rally* successfully with him.

To describe with effect the dispositions of the *great* and *little* amateurs, and the scenes which were produced on the road to the field of combat, would be impossible; but at twelve o'clock the motley group had assembled on the Downs, and shortly after the combatants arrived at the ring, an inner one of twenty feet having been roped off to perform in.

The seconds were, Mendoza and Clark for Belcher, and Cropley and Dick Hall for Dogherty. Betting at setting-to was precisely six to four on Belcher.

THE BATTLE.

Round 1. After sparring for half a minute, each of the combatants made a hit at one instant : Belcher stopped, and his blow fell short, when they closed, after an irregular rally; they disengaged, and Belcher hit his man a slight blow at half arm, and Dogherty, attempting to return it, closed, and threw his man. Betting, the same as at the commencement.

2. Dogherty made play without ceremony; by attempting a left-handed hit at his opponent's head, but Belcher stopped it skilfully; and after Dogherty had made a rally, which did not harm his adversary, he was hit off his legs with great dexterity. Two to 1 on Belcher.

3. An exceedingly well-contested round, and all the skill and strength of the combatants was shewn. Dogherty commenced at a rally within distance with determined courage, but he had the worst of the conflict throughout,

although he made some dexterous stops; but Belcher, by hitting and stopping at the same moment, had his fists, one or the other, constantly in Dogherty's face; but he was at length thrown.

4. Dogherty made a left-handed feint, when Belcher, within distance, hit him a severe facer before he recovered his guard, and for the first time commenced a furious rally, which was well opposed by Dogherty, who, however dexterously he made some stops, could plant no hits, but rather received them in a manner to have put an end to a combat with an ordinary taker. He followed Dogherty round the ring, constantly hitting him with all imaginable ease on the head only, and at length dropped him, by a blow under the right jaw. Three to 1 on Belcher.

5. Belcher hit his adversary a tremendous blow on the throat with his left hand through his guard, which left Dockarty so much abroad, that he received three others on the head, which resounded through the ring. An irregular fall closed the round.

6. Belcher hit his opponent two blows at setting to, the last of which dropped him.

7. This round was not so much in favour of Belcher as those preceding, for although he rallied his adversary, he was well stopped, and slightly hit, but Dogherty fell on one of his blows.

8. Dogherty went in very intemperately, and fought in a determined manner. Belcher's time was wholly occupied in stopping, and attempting to stop, for some blows were scientifically aimed by Dogherty, but he had lost his distance; the combatants closed, and Dogherty threw his adversary on the ropes with apparent ease. In

this

this round, betting was reduced to about six to four, for although Dogherty appeared much *pinked*, he was strong on his legs, and fresh, and consequently worth the risk of backing against Belcher, where stamina rendered success doubtful.

9. Although Belcher had the best of this round, he threw some hits away, and was hit himself, and after closing, he fell undermost.

10. Dogherty eagerly followed his adversary, who as cautiously retreated, to take his advantage of skill in planting hits, two of which were effectual, and Dogherty was thrown.

11. Belcher gave his adversary two other hits in the face, and both fell out of the ring.

12. Belcher performed precisely the same as in the last round, and after *jobbing* him, threw him.

13. Dogherty received a heavy fall in attempting to rally. Any odds, but no takers.

14. Belcher hit his adversary down when attempting to rally.— Five to one.

15. This round was considered decisive of victory for Belcher.— Dogherty's head was frightful in appearance, and although he seemed to maintain the same resolution as at setting-to, he had not power to place a blow. When he rallied, Belcher met him by a well-measured distance, and the goodness of the other brought a close, in which Belcher punished him by under half-arm hits, and at length dropped him from between his arms.

16 and 17. These rounds were, as usual, so much in favour of Belcher, that in the latter round, so confident was he in not giving a chance away, that he left his adversary in a feeble posture, without hitting him.

18 and 19. These rounds were also in favour of Belcher, although Dogherty had made a slight turn in the odds, by some gaiety ; but it was of short duration. He stopped his adversary very cleverly, but he had not power to hit him.— Both fell in the latter round, as if weak.

To detail further particulars of this combat would be only to state, that Belcher's fists were never away from Dogherty's face, and the blows of the former were put in with as much strength as at the commencement. Dogherty was fighting under heavy hurts, as his figure demonstrated, and Belcher was amusing himself, as if sparring in the Fives Court. The 24th round reduced the battle to a certainty, notwithstanding Dogherty appeared determined not to resign till nature compelled him. In this round Belcher hit him three or four severe blows in the face, and at length, by a blow in the wind and neck at the same moment, doubled him together so scientifically, that he fell like a helpless infant. Nine other rounds were fought, in which Dogherty only faced his adversary to fall without ever being hit. Belcher threw a *summerset* at the close of the battle, which lasted thirty-five minutes, and ran to the Rubbing-house, where he was trained, without stopping to dress himself.

REMARKS.

Belcher fought this battle with more gratification to the beholders, than he had ever done in his several well-contested combats. He measured well his distance, and every hit told well. His science and courage gave him so decided an advantage from the first round, that nothing but Dogherty's determined

mined resolution could give him a chance, and that chance was in staying too long. Dogherty hits often open-handed, and measures his distance badly, but he shewed himself a real game man, labouring under these disadvantages. This match was for fifty guineas. Belcher had not even a hit which made any visible impression.

A second battle was fought for a subscription plate between Richman the black and a West countryman, who was a candidate for the list of pugilists, but who failed in his attempt. At the commencement of the battle, Richman had the worst of it, his adversary being a man of size and strength much superior to him, by going in and rallying. Richman was at a loss frequently, until the countryman, who appeared rather tired, stood and sparred with his adversary, when he met Richman's science by some severe left-handed facers, which ultimately so much displeased him, that he took Richman by the legs, and hit him over his head. There were, however, some rallying rounds, and the countryman was so full of gaiety at the commencement, that he had lost more strength in bravado to the spectators, than in hitting Richman, which occurred but seldom. The countryman shewed a little *white feather* towards the end of the battle, and prudently declined being punished much.—Tom Jones seconded the winner.—The ring was well attended as usual.

THE PHILOSOPHICAL GAMESTER.

" THE loss of four hundred pounds to one in your circumstances must have been a dreadful misfortune."

" Their loss was one of the luckiest things that ever happened to me. I was obliged to pinch so hard to make it up, that I have thought myself in affluence ever since."

" You are a philosopher, and bear misfortunes with great fortitude."

" I have hardly any to bear."

" I am surprised to hear you say so; for I have heard you lost near seven hundred pounds in the space of a month, being in a very persevering run of ill-fortune."

" Thereabout."

" And what, in the devil's name, do you call that? a man who loses such a sum must think himself very unfortunate."

" Not if he previously won it all in the course of a week's play."

" That is not the way in which men calculate their own misfortunes."

" It is the fair way, however; for the most fortunate man that ever existed will be proved to be unfortunate, if you throw out all the lucky incidents of his life, and leave the unlucky behind."

PEDIGREE AND PERFORMANCES
OF
DITTO.

Bred by Sir H. P. Hoghton, Bart. of Walton, Lancashire, and sold to Sir Hedworth Williamson, Bart.

HE was got by Sir Peter Teazle; his dam, (bred by his R. H. the Prince of Wales) by Dungannon; grandam,

grandam, (Grey St. George and Fancy's dam) by Prophet; great grandam, Virago, (Saltram's dam) by Snap, Regulus, out of an own sister to Black-and-all-Black, by Crab.

At Epsom, 1803, *Ditto* won the Derby Stakes of 950gs, the last mile and half, beating Sir Oliver, the brother to Stamford, Dreadnought, Discussor, and Wheatear: 7 to 4 against the brother to Stamford, and 7 to 2 against Ditto, who won very easy. At this time, his owner refused 3000gs for him.

At Newmarket First Spring Meeting, 1804, *Ditto* won the Claret Stakes of 700gs, Ditch-in, beating the brother to Stamford, and Discussor :—7 to 4 on Ditto, who won very easy.

At Newmarket Craven Meeting, 1805, *Ditto* won the Craven Stakes of 130gs, across the Flat, beating Castrel, Agincourt, Aniseed, Dora, Quiz, Mary, Stockton, Sir Harry Dimsdale, Goosecap, and Lady Brough :—13 to 8 against Lady Brough, 7 to 2 against Ditto, and 4 to 1 against Castrel. A most excellent race between Ditto and Castrel, and won by a head. On Thursday, in the same Meeting, he was beat, (for the first time) by Sir Harry Dimsdale, same age, to whom Ditto allowed 9lb. over the B. C. At Guildford, in June, *Ditto* won the King's Plate, beating Mr. Emden's Gipsy, who was drawn after the first heat.

At Newmarket Second Spring Meeting, 1807, *Ditto*, 8st. 10lb. received 20gs. compromise from Mr. Howorth's Hedley, 7st. Ab. Mile, 50gs. He was beat in the same Meeting, in a Handicap Stakes, won by Hippomenes. The above were the only times of his running.

Ditto is 15 hands and half high, with great bone and powers, has very superior action, free from all natural blemishes, and is perfectly sound and healthy. He was allowed to have more speed than any horse of his day.

Ditto is own brother to *Walton* and *Lancaster*.—In 1801, *Lancaster* won 50gs at York; twice 50l. and 100gs at Morpeth. In 1802, he won 50l. at Middleham; 50l. at Manchester; at York Spring Meeting, he won 200gs, beating Belleisle, and Dr. Solander :—6 to 4 against Lancaster, who was sold to John Clifton, Esq. and at Preston, in September, he won a 50l. Plate, and one of 50gs. He died of a mortification in his foot, occasioned by a prick of a thorn, in the Spring of 1803.

At Epsom, in 1802, *Walton* won 50l. beating Dotterel, Wilkes, Pacificator, and Morgan Rattler. At Newmarket Craven Meeting, in 1803, he won the third class of the Oatlands' Stakes, beating Duxbury and Eleanor. In the First Spring Meeting, he won 50l. beating Lignum-Vitæ. In the First October Meeting, he won the King's Plate, beating Orlando and Allegranti. In 1804, he won the King's Plates at Newmarket, Guildford, Salisbury, Winchester, Warwick, and Litchfield; also, 100gs at Newmarket, and 60gs at Winchester. In 1805, he won 200gs, 100gs, 50l. and a King's Plate at Newmarket; also 50l. and 60gs at Lewes. In 1806, he was a stallion at Newmarket. And in 1807, he was second to Selim for the Craven Stakes, beating Currycomb, Jerboa, Stripling, and six others.

He is now a Stallion at Mr. Perren's Stables, Newmarket, at 10gs. a mare, and half-a-guinea the groom.

FEAST

FEAST OF WIT.

AT the Huntingdon Assizes, an action was tried for the recovery of the sum of 33l. for the price of three heifers. The sale took place at a public-house, and the landlady was brought up to prove the contract; and who stated to the Court, that previous to the bargain being struck, there was a good deal of " *botheration.*" Mr. Serjeant Sellon, on cross-examining one of the witnesses for the defendant, said to him, " you have heard what Mrs. Bird has said about this contract, and that she says that there was a good deal of *botheration* before it was concluded; I will thank you to inform the Court what is the meaning of the word " *botheration.*" " Why, Sir," says he, " it is something like what is passing between you and me.

Mr. ———, a wretched artist, telling a friend that he meant to white-wash the ceiling of his room, and then paint it—the gentleman observed, that he thought he had better paint it first, and then white-wash it!

A Quaker, a few days since, having been cited as an evidence at a Quarter Sessions, one of the Magistrates, who had been a blacksmith, desired to know why he would not take off his hat? " It is a privilege," said the witness, " that the laws and liberality of my country indulge people of our religious mode of thinking in." " If I had it in my power," said the angry Justice, " I would have your hat *nailed* to your head." " I thought," said Obadiah, " that thou hadst given over the trade of *driving nails.*"

A clown, in Berkshire, employed to draw timber from a wood, met with an oak trunk of so large a size, that the tackle he made use of to place it on the carriage broke twice on the trial. *Hodge* slung his hat on the ground, and scratching his head with much vexation, exclaimed, " D——n the *hogs* that did not *eat thee*, when thee was an *acorn*, and then I should not have had this trouble with thee."

A gentleman, a few days since, having brought an action for an assault, his servant was called as a witness to support it; who, after a few questions, observed, that he was certain if his master had not a very *thick* head, the blow which the defendant gave him would have cracked his skull.

A few days ago an undertaker was observed to shed tears at the interment of a *quack*—a friend asked him the cause of it—" Why," said he, " you see I have just buried one of my best friends."

Refinement of Language.—A match vender now calls himself a *timber* merchant; a poulterer, a *Turkey* merchant; a distiller, a *chymist*; a two-penny-post man, a *man of letters*; a grave-digger, a *banker*; a vender of old clothes, a *dealer in wall flowers*; a gardener, master of the *mint*; a barber, a dealer in *logwood shavings*, &c.

A YOUNG

A YOUNG Lady advertises, that she has had the *management* of an *old man* for some time, and that she wishes for a similar situation.

———

THE following curious advertisement we have copied from a provincial paper:—

"Wanted, a person qualified to conduct the performances at Oversley Green Wake, near Alcester, which will be celebrated on Easter Monday, Tuesday, and Wednesday, the 18th, 19th, and 20th of April instant. It is requisite that he should have a complete knowledge of poney and donkey racing; wheelbarrow, boat, bag, cock, and pig racing; archery, single-stick, quoits, cricket, foot-ball, cocking, wrestling, bull and badger baiting, dog fighting, goose fighting, bumble puppy, &c. He must be also competent to decide in dipping, mumbling, jawing, grinning, whistling, jumping, jingling, skinning, smoking, sealing, knitting, bobbing, bowling, throwing, dancing, snuff-taking, singing, pudding-eating, &c.

———

THOMAS Bastard, Esq. educated at Wykeham's School, admitted Fellow of New College, 1588, wrote the following Epigram on his three wives:

Though marriage by most folks be
    reckon'd a curse,
Three wives did I marry for better or
    worse;
The first for her person—the next for her
    purse—
And the third for a warming-pan, doc-
    tress, and nurse.

———

THE GHOST.—The late Dr. Fowler, Bishop of Gloucester, and Justice Powell, had frequent altercations on the subject of ghosts. The Bishop was a zealous defender of their reality—the Justice somewhat

sceptical. The Bishop one day met his friend, and the Justice told him, that since their late conference on the subject he had had an ocular demonstration of the existence of ghosts.—"I rejoice at your conversion (replied the Bishop); give me the circumstances that produced it, with all the particular ocular demonstration you had.'——
"Yes, my Lord:—As I lay last night in my bed, about the twelfth hour, I was awakened by an uncommon noise, and heard something coming up stairs—(Go on)—Alarmed at the noise, I drew my curtain—(proceed)—and saw a faint glimmering light enter my chamber—(of a blue colour, was it not?) —of a pale blue; the light was followed by a tall, meagre, stern figure, who appeared as an old man of 70 years of age, arrayed in a long light-coloured rug gown, bound round with a leathern girdle, his beard thick and grisly, his hair scant and straight, his face of a dark sable hue, on his head a large fur cap, and in his hand a long staff—terror seized my whole frame—I trembled till the bed almost shook, and cold drops hung on every limb; the figure, with a slow and solemn step, stalked nearer and nearer—(Did you not speak to it? There was money hid; a murder committed, without doubt) —My Lord, I did speak to it; I adjured it, by all that is holy, to tell whence it came, and why it thus appeared—(And, in Heaven's name, what was the reply?)—It was accompanied by three strokes of his staff on the floor, so loud that they made the room ring, when, holding up his lanthorn, and holding it close to my eyes, he told me—*he was the watchman*, and came to give me notice that my street door was wide open, and, unless I arose and shut it, I might
    chance

chance to be robbed before morning." The Judge had no sooner concluded than the Bishop disappeared.

———

BRAND, in his history of Shetland, says, that in this year (1640) there were three luxuries introduced into that island; namely, soap, with which some of the Lairds had their shirts washed, pewter spoons, and coarse table-cloths.

———

THE following is probably as good a *punning rebus* as any that female ingenuity has lately produced:— *Quere:* "Why is *Ireland* likely to become one of the richest islands in the universe?—*Answer.* Because her capital is always *Dublin.*"

———

WHEN is a door not a door?— Answer—when it is a *jar*.

Why is Athens like the wick of a tallow candle?—Answer—because it is in the midst of *Greece.*

———

A CORRESPONDENT observes, the events of Miss Farren and Miss Brunton becoming Countesses, will animate the hopes of Misses P. T. S. &c. &c. as virtue like wine should become more valuable the longer it is kept—*should* we say, for we fear that it is not quite so much in the general *taste*. The *Derby* stakes and the *Craven* plate are gone, but there are doubtless many good *matches* yet to be won by our theatrical *fillies*, if they will be managed by prudence, and not prematurely run *out* of the *course.*

———

A SMART Retort.—A purse-proud fellow, who, pluming himself on his property, was rebuking an honest tradesman for not attending to him so much as he expected, saying, "Why fellow! do you know that I rise every morning worth ten

thousand pounds?" "No," answered the man, archly, "I really did not exactly know, before you told me; but, by G—d, that is *all* you are worth."

———

THE Puff Military.—" Militia, &c.—Forty guineas bounty will be given immediately, paid to men and boys, five feet two and upwards, from eighteen to forty-five.

"Now my boys, the door is open to a service congenial to an Englishman's feelings, the old constitutional force of the country, short in its duration, limited in its operation, with ample provision for the wives and families of the married men, and a glorious opportunity for the dashing and aspiring single hero, clothed in his scarlet and fine linen, faring sumptuously every day, to *brush* (run away) with a rich heiress, or get *swished* (married) to some buxom widow, and seal his happiness for ever. Rouse then from your lethargies, shake off the galling yoke, fly from your moping pestilential employment, breathe the fragrant air, and it will not only add a cubit to your stature, but add twenty years to your natural lives!!!"

———

A FOREIGNER says, that *old maids* in England are buried in *crab-tree*, cowards in *trembling* aspin, the honest tar in sturdy *oak*, and bruisers in *box-wood.*

———

AN actor of Manchester, lately performing *Careless*, in the *School for Scandal*, said to *Charles*, in the picture scene, (according to the text)—" What shall we do for a hammer?" A carpenter in the gallery, happening to have one stuck in his apron string, threw it on the stage, saying, "Now, go on, my lad, there's a hammer for you."

F   CLERICAL

CLERICAL ARITHMETIC.——A gentleman has made the following calculation—thirty Welsh curates make one rector, ten rectors one pluralist ; five pluralists one dean ; two deans one bishop.

MR. Caleb Whitefoord was at an entertainment, in which Madeira of a fine flavour was plentifully served during dinner. After dinner a bottle of Cape wine was introduced—so excellent, that the company gave several hints that another bottle would be very gratifying. The hint was not taken: on which Mr. W. said, " Well, if we cannot *double the Cape*, we must return to *Maderia*."

A CERTAIN Quack Doctor being indisposed, sent for a physician, who expressed some surprise at being called in on so trifling an occasion :—" Not so *trifling*, neither (said he) for, by mistake, I have taken some of my own cordial!"

A GERMAN Journalist observes, that the sale of *Divinity* at the last Leispsic book-fair was *dull*, and that books of *Physic* were a mere *drug*.

THE Frenchman who has taken out a patent for *allaying storms*, says, the discovery will be of the utmost importance to many families.

A MODERN Tourist says, " they make as good *Cheshire*-cheese in Ireland at present as in *any other* part of England!"

A COUNTRY gentleman a few days since asked his son, who was at college, what was meant by a *Bachelor of Arts ?*—" One (said the student) who *woos* the Arts, but never weds them!"

THE Constable hoaxed.—The Constable of Wolverhampton, when taking down the names for the late militia ballot, called at the house of an old man, named Thomas Evans, who kept an ass to carry coals from the pit for sale ; and enquiring of his wife, a very deaf old woman, if she had a son, she answered, through mistaking the question, " *Hey ! what do you say ?—There's our Tommy*," the name by which they called the ass. The Constable asked her how old *Tommy* was ? She replied about *twenty* ; the name of *Tommy Evans* was put in the list ; and so it happened that *Tommy* was drawn.—When the Constable went to serve the summons, saying *he had a bit of paper for Tommy*, the old woman said he was in the garden, and shewed the place where he was feeding. The Peace-officer's chagrin, and the merriment of the town at his expence, when the donkey was actually dressed up with the cockades of the recruits, and led through the streets, may be readily conceived.

———

A YORKSHIRE HOAX.—An advertisement lately appearing in one of the London papers for a wife, it was answered, we understand, by an arch wag from the country : and after a short correspondence, the advertiser arrived in Yorkshire, tiptoe on expectation, to meet an angel of sixteen, and a copartnership in a lucrative concern in trade. His surprise, however, may be easily judged, when it turned out that he could find no other angel than the sign of the inn where he put up, (his charming *incognita* being only *in nubibus*) and that a journey of one hundred and sixty miles to the north was the extent of his speculation!

CARAC-

ELEANOR.

CARACTACUS;

A NEW PANTOMIME.

DRURY-LANE, FRIDAY, APRIL 22.

THE story of Caractacus, as narrated in the annals of Tacitus, lib. cap. 33—37, is shortly this: He was one of the Kings of Britain, who distinguished himself so remarkably by his skill, intrepidity, and perseverance, in defending his country against the Romans, that his fame was celebrated not only in the adjacent provinces, but in Italy, and even at Rome. The historian adds, that his name was held in considerable repute. After nine years effectual resistance, he was at last defeated, when fighting at the head of the Silures, or ancient inhabitants of South Wales, and was carried by his conqueror, Ostorius Scapula, together with his brother, wife, and daughter, prisoner to Rome. There he was shewn in triumph to the people; and while his relations seemed to sink under the weight of their misfortunes, Caractacus, still retaining a noble firmness and dignity of character, at the moment when he was exposed in public spectacle, addressed himself to the Emperor Claudius in the following terms :—" Had my moderation been equal to my birth and power, I would rather have come to this city as a friend than as a captive, and in that case you would not have disdained to enter into pacific engagements with the descendant of illustrious ancestors, and the ruler of several nations. My present lot is as humiliating to me as it is proud for you. I was in possession of men, horses, arms, and wealth—and where is the wonder that I should be unwilling to lose them?—because you wish for universal dominion, does

it follow that all should voluntarily become your slaves? Had I surrendered without resistance, neither my fortune nor your glory would have been conspicuous; and oblivion would have followed on my punishment. If you spare me, I shall be an eternal monument of your clemency."—Such was the impression which this address made upon the mind of the Emperor, that he instantly granted his pardon to Caractacus and all his family.

This is the story of Caractacus, as related by Tacitus; but the program of the Pantomime differs materially in the exhibition, though the principle is preserved. The invasion of Great Britain is successful, our patriot-chief is made prisoner, and conducted in chains before the throne of the Roman conqueror.

This ballet, being one of the grandest that ever graced an English stage, reflects the highest honour on D'Egville's taste and genius. It is very interesting throughout; and Miss Bristow's character of Hengo was one of the most attractive and impressive we ever saw.—It was received with great applause.

ELEANOR,

From a Painting by Mr. Clifton Tomson, of Nottingham.

THE pedigree and performances of this celebrated mare will be given in our next Number. At present we shall only cursorily state, that Eleanor was bred by Sir C. Bunbury, got by Whiskey out of Young Giantess, and foaled in 1798. Giantess was bred by Lord Bolingbroke, foaled in 1769, got by Matchem; her dam, Molly Longlegs, by Babraham.

SPORTING INTELLIGENCE.

NORBROOK Races, Oxon, on Wednesday the 6th instant, notwithstanding the unfavourable state of the weather, were numerously attended. We noticed the following distinguished characters in the hunt, on the Downs :—Sirs T. Mostyn, H. Peyton, and E. Lloyd ; —Messrs. Whitmores, Harrison, Drakes, Dorrien, Lloyd, Peyton, Villebois, Pope, Pryce, Rush, Grey, Dolphin, Holloway, Farrel, Lawrell, &c. &c.

Mr. Weller's br. m. beat Mr. Dillon's b. m. a match for 50 guineas.

A Sweepstakes for hunters, rode by members of the hunt, three miles, was won by Mr. Dorrien's bl. h. beating two others.

The Cup given by the hunt for farmers' horses, resident within the limits of the hunt, was won at two heats by Mr. Hitchcock's horse, beating seven others.

A Sweepstakes for hacks, the property of gentlemen of the hunt, one mile heats, was won by Mr. Cope's Fly-by-night, beating Mr. Dorrien's Plenty, at three heats.

THE great main of cocks fought on Thursday and Friday, the 7th and 8th instant, at Wheatley, Oxon, was won by Berkshire as follows:

OXFORDSHIRE.		BERKSHIRE.	
	M. B.		M. B.
Thursday	2 1	Thursday	6 4
Friday	0 0	Friday	0 0

A TROTTING match for 50l. took place this month on the Romney road, between two horses, the property of Mr. —— Longley of Tenterden, and Mr. —— Hodges of Appledore, Kent ; the distance three miles, which was performed in nine minutes and a half, and won by Mr. Hodges.

A RACE between Capt. Emerson and Mr. Hunt's galloway, took place on Tuesday the 12th, at Kingsweston, near Bristol, and was won hollow by Mr. Hunt. The evening's amusement terminated by a well-contested boxing match, of an hour and a half, for a subscription purse of ten guineas.

WE are informed that Lord Darlington's celebrated horse Haphazard, by Sir Peter, one of the best bottomed horses in the kingdom, has been purchased at 1050gs. by a farmer and breeder at Finchley ; who some time ago purchased Eagle, the finest and speediest horse on the turf, at 1000 guineas. They are kept as stud horses to serve the public ; and from the number of visitors they have lately had, promise to remunerate this bold farmer.

MR. Mellish has exchanged from the Prince's regiment, for a company in the 87th regiment.

IN the course of a trial at Buckingham assizes, Mr. Wilson, counsel for the plaintiff, observed to the jury, that if a horse was bought and warranted sound, but which afterwards proved unsound, it was not necessary (as was generally supposed) for the purchaser to return the horse, in order to support an action for recovery of damages for such unsoundness. He need not return the horse at all, and yet might bring

bring the action and recover damages. In this opinion, Judge Grose coincided.

LAST week, a valuable mare belonging to Mr. Podmore, farmer, near Hawarden, Flintshire, was suddenly taken ill, after drinking some water in a pond, and all efforts to swallow any thing proved ineffectual. She swelled remarkably large, and lived two or three days in the most excruciating agony, when she died. On opening her, nothing was found in her bowels that could occasion her death ; but on cutting open the windpipe, a large toad was discovered alive! which she is supposed to have taken into that orifice on drinking the water.

THERE are now living, at Barkley, in the county of Northampton, a horse and its owner, whose ages together amount to 121 years.— This aged animal was bought by the present possessor, June 29, 1769, at a village in Warwickshire, and since that time he has never used any other horse.

MALTON FAIR.—The show of horses of every description was uncommonly numerous, and the attendance of London dealers tolerably great ; but the best horses only found ready purchasers—and even those were bought at least fifteen per cent. under last year's prices ; so the London customers of these gentlemen have a right to a *similar abatement.* Horses of large size, fit for carriages, had the most ready sale.

BOXING.—A severe pugilistic contest took place on Monday, the 18th, at Braybrook, Hants, between Holden, better known by the name of the *Country Diamond,* and George Sheen, groom to Cap-

tain Strathmore, of Colney, Hants, for 100gs. - Holden is a regular teacher of boxing, and has won several battles ; and this contest originated in a dispute between the combatants. Sheen, although inferior to his adversary in skill, went in, rallied, and never left his man until he was hit down. Holden, on the contrary, kept his distance, and fought shy ; but he grew weak after fighting forty minutes ; and at this stage of the battle the groom was hideously disfigured, but he never exhibited any symptoms of weakness ; and by his determined mode of fighting he won the battle in two minutes less than an hour. He never hit Holden down during the first forty minutes, but often closed, and threw him heavy falls. There were about two thousand spectators ; and a liberal subscription-purse was given to the loser.

A GENTLEMAN of fortune, who, perhaps, sports as much money as any other on the turf, has booked bets on Gregson against Gully, to the amount of 5000l. The combat will take place, as is supposed, in Worcestershire, the beginning of May, play or pay. The pugilists have been in steady training upwards of two months.

PIGEON SHOOTING.—A match at single birds was decided lately, on Hounslow Heath, for twenty guineas, between Messrs. Holliday and King, the keeper. The parties killed six successive birds, and each missed the seventh. Holliday missed his ninth bird, which King killed, and won the match. The sportsmen next shot at sparrows, for ten guineas, which match was also won by Mr. King, who killed four from six.

A PIGEON match took place on Thursday,

Thursday, the 14th instant, at Blackheath, between Captain Johnson, of Greenwich, and a Mr. Kingston, by turning out at once two birds from a basket, and shooting at them with a double-barrelled gun; each was allowed twelve birds. The Captain killed his first two, and one each time till the sixth fire, when he again killed both birds, which gave him eight in the whole. Mr. Kingston missed his two first birds, one in the second, killed both in the third and fourth fires, one in the fifth, and one in the sixth, which gave him seven. The match was for ten guineas aside, and the Captain was declared the winner.

It is not with us to decry any species of sporting; at the same time men of honour should not be wholly indifferent from whence, and *how*, the objects of their sport are obtained; for at the last Old Bailey Sessions the following trial took place:—Jonathan Neale and Richard Norris were indicted for stealing five dozen and four pigeons, the property of W. Pope, Esq. The prosecutor, Mr. Pope, was a gentleman residing at Hillingdon, near Uxbridge; and on the morning of the 18th of March, he found that his dove-cote had been broken open, and all his pigeons stolen. It occurred to him, that as there were continual matches of pigeon-shooting at the Old Hats, a public-house on the Uxbridge road, it was probable the thieves had sold some of the pigeons at that house. He accordingly went and enquired of Mr. Fox, the landlord, if he had bought any pigeons that day? Fox immediately said that he had, and shewed him the pigeons, telling him, that he had bought them that morning of a man of the name of

Neale, and by his directions a constable went in pursuit of them, and both Neale and Norris were apprehended. But the principal evidence against the prisoners was an accomplice of the name of W. Griffin, who stated, that the two prisoners and himself, on the night of the 17th of March, went to the dove-cote of Mr. Pope, and got into it by means of a ladder which they found in the orchard, and having stopped the holes with straw to prevent the flight of the pigeons, they stripped the house. The Jury found them both Guilty.

Rowing-match against Time.—On Monday, the 18th, fourteen persons (inexperienced rowers) undertook for a wager to row a six-oared boat from Boston to Lincoln, and back, a distance of seventy-two miles, in eighteen hours, which they performed two hours and three quarters within the given time.—Much money was sported on the occasion.

William Elvey has been committed to St. Dunstan's gaol, Canterbury, charged on suspicion of having, in the night of the 17th, or early on the morning of the 18th instant, broken into the stable of Mr. James Fassell, of Wye, and damaged and disfigured five of his waggon horses therein, by cutting off the hair from their manes and tails, and stealing the same.

Lesson to Poachers and Buyers of Game.—John Chapman and W. Fuller, executed at Norwich, are melancholy victims to an offence arising out of a breach of the game laws. If any man who suffers under the just judgments of English jurisprudence may be considered pitiable, these unhappy men may be said truly to have merited commiseration,

miseration. They were poachers, and in an encounter with Lord Cholmondeley's watchers, they fired upon and wounded William Bussey, the principal keeper. They were convicted under Lord Ellenborough's Act, and condemned to die. After their sentence, they conducted themselves in the most exemplary manner, and considerable efforts were made to obtain their reprieve, but without success.—We cannot avail ourselves of a more awful opportunity to impress upon the minds of the purchasers of game the miserable consequences to which they seduce their instruments, than the present. There is in the mind of man an impulse which prompts him to the pursuit of wild nature; it is one of the earliest and strongest passions. How cruel, then, is it to add the stimulus of gain to this natural temptation. The consequences of poaching are almost uniformly—disgust to honest industry—habits of intoxication and vice—disregard of the laws, arising out of this first violation—fowl-stealing, next general robbery, and, as in the above instance, not unfrequently a contemplation of murder. The cause and the effects are inseparable; and we shall rejoice if the lamentable end of these wretched men should operate as a warning to the sellers and buyers of game. It ought also to lead country gentlemen to reflect, that a too rigid enforcement of the game laws contributes, in no small degree, to the commission of this offence.

A FOOT-RACE of 100 yards, for 50 guineas, was run on Monday the 18th, in St. James's Park, between Mr. James, the Piccadilly pedestrian, and Mr. Foxall, of Carnaby Market. The match had been for some time in agitation, and there were more bets depending on the event, than is usual on such occasions. At starting, Mr. James took the lead, but the race was so well contested, that it was won only by half a yard, by Mr. Foxall. The winner weighs 16 stone, and the loser eight pounds more.

EXTRAORDINARY Walking.—It has been stated that a Mr. Paul had matched himself for 100 guineas on the first event, and 50 guineas on the second, to go from Knightsbridge to a spot near Windsor, in two hours and a half, a distance of something more than 20 miles, and to return to Knightsbridge in three hours (within twelve hours). He started at eight o'clock on Wednesday morning the 20th, and was nine miles within the first hour, and he had arrived within a mile and a half of Slough at the expiration of the second hour.—He had then two miles and three quarters to do in the other half hour, which he walked with ease. After lying on a straw bed between blankets four hours, he started on the next match, to return in three hours, but the rain fell in torrents, and he went seven miles in the first hour with an umbrella. He would in fair weather doubtless have won both matches, but on his arrival on the second, at Hounslow Heath, with wind and weather against him, he prudently resigned, but won 50 guineas by his day's fatigue.

Mr. Podgers, who engaged to walk 400 miles in eight successive days, finished his task on Tuesday the 15th inst. He started at Basingstoke; and from Hampshire walked into the counties of Wilts, Gloucester, Somerset, Sussex, and Kent, finishing at Maidstone. He

weight

weighs 14 stone, walked twelve hours each day, and slept eight. He did not appear to be in the least fatigued, at any period of his journey. He had himself betted 200 guineas on the performance.

Mr. Chapman, on Friday the 15th, concluded his pedestrian feat, of one mile an hour for 100 successive hours, near Canterbury, with great ease. Some of the latter miles he walked in thirteen minutes and a half and fourteen minutes.

During the last month, a man who is 48 years of age, and weighs near 16 stone, undertook for a wager of 20 guineas, to run 400 yards, while tied in a five bushel sack, in six minutes, in Windsor Park. He started about seven o'clock, in the Long Walk: he performed his undertaking in three minutes and forty-nine seconds, to the astonishment of several hundred spectators, who were assembled on the occasion.

The 31st ult. a walking match against time was made between Mr. John Watkins and Mr. Benjamin Brookman, both butchers, of Leadenhall Market. Mr. Brookman betted Mr. W. twenty guineas that his brother-in-law walked fifty miles in eleven hours, at one start. The pedestrian accordingly started at six o'clock in the morning, at the three-mile stone on the Lee-Bridge road, to go to the fifth mile stone and turn, amongst some thousands of spectators. He went the first six miles in one hour and one minute, and kept on till he had performed upwards of twenty-one miles in four hours and ten seconds, when a severe pain coming on in his right side, he dropped down apparently dead; upon which

his friend relinquished the wager. Considerable sums were lost on the occasion, six to four being freely betted on the performance.

About a week since, a Nobleman's gamekeeper shot a hare, which on taking up he found to be very big with young, he therefore opened her with care, and drew forth two living leverets, which, on being wiped dry, skipped about the dead animal, and actually sucked her as long as warmth would admit the flow of milk, one of them died soon afterwards; but the other, we believe, is in a fair way of being reared.

On Wednesday morning, the 20th, died, in the 42d year of his age, Benjamin Burton, Esq. of Walcot, near Stamford. Some months ago, Mr. Burton fractured his scull by a fall from his horse whilst hunting: he had, however, nearly recovered from a most painfull illness, the consequence of the accident, when, venturing too ardently in pursuit of his favourite amusement, he brought on a brain fever, which terminated his life in a few days, to the infinite regret of every body who knew him.

A fine young lioness was this month landed at the Tower, as a present to his Majesty, by the Hon. Captain Paget.

The Burton Hunt Races took place the 5th instant, under the auspices of the Noble Lord of Burton, and the Stewards, Charles Chaplin, Esq. in the absence of Mr. Kent, Conningsby Sibthorpe, Esq. The weather was most unfavourable for the morning sports; but on the second day of the race, a most elegant ball and supper was given by the gentlemen of the Hunt,

Hunt, and attended by all the beauty and fashion of Lincoln and the neighbourhood. A numerous party from Burton graced the rooms at an early hour, when the ball was opened by Lady Monson and Mr Charles Chaplin, to the tune of *The Burton Hunt*. Her Ladyship's dress was of the most magnificent kind, but nothing could equal the bewitching affability of her manners, or the beauty of her person. About two o'clock the company partook of a supper, which did high credit to the managers; after which the dancing recommenced, and continued till near seven o'clock, when all retired, gratified with their evening's entertainment. — On Wednesday last, a most splendid dinner was given by Lord Monson, to the Mayor, Corporation, and Sheriffs of Lincoln. Burton presented that most finished scene of magnificent hospitality, for which its noble possessors have been from one generation to another renowned—all was cordiality and satisfaction— and all united in admiration of that elegant mansion which has lately undergone, and is still undergoing, such judicious and tasteful improvements.

An Old Sportsman.—On the 26th of March died, in his 63d year, at the Black Jack Tavern, in Clare-Market, London. Mr. James Featchum, well known on the turf, and much respected as a very worthy, well-disposed, and inoffensive sportsman.—He was a constant attendant at the meetings at Newmarket, Epsom, York, &c. for upwards of 40 years. Dying without a will, almost suddenly, his property, which is very considerable, will be divided between his three surviving brothers.

Mr. Mellish has sold Weaver for 1000gs. to Mr. Haworth.

At Newmarket Craven Meeting, Lord Lowther purchased the two favourite horses, Brainworm, by Buzzard; and Trafalgar, by Gohanna.

The Annual Easter Plate was run for on Tuesday the 19th, on Barham Downs, and won with ease by Mr. Thomas Cramp's b. h. Driver, beating Mr. John Palmer's b. m. Molly.

The following Match was made a few days ago, to be run on Monday, May 23, in the next York Spring Meeting. — Mr. Wentworth's Centurion, 8st. 4lb. agst Mr. Brandling's Smasher, 7st. 12lb. four miles, 200gs.

The following three-year old colts and fillies, got by Sir Peter Teazle, are named to run in the present year:

Duke of Hamilton's Petronius, and Peter Little.
Duke of Grafton's Vandyke.
Lord Fitzwilliam's Charcoal, and colt, out of Evelina.
Lord Stanley's Jacobus.
Lord Grosvenor's Chester; filly, out of Ibis; and filly out of Popinjay's dam.
Lord Foley's Petrowitz.
Sir F. Standish's filly, out of Eagle's dam; and filly, out of Storace.
Major Wilson's colt, out of Brown Charlotte.
Mr. Hewett's Teazle Evitch.
Mr. Sitwell's Clinker.
Mr. Bettison's filly, dam by Alfred.
Mr. Lockley's filly, out of Queen Charlotte.
Mr. Clifton's Poulton, (late Alexander the First.)
Mr. R. Benson's Dimple.

G   Mr.

Mr. M. Benson's filly, dam by Sweetbriar.

THE following Match was made at Catterick Races, in Easter Week; to be run on the Saturday before the York August Meeting next:—Mr. W. Hutchinson's Silvio, by St. George, against Mr. J. Acred's Wansford, by Stamford, 8st. each, two miles, 200gs, h. ft.

A SINGULAR instance of canine sagacity occurred a few days since in the Thames, below Blackwall:—Mr. Turnbull, the master of a coasting trader, kept a Newfoundland dog on board. Whenever the vessel dropped anchor in the river the dog swam to shore, and generally swam on board again the same evening. Having recently attempted to get to the ship in his usual way, the tide drifted him with so much velocity that he could not reach the vessel: he was consequently forced to re-land, and to the astonishment of all who witnessed the sagacity of the animal, he went near half a mile from the spot where he had first started, up the bank, and by swimming across the stream, made an angle, which enabled him to gain the ship. The master of the dog does not say the animal is a mathematician, but he asserts, with reference to this instance of sagacity, that no Waterman on the River could have reached the ship with more judgment.

METHOD of discovering Canine Madness.—When a person has been bitten by a dog, apprehended to be mad, it commonly happens that the dog is killed before any one is assured of his condition. M. Pettitt, an eminent surgeon, of France, has discovered an expedient for putting an end to this uneasiness: He rubs the throat, teeth, and gums, of the dead dog with a piece of meat that has been dressed (taking care that there has been no blood to stain it), and then offers it to a living dog; if he refuses it with crying and howling, the dead dog was certainly mad; but, if it is well received, and eaten, there is nothing to fear.

A CORRESPONDENT complains of the obstacles thrown in the way of destroying rabbits by the new laws respecting game licences. He says, where the soil is dry and light, if these animals are suffered to abound, the mischief they do is incalculable, not only by devouring corn, turnips, clover, &c. but still more, by undermining and thereby destroying the fences, and eating down the young quick and newly-planted trees of every description; and it is well known that such is the prolific nature of the animal,* it is only by continual attention, and no inconsiderable degree of labour, that they can be prevented from swarming where they once gain a footing. Now even losing sight for a moment of the injustice of compelling a farmer to pay for a licence to kill vermin which is running his farm, it is impossible that his individual exertions, without the aid of his labourers, can subdue this enemy; from which it results that he must either take out licences for his whole household, or quietly submit to see his crop devoured and his fences destroyed.

* Naturalists have calculated that a single pair may, in four years, increase to the astonishing number of 1,274,340.

POETRY.

POETRY.

THE HIGH COURT OF DIANA.

EPILOGUE

TO THE NEW COMEDY OF
THE WORLD.

THE scene is clos'd—and now a pause
    ensues
Before your verdict saves or damns the
    muse ;
An awful pause ! for which of you can
    hear
That verdict giv'n, and not turn pale
    with fear ?
When from yon roof the cloth of green
    shall fall,
Which from your sight divides us, surely
    all
Must feel their brows with Terror's dews
    impearl'd,
To see the curtain clos'd upon the *World !*
Yes, ladies, yes, my blood runs cold to
    say,
Perhaps, some few short moments roll'd
    away,
Perhaps those words, those dreadful
    words may rend
Your ears and ours—*The World is at an
    end !*
How shall I ward its fate? Oh, deign to
    hear,
Ye lovely nymphs ! my suit with fav'-
    ring ear ;
For from your grateful breasts be censure
    hurl'd,
'Twould shock us all to hear you *damn
    the World*—
The *World,* th' adoring *World,* which joys
    to view
Its brightest gems and sweetest flow'rs in
    You.
Ye thrifty fathers, who would gladly shun
The dread expences of a travelling son,
Now clear your brows, and be your
    purses furl'd,
Here, for six shillings, all *may see the
    World !*

And you, ye dashing dames ! whose rul-
    ing passion
Is to collect at routs the mob of fashion,
And see all London in your chambers
    cramm'd,
Crush'd, crowded, squeez'd, squash'd,
    jolted, jostled, jamm'd,
When beau to belle, and belle to beau
    opposes,
The war of elbows, and the shock of
    noses ;
Where none can tell (so close their
    union's grown)
Which is his neighbour's nob, or which
    his own,
Oh ! if a crowd's your wish, to Drury-
    lane
Drive—nightly drive—nor fear to drive
    in vain
While our play lives ; behold your pro-
    per sphere !
For rest assur'd, you'll say, the *World* is
    here.
You all, no doubt, have often sought to
    view,
In Fancy's glass, what the *World* thinks
    of *you ;*
But now, we'll know, from Gallery,
    Boxes, Pit,
Not what it thinks of you, but what *you*
    think of it.
If o'er your bosoms self-love holds its
    sway,
You'll surely shew some mercy to this
    play ;
Repressing hiss and hoot, and cough and
    groan,
For know this Drama's fate involves your
    own.
Then while applause our anxious doubts
    dispels,
Applaud ye beaus! make them applaud,
    ye belles !
For if with frowning faces now we sever,
We all to-night shall *leave the World for
    ever !*

SONG

SONG,

SUNG BY MR. MUNDEN, IN
'TRAVELLERS IN SWISSERLAND.'

EV'RY night (a little mellow)
  Dan was thought a merry fellow;
And so frolicsome they found me,
All the lasses flock'd around me,
    Jesting, joking,
    Gig provoking,
  While the Vicar's red nose smoking!

Then our liqu'rish lips would wag on
Cockles hot! or *blue snap-dragon!*
And of this when we'd enough,
Up we jump'd to *blindman's buff!*
That's the pastime, sure and certain,
-For a kiss behind the curtain;
    " Fie upon you, don't do so!
      " Sure as death
      " You'll stop my breath!
    " Wicked creature, let me go."—
Thus our minutes pass'd away,
Sweetly as the flow'rs in May.

Then sometimes in frosty weather,
Squatting on the floor together,
Hands in busy motion gliding,
Where the funny *slipper's* sliding,
Scarce an inch of candle's burning,
While the maids the game are learning;
And, lest sland'rous tongues should
      wrong us,
Master making one among us:
    " Have you caught it, Daniel?"—
      No, Sir!
    " Lasses, sit a little closer;
      " Round it goes,
      " Smooth your clothes;
    " Kitty, don't turn in your toes!"
Thus our minutes pass'd away,
Sweetly as the flow'rs in May!

BULL-BAITING.

SEE yonder crowd assembled in the
    field,
With looks ferocious, and with hearts
    well-steel'd:
What boist'rous shouts, what blasphe-
    mies obscene,
What eager movements, urg'd with
    threat'ning mien,
Present the spectacle, of human kind
Devoid of feeling, destitute of mind;
With ev'ry dreadful passion rous'd to
    flame,
And sense of justice lost, and sense of
    shame.

What mighty project, cent'ring in the
    place,
Attracts the village rabble, vile and base,
Drains from the plough, the flail, the
    shop, the stall,
The idle and the drunken, one and all?
What but the pleasure cruelly to treat
A noble beast, the sire of milk and meat!
Bound by the treach'rous cowards to the
    stake,
His goaded sides with indignation shake.
The strong-mouth'd dogs let loose (of
    fiercest sort,
Train'd by their masters to the barb'rous
    sport)
Around the trammell'd bull they teasing
    ply,
Provoke his rage, and watch his vengeful
    eye.
Yet oft his sinewy neck and pointed horn
Throw high his puny enemies, in scorn;
Thence, sprawling on the ground, they
    mangled lie,
Or, dash'd to-pieces, in an instant die.

Gall'd by his bonds, and worried out, at
    length
The fruitless toil exhausts his mighty
    strength;
Beset with numbers, friendless and for-
    lorn,
His nostril pinion'd, and his dewlap
    torn,
He sinks confounded, groaning deep and
    loud,
While shouts of hellish joy inspire the
    crowd.

These are exploits design'd to keep alive
Our rustic mirth, and make the country
    thrive!
Sanction'd by law, these dastard scenes
    shall breed
A harden'd race, prepar'd for daring deeds
'Tis granted such amusements may im-
    part
A love of *cruelty*, a *flinty heart*;
May make men hate their work, and
    join the roar
Of drunken squabblers at the ale-house
    door.
The Army and the Navy hence may
    draw
Large levies of tough boobies, tough and
    raw;
These may stand shooting at, though fit-
    ter far
For mutiny and plunder, than for war;
They may be marshall'd, but with whip
    and goad,
As stubborn asses trudge a sandy road.

THE
SPORTING MAGAZINE
OR,
MONTHLY CALENDAR
OF THE
TRANSACTIONS
OF
THE TURF, THE CHASE,
And every other Diversion interesting to
THE MAN OF-PLEASURE, ENTERPRISE, AND SPIRIT.

MAY, 1808.

CONTAINING

Memoirs of the Life of G. Stubbs, Esq. the celebrated Painter of Horses .... *Page* 55
Races appointed in 1808..... 57
Disputes between Gentlemen, on Points of Honour, &c. &c. 57
York Spring Meeting 59
The Derby and Oaks' Stakes at Epsom 60
The Amusements of Paris described.. 61
  Literary Booths 61
  Jewellers' Shops 62
  Lotteries, &c. 63
  The Pont Neuf 64
  The Place de Greve 64
The Philosophical Sportsman, No. VI. 65
Sporting Anecdotes of Colonel John Mordaunt..................... 67
Pedigree and Performances of Eleanor 71
Grand Pugilism 73
Court Martial on Richard Corrall, of the 15th Light Dragoons 79
Harmonious Change-Ringing 81
Wild Cats—a Caution to Farmers.... 82
Sporting Subjects in the Exhibition of the Royal Academy, 1808 83
Colonel Thornton and his Attornies.. 84
Alphabetical List of Stallions to Cover in 1808 85
May in London 86
Fashionable Gaming Table 87

Feast of Wit.......... .... *Page* 88
  Sailor's Journey in a Stage-coach .. 88
  Queer Pun.................. 89
  On a late Senatorial Sermon 90
  Epitaph on John Bully 90
  Lineal Descent.................. 90
  The Dilemma 90
  The Retort Courteous............ 91
  Impromptu 91
  Singular Advertisement 91
Court Martial on Assistant-Surgeon Talbot, of the 60th Regiment. ... 92
The Shepherd's Dog 93
Match against Time 93
Mr. Samuel Burder 93
Sporting Intelligence 94
  Cocking 95
  Certificates for Shooting 96
  Cruelty to Horses 97
  Sports of Plowden Fair 98

POETRY.

Lines to the Memory of my Spaniel, Dash 99
The Rustic's Creed 99
Quintetto, from the Farce of Who Wins? or, the Widow's Choice 100
Song from the same 100
Epigram....................... 100
Racing Calendar 13

Embellished with—I. An exquisite Engraving of the Horse and the Lion, from a Painting by Stubbs.—II. The Shepherd's Dog, an Engraving.

LONDON:
PRINTED FOR THE PROPRIETORS,
By J. Pittman, Warwick Square;
AND SOLD BY J. WHEBLE, 18, WARWICK-SQUARE; C. CHAPPLE, 66, PALL-MALL; J. BOOTH, DUKE-STREET, PORTLAND-PLACE; JOHN HILTON, NEWMARKET; AND BY ALL THE BOOKSELLERS IN TOWN AND COUNTRY.

TO CORRESPONDENTS.

THE Communication from Scotland relative to the new-invented Patent Gun-Lock, shall be attended to next month.

A Letter and Hand-bill previously received from Edinburgh, on the Construction of Manton's New Patent, shall likewise have consideration at the same time.

Irish Stallions—in our next.

W. W.'s favours are some of them used—the rest are deferred.

J. M. L.'s Poetry, and numerous other Communications, shall have due attention in next Number.

Gentlemen disposed to favour the Publisher of this Magazine with Original Paintings of Sporting Subjects, are assured that the utmost care shall be taken of them, and of their being safely returned. The Engravings thus taken, will be executed by the most approved Artists, and in the first style of excellence.

THE ·

SPORTING MAGAZINE;

FOR MAY, 1808.

MEMOIRS

OF

GEORGE STUBBS, ESQ.

THE CELEBRATED PAINTER OF HORSES.

One of whose fine enamel Pictures (the HORSE *and* LION) *we have been permitted to copy, and here respectfully present to our Readers.*

MR. STUBBS, the subject of these memoirs, was born at Liverpool very early in the last century. His father was a currier and leather-cutter in that town, of extensive business and great respectability. Young George was intended to succeed to his father's trade, but being rather of a delicate constitution, he was excused from the manufacturing part of the business, and principally employed as a clerk to the concern, for which, it will appear, George had no great inclination.

Stubbs, from his childhood, had evinced a taste for the imitative arts, and such was his predilection for them, that it soon overturned every other consideration, though it might tend ultimately to the highest fortune. His deep study of nature, and his fine pencil, together with his exquisite correctness, enabled him, before he had acquired the age of fifteen, to produce many high-finished performances, and to become the admiration of all the ingenious men in that part of the country. His

father, however, was his greatest enemy in these pursuits, and it was sometimes the case that correction of a very unpleasant nature took place, when the elder Stubbs found his books neglected, for what he would call an idle and unprofitable employment; but regardless of his father's leather-cutting attachments, Mr. G. Stubbs followed the bent of his genius, and would often steal from the compting-house to the close, to delineate the actions of a favourite horse, even at times when he knew that a discovery would provoke the whip, or the severity of parental indignation.

Every effort was now used to dissuade Stubbs from the use of the pencil, but in vain. The same cause (says the philosopher) will still produce the same effect. Our painter was determined, at all hazards, to venture for the wreath of fame, and to encounter every obstacle in his way, although he might lose for ever the friendship of his too rigid father. At length, by the persuasion of some who knew his merit, the elder Stubbs was prevailed on to give his son a sum of money, and to let him quit the ledger for the quiet pursuit of his more favourite study of animal nature. His first effort was the model of a horse, which he presented to the Society for the Encouragement of Arts in the town of his nativity. It so far met the appro-

bation

bation of the members, that they awarded Stubbs the gold medal, with a letter of compliment, and an order was given to preserve this effort of youthful genius among their best specimens, which was accordingly obeyed; and it is at this moment to be seen, with a modest eulogium on the base.

The fame of young Stubbs became the general talk of polished society, and several gentlemen of the highest respectability became his patrons, particularly the Earl of Grosvenor, who, with others, mingled purses, and sent the young artist to Italy, an arrangement the most congenial with his wishes, as he could there study, without interruption, Nature, and the productions of the greatest masters of the approved schools. Mr. Stubbs was now indefatigable in his endeavour to obtain the end for which he had left his native country; he frequently obtained prize medals, and his works were always admired and justly applauded. Having remained the time necessary for his improvement, Stubbs embarked for England, and during his passage he became acquainted with a gentleman, a native of Africa, whose taste and pursuits in life were similar to his own. This gentlemen had been to Rome, and was returning to his family: he was liberally educated, and spoke the English language with accuracy. His information made him a delightful companion to Stubbs, who had often expressed how much it would add to his gratification if he could but behold the lion in its wild state, or any other wild beast. —His friend, on one occasion, gave him an invitation to the paternal mansion he was about to visit. The offer was accepted with pleasure, and Stubbs landed with his friend at the fortress of Ceuta. They had not been on shore many days, when a circumstance occurred most favourable to the wishes of our painter. The town where his friend resided was surrounded by a lofty wall and a moat. Nearly level with the wall a capacious platform extended, on which the inhabitants occasionally refreshed themselves with the breeze after sun-set. One evening, while Stubbs and his friend were viewing the delightful scenery, and a thousand beautiful objects, from this elevation, which the brilliancy of the moon rendered more interesting, a lion was observed at some distance directing his way, with a slow pace, towards a white Barbary horse, which appeared grazing not more than two hundred yards distant from the moat. Mr. Stubbs was reminded of the gratification he had so often wished for. The orb of night was perfectly clear, and the horison serene. The lion did not make towards the horse by a regular approach, but performed many curvatures, still drawing nearer towards the devoted animal, till the lion, by the shelter of a rocky situation, came suddenly upon his prey. The affrighted barb beheld his enemy, and, as if conscious of his fate, threw himself into an attitude highly interesting to the painter *(vide plate)*. The noble creature then appeared fascinated, and the lion, finding him within his power, sprang in a moment, like a cat, on the back of the defenceless horse, threw him down, and instantly tore out his bowels.

This was a grand study for our artist, and he has since made the most of it, having favoured his country with three fine pictures in enamel, perfectly descriptive of what he beheld. The first is the barb,

barb, with the distant appearance of the lion; the second, the horse affrighted at the lion's appearance from the rock; the third is the lion seizing his prey: all of which are generally admired.

Mr. Stubbs, on his return to England, became exceedingly attentive to his profession, and was soon patronised by the nobility and gentry. His Grace the Duke of Richmond delighted much in his productions. Gentlemen of the turf were eager to possess a picture by Stubbs, and the sums he acquired are almost beyond probability. His four shooting pictures, in the possession of General Stibbert, of Mount Bevis, were sufficient to establish his reputation as a great painter, had Stubbs never covered another piece of canvas.

To recount all his beautiful productions, would outstep the limits of this memoir; indeed they are so well known in those circles where they are likely to flourish, that further description is unnecessary. Mr. Stubbs has left behind him enough to prove him an honour to the art in which he delighted.

He was a liberal and faithful friend, a good companion, and left the world respected by all who had the pleasure of his society. Paul Sandby, Esq. his beloved friend, followed him to the grave, and saw the end of one who was so dear to the lovers of the turf, the admirers of rural sports, and the sons of Apelles.

Mr. Stubbs has left many pictures, which have become classical in the great schools of Europe.—His anatomy of the horse is particuly preferred in the foreign Seminaries; and he has left this lesson to posterity, that whenever Providence bestows the gift of genius,

opposition to its operations is futile and ridiculous, for, like the great luminary of nature, though clouded during a short period, it will repel all obscurity, and shine out with redoubled lustre.

T. N.

RACES APPOINTED IN 1808.

EPSOM............... *June* 1
  Guildford 7
Bogside, (North Britain)...... 7
Manchester 8
Maddington 8
Newton 15
Newcastle 20
Ascot-Heath 21
Tenbury 22
Cardiff, Glamorganshire 29
Bibury...............*July* 4
Newmarket.................11
Canterbury 19
Exeter 26
Swansea ....*Aug.* 9
Warwick, ...*Sept.* 6
Kingscote..................20
Lincoln 21
Newmarket First October Meeting .... *Oct* 3
...... Second October Meeting 17
...... Houghton Meeting 31

DISPUTES
BETWEEN GENTLEMEN,

On Points of Honour, &c. &c. &c.

The King *v.* Richard Watson.

IT will be recollected, by our readers, that the defendant, in this case, had been dismissed from his Majesty's service, in which he held the rank of Lieutenant-Colonel, by the sentence of a court-martial,

martial, of which the prosecutor, General Gwynne, was the President.

The defendant was charged with having written some anonymous letters to the General, with an intent to provoke him to fight, and with having personally insulted him in public, in consequence of that dismissal, on which occasion he was found *guilty*.

With the sentence which the law may inflict we have no business, but we shall presume to offer some remarks on the nature and spirit of such violations of the peace.

Agreeably to this case, as published, General Gwynne merely acted as the president or organ of a court martial, convened for the immediate purpose of investigating the alledged misconduct of the defendant, and for the ultimate purpose of preserving the discipline of the British army. If, under these circumstances, it were possible for the accused person, on conviction, to challenge the primary organ of that military commission, for an act of particular malice, which was *bonâ fide* the result of an unanimous and concurring opinion in that court; then we aver, that no gentleman could be found, sufficiently willing to hazard his public reputation, or his private peace, upon the issue of a question of such a nature. We can make great allowance for personal irritation, when the honour of an officer is accused on slight grounds, but when the nation understands, from the common bearing of the case, that the accused has been guilty of misdemeanors, in a situation where the responsibility of the offender comprehends the safety and dignity of the state in a greater or lesser degree; and, when the *fiat* of the sovereign puts the validity of the verdict beyond all question; the nation will expect a silent and decent acquiescence on the part of the criminated individual; and every attempt that he may eventually make, with a view to cast an odium on that tribunal of honour, before whom his infirmities or his guilt may have been investigated, will but operate to plunge him deeper in that species of popular discredit which he would appear as anxiously wishing to avoid.

The preservation of manners in civil life, forms the amount of social security and happiness; and, in pursuance of this conviction, all well-regulated and thinking persons agree in repelling rude and irregular people from a seat in their selected circles of friendship; being conscious that the practice of rudeness would endanger the harmony of the establishment; and when the evidence of such rudeness has been duly exhibited, there are few who would be hardy enough to plead for the re-admission of such an offender. As this position is undeniably true in regard to the usual forms of private life, how much more forcibly does it apply to situations of military trust, where the influence of an improper example becomes widely pernicious, and where the supposition of dishonour in an officer must be held above the sphere of a soldier's imagination.

The retrospective glances at General Gwynne, on his ascribed conduct, while on duty in America, could not come with a good grace from a person under Colonel Watson's circumstances. It doth not appear that they are supported by any correspondent authorities: and, what renders them at once suspicious and odious is, that they were

were urged and conveyed under an anonymous mark !—What character would be safe for a single day if it were possible for an anonymous writer to circulate his calumnies with effect, under such a villainous and dastardly mode of security? The slanderer, like the murderer, shuns the light, as long as possible; he aims his deadly blows at the victim of his antipathy, from the shades and fastnesses of concealment, and values himself on his diabolical address, in wounding innocence without danger or exposure. The manifestation of such a base spirit, in an ordinary member of society, is sufficient to insure him general detestation; but when it is called into action by a British officer, the emotions of the brave and the generous become too indignant for language to express: The iniquity is doubled by the meanness which accompanies its promulgation, and all consequent pity is withheld from the perpetrator in his disgrace, because his brother soldiers are not more disgusted with his want of spirit, than his want of integrity and moral honour.

In quitting a subject on which there is no pleasure to dwell, we merely add the sentence of the Court of King's Bench on Colonel Watson, passed the 23d instant, which was, that of one year's imprisonment in the King's Bench prison, and to enter into a recognisance in 200l. to keep the peace for two years.—Mr. Justice Grose, who passed sentence, said, that society would be in a lamentable state, if every Officer who gave his opinion upon a Court-Martial was compelled to answer for the same at the point of the sword.

W.

YORK SPRING MEETING.

THE following is an abridged account of the sport at York Spring Meeting : the details will appear in our next month's Racing Calendar.

Monday, May 23.

Sweepstakes of 20gs. each, for all ages, two miles, seven subscribers, was won by Mr. Duncombe's br. f. Ceres, beating Lord Strathmore's br. h. Cassio, and Mr. Wentworth's b. f. Margaret.— Even betting between Cassio and Margaret, and 8 to 1 against Ceres. Won by a neck, and run in four minutes two seconds.

Mr. Goulburn's gr. h. Grimaldi, beat Mr. Benson's gr. h. Atlas, 500gs. h. ft.—Six to 4 on Grimaldi; won easy.

Mr. Brandling's br. h. Smasher, beat Mr. Wentworth's b. h. Centurion, 200gs. h. ft.—Six and 7 to 4 on Smasher : won easy.

Tuesday, May 24.

Sweepstakes of 20gs. each, for three-yr old colts and fillies, last mile and three quarters, ten subscribers, was won by Mr. Garforth's ch. c. by Hyacinthus, beating Mr. Garforth's b. c. by Hambletonian, the Duke of Leeds's ch. c. by Pandolpho, Mr. Hewett's b. colts St. George and Stilton, Sir E. Smith's gr. c. by St. George, Sir T. Gascoigne's ch. c. by Hambletonian, and Lord Strathmore's b. c. by Hambletonian : 22 to 10 agst the winner, who won very easy, running the distance in three minutes and 35 seconds.

Sweepstakes of 20gs. each, for three-year old fillies, last mile and half, was won by Mr. W. Fletcher's bay, Miss Staveley, beating Mr. W. Sawdon's br. by Warter, Mr. F. Watt's bay, by Stamford, and

and Mr. Duncombe's ch. Laurel Leaf: 7 to 4 on Miss Staveley; won very easy, in three minutes and seven seconds.

Sweepstakes of 30gs. each, h. ft. for two-year old colts and fillies, two-yr olds' course, six subscribers, was won by the Duke of Hamilton's ch. c. Middlethorpe, beating Mr. Dinsdale's b. f. Fair Candidate, Mr. Garforth's b. c. by Hambletonian, and Col. Childers's ch. c. by Waxy. Six to 4 on the Waxy colt, and 2 to 1 against the winner, who won it easy; run in one minute and twenty seconds.

The Oatlands' Stakes of 30gs. each, h. ft. for horses, &c. the last mile and half, eight subscribers, was won cleverly by Lord Darlington's b. c. by Archduke, beating Sir M. M. Sykes's b. f. Harriet, Lord Scarbrough's br. c. Hospodar, and his br. c. by Sir Solomon, Lord Darlington's br. c. brother to Expectation, Mr. Wentworth's gr. f. Irene, and Sir J. Lawson's b. c. Presentation. Six to 4 that the winner or the brother to Expectation won.—Run in three minutes and one second.

Wednesday, May 25.

The Stand Plate of 50l. for all ages, four miles, was won by Ld Strathmore's br. h. Cassio, beating Mr. Goulburn's gr. h. Grimaldi: 5 to 2 and 3 to 1 on Cassio; a good race, and run in eight minutes and five seconds.

DERBY AND OAKS' STAKES.

THE following are expected to start for the Derby Stakes at Epsom, on Thursday, June 2:—

His R. H. the Prince of Wales's ch. c. Rubens, brother to Castrel
Lord Egremont's b. c. Brother to Trafalgar, by Gohanna

Duke of Grafton's br. c. Vandyke, by Sir Peter Teazle
Ld Stawell's ch. c. by Sorcerer
Mr. Sitwell's br c. Clinker, by Sir Peter Teazle
Mr. Mellish's b. c. Bradbury, by Delpini
Mr. Ladbroke's b. c. Tristram, by Teddy the Grinder
Lord Derby's br. c. Jacobus, by Sir Peter Teazle
Lord Grosvenor's b. c. Chester, by Sir Peter Teazle
Sir H. Williamson's ch. c. Pan, by St. George
Mr. Lake's b. c. by Sorcerer, or b. c. by Trumpator
Mr. Fermor's b. c. Jason, by Expectation.

BETTING AT TATTERSALL's.

7 to 2 agst Rubens
4 to 1 agst the Brother to Trafalgar
4 to 1 agst Vandyke
9 to 1 agst Ld Stawell's colt.
10 to 1 agst Clinker
12 to 1 agst Bradbury
10 to 1 agst Tristram
14 to 1 agst Jacobus
25 to 1 agst Chester
6 to 5 the field agst Rubens and Vandyke.

The following are expected to start for the Oaks' on Friday.

Duke of Grafton's ch. f. Morel, by Sorcerer
Mr Sitwell's b f Gooseander, by Hambletonian
Mr. Lake's bl. f. Oberea, by Sorcerer
Lord Barrymore's br. f. Miranda, by Sorcerer
Ld Egremont's br. f. Sister to Mouse, by Gohanna
Mr. Fermor's br. f. by Stamford
Mr. Howorth's b. f. Sister to Elizabeth, by Waxy
Lord Foley's f. by Vermin, dam by Highflyer
Sir F. Standish's b. f. by Sir Peter
Mr C. Browne's b. f. Anna, by Coriander
Gen. Grosvenor's b. f. by Stickler.

BETTING.

4 to 1 agst Morel
4 to 1 agst Gooseander
6 to 1 agst Oberea
8 to 1 agst Miranda, by Sorcerer.

THE AMUSEMENTS OF PARIS DESCRIBED.

Continued from Page 33.

JUGGLERS AND TUMBLERS.

BUT it does not rain now, and I had almost forgotten that we are to see the bustle in the streets. Should you not think that something very remarkable is going forward in yonder crowded circle of people? An old rope-dancer, perhaps superannuated, has taught some idle, blackguard boys, to tumble head over heels. A couple of his pupils seem to have escaped, with a view of carrying on business on their own account. At the corner of yon street they have spread a piece of carpet, so full of holes that it scarcely hangs together. They have endeavoured to give to their own rags the look of those worn by tumblers; and while one is rolling and tumbling about the carpet, the other endeavours to imitate the drollery of a buffoon.

That fellow with his cups is as little worth attention; he is a common juggler. But if you step behind the curtain for a moment, you will not repent it. You will find an extraordinary female, to whom nature has granted the ornament of man—a long, thick, black, capuchin beard. It is no deception, for I examined it closely. She is between twenty and thirty, has weak eyes, shaded by a pair of very bushy and coal-black brows. If you fancy to yourself a face thus decorated, covered above with a dirty white turban, with two full, white breasts; and the arms, feet, and neck, thickly overgrown with hair, you certainly will not think it a tempting figure. Were it not for her bosom, and her singing in such a clear and

shrill voice, as to make people run away, no one would think he was looking at a woman. "She is a native of Norway," said her keeper, "and was born five hundred leagues beyond Bergen!!"

I pretended to be a Dane, and questioned her in her native language. This quite puzzled the poor bearded lady. "I was brought to Paris by my father, when only three years old," replied she, in a Parisian accent. Let us quit this object, to whom the petulance of nature has refused the usual attributes of feminine beauty. Let us rather cast a transient look on the numerous articles exposed to sale. We shall often find the most singular contrasts:—here you are offered baskets full of dogs of various breeds; there, portraits of our Saviour, consisting only of a sheet of paper, containing the well-known spurious passage in Josephus.

LITERARY BOOTHS.

In this small portable booth, filled with a great variety of articles, each is sold for eighteen sous—in that for twenty-five; and you find many things among them which you can scarcely conceive it possible to sell at so low a price. Close to them are laid upon a cloth a whole mountain of books of every description. "Buy, gentlemen!" cries the owner, "take your choice! six sous apiece!" Another envious hawker, to spoil his trade, offers his heap of literary productions at four sous. They generally consist of insipid novels; yet I have frequently found many good things among them: such as odd volumes of Madame de Sevigné's Letters, &c. I have put my hand on them the second or third touch. If one were to take time, and a little trouble, a small collection of good books

books might be formed for a few livres.

The old books on the balustrade of the Pont Neuf, and on several of the quays, are more conveniently exposed, but dearer, though dog-cheap, according to the vulgar phrase. To judge from the very handsome manner in which most of them are bound, they are the remains of libraries that have been destroyed. Here the most valuable works are often found complete, in excellent condition, and at very moderate prices.

THE JEWELLERS' SHOPS.

I perceive that the jeweller's glittering shop attracts your eyes :— your taste is good. More elegant workmanship is found neither at Augsburgh nor Vienna. I have no where met with works of art that can be compared with these, except in the manufactory of the excellent counsellor of state De Busch, at Petersburgh. It is difficult to leave this place without purchasing something. It is here that you feel tempted to envy the rich. But you doubtless perceive something characteristic of the present time in France, in the contents of that window, which is full of gold or gilt shrines for the host ; a proof that there now is a great demand for this sacred article. Who has gained most by the temporary suppression of the Roman catholic religion ?—The goldsmiths.

STUFFED BIRDS AND BEASTS.

I entreat you to go a step farther, for the man who exposes such a variety of stuffed animals, deserves admiration as an artist, and has certainly attained perfection in his art. Every thing lives and seems to move. You stretch out your hand to rescue the fowl from that fox, which is carrying it off

in his jaws : you feel pain at seeing that hawk stick his talons in the defenceless fieldfare : you stop delighted before the cage in which the canaries are hatching, and the hens feeding their brood :— you smile at the fine shaggy spaniel carrying a lanthorn in his mouth ; you fancy he stops only because the person whom he is lighting is not quite close enough to him. A great number of single birds decorate the back part of the shop. This charming art affords the Parisians this advantage, that a person who possessed a faithful dog, a favourite bird, or any other animal he was fond of, does not lose it entirely after its death. For a trifling consideration he preserves its exterior figure as natural as life. The prices of these curiosities are very low. The stuffing of a small bird, for instance, costs only three francs, if the bird is furnished by the customer ; otherwise a little more, in proportion to the rarity of the animal.

AN AVIARY.

This theatre of inanimate bodies is, in some measure, preferable to that which swarms with living creatures, but which is rendered offensive by the disagreeable exhalations. If, however, you can stay a few moments in the latter shop without feeling indisposed, you will obtain some idea of Noah's ark, which could scarcely have been celebrated for its pleasant smell. Here you see lodged in a vast number of cages, grey, green, and party-coloured parrots, white cockatoos, superb India ravens, all of which scream at once, in such a manner as to deafen you. But you must not think that because birds are so plentiful, they are to be bought cheap ; no : you could not purchase.

purchase any of these for less than eight louis, unless it were yon sparrow-like parrot, that cannot speak, and never will learn; that you may perhaps buy for three louis. These foreigners with variegated plumage justly occupy the first row in the aviary. Next to them come pigeons and fowls of the rarest species, in great numbers; Turkish ducks, pearl hens, gold and silver pheasants, singing birds of every kind, from the nightingale to the greenfinch. Between these are placed spaniels, pug-dogs, squirrels, guinea-pigs, hares, and rabbits.—And here pigeons and young weasels, birds and Angora cats, are seen living in the greatest harmony by the side of each other. The walls are hung with cages from top to bottom, and even the whole outside of the shop next the street, is covered with them. Now let us enter this beautiful repository of household furniture, in which taste is subservient to luxury, and sometimes the contrary. But why should we trouble ourselves concerning this? we foreigners, who can carry nothing along with us! How great houses are here furnished, I shall not shew you in the street. For the same reason let us quickly pass this china warehouse, glittering with gold, where the brittle materials exhibit the most pleasing variety of colours. A charming sight indeed, indeed! and which has attracted my notice many a quarter of an hour.

LOTTERIES, &c.

Don't mind the woman, who absolutely wants to force upon you a ticket of the national lottery.—" Seventy-five thousand livres to be gained for a trifle," she incessantly cries, as if she had been taught by a Brunswick lottery-

office keeper; but more modest than the latter, she does not pester you with letters, but only follows you to the corner of the street. Now you have got rid of her, a good-natured savoyard, who, if you please, will clip, wash, and comb, your dog—offers to clean your shoes. But you like to trust your feet only to female hands, and by proceeding a few steps farther, you may satisfy that modest scruple.

GAMBLERS, WASHER-WOMEN, &c.

I now propose to walk slowly down the Quay l'Ecole, and thus to terminate this day's excursion. We shall leave to the left all the coffee-houses and restaurateurs, however inviting may be the inscriptions, painted in large characters on the glass doors and windows: cold and warm breakfasts, fork breakfasts (dejeuners 'à la fourchette), rum and rack punch, ice-cheese, milk-coffee, chocolate, &c. The next-door neighbour invites us to a game à la poule; the next to him offers a game at billiards; and a third offers capital March beer. But all in vain: we will walk on. Nor will we suffer ourselves to be tempted by the chesnuts roasted in the streets, nor the apples and grapes, nor the dirty ganymedes, who fill tin pots with an insipid beverage resembling the sbit in Russia. Such a potful, indeed, costs only one sous; but I shall advise you rather to drink clean water, which you may have for nothing. Ah! how lively is the street which leads along the Seine! to the left is a row of elegant shops, where the productions of every part of the world, nay, even those of other worlds (for even the celebrated stones which dropped from the moon can be bought here) are exposed for sale. And then the motley multitude of people, hackney coaches, and cursed cabriolets !— Now look down the river on the right. All the washerwomen in the world seem to be collected here. Ranged in rows, in long boats, covered with roofs; they are employed in mercilessly beating each separate piece of linen, which they afterwards throw into heaps. They brandish their thick muscular arms, and deal powerful blows, yet little noise is heard from their strokes, because they drown it with their charming prattle.

What this group wants in beauty is supplied by the different floating baths on the Seine, of which those of Vigie are particularly worthy of notice. In point of order and elegance, they are, however, in my opinion, far inferior to the floating bath at Berlin: but the superior magnitude of the Parisian is more striking, and some of them are rendered more agreeable by being surrounded by odoriferous flowers and shady trees.

THE PONT NEUF.

Let us, for a moment, ascend this new bridge, of which the government have made a superb present to the Parisians for their convenience and pleasure. Its pavement is as level and even as the floor of an apartment. As a flight of steps leads up to it at each end, so that neither horsemen nor carriages can annoy the pedestrians, it will become one of the most pleasant promenades in spring and autumn for the fashionable world.— It possesses another advantage, which is, that one sous must be paid for the liberty of walking on it, so that you are certain of not being molested by beggars.

What a charming view on both sides of this bridge ! Every morning you may here see the curious spectacle of flat-bottomed boats, intended for the invasion of England, manœuvring on the Seine. The soldiers, it is true, are still very indifferent hands at rowing ; and if the drummer, who is stationed on an elevated part of the boat, does not beat time, the vessel, with its numerous oars on each side, sometimes resembles a waggon going over a bridge composed of loose planks, which successively rise and fall as the vehicle proceeds. With a little more practice the men will do better, if the sea be only as patient an element as the Seine.

Industry and activity every where accompany this river. Hence it turns mills to furnish the inhabitants with food ; higher up it carries vessels laden with charcoal, to warm them ; farther down, the water is drawn from its centre to the shore, and there pumped through linen strainers into casks, to afford a pure beverage to the thirsty. These heaps of corn have likewise been borne up its bosom, and it conveys those pipes of wine unadulterated into the cellars of the anabaptists. Here you see a motley mixture of buyers and sellers. Take care not to go too near those black coal-heavers with your white robe ; and keep out of the way of those merry quarrelsome Auvergnats, who are fighting for fun so seriously hard, that the blows would kill either you or me, if we were to receive such a drubbing.— They likewise speak a gibberish, of which we do not understand a syllable.

THE PLACE DE GREVE.

Let us retire from this confused crowd into that square. Alas ! it is is the Place de Grève, where, formerly, criminals only suffered death, but which, during the reign of terror, was stained with the blood of many illustrious characters. Here is the spot on which the guillotine was long permanent, and in yon corner is the lamp-post on which Foulon was hanged.— We will quit this place, which a few days previous to the last execution, served for the exhibition of shows. For future executions, government has provided another place, in a different quarter of the town; where, I did not take the trouble to enquire, for I am not fond of such spectacles.

ITALIAN MOUNTEBANK.

In order to draw your lively imagination from these melancholy subjects, we will mingle with the crowd surrounding that mountebank dressed in scarlet. This man, with his aquiline nose, pretends to speak French with an Italian accent. " I am just arrived from Naples," says he; " I have heard of the good people of Paris. It is not interest that brings me hither : no, it is only the desire to be of service to the great nation, and the good people of Paris. Look here, gentlemen, at this invaluable medicine : every bottle of it costs, upon my honour, six livres, but I am satisfied if I can administer relief to suffering humanity. I ask nothing, nothing at all; I give away my bottles—yes, yes — I give them away. How? does nobody call? Indeed the people of Paris are better than they have been represented to me; they are too proud, too generous; they will have nothing given them. Well! not to offend your delicacy, I will set a price upon it. Instead of six livres, I ask only six sous. Buy! buy!

buy !" And behold multitudes rush forward to purchase. Now we go home laughing; don't we, my sweet friend?

To be continued.

THE
PHILOSOPHICAL SPORTSMAN.

NO. VI.

But most by numbers judge a poet's song,
And smooth or rough with them is right or wrong.

Essay on Criticism.

WHILE a fashionable young man was endeavouring to amuse me the other day, by playing two or three tender airs on the harpsichord, which he accompanied with his voice, I was more agreeably amusing myself in turning over a fold of loose papers, lying in the box from which he had taken out the music and songs before him. The bundle of papers consisted of manuscript music and old songs, some with and others without notes to them. One of these, called " *A Song for those that love hunting,*" attracted my notice more particularly, as it appeared to have been long written, the orthography defective, and the hand-writing indifferent.

My musical companion having finished his song, I made enquiries about the manuscripts. " They are old scraps of my late father's," said he. " I have not looked them over yet, but intend to do it soon, and to clear the place. I do not suppose that there is any thing worthy of notice or preservation among them; for my parent was a slave to the chase, and whatever had a relation to it in the song way,

way, he was sure to get; that is, provided it was couched in coarse language, and stuffed with gross ideas."

"A song," returned I, "may be composed in coarse inelegant language, and filled with gross ideas, and yet contain much matter, and convey a pleasure to the mind by that very strength and grossness of the ideas. Such compositions excite attention, and, I think, have their merit. As to slavery, we are slaves if our minds are wholly absorbed by any one particular object, for he whose mind is entirely absorbed in matters of taste, elegance, and refinement, is as equally a slave as he whose mind and affections are wrapped in hounds, and buried in the chase. Every thing ought to have some portion of our attention, that every thing may have its due; but the man who is devoted solely to one particular concern or object, is criminally unjust to all others. The flower which has elegance of symmetry without perfume, must be praised for its simplicity and agreeableness; that which has a variety of varied colours, and some little sweetness, must be admired for its beauty, and praised for its agreeably mild perfume; but the plant that diffuses around it a strong richness of perfume will ever have the most admirers; and those in particular who admire intrinsic qualities above those which have only extrinsic perfection.—There is something in high seasoning that gives an edge to the appetite, and renders ordinary things more palatable than better are without it; as insipidity, even in the best of provision for either body or mind, is relished by a few only, while a due portion of attic salt will force the coarse morsel

down." "Very well," said he; "pray have the goodness to read the song in your hand, which you seem to admire so much for its seasoning. To this request I gave a ready compliance.

A SONG FOR THOSE THAT LOVE HUNTING.

MAY I live to grow old, in a neat country town,
Where drinking and hunting may never go down;
May I ever be happy in Bradly and Brett,
John Deal and John Ford, and a true jovial set.
   May I live in good fashion, not too rich nor too poor,
   Nor tortur'd with care, nor dunn'd at my door,
   But ale and good claret, enough and no more.

On a fine spacious plain, with a plenty of game,
Remote from all gentry, and men of ill fame,
With a gallopping horse, and a pacing-pad nag,
To chase the fat deer, the hare, and the stag.
   May I live in good fashion, &c.

There was Cupper, and Tomboy, old Ruler, and Flutter,
There Roman, brisk Osbis, stout Toper, and Sutter;
There Jocky and Juno, brisk Lady and Mary,
Whose tongues are agreeing to Countess and Perry.
   May I live in good fashion, &c.

With a pudding on Sundays, and stout humming liquor,
With tobacco and pipes for to cheer up the vicar,
With a cleanly young girl to serve up my dinner,
Not twenty years old, yet a brisk tempting sinner.
   May I live in good fashion, &c.

Let pot-hunters starve, and snarers be flamm'd,
Let poachers be cuckolds, and greyhounds be d——d;
Let death take their horses, and murrain their hogs,
              And

And all to make pottage and meat for our
    dogs.
    May I live in good fashion, &c.

With courage undaunted may I halloo all
    day,
And when I am gone may the better sort
    say,
That he drank with discretion, yet ne'er
    left a drop,
Till he laid himself down, and then slept
    like a top.
    That he liv'd in good fashion, &c.

" Well, now you have read it,"
said he, " put it in your pocket;
you are welcome to it, and as many more of the kind as you may
think worth the carriage. They
are of no use to me; I love soft
music, and delicate smooth language." " But variety," returned
I, " is charming. I grant that
nothing can be more agreeable than
the plaintive songs and soft sweet
notes of the ladies; they are like
the fanning breezes of the grove or
umbrageous walk; but after having
been so tenderly entertained, it is
reviving to my heart when a
hearty old buck of a sportsman
breaks out humorously in a sono-
rous voice, and gives his companions a song similar to the above,
which is like the warm vivid rays
of the sun; and it is his rays that
invigorate and stamp the manly
character, and such, no doubt, was
your father. I have heard that he
loved staunch october, wine, and
brandy.—" True," said he, " he
did, particularly his october; one
pint of what he called his own
beer would make my head ache for
a week;"—" A striking indication
that," returned I, " that your
head is weakly." " That is excellent," said he, much delighted with the play on the word.—
" Your father, as I have heard, did
not give up all his time to pleasura-
ble exercise and joviality, but managed his business so well that he

has left you in it, and in tolerable
easy circumstances. He was no
churl, he not only drank freely himself, and gave as freely to his companions, but he frequently made
glad the hearts, and renewed the
spirits and vigour of his labours,
with a reviving draught of his
brown stout; and the man who
manages his business properly, sees
that his men do their work, and
pays them liberally for it, and
withal cherishes their hearts occasionally to encourage them in well-
doing, shall have success in his
affairs, he may take his pleasure,
and shall never want the means of
doing it.   M.

SPORTING ANECDOTES
OF THE LATE
LIEUT. COL. J. MORDAUNT,
*Of the Honourable East-India Company's
Madras Establishment.*

Continued from Page 13.

MORDAUNT was little ac-
quainted with the small sword,
but was an excellent marksman,
either with ball or small shot.—
With the latter, he scarcely ever
was seen to miss, and I have known
him to come off winner when he
has wagered to kill twenty snipes
in as many shots; although he
missed one bird, he made up for it
by killing two that were sprung at
the same moment, and which, flying across each other's directions,
were shot at the point of intersec-
tion. He was one of three who,
during one day, in the year 1786,
shot such a quantity of game,
chiefly snipes and teal, as loaded
a small boat which conveyed the
birds from Gowgautchy to Calcutta. His favourite sport was tiger
shooting, in which he was often
very

very successful, being vigorous, spirited, and expert; all which qualifications are indispensably requisite in that noble branch of the chase.

With respect to his use of a pistol, it was wonderful. I have often competed with him, but without the smallest chance of winning; he has frequently laid five to one, though he confessed I sometimes trod close on his heels. I have, more than once, seen him hit a common brass-headed nail at fifteen yards; and I would always have wagered on his side, when the object was an inch in diameter!

A curious circumstance happened to him while at Lucknow: An officer had taken offence at something he had said, and talked much of calling him to an account. He went to Mordaunt's with a friend, and there detailed the cause of his visit, in terms not cloathed in all the politeness the dictionary could have helped him to. He was heard very patiently, and after a very short explanation, found himself to be in the wrong. Mordaunt convinced him of his error, and reprimanded him for his manner of delivering himself on the occasion. After the matter was concluded, and they were perfectly reconciled, I happened to drop in to take a few shots, when the ability displayed by Mordaunt made his visitor look pale; he afterwards confessed to me, that it was well all was settled.

Yet, strange to say, when, a few years after, Mordaunt and another gentleman engaged in a quarrel of a very serious nature, with a third, whom they had accused of some improper conduct at cards, he missed his adversary, who, on the other hand, wounded both Mordaunt and his friend desperately. This was not owing to agitation, but as Mordaunt expressed, in very curious terms, at the moment of missing, to the pistol being too highly charged.

While speaking of cards, I must again state, that he was acquainted with all the ordinary tricks in the shuffling, cutting, and dealing way. Of this an instance is well known. Mordaunt observed, that one of his adversaries, at whist, was remarkably fortunate in his *own* deals; and, as he was rather a suspicious character, thought it needful to watch him. When Mordaunt came to deal, he gave himself thirteen trumps! This excited the curiosity of all, but particularly of the gentleman in question, who was very pointed in his observations on the singularity of the case; Mordaunt briefly said, " Sir, this was to show that you should not have all the fun to yourself," and, rising from his seat, left the blacklegs to ruminate on the obvious necessity of quitting India! Here, however, Mordaunt's goodness of heart was prevalent; for he obtained a promise from the whole party to keep the secret, provided the offender instantly left the country; which he accordingly did by the first conveyance.

With respect to the ordinary rules of arithmetic, no man could be more ignorant than Mordaunt; at least he never shewed the least knowledge of any thing relating thereto. He kept no books, but all his money concerns were on scraps, and under terms and figures intelligible only to himself. He had many extensive claims on the Nabob, and he had immense losses and gains to register in the I, O, U, way. Yet, even the most intricate cases never puzzled him; and, at settling times, he was rarely, if ever,

ever, found to be in error. This was one of the points in which he was apt to be peremptory ; for no sooner did he hear a claim stated, which did not tally with his own peculiar mode of accounting, than he condemned it, in round terms, and would scarcely hear the attempt to substantiate, what he so decidedly denied.

It was well known that he could arrange the cards according to his pleasure, yet such was the general, I may say universal opinion of his honour, that no one hesitated to play with him, sober or otherwise, for their usual stakes. His decision, in cases of differences, was generally final ; and many references have been made to him, by letter, from very distant situations, regarding points in gaming.

Mordaunt was so much master of his racket, and was so vigorous, that he would always wager on hitting the line from the over-all, a distance of thirty yards, once in three times. He could beat most people with a common round ruler.

If he ever did indulge in mischief, it was at this game, when his best friends were sure to receive some smart tokens of remembrance ! I have had a ball or two from him, occasionally, which kept my back in a glow for hours. But he used to be terribly severe on a very worthy, good-natured civilian, Mr. Marcus Sackville Taylor, deputy to Colonel, now Major-General, Palmer, who was for some years resident at the Nabob's court.

Mordaunt never allowed the Nabob to treat him with the least disrespect, or with hauteur ; indeed, such was the estimation in which he was held by that prince, that, in all probability, the latter never found any disposition towards exerting his authority. Something

may be gathered from the following anecdote. The Nabob wanted some alterations to be made in the howdah of his state-elephant, and asked Mordaunt's opinion as to the best mode of securing it : the latter very laconically told the Nabob, he understood nothing of the matter, he having been born and bred a gentleman ; but that probably his blacksmith, (pointing to Colonel Martine,) could inform him how the howdah ought to be fastened.

This sneer, no doubt, gratified Mordaunt ; who, though extremely intimate with Martine, and in the habit of addressing him by various ludicrous, but sarcastic nicknames, seemed not to relish that fondness for money, and those various practices, of which he was said to be guilty.

Marquis Cornwallis was either unwilling to compel Mordaunt to return to the Madras establishment, or was prevailed on by the Vizier to let him remain on his staff. The Marquis, one day, seeing Mordaunt at his levee, asked him, " if he did not long to join his regiment ?" " No, my lord," answered Mordaunt, " not in the least." " But," resumed the Marquis, " your services may be wanted, perhaps." " Indeed, my lord," rejoined Mordaunt, " I cannot do you half the service there, that I can in keeping the Vizier amused, while you *ease* him of his money."

As a *bon vivant,* as master of the revels, or at the head of his own table, few could give greater variety, or more complete satisfaction, than Mordaunt. He had the best of wines, and spared no expence, though he would take very little personal trouble, in providing whatever was choice or rare.

K He

He stood on little ceremony, especially at his own house; and, at his friend's, never allowed any thing to incommode him, from a bashful reserve. Whatever was in his opinion wrong, he did not hesitate to condemn.

These observations were very quick, and generally not devoid of humour. His old friend, Captain Waugh, dining with him one day, made such a hole in a fine goose, as to excite the attention of Mordaunt; who, turning to his head servant, ordered aloud, that, "whenever Captain Waugh dined at his house, there should always be *two* geese on table; *one* for the captain, *the other* for the company."

The following anecdote will exhibit, that the above directions were not misapplied.

Captain Waugh commanded one of the six battalions, which, under the immortal Goddard, penetrated through the heart of the Mahratta country, though opposed by at least one hundred thousand men, chiefly cavalry. When the peace was concluded with that power, in 1782, Captain Waugh took his passage from Bombay to Bengal, in a vessel which was captured off Tranquebar, by Suffrein. That Admiral treated him with great politeness, and invited him to his table. The French, according to their custom, began with their soup, &c. while Waugh commenced his attack upon a goose, which happened to be near him. The bird was soon disposed of, and Waugh had just stuck his fork into a duck, when Suffrein, with great good nature, but under no small astonishment, observed, that he had forgot the English captain's name, but requested that he would take a glass of wine. "My name is Waugh, and I will drink with you with all

my heart," answered the Captain. " *Bon, bon*," said Suffrein, delighted at what he thought was a joke of his guest's; *mais, Monsieur Waugh, si vous resterois ici, nous n'aurions pas une oie* (a goose) *dans toute l'escadre.*"

The pun was rather a fortunate one for Waugh, who played such a tune with his knife and fork as made all the Frenchmen stare, and induced Suffrein to set him ashore, on parole, at the first port.

After the arrival of the two brothers, Harry and John, in Bengal, they had but little intercourse. Harry seemed to be jealous and envious of his brother's qualifications, and of the general partiality in his favour; which was by no means the case with himself. He was haughty, reserved, tenacious, and satirical; consequently was not very likely to be much respected, or relished as a companion. His appearance was not calculated to prepossess either sex in his behalf. John always treated him with particular consideration; but when having attempted to oppose, or to argue against him, used briefly to put him down with, " Hold your tongue, Harry, you are a puny little fool, and fit for nothing but to be a lord." Nevertheless, John never allowed any person to speak disrespectfully of him.

Harry died of diseases which seemed to have been rocked with him in his cradle; while John, though possessed of a vigorous constitution, seemed to descend, as it were, down a precipice, into his grave. He never, indeed, got completely better of the pistol-shot in his breast; and, probably, actuated by that mistaken pride generally urging men who have done wonders, not to allow their decrease of vigour to be noticed or suspected, he he neglected the warnings given him by one or two serious attacks on his liver, and thus hastened that end which we may call untimely !"

He died in the 40th year of his age, beloved and regretted by a numerous circle.

Such are the outlines of a man, who, had he been bred in courts, would probably have been the Rochester of his day ; for he was inordinately fond of women, and seemed, when ill, to regret his situation chiefly as depriving him of their society.

PEDIGREE AND PERFORMANCES
OF
THAT WELL-BRED RACING MARE,
ELEANOR,

(Own Sister to Clarissa, Julia, Young Whiskey, Lydia, &c. &c.—Bred by Sir T. C. Bunbury, Bart. of Barton, near Bury St. Edmund's, Suffolk:)

ELEANOR was got by Whiskey; her dam, *Young Giantess* (Sorcerer's dam) by Diomed ; grandam, *Giantess*, (Volatile, Pharamond, Gawkey, and Grey Gawkey's dam) by Match'em ; great grandam, *Molly Longlegs*, by Babram ; great great grandam by Mr. Cole's Foxhunter ; great great great grandam, (own sister to Mr. Panton's Cato) by Partner, out of an own sister to the noted *Roxana*, that bred Lath, Roundhead, and Old Cade.—*See Pick's Turf Register.*

At Newmarket First Spring Meeting, 1801, *Eleanor* won a Sweepstakes of 100gs. each, h. ft. (4 subscribers) across the Flat, beating Miss Fury and Gaoler—2 to 1 against Eleanor. At Epsom, May 21, she won the Derby Stakes of 50gs. each, h. ft. (3 subscribers) the last mile and a half, beating Mr. Wyndham's br. c. by Fidget, out of Cælia ; Remnant, Gaoler,

Matthew, Belleisle, and five others ! 5 to 4 against Eleanor. And the next day, she won the Oaks' Stakes of 50gs. each, h. ft. (18 subscribers) the last mile and a half, beating Daisy; Crazy Poetess, Remnant, Thaïs, &c.—7 to 4 and 2 to 1 on Eleanor. At Ascot-Heath, June 9, *Eleanor* (carrying 7lb. extra) was beat by Teddy the Grinder, beating Dissenter and Daisy. On Monday, in the Newmarket First October Meeting, she won a Sweepstakes of 200gs. each, h. ft. (7 subscribers) Across the Flat, beating Miss Fury :—15 to 8 on Eleanor. And on Thursday, she beat Flambeau, 8st. 2lb. each, Across the Flat, 200gs.—13 to 8 on Eleanor.

On Tuesday, at Newmarket First October Meeting, 1802, *Eleanor* won one-third of a subscription of 25gs. each, (15 subscribers) with 50l. added by the Jockey-Club, Ditch-in, beating Penelope and the Sister to Gouty :—6 to 4 on Penelope, and 7 to 4 against Eleanor. And on Thursday, she won the King's Plate for four-year olds, 10st. 4lb. five-year olds and aged, 12st. 2lb. R. C. beating the Sister to Gouty, 4 years old ; Aniseed, 5 years old ; Warter, aged ; Hospitality, 4 years old ; and Malta, 4 years old :—6 to 5 on Eleanor. In the Second October Meeting, she won the Subscription Plate of 50l. for three-year olds, 7st. 10lb. and four-year olds, 8st. 10lb. Across the Flat, beating Shock, 3 years old ; Northampton, 3 years old ; and Harefoot, 3 yrs old :—10 to 1 on Eleanor.

At Newmarket Craven Meeting, 1803, *Eleanor* received 50gs. compromise from Fieldfare, 8st. 7lb. each, the last three miles of B. C. 200gs. h. ft. At Ipswich, July 7, she won 50l. beating Peace-Maker,

At Oxford, July 25, she won the Gold Cup, value 100gs. with 50gs. in specie, four miles, beating Julia, Pyrrhus, and Frolic :—5 to 2 on Eleanor. And on the 27th, (same Meeting) she won 50l. beating Garnerin and Gazer :—20 to 1 on Eleanor. At Huntingdon, August 2, she won 50l. beating Field-fare, Bob Handy, &c. And the next day she won 50l. beating Pi-pylin. At Lincoln, September 14, she won the King's Plate, beating Primrose.

At Newmarket First Spring Meeting, 1804, *Eleanor*, 8st. 10lb. won a Handicap Plate, of 50l. Clermont Course, beating Rebel, aged, 8st. 7lb.; Chippenham, aged, 8st. 8lb; and five others :—6 to 5 on Eleanor. In the Second Spring Meeting, at 9st. 2lb. she won a Handicap Plate of 50l. Across the Flat, beating Quiz, 6 years old, 8st. 9lb.; Duxbury, 5 years old, 8st. 7lb.; and Gaoler, 6 years old, 8st. 9lb.—6 to 5 against Eleanor. She also, at 8st. 10lb. received 40gs. compromise from Surprise, 8st. 7lb. Two-year Olds' Course, 50gs. At Ipswich, July 5, she won 50l. beating Fly, by Pot8o's. At Newmarket July Meeting, at 8st. 12lb. she won 50l. Ditch-in, beating Heathpolt, 3 years old, 6st. 9lb.; Captain Absolute, 5 years old, 8st. 8lb.; The Carpenter, 3 years old, 6st. 9lb.; and Miss Brocket, 3 years old, 6st. 9lb.—9 to 4 on Eleanor. At Chelms-ford, July 25, she won 50l. beating Coaxer, by Pot8o's. At Huntingdon, August 8, she won 50l. beating Capella, by Buzzard. At Bedford, September 13, she received a premium of 20l. no horse entering against her. At Newmarket First October Meeting, *Eleanor*, 9st. 1lb. won the Gold Cup, value 80gs. and 90gs. in spe-

cie, Across the Flat, beating Vir-tuosa, 3 years old, 5st. 10lb.; Lig-num-Vitæ, aged, 8st. 10lb.: Ani-seed, Lenox, Castrel, Elizabeth, and seven others, also started, but were not placed :—4 to 1 against Eleanor; 5 to 1 against Lignum Vitæ, and the same against Castrel. In the Second October Meeting, she won one-third of a Subscrip-tion of 25gs. each, (16 subscribers) with 50l. added by the Jockey-Club, for five-year olds, 8st. 5lb, six-year olds and aged, 9st. B. C. beating Orville, 5 years old; and Lignum-Vitæ, aged :—7 to 4 on Eleanor.

At Egham, September 3, 1805, *Eleanor*, 8st. 12lb. won the Gold Cup, value 100gs. and 100gs. in specie, four miles, beating Miss Coiner, 4 years old, 7st. 8lb.; Prospero, 4 years old, 7st. 10lb.; Houghton-Lass, 4 years old, 7st. 8lb.; and Quiz, aged, 9st.— 2 to 1 against Houghton-Lass, 2 to 1 against Quiz, and 6 to 1 against Eleanor. September 5, (same place) at 9st. 6lb. she won 50l. two-mile heats, beating Quiz, aged, 9st. 6lb.; Cerberus, 3 years old, 6st. 8lb.; and Little John, 5 years old, 8st. 13lb.—6 to 4 on Eleanor. And the same day, at 9st. 2lb. she beat Wormwood, 3 years old, 6st. 12lb. the New Mile, 100gs. :—7 to 4, and 2 to 1, on Eleanor. At Newmarket First October Meeting, at 9st. 7lb. she beat Czar Peter, 8st. Ditch-in, 100gs. :—5 to 4 on Eleanor. This was the last year of her running. She is now a brood mare in Sir C. Bunbury's Stud.

Whiskey, (sire of *Eleanor*, &c.) was bred by His Royal Highness the Prince of Wales. He was got by Saltram; his dam, Calash, (Pa-ragon, Louisa, Aston, and Kite's dam) by King Herod; grandam, Teresa,

Teresa, by Match'em, Regulus, out of an own sister to the Duke of Ancaster's Starling, by the Duke of Bolton's Starling.

At Newmarket, in 1792, *Whiskey* won a stakes of 1200gs; a Produce Stakes of 3000gs; the Subscription of 1400gs; a Subscription of 120gs; a Match of 100gs; and a 50l. Plate at Bedford. At Newmarket, in 1793, he won the Jockey Stakes of 750gs; a Match of 200gs; a 50l. plate; and a Stakes of 60gs. He was sold to Sir Charles Bunbury for a Stallion, and is sire of Clarissa, Pamela, Julia, Froth, Gig, Orlando, Whirligig, Tinsel, (afterwards Sir Ulic M'Killigut), Prospero, Lydia, Orangeade, Snug, Whiskerandos, Rumbo, Trumper, Pelisse, Handicap, Midas, Moustache, Rosabella, Charmer, Tamburro, Tim, Chaise-and-One, Grampound, Juniper, L'Huile de Venus, Matilda, and several other winners.—*Whiskey* now covers at Great Barton, near Bury St. Edmunds, Suffolk, at 10gs. a mare, and 10s. 6d. the groom.

GRAND PUGILISM.

THURSDAY, MAY 12.

FOR several days past, the sporting world has been in a state of great ferment and agitation, an extraordinary degree of expectation having been excited by the great match between Gregson and Gully, which was fixed for yesterday. Two other matches, one between Cribb and Horton, the other between Dutch Sam and Cropley, were announced for the same field, and at the same time, being triumvirate against triumvirate, of the crack men of the day, the whole presenting the most elegant bill of fare ever presented to the amateurs of pugilism.

On Saturday the 7th, it was whispered confidentially, to the chosen few in the gymnastic circles, that a common, on the confines of Bedfordshire and Buckinghamshire, was to be the scene of action. It was scarcely to be expected, that a secret of such interest and importance would not transpire. The Marquis of Buckingham, apprised of the arrangement, gave public notice, on Monday, in some of the London papers, of his intention to frustrate the sport. A great number of persons had, however, previously left town on Saturday and Sunday, and secured beds and stables on the road, and in all the villages and hamlets between London and Woburn. About two miles and a half beyond the latter place, Ashley Common, the proposed scene of action, is situate. A crowd so great and unexpected, pouring down in that direction, excited no little alarm. Some of the ignorant took it into their heads that the French had landed, and that the Londoners were flying to their country friends. The appearance of the Dunstable volunteers, under arms, with drums beating, colours flying, double cartouche boxes, doubly provided, muskets loaded, and fixed bayonets, tended to encourage these fears, and excited no trifling degree of terror and confusion. The alarm of invasion, however, was transitory, and the people were soon informed of the real cause of all this terrible tumult and uproar. It appeared that Ashley Common was selected for this grand exhibition of the pugilistic art, and that the magistrates of Bedfordshire and Bucking-

Buckinghamshire, at the head of their constables, and *posse comitatus*, with a subsidiary force of volunteers from the neighbouring districts, were determined to resist this unlicensed incursion into their territories. The Dunstable volunteers were out under arms so far back as Monday, by which time the concourse of people was so great in that vicinity, that thirty shillings were asked for a bed; and in one house three beds were let upon those terms, producing 4l. 10s. All the lofts, barns, and outhouses were filled, and happy were they who had their carriages to sleep in. Some idea of the crowd may be formed, when it is considered that it was formed of persons from within a circle of 200 miles, consisting of several from Manchester, Birmingham, Bristol, Liverpool, and Yorkshire.

During the whole of Monday night, the town of Woburn was in continual motion; all was uproar and confusion, with people arriving on foot, on horseback, and in carriages, all seeking that accommodation which only a few comparatively could find; few knowing which way to go, and all dreading disappointment, from the reports of the day, or the decided interference of the magistracy. So strong was this latter impression, that from betting upon the battle, they began to bet that there would be no battle at all, and ten to one were bet over and over again that there would be no fight. In one room at Woburn fifteen gentlemen lay upon the floor and chairs, and were happy to pay for their hard fare, upon the same terms as if they lay upon the softest feather beds; and in many instances the horses, although the weather was severe, were obliged to stand without covering. This was the state of Woburn town on Monday night.

About five o'clock yesterday morning, the visitors began to move, and the inhabitants of Woburn to be on the look out after them; having taken, however, the precaution, as their guests arrived, to secure their boots, or some part of their property of equal value. Between six and seven, several carriages and four arrived direct from London, with the most dashing and fashionable amateurs. The famous pugilist, Richmond, commonly called the Black Diamond, was their finger-post—he was smartly dressed in a blue coat, white pantaloons and waistcoat, and white hat lined with green, and took his station, in consequence of a preconcerted plan, at the Magpie, to give his fashionable friends the clue to the wished-for spot. The people in general soon caught the hint, and followed these leaders to the intended scene.

The ring was formed upon Ashley Common, about two miles to the left of Woburn, on the Manchester road. It was a complete 40-feet ring, raised with sods about twelve inches from the ground. Hundreds of amateurs had viewed it before nine o'clock, and were greatly pleased with its appearance. A great many carriages had arrived at that time, and were penned off safely; and a cart, loaded with ropes and stakes, to complete the circumference of the ring, was within sight of the place. An express, however, at this moment arrived, to inform the people that the Magistrates were aware of what was intended; that some of them had ridden over the ring early in the morning (and indeed it bore the marks of horses' feet), and that they

they would not suffer the matches to be fought there.

Some of the knowing ones, suspecting that this was a hoax, sent off an express to Hogstall, a public house about a mile off, where Gregson held his head-quarters,— Before the answer arrived, however, Mendoza, dressed in green, and mounted in a dashing style, came up with two or three gentlemen amateurs, and assured them that the battle would not be fought at that place. Upon this assurance, the whole crowd rushed down the hill, on their way to Gregson's lodgings, where they found this champion seated in the Earl of Barrymore's barouche, with the horses' heads turned to Woburn, and escorted by about one hundred and fifty noblemen and gentlemen on horseback, the rear brought up with an immense string of gigs, tandems, &c. Many persons, not apprised of the change of scene, were, in the mean time, advancing from Woburn to the Common.— The two tides soon met, and both came, with their accumulated force, into Woburn, the knowing ones who led the mass having been apprised, that in case of any unforeseen disappointment at the original spot, they were to rendezvous at several places in reversion, the first of which was Sir John Sebright's park, in Hertfordshire, about seventeen miles distant from the original spot.

The spirits of the fondest admirers of the art now began to flag, and before they reached Dunstable, many had repented of their expedition. Several, tired of the journey, returned home, concluding there would be no fight; but the multitude was so great, they did not appear to have suffered any diminution. For sixteen miles, the road was covered with one solid mass of passengers; and in Dunstable, and for half a mile on each side of that town, there was a string of carriages in a triple row, as close as ever was seen in Hyde Park. Several carriages were broken in the pressure, and many of the horses knocked up, the owners of which now offered a guinea a mile for conveyance to the real scene of the fight. Neither horses nor decent carriages, however, were to be procured for any money, and many gentlemen were glad to stow themselves in butchers' carts, at the rate of a shilling a mile.

About two o'clock, a considerable part of the crowd had arrived in Sir John Sebright's park, where a flat spot was selected within the paling, in front of the house, and about half a mile from it. The paling was broken in a few places for admission, but there was no wanton mischief committed, and these uninvited guests behaved in an orderly manner. Progress was immediately made in forming the ring. The exterior circle was nearly an acre, surrounded by a triple ring of horsemen, and a double ring of people on foot, no carriages having presumed to enter. About three o'clock the day overcast, a torrent of rain began to pour down, and every one became impatient for the fight. Shortly after, Gregson, Gully, Mendoza, Harry Lee, Joe Ward, the Chicken, and several other first-rate heroes, made their appearance. A slight ring was immediately formed, and the sports commenced.

GREGSON AND GULLY.

It is impossible to describe the delight of the spectators on beholding these two champions enter the

the ring. Although the ground was almost flooded with the rain, the people lay down with the greatest pleasure, and a forty-feet ring was soon formed in complete style. Captain Barclay was the umpire. Harry Lee was second to Gregson, and Joe Ward to Gully. The combatants fought in silk stockings, without shoes, and white breeches. After they had stripped, their great coats were thrown over them to keep off the rain, in expectation that it would soon prove fair.

But though the second in order of time, as the battle between Gregson and Gully was of the first consequence, with this we shall commence our narrative.

ROUNDS.

1. The utmost silence prevailed in every part of the ring, and each had his eye stedfastly fixed on the combatants, who sparred for above a minute without approaching within length. This silence was soon turned into peals of applause by the admirers of Gully. He perhaps gave one of the most signal specimens of the art of boxing ever witnessed, by putting in two dexterous hits at the same moment through Gregson's guard on the throat and mouth. Gregson fell as if he had lost his legs, and he was covered with blood.—6 to 4 on Gully.

2. Gregson made an ineffectual hit at his adversary's head ; Gully shifted it, and pointed his finger at him—Gully commenced a rally, and some blows were exchanged to the advantage of Gully. In the rally, Gregson turned round, and hit his adversary a back-handed blow on the loins ; both fell.

3. Gregson planted a right hit on Gully's breast, and a rally followed, most decidedly in favour of Gully, who kept hitting, and getting away from his man, but was ultimately thrown.—Gregson bled copiously, and his head began to swell—2 to 1 on Gully.

4. Gully made play, and planted two other blows on his adversary's head, and slipped up.

5. Gregson made a determined hit, which was scientifically stopped, and he ran upon his man, grasped him by the thighs, held him in his arms, and hit him down—Some disapprobation.

6. Some obstinate rallying, but so decidedly in favour of Gully, that Gregson was hit about at pleasure. Gully received a tremendous blow on the right side of his head at the close of this round, and both fell out of the ring.

7. Gully rallied his man in this round, and hit him about six blows on the head with great ease, and he also stopped those of Gregson, whose left eye was closed, his nose broken, and his face hideously disfigured ; Gregson was at length hit off his legs.

8. A round somewhat in favour of Gregson, as far as regarded slight hitting. In closing, he threw Gully a heavy fall.

9. This round was pretty decisive of the result of the battle, for Gregson manifested a falling off in strength, and was grievously hit again in the face ; he, however, shewed good, but fell on his knees on one of his adversary's blows.

10. The blood flowed in torrents from Gregson's face, and he acted very shy, his eyes being nearly closed, and every other part of his face as badly hit. A blow was exchanged, and Gully was thrown —a fall of his own choosing.

11. Gregson, on setting to, put his hand to his left eye, and looked

at

at it. He commenced a rally, which ended again in his discomfiture; and on receiving a knock-down blow, he hit Gully a back-handed blow, whilst falling.

12. Gregson was hit down, in return for a blow planted on his adversary's breast.

13. Gully fell down in making play.

14. Gully hit his adversary through his guard within distance, right and left, one of which blows alone would have dropped him.

15 and 16. Gregson made ineffectual rallies in each round, but in the latter it was evident he could not rise, and he was weak; he ran in upon Gully and bored him down.

17. There certainly was something like a Whitelocke in Gregson's conduct in this round, although it might have arisen from blindness or pain. He lost his temper, and run in upon his adversary, who kept hitting and getting away from him in a manner which excited astonishment. He turned his back to his man twice in the round, and made towards the ropes, but Gully changed his front, fibbed him, and kept him from falling, until he had ruffianed him into an apparent senseless state, and then dropped him quietly between his arms.

18. A similar round to the former, and Gregson was as badly punished when he retreated.

REMARKS.

The battle excited some disappointment, inasmuch as it was generally understood, although not by judges, that Gregson had been taught the science of fighting; but it turned out diametrically opposite. He was a resolute novice at the late battle with Gully, at Newmarket, and by instinct he threw in several tremendous blows at length.

It will not be wondered at that the spectators were surprised when they saw the man, who in the late battle never could approach until he made play, in this instance make play too, hit him through his guard, and doing almost any thing with him. It was evident this all arose from the very attempt of teaching a novice, on the wrong side of thirty, to box. He was constantly abroad too, in rallying, which was not the case in the last battle.

Ten other rounds, if they might be called so, were fought, and in this way Gregson never planted one hit, but was constantly receiving tremendous blows on the head and loins; he was fighting under every disadvantage of weakness, blindness, achings, &c. and consequently unable to turn the career of his adversary. In the 25th round he received two as tremendous blows as any in the battle, and which decided it in the 28th round, when Gregson could not be brought to the mark of setting to in time; he also received a tremendous hit in the ear in the 27th round.

Gully fought him with studied caution; and when he had him at rallying, there was not one instance in which Gully failed. The Champion was also in much better condition than when he fought at Newmarket, and never betrayed symptoms of weakness.

After the battle Gully addressed the ring, and informed them publicly, he was so situated that he never intended to fight again, nor would he have done so in this instance, had he not been bound in honour to comply with Gregson's challenge. He had in this instance fought

fought with a lame left arm, and Gregson surely would not desire to combat with him again. The battle lasted one hour and a quarter.

CRIB AND HORTON.

The combatants entered the ring the same moment. Before setting to, bets were 5 to 4 on Crib. They were both in fine condition, and excellent spirits.

Horton's manner of fighting is different to any other boxer. He did not attempt to stop much, but generally made play. He did not seem a judge of his distance, and when he hit at his proper length he was generally stopped. He is a young man, full of health and vigour, but something shorter and lighter than Crib, and much inferior in skill. Crib is a known safe fighter, but he was particularly so in this instance, for he threw but few blows away, and continued to keep the blood constantly flowing from the head of his adversary, by superior skill, without going into a rally. The battle was safe from the first round, and the cognoscenti made a good harvest.

Horton is a bad hitter; he cannot stop at all; but he is a bottom man. He will never rank as a first-rate boxer. He was much disfigured, and the battle was won easily by Crib.

DUTCH SAM AND CROPLEY.

This was a scientific battle betwixt two very good men, but Sam was the favourite after the first round, in which he got a black eye. Cropley tried by every pugilistic stratagem to get at Sam's head in vain, for the latter was even a better fighter than Cropley, although a stone lighter; Cropley was a good deal punished about the head,

and his eyes were closed. He fell weak after fighting 25 minutes, and after making a good stand, he resigned by the call of nature in ten minutes after. Sam is a man capable of beating any man of eleven stone, and he never fought better than in this instance.

The fighting was not over till near seven in the evening.

———

Gregson, it seems, though abandoned for the moment by most of his former friends on the day of defeat, afterwards met with more generous treatment. He arrived on Saturday the 14th at Highgate, and on the following Monday, he was visited by several noblemen and gentlemen amateurs, several of whom, the Marquis of T—— setting the example, made the fallen champion some handsome presents. He spoke highly of Gully's perfection in the art of boxing, and said, that during the whole battle he never recovered the tremendous right-handed hit, in the left jaw, during the first round, which produced an effusion of blood, loosened his teeth, disfigured his eye, and disordered his head in every part. —It is added, that soon after the battle, several gentlemen, among others, Captain B——, Gully's backer, called on Gregson, and left him something handsome, and that a subscription was also made in the ring.—If Gregson could have had his choice, he would have fought at some place in Lincolnshire.—In the course of a few days, it is reported, he will be matched against Crib. Other matches are to be made; viz. between Jem Belcher and Horton; Young Belcher and Cropley; and Dutch Sam and Nichols, who beat Crib about two years since at Blackwater.

COURT

COURT MARTIAL

ON RICHARD CORRALL, ESQ.

AT a General Court-Martial, held at Woodbridge, on the 6th of January, 1808, and continued by adjournment to the 28th of the same month, Richard Corrall, Esq. Paymaster of the 15th (or King's) Regiment of Light Dragoons, was arraigned on the undermentioned charges; viz.

" 1st, For malversation in his office of Paymaster of the 15th (or King's) Regiment of Light Dragoons, in having, contrary to his duty, and in disregard of the third Article of the Additional Instructions and Regulations respecting the conduct of Regimental Paymasters and others, dated the 11th of May, 1801, drawn on the public account, upon the regimental agents, for the sum of three thousand five hundred pounds fourteen shillings and eight-pence, or some other large sum or sums of money, beyond what was actually required for the regular services of the said regiment, between the 24th December, 1806, and the 25th October, 1807.

" 2d. For neglect of duty, in not having rendered his accounts at the periods prescribed by the established regulations and official orders, and particularly by the instructions to Regimental Paymasters, dated the 19th January, 1798; the circular letter from the Examiner of Army Accounts to Regimental Paymasters, dated 14th February, 1806, and 7th August, 1807; and the Secretary at War's circular letter to Regimental Paymasters, dated the 22d July, 1807.

" The accounts herein referred to, are the Monthly General Abstracts for the period, from the 25th December, 1806, to the 24th October following, both inclusive and the Quarterly Accounts for the periods from the 25th June, 1806, to the 24th September, 1807, both inclusive."

Upon which charges the Court came to the following decision :—

The Court, having considered the evidence for and against the prisoner, with the whole of his defence, and the accounts given in by him, are of opinion, that he has drawn, between the 24th December, 1806, and the 25th October, 1807, for the sum of three thousand five hundred pounds, fourteen shillings and eight-pence, stated in the charge, beyond the money actually expended by him for the public service.

The Court is further of opinion, that the prisoner has not accounted, by any expenditure stated in his abstracts, for the sum of money so over-drawn; and although it were proved (which it is not) that the prisoner had debited himself in his abstracts, from error, with the sum of one thousand pounds or thereabouts, expended for the service of the regiment, which ought to have been charged to the Colonel's private account, yet there would still remain the sum of two thousand five hundred pounds, fourteen shillings and eight-pence, over-drawn on the public, of which no satisfactory account, supported by proper vouchers, has been given to this Court.

The Court do therefore find the prisoner *guilty* of malversation, as far as the word applies to the improper expenditure of public money, but whether it has been applied by the prisoner to his private use, or advanced on the charges of others, without due examination, and without the care and caution which it is the duty of every per-

L 2   son

son intrusted with the disbursement of public money, they are not enabled to determine.

The Court do also find the prisoner *guilty* of having drawn beyond his estimates, in breach of the third Article of Additional Instructions of the 11th of May, 1801.

With respect to the second charge, the Court are of opinion, that the inconveniences experienced on the march of the regiment, might have delayed for a short time the sending in of the monthly estimates and abstracts. It does not appear to the Court, that the want of sanction of the allowance of corn for the horses at grass, should have prevented their being transmitted, as a remark might have been added on that charge. The Court admit, that the time during which the prisoner was absent from the regiment, attending to the clothing and other concerns of the regiment, was a considerable impediment to his fulfilling his duties as Paymaster; but they are of opinion that the first duty of every man is to execute the business of the office in which he is placed; and although, if the prisoner had cleared himself from the first charge, the Court would have received with great indulgence the excuses advanced for the breach of the regulations in the second, yet, from what has appeared before them, they consider the inability to account for the expenditure of the money drawn, to have been a greater impediment to the regular transmission of the estimates and abstracts, especially for the latter part of the period, than any thing which the prisoner has stated.

The Court do therefore find the prisoner *guilty* of the second charge.

The Court, therefore, having found the prisoner *guilty* on both charges, do adjudge, that he, the prisoner, Richard Corrall, Esq. shall be dismissed his situation of Paymaster of the 15th (or King's) regiment of light dragoons; and the Court do farther adjudge, that the prisoner shall make good the whole of the money drawn beyond the expenditure, not only of the sum of three thousand five hundred pounds fourteen shillings and eight-pence, stated in the first charge, but also the money received for the sale of cast horses, viz. the sum of four hundred and sixty-two pounds eleven shillings and eight-pence; and further, whatever other money the prisoner may have received by stoppages from the men, or any other public money, the application of which has not been clearly accounted for: and they direct that an account of such stoppages be transmitted by the Commanding Officer of the 15th regiment of light dragoons, to Messrs. Greenwood, Cox, and Co.

The Court have received with great respect the testimony of his Royal Highness the Duke of Cumberland to the zeal, attention, and long good conduct of the prisoner, and though by the fact in the first charge being proved, they are precluded from taking it into consideration in their sentence, they earnestly wish that that testimony may be attended to, and that it may benefit the prisoner in any other situation.

His Majesty having been pleased to confirm the opinion and sentence of the Court, and to direct that the same shall be carried into effect, his Royal Highness the Commander in Chief is pleased to direct that the charges, together with the sentence

sentence of the Court, shall be inserted in the orderly books of every corps.

HARRY CALVERT, Adj.-Gen.
Horse Guards, April 14, 1808.

HARMONIOUS CHANGE RINGING.

CONTESTED.

To the Editor of the Sporting Magazine.

SIR,

ANNEXED I have sent a true and correct account of Contested Harmonious Change Ringing, in the northern part of England, which is particularly requested you will insert in your interesting and valuable Magazine, as early as possible; and you will greatly oblige, Sir, your most obedient, and most humble servant,

JOHN PARNELL.
Manchester, April 21st, 1808.

[*We should notice, that an article embracing a part of this communication appeared in our Magazine for February last, Page 236.*]

On Tuesday, the 5th day of January, 1808, Joint Societies of Change Ringers, consisting of three Ashton-under-line College Youths, four Oldham Youths, and an honest Yorkshireman, ascended the venerable and gothic tower of St. Michael's Church, at Ashton-under-line, in the county palatine of Lancaster, and in the quick time of three hours and five minutes they completely brought round a sprightly and harmonious well-rung peal of BOE MAJOR, containing 5040 changes, to the general satisfaction of thousands of delighted hearers. The ringing artists were as follow; viz.

Treble Bell.—Mr. Joseph Newton.
2. Mr. Thomas Dewsnap.
3. Mr. Henry Hindle.
4. Mr. Aaron Walker.
5. Mr. William Rigby.
6. Mr. Jonathan Wild.
7. Mr. John Parnell.
Tenor.—Mr. John Whitehead.

And was conducted by Mr. Joseph Newton, the treble bell ringer.

A complete new peal of eight bells were opened at Flixton, seven miles from Manchester, in Lancashire, on Monday, the 25th day of January last, by the Manchester Society of Change Ringers, who completed a peal of Mr. John Holt's grandsire tripples, in ten courses, containing 5040 changes, in the time of three hours and four minutes, and was conducted by Mr. Holden.—Then came forward the Oldham Youths, and rang a complete fine peal of Mr. John Holt's grandsire tripples, also in ten courses, containing 5040 changes, which was completely brought round in the quick time of two hours and forty-seven minutes, and was conducted by Mr. Joseph Newton, who rung the fourth bell.

The College Youths from Ashton-under-line, ushered in Tuesday morning, with ringing a fine peal of Mr. John Holt's grandsire tripples, in ten courses, containing 5040 changes, which was completely brought round in the quick time of two hours and forty-five minutes, and gave general satisfaction to all attentive hearers. The amateurs in the art of Change Ringing, who attended this Flixton opening, amounted to 152 persons. —Weight of the tenor, 14cwt. 2qrs. 24lb. bell metal.

N. B. The above peal was conducted by Mr. Jonathan Wild, who rung the treble bell.

On

On Tuesday, the 5th of April, the Union Society of Change Ringers, at Shrewsbury, ascended the modern tower of St. Chad's Church, in that town, and in the time of six hours and fifty minutes, completely brought round a fine-rung peal of grandsire caters, composed of 10,097 harmonious changes; being the greatest performance ever achieved in that part of the kingdom.—Weight of the tenor, 34cwt. bell metal.

On Easter Monday last, the Oldham Youths paid a visit to the village of Mottram, in Cheshire, and rung a fine peal of Mr. John Holt's grandsire tripples, in ten courses, containing 5040 changes, which was brought round in the quick time of two hours and thirty-nine minutes, by the following youths; viz.

Treble.—Mr. James Taylor.
2. Mr. Robert Coope.
3. Mr. Henry Hindle.
4. Mr. Joseph Newton.
5. Mr. William Rigby.
6. Mr. Joshua Kershaw.
7. Mr. John Whitehead.
Tenor.—Mr. James Gartside.

The peal was conducted by Mr. Joseph Newton, who rung the fourth bell.—Weight of the tenor 13cwt. bell metal.

WILD CATS.

A CAUTION TO FARMERS.

THE following most singular instance of ferocity in the cat species, may be relied on as a fact :

Mr. G. Burton, steward to John Gurney, Esq. of Earlham, lately had an ewe die, that suckled a very fine lamb; he took the ewe away, and the lamb did not seem to regret the loss of its dam, but fed on the turnips, with the other large lambs; going his rounds early the next morning, he perceived this lamb lying dead, with its neck bloody, and its eyes out, which much surprised him, having left it quite well at dusk the preceding evening; supposing it too early to be done by crows, he took it home and flayed it, when it was found to have a small hole in its neck, about the size of a goose quill, and just below it a small place about the size of a six-pence, with the wool off, and apparently about half through the skin, and the wool, with part of the skin, scrabbled off the hind quarter, about the size of his three fingers, the wool lying in small lots by it when found. On looking amongst the others, he found there were two more living, and following their dams, with their necks bloody, and in the same state as before described in the dead one.

In the afternoon of Wednesday, the small one of the other two died; on flaying it, its neck was found to be in the same state, swelled and much gangrened, the blood much settled in its neck.—In the afternoon, Mr. John Scarnell, a near neighbour, to whom Mr. Burton had related the above circumstance, sent his two servants down to him with a large male cat, as judging him to be the murderer, by the following circumstance :—His servants having two kittens on the hay-loft, nearly half grown, and as they had always been in the habit of coming down into the stable the time of feeding the horses, and not having seen them in the course of the day, one of the men went up to see if he could find them, and feeling where they used to lie, this cat was found lying by them, and running down into an out-

out-house, they shut the door and secured him (he having been seen for three or four years on different premisesin Earlham) : on taking the kittens, they were found to be sucked just under the ear in the same way as the lambs were, and one of them having the hind part and half the body, with its inside eaten up; on opening the cat's body, a part of the skin of the kitten was found in its stomach, and a foot of it whole, and some small pieces of wool; Mr. Burton had observed before, (when the ground was covered by snow) the footing of a cat quite round the turnips, and among the ewes and lambs, but yet he never thought a cat would interrupt the lambs; and had not the above circumstance occurred, he believes it would never have been discovered, unless he had absolutely seen him attack the lambs. He therefore advises all persons seeing these wild cats strolling about, to destroy them, as the above circumstance is a proof of their pernicious qualities.

SPORTING SUBJECTS
IN THE
EXHIBITION OF THE ROYAL ACADEMY, 1808.

THE dead hare. — W. Mulready.

Morning, with a mill and cattle.—P. J. De Loutherbourg, R. A.

Trap-ball; portrait of a young gentleman.—H. Thomson, R. A.

Draught-player.—J. Burnett.

A shepherd with his flock.—Sir F. Bourgeois, R. A.

Boy and dog.—T. Clarke, A.

Sir David, by Trumpator, with Samuel Chifney; the property of his R. H. the Prince of Wales.—H. B. Chalon.

Card-players.—D. Wilkie.

Flying leap; fox dying.—J. N. Sartorius.

Orville, by Beningbrough, and Smallman, the groom; the property of his R. H. the Prince of Wales.—H. B. Chalon.

Barbarossa, by Sir Peter, the property of his R. H. the Prince of Wales.—H. B. Chalon.

Portrait of Pilot, formerly the property of Mr Lade.—D. Wolstenholm.

Portrait of a pointer.—J. Emery, H.

Fighting horses.—J. Ward, A.

Landscape: horse and figures.—R. B. Davis.

Portraits of a foreign nobleman and his horses.—B. Marshall.

Carlo; a portrait of a famous spaniel, the property of Mrs. Kennedy.—H. B. Chalon.

Portrait of an Irish mare.—J. Emery, H.

Cattle sheltering from a storm, with an effect of a rain-bow : Kitcat.—G. A. Grainger.

Portrait of a stallion.—J. N. Sartorius.

The favourite rabbit.—S. Drummond.

Dick Andrews, the property of Viscount Sackville.—J. Whessell.

Violante, the property of Earl Grosvenor.—J. Whessell.

Boar-hunting.—E. A. Spilsbury.

Portrait of a long-horned bull, the property of the Right Hon. Lord Viscount Anson.—T. Weaver.

The Sportsman's song.—G. Turner.

Portraits of Mr. Johnson's children, with a favourite poney.—J. Allen.

Children with wood-pigeons.—Miss Spilsbury.

Portrait

Portrait of a pug dog.—J. N. Sartorius.

Portrait of a favourite mare, belonging to the Right Hon. Viscountess Anson.—T. Weaver.

Tigers.—J. Ward, A.

View in the gardens of the Prince Borghese, near Rome, exhibiting a race between two English hunters, which took place in the Circus, in 1795.—J. Frearson.

Portrait of a dog, the property of Lord Viscount Sedley.—T. Highton.

The red grouse, or moorcock.—J. Sillett.

Rabbits.—J. Ward, A.

The young flageolet-player.—T. Stewardson.

Portrait of a sportsman, with setters.—W. Brown.

Girl with a nest.—W. Walker.

View of the interior of the six-stall stable at the Finsbury Repository.—D. Wolstenholm.

Dead game, from Nature.—Miss Dubuisson, H.

MODEL ACADEMY.

A study of a greyhound, from nature.—J. Coffee.

In the reference list of the catalogue, we notice the omission of the name and numbers of Mr. Emery's pictures. Of Mr. Emery it may be said, " he can soar with the eagle, or sit with the wren." —To notice his broad vacant humour on the stage, and his plain unaffected manners in private life, it might be supposed that he possessed no ideas beyond those which he gives life to on the boards of a Theatre : yet this said Mr. John Emery, comedian, of Covent Garden Theatre, to a strong mind adds a very correct taste in painting, music, &c.; his horses in this Exhibition are very well executed, for though they approach not to the excellence of his friend Marshall, they are nevertheless very respectable.

The other exhibitors in the sporting line, particularly Mr. Sartorius and Mr. Chalon, have each of them established characters, and require no eulogium from us.— Marshall's single picture is a most incomparable performance; he, likewise, wants not the aid of praise—look at No. 248, that is sufficient.

COLONEL THORNTON, ### AND HIS ATTORNIES.

THE following report of a cause in Chancery has been mislaid, or should have appeared sooner :—

IN CHANCERY.

Col. Thornton v. Harvey and Robinson, Attornies.

The defendants were called upon by the complainant to account for various sums of money, amounting to 14,000l. placed in their hands by him, for the purpose of paying his then existing debts, but which it was alledged the defendants had neglected to do; one of whom (Mr. Harvey) in an answer to the complaint, stated in excuse, his having, subsequent to the transaction, slept one night at Thornville Royal, and left certain papers containing the account of monies in his bed-chamber; and that he had applied several times to the Colonel for those papers, but had never been able to obtain them. The Colonel then addressed the Court, in person, and pledged himself that the excuse was an absolute fiction, never having heard any such circumstance until that moment, and earnestly requested the business might be immediately gone into.

The

The Chancellor assented, and said, he thought the Colonel acted very fairly and honourably, and ordered the affair to go immediately before the Master—And the Colonel is now using every means to facilitate a final settlement of this business.

COLONEL THORNTON MISREPRESENTED.

IN the newspapers there has lately appeared the following article :—.

"Suicide and duelling have been this winter in vogue; we understand a meeting took place between the sporting Colonel T— and Mr. P—, which was honourably settled by Major T—, who attended Colonel T—, and Lieutenant B—, who attended Mr. P—. Chalk Farm was the place fixed on, but as there was reason to believe that the parties would be watched, it was fixed by Colonel T—, at an early hour, in Kensington Gardens; the subject of dispute was cards."

But here we have an opportunity of doing justice to the Colonel, who is considered as a man that plays deep, and, as stories go, is said to have won Thornville Royal of the D— of Y—, a large sum of the Earl of C—e, and a still larger of L— G—n; whereas the fact is, he never played with the above personages, or any other; and further, a tablet of *verde-antique* marble, was put up on his arrival to his estate, with this inscription, "*Utinum hanc domus hanc veris amicis implean*," perfectly conspicuous; further adding, that no play, of any kind, was permitted in his house, which was consigned to hilarity, hospitality, and conviviality; and we have reason to believe, that the Colonel's determination to the observance of this rule, was the ground of the dispute alluded to above.

ALPHABETICAL LIST
OF
STALLIONS TO COVER IN 1806.

Continued from page 94.

AGRIMONY, at Battlesden, near Woburn, Bedfordshire, at 3gs. and 2s. 6d.—By Asparagus, out of an own sister to Trumpator, by Conductor.

ALLWORTHY (late Whitley) at Newark, at 1g. and half, and 2s. 6d.—By Orpheus, out of Beningbrough's dam.

ARTICHOKE, at Rutham, Cheshire, at 1g. and 2s. 6d.—By Don Quixote; dam by Dungannon, out of Lady Teazle, by High-flyer.

CENTRIPETAL (late Young Justice) at Sleaford, Lincolnshire, at 2gs. and 5s.—By Justice, out of Dido, by Eclipse.

CLEVELAND, at Burton, two miles from Lincoln, at 5gs. and 10s. 6d. — By Overton; dam, Charmer, (Saxoni and Cardinal York's dam) by Phenomenon.

CRYER, at Normanton, near Stamford, at 2gs.—By Alexander; dam by Sweetbriar, King Herod, out of Monimia's dam, by Alcides.

DOTTEREL, at Becket, near Faringdon, Berks, 3gs. and half, - and 5s.—By Buzzard; dam, Drowsy, by Drone, out of the late Mr. Goodricke's Old England Mare.

GOLDFINDER, at Gunby-Park, Lincolnshire, 1g. and half,

M   and

and 2s. 6d.—By Stamford; dam, Young Juno, by Old Goldfinder, out of Lord Lincoln's Juno.

HYPERION, at Wyke-Farm, near Brentford, at 7gs. and 10s. 6d. —By Highflyer; dam, Co-heiress, by Pot80's; grandam, Manilla, by Goldfinder, out of the late Mr. Goodricke's Old England Mare.

MARSK, at Newark, at 2gs. and 5s.—By Young Marsk; dam, Cora, (Timothy's dam) by Match-'em, Turk, Cub, out of A-la-greque's dam.

MONARCH, at Tring Grove, Herts, at one guinea and a half.— Bred by his Majesty, and rode by him as a charger for three years.— He is a dark chesnut, upwards of 16 hands and a half high, and got by Arrogant; dam by Bijou, out of a true Arabian mare.

PILGRIM, at Newark, at 3gs. and 5s.—By Restless; dam, Rosaletta, by Nabob, out of Rosetta, by Squirrel.

QUICKSILVER, at Bolingbroke, Lincolnshire, at one guinea and half.—By Quicksilver (son of Mercury); dam by Young Candidate; grandam by Mr. Turner's Spot, out of a daughter of Mr. Hunt's Jigg.

QUILTER, at the Manor Farm, Friern Barnet, near Whetstone, at 3gs. and 10s. 6d.—By Standard; dam by Young Sir Peter; grandam by Engineer, Mr. Wilson's Arabian.—Young Sir Peter was got by Doge, out of a sister to Mambrino by Engineer.

SAXE COBOURGH, at Netley, near Shrewsbury, at 5gs. and 10s. 6d.—By Boudrow; dam by Le Sang; grandam by Careless, out of Miss Barforth, by Snap.

TROWSERS, at Edmonthorpe-Hall, Leicestershire, 1g. and half, and 5s.—By Traveller; dam, Maria, by Carabineer, Priam, Cadee,

out of a daughter of Lord Gower's Stallion.

YOUNG CICERO, at the Red-Lion Yard, Gray's Inn-Lane, London, at 2gs.—He was got by Old Revenge; dam by Old Cicero, out of Sappho, by Turf.

YOUNG SIR PETER, at Bovingdon-Green, Herts, at 5gs.— By Sir Peter Teazle; dam by Woodpecker, Sweetbriar, out of Buzzard's dam, by Dux.

YOUNG TRUMPATOR, at Holme, next the sea, Norfolk; thorough-bred mares, which have won the value of 50l. gratis.—By Old Trumpator; dam by Conductor, King Herod, Match'em, Snap, Lord Cullen's Arabian.

MAY IN LONDON.

THE passing month is that which is most distinguished in the metropolis for the variety and gaiety of its amusements. Whoever has passed his days in distant retirement, and wishes to know what London can produce, must visit it in the month of May. Whoever would know the full tide of the happiness of town life, of all that fashion prescribes, and all that crowds follow, must come to London in May. London is the world, and May the sun that cheers, enlightens, and invigorates, all that can make life tolerable.—Sorrow is now banished by universal consent.—Time flies in a perpetual circle of delight, and the diversions of night and day are no longer acknowledged.

In May, the votaries of pleasure agree to assemble in general congress. Every town and every village send up their deputies and represenpresentatives, to assist in the councils of fashion, and to bring down the last intrigue, and the newest cap. On their return, they animate rustic conversation by a detail of wonders, of plays and operas, concerts and exhibitions, routs and panoramas. They demand attention, and ensure submission, by the superiority of having seen and heard all that with which London gratifies the eye and ear. They shew, by the rapid circulation of a thousand private surmises, and a thousand confidential hints, how little can be learned from the printed reports of the papers, and how frequently a fashionable event is in danger of being mutilated by ignorance or suppressed from fear.

Then the parks on a May-Sunday! What a delightful *pele-mele*! To elbow all whom one wishes to know—to be admitted gratis to see *live* lords and ladies—and on *one's* return to be able to say that *one* actually saw all this with *one's* own eyes! What a triumph over rural ignorance! How little qualified are they to live in the world, and how shockingly unprepared to leave it must they be, who have not visited *London* in May—the *whole world* in May—*every body* in May!

FASHIONABLE GAMING TABLE.

"I Cannot conceive," said Lady Alspice to her partner, "what is the meaning of your holding such very bad cards."

The gentleman confessed, with every mark of contrition, "that his cards had been very bad."

"Bad," rejoined she, "they were detestable, Sir!—I never saw any body hold such; I own I do not understand it."

"Why, Madam," said he, "that my cards were bad was my misfortune, as well as your ladyship's."

"That is nothing to the purpose," rejoined she.

"I really do not know what apology would satisfy you," resumed the gentleman, "but I may safely assure your ladyship, upon my honour," laying his hand on his breast, "that I have all the inclination in the world to hold good cards."

"Sir," replied she, with a look of dignity, "I would not willingly call any gentleman's honour in question, but I cannot help remarking, that you had good hands when you were her Grace's partner; it was not till you became mine, that you had bad cards. This you will permit me to say, seems a little unaccountable."

"However unaccountable it may seem, I think I can explain it," said the Duchess, interfering. "The gentleman's having held honours when he was my partner, and not when he was your's, may have proceeded from my being at present in a run of good luck."

"That will account for it, unquestionably, but I wish your Grace had been so good as to have informed me of it a little sooner."

"Why truly, I only began to suspect it myself after I had won the second rubber, and I was not absolutely certain until after I had won the third."

FEAST OF WIT.

THAT eccentric preacher, Orator Henley, once, by advertisement, invited the licensed victuallers to a lecture on "social morality," after which he promised to inform them "how they should sell more porter than they usually did."—It is little to be doubted but that the oratory was on this important occasion crowded with publicans. The orator was particularly animated and entertaining ; he explained to them the nature of their situation and duties, descanted on the various characters of their guests, and many other collateral circumstances : at last he said, "My brethren, to perform my promise, and, by explaining to you how you shall sell more beer, endeavour to inculcate a moral duty, I must apprise you that my instructions can never be forgotten. because they are comprised in three words, "*Fill your Pots!*"

A SAILOR's Account of his Journey in a Stage-Coach :—Hove out of Portsmouth on board the Britannia Fly—a swift sailer—an outside birth—rather drowsy the first watch or two—like to have slipped off the stern—cast anchor at the George—took a fresh quid and a supply of grog—comforted the upper works—spoke several homeward-bound frigates on the road, and after a tolerably smooth voyage entered the port of London at ten minutes past five, post meridian —steered to Nan's lodgings, and unshipped my cargo—Nan admired the shiners—so did landlady —gave them a handful a-piece—

emptied a bowl of the right sort with landlady and Nan to the health of my Admiral.—All three set sail for the play—got a birth in a cabin on the larboard side—wanted to smoke a pipe, but the boatswain would not let me—Nan, I believe, called the play Poll-zaro, with Harlekin Hamlet—but d—n me if I knew stem from stern—remember to rig out Nan like the fine folks in the cabin right a-head— saw Jack Junk aloft in the corner of the upper deck—hailed him— the signal returned—some of the lubbers in the cockpit began to laugh—tipped 'em a little forecastle lingo till they sheered off—emptied the grog-bottle—fell fast asleep— dreamt of the battle of Trafalgar— Nan told me the play was over— glad of it—crowded sail for a hackney-coach—got on board—squally weather—rather inclined to be sea-sick—arrived at Nan's lodgings— gave the pilot a two-pound note, and told him not to mind the change—supped with Nan, and swung in the same hammock— overlooked my rhino in the morning—great deal of it to be sure— but I hope, with the help of a few friends, to spend every shilling of it in a little time, to the honour and glory of Old England.

The *Johnsonian style* is not yet worn out in our familiar addresses. The projector of a Sunday paper informs his readers, that he will admit no quack advertisements.— "Their vile indecency shall not *gloat* through the mask of philanthropy ; sickness shall not be flattered

tered into *incurability;* nor debauchery indulged to the last gasp by the promises of instant restoration!"

As Mr. Fox was going down upon a visit to Lord Albemarle, at Elvedon, some time in the year 1805, his chaise broke down at Barton Mills; he was extricated from his perilous situation by a young gentleman, who resided near the spot. Enquiring, afterwards, to whom he had been so much indebted, he learnt that the gentleman's name was Buck. "Buck," said the distinguished orator, "then I am the more obliged to him; many a *Buck* has led me *into* a scrape, but few have extricated me *from one.*

Notwithstanding Napoleon's avowed fidelity to his *Empress,* he has been long hankering after the possession of a *Foreign Queen.* But with a noble spirit she has resisted, and will never submit to his wishes. From her situation and dignity, she is called *the Queen of the Ocean.*

A DRAGOON in Dublin was shot for desertion, and taking away his horse and accoutrements at the same time. When on his trial, an officer asked him, "What could induce him to take away his horse?" To which he replied, "He ran away with me."—"What," said the officer, "did you do with the money you sold him for?"—"That," said the fellow, "please your honour, ran away too."

WHEN the fight was on Epsom Down, between Belcher and Dogherty, there was, as is usual, a plentiful supply of erections for the spectators to witness it: amongst the number, Mr. Pierce, the carrier, of Epsom, brought his waggon, and finding a more numerous company than he expected, went back to Epsom to fetch another waggon, but while he was so doing, one of the London *Gemmen,* who came to make a harvest, shewed the spectators up into the one he had left, at two shillings per head. Mr. Pierce, after a short time, arrived with the other waggon, and began to bully and abuse the people for getting into his waggon, and desired them to get out, or give him half-a-crown; they would, of course, do neither, and told him they had paid two shillings already; he asked them who they had paid it to, when they pointed to the cockney, and Pierce says, "Come Sir, you hand over," the cockney answered, "he had spent it all." Pierce, of course, was obliged to put up with the joke, and content himself with the benefit of the other waggon only, after a hearty laugh from the people who heard the dialogue.—The money the cockney took amounted to between thirty and forty shillings.

THE word *bother* was first used by a serjeant, who being exposed to the volubility of two Irishmen, *one at each ear,* cried, "don't *both ear* me!"—Hence the verb *to bother.*

QUEER Pun. — Two cocknies reasoning upon the cause of the late prevalence of *wet weather,* one of them said he had no doubt that it was owing to the *number of Kings* lately created by BONAPARTE. How can that be, enquired the other? why because there are now more people *raining* (reigning) than ever.

ON A LATE SENATORIAL SERMON PREACHED BY A NEW-MADE BISHOP.

'TWAS *well enough* that *Goodenough*
Before the House should preach;
For *sure enough* full *bad enough*
Were those he had to teach!

THE Ruling Passion strong in Death.—When Hal Spedding, the celebrated gambler, was on his death-bed, he addressed his physician in these words—" Doctor, I know your skill, and I believe you are an honest man ; I am about to put a question to you, the answer to which will not alarm me, be it what it may—How many days do you think I may live ?" " *Three,*" said the doctor.—" I'll bet you twenty guineas," cried the patient, " that I will *four.*"—Spedding died the next morning.

EPITAPH ON JOHN BULLY, IN WELSTED CHURCH-YARD.

OLD purse-proud Bully lieth underneath,
Who *bully'd* poor folk far and nigh him;
Nay, more, he thought to bully Death,
But Death would not be *bully'd* by him.

THE Dublin Corporations are all resolving against the union. The *Tailors* declare it does not *suit*, and requires to be *trimmed*. The *Butchers* are *carving* away at it, and declare it ought to be entirely *cut up.* The *Smiths* have much *striking* opposition upon the *anvil*, and are of opinion that the " *iron* ought to be struck while *hot.*" The *Shoemakers* say it must be *awl* over with them if it obtains a further *footing.* The *Musicians* declare that all *harmony* is lost, and are fretting themselve to *fiddle-strings ;* and the *Barbers* vow, that the *shavers* who support it must be well *lathered.*

LINEAL DESCENT.—A late publication gives the following anecdote on heraldic honours:—A man applied at the College for a coat of arms, who was asked if any of his ancestors had been renowned for any singular achievement ? The man paused and considered, but could recollect nothing.—" Your father," said the herald, aiding his memory; —" your grandfather, — great grandfather ?"—" No," returns the applicant, " I never knew that I *had* a great grandfather or a grandfather !"—" Of yourself ?" asks this creator of dignity—" I know nothing remarkable of *myself,*" returned the man, " only that once being locked up in Lud gate prison for debt, I found means to escape from an upper window; and that you know is no honour in a man's 'scutcheon."—" And how did you get down ?" said the herald : " Odd enough," retorts the man—" I procured a cord, fixed it round the neck of the statue of King Lud, on the outside of the building, and thus let myself down."—" I *have* it," said the herald—" No honour ? *Lineally descended from King Lud !* and his coat of arms will do for *you !*"

THE DILEMMA.

WHEN I'm afflicted with the *gout*,
My wife she scolds me night and day,
Right well she knows what she's about,
She knows I cannot *run away* !

DURING a recent debate in the House of Commons, about *four* in the morning, a member was called to order for *snoring*; while a very eminent orator was addressing the House.—When a division took place, the Speaker, as usual, put the question—" Those who are for the amendment say *aye*, and those who are of a contrary opinion say *no.*"—A gentleman who was near the snoring

snoring member, exclaimed from the gallery the *nose* had it.

Two *white* rooks have lately been discovered in a rookery, in Cambridgeshire. The owner may make a fortune by showing them at *Newmarket!*

THE Retort Courteous.—The late Mr. Charles Fox, who possessed no small portion of eccentricity of character, once hastily told an impertinent fellow he would " *kick* him to *hell!*" " If you do, (said the intended *kickée*) I'll tell your *father* how you are spending his money!"

IMPROMPTU.

DICK, known for a libertine, drunkard,
   and rake,
  Was heard by his friends with great
    wonder;
(Who knew with religion he'd liberties
    take,
And call each good parson a dunder)

To assert with an *oath* and a *serious* face,
  That a penitent grown and converted,
He long'd to his soul, for a *calling to
    grace,*
And that all his old sins he'd deserted.

" How Dick!" cried a friend, quite asto-
    nish'd to hear
  Love of grace from the mouth of a
    sinner,
But Dick stopp'd him short, with " My
    boy, never fear,
'*Tis the calling to grace before dinner!*"

STELLA Magiora, or Living Phenomenon.—We entertain our readers with the description of a most strange production of nature, consisting of an animal apparently a handsome black heifer, with a surprising branch growing from the shoulders, one part whereof measures sixteen inches in circumference, rising above three feet from the body, at the end of which is a singular horny substance, resem-

bling a lobster's claw, another distinct limb growing also from the same projection, in the shape of a deer's leg, at the end of which, in lieu of a deer's foot, is a full-sized goat's-horn: this surprising and truly astonishing curiosity, was bred on the Alps, in Italy, near Genoa, and lately landed at Portsmouth from Holland, and has been exhibited before the Hon. Company of the Agricultural Society, patronised by his Grace the Duke of Bedford, Lord Somerville, &c. in London, who, with high satifaction, pronounced it to be the greatest natural curiosity of the present æra.

SINGULAR ADVERTISEMENT.— Ten Guineas Reward.—Dropped Child.—Parish of St. James, Westminster.—Dropped on Saturday night last, about twelve o'clock, at the Marquis of Buckingham's door, Pall-Mall, a female child, in a new flag basket, supposed to be about three weeks old; had on when found, a cambric muslin frock, a white dimity petticoat, a spotted lace muslin cap, a white calico bedgown, and a blanket; and a small gold seal, with a garter of blue ribbon was tied round its waist. Also in the basket, three damask napkins and a blanket: was directed on the basket, to the Marchioness of Buckingham. Also a copy of verses, the first and last stanza as follow:—

  In me, sweet lady, here you see
    An helpless orphan child,
  The offspring of a guilty love
    Indulg'd in transport wild:
  Transport me to some lonely cot,
    Where I may live unknown,
  Far from the purlieus of the town,
    To vice and folly prone.

THE Corporation of *Cooks* in Dublin, have agreed to petition for a repeal of the Union. The petition is well seasoned with *attic salt,* and is *dished* up in a very neat style.

COURT

COURT MARTIAL

ON

ASSISTANT-SURGEON THOMAS TALBOT,

As reported in General Orders.

Horse-Guards, May 21, 1808.

AT a General Court Martial, held at Kingston Barracks, Jamaica, on the 1st of September, 1807, and continued by adjournments to the 7th of December following, Assistant-Surgeon Thomas Talbot, of the 1st Battalion of the 60th Regiment, was arraigned on the following charges; viz.

" 1st. For writing a highly disrespectful and insubordinate memorial to the Commander in Chief at Jamaica, in which he accuses his Excellency of having prejudged and treated him with injustice.

" 2d. For writing a mutinous and seditious letter to the Deputy Adjutant-General.

" 3d. For writing another memorial to the Commander in Chief, falsely accusing Brigadier-General Carmichael of oppression and injustice in the execution of his duty.

The 4th, 5th, and 6th charges, are of a similar nature.

" 7th. For seditiously attempting to excite a spirit of discontent and disaffection to his Majesty's service, by endeavouring to impress an opinion, that the troops had been tyrannically used, oppressed, and treated with injustice.

" 8th, For conduct extremely prejudicial to his Majesty's service, by preferring charges against his superior Officers.

" 9th. For mutiny on the evening of the 16th April, 1807, at the barrack, Montego Bay, first, by threatening to kick his Commanding Officer, Captain Graw, out of the mess-room, when in the execution of his duty, making use of

scurrilous language to him, and drawing, or offering to draw, his dirk or dagger, and attempting to assault him (Captain Graw) in presence of the Officers and men ; secondly, by not retiring, when ordered so to do by Captain Graw, his Commanding Officer, after having been put in arrest, and continuing to offer personal insult to him in the presence of Officers and men, whom he excited by his example, and instigated, to join in a party or combination against Captain Graw."

He was found guilty of seven of these charges.

" The Court sentences the prisoner, Assistant-Surgeon Talbot to be cashiered.

" And the Court further adjudges him unworthy to serve his Majesty in any military capacity. This sentence to be publicly read to him, and his sword broken over his head.

" The Court, considering this sentence inadequate, regrets the Mutiny Act does not authorise transportation to be awarded on crimes of such magnitude, a punishment which appears to it peculiarly applicable to an offender of this dangerous description, when the circumstances of the case may not incur the forfeiture of life."

His Majesty has been pleased to approve of the finding and sentence of the Court, and to command the same should be carried into effect, in the presence of the whole garrison where the prisoner is stationed.

His Majesty has been further pleased to command, that the conduct of Lieutenant-Colonel Rainey may be immediately investigated by a General Court Martial, in order that Lieutenant-Colonel Rainey may have an opportunity of accounting for the peculation and
other

J.Ward pinx.   H.R.Cook sculp.

The Shepherds Dog.

other abuses which appear to have existed in the battalion under his command, in which it also appears the Lieutenant-Colonel was materially concerned, and which it must be considered to have been his duty as Commanding Officer to have prevented and detected, and to have brought the authors to punishment.

HARRY CALVERT, Adj. Gen.

THE SHEPHERD'S DOG.

An Engraving, by H. R. Cook, from a Painting by Mr. Ward.

ALTHOUGH we cannot compliment ourselves on the choice of this subject, as connected with sporting, we nevertheless most chearfully admit of the merit of the painter and engraver in the design and execution of it. We shall not take up much time or space in a description of this *elevated* class of the canine race, but only observe, that the Shepherd's Dog has many claims to the respect of his master, being generally found a prompt, vigilant, and faithful servant.

MATCH AGAINST TIME.

To the Editor of the Sporting Magazine.

SIR,

THE nonpareil (and, I believe, the *Ne plus ultra)* of all trotting performances in harness, was this morning accomplished by a horse belonging to Mr. Michael Weston, stable-keeper, near Moorfields. I attended to keep the time. He started to perform fourteen miles within the hour, which he performed in fifty-nine minutes and forty-three seconds, leaving seventeen seconds to spare; he scoured very much, and exhibited evident marks of distress for the

last four miles. Bettings were considerably against him, and, but for the masterly driving of Mr. Charles Hull, of Little Moorfields, must have been beaten. It has often been tried by the best horses for the last twenty years, but never completed.—Your's,

H. OLDFIELD.

Fenny Stanton, Saturday Morning, May 21.

Seven miles out and seven miles in, between Cambridge and Huntingdon.

IN addition to the above we learn, that the bet was 250l. to 50l. against the horse. The match had occupied the attention of the sporting world in a manner but seldom heard of; and, although decided so far from London as between Cambridge and Huntingdon, there were thousands of spectators to witness it. The horse kept a steady winning pace the whole way, without once breaking into a gallop.

MR. SAMUEL BURDER.

IN St. Mary's Church-yard, Suffolk, is a tomb-stone, on which is engraved the following inscription :—

TO THE MEMORY OF SAMUEL BURDER,

Who unfortunately lost his life in riding a match for Mr. Fortescue, at Newmarket, 17 April, 1770, aged 29 years.

The above-mentioned Mr. Samuel Burder was Jockey to the late Lord Clermont. In riding a match over the Beacon Course, he was driven against a post, and died a few hours after.—Since the above accident, (occasioned by crossing and jostling) the practice is forbidden by the Jockey Club. G. T.

N   SPORT-

SPORTING INTELLIGENCE.

GOODWOOD Races commenced on Tuesday the 10th instant, when the Hunters' Plate of 50l. was won by Mr. Gage's Pic Nic, by Ramsden, out of Skyscraper.—Wednesday, the Silver Cup, value 50gs. was won by Mr. Trevanion's Bucephalus, by Alexander, beating Sir Launcelot, &c.—This was a great betting race.—The Hunters' Plate of 50l. was won by Mr. Gage's Pic Nic:—And the Ladies' Plate of 60gs. by Lord Egremont's Election, by Gohanna; beating Mr. Buttler's Epsom, and Captain Haffenden's Tom Pipes, (who ran the Three-mile Course by mistake, and was distanced the first heat.)—The betting was high on Election, who won easy.—A more particular account will be given in our next Number.

At a meeting of the inhabitants of Boroughbridge, Yorkshire, held in the last week of April, it was agreed, that the Horse Races usually held there, should in future be discontinued.—These races first commenced in April, 1757, when there were three 50l. plates run for; the first of which was won by Mr. Smith's Careless, by Traveller; the second by Mr. Stanhope's Short-hose, by Regulus; and the third by Mr. Hunt's Poor Farmer, by Sloe.

The Races at Catterick Bridge were not so numerously attended this year as usual, on account of the severity of the weather. A great quantity of snow fell during the second day, which was allowed to be one of the most stormy we have had this last season.

SKIPTON Meeting was also thinly attended.—In running for the Hunters' Stakes, the first day, Lord Ribblesdale's Horse, Neighbour, broke his bridle, and his rider, Mr. Simpson, pulled him up luckily at the distance post. In the second heat, Neighbour made severe play, and won easy.—In the second day's race for the Plate, Clotilda fell over a post, when supposed to be winning.

DURHAM Races were attended by the most numerous and fashionable company ever known at that place.—The Lambton-hunt Stakes, and several Hunters' Stakes and Matches, ridden by gentlemen, afforded great amusement. Mr. Tatton Sykes, as usual, was allowed to be the best rider.—He rode the winner of the Hunters' Stakes at Skipton, on Thursday, and came a distance of near ninety miles, to ride at Durham next day.

On Thursday the 5th instant, the gentlemen of the H. H. C. held their anniversary on Soberton Down, Hants; there was much sport, and the fineness of the day, together with the beautiful scenery of the country, attracted a numerous and respectable company.—A cup, given by Mr. Powlett, value 50gs. was won by Mr. Aylward's bay mare; a cup of the same value, given by the officers of the Portsdown, or South-East Hants Yeomanry Cavalry, (run for by the corps) was won by Mr. Stewart's brown mare Cottager; and the members' subscription cup, of the like

like value, was won by Mr. Minchin's brown horse. A subscription has commenced to purchase two 50l. plates for the next year.

THERE are now ten subscribers to the sweepstakes of 10gs. each, the first morning of Worcester races, and ten horses named; to the sweepstakes of 5gs. each (in addition to the hunters' purse) there are eight subscribers.

DOTTEREL have been very scarce on the Wolds this year, and wild geese equally so through the winter. The great improvements that have been made in the agriculture of these parts may account for this; and the drainage of the Carrs has nearly annihilated snipe-shooting.

IT is supposed that there has been a greater mortality amongst the foals this year than ever was known. Many gentlemen have lost half their stock. Lords Grosvenor and Egremont have been the principal sufferers.

IT has been decided, and which is useful to be known, that a huntsman is liable to be informed against and pay the penalty, who goes out with hare-hounds, if his master be not present. This does not involve the case of fox-hounds.

SIR Charles Bunbury has sold Rambler to the Duke of Rutland for 400gs.

COCKING.—A Long Main of Cocks was fought at the Cock-pit Royal, Essex-street, Dublin, on Monday, March 14, and the five following days, between the gentlemen of the county of Armagh, (Gallagher, feeder and setter) ; and the gentlemen of the King's County, (Archy, feeder and setter) for 20gs. a battle, and 1000gs. the main, which was won by the former, viz.

Gallagher.	M.	B.	Archy.	M.	B.
Monday,	3	2		2	0
Tuesday,	4	1		1	1
Wednesday,	4	0		1	2
Thursday,	2	1		3	1
Friday,	4	2		1	0
Saturday,	3	1		2	1
Total	20	7		10	5

A very good and well-fought main, and great betting.

WE are informed, that Sir Henry Tempest Vane and Mr. Brandling have engaged to fight two mains, (three seasons each) one of the engagements at Durham, and the other at Newcastle.—To commence next spring.

Two *white* rooks were lately taken from the rookery of Edward Curtis, Esq. of Dutton, near Cambridge. They have not a black feather about them ; their legs and beaks are also white. They are both now alive.

A FINE swan, on a piece of water belonging to the Marquis of Stafford, was lately observed to be struggling and very much agitated, with its head under water, in which state it continued till the bird was completely lifeless. Upon approaching it with a boat, and lifting up the body of the swan, a large pike, of about 12lbs. weight, was drawn up, suspended at the neck, near the head, its voracity proving fatal to both.

TEN lambs were killed at Moorside Park, belonging to Mr. Dickinson, near Whitehaven, by two eagles, a few days since.

A FEW days ago, a litter of six young foxes was found amongst the ivy upon the wall just over the gates that lead from the inner court into the gardens, at Warwick Castle.

N 2   AT

AT the end of the Hunting Season, the Westfield hounds unkennelled a fox on Fairlight Down, which, after a long and gallant chase, they killed in good style. The gentlemen who were in at the death retired from the field to the Hare and Hounds, near Hastings, where they regaled on the heart of poor Reynard, and, like true sons of the chase, washed down the delicious morsel with bumpers of punch, highly flavoured with the perfume of his brush.

CERTIFICATES for Shooting.—A clause has been introduced into this Bill, which exempts persons from the game duty who use guns to shoot rabbits on their own grounds.

THERE is, within two miles of Couper Angus, Forfarshire, in the possession of a gentleman farmer, a tame otter, which has been in a domestic state these two years, This animal is as tame as a dog, and sleeps every night in bed with one of the farmer's sons.

THE following passage is not the production of any obscure pugilist of the present day, but from the pen of one of the most enlightened philosophers and most powerful writers that now adorn this country :—" The frequenters of our boxing-matches would probably feel as much horror and disgust as any other persons, were they to see men deprived of the power of resistance, or opposed to very unequal force, beaten as the several combatants beat each other ; but the display of manly intrepidity, firmness, gallantry, activity, strength, and presence of mind, which these contests call forth, is an honour to the English nation, and such as no man needs to be ashamed of viewing with interest, pride, and de-

light : and we may safely predict, that if the Magistrates, through a mistaken notion of preserving the public peace, succeed in suppressing them, there will be an end of that sense of honour and spirit of gallantry, which distinguishes the common people of this country, from that of all others ; and which is not only the best guardian of their morals, but perhaps the only security now left, either for our civil liberty or political independence. If men are restrained, from fighting occasionally for prizes and honorary distinctions, they will soon cease to fight at all, and decide their quarrels with daggers instead of blows ; in which case the lower order will become a base rabble of cowards and assassins, ready, at any time, to sacrifice the higher to the avarice and ambition of a foreign tyrant."—*Knight on Taste, part* 3, *ch.* 1. *sect.* 13.

THE following notice was published in the *County Chronicle* the day on which it is dated :—

Buckingham - House, London, May 8.—Information having been transmitted to me, his Majesty's Custos Rotulorum in and for the county of Bucks, of an intended riotous assembly, aiding and assisting in breach of the peace, by a boxing match, within that part of the county of Bucks which touches or joins on the counties of Bedford and Herts, near the town of Dunstable ; and that the said illegal and riotous assembly will take place on Tuesday the 10th instant, notice is hereby given, that proper steps have been taken for the detection and punishment of all persons acting as aforesaid, in breach of the peace, by the attendance of the magistrates, high constables, petty constables, and other peace-officers,

officers, entrusted with the execution of the law within the said county.

"NUGENT BUCKINGHAM,
Custos Rotulorum of
Bucks."

THURSDAY, May 19, a pitched battle was fought on Wilsden-Green, by two men, who possess a deal of science in the pugilistic art, though young, and will shortly be better known among the fashionable bruisers. The one is of the name of Jerry, better known by the name of My Lord, as being rather diminutive in stature, but well-built for a pugilist—the other named Hockley, known by the nick-name of Little Dicky. Jerry shewed a deal of play in the first round, but by a sudden and well-timed hit, he threw Hockley off his guard, and gave him a most tremendous blow in the throat, which he did not seem to relish. They both shewed a deal of pluck, and after severe fighting for twenty-five minutes, My Lord was declared the victor. Several gentlemen amateurs were present, who declared they fought admirably.

On the night of the Countess of Essex's grand rout, the Earl of T—lle's and the Earl of C—l's carriages drove up at the same time. The Earl of T—lle's reached the door first, and received him, his Countess, and daughters. The Earl of C—l, dissatisfied with his coachman, ran down the steps, seized the reins of the horses, and backed his own carriage, endeavouring, at the same time, to take the coachman from the box. The servants took the part of their brother of the whip; the Earl of C—l was very roughly handled, and obliged to sound a retreat, after

having fallen under the horses' feet.

A Fracas arose on Newmarket course, between Mr. M—ish and Mr. C. B—wn, in consequence of their both riding in with their horses that were running with a precipitancy that brought them into a kind of contact that produced some personal altercation, and which was expected to take a very serious turn; by the timely interposition of turf friends, however, it was agreed, that neither should have the whip hand of the other, so that mutual apologies were given and received, to prevent the owners of blood horses spilling their own blood unnecessarily.

AT the last quarter sessions of the peace at Salisbury, John Pretejohn, Esq. and his coachman were fined, the master 50gs. and the servant 1l. for an assault upon John Lane, an old and infirm but respectable farmer, at Hurst, near Reading.

CRUELTY to Horses.—Little as we are inclined to feel or express satisfaction at the punishment of our fellow-men, yet when their conduct towards inferior animals degrades them below the suffering objects of their cruelty, we conceive it our duty to apprise those whose brutal propensities are not subjected to the controul of reason, that nevertheless they are amenable to the laws of their country, which are founded in wisdom and humanity. Thus, with the view of preventing the recurrence of shocking barbarity, we insert the commitment to the Northampton county gaol of the two following delinquents:—Joshua Pointer, and William Hill, boatmen, servants to Messrs.

Messrs. Pickford and Co. were convicted before J. P. Clarke, Esq. of Welton-Place, of over-driving and cruelly treating the horses entrusted to their care, while employed in towing the boats upon the Grand Junction Canal. Pointer was ordered to be confined 21, and Hill 14 days. These sentences, comparatively mild, we trust will have due effect toward inducing proper treatment to that nobly useful, but ill-fated animal, the horse; and particularly as the magistrates in that quarter have expressed their determination to make examples in future of all persons who may be found guilty of similar practices.

ANOTHER instance similar to the above occurred during the present month, when John Lumb, of Wakefield, was apprehended by a warrant, for beating his horse in a most unmerciful and cruel manner, and put in prison all night. Next morning a committal was ordered to be made out, but in consideration of his family, and his penitent behaviour, he was suffered to depart on payment of the expences, and promising not to be again guilty of such cruelty.

THURSDAY morning, May 5, at twenty-one minutes after five o'clock, Captain Thompson, of the 74th regiment, started at the 7th mile-stone, on the Ellon road, near Aberdeen, returning to the 4th, till he should perform a distance of one-and-twenty miles, in a given time of three hours. He accomplished the task in four minutes and a half less than the time. The first fifteen miles he went in two hours. This may be considered as an instance of the greatest exertion, and as one of the most uncommon sporting feats ever performed

in Scotland. Much money was depending on the match.

ON Monday, the 9th, a pedestrian match against time took place on the Margate road, when Mr. Samuel Morrell, of Canterbury, for a wager of forty guineas, undertook to walk twenty miles in four successive hours, which he performed within twenty-one minutes of the given space. The first five miles were walked in sixty minutes, the second five in forty-eight minutes, the third five in fifty-six minutes, and the last five in fifty-five minutes.

SPORTS of Plowden Fair.—The Saturday of Plowden Fair, Hants, afforded plenty of amusement to the lovers of athletic sports. Previous to the usual diversion of donkey-racing, grinning through a horse's collar, virgins racing for shifts, &c. a match of single-stick playing between Hants and Somerset counties, and a pitched battle between two provincial professors, took place. The amusement began as early as eight o'clock in the morning, when Hasell and Grey contended for a prize of twenty guineas at single-stick, which was won by Grey, who contended with Davies, and was beat by him. Hasell, and another man of the name of Curtis, who belonged to Hants, with Davies, contended for the prize, which was won with difficulty by Curtis, and Hants was the successful county. The battle for a subscription purse of twenty guineas took place at ten o'clock, and after an obstinate contest of ten minutes only (no time being allowed), Godden, the favourite before setting to, beat his man, a miner of the name of Oldfield. The fair was not over until dusk in the evening.

POETRY.

POETRY.

THE HIGH COURT OF DIANA.

LINES
TO THE MEMORY OF MY SPANIEL,
DASH.

WOODCOCKS, pheasants, snipes,
　　rejoice,
No more you'll hear poor Dash's voice;
Gun! thou now may'st lie to rust,
For Dash is number'd with the dust.

How oft, with wriggling tail, so blest,
I've mark'd thee 'midst the cover quest,
And never knew thee fail to say
Where ev'ry feather'd trembler lay.

And when, by well-directed gun,
I kill'd my bird—how thou would'st
　　run!
And take it up so clean and neat,
Then lay it at thy master's feet.

Exulting now, with speaking eye,
Silent and still, thou down would'st lie,
And staunch as any pointer stay,
Until the word was given—Away!

I do not think that often, Dash,
Thou felt from me the odious lash,
But I had little cause to use it,
And am not one who would abuse it.

I own I've chided thee when, flush'd
With heat of chase, thou'st rashly rush'd,
And sprung at pheasant, now for in-
　　stance,
When I have been far out of distance.

And this thou know'st was very wrong,
For this thou sometimes felt the thong;
Yet we continued friends to th' last,
And never dwelt on what was past.

Fare, fare, thee well! I ne'er shall find
An equal thou hast left behind;
Ne'er more shall view thy honest face,
Thou first of all the spaniel race.
　　　　　　　　　　R. S.
B. Warwick-Lane, May 25, 1808.

THE RUSTIC's CREED.

LET Kings be clad in robes of state,
　　And Lords in lace upon them wait,
And bend the knee and bow the pate,
　　And teach their tongues to flatter;
Far happier I, in Skiddaw Grey,
With angling rod to haste away,
On Weisa's banks to sing and play,
　　Than Kings with all their clatter.

Let courtiers jostle in the race
That's run for pension and for place,
Take the whip-hand, or cross the chase,
　　To gain the loaves and fishes:
To me it matters not a pin,
Or who is out, or who is in,
I eat my crust with little din,
　　And circumscribe my wishes.

Let Aldermen, with wond'rous glee,
Bolt Calipash and Calipee,
And rich ragouts unknown to me,
　　Confections, tarts, and jelly;
Less luscious meats me better suit,
A mess of beans, or parsnip root,
Will guard my great toe from the gout,
　　From spasms protect my belly.

Let gentry in their coaches ride,
And, lolling, look with mickle pride,
And lacquies caper by their side,
　　With many a crack and quaver;
My heart far nobler pleasure feels,
With honest Bawty at my heels,
Whilst angling for my trouts and eels
　　In Wampool or in Waver.

Let misers cent. per cent. their store,
And starve in want, to make it more,
Pile up their guineas score by score,
　　And idolise their riches;
I envy not their heaps—not I!
Life's comforts I contrive to buy
With forty pounds' annuity,
　　And wear undarned breeches.

Oft have I mus'd, and mus'd again,
(And still the thought inflicted pain)
　　　　　　　　　　　　That

That oft the rich the poor disdain,
  And frown them from their dwelling;
While men less rich we may descry,
Who ne'er poor beggar-man deny,
Where want speaks from his pleading
        eye;
  This tale is worth the telling!

QUINTETTO,

FROM THE FARCE OF " WHO WINS?
    OR, THE WIDOW'S CHOICE."

*Trust, Matthew, Extempore, Caper, and
    the Widow Bellair.*

Trust. THE dice-box take, the terms you
        know—
      He wins, who throws the high-
        est throw.
Mrs. B.—O fortune favour my request,
(aside)   And let him win, who I like best.
Extemp. I always lost at ev'ry game,
      And now expect to do the same.
Caper.   I never lost in all my life,
      So now for riches and a wife.
Matthew. I well know which I wish to
        win,
      O Fortune, take the merchant in!
Mrs. Bel. Now, fortune with my hopes
        keep pace.
Extemp. (after What is my throw?
  throwing)   Is it high?
Caper.   Or is it low?
Matthew. It is deuce ace!
All.   It is deuce ace!
Mrs. Bel. (aside) Deuce ace!—ah me!
Caper.   Deuce ace! ha, ha!
Matthew. Deuce ace, I see—
All.   He'll lose, I see—
Mrs. Bel. How the odious wretch gri-
        maces!
Caper.   Come, the box, and take your
        places;
      What is my throw?
        Is it high?
Extemp. Or is it low?
All.   High or low?
Matthew. He has thrown aces!
Extemp. Aces! then I've won!
Mrs. Bel. (aside) Aces—ho! ho!
Caper.   I have lost and am undone!—
All.   He has lost, and is undone.
All.   Now if the lady should but
        prove,
      Kind, gentle, fair, and form'd
        for love,
      Thrice happy he, by fortune
        blest,
      Of ev'ry joy in life possess'd.

SONG—*(Extempore).*

(FROM THE SAME.)

I'LL write a play, an opera, pantomime,
Farce, comedy, deep tragedy in rhyme—
Scenery, music, dancing and action,
All shall be combin'd without distraction.
  The farce to make 'em grin,
  The tragedy all glum;—
Drums and trumpets, what a din!
  And pantomime quite dumb.
Harlequin and Columbine,
Kings and queens in dresses fine.
Scenery, machinery,
Declamation, decoration,
Dancing and speaking,
Singing and squeaking,
Puppets work'd by wire,
Real water, real fire,
A large dromedary dancing,
And some little ponies prancing.
Then I'll have a fiery dragon,
Harness'd to a broad-wheel'd waggon.
Scenery, music, dancing, action,
All shall blend without distraction.
Now the prompter rings his bell,
And the band begin pell-mell!
Clouds, lightning, and loud thunder,
Large trees are cleft asunder!
Rain, hail, tempest, rattle,
Cannon bang!—A battle—
A mighty crash!
And now the fell enchantment's broke,
Away with thunder, fire, and smoke!
Tempest subsiding,
Moon gently rising,
Night fine and serene,
All the stars are seen;
Conflagration—consternation,
  All the ocean in commotion!
Flash, splash, a mighty crash!
  All is in commotion!
Rain, hail, tempest, rattle,
Cannon bang!—a battle!—
  A mighty crash!
Oh! what a most delightful jumble!
If people come, let critics grumble.

EPIGRAM,

From the Latin of Naugerius.

A Woman once, as it is sung,
  Could speak so loud without a tongue,
That you could hear her full a mile
        hence:—
A greater wonder I can tell,
I knew a woman very well,
  That had a tongue, and yet *kept silence!*

THE

SPORTING MAGAZINE;

OR,

MONTHLY CALENDAR

OF THE

TRANSACTIONS

OF

THE TURF, THE CHASE,

And every other Diversion interesting to

THE MAN OF PLEASURE, ENTERPRISE, AND SPIRIT.

JUNE, 1808.

CONTAINING

On the late Trotting Match in Harness ....*Page* 103
Summary of Sport at the Ascot-heath, Newton, and Newcastle Races.. 105
Thoughts on Disputes between Gentlemen, on points of honour, &c. 107
The Amusements of Paris described 109
Cruel Abuse of Horses 114
The Sailor turned Pedlar............115
Of the Ass 116
Apology for fortunate Gamesters....117
The Earl of Derby's Stud..........118
The Mysterious Bride 121
An Epistle from a Pedestrian........122
Friendship in the Feathered Race....123
Pedigree and Performances of the Brother to Vivaldi 124
Stallions that cover in Ireland in 1808 125
Alteration in the Game Laws 127
Extraordinary Irruption 128
FEAST OF WIT.......... 129
Spanish Pride................130
On a Printing Office............132
Epigram on a late Battle.........132
Hints to the Bearers of Walking-Sticks and Umbrellas 133
Breach of the Game Laws..........136
Boxing 137
Remarkable Yew Tree 137
Pedigree and Performances of Stamford 138

Races appointed in 1808 ......*Page* 139
Viper, an Etching 140
The Metamorphose of a Bashful Man 140
Cricket Matches 141
Attachment in Brutes 141
SPORTING INTELLIGENCE..........142
Cocking, at the Royal Cockpit, Manchester, and Newton......143
Wrestling 143
Bettings at Tattersall's for the St. Ledger Stakes 144
Trotting Match 144
Sparring Exhibition 144
Pedestrianism 145
The Driving and Whip Clubs 147

POETRY.

The Kilruddery Fox-Chase 149
Jeu d'Esprit, circulated at a late Masquerade 150
Poor Barley-Corn................151
To the much-distressed Members of the Society of decayed Guide-Posts 151
Lines to Mary 152
Content......................152
Epitaph 152

RACING CALENDAR 28
Racing Intelligence Extra 39

Embellished with—I, An excellent Engraving of the Brother to Vivaldi.
II, Viper, an Etching,

LONDON:

PRINTED FOR THE PROPRIETORS,
By J. Pittman, Warwick Square;

AND SOLD BY J. WHEBLE, 18, WARWICK-SQUARE; C. CHAPPLE, 66, PALL-MALL;
J. BOOTH, DUKE-STREET, PORTLAND-PLACE; JOHN HILTON, NEWMARKET;
AND BY ALL THE BOOKSELLERS IN TOWN AND COUNTRY.

TO CORRESPONDENTS.

Our correspondents in the West will perceive that we have at length succeeded in procuring the Old Hunting Song of Kilruddery, &c. which has a place in our poetical department this month.

A. B. and other favours have been attended to.

On the cover of our present month's Magazine, are the proposals of Messrs. Random and Sneath, for publishing a set of the most elegant sporting prints.—From one of these beautiful copper-plates the Ptarmigan, given in our Magazine for January last, was copied, and which should have been mentioned in the article describing the bird; we have been highly favoured by the loan of many pictures, and, with permission, occasionally to copy from valuable prints, in all which cases it is our wish, explicitly and gratefully, to acknowledge the sources from which we derive those ornamental parts of our work.

Gentlemen disposed to favour the Publisher of this Magazine with Original Paintings of Sporting Subjects, are assured that the utmost care shall be taken of them, and of their being safely returned. The Engravings thus taken, will be executed by the most approved Artists, and in the first style of excellence.

BROTHER TO VIVALDI.

THE

SPORTING MAGAZINE;

FOR JUNE, 1808.

ON THE LATE
TROTTING-MATCH IN HARNESS,
On Fair Usage, and a Reprobation of Cruelty to Sporting Horses.

To the Editors of the Sporting Magazine.

GENTLEMEN,

OUR London newspapers of late have rung with accounts, to all appearance desseminated with much industry, of that most wonderful and surprising performance—a gelding trotting in harness fourteen miles in one hour, or seven miles out and seven miles in, upon the level road between Cambridge and Huntingdon. These accounts were signed with a name, which, perhaps, we might have supposed to have been that of a sportsman, had they been in a less flourishing style.

" A performance to which nothing was ever equal to it, either in memory or tradition ! the wonderful animal ! and he made play at starting, and all that ! and must have been beat, but for that excellent whip, young Mr. Hull (not Young Roscius) and, Lord have mercy ! what a pity that would have been, and how it must have affected Mr. M'Lean !!"

Seriously, Gentlemen, I wish to bring the *rationale* of this matter before your's, which is the proper tribunal, and if my memory do not immediately furnish me with actual precedents, I hope my expe-rimental practice will with analogies, or, in plain English, probable reasonings, on the case, and such as I trust, will fully satisfy both you and all sufficient judges of the matter.

I have a confused recollection of trotting in harness at various periods, but cannot just now ascertain what the events were; I will nevertheless stake whatever credit I may be supposed to have in respect to judgment in the practice, that a horse is very well able to trot upon the even turnpike, fourteen miles in one hour, drawing a light weight, and I have no doubt but many have and will be able to perform such task, with a common light gig, carrying two persons. Hereafter follow my reasons for such assertion, and without the least fear of difference, I submit them to Marsden, to Aldridge, to Bishop, to Johnson, and the rest of our experienced trotting-jockies.

In the first place, it is well known, that some horses will trot nearly as fast in light single harness as out. As an instance :—I once saw a trotter, in a light gig, carrying two persons, keep company above a mile with Cartwright's old chesnut horse, well known to be one of the speediest of his day. About 1798, it was published in the papers, that a gentleman's hackney (of the Admiralty) trotted in harness one mile in three minutes. For the correctness of that fact I cannot answer. Not only do we know that horses will trot fast enough in harness to complete the feat required, but we know with equal certainty, that at any rate slow horses will trot *up to their foot in harness*, and by a parity of reasoning I have a right to judge, that speedy ones will likewise. It has come within the observation of most buggy-drivers, that many hacks will trot nine or ten miles in one hour in harness, which they can do at most but a mile or two more with the saddle. I have myself timed a little weak mare, on a mixed road, good and bad, twelve miles in less than one hour, without even the thought of preparation; another person about my own weight (9st. 5lb.) being with me in the gig; the mare never in her life had been able to trot fourteen when ridden.

Now as it is proved that horses can make use of their speedy trot in harness, and trot up to their speed, in what can possibly consist the vast difficulty of trotting fourteen miles in a light carriage, within the hour? It most probably does consist, whenever there is either failure or great difficulty in such a case, in the horse's being no trotter, a speedy jade, or one with weak loins, or otherwise unfit for harness. Can any horseman doubt the ability of a hack, master of fourteen stone, and capable of trotting sixteen miles within one hour, to trot fourteen in light harness? Such a notion is incredible, nor can I bring myself to believe, that any of our stout, that is to say, lasting capital trotters, would have suffered damage, pain, or even inconvenience in the performance.

As foils to set off the wonderful powers of our great trotter in harness, we have lately had two of the most dreadful humbug matches that ever disgraced Old Time, by entering into a competition with him. Yet the *harnessed animals* in these matches were not jack-asses. One, the Lord help it! could not manage to trot six miles and half, in harness, in half an hour! the other, unable to perform thirteen within a whole hour, was wisely pulled up at the end of fifty minutes. Somehow, a set of people have got possession of our newspapers on the subject of trotting, who do not themselves trot very smoothly, and without hoisting either one way or the other. Lately out-popped a paragraph to tell us, that a young mare had trotted eight miles in half an hour, and it truly was such a thing as was never before heard of, that is to say, by said publishers. But on the other side of the question, a most successful and truly wonderful match was trotted, some years ago, *in the newspapers*, by a gentleman's horse, in Billiter-square, THIRTY MILES IN AN HOUR AND HALF!!! The *hoax* was indeed most successful, and copied into Bewick's Quadrupeds, Encyclopedias, Sportsman's Dictionaries, and into the various publications of those authors, who are in the laudable habit of writing about horses, because they may only have *seen* such things.

Before we part on this occasion, Gentlemen, let me assure you and your numerous readers, that however gratified I ever am, in witnessing the exertions of a noble, generous, and useful animal in the race, my gratification can be genuine only when the animal is well capable of his task, and fairly and humanely used; and that I hope not to be classed with that execrable and

and inhuman set of blackguards, well indeed deserving a few gentle stretches upon the rack, who can torture out the life of a wretched creature, endowed with feelings equal to their own, to forward their dirty interests, or excite their spurious, unmanly, and unnatural gratifications.

I have not yet forgotten the heart-rending story of the poor old flea-bitten horse, his entrails cut out with the whip, and trailing after him upon the turnpike-road, where, with his last expiring sobs, he had, a second time, for the profit of a knot of miscreants, (who, if now in Hell are its foul disgrace) won a gallop-match of twenty-two miles within the hour. He was the only horse, not thorough-bred, which ever ran that distance within the hour, and he performed it between London and Windsor, and was really able to perform it whilst in his prime, sound, and fairly used. Happily I did not witness his miserable end, and most barbarous usage; but the account of it came to me from too authentic a source for me to refuse it credit.— More happy still it is that I am assured, the times are so much more humanised, that few would be inclined, and none would dare, to exhibit such a tragedy on our roads at the present day.

I remain, Gentlemen, your old friend and servant, and (under the above salvo)

A PROTTING JOCKEY,

June 14.

P. S. Give me leave to observe in addition, that no horse should be tried at the above performance, but one which is able to trot full fifteen miles in one hour, with a pretty high weight.

SUMMARY OF THE SPORT

AT

THE ASCOT-HEATH, NEWTON, AND NEWCASTLE RACES.

ASCOT-HEATH.

ON *Tuesday,* the 20th instant, his Majesty's Plate of 100gs. was won by Mr. Shackel's Felton, beating Mr. Deane's Le Maitre, and the Hon. Mr. Villiers's Strideaway. —The Sweepstakes of 100gs. was won by Sir C. Bunbury's Sorcerer, beating four others.— Renewal of the 10gs. Stakes for all ages, for the years 1808 and 1809, was won by Mr. Ladbroke's Corsican, named by Mr. Wyndham; beating Captain Haffenden's Sir Launcelot, and Mr. Batson's Charmer (named by Sir C. Bunbury). Bets, 8 to 1 against the winner.—Lord Jersey's b. c. by the Wellesley Arabian, out of Bowling's dam, beat Mr. Freemantle's ch. c. by the same stallion, dam by Prospect; last mile, 100gs. h. ft. a fine race.— Lord Jersey's b. h. Poke, 9st. beat Mr. Lake's Silvermere, 7st.; last half mile, 25gs.—Her Majesty, the Prince of Wales, Duke of York, and the rest of the younger branches of the Royal Family, were present.

Wednesday, his Royal Highness the Duke of York's Plate of 50l. for all ages, was won by Sir J. Honywood's Hawk, beating Mr. Fenwick's Sir Launcelot, and three others.—The Swinley Stakes of 25gs. each, 15gs. ft. was won by Lord Egremont's Election, beating Mr. Fermor's Stripling only by half a head.—A Sweepstakes of 15gs. each, for horses of all ages, that never won more than 50gs. at any one time before the day of naming, was won by Mr. Fermor's Bantam, beating Lord C. Somerset's White-Rose,

Bess, Sir J. Honywood's Delville, and Lord Egremont's brother to Hedley. — Her Majesty and the Princesses again honoured the course with their presence, as did also the Dukes of York and Cumberland.

Thursday, the renewal of the 10gs. Stakes, for three-year olds, for the years 1808 and 1809, was won by Mr. Ladbroke's Trimbush, (named by Mr. Wyndham) by Teddy, beating Lord Egremont's b. f. by Gohanna.—The Gold Cup of 100gs. value, the surplus to be paid to the winner in specie, a subscription of 20gs. each, for horses that never won above 100gs. at any one time before the day of naming, was won by Mr. Fermor's Brighton, beating Mr. Buller's Epsom, after running a dead heat.— Lord Foley's f. bought of the Prince, paid forfeit to Lord Egremont's f. by Gohanna, the last half mile, for 100gs.—Lord G. H. Cavendish's Pagoda, beat Mr. Craven's Beau Nash, last half mile, 100gs.—Lord Jersey's colt, by the Wellesley Arabian, dam by Pot8o's, beat Ld Foley's f. by Vermin, out of a Highflyer mare, last mile, 100gs.—For the Plate of 50l. for yeomen prickers and keepers, Mr. Starling's Blenheim walked over the course.

Friday, for the Sweepstakes of 20gs. each, five subscribers, Lord Egremont's Canopus walked over. —Sweepstakes of 30gs. each, for two-year olds, was won by the Duke of York's ch. c. Silvermere, beating Mr. Fermor's b. f. by Gohanna, Mr. Emden's Miss Seedling; and Mr. Ladbroke's b. f. sister to Election.—Handicap Plate of 50l. for all ages, was won by Mr. Batson's Gladiator, beating Lord Jersey's Poke. — Sweepstakes of 20gs. each, three subscribers, was

won by Mr. S. Batson, jun.'s Gladiator, beating Mr. Turner's Drake.

NEWTON.

On *Wednesday*, June 15, the Maiden Plate of 50l. three-mile heats, was won by Lord Wilton's b. f. by Alexander, 3 yrs old, beating Sir T. Stanley's bl. g. by Sir Harry, 4 yrs old ; Mr. Richardson's Cleopatra, 3 yrs old; and 3 others. —The Gold Cup was won by Julius Cæsar, by Alexander ; beating Baron, Belinda, Phlebotomist, and Newton.

Thursday, the 70l. was won by Miss Prisle, by Sir Peter, beating Honest Bob, and 3 others.—The Sweepstakes of 15gs. each, was won by Dimple, by Sir Peter Teazle, beating the Sister to Bucephalus.

Friday, the Sweepstakes of 10gs. each, with 20gs. added, was won by Baron, by Stamford, beating Baronet and Josephina.—And for the 70l. there was no race ; General Benningsen received the premium.

NEWCASTLE.

Monday, the Produce Stakes of 50gs. each, was won by Sir W. Gerard's ch. c. by Hambletonian, beating Mr. Riddell's f. by Expectation, and Mr. Hutchinson's Dorimond. — Sweepstakes of 20gs. each, was won by Colonel Horton's b. c. by Bustard, beating 3 others.—Sweepstakes of 20gs. each, for four-year olds, was won by Cardinal York, beating Oran and Silvio.

Tuesday, the King's Plate was won by Cardinal York, beating Ranger.—The Maiden Plate of 50l. was won by Mr. Riddell's b. f. by Expectation, beating three others.

        One

On *Wednesday*, the Silver Cup was won by Silvio, beating several others : and the 50l. Plate was won by Cramlington.

THOUGHTS

ON

DISPUTES BETWEEN GENTLEMEN,

On Points of Honour, &c.

AMONG those disagreeable events of life which create disunion in society, there are, perhaps, none more deeply to be lamented than those connubial irregularities; which too forcibly mark the character of the present age. There are but few offences against the principles of civil order which bear more heavily upon the heart, or carry, in their stream of action, a disposition to resentment more indelible. The emotions arising from an ordinary insult may be becalmed by atonement, or obliterated by the punishment of the aggressor : but in this species of injury the consequences are materially different ; the mind is tinged with a sorrow that only ceases with existence; and a whole family are doomed to participate in a dishonour to which they bore no active part, and which calumny will not suffer to sink in oblivion !

We are more immediately led to these remarks, by a recent affair of fashionable notoriety, where the wife of a Nobleman eloped with her paramour in the full face of day; exhibiting such symptoms of indifference to the opinion of the world upon moral rectitude, as do not frequently occur even in these days of degeneracy, when the God of Love is wantonly and surreptitiously effacing the immemorial privileges of Virtue and Hymen.

We can scarcely peruse a modern newspaper, without perceiving some novel instance of illicit gallantry in the *beau monde*, or some deed of indiscretion in a spinster, which compromises the indispensable delicacy of the sex : for we must insist upon it, that a lady without delicacy will soon lose her required importance in life, be her rank or title what it may.

The number of duels that have been fought, and lives that have been lost, in consequence of similar immoralities, renders it a theme of national concern to enquire into the causes of this increasing evil— and which is scarcely now accompanied with a sentiment of shame, from the incessant repetition of example !—Is this propensity to matrimonial infidelity sown in the elements of a *stylish* education ? or is it awakened and enforced by that flippant tone of conversation in which licentious coxcombs are permitted to indulge, with scarcely any reference to decency, but what consists in verbal distinctions, making the zest poisonous, though the medium is not disgusting ?

Or does it arise from that pernicious but fallacious idea, that a reformed rake makes the best husband ? There is a prevailing notion among the mass of our young men of distinction, that the ladies are more readily captivated by what are termed *dashing fellows ;* and this notion has produced innumerable extravagancies and eccentricities of action, which were utterly repugnant to the natural dispositions of the blockheads who assumed them. Many do not hesitate to violate truth, in the ardent hope of being thought more absurd than they really are ; and proudly brag of a head-ach from a debauch, where they have never been !—Mr. Cumberland has truly depicted this wretched

wretched passion to be nominally vicious, in his comedy of *The Wheel of Fortune*, where Governor Tempest thus rebukes Sir David Daw, for wishing to be thought moral, when paying his addresses to his daughter Emily: "If you wish to succeed with the ladies, Sir David, keep that sentiment to yourself; as the world is now so fashionably depraved, that a man is forced to *affect* vices to keep well with it."

We trust that our fair country-women will consider this subject as infinitely more interesting to them than to the gentlemen; inasmuch as whatever takes from that dignity and decorum, which should be in-alienable to the marriage compact, is lamentably depriving them of a legal and due share in the higher delights of civilized society.—Man, in his nature, as well as in the ad-mitted order of things, possesses a latitude in agency which is neces-sarily denied to the softer sex; as involving more purity of character: and whenever a female deserts the standard of her own honour, she not only degrades herself for ever, but commits an act which abridges the wholesome privileges of beau-ty, by making men repugnant to enter into that state which was the behest of the Almighty, and should be the universal desire of mankind.   W.

DUEL.

On Saturday the 11th instant, a meeting took place on Epping Fo-rest, between Captain R——ds, of the Northampton militia, and Lieu-tenant H——n, of the 15th light dragoons. The parties fired toge-ther, and exchanged three shots (the second pistol of Captain R. missing fire,) and in the third shot Captain R. received his adversary's ball in the leg, which shattered the shin-bone, and although it was immediately extracted, it is appre-hended he must suffer amputation. —They were attended to the field by their seconds and surgeons.—The principals were a short time ago quartered together in Wood-bridge Barracks, when an intimacy ensued; and the cause of the meet-ing was produced by a Capt. R. ha-ving lately suspected that Lieut. H. had been carrying on an improper correspondence with his wife, the particulars of which, we are given to understand, will be very soon disclosed by a legal investigation.

COURTS-MARTIAL.

A Court-Martial was lately held at Portsmouth on Lieutenant W. Pitcher, of the Royal Marines, of His Majesty's ship Isis, who was ordered to be tried for having de-graded himself while on shore, by grossly insulting a Gentleman, and suffering himself to be repeatedly thrashed; and for disobedience of orders. The Court did not inquire into the first charge, as it did not happen within the jurisdiction of the Admiralty: he was found guilty of the disobedience of orders, and sentenced to be dismissed from the ship, and put at the bottom of the list of Second Lieutenants.—Rear-Admiral Tylar, President.

The 31st ult. Lieut. Mopps, of the Turbulent gun-brig, was tried by Court-Martial at Sheerness; for taking four guineas from a Danish Master; but as the money was not appropriated to his own use, he was ordered to make good the same, and to be more circumspect in future.

THE

THE AMUSEMENTS OF PARIS DESCRIBED.

Continued from Page 65.

LIVES AND MANNERS OF EUROPEANS.

I Lately mentioned to you, my dear lady, the portrait of our Saviour, which may be had for one sous, on the Boulevards; to-day I will make you acquainted with a similar speculation. Look at that sheet of paper, decorated with large wooden cuts, and printed only on one side; it contains, notwithstanding, nothing less than the "Lives and Manners of the Nations of Europe: *Vies et Mœurs des Nations de l'Europe*," says the superscription. For my part, being a German, and only knowing the manners of nations from thick volumes in quarto, my curiosity is naturally excited, and I read with pleasure the quintessence of the judgment and prejudices of Frenchmen respecting themselves and their neighbours. The following are examples:—

"In religion, the German is unbelieving, the Englishman devout; the Frenchman zealous; the Italian ceremonious; the Spaniard a bigot.

"In keeping his word, the German is faithful; the Englishman safe; the Frenchman giddy; the Italian cunning; the Spaniard a cheat.

"In giving advice, the German is slow; the Englishman resolute; the Frenchman precipitate; the Italian nice; the Spaniard circumspect.

"In love, the German does not understand it; the Englishman loves a little here and there; the Frenchman every where; the Italian knows how one ought to love; the Spaniard loves truly.

"In external appearance, the German is tall; the Englishman well made; the Frenchman well looking; the Italian of the middle size; the Spaniard frightful.

"In dress, the German is shabby; the Englishman superb; the Frenchman changing; the Italian a tatterdemalion; the Spaniard decent.

"In manners, the German is clownish; the Englishman barbarous; the Frenchman easy; the Italian polite; the Spaniard proud.

"In keeping a secret, the German forgets what he has been told; the Englishman conceals what he should divulge, and divulges what he should conceal; the Frenchman blabs every thing; the Italian does not utter a word; the Spaniard is mysterious.

"In vanity, the German boasts little; the Englishman despises all; the Frenchman praises every thing; the Italian values little what is of little value; the Spaniard is indifferent to all.

"In eating and drinking, the German is a drunkard; the Englishman a lover of sweets; the Frenchman delicate; the Italian moderate; the Spaniard niggardly.

"In offending and doing good, the German does neither good nor harm; the Englishman does both without reason; the Italian is prompt in beneficence, but vindictive; the Spaniard indifferent in both respects.

"In speaking, the German speaks little and badly, but writes well; the Frenchman speaks and writes well; the Englishman speaks badly, but writes well; the Italian speaks well, writes much and well; the Spaniard speaks little, writes little, but well.

"In address, the German looks like a blockhead; the Englishman resembles

P

resembles neither a fool nor a wise man; the Frenchman is airy; the Italian is prudent, but looks like a fool; the Spaniard is quite the reverse.

"In laws, the German laws are indifferent; the Englishman has bad laws, but observes them well; the Frenchman has good laws, but observes them badly; the Italians and Spaniards have good laws; the former observes them negligently, the latter rigidly.

"Servants, are companions in Germany; slaves in England; masters in France; respectful in Italy; submissive in Spain.

"Diseases—Germans are particularly infested with fleas; the English with whitlows; the French with the small-pox; the Italians with the plague; and the Spaniards with wens.

"The women are housewives in Germany; queens in England; ladies in France; captives in Italy; slaves in Spain.

"In courage, the German resembles a bear; the Englishman a lion; the Frenchman an eagle; the Italian a fox; and the Spaniard an elephant.

"In the sciences, the German is a pedant; the Englishman a philosopher; the Frenchman has a smattering of every thing; the Italian is a professor; and the Spaniard a profound thinker.

"Magnificence — In Germany the princes; in England the ships; in France the court; in Italy the churches; in Spain the armories, are magnificent.

"Husbands (make the conclusion), in Germany they are masters; in England servants; in France companions; in Italy schoolboys; and in Spain tyrants."

I will readily grant you, my dear madam, that one-third of these singular characteristics is untrue, and sometimes absurd; but the other two thirds I could vouch to be true. With regard to us Germans, we have the least reason to complain of the painter; if he had but omitted the horrid libel that we do not understand how to love, and that among us husbands are masters, we might then be well satisfied with him.

PICTURES AND CARICATURES.

Now let us, if you please, walk further up this library suspended by threads; it borders on another of musical productions, which is followed by a third, consisting of pictures; among the musicals, you find all the new ariettas, duets, &c. from the most popular French and Italian operas; among the pictures, a representation of every thing that is most interesting to the Parisians; for example, Fanchon, the lute girl; the fine drum-major of the consular guard, with his enchanting whiskers; the First Consul's superbly-dressed Mameluke; and, of course, the First Consul himself, in a thousand different attitudes, especially with his drawn sword in his hand, replanting the cross. Faith presenting him with a palm branch, and the other two Consuls by his side; or the beautiful Madame Recamier, with her face half veiled.

Plenty of caricatures are likewise to be met with here, and the King of England is at present the general mark at which the French direct the shafts of their satire; for which they are, however, not only more abundantly, but even more wittily, requited by their transmarine neighbours; for it must be confessed, that among twenty French caricatures, there is scarcely one that has any claim to wit.—

Here

Here you see the king between his good and evil genius, throwing himself into the hands of the latter; there an Englishman riding upon a Calcutta turkey; on the pommel of the saddle are wine-hampers with bottles, and below is written, " the attack." The companion to this print is the defeat, where the same Englishman is seen flying on a fleet stag, losing his hat and tobacco-pipe. Here the Duke of C—mbr—ge is driving the Hanoverian post-waggon, and behind it is a cask, on which is written, Hanoverian blood; there an army of frogs, whose general wears British regimentals, and rides on a lobster, while a Frenchman takes up one frog after the other, and cuts them in two with his broad sabre. At other times, an elephant is laying hold of the king's cup, and dashing it with his trunk into a well; on the cup is to be read this inscription, " Thou must go to pieces after all."

In some of these wretched productions, Mr. Pitt is represented riding on his M—j—ty's back, on the sea-shore, peeping at the French ships in the offing; here the sovereign leaps over the channel, and in his jump loses his crown: there he picks up a number of paper cases, on which the names of his dominions are written; but, unable to hold them all, he lets some of them fall. Hanover is already on the ground, Ireland just tumbling, and Malta appears very loose. Here the English are seen flying before a cloud of dust, raised by a flock of sheep; and there Mr. Pitt exercising his troops, all of whom have pig's heads. The caricature which may perhaps be called the wittiest, is the following: a maker of trusses for ruptures presents the king with a new truss,

on which is written—" observation des tratiés—the observance of treaties." At his Majesty's feet lie two broken bandages, one bearing the inscription, " forces navales—or, naval forces;" the other, " levée en masse—raising in a mass."— Thus you see that politics are the axis round which every thing turns. A few only of these distorted figures attack the manners of the English; such as, for instance, the English family in Paris, where a huge, clumsy Englishman, stuffed with roast beef, leads two stiff misses by the arm, who make a very awkward curtesy, &c. &c.

THE CAPUCHIN'S GARDENS.

If you are by this time tired of the squalling of the ballad-singer, we will saunter about the garden of the Capuchins, where there are tigers and monkeys, where Franconi exhibits his equestrian feats, where the spirits appear at night, and where, in a word, a thousand different spectacles are to be gazed at from morning till night. Here stands for a moment a portable booth, hung with old carpet, in which my dear punchinello is very amicably fighting with the devil.— Two hocus-pocus men attract crowds on both sides; one by cups, the other by tricks with cards. A much greater concourse of people gathers round a man, whose whole apparatus consists of a chafing-dish full of glowing charcoal, and about half a dozen small pieces of asbestos. He begins with an impressive account of the expedition to Egypt; whilst his neighbour represents at the same time in his show-box, to those who like to see it, what heroic exploits were achieved by his assistance in that country against Mamelukes and crocodiles; and how he once strip-

ped

ped one of the slain men of his shirt, and found that it did not consist of linen, as usual, but of a fossil fabricated into cloth, which the Egyptians use for the sake of convenience, as they need not wash or dry their shirts, but only throw them into the fire in the evening, and take them out again in the morning as white as snow.

In order to impress on the minds of his hearers a conviction of the truth of what he says, he seizes one of the needles, to which he has fastened a small bit of asbestos, and turns it round in the mud till the original colour cannot be distinguished: he then throws it into the chafing-dish, and while it is glowing, continues to harangue his audience for a few minutes longer, when he draws it out of the fire, and, to the great astonishment of all the spectators, quite purified by the fiery element.

One of my neighbours, who seemed to be a wit, compared the whole process to the French revolution, which likewise arose pure, new, and brilliant, out of the glowing fire I wish, with all my heart, that nobody could dispute the truth of this assertion.

THE STRONG WOMAN,

' Who is to be seen in this hut of planks, is still more disgusting than the female with the long black beard. With the latter, pity gains the upper hand: for how can the poor creature help being obliged to wear a beard so immensely long? but with the former, disgust and indignation get the better of compassion. The one merely obeys nature, the other sets her at defiance. She suffers three men to tread upon her body, which is stretched out in a hollow posture; she suffers iron to be forged upon

it, and exhibits other *tours de forces*, from which you, my dear, very properly turn away. But how can I help it? You must creep with me into another hut of this kind, to see the incombustible Spaniard, who really excites as much horror as admiration. Do you see the jar of oil, bubbling and boiling over a coal fire? the young man, who takes it off, drinks a hearty draught of its burning contents without distorting a feature, rinses his mouth for a long time with it, as if it were fresh water, and spits it out still boiling; he then, with the remainder of the oil in the pot, washes his hands, arms, face, and even eyes, which, however, he shuts. Having been purified by the fire, like the asbestos, he takes a walk, by way of change, with his naked feet, upon a piece of red-hot iron, and, to refresh himself, he even licks the glowing metal with his tongue. If this poor youth be equally insensible to the flames of love, he is undoubtedly to be pitied. All this is no imposture, but really happens as I have now related; but whether, as some assert, he causes a kind of salamander-ointment to be rubbed into his skin, which is not to be perceived, I shall leave undetermined.

A NEW GAME AT NINE-PINS.

To efface these unpleasant impressions, let us for a few minutes step before this little fortress, of which you find many patterns on the Boulevards. It is a new kind of game at nine-pins, at which you not only see boys, but even respectable-looking citizens, delight to play. It is, indeed, preferable to the usual game; as it takes up much less room, and may be removed from one place to another. This little fortress is about the height of of a man, built in the form of an amphitheatre; below, it has a draw-bridge, over which the walls are gradually raised, and on them a number of soldiers stationed at intervals. Eight or ten yards from the fortress, a wooden mortar (or even a cannon) is planted, from which, as with the children's guns, a ball is discharged. The force of the mortar is calculated exactly according to the distance, from eight to ten paces. The skill in this play consists in taking so good an aim, as to knock down one or more soldiers at once, or even in accurately hitting the very centre, in which case the draw-bridge falls, and by means of the spring, which has been touched by the ball, a state coach with six horses comes out: in others, a white flag is hoisted at the top of the fort; the ball is lost within, and comes out again at the bottom. This pretty game has manifold advantages over the common game at nine-pins; it can be exhibited in the smallest garden, nay, even in any room in the least spacious. It requires but trifling bodily exertion, so that even ladies may play. It is interesting, because the aiming and hitting premises a certain dexterity and practice: in short, by describing this game, I hope to have furnished a pleasing supplement to the gymnastic exercises.

CANARY BIRDS.

Decorum not permitting us, my dear friend, to partake of this game on the Boulevards, we had better look awhile at those poor little canary birds, who are instructed in yonder booth in all sorts of arts, directly contrary to their nature.—Here one turns a spit; another drives his fellow in a wheelbarrow; a third stands sentry with his gun,

sword, and grenadier's cap; a fourth does not stir from his master's shoulder, though he beat the drum loud enough to make one run away; a fifth fires a cannon, the burning cork of which knocks a sixth down from the table, and leaves him on the ground for dead. A seventh sits in the very middle of a flaming wheel, as quiet and merry as if perched upon a rose-bush in its native island. You have probably often seen such things in Germany, though not in equal perfection; but one observation relative to these birds you have, perhaps, never heard. It was made by their teacher and master, and affords matter for reflection. " The hen," said he, " certainly takes every thing much quicker than the cock, and I can generally render them very skilful at the expiration of a few weeks, but they soon forget, and soon die." Methinks his argument respecting the feathered tribe may be equally applied to its tormentors, man; for if our belles learn moral or æsthetic arts, they do not indeed die of it, but their loveliness generally finds its tomb in them.

THE PUBLIC FOUNTAINS.

Having yet half an hour to spare, let us make use of it to see two celebrated fountains. The fountain in the Rue Grenelle is really very fine, but the street very narrow and obscure; the fountain has not a free exposure on all sides, and the great building is, besides, deformed by all sorts of signs. On the right is a large painted cow, because milk is sold there; on the left is a carpenter's sign, &c. To me, pardon the heresy, if it really be one, it will always appear ridiculous to raise such a building with two wings to such a height as three stories,

stories, to decorate it with columns and statues, and all this on account of the two lions' heads below, a few feet above the ground, which you do not even perceive, because there is no stream of water, but what little remains must be brought up by pumping.

Of the inscription, which is for the most part erased, only these words remain: "For the use of the citizens, and for the ornament of the city." The conclusion alone is true, and that only in part. This end might have been obtained much more splendidly in another manner.

Now we are in the *marché des Innocens.* The fountain may be fine when the water flows; but it is still worse than that in the Rue Grenelle, as not a single drop can be pumped out, it being quite dry. The large bason, which stands at a considerable height in the centre, looks like a round tea-table, which has just been placed there, and forms an odd contrast with the surrounding objects. Upon the whole, this monument is altogether extremely filthy, and out of repair. To indemnify you, however, for being disappointed in your expectation, please to cast a look on the fine market-place, which, by its spaciousness, and bustling scenes, is far more interesting than that useless piece of architecture. There, in numerous rows, monstrous fat women, called poissardes, or fish-women, are seated under large umbrellas, between eight and ten feet in diameter, forming, if viewed from above, a roof resembling that of the ancient Roman soldiers; when advancing with their shields thrown over their heads, in a manœuvre, called the testudo. These umbrellas are not the property of those women, but hired in the market for a few sous. Thus screened

from the rain and the sun, you may here admire mountains of butter, shoals of fish, stores of eggs, towers of apples and pears, gardens of flowers, and great quantities of grapes and other sorts of fruits, together with a party-coloured mixture of vegetables, among which, the large dazzling white, and neatly raised heaps of cauliflowers, afford a spectacle particularly pleasing. Listen a little, meanwhile, to the energetic *patois* (gibberish) of the stout market women, an energy from which you have now nothing to fear; and if the view of so many dainties has created an appetite, let us quickly throw ourselves into a *fiacre* (hackney-coach), and drive to the *Restaurateur.*

CRUEL ABUSE
OF
TROTTING MATCHES, &c.

(From the Morning Advertiser.)

MR. EDITOR,

MANY readers of your paper were shocked at the account it contained of a bet on a wonderful horse, who was obliged " to perform the distance of fourteen miles within an hour in harness, at a trot." We are told that the animal " *made play* at a winning rate." This technical phrase may be intelligible to the *knowing ones,* as they are called, and may possibly mean that the poor creature appeared to run with ease. But we are told also that it was " driven by an *expert whip* of eleven stone," and this *expert whip,* if it was not exercised on the body of the unfortunate beast all the time, was doubtless employed in such a manner

ner as to keep up his speed by the force of terror. What must be the feelings of men, who, for the sake of a little paltry cash, could inflict upon a poor beast, much more harmless than themselves, an hour of such torture and apprehension? But this is not all, for it is said, "the animal was offered to be backed to perform the same distance *within an hour*, and to *draw 20st.*" Good God, Mr. Editor, is it possible that there can be so much cruelty in a country which prides itself on its humanity! it was not enough that the horse had performed so laborious a task, and endured such an hour of alarm and agony, to augment his pace, but before it could be supposed to have hardly recovered from the heat, to say nothing of the fatigue of such a dreadful exertion, it was offered for a still greater effort, and would most probably have been put to the trial, if a fear of his success, not an impulse of humanity, had not prevented any body from accepting the proposal. We may surely say with Othello, "Are we turned Turks?" when we hear of such horrid violations of every feeling that ought to characterise mankind. Nay, though the Turks are ferocious enough to each other, and particularly to those who differ with them in religion, it is not probable that a poor dumb animal, which is so useful, and indeed so necessary to man, when properly employed, would be treated by them with so much ingratitude and injustice.

The accounts of the contests which take place among the pugilistic professors, however disgusting, are read with less horror than the recital of the miseries which are so often inflicted on the inferior race of animals; because in those contests, each party has a will of his own, and exposes himself from motives of interest or ambition to all that befalls him; but the poor horse is obliged to submit to the tyranny of man, against whose cunning his strength is of no avail. It is surely time to put an end to these odious practices, which, if not checked by the indignation of mankind in general, will become as fashionable as any vice or folly, and which will degrade the national character, as well as blunt those feelings which have raised it above that of any other people on the face of the earth.

A CONSTANT READER.

Thatched-House, May 24.

P. S. If the patrons of these inhuman sports were ever likely to hear of Pythagoras and his doctrine, they might possibly be brought to think of *retribution*, and fear that a *brute* in the *human shape* might hereafter be consigned to one more fit for his savage nature, and receive due punishment from the very animal which he had tortured, when the latter may be exalted to the state for which he might be much better qualified than his former tyrant.

THE SAILOR TURNED PEDLAR.

MR. EDITOR,

IN travelling along the public road, I lately overtook a sailor, hobbling away upon a wooden leg and a crutch, who asked charity in the usual way.—He told me he had been fighting for his King and country ten years, and had crippled and destroyed as many French dogs as he could, and had he not in turn been

been crippled himself, would still
have been fighting away as usual.
Of course I praised his valour, and
informed him, that besides the
cause he had been engaged in, he
had been fighting for *social order*,
and *religion*, and that he should be
always careful to mention this when
he solicited charity of the old women, or the clergy.—Jack swore I
was right, for he remembered his
mother had taught him the Lord's
Prayer when he was very young,
and that the parson had given him
a half-penny for saying part of
the *Belief*.—But, says he, if they
should ask me who this *social order* is, and what post he holds,
what must I say? for I never
heard of him before.—Oh, says I,
you must tell them he is Lord High
Admiral to the King of Sweden,
and that he will come soon with a
great fleet to assist us.—I will,
please your honour, says Jack, but
mind what I say, " he will never
fight better than Old Nelson, for all
that."

The old tar now seemed to wish
to drop the subject, and advert to
his own case.—I have fought de-
vilish hard, said he, many a glass,
but the lubbers have crippled me
now, so that I can fight no more,
and I am trying to get an honest
penny, by selling a few articles of
hardware, and a few godly books.
If your honour will shorten sail
and lay me along-side, you shall
overhaul my stores.—Accordingly
I lay to, while Jack handed me his
basket, which contained the whole
stock in trade, such as coarse hardware, some inkle, garters, brimstone, matches, &c. &c.—The literary department was enriched
with the History of Jack the Gi-
ant-killer, Tom Thumb, An Account of the last Illness of Mr.
Pitt, and the dying speeches of

some of the most celebrated heroes of the Old Bailey. He had
also a collection of love songs for
the amusement of the village girls,
and to complete the venture, had
laid in a few dozens of prayers for
the fast-day.

As he seemed to expect I should
purchase something, I took a pen-
knife, leaving him the change, by
way of increased profit. I then
asked him if the prayer-trade was
brisk and profitable? Ah, no, said
he, I can sell a hundred of any
other books for one of my prayers;
and if I cannot rid my stock of
prayers off in a few days, I shall be
aground, and be obliged to throw
the remainder in among the old
stores, for another twelvemonth.
I did all I could to comfort Jack, as
to his prayer-speculation, by hint-
ing that if many of his stock
should remain on hand, he might
cut it into small slips, and sell it
along with his brimstone matches,
to the masters of public-houses, to
light their candles, or the pipes of
their guests with. Jack thanked
me kindly, for the suggestion, said
he would practise it if needful,
and then we parted.

OF THE ASS.

THE ass is an ass, and not a de-
generated horse; a horse with
a naked tail; he is not outlandish,
nor an intruder, nor of spurious
origin; he has, like all other animals, his family, his species, and
his rank; his blood is pure, and
though his family distinction is
less illustrious, it is altogether as
good and as ancient as that of the
horse. Why then so much contempt for an animal, so good, so
patient, so sober, and so service-

able? Would then despise, even among the brutes, such as serve them with too much fidelity, and too cheaply? The horse receives an education, is taken care of, is instructed, we give him exercise; whilst the ass, abandoned to rough treatment by the meanest of servants, or to the unluckiness of children, far from gaining, can only lose by his education, and if he had not a great store of good qualities, would certainly hate them for the manner in which he is treated; he is the sport, the butt, and the scoff of the peasantry, who lead him with a stick in their hand, beat, overload, and maltreat him, without consideration, and without mercy.

They do not reflect that the ass, both of himself (if there were no horse in the world) and with regard to us, would be the first and most distinguished of animals; but instead of being the first he is the second, and, for that reason only, seems of no consideration. It is the comparison that degrades him. He is regarded and judged of, not absolutely, but by the relation he bears to the horse; it is forgotten that he is an ass, who has all the good qualities of his nature, all the endowments peculiar to his species, and nothing is thought of but the figure and qualities of the horse, of which the ass is destitute, and ought not to be possessed.

In disposition, he is as humble, meek, and patient, as the horse is spirited, fiery, and impetuous; he suffers with firmness, and endures with fortitude, chastisement and blows: he is moderate both in the quality and quantity of his food, he is very nice with regard to his water, he will not drink but of the clearest, and of streams he is acquainted with: he drinks as mo-

derately as he eats. As he is never curried, he frequently rolls upon the grass, upon thistles and fern, and by this seems to reproach his master with the little care that is taken of him; for he never plunges like the horse, into the mire and water, he is even afraid of wetting his feet, and turns aside to avoid the dirt; he has also a drier and a cleaner leg than the horse. He is capable of education, and some have been sufficiently well taught to be exhibited for a show.

APOLOGY FOR FORTUNATE GAMESTERS.

WE must not suppose that all of the very fortunate gamesters have used those means to collect fortunes which are generally reckoned fraudulent; but we may suppose, that among a great number of careless inattentive people of fortune, a few wary, cool, and shrewd men are mingled, who know how to conceal real caution under apparent inattention and gaiety of manners; who have perfect command of themselves, push their luck when fortune smiles, and refrain when she changes her dispositions, who have calculated the chances, and understand every game where judgment is required.

If any of those fortunate people were brought to trial, and examined by what means they had accumulated such sums, they might answer in the words of the wife of Concini, Mareschal d'Ancre, when she was asked what charm she made use of to fascinate the mind of the Queen—"That ascendancy which a superior mind always possesses over a weak one."

Q   THE

THE EARL OF DERBY—HIS STUD.

THE Earl of Derby commenced upon the turf in 1774, and was the owner and breeder of a great number of very valuable and successful racers. In 1793, his Lordship reduced his Stud, and afterwards had seldom above one or two in training at a time; but regularly named a colt or filly for the Derby and Oaks' Stakes at Epsom, and generally for Preston, Lancashire.—But, notwithstanding, his Lordship retained his choicest mares, for breeding, along with that celebrated stallion, *Sir Peter Teazle,** who has been unparalleled for upwards of twelve years, and whose produce is so well known to sportsmen and breeders, as to need no comment.

THE STUD.

Horses, &c. Names.	Sires.	Dams, and what got by.	Year when foaled.
Prospero	Syphon		1770
Candidate	Dainty Davy	Regulus	1771
Young Fellow	Fellow	Regulus, Sedbury, Grenadier's dam	1772
Juliet	Dainty Davy	Regulus	1774
Laburnum	King Herod	Young Hagg, by Skim	1774
Turnspit	Mr. Vernon's Arabian	Sister to Alexander, by Lot	1774
Ægis	Young Snip	Emma, by Spectator	1775
Guildford	King Herod	Tulip, (sister to Pacolet) by Blank	1775
Bridget	King Herod	Jemima†, by Snap	1776
Choice	Fitzherod		1776
Fame‡	Pantaloon	Diomed's dam, by Spectator	1776
Geranium	Syphon	Lofty	1776
Ugly	Syphon	Candidate's dam, by Regulus	1776
Aladdin	King Herod	Jemima, (Bridget's dam) by Snap	1777
Beauty	King Herod	Ugly's dam, by Regulus	1777

* In 1790, he covered (his first season) at Knowsley, Lancashire, at 10gs. and 10s. 6d.—The first of his get that started was Mr. Fox's Shuter, who ran at Newmarket in July, 1793; the second was Lord Fitzwilliam's dark brown, or grey filly, out of Desdemona, that ran a match against Mr. Garforth's Bradamanta, at Doncaster, in the same year. In 1794, Mr. Clifton's Mary-Ann (the first winner of his get) won a Stakes at Catterick, and one at Knutsford:—Lord Derby's Hermione received 80gs. forfeit at Newmarket Craven Meeting, and won the Oaks' Stakes at Epsom in June, 50gs. at Lewes, and 50l. at Reading:—Also, Mr. Tarleton's br. filly, (Jack Tar's dam) won a match at Preston, and a Stakes at Nottingham. His produce afterwards proved themselves superior to the get of any other stallion in the kingdom.

† Jemima, (foaled in 1769) was bred by Mr. Shafto, and sold to Lord Derby for a brood mare before she bred Bridget. She was own sister to Mexico, by Snap; her dam, Match'em Middleton, by Match'em, out of Miss Middleton, by Regulus.

‡ Fame was bred by Mr. Vernon, and sold to Lord Derby when four years old.

Horses, &c. Names.	Sires.	Dams, and what got by.	Year when foaled.
Spitfire	Eclipse	Lord Orford's Barb	1777
Faith	King Herod	Curiosity, by Snap	1778
King William	Florizel	Milliner, by Match'em	1778
Paulina*	Florizel	Captive, by Match'em	1778
Achilles	Eclipse	Countess (Delpini's dam) by Blank	1779
Oliver Cromwell	Protector	Flippanta, by Snap	1779
Peru	King Herod	Jemima, (Bridget's dam) by Snap	1779
Fortunatus	Mr. Vernon's Arabian	Bridget's dam, by Snap	1780
Collector	Conductor	Capella †, by King Herod	1781
Dancer	King Herod	Marotte ‡, by Match'em	1781
Lady Teazle	Highflyer	Papillon §, by Snap	1781
Noodle	Magnet	Clara, by Careless	1781
Blandish	Il'mio	Marotte, by Match'em	1782
Inca	Highflyer	Jemima, (Bridget's dam) by Snap	1782
Little Anthony	Conundrum	King Herod, Regulus	1782
Mulberry	Florizel	Match'em	1783
Wren	Woodpecker	Papillon, by Snap	1783
Zilia	Eclipse	Jemima, (Bridget's dam) by Snap	1783
Active	Woodpecker	Laura, by Whistlejacket	1784
Annette	Eclipse	Virago, (Saltram's dam) by Snap	1784
Paul	Trentham	Paulina, by Florizel	1784
Rose	Sweetbriar	Jemima, (Bridget's dam) by Snap	1784
Sir Peter Teazle	Highflyer	Papillon, by Snap	1784
Altamont	Garrick	King Herod, by Squirrel	1785
Director	Conductor	Paulina, by Florizel	1785
Georgiana	Sweetbriar	Capella, by King Herod	1785
Nutmeg	Mambrino	Marotte, by Match'em	1785
Miss Guildford	Guildford	Paulina, by Florizel	1786
Bab	Bourdeaux	Speranza ‖, by Eclipse	1787

* Paulina was also bred by Mr. Vernon, and sold to Lord Derby when two years old. Her dam was out of Calliope, the dam of Mr. Burdon's Orpheus and Duchess.

† Capella (foaled in 1773) was bred by General Parker, and sold to Lord Derby after racing, (four years old) for a brood mare.—Capella's dam was Miss Cape, by Regulus, out of Mr. Routh's Blackeyes, by Crab.

‡ Marotte, (foaled in 1766) was bred by Lord Bolingbroke, and sold to Lord Derby before she bred Dancer. She was also the dam of Mr. Hamilton's (of Ireland) famous racer and stallion Bagot, (own brother to Dancer)—Marotte's dam was got by Old Traveller; grandam by Mr. Hartley's blind horse, out of Mr. Routh's Northern Nancy, by Highland Laddie.

§ Papillon (foaled in 1769) was bred by Mr. Shafto, and was a brood mare in Lord Grosvenor's stud, and afterwards sold to Lord Derby before she bred Lady Teazle.

‖ Speranza, (foaled in 1778) was bred by Mr. Parker, and sold to Lord Derby after racing, at four years old. She was own sister to Saltram, by Eclipse; dam, Virago, by Snap, Regulus, out of a sister to Black-and-All-Black.

Horses, &c. Names.	Sires.	Dams, and what got by.	When foaled.
Lee Boo	Florizel	Ruby, by Pantaloon	1787
Mrs. Candour	Woodpecker	Papillon, by Snap	1787
Dancing-Master	Woodpecker	Madcap, by Snap	1788
Malespinner	Guildford	Jemima, (Bridget's dam) by Snap	1788
Pigmy	Florizel	Ruby, by Pantaloon	1788
Wagtail	Woodpecker	Papillon, by Snap	1788
Brown Bess	Highflyer	Papillon, by Snap	1789
Bustard	Woodpecker	Matron*, by Alfred	1789
Hotspur	Volunteer	Bridget, by King Herod	1789
Kidney	Pot8o's	Paulina, by Florizel	1790
Eustatia	Highflyer	Wren, by Woodpecker	1791
Hermione	Sir Peter Teazle	Paulina, by Florizel	1791
Miss Piper	Sir Peter Teazle	Fame, by Pantaloon	1791
Shuter	Sir Peter Teazle	Zilia, by Eclipse	1791
Brass	Sir Peter Teazle	Paulina, by Florizel	1792
Fair Helen	Sir Peter Teazle	Bridget, by King Herod	1792
Zenobia	Sir Peter Teazle	Zilia, by Eclipse	1792
Black George	Sir Peter Teazle	Bab, by Bourdeaux	1794
Go-By	Sir Peter Teazle	Paulina, by Florizel	1794
Henrietta	Sir Peter Teazle	Matron, by Alfred	1794
Bellissima	Phenomenon	Wren, by Woodpecker	1795
Knowsley	Sir Peter Teazle	Capella, by King Herod	1795
Sir Harry	Sir Peter Teazle	Matron, by Alfred	1795
Sir Thomas	Sir Peter Teazle	Bridget, by King Herod	1795
Telegraph	Sir Peter Teazle	Fame, by Pantaloon	1796
Countess	Sir Peter Teazle	Fame, by Pantaloon	1796
Expectation	Sir Peter Teazle	Zilia, by Eclipse	1796
Lady Jane	Sir Peter Teazle	Paulina, by Florizel	1796
Robin Redbreast	Sir Peter Teazle	Wren, by Woodpecker	1796
Agonistes	Sir Peter Teazle	Wren, by Woodpecker	1797
Attainment	Sir Peter Teazle	Zilia, by Eclipse	1798
Ealleisle, after- wards Cheshire Cheese	Sir Peter Teazle	Georgiana, by Sweetbriar	1798
Hind	Sir Peter Teazle	Paulina, by Florizel	1799
Miss Zilia Teazle	Sir Peter Teazle	Zilia, by Eclipse	1799
Maud, alias Pan- dora	Sir Peter Teazle	Brown Bess, by Highflyer	1801
Tiney	Sir Peter Teazle	Wren, by Woodpecker	1801
Milo†	Sir Peter Teazle	Wren, by Woodpecker	1802
Stranger	Sir Peter Teazle	Georgiana, by Sweetbriar	1802

* Matron, alias Betsy, (foaled in 1785) was bred by Sir Harry Harpur, Bart. and sold to Lord Egremont, who raced her in 1790 and 1791; she was then hunted two seasons, and afterwards was a brood mare in Lord Derby's Stud. Her dam was got by Marsk, Regulus, out of Wildair's dam, by Steady.

† Milo is kept by Lord Derby for a stallion, and covers at Knowsley, at 4gs. and 5s.

Atlas,

Horses, &c. Names.	Sires	Dams, and what got by	Year when foaled.
Atlas........	Sir Peter Teazle	Bab, by Bourdeaux	1803
Grazier........	Sir Peter Teazle	Sister to Aimator, by Trumpator	1803
Knowsley......	Sir Peter Teazle	Bab, by Bourdeaux	1804
Margaret	Sir Peter Teazle	Brown Bess, by Highflyer......	1804
Jacobus	Sir Peter Teazle	Brown Bess, by Highflyer......	1805

Lord Derby was the breeder of several others beside the above, which were sold when young, as were also nearly the whole of Sir Peter Teazle's get that were bred by his Lordship.

THE MYSTERIOUS BRIDE.

THIS new play, the production of Mr. Skeffington, a gentleman well known in the fashionable world, has repeatedly continued to attract numerous audiences to Drury-Lane Theatre. The characters were—

Almaric	Mr. Putnam.
Oswald..............	Mr. Raymond.
Armanski	Mr. Siddons.
Bolmann	Mr. Palmer.
Miesco	Mr. De Camp.
Store	Mr. Maddocks.
Orloff	Mr. Cooke.
Elisena	Mrs. H. Siddons.
Olfrida	Mrs. Harlowe.
Gertrude	Mrs. Sparks.
Marian	Mrs. Bland.

SCENE—*Transylvania.*
TIME—*Fourteenth Century.*

THE FABLE.

Elisena, daughter of the Bohemian King, has been sent under the care of an Officer, called Armanski, to be united in marriage with Almaric, the Prince of Transylvania. Previous to her departure, the Bohemian Monarch had given a medallion to Armanski, with the name of Elisena marked in diamonds.—Elisena is ignorant of this circumstance, as the present is intended as an agreeable surprise to the Prince on the day of marriage. Oswald, an ambitious favourite of the Prince, had conceived a daring design of imposing his sister Olfrida on his master for the long - expected Princess. Enamoured by the portrait artfully presented by the brother, the Prince hails Olfrida as his long-expected bride.—In the mean time, the ruffians of Oswald attack Armanski and his train in the Forest of Moldavia, rob him of the medallion, and every other proof; they seize the Princess, and plunge Armanski into the river. When Elisena arrives, two ruffians are about to murder her; touched with pity, they spare her life, and disguise her as a peasant. She is hired as a servant at the inn by Bolmann, and his waiter, Miesco, a generous rustic. She here meets the Prince, and captivates him at a *fête*, yet dares not disclose herself, dreading the vengeance of Oswald and Olfrida. Miesco is shortly enamoured of Elisena, but when she discloses her real situation, wholly renounces his passion, and devotes himself with zeal to her welfare. As the Prince and Olfrida are about to be united, Armanski, who had been saved by the care of peasants, arrives at the moment. He accuses Oswald and Olfrida, who retort the charge of imposture. Armanski asks the Prince for the medallion

lion in which the portrait of Elisena is concealed by a secret spring.
He then urges the false Elisena to
prove herself the daughter of his
master, the Bohemian King, by
shewing the diamond which opens
the medallion. She faulters. Elisena points to the letter E. The
Prince opens the medallion, and
the title of Elisena is confirmed.—
The piece ends with the defeat of
the impostors, and the union of
Almaric and Elisena.

Exclusive of the panegyrics bestowed upon the piece by the newspapers, we have to add, the language was always correct, perfectly
natural, and, when occasion required it, sufficiently dignified.—
The interest was kept alive during
the whole piece, and increased as
it approached the *denouement*.—
The scene between the innkeeper
and his wife, in which goodness of
heart and jealousy seem contending
for the ascendancy, is well conceived, and the author has displayed no inconsiderable knowledge
of human nature.

We must offer our testimony of
approbation to Mr. Siddons, whose
developement of the plot was admirably delivered; and the author's
language, which was here particularly strong and appropriate, was
correctly conceived, and given with
spirit. The performance of Mrs.
H. Siddons was chaste and pleasing; and in the scene where she
attracts the notice of the Prince by
the elegance of her language, and
dignity of deportment, she was
particularly happy.

The prologue, by Mr. Skeffington, was spoken with uncommon
energy by Mr. Putnam.

The epilogue, by Mrs. Piozzi,
was spoken by Mr. Russell.

Mrs. Bland sung a Neapolitan
air, which was much applauded.

An EPISTLE from A PEDES-TRIAN.

To the Editor of the Sporting Magazine.

SIR,

I Wish very much that you
would just *row a queer homo* or
two, who have taken upon themselves in several newspapers, to
quiz us, who are upon a better *footing* in the world than themselves; I mean we gentlemen who
have made ourselves famous for
walking against time, and whose
time being our own, we think we
have a right to do with it as we
please. These geniuses, Sir, have
never been admitted into company
that are quite the *go*, and therefore
can stand no chance with us who
have a *feed* now and then at the
first tables. It will not be a difficult matter for you, Mr. Editor,
who are up to the trick of it,
to say a number of good things
in our defence; for instance, that
we have a right to *put the best
leg forwards*, that we must *keep
moving*, that we have more occasion (our habits in life being gen-
teeler) for *leg-bail* than they have;
that we are used to out-run the
constable, and that we don't *stand*
at a trifle. It is true, that some
queer fellows among them may
reply, that though we *go on* at the
d—l of a rate we never get *forward*, and that *the more haste the
less speed.* However, Mr. Editor,
do the best you can to keep us *in*
countenance, and I'll in return for
the favour, introduce you to some
of us, who will put any body else
out of countenance. There's my
friend, Captain Clodhopper, of the
light infantry, who is as high-
finished in the fancy as you can
desire; he shall teach you the *hopp
and wheel, jumping the butts, hopping*

ping *the furlongs*, and all the fashionable sports; he is a great *goer;* he's the boy for the seven leaguers; we call him in the mess, *Father Long-legs;* and it is astonishing the wit that sometimes passes about *post shoes, Shanks's nag,* and so forth.

We go off in great style, when we have finished our education, I assure you; and we havn't been *hand in glove* with Gulley and the Game Chicken for nothing, so that I think, that after a *set-to* with those slow-moving geniuses, they will stand no more chance with us than *Bob Waddle* against *Bill Scamper,* as my honest friend, *Pat Flyaway,* says. There, now, is another good fellow; his race is generally against the bailiffs, and sometimes a hard match it is. Matters run at times very cross with Pat; it is a plaguy thing to be poor, and to be *cut* by the money-lenders. Pat is a fellow of great humour, and he and I are as friendly as *Sudbury* and *Monkey,* mentioned in your Magazine for December last.

Now, Mr. Editor, having said thus much, I hope that you will give these critic *curs,* a lecture in the *Sporting Magazine,* that they may give us a little more elbow room in the world: so that they may keep the *course* clear, and let us go our *own* way, I have no objection to their going their's; and that's the way most people like to go, after all. So I subscribe myself, Mr. Editor, your's truly,

ENSIGN AMBLESIDE.

Harrow-road, June 1, 1808.

FRIENDSHIP IN THE FEATHERED RACE.

DR. Lettsom has lately published a letter, "on the inhumanity of confining song-birds," in which he relates the following very extraordinary instance of affection between two linnets:—

" That the feeling and sentiment of birds, by whatever name we may designate them, are tender and sympathetic, their conjugal and parental conduct amply testifies.

" I well remember, when a school-boy, there was not one among us without his bird. There were two male linnets, who preserved during their lives, which were protracted for some years, the most inviolable attachment and friendship. These linnets were named Robert and Henry; they had not been brought up together, nor did they both belong to the same person. It was early observed, that whenever one of the birds sung, the other joined it, and at night each slept on that side the cage next its friend's. At length their attachment was more fully ascertained by this incident:—It was customary to allow the birds to fly about the chamber in which they were kept, on cleaning the cages. On one of these occasions, one of the linnets, being at liberty, flew to the cage of the other, and they were afterwards now and then indulged with the privilege of being together in one cage, when they uniformly expressed their high gratification, by fluttering towards each other, joining their bills together, and alternately gently picking the tongue of their friend. At length it was resolved to allow one of these birds to fly abroad in the open air, whilst the other was placed out in its cage. I have known the friend left at liberty to mix for some hours with the wild linnets, for this was on a heath, or common, near the school-house, and regularly return in the evening

ing to his vacated cage, placed near his confined friend. This indulgence of the common, was conferred alternately on Robert and Henry, and with the same undeviating attachment. They never were allowed this liberty together; and probably had it been suffered, they would not have returned; for each seemed to enjoy the company of the wild linnets, but so indelible was their mutual attachment, that they preferred imprisonment together, rather than separation.

"One of these friends at length died, and the other pined away and soon followed his deceased friend—*ad sedes illuc negat redire quemquam.*"

PEDIGREE AND PERFORMANCES OF

That well-known Bay Horse,

BROTHER TO VIVALDI.

Of which an Engraving, from a Painting by Clifton Tomson, is here given.

THIS celebrated racer was foaled in 1799, bred by the Earl of Egremont, and for some time in the possession of his Royal Highness the Prince of Wales; and afterwards became the property of Major Wilson.

He was got by Woodpecker; his dam, (Paulo and Palermo's dam). by Mercury; grandam, Cytherea, (own sister to Drone) by King Herod; great grandam Lily, (own sister to Jethro) by Blank; Peggy, by Cade, out of an own sister to the Widdrington Mare, by Partner. *Woodpecker* died in 1798.

At Bibury, in June, 1805, *Brother to Vivaldi*, 11st. 10lb. won a Handicap Stakes of 10gs. each,

(8 Subscribers) two miles, beating Young Eclipse, six years old, 11st.; Chilton, aged, 11st. 3lb.; Lismahago, 6 years old, 12st.; and Little Printer, aged, 11st. 7lb.—Seven to 4 against the Brother to Vivaldi, who was rode by Mr. Delmé Radcliffe; and 2 to 1 against Young Eclipse.

At Ascot-Heath, in June, 1806, at 9st. he won a Sweepstakes of 10gs. each, with 25gs. added (11 Subscribers), two miles and a half, beating Agincourt, 3 years old, 8st. 5lb.; Watery, 5 years old, 8st. 3lb.; and Victory, 4 years old, 7st. 9lb.—Five to 4 against Agincourt, 5 to 2 against Watery, and 7 to 1 against the Brother to Vivaldi.

At Ipswich, in July, at 9st. 3lb. he won 50l. two-mile heats, beating Mr. Browne's Laura, 5 years old, 9st. 4lb. who was drawn after the first heat.

At Northampton, in August, at 9st. 3lb. he won 50l. four-mile heats, beating Zodioya, 4 years old, 7st. 5lb.; and Enchanter, aged, 9st. 5lb. who was second, and drawn.

At Stamford, in July, 1807, at 9st. 2lb. he won 50l. for all ages, four-mile heats, beating Wildair, 3 years old, 6st. 6lb.; Buzzard, 4 years old, 8st. 3lb.; and Eliza, 4 years old, 7st. 11lb.—Even betting; and after the heat, 6 to 4 on the Brother to Vivaldi.

At Bedford, September 11, at 9st. he ran four very severe heats (4 miles each) against Sir Launcelot, 5 years old, 8st. 12lb.; beating Dodona, 5 years old, 8st. 5lb.

At Leicester, September 17, he was beat by Grimaldi and Coiner; notwithstanding, the same day, at 9st. 3lb. he won the Burgesses' Purse of 50l. four-mile heats, beating Buzzard, 4 years old.

old, 7st. 8lb.; Margaret, 3 years old, 5st. 10lb.; and Mr. Fisher's Waxy colt, 3 years old, 5st. 10lb.—Five and 6 to 4 on the Brother to Vivaldi.

He has run hard for a great many other plates, &c. and though beaten, few horses have better supported travelling and running, especially at high weights, than the *Brother to Vivaldi.*—He is yet in training, though nine years old.

STALLIONS WHO COVER IN IRELAND, 1808.

AMETHYST, at Blarney-Castle, near Cork, at 5½gs.—By Diamond; dam, Sweetmarjoram, by Sweetbriar, out of Dizzy, (Pilot's dam) by Blank.

AUGUSTUS, at Higginstown, near Kilkenny, at 5gs. and a crown. —By Tantrum; dam, (Nottingham's dam) by Sampson; grandam by the Godolphin Colt, out of Flora, (Marquis's dam) by Regulus.

BACCHUS, at Tuam, at 4gs. and a crown.—By Bacchus, (son of Apollo) out of a daughter of Gamahoe.

BLACKLEGS, at Grange, within a mile of Boyle, at 3gs. and a crown.—By Deceiver, (Son of Chocolate.)

BRUISER, at Waterford, at 2gs. and a crown.—By Boxer, (a Son of Old Bagot); dam by Pot8o's; grandam, Heifer, by Woodpecker; great grandam, (Lord Egremont's Matron's dam), by Marsk, Regulus, out of Wildair's dam, by Steady.

BUFFER, at Mr. Whaley's Stables, on the Curragh, at 10gs. and a crown.—By Prize-fighter; dam by Highflyer; grandam, Shift, by

VOL. XXXII.—No. 189.

Sweetbriar; Black Susan, by Snap, out of Lord Bruce's Cade Mare.

CAPTAIN, at Johnstown-Bridge, County of Kildare, at 4gs. and a crown.—By Commodore; dam by Master Bagot; grandam, by Old Bagot, out of Comfort, the dam of Belisarius, Soldier, Cornet, Duncan, Consolation, and Honest Ralph, all good runners.

COMMODORE, at Mr. Edwards's Stables, on the Curragh, at 8gs. and a crown.—By Tugg; dam, Smallhopes, (Admiral's dam), by the Duke of Kingston's Scaramouch, Blank, Traveller.

DRONE (Old), at Birr, at 5gs. and a crown.—By Old Bagot; dam Flirt, by ————, out of Old Mother Browne, by Trunnion.

EBONY, at Mark Daly's, Thomond-Gate, at 3gs.—By Prize-fighter; dam, Harriet, (Loyal's dam) by Dungannon, out of Miss Euston, by Snap.

FAUNUS, at Berry-Kerry, near Carlow, at 5gs. and a crown.—By Master Bagot; dam, Miss Doe, by Young Gamahoe; grandam by Old England.

GLUTTON, at Purse-Lodge, near Longhrea, at 3gs. and half-a-crown.—By Maximin, out of the Maid of Derry-O!

JERRY SNEAK, at Swinburn's Hotel, Limerick, at 4gs. and a crown.—Own Brother to Old Toby, by Chocolate, out of Old Mother Browne, by Trunnion.

LOYAL, at Seaview, Wicklow, at 6gs. and a crown.—By Old Bagot, out of Harriett, (Ebony's dam) by Dungannon.

MASTER EAGLE, at Mr. Brownrigg's, of Tubber, near Dunlavin, at 6gs. and half-a-crown. —Own Brother to Sir Frank Standish's Spread-Eagle, Split-Pigeon, and Eagle, by Volunteer; dam

B

dam by Highflyer, Engineer, Cade, out of Lass of the Mill, by Traveller.

RICHMOND, at Coolrain, between M'Ram and Burriss, in Ossory, at 4gs. and a crown.—By Swindler, dam Mrs. Dawdle, (own Sister to Mr. D. B. Daly's Dawdle) by Master Bagot, out of Twilight, by Lenox.

RUGANTINO, at Mr. Whaley's Stables, on the Curragh, at 2gs.—Own Brother to Escape, by Commodore; dam, La-la, (Young Pipes and Georgina's dam) by Old Bagot; grandam, Lottery, by Gamahoe, out of Shepherdess, one of the highest bred mares in England, and a good runner.

SELIM, at Prospect-House near Newtown, Mount Kennedy, at 3gs. and half-a-crown.—By Honest Tom; dam by Lenox; grandam by Paymaster.

SIR WALTER, at Higginstown, near Kilkenny, at 5gs. and a crown.—By Waxy; dam, Woodcot, by Mentor; grandam, Titania, by Shakspeare, out of Mr. Latham's Snap's dam, by Cade, Partner.

SOLDIER, at Belleny, County of Meath, at 3gs. and a crown.—By Chocolate; dam, Comfort, (Cornet, Belisarius, Dunean, Consolation, and Honest Ralph's dam), by Banker, out of Lady Bountiful, by Old England.

STICKLER, at Derry-Allen, near Tanderagee, at 4½gs.—Own Brother to Diamond and Screveton, by Highflyer; dam by Match'em; grandam, Barbara, by Snap; Miss Vernor, by Cade, out of an own sister to the Widdrington Mare, by Partner.

SWEETWILLIAM, at Saddleston, near Bellewstown, County of Meath, at 5gs. and a crown.—By Tugg; dam, St. Bridgett (own

sister to Master Bagot) by Old Bagot, out of Harmonia, (own sister to Mr. O'Kelly's Soldier and Gunpowder) by Eclipse.—Old Bagot was own brother to Lord Derby's Dancer, by King Herod, out of Marotte, by Match'em.

SWINDLER, at Mr. Hamilton's Stables, on the Curragh, at 6gs. and a crown.—By Old Bagot; dam, Ariel, (The Hank's dam) by Highflyer; grandam, (own sister to Figurante) by Regulus, Bolton, Starling, out of Snap's dam, by Fox.

SWORDSMAN, at Castle-Plunket, within ten miles of Roscommon, at 8gs. and a crown.—By Prize-fighter; dam, Zara, (own sister to Isabella) by Eclipse; grandam, (Lance's dam) by Squirrel, out of Ancaster Nancy, (own sister to Ancaster) by Blank.

SYMMETRY, at Linville, between Clonmel and Carrick, at 8gs. and a crown.—Own Brother to Mr. Creed's Noblessa, by Diamond; dam, Jane Harold, by Friar; grandam, Noblessa, (own sister to Noble) by Gamahoe, out of Coquette, by the Duke of Bolton's Sloven.

THE HANK, at Flanstown, two miles from Mullingar, at 4gs. and a crown.—By Master Bagot, out of Ariel, (Swindler's dam) by Highflyer, &c.

THRESHER, at Tullamaine, near Cashel, at 6gs. and a crown. —By Commodore; dam, Gaylass, by Highflyer; grandam, Leonora, by Shakspeare, out of Diomed's dam, by Spectator.

TOM PIPES, at Mr. Caldwell's Stables, on the Curragh, at 8gs. and a crown.—By Commodore; dam, La-la, (Young Pipes and Georgina's dam) by Old Bagot; grandam, Lottery, by Gamahoe, out of Shepherdess, one of of the highest bred mares in England, and a good runner.

WASHINGTON, at No. 22, Aungier-street, Dublin, at 3gs. and a crown.—By Sir Peter Teazle; dam, (His Lordship and Shittlecock's dam; also, own sister to Trumpator) by Conductor, out of Brunette, by Squirrel.

YOUNG LAMBINOS, at Castletown, near Carlow, at 2gs. and a crown.—By Lambinos; dam by Gamahoe; grandam by Tim, out of the Patch Mare, (Hippolitus's dam) bred by the late Sir Edward O'Brien, and got by Old England.

YOUNG PIPES, in Tipperary, at 4gs. and a crown.—By Cornet, out of La-la, the dam of Tom Pipes, &c.

GAME LAWS.

THE following is a copy of the Bill recently passed, "to repeal so much of an Act of the First Year of King James the First, as relates to the Penalties on Shooting at Hares; and also to alter the Provisions of an Act of the Year of King George the First, so far as relates to the appointment of Gamekeepers.

"Whereas an Act was passed in the second year (commonly called the first year) of the reign of King James I. intituled, 'An Act for the better executing of the intent and meaning of former statutes made against shooting in guns, and for the preservation of the game of Pheasants and Partridges, and against the destroying of Hares with Hare-pipes, and tracing Hares in the snow,' whereby it was amongst other things enacted, that every person who should shoot at,

kill or destroy, with any gun, cross bow, stone bow, or long bow, any hare, should be subject to the penalties therein mentioned:

"And whereas it is expedient that the said provision should be repealed so far as relates to persons qualified to kill Game:

"And whereas it is also expedient that a certain other Act, passed in the third year of his late Majesty King George the First, intituled, 'An Act to explain and amend several laws therein mentioned, for the better preservation of the game,' should also be repealed:

"Be it therefore enacted by the King's Most Excellent Majesty, by and with the advice and consent of the Lords Spiritual and Temporal, and Commons in this present Parliament assembled, and by the authority of the same, That the said provision of the said recited Act, of the second of James the First, and the said recited Act of the Third of George the First, relative to the qualification of gamekeepers, and regulating the appointment thereof, shall be, and the same are hereby repealed.

"And be it enacted, That the said statute shall not extend to prevent any person, duly qualified by any law now existing, to kill game, from shooting at or killing any hare, with any gun, cross bow, stone-bow, or long bow, but that it shall be lawful for such qualified person to shoot at or kill any hare, by any of the means aforesaid; any thing to the contrary, in the said recited statute, notwithstanding.

"And be it further enacted, That it shall be lawful for any Lord or Lady of any manor to appoint and depute any person whatever, whether acting as a gamekeeper to any other person or not, or whether retained and paid for as a male servant of any other person or not, or whether a qualified person or not, to be game-keeper to any such manor, with authority to such person, as game-keeper, to kill game within the same, for his own use or for the use of any other person or persons whatever specified in such appointment or deputation, whether qualified or not ; and no person so appointed game-keeper as aforesaid, and empowered to kill game for his own use, or for the use of any other person, and not killing any game for the use of the Lord or Lady of the Manor, for which such deputation shall be given, shall be deemed or taken to be, or entered or paid for as the game-keeper or male servant of the Lord or Lady making such appointment, or giving such deputation as aforesaid ; any thing in any Act or Acts of Parliament to the contrary notwithstanding.

" And be it further enacted, That any person appointed game-keeper, under the authority of this Act, to kill game for his own use or the use of any other person, shall have the same rights, privileges, power, and authority, as if he had been legally qualified and appointed to act as game-keeper, or kill game for the use of the Lord or Lady of the manor appointing such game-keeper, under any laws in force immediately before the passing of this Act."

EXTRAORDINARY IRRUPTION,

(From a New-York Paper of December last.)

A Letter from Johnstown, Montgomery County, mentions, that the country in the vicinity has, this autumn, been uncommonly infested with bears.—About 250 have been killed within the circuit of eight or ten miles. The cause of this irruption, as it may be termed, is supposed to be the scarcity in the back part of the state, of chesnuts and beech nuts, which compelled the bears and squirrels to resort to the more southern and productive tracts. Instances have been known of a whole corn-field being stripped by these *marauders* in the course of a night.—A singular instance of strength in a bear, occurred lately in the neighbourhood—A young one, nearly full grown, was taken in a steel trap of 21lbs. weight, to which was annexed an iron chain of 23lbs.—his hind leg was broken, notwithstanding which, he dragged both trap and chain above two hundred yards, to a large hemlock tree, up which he climbed, until the chain became entangled in the branches, and checked his progress. In the morning he was traced to his retreat, and shot, and it was found necessary to cut the tree down, to get possession of the body.—A panther of considerable size has likewise been seen by several country people, lately prowling in the vicinity of the town. A farmer, when in the middle of a field, was alarmed by the approach of this unwelcome visitor : his only refuge was the stump of a tree, on which he mounted, and with a rope halter that he had in his hand, kept up a constant noise, by beating the same against the trunk ; whether deterred by this or not, the panther contented himself with walking several times around him, and then, without any particular *congé*, took a French leave, and retired to the woods.

FEAST

FEAST OF WIT.

THE following anecdote may, perhaps, serve to shew the absurdity of the practice of duelling better than the most serious argument.—The brave Dutch Admiral, Van Tromp, who was a large heavy man, was challenged by a thin active French officer. "We are not upon equal terms with rapiers," said Van Tromp, "but call upon me to-morrow morning, and we will adjust the affair better."—When the Frenchman called, he found the Dutch Admiral bestriding a barrel of gunpowder: "There is room enough for you," said Van Tromp, "at the other end of the barrel; sit down, there is a match; and as you were the challenger, give fire." The Frenchman was a little thunderstruck at this terrible mode of fighting; but as the Dutch Admiral told him he would fight in no other way, terms of accommodation ensued.

THE following circumstance occurred with the Exminster Volunteers, on his Majesty's birth-day. The regiment having paraded in Powderham Park, Devonshire, under the command of Major Rainsworth, received their ammunition, and were then marched on the hill near Lord Courtenay's Belvidere, for the purpose of firing three vollies, which should "make the welkin resound." The muskets were primed and loaded—the word was given to *make ready !—present !—* when one of the privates exclaimed, "Sir, we have got no flints." On this an examination took place, and it was found that not a single man had a flint in his musket, the hammers being merely charged with a small piece of wood. What was to be done ? the flints were locked up in store in the Belvidere, the person who kept the key was not to be found, and the door could not be forced. Under these circumstances, the Commanding Officer thought it proper to take the only step which prudence could dictate, and that was, to order every man to draw his cartridge, and throw the priming from the pan; which being done, the regiment then *went through the motions*, and reserved the *real fire* for a future opportunity.

A PERSON who had resided for some time on the coast of Africa, was asked if he thought it were possible to civilise the natives ?— "As a proof of the possibility of it," replied he, "I have known some negroes, who thought as little of a *lie* or an *oath* as any European."

A SCENE-PAINTER at a provincial theatre, lately daubed a fleet of ships for the *English Fleet*. His performance was so indifferent, that the same scene was afterwards used for the *Forest of Arden*, in the play of *As You Like It*. On being told by the manager that his *ships* were like *trees*, he observed, "then I am correct in my delineation, for Homer says, a fleet is a moving wood."

THE following hand-bill was distributed at a late masquerade, by Sir

Sir T. Gage, in the character of Sylvester Daggerwood:—

" Grand Histrionic Rooms, up ten pair of stairs, at the sign of the Cow and the Snuffers, in Billingsgate.

" For the benefit of Mr. and Mrs. Daggerwood, will be performed (by particular desire of several ladies and gentlemen of the very first distinction) the grand serio-comico-farcico-pantomimico Melo-Drama, called *A Whale in a Butter-Boat*. In seven acts and a half.—King of the Pigmies, Mr. Daggerwood; the Irish Giant, Mrs. Daggerwood; John Roast Beef, Mr. Apollo Daggerwood; Lady Dandlecub, Mrs. Tag; and the Butter-Boat, by Miss Melpomene Daggerwood, who will sing the admired song of *Nobody coming to marry me*, to a full band of marrow-bones and cleavers.

" After which will be represented, Shakespeare's Tragedy of *Macbeth*. In one short act.—Macbeth, King of Scotland, Mr. Daggerwood, in which he will introduce a favourite *pas seul*.—Lady Macbeth, (with a candle) Mrs. Daggerwood; Candle Snuffer, Master Daggerwood; Extinguisher, Miss Melpomene Daggerwood:—Sun, Moon, and Stars, Ghosts, Devils, and Witches, by the rest of the company.

" To begin at six o'clock.—Boxes, 6d.—Pit, 3d.—Gallery, 1½d. Tickets delivered by Mr. and Mrs. Daggerwood, at the Cow and the Snuffers, and at all other places of fashionable resort in this metropolis.—God save the King."

A GRAVE BULL.—The following epitaph is to be found in Kirkeel church-yard.—" Here lie the remains of Thomas Nicolls, who died in Philadelphia, March, 1758.—

Had he LIVED, he would have been buried here."

SPANISH PRIDE.—A Florentine, walking with a Spaniard in Florence during the time of the Medici, they met the Grand Duke, with his brother, the Cardinal.—The Florentine asked his companion if he was not highly delighted with seeing those two Princes? The Spaniard, after being repeatedly asked, at length replied : " In Spain, we have forty equal to your Cardinal ; ten equal to your Grand Duke ; two equal to the Pope, and one equal to God.—The forty, are the forty Canons of Toledo ; the ten, are the ten Grandees of Spain ; the two equal to the Pope, are the Archbishops of Toledo and Seville ; and the one equal with God is our King."

THERE are two Members in the House of Commons, named Montagu Mathew, and Mathew Montagu ; the former a tall handsome man, and the latter a little man. During the present Session of Parliament, the Speaker, having addressed the latter as the former, Montagu Mathew observed, it was strange he should make such a mistake, as there was as great a difference between them as between a Horse-Chesnut and a Chesnut Horse.

A POLITICAL Fishmonger is happy to find, that the brave Fins go on swimmingly, and has no doubt the dear soles will very shortly plaice the Russians, so as to beat them like stock fish.

At a late review of a volunteer corps, not twenty miles from York, the Major, who gave the word, not finding the men so expert as he he wished, was perpetually calling, " *As you were—As you were*,"— and putting them twice through the ordered manœuvre; the Inspecting Officer at length losing all patience, exclaimed, " *As you were!*—No; I'll be d—d if you are as you were; for you are not half so good as you were the last time I saw you."

In a field by the road-side, near the Holmwood Common, between Horsham and Dorking, is set up a board with the following inscription :—

Who so Ever
Is Fond stilling
Turners In this Ground
Will be perse
Cuted as the Law Directs

A few days ago, a respectable druggist at Blackburn received the following curious epistle :—" Will you Send me help for Babey That is 9 weeks of age it is Greatley fulfild with a Cough and if it Please your honour Sir Will you Right it down how it must Be taken."

EPITAPH.

HERE lies *Thomas Cole*,
Who died, on my soul,
After eating a plentiful dinner:
While chewing his crust,
He was turn'd into dust,
With his crimes undigested, poor sinner!

A few days ago, in the neighbourhood of Midhurst, a man took up and carried away one of the mile-stones; he was had before a magistrate, who, during the examination, enquiring of him what he intended to do with it, the man innocently replied, he was going to make a hog-trough; upon hearing of which, the magistrate committed him to Petworth Bridewell,

there to remain, and take some rest before he set about so arduous a task.

Towards the latter end of the seventeenth century, it was the custom, (as Lord Molesworth informs us, in his Account of Denmark) at the end of every royal hunting-match, in order to conclude the entertainment with as much festivity as it had begun, to issue a proclamation, enjoining every one to stand forth and accuse such as had transgressed the known laws of hunting. As soon as the contravention was ascertained, the culprit was made to kneel down between the horns of the stag that had been hunted; two of the gentlemen then removed the skirts of his coat, when the King, taking a small long wand in his hand, laid a certain number of blows, which were proportioned to the greatness of the offence, whilst, in the mean time, the huntsmen, with their brass horns, and the dogs, with loud openings, proclaimed the King's justice, and the culprit's punishment.

A player, in a theatrical barn, having undertaken a great *tragic character* for his *benefit*, after ranting and strutting through the first act, addressed the audience in his own character, in words to the following effect :—" Ladies and Gentlemen, I am assured by some of my best friends, that they came here to *sarve* me, not to *see* me; and that *you* would rather see *any body* else in the *part* than myself; —I shall, therefore, (as it is my duty to please you as far as lies in my power) just put off my *whiskers*—wipe my face, and give you the *wooden shoe dance*."

ON

ON A PRINTING OFFICE.

THE *World's* a *Printing-Office, our words*
    are *thoughts,*
Our *deeds* are *characters* of several sizes;
Each *Soul* is a *Compositor,* of whose
    faults
The Levites are *Correctors,* Heav'n
    revises.
Death is the common *press,* from whence
    being driven,
We're gather'd *sheet* by *sheet,* and bound
    for *Heaven.*

ANECDOTE, from the Spaniard's
Letters from England.—Speaking
of the plunder and animosity which
so long subsisted between the English and Scotch borderers, this entertaining writer says—" Though
their plundering habits are laid
aside, they retain much of their old
rude manners and barbarous spirit.
An instance of this we hear from
our companion :—A borderer, of
the name of Taylor, who was at
mortal enmity with one of his
neighbours, fell sick, and being
given over, sent for his enemy, that
they might be reconciled. ' Ah,'
said he, when the man entered the
room, ' I am very bad, very bad
indeed—d'ye think I shall die ?'—
' Why, hope not, (replied his visitor) hope not ; to be sure you are
very bad, but for all that, perhaps,
you may do yet.' ' No, no, (said
the other) I shall die, I know I
shall die—and so I have sent for
you, that I may not go out of the
world in enmity with any one. So,
d'ye see, we'll be friends. The
quarrel between us is all over—all
over—and so give me your hand.'
Accordingly, this token of reconciliation was performed, and the
other took his leave ; when, just
as he was closing the door after
him, the sick man cried out—' But
stop, if I should not die this time,
this is to go for nothing : mind
now—it's all to be just as it was
before, if I do not die.'

EPIGRAM ON A LATE BATTLE.

BEHOLD, great King, at Fate's com-
    mand,
(Thus sung the leader of the band)
    Where sleeps poor old Darius !
On the bare earth repos'd he lies,
Without a friend to *close his eyes*—
    When dead, none e'er come nigh us.

Poor Pagans, ignorant and rude !—
Thank Heav'n ! such base ingratitude
    Our Christian age can't sully :
GREGSON, for thee kind Fate supplies
A pious friend to *close thy eyes,*
    And that dear friend is—GULLEY.

AN Irish footman having carried
a basket of game from his master
to a friend, waited a considerable
time for the customary fee, but not
finding it likely to appear, scratch-
ed his head, and said—" Sir, if
my master should say — Paddy,
what did the gentleman give you ;
what would your honour have me
to tell him !"

THE principal emulation of the
present day, is between the *Funny
Club,* the *Whip Club,* and the *Pedestrians.* The merit of the first
is in the *skull,* of the second in the
hand, and of the third in the *leg.*

A *German* dramatic author has
published a new play, entitled,
" *The Benevolent Cut-throat,*" in
which he has a most felicitous idea,
that of the *Moon fainting away.*—
This is certainly an improvement
on Shakspeare (who, by the bye,
must be allowed to have had a
pretty knack at writing), for he
only makes the moon sleep.

Five Plagues of a Village.—A
Lawyer with great knowledge and
no justice :—A Physician with little skill :—A Methodist Preacher :
—A Democratic Politician :—and
a dogmatic Man of Letters !

HINTS
TO THE
BEARERS OF WALKING-STICKS
AND UMBRELLAS.

Illustrated with Six Engravings. Price Two Shillings and Sixpence.

THIS new work possesses an uncommon degree of humour, both for the eye and the ear. The learning, too, of the author, is truly recondite, in his notices of the derivations and variations of the simple staff to the sceptre of the monarch, the spear of the warrior, the javelin of the hunter, the shepherd's crook, the Bacchanal's thyrsus, the Bishop's crosier, the magician's wand, canes, switches, sword-sticks, bamboos, supple-jacks, &c. &c.

In the second chapter the author treats of the various modes of miscarrying walking sticks and umbrellas, to the general annoyance of all passengers in the streets, as follows:

Not few are the inventions which plain utility recommend in their origin, but which in the process of time the power of fashion has debased into useless decoration. The shield that protected the hardy limbs of the ancient hero, now decorates the coach-door of his effeminate descendants. The walking stick, designed, as I have shewn above, for the support of the weary and infirm, is now borne in the hand by millions, who pretend not to consider it as an article of use, but as a mere ornament. It is still employed by many, I must own, for the very purposes to which it was originally destined, but to those the following remarks will be rarely found to apply.

Every one, who has ever walked through the crowded street of any town, must have met with considerable obstruction and annoyance.

from the awkward manner in which the greater part of mankind carry both walking sticks and umbrellas. The pavement is a free common, of which all have a right to partake, but it is not without stint; and if one, by his inattention to the convenience of others, unnecessarily occupies the space of four or six, he is justly to be regarded as a common nuisance, which every one has a right to abate, committing as little violation of the King's peace as possible. The selfish and stupid indifference to the feelings of others, displayed by men of all ranks, from the lounger of noble blood to the common brandisher of a cart-whip, in this particular, must continually strike the observation of every one who finds leisure to reflect in the street upon the passing multitude. One man, a gentleman not wilfully rude, not malicious, but without reflection, dips his cane into the mud, and then wipes the dirty ferule on the clean dress of the next woman who passes. Another twirls his stick in the air, though sure to strike some one near him, to break a lamp, or to jerk the dirt over the backs and faces of passengers before and behind. A third fixes his cane or umbrella under his arm: if he moves strait forward, the ferule behind impales the eye of one who follows with a brisker step; or if it should slope downward, stabs his breast, and soils his dress. If the bearer of the stick so placed turn himself sideways in the street, he becomes a sort of turnstile; his stick extends over the whole pavement, the near-sighted are struck in the neck or face, and all are obliged to remove it, or remonstrate. The more common inconvenience to passengers in a hurry arises from the oblique direction in which the generality place their sticks upon the ground, engrossing thereby an undue portion of the pavement, and infallibly tripping up those who do not narrowly look to their steps. I shall endeavour to display, in a series of distinct propositions, the quantum of encroachment on the public right of way, and consequent injury to passengers in general, from some of the principal instances of stick nuisances, and occasionally suggest such methods of handling both walking sticks and umbrellas, as seem most consonant to graceful attitudes, most convenient to the ease of the walker, and least likely to incommode the public.

The author then enumerates, as follows, some of the principal encroachers on the public way, thus: —the fencer, the twirler, the arguer, the trailer, the Parthian, the unicorn, the turnstile:—umbrella-bearers he distinguishes by the characteristic names of shield-bearers, sky-strikers, mud-scoopers, and inverters.

1. The fencer is commonly a boy just presented with a gaily varnished cane or stick, by some kind aunt or godmother, or grandmama, or bearing their first purchase with their present in money. He has perhaps seen fencers on the stage. The shining ferule reminds him of a sword, and he pokes it with an awkward flourish between the legs, against the breasts or faces of all he meets. It is soon broken by some petulant passenger, or between the spokes of a coach-wheel, or the rails of an area.

2. The twirler is usually some gay youth, just allowed to walk in the streets without an attendant, in his first vacation from college. Ambitious to exhibit an easy *non-chalance*, he whirls his cane in the air by means of a ribbon or leather passed through a hole in the head. He thus dashes off the hat or bonnet of one, throws dirt over another: a broil is excited—the youth is resolute—he receives a drubbing, and talks of a challenge.— Men-milliners, linen-drapers' apprentices, and bankers' and attornies' clerks, are commonly twirlers. For a charming description of the effects of twirling, see the story of the Little Notary, in Sterne's Sentimental Journey.

3. The arguer endeavours to supply with the head of his cane, some deficiency in his own. I do not allude to that species of baculine argument, in the course of which the disputant knocks down his opponent, but to that milder sort, in which the head of the stick, held in the right hand, is pressed into the palm of the left with force proportionate to the supposed cogency of the position. In this case, the lower end of the cane is thrown out sideways, to the great impediment of passers. More vehement orators occasionally brandish the cane like a truncheon, or scroll of the leader of a band, smashing thereby a projecting shop window, together with the exhibited specimens of Sève or Shropshire china.

4. The trailer indolently drags his stick after him. Most loungers, men whose thoughts are never engaged in any thing, and men whose minds are fully occupied, are equally liable to err in this way.— The stick extends nearly a yard behind them. When they cross a street, the wheel of a carriage frequently passes over the trailed stick, and breaks it. This is a fortunate accident, but it is no compensation to the many passengers, who, in their haste, have been tripped up

up by it, and thrown into the mud.

5. The Parthian, as every body knows, while his horse galloped, shot his arrows with dexterous aim behind him. Thus many fix the head of their cane or umbrella close under their arm, preserving it firm in a horizontal position, or somewhat inclining upwards: hence, an inadvertent or dim-sighted follower receives the dirty end in his mouth, or stabs his eye against the pointed ferule, which, like a reverted spear, wounds those who follow, instead of those who meet its bearer.

6. The unicorn is the converse of the Parthian. His formidable horn projects, and forces a passage through the crowd for the resolute charger. The stick grasped by the head, with the end advanced in the manner of a spear or bayonet, characterises the bullying buck, and many varieties of vulgar swaggerers. There is, moreover, a species of unicorn, destitute of ferocity in appearance, but not less incommoding to passengers; he may be called the unicorn au corne baissé, as he drives the point of his cane like a plough before him on the pavement.— This is an awkwardness of men who are subject to abstraction or absence of mind, or who wish to assume an air of reverie.

The turnstile, instead of fixing his cane or umbrella, like the Parthian, so that it may extend its whole length behind, or advancing it wholly before like the unicorn, places it under his arm in such manner, that it may extend equally both behind and before. Now, though it does not extend nearly so far in either direction as in each of the former instances, it produces the united inconvenience of both. In

fact, a man so circumstanced engrosses the rightful portion of three men at least on the pavement; and when he turns round, his stick describes a circle of space which might fairly be occupied by five.—An absent man, of the turnstile species, was walking through a street, when two men, with coal sacks on their shoulders, endeavoured to pass on either side; the elbows of the coal-heavers struck against the extremities of his umbrella; the force of their advance rolled him into the gutter; the shock overthrew the coal sacks from the heads of the bearers; the unfortunate turnstile wallowed in the mud, was sorely bruised, and nearly buried and stifled under six bushels of small coal.

Common sense, and a small degree of sympathy with general distress, point out an easy method of avoiding all the above disorders, viz. that the cane or closed umbrella should be borne as close to the body, as near to the front as possible, and constantly in a perpendicular position. I take leave to suggest, to young gentlemen in general, that nothing is truly graceful, which is manifestly in direct opposition to utility.

A word or two on expanded umbrellas. The shield-bearer drives his umbrella before him, covering completely his head and body. He can see nobody in front, and he occupies the whole pavement: he either runs against every one before him, or compels them to step into the gutter. If, however, he should meet with a unicorn, the cane of the latter pierces and rends the silk or varnished cover of the umbrella. Thus rival follies and contending vices mutually annoy each other to the furtherance of justice, and to

the

the advantage of the community. When two passengers meet and wish to pass, with spread umbrellas, each should incline his pole in the angle 45, to his proper side; thus neither will be incommoded. When two meet a third, the centre should elevate, and the outside slope umbrellas. The generality are sky-strikers or mud-scoopers. Every passer either jirks up his umbrella to the sky, whereby the shorter endangers with the points of his whalebone the eyes of the taller, or dashes it to the ground so as to impede all passage; the latter case is the last degree of awkwardness, and chiefly occurs amongst the most vulgar servant-maids and young children. These are called mud-scoopers, from plunging the edges of their instrument by such means into the dirt.

Inverters are those careless beings who present the inside of the umbrella to the wind, whereby the cover is turned inside out, and commonly much lacerated, while they impede the progress of many a time-pressed citizen during their awkward attempts to re-arrange it.

BREACH OF THE GAME LAWS.

COURT OF KING's BENCH.

ON Wednesday, May the 4th, Mr. Park moved for leave to enter a nonsuit in a case entitled *Wornford* v. *Kendall*, tried at York assizes, and a verdict obtained for the plaintiff. It was an action arising out of a breach of the Game Laws, for exposing a hare

to sale, and it appeared that the defendant had been appointed by the steward of the manor to look after some poachers.

The plaintiff coursing one day, killed a hare, and the animal fell dead near the defendant's feet; he took the hare up, and walked away with it, and it was for this act the present action was brought, the Game Laws authorising the conclusion that the having game in possession improperly, is an exposure to sale; it was, however, further proved, that the defendant took the hare to the steward.

Mr. Justice Lawrence was of opinion that the action would not lie; but the plaintiff's counsel quoted the case of *Molton* v. *Cheesely*, from *Mr. Espinasse's Reports, p.* 123, wherein a man was held by Mr. Justice Buller to have committed an offence against the Game Laws, by picking up a pheasant that had been accidentally killed by his dog, and carrying it away; Mr. Justice Buller upon that occasion said, " if it appeared that the bird was killed by accident, that that was no offence, but that in such case it should be left where the bird was killed, for if it was taken away, it subjects the party to a penalty for having game in his possession."—And the plaintiff in this case recovered 5l. for the offence.

Mr. Justice Lawrence said, if that was the law, certainly the plaintiff was entitled to a verdict, and therefore ordered a verdict to be entered accordingly, subject to the opinion of the Court, upon the accuracy of the case cited.

Mr. Park said, if what he had stated was to be construed an offence, game of all kinds, if found dead on the land, must in future be left to be crushed in high roads, by by carriages, rather than be taken up by unqualified persons.

The Court seemed to think the report of *Molton* v. *Gheesely* inaccurate, and desired Mr. Park to take a rule to shew cause.

BOXING.

THE battle between *Dockarty*, of pugilistic note, and a Scots baker, of the name of *Peatikin*, the former having been backed 40 guineas to 20 against his adversary, was decided on Saturday, June 11, at Goolder's Green, on the Hendon-road, in the presence of a miscellaneous company of several hundreds, from the duke, marquis, and lord, down to the costermongers and kids of the metropolis. Dockarty is known to the public as a professional fighter, who was beaten by young Belcher a few weeks since on Epsom Downs. The Scots baker, who has recently beaten a couple of novices, entered the lists with no very favourable omen, as the result of the contest verified; he had to contend with a good fighter, in speaking generally of Dockarty, because he possesses, in a certain degree, a little of every requisite, and added to this he was a tried bottom man. The combatants set to at one o'clock, and bettings were seven to four on Dockarty. It would not gratify even the amateur to detail the rounds of the battle, for although Dockarty evidently was not in fighting condition, his adversary never gave a turn to the betting.—Dockarty had something the best of the first round after the baker had made play, and the second round also ended very materially in Dockarty's

favour.—The combatants rallied in this round, and exchanged hits, and whilst thus contending, Dockarty took most of the fight out of his adversary, by a well planted hit at length, on the baker's head, which dropped him dexterously. Bets were offered three to one, and this odds was never lessened during the combat. Peatikin often hit his adversary, but his blows, even in vigour, were inoffensive. He appeared before Dockarty (who never fought so bad) a greater novice, than even these novices he had beaten, appeared before him; and in the latter rounds of the battle he shewed some currish manoeuvres. The baker had received a hideous black eye in the second round, and he had some body hits. He gave in after fighting three quarters of an hour, without taking any material harm, and if not entirely to the satisfaction of his friends, he displayed more judgment than he had done in any part of the combat.

As the day was fixed on for *elegant* pastime, so it finished with the baiting of the bull.

REMARKABLE YEW TREE.

PERHAPS there is one of the greatest curiosities, in a yew tree, at Grasford, in Denbeighshire, North Wales, (eight English miles from the city of West Chester) that ever was recorded in the annals of history.

In the church-yard, at this village, are growing nineteen yew trees, one of which has been an evergreen upwards of four hundred years, at the will of its owners, in that sacred ground,

Its

Its circumference was taken by a curious traveller in antiquity, on Wednesday the 11th of May, 1808, and is of the following dimensions. —The circumference of the body (or bole) of this said yew tree, one foot from the ground, is the enormous size of *seven yards eighteen inches* ; and its circumference, five feet from the ground, is *nine yards nine inches* ; two of the great arms are dead, and two more are following very rapidly, yet there still remain a sound body, and seven great arms that are still in a thriving state ; and it is supposed will *pilot old age*. through another long century, before it will resign itself, drop into, and amongst the graves of the ancient dead, which it has so many long centuries shaded.

This tree has stood in the reign of *seventeen kings, three queens, and the commonwealth of Oliver Cromwell* ; viz. from the reign of Henry IV. 1399, to the present time.

PEDIGREE AND PERFORMANCES
OF
STAMFORD.

STAMFORD is own brother to *Mr. Teazle, Archduke*, and *Paris* ; was bred by Sir Frank Standish, Bart. and sold, after racing, to Colonel Childers, for a stallion.

Stamford was got by Sir Peter Teazle ; dam, Horatia, (own sister to Greybeard and Achilles) by Eclipse ; grandam, Countess, (Delpini's dam) by Blank, Rib; Wynne's Arabian, Governor, out of an own sister to the Duke of Ancaster's Gentleman, by Mr. Alcock's Arabian,—Lord Bristol's Grasshopper, a son of the Byerley Turk.)

At Newmarket Craven Meeting, 1797, *Stamford*, 8st. beat Emigrant, 8st. 3lb. R. M. 200gs. —Seven to 4 on Stamford.—And received 150gs. from the Duke of Bedford's Mufti-colt.

At Epsom, in June, (after being beat for the Derby Stakes) at 8st. 7lb. he beat Louisa, 8st. 4lb. the last mile and a half, 200gs.— Three to 1 on Stamford.

At Stamford, in July, at 8st. 7lb. he won a Sweepstakes of 20gs. each, (15 subscribers) once round and a distance, beating Razor, 8st. 2lb.; Plaistow, 8st. 5lb.; Petworth, 8st. 2lb.; Niké, 8st. 5lb.; and Peeping Tom, 8st. 7lb.—Even betting on Stamford.

At Doncaster, on Tuesday, he was second to Lounger, for the St. Leger Stakes.—On Wednesday, he won the Gold Cup, four miles, beating Patriot, Moorcock, Trimbush, Garswood, &c.—Five to 1 against Stamford.—And the next day, he ran four two-mile heats, against Warter, Pepperpot, &c.— *Stamford's* racing and travelling this year (three years old) has not hitherto been equalled.

At York August Meeting, 1798, *Stamford* won the Subscription-Purse, of 175gs. for four-year old colts, 8st. 7lb.; fillies, 8st. 4lb. four miles, beating Tartar, Razor, Lopcatcher, &c.—Seven to 4 agst Stamford.—And the next day, at 7st. 7lb. he won the Ladies' Plate, for horses, &c. four miles, beating Lounger, 4 years old, 7st. 7lb.; Harry Rowe, 5 years old, 8st. 5lb.; and Dapple, 4 years old, 7st. 7lb. —Five to 4 against Stamford.

At Doncaster, at 7st. 11lb. he won the Gold Cup, for all ages, four miles, beating Timothy, four years old, 7st. 7lb.; Warter, four years old, 7st. 7lb.; Honest John, four years old, 7st. 7lb.; and three others.

others.—Stamford and Timothy ran a dead heat, but being run over again, was won cleverly by the former, who carried 4lb. extra, for winning at York.—Thirteen to 8 on Stamford; after the dead heat, 2 to 1 he won.—And the next day, at 8st. 11lb. he won the 100l. Plate, beating, at three two-mile heats, Knowsley, 3 years old, 7st. 9lb.; Quatorze, 3 years old, 7st. 3lb.; Tartar, 4 years old, 8st. 7lb. &c. —Six to 4 against Stamford; after the second heat, 7 and 8 to 1 he won.

At York August Meeting, 1799, *Stamford*, 11st. 6lb. won the King's Plate, four miles, beating Agnes, 4 years old, 10st. 4lb.; and Camperdown, 4 years old, 10st. 4lb. —Seven to 4 against Stamford.— On Wednesday he ran a very severe heat against Timothy, beating Tartar and Wonder.—And on Saturday, at 8st. 5lb. he won the Ladies' Plate, 4 miles, beating Camperdown and Collector, both 4-year olds, 7st. 9lb. each.—Two and 3 to 1 on Stamford.—He started several times in 1800 and 1801, but proved unsuccessful.

In 1802, 3, 4, 5, and 1806, he covered at Carr-House, near Doncaster, at 5gs. and 5s.; in 1807, at Cantley, near Doncaster, at the same price; and in 1808, at Cantley, at 10gs. and 10s. 6d.—He is a dark brown, 15 hands 2 inches high, with great bone, and was a stout honest racer, and is sire of the following winners, viz.

Mr. Mellish's Luck's-All, and Comrade.
Mr. Clowes's Bessy Carr.
Sir M. M. Sykes's Sir Sacripant, and Anna-Maria.
Mr. Marris's Sir Sampson.
Colonel Childers's Baron.

Mr. T. Duncombe's Laurel-Leaf.
Mr. Elwes's Miss Sophia.
Mr. Wilson's bay filly, out of Miss Judy.
Mr. Uppleby's bay filly, dam by Toby.
Mr. Robinson's br. filly, out of Belle-Fille.
Mr. Acred's Wansford.
Mr. Richardson's bay filly, out of Coriolanus's dam; and
Mr. Vansittart's Burleigh.

RACES APPOINTED IN 1808.

BIBURY............. *July* 4
Ipswich................. 5
Nantwich................. 6
Newmarket July Meeting.... 11
Preston.................... 12
Stockbridge................ 14
Canterbury 19
Winchester 19
Chelmsford 19
Knutsford.................. 20
Salisbury 20
Newbury ....*Aug.* 2
Swansea 9
Nottingham................. 9
Blandford.................. 9
Newcastle, Staffordshire ... 10
Derby...................... 16
Reading 16
Exeter..................... 16
York August Meeting, (Saturday the entrance day)...... 20
Egham...................... 23
Warwick, ... *Sept.* 6
Air, Scotland 19
Kingscote.................. 20
Lincoln.................... 21
Newmarket First October Meeting................ *Oct.* 4
.... Second Ditto...... 17
.... Houghton Meeting 31
VIPER.

VIPER.

THE picture from which our etching is taken is from the much-admired pencil of Mr. Ward, a gentleman well known for his excellence as an animal painter; this circumstance, and the singularity of the dog himself, entitles him to a place in our Magazine.

The colour of Viper was a brown tan, and the qualities usually belonging to terriers he possessed in a very great degree; but what makes him most remarkable is, his uncommon courage, of which Mr. Ward, to whom he formerly belonged, had frequent opportunities of witnessing, having at the same time a large bull-dog, much superior in size and strength to Viper, but notwithstanding this, they never met each other without a battle being the consequence; and when this happened, no beating whatever would separate them, nor was there any way of effecting it, but by rolling them both in a pond, and even then they would continue to hold each other as long as they could keep together above water; he was extremely faithful to his master, and would take a moderate chastisement from him, but if continued too long and too severe, he would be sure to retaliate, and on these occasions was no less remarkable for his obstinate courage, as he could not be compelled to be the first to give up the dispute.

He was very fond of going out with horses, and at such times was accustomed to take such violent exercise, as frequently to throw him into fits, which, however, were attended with no other inconvenience, than retarding his progress for a short time.

THE METAMORPHOSE OF A BASHFUL MAN.

Verbum sapientiæ sat est.

I Am the son of a Sussex farmer, and was naturally of a *timid* and *bashful* disposition, which circumstance made my father very averse to my being of his own profession, as it was his maxim that no one could make a good farmer, who could not leap hedges and ditches, and keep up close with the fox-hounds. So, after some consideration, it was determined among my friends that I should be of the medical profession, to which I readily assented, as I thought at that time, that doctors had nothing to do (comparatively speaking) but to take the money and put it into their pockets; so, after a proper education, I settled as surgeon and apothecary in a small town about twenty miles from London. My first customer was one of those fine ladies commonly called *Ladies' Maids*, who, accompanied by half a dozen of the same description, came bouncing into my shop, and, with such an air of impudence and assurance, that I really believe would have abashed even B——d himself, asked me if I sold hartshorn, which, after answering in the affirmative, I proceeded to serve her with; but their presence had put me into such a confusion and flustration, that instead of taking the hartshorn bottle, I took the one next to it, and which (as I afterwards discovered) contained *aqua fortis*, or, pump-water; but that I suppose answered her purpose, as, after smelling to it, and turning up her nose, she declared that it was the best hartshorn she ever smelt to in her life; which plainly shewed

shewed she did not come for harts-horn, but to see the new young doctor and his shop; they then left me, and as soon as they had got out of the house, I heard one of them exclaim,—" What a poor little bashful thing it is!" I was not left long to reflect on this, before I was summoned to wait on and to bleed my Lady B———, who resided about a mile from the town. I instantly mounted my horse, and having arrived there, I was ushered into my lady's dressing-room, where I found her lying on a sofa, with two of her fine ladies standing by her; I was desired to proceed with the operation, but the impudent eyes of the ladies had again put me into such confusion, and made my hand shake to such a degree, that I could scarcely hold the lancet; and when I came to make the incision, a sudden jerk of my lady's arm, together with the shaking of my hand, had such an effect on the lancet, as to drive it in about half an inch farther than was necessary; of course the blood spouted forth, my lady fainted, and in a minute, the whole house was in an uproar, in the midst of which I mounted my horse, and rode off for this metropolis, resolved never to return to the place or the lancet again. I am now waiting a favourable opportunity to become a farmer, and consequently a useful member of society; among which class of men I am at present.

IGNOTUS.

London, April 19, 1808.

CRICKET MATCHES.

THE grand match at cricket, in Lord's Ground, which commenced playing on Monday the 30th ult. between ten gentlemen of

the Mary-le-bone Club, and Howard, against eleven of the county of Middlesex, for five hundred guineas aside, was decided the following day, in favour of the latter, by eighty-three runs.

THE grand match on Lord's Ground, on Monday the 6th instant, and two following days, for one thousand guineas aside, between eight gentlemen of the Mary-le-bone Club, with Beldam, Robinson, and T. Walker, and seven gentlemen of the Homerton Club, with Lambert, Hammond, Bennett, and Small, was decided in favour of the former by 156 runs. The following is a state of the innings:—

Mary-le-bone Club.	Homerton Club.
First Innings - 264	First Innings 84
Second Ditto - 141	Second Ditto - 165
405	249

ON Thursday the 16th instant, a match was played on Streatham Common, between eleven gentlemen of the Streatham Club and eleven gentlemen of the Berkeley Club, which was decided in favour of the latter by eight wickets.

ATTACHMENT IN BRUTES.

AS a milkman, at Manchester, who has a small horse for the purpose of carrying the pails, and is likewise followed by a terrier dog, was going his round lately, the dog was attacked by another of his species, when a fight ensued; and, strange to say, in the violence of the contest, the little horse run at the dog opposed to his friend, and seizing him by the back of the neck, gave him a violent shake, and threw him over his head:—a most singular instance of sagacity and attachment in the brute creation

T   SPORT-

SPORTING INTELLIGENCE.

ON Tuesday March 8, the Rathfarnham Hunt enlarged a bag fox on the commons of Crumlin, Ireland, when Reynard, tardy to begin a new journey, was obliged to be hooted and whipped into motion; he at length resolved to run his chance as to the future, by escaping from present evils, and accordingly set off in full career.—After affording an animated run for twelve miles, he took to the hills, crossing Cappure, and the mountains in the vicinity; the horsemen were thus thrown out.—The hounds, staunch, vigorously and closely continued the pursuit:—On the Wednesday evening the hounds had not returned; the huntsman attempted to follow on foot, but was bewildered in the course.—This was the fourth hunt the same fox had given, and at each afforded admirable good sport.

THE following remarkable circumstance took place at the last Epsom races:—*Comrade* won the three 50l. Plates, viz. on Wednesday, at four two-mile heats; on Thursday and Friday at three two-mile heats each; a performance never before equalled in the annals of the turf.

IT was allowed by superior judges, that F. Collinson, who rode *Pan*, for the Derby Stakes, won the race by good riding and his excellent judgment in waiting.—After the race, the owners of *Vandyke*, *Rubens*, and *Clinker*, offered to run *Pan* single, at the same weight and length, which was not accepted.

MONDAY, June 6, being settling day at Tattersall's for the sporting concerns at the late Epsom races, the *Turf Exchange* was crowded at an early hour, and bets to the amount of thousands were finally settled; the most distinguished *legs* were present, and proved the principal *receivers-general*; but two or three of the inferior order, who went on the *wrong side of the post* on Epsom Downs, were looked for in vain.

WILLIAM Garforth, Esq. has sold the three following three-year old colts to Sir Charles Turner, Bart. for 2000gs. viz. Bay Colt, by Hambletonian, out of Caroline, (Evander's dam), by Phenomenon;—Chesnut Colt, by Hyacinthus, out of Flora, (Lismahago's dam), by King Fergus;—Chesnut colt, by Hambletonian, out of Rosalind, (Hyacinthus's dam), by Phenomenon.—*Caroline* was out of Faith, by Pacolet;—and *Faith* was out of Atalanta, by Match'em.—*Flora* and *Rosalind* were both out of Atalanta.—Sir Charles Turner has matched the above three colts to run at Newmarket, in October next, for which *see our Racing Intelligence Extra, page* 40.

LORD Stawell has sold Deceiver, by Buzzard, to Lord Sackville, for 1000gs.

LORD Darlington has purchased Rubens (brother to Castrel and Selim), by Buzzard, of the Prince, for 1200gs.

MR. Sitwell refused 2000gs for Clinker, before starting for the Derby

Derby Stakes.—He is the first favourite, (in the south) and Mr. Clifton's Poulton (in the north) for the St. Leger Stakes at Doncaster:—and 5 to 1 has been taken but Peter Plimley wins the St. Leger Stakes.

Sir Charles Turner has purchased Mr. Perren's Stables, at Newmarket, for Mr. Dixon Boyes.

Mr. Wentworth has sold Irené, by Zachariah, to Mr. C. Fothergill, of York, for a brood mare.—She has since been covered by Ditto, by Sir Peter Teazle.

Jerry Clifton, Esq. and John Parker (jun.) Esq. are appointed Stewards for Manchester Races next year.

Mr. Kerby has sold his chesnut colt Fancy, by Delpini, dam by Rockingham, to the Duke of Leeds.—He is engaged in a Stakes at York August Meeting, 1809.

Cocking.—On Monday, the 30th ult. commenced fighting, at the Cock-Pit Royal, the South-side of St James's Park, London, the first year of the Great Main, between the gentlemen of Northamptonshire and those of Yorkshire, for 20gs a battle, and 500gs the main.—Feeders, Potter for Northamptonshire, and Gilliver for Yorkshire. The following is a statement:—

Potter.	M. B.	Gilliver.	M. B.
Monday,	8 0		2 2
Tuesday,	4 1		1 2
Wednesday,	2 0		3 3
Thursday,	0 0		6 2
Friday,	2 1		4 1
Saturday,	2 0		4 2
Total	13 2		20 12

Manchester Cocking.—In the race-week, a long main of cocks was fought between Potter and Harrison, which was won by the former by 4 a-head.

Newton Cocking.—In the race-week, a main of cocks was fought between Lord Derby and Richard Legh, Esq. for 10gs. a battle, and 200gs. the main, consisting of 39 main and 8 byes. Goodall and Gilliver feeders, which was won by the former by 7 a-head.

Wrestling.—The wrestling at Falmouth, this month, was one of the greatest ever known in Cornwall. The company was numerous and respectable beyond example in latter times, and most of the first champions of the county exhibited. Mr. Higgs, of Probus, and Absalom Bennetts, of Gwennap, were the sticklers. [The latter of these veterans has won in his time 22 gold-laced hats, beside a great number of other prizes. He bore off the prize seven years successively at Probus games.]—The sport at Falmouth lasted two days; the silver goblet was won by Richard Jolly, of St. Enoder; the cup by Henry Chipman, of Redruth; the gold-laced hat by Stephen Symons, of Redruth; and the silver-laced hat by Stephen Mitchells, of Gwennap. A bye-match between Uren, of Penryn, who challenged the field, and Chapman, for 10gs. aside, and considerable sums in bye-bets, excited much interest; but on the fourth spar, Uren complained that he had sprained his wrist, and gave in.—A gold-laced hat was also wrestled for on Tuesday, on Feock Downs, and won by James Barry, of Mawgan in Pyder.—A hat was also wrestled for on Wednesday at Truro, and won by —— Crapp, of Padstow, a seaman belonging to his Majesty's ship Tromp.—On a stage erected in Illogan, six persons danced for a prize, to the no small amusement of more than 2000 persons.

WE have the pleasure to inform the amateurs in the art of change ringing, that the Oldham Youths, of Lancashire, have challenged the College Youths of Ashton-under-Line, in the said county, to ring them Mr. John Holt's Ten-Course Peal, of 504 changes, each course of Grandsire Tripples.—The College Youths have accepted the challenge to ring them for 40gs. a peal, in the above method, containing a true and complete peal of 5040 changes *only*, at St. Michael's Church, Flixton, near Manchester, all in the said county, on the 25th day of June inst.—Weight of the tenor, 14 *Cwt.* 2 *Qrs.* and 24 *Lb.*

BETTING for the St. Leger Stakes, at Tattersall's, Monday, June 20 :—

9 to 2 against Peter Plimley, by Hambletonian.

6 to 1 against Poulton, by Sir Peter Teazle.

6 to 1 against Clinker, by Sir Peter Teazle.

8 to 1 against Laurel-leaf, by Stamford.

8 to 1 against Mr. Peirse's colt, by Expectation, out of Rosamond.

55 to 50 field against any three.

TROTTING Match.—It has been made known that a horse, the property of Mr. Progers, which, a few weeks since, was sold to trot seven guineas, was backed to trot seventeen miles in one hour. The distance has very rarely been performed, although the wonderful mare, called the Phenomena, once did nineteen miles within an hour. The stake for this match was 250l. to 100l.

The horse started, with a severe stone jockey, at eight o'clock, on Saturday morning, June the 18th, as Hollesgreen, Herts, to go over some picked ground. The animal went half the distance in two minutes above half the time, and the next two miles were performed at a winning rate. After the horse had done twelve miles he began to lag, and the match was lost after fourteen miles had been performed in fifty-two minutes.

SPARRING Exhibition.—The beginning of the present month, Gully and Crib had a benefit, it being the first of this season, at the Fives Court, in St. Martin's-street, which was filled with company of the first order previous to the hour appointed for the bloodless exhibition. Tickets of admission were 3s. 6d. per head; and such was the anxiety to witness the pugilists since their successful combats in Hertfordshire, that it was difficult even to press through the crowd to approach the door. The court was never seen so full of *distinguished characters* as in the present instance, and the amusement afforded *high gratification*. Several of the most distinguished pugilists of the day set to, but the couples which afforded most amusement were, Gully and Jem Belcher, and Young Belcher and Crib; the other couples which engaged were Cropley and Dogherty, Jones and Blake, Crib and Wood, &c. &c.

BOXING Matches.—On Saturday the 11th instant, two matches were made; the first between Jem Belcher (the late champion) and Crib, whose name is also sufficiently known in the sporting world. The battle will be for 200gs. aside, half forfeit. The combatants will go immediately into training, and the contest

test will take place in two months. It will be remembered, that the parties fought a closely-contested battle at Moulsey, in April, 1807, when Crib, although terribly disfigured, was the victor, Belcher's strength and vigour having failed him. Cropley is also matched to fight Edward Belcher, the elder of the three brothers, in six weeks, who is but little known as a fighting man, for 100gs.

A most obstinate pugilistic contest took place on Thursday the 9th, in the parish of Holton, near Wincanton and Cheriton Hill, between Hazard, a butcher, and John Perry, an athletic young man. They fought 87 severe rounds, when Hazard, being beaten blind, the remaining rounds were entirely in favour of Perry, who came off victor. Notwithstanding the thinness of the population in that neighbourhood, and the challenge being given only the night before, it is supposed there were nearly 1000 spectators.

A few evenings since, as Dutch Sam, the noted pugilist, was in company with a fair pugilist, of the name of Jane Egg, of Grey's-street, St. George's-fields, spending the evening at a public-house in that quarter, some difference arose between the parties, who came to blows. The lady maintained the contest during several rounds with great spirit, but at last the combatants were parted by their friends. Sam has since obtained a warrant against his antagonist, who at the same time got one against him, and this reciprocal charge of assault and battery is not yet decided.

On the 9th of this month, Thomas Jameson, of Wandsworth, a person near 50 years of age, for a wager of one guinea, ran upon the Clapham-road seven miles in the space of fifty-eight minutes, carrying at the same time a box on his back, weighing 24lb.

PEDESTRIANISM.—By accounts which arrived in town on Friday the 24th instant, it appears that the Highland gentleman, who undertook to walk, on Sunday morning the 19th, from Vauxhall to Manchester, in 69 hours, for a bet of 500 guineas, arrived at the Bridgewater Arms, Manchester, at nine o'clock on the Wednesday evening, being one hour within the time limited.—He performed the journey in the following manner :—He arrived at ten o'clock on Sunday evening at Daventry, being at the rate of 72 miles in 21 hours, including stoppages. There he slept for six hours, and resumed his journey with alacrity. On Tuesday evening, by eleven o'clock, he arrived at Sandon, having walked at the rate of 64 miles in 19 hours and a half. Having rested here for six hours, he proceeded with full confidence of success, and arrived at Manchester, as already stated, by nine o'clock, having walked the third day 52 miles in fifteen hours and a half. Notwithstanding the precaution he used in keeping a quantity of oil in his shoes, the soles of his feet were a good deal blistered, and he was altogether very much fatigued ; the cause of which he ascribed more to the heat of the weather than to any over exertion. This pedestrian's name is Macraw, a native of Kintail, Ross-shire. The principal bet is between two officers in the guards, an Englishman and a Scotsman.

On Monday morning, the 27th instant, Lord Alvanley ran a match against

against time on the Edgware road. The bet was, that he could not run a mile in six minutes; but he performed it in twenty-one seconds less than the given time. Lord F. Beauclerck was umpire. The original bet was fifty guineas, with Arthur Shakespeare, Esq.: considerable sums were betted on the occasion.

New Game Act.—By the Act which passed the Royal Assent on the 1st instant, the duties on Game Certificates are taken from the Stamp-office, and are in future to be collected by the Tax-office.— The money, viz. 3*l.* 3*s.* to be paid by every gentleman using any dog, gun, net, or other engine, for the purpose of taking or killing any game whatsoever, or any Woodcock, Snipe, Quail, or Land-Rail, or any Conies, in any part of Great Britain, to the Collector of the Assessed Taxes for the parish or place in which he shall reside; such collector, on receiving the said duty, and one shilling for his trouble, shall make out a receipt, which the gentleman applying is to take to the Commissioners' Clerk, who must give him in exchange, without fee or reward, a certificate, which certificate is to be produced when demanded, as heretofore.— *Game-keepers,* for whom the servant's duty is paid, 1*l.* 1*s.* each; but persons shooting under deputations, not servants, to pay 3*l.* 3*s.*— The taking Woodcocks or Snipes with nets or springs, or Conies in warrens, or by proprietors in any inclosed lands, to be *excepted* from the said duties.—The above Act declares, that neither the foregoing assessments, nor the payment thereof, nor the certificate, nor any thing in this Act contained, shall authorise any person to use any

dog, gun, &c. unless such person shall be, by previous laws, qualified so to do.—Nor shall any person shooting under a deputation or deputations be hereby authorised to use any dog or gun off the manor, &c. for which he shall be deputed.

A WRIT of enquiry of damages was lately executed, at the Black Swan Inn, Hereford, between John Dutton Cott, Esq. plaintiff, and William Davies and Thomas Fenner, defendants, the former being game-keeper to Samuel Peploe, Esq. of Grbystone, and the latter coachman to Mr. Peploe, for assaulting the plaintiff in November last, in the manor of Weebley, and forcibly taking his gun from him.— The Jury, after hearing the evidence on the part of the plaintiff, assessed the damages at 60*l.*

MR. Western's Bill, for making it felony to commit depredations on oyster beds, puts the oyster under the immediate protection of the law. Tilburina, in *The Critic,* says, that " an oyster may be crossed in love." But this bill being passed, they cannot now be attacked with impunity. It is certain that the Romans, who highly valued the oyster, made severe regulations for their protection. Lucellus and Pollio were at an incredible expence in their lakes of sea water for fattening oysters. The former, at his villa near the promontory of Misenium, on the shore of Campania, fed and kept immense quantities of them. The famous epicure, Apicius Calius, who lived under Augustus, in his work, *De Arte Coquinaria,* or, *The Culinary Art,* treats particularly of the oyster. They were even conveyed to Rome, from the coast of Kent, under the Cæsars. These circumstances, which seem to make the
oyster

oyster a classic shell-fish, may justify the British Legislature in enacting laws for their preservation.

THE DRIVING CLUB set out from London, on Thursday, the 9th instant, and made a most noble display of horses and carriages, in the following order :—

1 Sir Henry Peyton's barouche-landau, and four bays.
2 Mr. Annesley's ditto, four roans, (high bred.)
3 Sir Stephen Glynne, ditto, four bays.
4 Lord Ed. Somerset......ditto
5 Mr. Villeboy's.........ditto
6 Mr. Harrison's ....ditto
7 Mr. Whitmore's........ditto
8 Mr. O'Couver's ....ditto
9 Sir Henry Smith's ......ditto
10 Mr. Pierrepoint's.......ditto
11 Mr. Cox's ....ditto
12 Sir Thomas Mostyn's ....ditto
13 Lord Foley's ....ditto
14 Mr. J. Ward's.........ditto

In returning, after partaking of an elegant entertainment previously provided at Bedfont, they dashed home, in a style of speed and splendour equal to the spirit and judgment displayed by the noble, honourable, and respectable drivers.— We congratulate Mr. Harvey, of the Black Dog, Bedfont, (not Belfont, as ignorantly spelt by some of the editors of newspapers) in the accession of this honourable party to his house, as no one knows better how to cater, or has superior claims to encouragement, than himself.— The members of the above Club were to dine again at the same inn, on Monday, the 28th instant.

WHIP CLUB. — Another Club, called the Whip Club, in rivalship with the above, met on Monday morning, the 6th, in Park-lane, and proceeded from thence to dine at Harrow-on-the-Hill. There were fifteen barouche-landaus, with four horses to each ; the drivers were all men of known skill in the science of charioteering. Lord Hawke, Mr. Buxton, and the Hon. Lincoln Stanhope, were among the leaders. The following was the style of the set-out :—

Yellow-bodied carriages, with whip springs and dickey boxes ; cattle of a bright bay colour, with silver plate ornaments on the harness, and rosettes to the ears.

Costume of the Drivers.—A light drab-colour cloth coat, made full, single breast, with three tier of pockets ; the skirts reaching to the ancles ; a mother-of-pearl button of the size of a crown piece.— Waistcoat, blue and yellow stripe, each stripe an inch in depth ; small-clothes, corded silk plush, made to button over the calf of the leg, with sixteen strings and rosettes to each knee. The boots very short, and finished with very broad straps, which hang over the tops and down to the ancle. A hat three inches and a half deep in the crown only, and the same depth in the brim exactly.

Each wore a large bouquet at the breast, thus resembling the coachmen of our Nobility, who, on his Majesty's birth-day, appeared, in that respect, so peculiarly distinguished.

A SET of gentlemen, amateurs of the oar, have formed a Rowing Club, under the title of the *Funny Society.* The members are said to be all exceedingly expert, and eminently distinguished *skulls.*— The first meeting has taken place, each gentleman in his own funny.

MR. Daniel Lambert.—We hear that this well-known gentleman, certainly one of the heaviest persons in the kingdom, being upwards of forty-six stone weight, and only forty-seven years of age, has been visiting Manchester, and intends to go to York. This information to sporting gentlemen must be very agreeable, as few men are better versed in what relates to either the turf, the sports of the field, or the breeding and training of dogs: indeed Mr. Lambert's dogs are in high request, and have brought very great prices. What adds to the pleasure of his company, he is in every respect a gentleman in his conversation and manners.

SOME miscreant, on the night of the 7th instant, had the cruelty to cut the tongue of a fine horse, the property of the Rev. James Filewood, Rector of Sible Hedingham, Essex, in such a manner, as to endanger the loss of the animal.

AMONG the newly-invented *agricultural* implements exhibited at Woburn this season, was a *mantrap*, which, by means of a chain, detains the offender without doing him any material injury.

ON the Tuesday evening of Ascot-Heath races, as a stage-coach was on its return from thence, with *only twenty-one* passengers on the roof, box, &c. and six insides, it happened very aukwardly that one of the springs broke at the bottom of a hill, and close to a large pond ; the coach was not overturned, but the outside collection were every one launched into the water, and completely soused ; two females, of circumference equal to Lady Buckinghamshire, made a most ludicrous display of their *invisible petticoats* and Dutch foundations. With some difficulty, all scrambled on shore ; and, after a liberal dispensation of *Nelson's Cordial*, from a gentleman of *spirit*, or in the *spirit line*, they proceeded on their journey to the next inn.

AN accident, which luckily was not attended with any serious consequences, befell Mr. Allen, the brewer, of turf celebrity, on the last day of Epsom races. The above gentleman, who is considered one of the most dexterous whips of the day, was driving a tandem from Epsom to the race-course, when one of the wheels dropped into a deep rut on ascending the hill which approaches the rubbing-house, and the vehicle was upset. Mr. Allen was alone, and his bruises have occasioned a temporary confinement.

A LETTER from a very ingenious gentleman, a Fellow of the Royal Society, contains the following passage :—" When you do me the favour of coming to this part of Middlesex, and are inclined to sail on dry land, I can indulge your disposition, having built a sailing chariot, which, with a moderate wind, and four persons on board, will run fifteen knots an hour, close hauled."

A FEMALE antelope, which was brought, with its mate, from Tripoli, by the Hon Captain Boyle, fawned, about two months since, at Cowdray Park, in Sussex, the seat of W. S. Poyntz, Esq. and the fawn and its mother are doing very well. Mr. Poyntz has been so attentive in making their residence suitable to their nature, that they do not appear to suffer the least from the difference of climate. This is believed to be the first instance of the antelope's fawning in this kingdom.

POETRY.

POETRY.

THE HIGH COURT OF DIANA.

THE
KILRUDDERY FOX-CHASE.

An Irish Hunting Song.

HARK! hark, jolly sportsmen, awhile
    to my tale,
Which to claim your attention I'm sure
    cannot fail ;
'Tis of lads, and of horses, and dogs that
    ne'er tire,
O'er stone walls and hedges, thro' dale,
    bog, and briar.
A pack of such dogs, and a race of such
    men,
'Tis a shrewd chance if ever you meet
    with agen ;
Had Nimrod, the mightiest of hunters,
    been there,
'Fore George, he had shook like an aspin
    for fear.

In seventeen hundred and forty and four,
The fifth of December, I think 'twas no
    more,
At nine in the morning, by most of the
    clocks,
We rode from Kilruddery in search of a
    fox.
The Lochter-town landlord, the bold
    Owen Bray,
And 'Squire Adair, he was with us that
    day ;
Joe Debble, Hal Preston, that hero so
    stout,
Dick Holmes, a few others, and so we
    set out.

We cast off our hounds for an hour or
    more,
When Wanton set up a most tunable
    roar ;
Hark, hark, now to Wanton! the rest
    were not slack,

For Wanton's no trifle esteem'd in the
    pack.
Then Bonny, and Collier, came readily
    in,
And ev'ry hound join'd in the musical
    din :
Had Diana been there, she'd been pleas'd
    to the life,
And one of the lads got a Goddess to
    wife.

Ten minutes past ten was the time of the
    day,
When reynard broke cover—and this
    was his way :
As strong from Killegar as though he
    fear'd none,
Away he rush'd round by the house of
    Kilmone,
To Carlick-mine thence, and to Cherry-
    wood then,
He climb'd Sheepshank-hills, and to
    Ballymogden ;
Bray-common he cross'd, leapt Lord An-
    glesea's wall,
And seem'd to say, " Little I value your
    all."

He ran bushes and groves, up to Carbury
    Byrns,
Joe Debble, Hal Preston, kept leading by
    turns,
The earth it was open, yet he was so
    stout,
Tho' he might have got in, yet he chose
    to keep out.
To Malpas high hills was the way that
    he flew,
At Dalkey-stone common we had him
    in view ;
He drove on by Bulloch, and then by
    Glangary,
And so on to Mountown, where Larry
    grew weary.

N   Thre'

Thro' Roche's town-wood like an arrow
  he past,
And came to the steep hills of Dalkey at
  last,
There gallantly plung'd himself into the
  sea,
And said, in his heart, there's none dare
  follow me:
But soon, to his cost, he perceiv'd that no
  bounds
Could stop the pursuit of our staunch-
  mettled hounds;
His policy here did not serve him a rush,
Five couple of tartars were hard at his
  brush.

To recover the shore then again was his
  drift,
But ere he could reach to the top of the
  cliff,
He found both of speed and of cunning
  a lack,
Being waylaid and kill'd by the rest of
  the pack.
At his death there were present the lads
  that I've sung,
Save Larry, who, riding a garran, was
  flung.
Thus ended at length a most delicate
  chase,
That held us five hours and ten minutes
  space.

We return'd to Kilruddery's plentiful
  board,
Where dwelt hospitality, truth, and my
  Lord.
We talk'd o'er the chase, and we toasted
  the health
Of the man that ne'er varied for places or
  wealth.
Owen Bray baulk'd a leap; says Hal, it
  was odd;
'Twas shameful, cry'd Jack, by the great
  living G——d:
Said Preston I halloo'd, get on, tho' you
  fall,
Or I'll leap over you, your blind gelding,
  and all.

Each glass was adapted to freedom and
  sport,
For party affairs we consign to the court.
Thus we banish'd the rest of the day and
  the night
In gay flowing bumpers, and social de-
  light;
Then till the next morning bid farewell
  each brother,
So some went home one way, and some
  went another.
As freedom befriended our earlier roam,
Bright Luna assisted in guiding us home.

JEU D'ESPRIT,

CIRCULATED IN CHARACTER AT A LATE
MASQUERADE.

To Private Theatricals.

MR. PARAGON PROLOGUE, Prof. Soc.
Busk. Prim. Dram. Pers. P. S. and
O. P. Emperor of all Actors, the greatest
man in the world, has the honour to
present a Prospectus of his new Histrionic
Academy, in which he engages to teach
Ladies, Gentlemen, and others, at all
ages, sizes, ranks, and condition, to become as truly great in the science and
practice of Acting as himself!!!

YE Private Theatricals, " lend me your
  ears,"
Be ye Margravines, Milliners, 'Prentices,
  Peers;
All ye who in Tragedy live to be dying,
In Comedy frisking, in Melo-drame sigh-
  ing,
Who warble in sing-song, in Farce who
  make faces,
Or in Pantomime bid heads and tails
  change their places;
I, PARAGON PROLOGUE, P. S. and O. P.
The very best actor that is, or will be,
Am come to instruct you by rules scien-
  tific,
To be gloomy, gay, comical, queer, and
  terrific.

To you, ye fair vot'ries, my bows are
  first due,
Sweet patrons of all that's eccentric and
  new:
Be ye fair, brown, or yellow, " blue spirits or grey,"
You shall teach me to love, and I'll teach
  you to play,
Your dimples or wrinkles shall live in
  renown,
As Thalia's arch smile, or Melpomene's
  frown;
Sage grandams in hoydens shall frolic so
  nimble,
While Misses, " blood-bolter'd," shall
  make the Gods tremble:
Frail Dames shine as *Imogene,* virtue
  adorning,
And Maids be made *Millwoods* at very
  short warning!

Ye Courtiers, who scenes of soft blan-
  dishment choose,
From me shall you learn how *Sir Pertinax*
  " boos;"
  Gouty

Gouty Peers shall look *Romeos*, love-sick
    and pretty,
And Masters from Harrow eclipse Mas-
    ter Betty ;
While beaux from Whitechapel and
    Mansion-house-street,
The Stage shall as *Rangers* and *Doricourts*
    greet ;
Turf heroes, in *Groom*, shall talk big of
    their cattle ;
Brave Colonels, in *Hotspur*, for once see
    a battle ;
Loud Lawyers shall quaver like Braham
    or Naldi,
And fat Common Councilmen vault like
    Grimaldi.

I'll teach you, moreover, new ways to
    pronounce,
To weigh out your words by the pound
    or the ounce,
And, when you'd give force to a tragedy
    swell,
To drawl, or to croak like a frog in a
    well :
With a brisk Irish brogue I'll enliven
    your *Spaches*,
If I don't, you may fill all my bones full
    of *Aitches*.

These feats (as my int'rest I never lay
    stress on)
I'll freely perform at five guineas a les-
    son ;
The terms are dog cheap : if my pupil
    be no log,
He'll not grudge his money to
        PARAGON PROLOGUE.

POOR BARLEY CORN.

From Farley's Bristol Journal.

THE following beautiful tribute to the
genial virtues of our old English beverage, likely soon to be known rather by
memory than taste, was written in the
days of Charles II. and has probably remained in MS. to this day.

When the chill north-east blows,
    And Winter tells a heavy tale,
When pies and daws, and doobs and
    crows,
Do sit, and curse the frost and snows,
    Then give me ale.

Ale, that the absent battle fights,
    And forms the march o' the Swedish
      drum,
Disputes the Prince's laws and rights,
What's gone and past tells mortal wights,
    And what's to come.

Ale, that the ploughman's heart upleaps,
    And equals it to tyrants' thrones,
That wipes the eye that ever weeps,
And lulls in soft and easy sleeps
    The tired bones.

Ale, that securely climbs the tops
    Of cedars tall, and lofty towers,
When giddy grapes and creeping hops
Are holden up with poles and props,
    For lack of powers.

When the Septentrion seas are froze,
    By Boreas his biting gale,
To keep unpinch'd the Russian's nose,
And save unrot the Vandal's toes,
    Oh! give me ale.

Grandchild to Ceres, Barley's daughter,
    Wine's emulous neighbour, if but stale,
Ennobling all the nymphs of water,
And filling each man's heart with laugh-
    ter,
    Hah! give me ale.

---

*To the much-distressed Members of the
honourable and very ancient*

SOCIETY OF DECAYED GUIDE-POSTS.

SIRS—we have look'd at your petition,
    And will attend to your condition;
We know of few who so deserve as
You Guide-posts do, for public service.
'Tis true, indeed, we can but own
You have been shamefully let down,
Have met, from many, treatment undue,
But justice shall be, shortly, done you ;
You shall not long have cause to rail
At justice's uneven scale,
Shall not, with reason, long complain
That she has " borne the sword in vain,"
As, very shortly, for your sake,
We will " *the sleeping Statutes*" wake ;
And when we Justices respect you,
Woe be to those who shall neglect you ;
Surveyors shall receive our precept,
That you may all in order be kept,
May all direct each wandering wight,
How to pursue the road that's right ;
        The

The wrong avoid—then, of the crew,
Those who use not " the friendly clue,"
Must blame themselves, not us, nor you.
You shall instructions place before 'em,
" By order of the Norfolk Quorum;"
" And this," (that you may ready be,
For your approaching Jubilee,
May have no more just cause to fear man)
" The Court assures you by
        THE CHAIRMAN."
April 27, 1808.

LINES TO MARY.

For the Sporting Magazine.

NO, Mary, no! it cannot be;
  My heart oppress'd, with anguish
    torn,
Still beats with ardent love for thee,
  Tho' doom'd thy *perfidy* to mourn.

When, circled in thy clasping arms,
  Rapture's full beam illum'd mine eye,
Oh! then, when madd'ning with thy
    charms,
  My soul dissolv'd in ev'ry sigh!
I swore to thee eternal love;
  The oath was register'd in Heav'n;
And never, should I faithless prove,
  Ah! *never* could I be forgiven.

By Him, whose word Creation hung
  Within the infinite of space,
I vow'd, as pleasure thrill'd my tongue
When folded in thy sweet embrace,
That never, from that happy hour,
  Thy Henry's breast should cease to
    love;
And Fate itself has not the pow'r
  My strong affection to remove.

No!—sooner from the realms on high
  The sun shall sink to endless night,
And ev'ry sphere that gems the sky
  Shine in full lustre without light!
Sooner the fix'd, unerring Mind
  Shall, wav'ring, bid his counsels jar,
And in one chain of order bind
  The solar orb and meteor star!

No, Mary, no! it cannot be!
  Till life's last breath my being end,
My heart shall fervent beat for thee,
  And in one dear idea blend
  The *Lover, Mistress, Wife,* and *Friend!*
        HENRY.

CONTENT.

DEAR Sam, who the camp and the
    pulpit have tried,
  You ask me what system of life I should
    choose;
To manage my own little farm is my
    pride,
  And to lounge where I like in my dir-
    ty old shoes.

In a patron's cold vestibule why should
    I freeze?
  Why dance up and down at the smiles
    of the great?
When to warm my own heart I can clip
    my own trees,
  And pursue my own game on my own
    small estate!

Who would angle for meals that can
    catch his own fish?
  As the honey unbought, what desert
    half so sweet?
Give me eggs of my own in a clean
    wooden dish,
  And my hind's lusty daughter to cook
    up the treat.

While for health I can plough, and for
    exercise dig,
  May the wretch who dislikes me my
    system forbear;
May he veil his grey locks in an Alder-
    man's wig,
  Grow gouty when Sheriff, and die
    when Lord Mayor.

EPITAPH
ON WILLIAM WILLIAMS,

Who died in consequence of bathing imme-
diately after Hunting, Sept. 24, 1782.

IN silence here, beneath, a youth is laid,
  By whom the sports of nature were
    survey'd;
With ravish'd breast, o'er meads he did
    pursue
The started hare, which thro' the land-
    scape flew;
By which pursuit, his heart oppress'd
    with heat,
Plung'd in the stream which nature
    thought so sweet:
But soon the stream a change to nature
    gave,
And plung'd the youth deep in the silent
    grave.
  Cheshunt, Herts.

THE
SPORTING MAGAZINE;
OR,
MONTHLY CALENDAR
OF THE
TRANSACTIONS
OF
THE TURF, THE CHASE,
And every other Diversion interesting to
THE MAN OF PLEASURE, ENTERPRISE, AND SPIRIT.

JULY, 1808.

CONTAINING

The Lion and Horse—engraved from a Painting by Stubbs ..... Page 155
Disputes between Gentlemen, on Points of Honour, &c. &c. 157
Races appointed in 1808 159
Cocking, at Nantwich 159
Preston 159
Newcastle 159
Stamford 159
Fox-Chase Extraordinary 160
The Philosophical Sportsman, No. VII. 161
Grand Divertisement and Spectacle, exhibited at Lisle in 1453 164
Philosophers Eclipsed by Sportsmen 168
Curious Particulars of Running Footmen 168
Theatrical Anecdote 169
Curious Anecdotes of a popular Performer 170
Action to recover the Value of a Horse 172
Anecdotes, from Hall's Travels 173
Fowling 175
Harmonious Change Ringing 176
Dialogue on a Dog between a Lady and a Lawyer 178
Extraordinary Duel 180
Female Pugilism 180
Feast of Wit 181
Extraordinary Apology 181
Royal Chastity 181
Anecdote of Lord Shaftesbury 181

On a late Publication ...... Page 182
Rigid Economy 182
Petition of the Tutelary Genius of Hyde Park 183
Epigram 184
Winners of Royal Plates at York, from 1710 to 1807 185
Young Ducks Alarmed—an Engraving 188
Eccentric Character 188
Rural Sports 188
Attachment in Dogs 189
Sporting Intelligence 190
Races at Stamford 190
Driving 191
Fatal Bet 192
Pugilism 193
Cricket Matches 194
Rowing Match 195
Singular Occurrence 196

POETRY.

Grouse Shooting 197
The Angler's Song 199
Lines on the Chancellor of the Exchequer's making Woodcocks and Snipes Game 200
The Greenland Hunter—a Masquerade Song 200

Racing Calendar 41

Embellished with—I, *The Lion and Horse, from a Picture of the late Mr. Stubbs.*
II, *Young Ducks Alarmed.*

LONDON:
PRINTED FOR THE PROPRIETORS,
By J. Pittman, Warwick Square;
AND SOLD BY J. WHEBLE, 18, WARWICK-SQUARE; C. CHAPPLE, 66, PALL-MALL;
J. BOOTH, DUKE-STREET, PORTLAND-PLACE; JOHN HILTON, NEWMARKET;
MAYNARD, PANTON STREET, HAYMARKET; AND ALL OTHER
BOOKSELLERS IN THE UNITED KINGDOM.

TO CORRESPONDENTS.

THE Article from Blandford, and a Child's Drawing, are laid aside, as unfit for publication.

We have received the Old Songs upon Cocking, Angling, &c. from a Country Correspondent, to whom we are much obliged ; one of them appears this month, and the remainder will receive due attention.

Further Communications upon Campanology in our next.

Gentlemen disposed to favour the Publisher of this Magazine with Original Paintings of Sporting Subjects, are assured that the utmost care shall be taken of them, and of their being safely returned. The Engravings thus taken, will be executed by the most approved Artists, and in the first style of excellence.

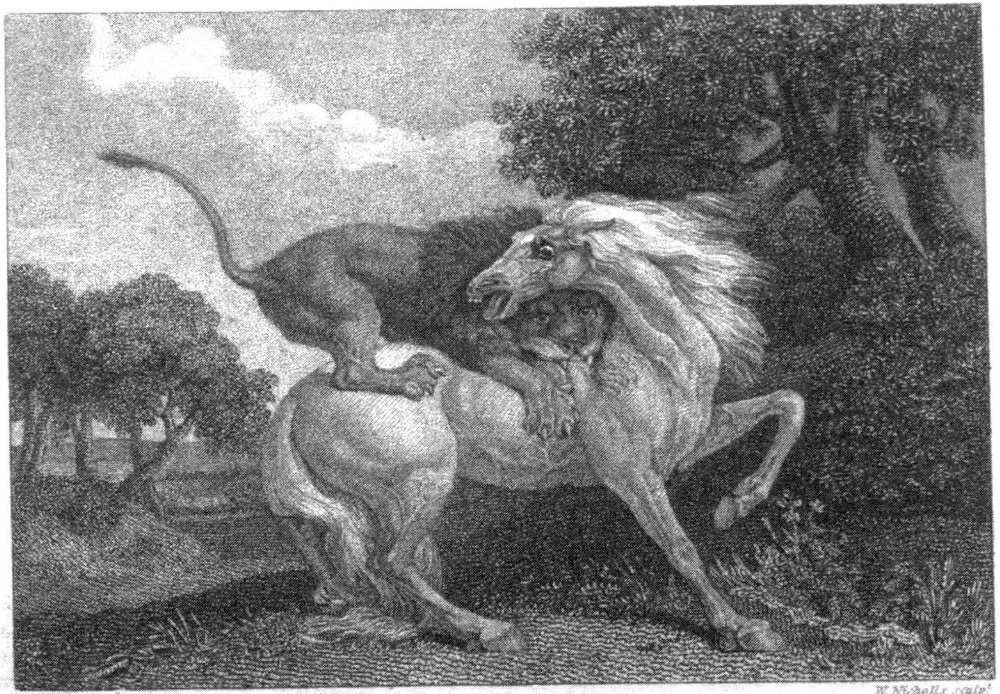

G. Stubbs pinx^t W. Nicholls sculp^t

THE LION & HORSE, FROM STUBBS.

THE

SPORTING MAGAZINE;

FOR JULY, 1808.

THE LION AND HORSE.

An Engraving from a Picture of the late Mr. Stubbs.

WE have this month the pleasure to present the readers of our Magazine with another subject from the works of that incomparable artist, the late Mr. George Stubbs. The engraving (as was that of the HORSE AND THE LION, in our number for May) is by Mr. William Nicholls, from a fine enamel picture, in possession of Mr. Stubbs's executrix, and esteemed a perfect *fac-simile* of the painter, who, after a study of three-score years, has kindly left the rising genius of his country a school to rival the pride of Athens:

" Nature, in her productions slow,
      aspires
By just degrees to reach Perfection's
      height: '
So mimic Art works leisurely, 'till Time
Improve the piece, or wise Experience
      give
The proper finishing."

That wise experience was peculiarly the painter's own, and although he has left a thousand proofs of the truth of this bold assertion, it was his last wish that his days might be lengthened, to enable him to add more to the honour of the British school.

The principal causes of Mr. Stubbs's surpassing his cotempora-ries in those studies to which he so warmly attached himself, were; his chaste delineation; his perfect knowledge of quadruped anatomy; and, if I may be allowed the expression, their passions; these were the charms that attracted his primal affections, and they reluctantly withdrew themselves at the verge of his grave. To dissect the body human was also his diligent pursuit, insomuch, that (as I have heard a relative of his declare) to procure subjects for his improvement, Mr. Stubbs has, an hundred times, run into such adventures as might subject any one with less honourable motives to the greatest severity of the law; and to shew clearly with what avidity he pursued this unsavoury study, I am enabled to state the following fact.

At the time Mr. S. lived in Upper Seymour-street, intelligence was brought him, at ten o'clock in the evening, that a dead tiger lay at Mr. Pidcock's, in the Strand, and that it was to be obtained at a small expence if he thought proper to apply for it; Mr. S. was undressing for bed when the news arrived; his coat was hurried on, and he flew towards the well-known place, and presently entered the den where the dead animal lay extended : this was a precious moment ; three guineas were given to the attendant, and the body was instantly conveyed to the

x 2   painter's

painter's habitation, where, in the place set apart for his muscular pursuits, Mr. S. spent the rest of the night, in carbonading the once tremendous tyrant of Indian jungle.

About this time our painter, in conjunction with Mr. George Townley Stubbs, began a publication of much interest to the sporting world; it was called "A Review of the Turf, from the Year 1750 to the Completion of this Work; comprising the History of every Horse of Note, with Pedigree and Performance;" which, from a cause I am not permitted to mention, after two numbers, fell abortive, and was heard of no more.

To shew at once the intention of our painter, and the loss his admirers have sustained in the failure of his undertaking, I shall present the sportsman with the introduction to his work, as written by himself, and make no doubt he will lament with me that any cause should prevent the completion of his enterprise.

"At a period when protection is daily solicited for embellishing editions of various authors, it may be deemed extraordinary to submit one of a different cast to the public consideration, where the chief merit consists in the actions, and not in the language of the heroes and the heroines it proposes to record, and with whom possibly literature may exclaim, ' She neither desires connection, nor allows utility.'

"As the history of an animal peculiar to this country, it surely may put in its claim 'to remembrance and notice; and although the numerous volumes of Cheney and Heber, downwards, may give critical knowledge to the diligent

and deep explorer, they certainly do not impart sufficient information to a superficial observer; yet both may regret that there is not a regular series of paintings and engravings of those horses, with their histories, which have been, or are now famous.

"This Review of the Turf will therefore comprise the history of every horse of note, with various anecdotes on the most remarkable races, and the whole will be embellished with upwards of one hundred and twenty prints, engraved in the best manner, from original portraits of the most famous racers, painted by Mr. G. Stubbs, at an immense expence, and solely for the above work."

It is not too late to take up the work where, the proprietor thought proper to decline it, as the sources from whence the pleasure was to derive, are still clear and uncontaminated; they are the property of a lady who has the greatest right to possess them, and who is by no means inimical to the plan, as the writer can aver, being in possession of her sentiments on the subject.

Plan of the Work as intended by Mr. Stubbs.

THE GODOLPHIN ARABIAN,

With great justice deemed the "FATHER OF THE TURF;" and those who are conversant in pedigree will allow, that no stallion, before or since his time, has contributed so much to the improvement of the breed of horses in this country.

He was sire of *Lath*, *Cade*, *Blank*, *Babraham*, *Bajazet*, and *Regulus*, who were all afterwards stallions of repute, and the latter (who won, in one year, seven

King's

King's plates, and was never beat) proved a most excellent one, having got Adolphus, Trajan, Spilletta, the dam of Eclipse, the grand-dam of Highflyer, and many other capital horses.

He was a brown horse, fourteen hands and a half high; was first the property of Mr. Coke, and was a gift from him to Mr. Williams, of the St. James's Coffee-house, by whom he was presented to the Earl of Godolphin.

The manner by which he became known as a stallion was rather singular, as for several years he was only teazer to Hobgoblin; but on the latter refusing to cover Roxana, she was put to the Arabian, and from that cover Lath was produced.

As no pedigree was brought over with him, he was reported, and generally believed, to have been stolen.

The cat is introduced in the picture by Mr. Stubbs, on account of the extraordinary affection shewn by this horse to that animal, and which was more particularly manifested by his extreme inquietude on the death of it.

He died at Gog-Magog hills, a seat of the Earl of Godolphin's, in 1753, at the age of twenty-nine, and was buried in a passage leading to the stable.

* Thus may the labours of our countryman be continued for the improvement of the arts, for the gratification of the sportsman, and the lovers of the turf, and in some degree for the advantage of one who was most respected by the subject of this paper, and who still fills the walks of life with great respectability.

I am, Sir, your's, &c.
T. N.

DISPUTES
BETWEEN GENTLEMEN,
On Points of Honour, &c. &c. &c.

AS we have recently had occasion to record very many instances of that serious order of social disputes which terminate in duels, we shall presume to offer some floating remarks on the establishment and infraction of that dignified principle of action, which is usually denominated *Honour!*

It has been asserted, in a French treatise on education, that honour, like light, has no definitive outline; that its boundaries are extended or narrowed agreeably to the operation of national prejudices; and that, even in a national point of consideration, it is farther subdivided by the pure or impure conception of those classes of life, who are more or less delicate in their agency, expression, and responsibility.

As *honour* cannot be said to exist without the accompanying aid of honesty and truth, it evidently relies for its basis upon the moral beauty of religion. No person, however exalted by adventitious events, or emblazoned by the decorations of heraldry, can duly claim the appellation of *honourable*, whose principle and whose action are not in perfect correspondence with the institutes of virtue.—To be thus honourably distinguished, is to be a *gentleman* in the just tenor of the word; or, in other terms, an exemplary person, whose importance is derived from the concurring homage of the wise and good, inasmuch as that homage is the result of thought, and cannot be purchased or bestowed without the impelling sanction of the heart.

Supposing an individual thus constituted

stituted and accomplished, he should certainly, deem the custody of his *honour* as a sacred obligation upon his nature : but to suppose that every flippant young man, with slip-shod manners and yielding morals, is under the same necessity, is to admit a solecism in the page of reason. Were mankind to deny the possession of *honour* to those who were not morally just, we might soon witness an increase of respect on the part of the public towards the real claimants on their esteem; and a proportionate diminution of those blatant coxcombs, who sully the genuine authority of a *gentleman*, by their gross misuse of the assumed character.

We have sometimes been inclined to desire, that a local *Court of Honour* should be raised, for the essential purpose of ascertaining the weight and extent of those infringements on decorum, which are sometimes urged by those who have some reputation to maintain, and, very frequently, by such as have no reputation whatever.— Were there a court of appeal of this sort, it would serve as a species of grand jury, whose awards might save many noble and generous spirits from trouble, when annoyed by the presumptuous and the unworthy : and tend considerably to check that career of arrogance, which threatens, in the present state of things, to overwhelm the better part of society with barbarous pretensions and unfounded argument.   W.

WE shall, under this head, present two occurrences for the consideration of the writer of the above excellent article, and to which we trust he will next month affix such comments as the subjects demand.

CRIM. CON.—Sir Arthur Paget having suffered judgment to go by default, in an action brought against him in the Court of King's Bench by Lord Boringdon, for *Crim. Con.* with Lady Boringdon, the assessment of damages took place before the Sheriff's Deputy, Mr. Burchell, and a Special Jury, on Tuesday, the 19th instant, at the office of the Sheriff of Middlesex.—Sir Arthur Paget is second son of the Earl of Uxbridge; Lady Boringdon, the second daughter of the Earl of Westmoreland.—At the time of Lord Boringdon's marriage he was thirty-two years of age; his wife, then Lady Augusta Fane, eighteen. After the statement of the dishonourable conduct of the defendant in the seduction of the plaintiff's wife, a number of witnesses were called, to prove the happy state in which Lord and Lady Boringdon lived, previous to Sir Arthur's becoming acquainted with the family; among these were, Lord Amherst, the Hon. George Villiers, who married Lady Boringdon's sister, Doctor Vaughan, Sir Wm. Elford, and particularly the Rev. Mr. Hayne, the Minister of Plympton, and Chaplain to Lord B. at Saltram, who spoke to Lord and Lady Boringdon's regular attendance at divine worship for three years, and to the perfect harmony and happiness that subsisted Lord B. he said, was uniformly a kind and indulgent husband—Lady B. a tender and affectionate wife.

Mr. Parke was Counsel for Lord Boringdon, and Mr. Garrow for Sir Arthur. The latter made a defence almost as bad as his client's cause. He concluded his speech by representing the defendant in no condition to pay large damages, and insisted it was a case that did not require them; but whether so or or not, Mr. Burchell summed up the evidence, and the Jury found for the plaintiff — Damages, *Ten Thousand Pounds.*

A few days previous to the above, an action was tried in the Court of King's Bench, wherein a Mr. Walker, a gentleman of fortune, was plaintiff, and Mr. Reader, the Counsel, defendant; this also was a *crim. con.* cause, and the damages laid by Mr. Walker at 20,000l.— The plaintiff's evidence not amounting to that *full proof* of criminality between Mr. Reader and Mrs. Walker which the law requires in such cases, the Jury, under the direction of the Judge, (Lord Ellenborough) pronounced a *nonsuit.*

RACES APPOINTED IN 1808.

NEWBURY .... *Aug.* 2
Taunton 2
Brighton 2
Worcester. 2
Tre Madock 2
Swansea 9
Nottingham 9
Blandford 9
Oxford 9
Newcastle, Staffordshire 10
Reading 16
Derby 16
Exeter 16
York 20
Egham 23
Southampton 25
Bodmin 30
Warwick, ... *Sept.* 6
Ayr, Scotland 6
Pontefract 13
Kingscote. 20
Beccles 20
Lincoln 21
Doncaster 26
Carlisle. 27
Dumfries .... *Oct.* 3
Newmarket First October Meeting .... *Oct.* 3
.... Second Ditto 17
.... Houghton Meeting 31

COCKING.

NANTWICH.

IN the race-week, a main of cocks was fought between the Gentlemen of Staffordshire, (Gosling, feeder) and the Gentlemen of Cheshire, (Harrison, feeder) for 5gs a battle, and 200gs the main; which was won by the former, 23 main and 4 byes, against 16 main and 2 byes.

PRESTON.

In the race-week, a main of cocks was fought between Lord Derby, (Goodall, feeder) and R. Legh, Esq. (Gilliver, feeder) for 10gs a battle and 200gs the main. —The following is a statement :—

Goodall.	M.	B.	Gilliver.	M.	B.
Monday,	8	3		5	1
Tuesday,	3	0		4	1
Wednesday,	3	0		4	1
Thursday,	2	1		5	0
Total	16	4		18	3

Before fighting, even betting on the main.

NEWCASTLE.

In the race-week, a long main of cocks, fought between the gentlemen of Northumberland and those of Durham, was a drawn one.

STAMFORD.

During the races, a main of cocks was fought between the gentlemen of Middlesex, (Fleming, feeder) and the Gentlemen of Lincoln-

Lincolnshire and Leicestershire, (Faulkner, feeder); consisting of 26 main and 15 byes, for 10gs a battle, and 100gs the main; of which the following is a statement:—

Fleming.	M. B.	Faulkner.	M. B.
Tuesday,	5 2		2 3
Wednesday,	2 4		7 1
Thursday,	6 2		4 3
	13 8		13 7

FOX-CHASE EXTRAORDINARY.

THE following Fox-chase, which took place about seven weeks ago, in the counties of Inverness and Perth, perhaps exceeds any thing ever known in the annals of Fox-hunting. On the 8th ult. near Dunkeld, Perthshire, there were seen on the high road, a fox and a hound, proceeding at a very slow trotting pace. The dog was about the distance of 50 yards behind the Fox: each was so fatigued and spent that the latter could not out-run the former, neither could the former overtake the latter. A countryman, who observed them in this state, very easily caught the fox by running. Both the fox and the dog were taken to a gentleman's house in the neighbourhood, where the dog received every mark of hospitality, to which his unwearied pursuit entitled him: and Reynard was placed in a garden, as a prisoner of war; but whether from over-fatigue, or from a determination not to out-live the loss of his liberty, he refused to take any sustenance, and the consequence was, that he died the day following. After the lapse of a week the dog seemed quite recovered from the fatigues of the chase; on which it was determined by the gentleman to tie a letter to the dog's neck, (for he had no collar) in which all the circumstances that passed in that place were stated; it concluded with requesting the owner of the dog, if ever he found his way home, to acquaint Mr. S—t, by post, where the fox started, in order that both the length of the chase, and the time employed in it, might be ascertained. In ten days after, Mr. S—t received a letter, informing him, that the dog had arrived safe at his master's house, in Badenoch, that he was one of the bounds of the Duke of Gordon's fox-hunter, in that country, and that the fox was started on the morning of the King's birth-day, on the top of those hills called *Mona-liadh*, which separates Badenoch from Fort Augustus. From this it appeared that the chase lasted four days, and that the distance travelled from the place where the game was sprung, to the place where it was caught, without making any allowances for *doubles*, *crosses*, and *tergiversations*, exceeded seventy miles. It is said that an application is to be made to the Duke of Gordon to enrol *Caro*, (the dog's name) among the list of his Grace's pensioners at Gordon Castle.

A chase, similar to the above, occurred in the year 1633, when a stag was run by a single greyhound out of Whinfield Park, Westmoreland, to Redkirk, in Scotland, and back again, a distance of near one hundred miles, when being both exhausted, the stag leaped over the pales and died; the greyhound, in attempting to follow it, fell back and died on the contrary side; in memory of which the stag's horns were nailed upon a tree just by, which to this day bears the name of " Hart's-horn Tree."

THE

THE PHILOSOPHICAL SPORTSMAN.

NO. VII.

Give me, by tender sympathy, to know.
The secret springs of ev'ry suff'rer's woe;
My heart shall share, my ready wish relieve,
And what I want in pow'r, in pity give.

ANON.

POOR JACK THE HUNTSMAN, A PATHETIC TALE.

IT has long and frequently been the theme of moral philosophers, that the life of mankind is filled up with vicissitudes, casualties, and uncertainties; that when their minds are elated with the pleasing prospect of near-approaching felicity, eager in their expectation of pleasure and fortunate occurrences, and ready to satiate their minds with joy and gladness, some unforeseen event intervenes, and disappoints all their hopes of pleasure and gratification. The prospect suddenly lours around them, and gloomy thoughts and corroding sensations fall, with a triple force and poignancy, on minds pre-occupied in the anticipation of approaching prosperity and pleasure. It, perhaps, no less frequently occurs, on the contrary, that when we are, with anxiety and dread, looking toward the approach of calamity and sorrow, magnifying troubles and evils, and harrowing up the soul about expedients, the prospect shall as suddenly brighten, the dreaded evil never arrive, and the apprehended sorrow never lay hold on us; thus we surmount difficulties, and get through evils with ease. The man of pleasure rises in the morning, and says, we shall have much sport to-day; the chase lies in a country where game abounds, and

is pleasant; esteemed and convivial friends are to join in it; the day promises fair; dogs and horses are in fine order.—The day, perhaps, proves stormy; the friends expected are detained; the dogs are unfortunate in starting the game, or, if soon started, the scent lies badly, or it takes such unaccountable turns in its progress, that the dogs are often at fault.—At the arrival of evening, he finds that the day has proved barren of amusement, that he has taken no pleasure; he is jaded and dispirited, not so much because he has had no sport, as from having been disappointed of that degree of it which he had promised to himself. But as the pleasures of the sportsman are liable to frequent contingencies, and depend so much on adventitious circumstances, he is not to be disheartened on account of one day's unamusing fatigue.

" Never, at morn, let him presume to say,
" That he shall have no pleasant sport that day."

For when amusement is least expected, the most agreeable and delightful may start up; friends drop into the chase, the object of their pursuit take the line they wish, the dogs follow in spirit without fault, and the day conclude with unwonted gaiety and conviviality.

Whoever makes any nice reflections on the occurrences of his days, will find that they are attended with similar vicissitudes and uncertainties; the philosophical sportsman meets with them as well as others, though, perhaps, not so frequently as younger men, of more active and enterprising pursuits. Some occurrence happens, or some object starts up, and affords food for his contemplative mind, at a time and place when he

X

he least thinks of it, as will appear at the commencement of the following tale of poor Jack.

Business called me a few miles from home, in May 1804, or 1805, and I was making my entrance on a pleasant green, prettily spotted with neat cottages and garden grounds. The morning was delightful, the sun resplendent; the larks were commencing their morning career, some nearly invisible, chaunting forth their melodious song, scarce audible, in the skies; others were just mounting, pleasing the ear more audibly and harmoniously; when, a little on my right, the voice of a man singing called off my attention from every other object; they were as sweet notes as I ever heard from a man's voice, full, made without constraint, or any attempts at art or embellishment, which gave them more native sweetness than if decorated with studied art. He seemed to be stationary while he sung the following lines:—

Bid care and sorrow keep away; .
The tender heart should still be gay;
Serenely o'er it time should roll,
Where no remorse can wound the soul.

Where wrong don't cause the heart to bleed,
Misfortunes such, should never heed;
For troubles past are troubles dead,
No more to raise their horrid head.

Then banish sorrow far away,
Smile as these cheerful days of May;
Jack now is happy, void of care,
And bids adieu to dark despair.

He can't abide a fixed home,
But, like the bee, abroad must roam;
So, farewell, mother; happy be;
You soon again poor Jack shall see.

The voice ceased, and a man made his entrance on the green in the dress of a huntsman, a scarlet coat, well worn, trimmed with green, with a leathern girdle about his middle, and a hunting cap; he was trotting over the road-way, talking to a fine hound which attended all his steps. Something peculiar and eccentric appeared in his manners, which indicated a mind not under the full force and government of reason; yet his whole countenance was mild, open, and simple, without a single trait of ill-nature or viciousness. Making over the way towards a pretty garden, he called to the mistress who was standing in the door-way, and begged a nosegay of her sweet lilies; "take as many as you please, and where you please, poor Jack," was her answer. Poor Jack tuned his voice again, entered the garden, and, while deliberately selecting such flowers as pleased, and fixing a fine branch of the white kind fancifully in his cap, and of the purple in his bosom, he sung the following song with great simplicity and native sweetness, whilst the old hound at his side appeared to be no less attentive to the song than myself.

The blackbird and linnet are offering their lays,
And the lark in the skies sounds his rapturous praise;
The ploughman is whistling, the lambs frisk and play;
All nature expands in the sweet month of May!

Sweet Spring! thou delight of the gay feather'd train,
Kind parent of plenty, the joy of each swain,
All nature around thee rejoice in thy day,
But Jack, crack-brain'd Jack, does not wish thee to stay.

Golden Summer, so rich, is now close in thy rear;
Come swiftly, so pass, and let Autumn appear;
Sober Autumn, that bends the weak shoots of the vine

With

With her dark blushing clusters, the
   fountain of wine.
Haste Autumn, serene, and then house
   up thy store,
That long tedious days with poor Jack
   may be o'er,
For Jack in the chase then contentment
   shall find,
And fatigue to his body bring peace to
   his mind.

Come, Autumn, and shower thy leaves
   on the plain,
Bring thy blue misty mornings, and soft-
   falling rain;
Bid the south-western wind shake the
   dew-spangled thorn,
And the huntsman shall rouse up the
   dogs with his horn:
Then the life-drops of Jack with emotion
   will spring,
When Ranter shall open, and make the
   woods ring;
To his voice I'll reply, as my heart
   bounds with joy,
And cry, " Ranter has nos'd him—that's
   it, my staunch boy."

Fox and dogs break the cover, they fly
   like the wind,
And Jack, panting Jack, shall come lag-
   ging behind :
But I'll aim to cross on ye, not sparing
   my breath,
And sometimes, thro' chance, may be in
   at the death. ,
Thus Autumn and Winter alone can
   impart
Those scenes to poor Jack which so glad-
   den his heart ;
Then with horses and hounds he can
   exercise find,
And at night sound repose, the relief of
   his mind.

Having finished this song, he put
on his cap, with the branch of
flowers nodding fantastically on the
left side, thanked the woman, and
set off on what is called a dog-trot.
It was curiously amusing to observe the looks and motions of old
Ranter, who seemed to understand
poor Jack's words as well as his
motions, for when he mentioned
him in the song, he gave tongue,
and put himself in motion.

" Poor Jack, as he styles himself," said I to the woman, " is not
an unpleasant fellow ; pray who is
he, for you seem to know him ?"
" Know him ! aye, master, that I
do, to be sartan ; why I know'd
him in his cradle.—His old father
and mother live only on t'other side
the green, just out of sight."—
" And pray, mistress, what is he
called besides Jack ?" " Why,
Jack Sendaway," said she ; " 'tis
strange you don't know him,
when every body knows him better than any body else, seeing he's
been all over the world running
a'ter the hounds. Why he was a
fine fellow once, man, and the old
folks were so proud of him as nothing can be like it ; and well they
might, for the matter of that, for he
set them up mainly, or they would
have been as poor, and no better
off, than their neighbours. But I
always said as how the longest day
will have a night, let folk set up
themselves as high as they will ;
and so it has com'd to pass—however, I'm sorry for poor Jack, for
he was a fine fellow when he went
with the great man's hounds ; but
I could not bear to see the old man
and woman so proud, and set up
about it : why, mayhaps, said I, he
may lose his place, and then he
may look long enough for sitch
another ; and only see how things
are turned about ! but I little
thought of his running a sort of
crazy, though I always thought
him a little windmill-headed, as
the saying is."—Having thanked
my informant, I pursued my way,
forgetting poor Jack for the time,
my mind being engaged in reflections on the speech just made.

Oh ! envy ! thought I, thou
jaundice of the eye, corroder of
minds, parent of foul detraction,
and nurse of scandal, how I hate
ye ! How oft from thee does
fame plume her wings, and scatter

her pestiferous breath, throughout the world, sowing discord and misery.—Horrid, yet wretched monster! to thee, this goodly scene of nature is a source of anguish and discontent; thy heart is gloomy, and thy days no better than those of the toad, that lives on the damp vapours of a dungeon.— Thou grudgest the prosperity of thy friends and neighbours, and thou blasphemously arraignest Providence with kindness and partiality, because the industry and attention of others are crowned with success, whilst thou reapest the fruits of thine own malignity, indolence, and neglect. Not so the liberal, candid mind, that joys in the prosperity of individuals, well knowing that it constitutes that of the public; that plenty makes cheapness; and that the poor man without a spot of land is a gainer by their prosperity, and in some degree becomes a sharer of the blessings annexed to good husbandry, timely industry, and attention. And why should man envy the appendages of riches, when he himself may view the sumptuous building, the gay equipage, the rising plantation, and the beautiful garden, with as great content and admiration, perhaps greater, than he who calls himself the proprietor?

From making farther reflexions on the cursed effects of envy, and the wretched condition of the envious, I was interrupted by the neat appearance of a garden and cottage at my side; a respectable-looking woman was standing just without the door, looking thoughtfully melancholy, and as though she was harkening to catch the sounds of poor Jack, which at times re-echoed across the field.—That woman, thought I, must be the mother of poor Jack; I stopped, and asked some questions, which gave her to understand that I had seen him on the green, that I had been amused with his manners and appearance, and interested myself in things relative to such singularities. This observation proving grateful to the feelings of a fond mother—" will you please to walk in, Sir," said she, " and rest you? I am able to tell you most things that have happened to poor Jack from his birth to this day."—I accepted her invitation, went in, and seated myself without ceremony, and Mrs. Sendaway, seating herself nearly opposite, began her pathetic tale, as shall appear in my next.

M.

GRAND DIVERTISEMENT AND SPECTACLE,

EXHIBITED AT LISLE, IN 1453, BY THE DUKE OF BURGUNDY,

Preparatory to the Crusade against the Mahometans.

IN an immense hall three tables were laid out, that might, perhaps, more justly be called theatres, considering the number of machines that were placed on each. That for the duke was square, and had four ornaments.

1. A church with its bell and organ, with four chaunters to play on it, and sing when their time of acting should require it.

2. A statue of a naked child, placed on a rock, who, from his " broquette pissait eau-rose."

3. A vessel larger than what would serve to navigate on the seas, having on board a numerous crew, who performed all the manœuvres as if they had been really at sea.

4. A ri-

... A rivulet that ran through a meadow, ornamented with shrubs and flowers; rocks, studded with sapphires and other precious stones, served as a boundary to it; and in the centre was a figure of St. Andrew, from the end of whose cross spouted out a stream of water.

On the second table were seen nine ornaments.

1. A sort of pasty, in which were inclosed twenty-eight musicians, men and children, who were each to play on a different instrument during certain interludes of the feast.

2. The castle of Lusignan, with its ditches and towers; from the two smallest, a stream of orangeade ran into the ditches; and, on the highest tower, Melusina was seen disguised as a serpent.

3. A windmill placed on a hillock. A magpie was fixed on one of the sails, which served for a mark to all sorts of persons, who amused themselves with shooting with cross-bows.

4. A vineyard, in the midst of which were placed two casks, as emblems of those containing good and evil. One held a sweet, and the other a bitter liquor. A man richly dressed, seated cross-legged on one of the casks, held in his hand a paper, by which he offered the choice of his liquors to all who might wish to taste them.

5. A desert country, where a tiger was represented fighting with a serpent.

6. A savage mounted on a camel, seeming on the point of making a long journey.

7. A man with a long pole, beating a bush, wherein many small birds had taken refuge. Near to it was an orchard inclosed by a trellis of roses, with a knight seated by his mistress's side, who caught and ate the birds the other drove from the bush. A kind of satirical allegory, ingenious enough, and which probably gave rise to the proverbial expression, " to beat the bush for another."

8. Mountains and rocks covered with hanging icicles, among which a fool was seen mounted on a bear.

9. A lake surrounded by various towns and castles. A vessel was on it, sailing with all her sails set.

The third table, smaller than the preceding ones, had but three decorations.

1. A travelling merchant, as passing through a village, with a pack on his back.

2. An Indian forest, full of automata of various animals walking about.

3. A lion fastened to a tree, near which was a man beating a dog.

On the right and left of the buffet, which was set off with vases of chrystal, cups ornamented with gold and precious stones, and an immense quantity of gold and silver plate, were two columns; one bore the statue of a naked woman, from whose right breast flowed hippocras during supper-time; the lower parts of her body were covered with a napkin, loaded with Greek letters of a violet colour.

To the other column, a living lion was fastened by an iron chain. He was there placed to guard the naked woman, as the inscription in golden letters on a shield announced — ' Do not touch the lady.'

It is probable the naked woman, with the Greek letters, was intended to represent Constantinople despoiled,—the lion, who forbade any one to touch her, the duke of Burgundy,—

dy,—and the man who beat the dog in presence of the lion, Sultan Mohammed.

Beside the number of machines I have described, the hall contained five scaffolds for those spectators who were not of the supper, and particularly for the great crowds of foreigners, whom the report of this feast had brought to Lille.

On the entrance of the duke and his court, he walked about for some time to examine the various decorations, after which he sat down to the table, and the maitres d'hôtel served up the supper.

Every course consisted of forty-four dishes, each of which was lowered down from the roof by machinery, on cars painted with blue and gold, and with the device of the duke.

The moment he was seated with his guests, the bell of the church tolled, and instantly three little choristers came out of the pasty and began to sing a very sweet air, by way of grace; they were accompanied by a shepherd on his pipe. Shortly after, a horse entered, escorted by fifteen or sixteen knights in the livery of the duke. He moved backward, and bore on his bare back two masked trumpeters, seated back to back; and in this manner he made the circuit of the hall backward, attended by the knights, the two trumpeters playing all the time symphonies.

When they had quitted the hall, the organ of the church was heard, and one of the musicians in the pasty played on a German horn,—A great automata, representing an enormous wild boar, now entered, having on his back a monster, half a savage and half a griffin; and this monster bore also a man on his shoulders. They had no sooner departed than the chaunt-

ers in the church sung an air, and three of the musicians in the pasty executed a trio; one played on the doucaine (dulciana, probably dulcimer), the second on the lute, and the third on another instrument.

Such were the different amusements that formed the accompaniments to the first course: all, excepting the music, were farces foreign to the feast. Those of the second course had as little connection; but they were preparatory to the last, in which the object of this entertainment was to be pathetically explained.

The entertainment of the second course consisted of a dramatic pantomime, that represented the conquest of the golden fleece, by Jason,—a kind of allegory that recalled to the spectators the order of the golden fleece, which the duke had instituted twenty-three years before.

For this spectacle, a small theatre had been erected at one end of the hall, and which a large green silken curtain had hid from the eyes of the assembly. On a sudden, a symphony of clarions was heard behind this curtain; it was drawn up, and Jason was seen fighting with, and bringing to the yoke, two bulls, that vomited flames of fire, to whom had been committed the defence of the garden of the Hesperides. The hero next combats a monstrous dragon, cuts off his head and tears out his teeth. He then ploughs a field with the bulls he had tamed, sows there the teeth of the dragon, and instantly an army of soldiers spring from the earth, who fight together most bitterly, and alternately kill each other.

The three acts of this sort of opera did not immediately follow: the spaces between each act were filled up by interludes in the taste of of those of the preceding. The first consisted of a youth, who entered the hall mounted on a large white stag, when they both sang a duo ; then a fiery dragon, who flew round the hall. A hawking scene was next presented, when two falcons were seen to strike down a heron, which was instantly presented to the duke. All these interludes were accompanied either by pieces on the organ, by the chaunters in the church, or by the musicians in the pasty, who every time executed an air on a different instrument.

These successive spectacles, however, were but, as I have said, a preliminary amusement, — or, to borrow the expression of the two authors from whom I make this extract, were but a ' worldly pastime,' given to the spectators to entertain them until the time of the grand scene, the scene which was to explain the subject of this feast, and the real cause of it.

It was opened by a giant dressed with a turban in the morisco fashion, and clothed in a long robe of striped green silk. He held in his left hand a guisarme of the antique mode, and with his right led an elephant. This animal bore on its back a tower, in which was a female to represent the church ; she had on her head a white veil, after the manner of nuns : her robe was of white satin, but her mantle was black, to mark her grief. When she was come near to where the duke sat, she sang a triolet to have the giant stopped, and then made a long complaint in verse, in which, having displayed the many ills she was suffering from the infidels, she implored succour from the duke and the knights of the fleece then present.

Different officers now entered with the king at arms of the order of the golden fleece, followed by two knights of the order, each leading a damsel, one of whom was natural daughter to the duke. The king at arms bore a live pheasant, decorated with a collar of gold and precious stones : approaching the duke he made a profound obeisance, and said, that it being the custom at grand festivals to offer to the princes and gentlemen a peacock, or some noble bird, for them to make a vow upon, he was come with two ladies to offer his valour a pheasant.

The duke, in reply to this proposition, gave to the king at arms a billet written in his own hand, that he had prepared before hand, the substance of which was read aloud, as follows : He there vowed to God pre-eminent, then to the glorious Virgin his mother, and afterward to the ladies, and to the pheasant, that if the king of France, his lord paramount, or any other princes, would undertake a croisade against the Turks, he would accompany or follow them ; and that he himself would combat the sultan body to body, if he would accept his challenge. The lady representing the church having thanked him, she made the circuit of the hall with her elephant, during which time almost all the princes and great lords present made vows on the bird of the most extravagant nature—such as not to drink wine, not to be seated at table, or not to lie down one day of the week, until they should have met the infidel army—or have been the first to attack it—or have overthrown the banner of the sultan—or to return to Europe without bringing with them a Turk prisoner. In short, one made a vow, (which will give an idea of the religion of these new croisaders)

croisaders) that if he could not obtain the last favours of his mistress before his departure, he would marry the first damsel he should meet that had twenty thousand crowns.

When the vows were ended, a troop of musicians entered, accompanied by a great number of lighted torches. Twelve ladies followed, every one attended by a knight; each personified a virtue. They formed a dance, and thus the festival ended.

All this noisy vain boasting had no effect. The duke levied large sums from his territories, under pretence of this croisade, and even advanced into Germany, when a convenient illness made him return home; and this pretended lion permitted Mohammed to beat the dog without any opposition.

PHILOSOPHERS ECLIPSED BY SPORTSMEN.

IN the Augustan age, the whole circle of arts and sciences comprised merely philosophy, rhetoric, mathematics, poetry, painting, sculpture, architecture, and music; but as mankind made progress in refinement, the circle was considerably enlarged. The appellation of arts and sciences was conferred on the *gladiatores*, or boxers; *saltatores* and *cantatores*, or dancers and singers; *rhedarii*, or charioteers; and on those performances called *equestres* and *pedestres*, or horse and foot races. It is true that all those performances were practised among the Greeks, but the credit of linking them with the arts and sciences is due only to the moderns, who have added several others of their own invention, such

as fire and stone eating, donkey-racing, gaming, duelling, calculating the long odds, quizzing a flat, and dressing in style. Our 'pugilists, players, opera singers, and dancers, whips, and black-legs, have all acquired or assumed the appellation of professional and scientific persons, and have almost superseded their predecessors in the patronage of great men. Philosophy can be of no use to men who have ceased to think or reason for themselves, except in the article of patience under their losses at play, and even that has given way to the bottle. All the strength and cunning of rhetoric could not parry a straight-forward hit from the arm of Belcher or Dutch Sam. Mathematics are become so familiar, that one of our stylish *whips* can imprint all the problems of Euclid with his coach-wheels on the sand, perform a curve within an inch of the edge of Dover cliffs, or cut out a fly's eye with his whip as it perches on the horse's ear; and our black-legs can calculate with the same mathematical precision the speed of horses, or the *quantum* of brains of the *flats* whom they mean to take in.

J. J. B.

Tottenham-Court-road.

CURIOUS PARTICULARS OF RUNNING FOOTMEN.

THE Romans had an *ante-ambulo*, whose express office it was to deliver messages; and also *veredarii*, who carried letters with wonderful speed; one or both of those gave birth to the *running-footmen*.

They were, however, rivalled in this nation: Mr. Smythe says, in his

his MS. Lives of the Berkelys. "Langham, an Irish footman of this Lord, (Henry Lord Berkely, in the reign of Eliz.) upon the sickness of the Lady Catherine, this lord's wife, conveyed a letter from Callowdon (near Coventry) to old Doctor Fryer, a physician, dwelling in Litile Brittaine, in London, and returned with a glass bottle in his hand, compounded by the doctor for the recovery of her health ; a journey of 148 miles, performed by him in less than 42 hours, notwithstanding his stay of one night at the physician and apothecary's houses, which no one else could have so well and safely performed."

Howell says, " You writ to me lately for a footman, and I think this bearer will fit you. I know he can run well; for he hath run away twice from me, but he knew the way back again; yet though he hath a running head as well as running heels, (and who will expect a footman to be a stayed man) I would not part with him, were I not to go post to the north. There be some things in him that answer for his waggeries; he will come when you call him, go when you tell him, and shut the door after him ; he is faithful and stout, and a lover of his master. He is a great enemy to all dogs, if they bark at him in his running, for I have seen him confront a huge mastiff, and knock him down.—When you go a country journey you must spirit him with liquor ; you must allow him also something extraordinary for socks, or else you must not have him to wait at your table; when his grease melts in running hard, 'tis subject to fall in his heels."

Lord Berkely's running footman was an Irishman. Running

has ever been a favourite and necessary accomplishment of barbarous nations, and is now of the American Indians. The heroes of Fingal were great runners; so were our ancestors the Britons. Giraldus Cambrensis says, that the Welch passed days and nights in running over the tops of hills, and penetrating woods.

From the above passage in Howell it appears, that he limits the term *footman* to these pedestrians. But one footman, and that a *running one*, was kept in families after the invention of coaches ; at least but one, to whom that term was generally, perhaps, applied. Taylor (the Water Poet) says, " all the serving men are converted into two or three animals, *videlicet*, a butterfly, a page, a *trotting* footman, a stiffe-drinking coachman, a cook, a steward, and a butler." In the English *Dictionarié*, or, an interpretation of hard English words, by H. C. Gent. 12mo. 1632, we have no *footman*, but a " *swift footman ceteripedian*."

The last running footman kept in London, was one by the late Duke of Northumberland ; this footman used to attend the Duchess to court. The writer of this article saw him preceding the chair of his mistress so late as the year 1763 or 4.

THEATRICAL ANECDOTE.

JUST as a performer at the Newcastle Theatre had announced his benefit, a stranger happened to arrive at Newcastle. No less a personage than the *Prince Annamaboo* was advertised to be seen at the small price of one shilling.— Tom, without delay, waited on the propri-

proprietor of this great Prince, and for a handsome sum prevailed on him to order his Highness to exhibit his royal person on the stage that evening. The manager, with much good humour, consented, and the bills of the day stated, that " between the acts of the play, Prince Annamaboo would give a lively representation of the scalping operation; he would likewise give the Indian war-whoop in all its varied tones, the tomahawk exercise, and the mode of feasting at an Abyssinian banquet." The evening arrived, and many people attended to witness these princely imitations. At the end of the third act his Highness walked forward, with dignified step, flourishing the tomahawk, and cut the air, exclaiming, " Ha, ha !—Ho, ho !" Next entered a man with his face blacked, and a piece of bladder fastened to his head with gum ; the Prince, with a very large carving knife, commenced the scalping operation, which he performed in a style truly imperial, holding up the skin in token of triumph.— Next came the war-whoop, which was a combination of dreadful and discordant sounds ; and, lastly, the Abyssinian banquet, consisting of raw beef-steaks ; these he made into rolls as large as his mouth would admit, and devoured them in a princely and dignified manner. Having completed his cannibal repast, he flourished his tomahawk in an exulting manner, exclaimed, " Ha, ha ! Ho, ho !" and made his exit. The manager, who possessed a penetrating eye, fancied this princely personage was an impostor, and his opinion was confirmed the following day ; for in the middle of the market-place he espied the most puissant Prince Annamaboo selling pen-knives,

scissars, and quills, in the character of a Jew pedlar. " What, (said Mr. K—), my Prince, is that you ? Are not you a pretty Jewish scoundrel to impose upon us in this manner ?" Moses turned round, and with an arch look replied, " Princh be d—d, I vash no princh; I vash acting like you. You vash kings, princh, emperors to night ; Stephen Kembles to-morrow ; I vash hampugs, you vash hampugs, all vash hampugs."

CURIOUS ANECDOTES OF A POPULAR PERFORMER.

From Ryley's Itinerant; or, the Memoirs of an Actor.

—— IS so well known as an actor, that my opinion can neither add to, nor diminish his fame ; were either in my power, panegyric would run through a dozen pages, and yet fall short of his merits. In some characters he is as much superior to any actor of the present day, as Garrick was to those of his time; but they are limited to such parts as suit his figure, which wants grace and proportion ; where these can be dispensed with, he has no competitor. As a man in private life, he is the gentleman, the scholar, the friend, the life of every party, an enemy to scandal and detraction, and benevolent even to imprudence.

Such is —— in his sober moments; but, when stimulated by the juice of the grape, he acts in diametrical opposition to all this. No two men, however different they may be, can be more at variance than —— sober, and —— in a state of inebriety.

At

At these times, his interesting suavity of manners changes to brutal invective, and the feelings of his nearest and dearest friends are sacrificed. Such are the unfortunate propensities of this singular man, unfortunate, I say, because he seems incapable of avoiding them, although they have a tendency to ruin his health, injure his property, and destroy his social connections. No one can more regret these failings than he does in his hours of sanity, or make more handsome apologies; and if at night he creates enemies, his conciliatory manners in the morning are sure to raise double the number of friends.

Of this great actor many ludicrous anecdotes are related. I shall point out a few which came under my own observation.

One evening, in Manchester, we were in a public bar amongst a promiscuous company, where —— was, as usual, the life of the party. Mirth and good humour prevailed till about ten o'clock, when I perceived a something lurking in his eye which foretold a storm. Anxious to get him home before it burst forth, I pressed our departure, under the plea of another engagement; but, instead of having the desired effect, it precipitated what I had foreseen. With a haughty supercilious look, he said,—"I see what you are about, you hypocritical scoundrel! You canting methodistical thief! am I, ——, to be control'd by such a would-be puritan as you? I'll teach you to dictate to a tragedian." Then taking off his coat, and holding his fist in a menacing attitude— "Come out," continued he— "thou prince of deceivers; though thou hast faith to remove mountains, thou shalt not remove me— Come out, I say." With much

difficulty he was pacified, and resumed his coat. There was a large fire in the bar, before which stood, with his coat skirts under each arm, a pitiful imitation of *buckism*, very deficient in cleanliness and costume. His face was grimy, and his neckcloth of the same tint, which, nevertheless, was rolled in various folds about his throat; his hair was matted, and turned up under a round greasy hat, with narrow brims, conceitedly placed on one side of the head, which noddled under it like a shaking mandarin. Thus equipped, the filthy fop straddled before the fire, which he completely monopolised. At length he caught the eye of our tragedian, who, in silent amazement, for the space of half a minute, examined him from top to toe; then turning to me, he burst into a horse laugh, and roared out, "Beau Nasty, by ——."—Perhaps intimidated by ——'s former blustering, this insensible puppy took little notice; but I knew he would not stop here, and indeed I thought the stranger fair game. —— now rose from his seat, and taking up the skirts of his coat, in imitation of the other, turned his back to the fire, "Warm work in the *back settlements*, Sir," said he; then approaching still nearer, as if he had some secret to communicate, whispered, though loud enough for every one to hear, —"Pray, Sir, how is soap?"—

"Soap?"

"Yes, Sir, soap; I understand it is coming down."

"I am glad of it, Sir."

"Indeed, Sir, you have cause, if one may judge from your appearance."

Here was a general laugh, which the stranger seemed not to regard, but noddling his head, and hitting his boots, with a little rattan, rang the bell with an air of importance, and enquired " if he could have a *weal killet*, or a *mutton chip?*"

" What do you think," said ———— " of a *roasted puppy?* because," taking up the poker, " I'll spit you, and roast you in a minute."

This had a visible effect on the dirty beau—he retreated towards the door, ———— following.— " Avaunt, and quit my sight; thy face is dirty, and thy hands unwashed; avaunt! avaunt! I say." Then replacing the poker, and returning to his seat, he continued, " Being gone, I am a man again."

It happened that Perrins, the noted pugilist, made one of the company this evening; he was a remarkably strong man, and possessed of great modesty and good nature. The last scene took such effect on his imagination, that he laughed immoderately. ————'s attention was attracted, and turning towards him with his most bitter look—" What do you laugh at, Mr. Swabson? hey? why, you great lubber-headed thief, Johnson would have beat two of you! laugh at me! at ————! come out, you scoundrel!!!"

The coat was again pulled off, and putting himself in an attitude, " this is the arm that shall sacrifice you." Perrins was of a mild disposition, and knowing ————'s character, made every allowance, and answered him only by a smile, till aggravated by language and action the most gross, he very calmly took him in his arms, as though he had been a child, set him down in the street, and bolted the door. The evening was wet, and our hero without coat or hat, unprepared to cope with it; but entreaty for admission was vain, and his appli-cation at the window unattended to. At length, grown desperate, he broke several panes, and, inserting his head through the fracture, bore down all opposition by the following witticism :—" Gentlemen, I have taken *some pains* to gain admission ; pray let me in, for *I see through my river.*" The door was opened, dry clothes procured, and about one o'clock in the morning we sent him home in a coach.

KILLING A HORSE.

COURT OF KING'S BENCH, JULY 19.

Before Chief-Justice Ellenborough.

Cumbers *v.* Gullan.

THIS was an action to recover from the defendant the value of a horse which he had hired of the plaintiff, and which, it was alledged, had died in consequence of excessive fatigue or improper treatment, which it had experienced while engaged in the journey for which it had been hired by the defendant.

The claim was two-fold— 1st, That the contract, which was to carry the horse only to Woolwich, had been improperly extended— 2d, That the horse had experienced improper treatment.

The young gentleman who rode the horse, being released from any responsibility, declared, that he had ridden him with the utmost care; that he had not over-ridden him, and that, except on one stage of the journey, when, in consequence of signal guns being fired on Woolwich Common, the horse had taken alarm, he had never whipped or spurred him to any excess. He had been going to the horse house of General Hulse, and had exceeded the journey to Woolwich. On opening the body of the horse, which exhibited marks of indisposition the following day, and died on the third day subsequent, there was observed a failure of the lungs, as if arisen from inordinate fatigue. To the time of his death, from the period of the journey in question, the horse had been unable to perform any work.

Lord Ellenborough was clearly of opinion, that the first point, as to the defendant's having exceeded his contract, amounted to nothing. A person entering into such an agreement did not stipulate that he should not go a mile or two beyond the place specified. As for instance, it could hardly be contended, that a person hiring a horse to Richmond was not entitled to cross the bridge to Twickenham. All that was meant was, to give some idea of the length of the journey to be undertaken. As to the other count, which regarded improper treatment and excessive fatigue, he left it with the Jury to consider of it.

The Jury, after deliberating for some time, found a verdict for the plaintiff. Damages, 32l. being the value of the horse.

ANECDOTES.

From Hall's Travels in Scotland.

A Petty practitioner of the law in Stirling, being proprietor of an estate in a neighbouring parish, sent his proportion of the stipend to the clergyman by the hands of the hangman. When the hangman, who, here, as well as in most other places, is neither a respectable nor a popular character, and who is seldom seen without the walls of the town where he resides, was approaching the minister's house, the servants and all in the house were much alarmed, except the clergyman: and when the hangman knocked at the door, it was like the sentence of death.—As every body had run with fear and trembling to hide themselves, no one could be found to let him in. However, he was at last admitted. Upon being desired by the clergyman, (Mr. Frame), of Alloa, to come in, he informed him he had been sent by Mr. J. C—l, with his proportion of the stipend. Finding the money good and the sum due, being asked for a receipt, Mr. Frame wrote, " Received from Mr. C—, through the hands of his agent and factor, the hangman of Stirling, the sum of 30l. sterling, &c." But it seems that, the year after, the gentleman judged it unnecessary to send his money by his former agent.

It was, and still is a custom in many places in the Highlands, that whoever comes into a house after a person dies, and before such person is interred, as also after a child is born till it is baptised, must eat and drink in the house before they leave it. This being the custom, to save expences, and because they think it disrespectful to God to have an unbaptised child in the house, poor people generally have their children as soon baptised as possible. But it happened once to a poor man in this part of the country, that a river, as is often the case, ran between his house and the clergyman's, so that neither the poor man could get to the clergyman, nor the clergyman to the poor man; in order to have the child

child baptised. The river was swoln by the gradual melting of the snow, and there was no bridge within twenty miles. The poor man's cheese, his bread, &c. was nearly expended ; he, therefore, on the one side of the river, and the clergyman on the other, consulting what was to be done, agreed that the child should be brought to the river side ; that the father, presenting the child, should take on the vows, as they term it, and the minister, with a scoop or Dutch ladle, should throw over the water ; which was done, though with difficulty, owing to the breadth of the river ; after which, the clergyman pronounced the name, prayed aloud, so as to be heard by the parent and his attendants on the other side, after which each went to their respective homes, perfectly satisfied with this new mode of baptism, and that, if the child died in infancy, it would go to heaven.

Being invited to dine with a gentleman, near Auldern, when I was praising the sallad, which I found extremely good, he said, smiling, " You need not be afraid ; it is not dressed with castor oil." Upon enquiring what he alluded to, he told me, that a gentleman and his lady in the neighbourhood, who sometimes, as is the case in inland places, where there are no resident doctors, when any of their tenants are sick, recommend an emetic, or the like, to them, and at their own expence afforded the medicine. This gentleman, having an appeal to the house of peers about a large estate, was at London ; and, as he gained the process, and was about to return to Scotland, he bought some gallons of castor oil, to lie at his house, and be served out as occasion should require. Upon his arrival in Scotland, as it is natural, all the nobility and gentry, who were acquainted with him, came to dine with him, and congratulate him and the family on so many thousand pounds yearly being added to their fortune. When mostly all the genteel families for twenty miles round had paid their compliments to him in this manner, and he and his lady found leisure to hear the complaints of those sick people that applied to them, he found that some castor oil might be useful to a person that had come to consult them. Upon this, he rang the bell for John, the servant, who appearing, and being desired to bring some castor oil, replied, it was all done. " Done !" replied the gentleman ; " do not you know there is a keg of it lately come from London ?" " Yes, but if it please your honour, that one is done too." " How can that be ?" replied the gentleman, in a passion ? " Why, sir, you have had such a round of company almost every day since it came, and always sallad at table, that it is all gone." " Don't you know it is castor oil I want ; and that the name is written in large letters on the cask ?" " So it is," replied the servant ; " but, as your honour knows, it was for the castors, and dressing the sallad : it is all gone."—It should be added, for the credit of the oil, that the gentleman and his family had never in their life a better summer's health, nor the people who visited him."

Effects of a Sermon.—The Rev. Dr. Thomas Bisset, late minister of Logie Rait, had been preaching to his congregation, against not only stealing, but all manner of fraud, circumvention, and roguery. A little after he had returned to the manse,

manse, a servant came, and told him that Rob Roy was at the door, and wanted to speak with him: this was a noted drover, or dealer in cattle. Robert being called into the parlour, immediately explained the purpose of his visit to the minister, before his son and some other persons who were present. Oh! sir, said he, you made that preachment against me. You have heard of my cheating that poor woman, Widow Robertson, in buying her only cow. I took advantage of her not knowing the price, and of her being in want of money, and I got it at little more than half value, as you clearly shewed this day. What shall I do to make her amends?—Give her back the cow, said the worthy pastor, and allow her time to pay you back the money you gave her.—Would that, reverend sir, make up for my cheatry, and save me from all the punishment on this account that you was preaching about?—I dare say it might.—Then, sir, said he, to make sure work, I will give back the cow without the price, and keep from such tricks hereafter.—This resolution he actually performed.

FOWLING:

A POEM, IN FIVE BOOKS.

Descriptive of Grouse, Partridge, Pheasant, Woodcock, Duck, and Snipe Shooting.

ANXIOUS to gratify our judicious readers, we have availed ourselves of this elegant little work, just published. We think it an excellent appendage to Somerville's Chase, as it improves upon the beauties of that writer, without adopting any of his blemishes.— With Mr. Somerville, the author observes, he has ventured to differ essentially; "he has not enlarged his work by the introduction of any foreign modes of shooting, and he has avoided all extraneous ornaments and classical allusions. It was a home scene he wished to delineate, and Nature and Sport were the only figures in the picture."— The author observes, he will not disgust the liberal mind by meanness and servility. The illiberal he is proud enough to deem beneath his notice; and were he to address them at all, he says it should not be in his own words, but in those of the author to whom he is already indebted for his motto:—

" Magnos canibus circumdare saltus."

The following are the contents of the first book; and, as a specimen of the author's manner of treating his subject, and his mode of versification, an extract will be found from his first book, in our poetical department for this month.

Contents.—Subject proposed and invocation of nature.—Address to sportsmen in general, and fowlers in particular.—Justification of fowling, and reproof of prejudice and false sensibility, with a short admonition to sportsmen not to suffer the prey to linger in dying.—Grouse shooting throughout the day described.—Morning shooting—Finding the pack, and killing.—Reproof of boastful and exaggerating sportsmen.—Breaking off at noon, retiring to shelter, and fowler's repast.—Vulgar superstition, and belief of the existence of the heath hounds.—Simple and pedestrian fowling commended.—The grouse described, with directions for shooting.

ing. Afternoon shooting—finding and killing.—Breaking off at sunset, and return home.—Summer evening, with rural sights and sounds.—Concludes with the close of day.

HARMONIOUS CHANGE RINGING.

THE Oldham Youths, some time since, challenged the College Youths, change-ringers of Ashton-underline, to ring them Mr. John Holt's ten-course peal of grandsire tripples, of 504 changes each, making a complete peal of 5,040 harmonious changes.—The Collegians of Ashton-underline accepted the challenge to ring the above peal for 40 guineas, which was staked, and who have since completed it in the finest style of ringing, and in the quickest time, on the new peal of eight bells, at St. Michael's church, Flixton, on Friday June the 24th, 1808.—Weight of the tenor bell, 14cwt. 2qrs. 24lb. net bell metal.

This wager had caused a spirit of emulation between these two fine and loft-ringing Societies; and various trials were made of their skill previous to the decision.

The College Youths of Ashton-underline took the lead first (in practice); on Sunday the 15th day of May, they rung at their village, a complete peal of Mr. John Holt's grandsire tripples, in ten courses, containing 5,040 changes, which was finely completed in the quick time of two hours and 33½ minutes.

On Monday the 16th day of May, the Oldham Youths rung at their village, a complete peal of Mr. John Holt's grandsire tripples, in

ten courses, containing 5,040 changes, which was well rung in the quick time of two hours and 38 minutes.

On Tuesday the 24th day of May, the Ashton College Youths ascended St. Michael's tower, at their villa, and rung well Mr. John Holt's ten-course peal of grandsire tripples, containing 5,040 changes, in the quick time of two hours and 34 minutes.

Early in the morning of the 29th day of May, in honour of the old English oak, the Oldham Youths ascended St. Paul's Gothic tower, at their villa, and rung a fine peal of Mr. John Holt's grandsire tripples, composed of 5,040 good pleasing changes, which was completed in the quick time of two hours and 29½ minutes.

On the morning of the same day, the College Youths of Ashton-underline, ascended St. Michael's fine Gothic tower, also in honour of the ancient English oak, and most nobly brought round a fine-rung peal of Mr. John Holt's grandsire tripples, in ten courses, containing 5,040 beautiful changes, in the quick time of two hours and 29¼ minutes.

On Saturday June 4th, in honour of his Majesty's birth-day, the Oldham Youths again ascended the Gothic tower at their village, and completed a fine peal of Mr. John Holt's grandsire tripples, containing 5,040 changes, which they finely rung in the quick time of two hours and 29¼ minutes—in the ten-course method.

On Thursday June the 9th, from a friendly invitation, the College Youths of Ashton-underline paid a visit to Mottram, in Cheshire, and a select eight of them ascended the neat and Gothic tower at St. Mary's Church, in that romantic village.

village, and rung a charmingly fine peal, in ten courses, of Mr. John Holt's grandsire tripples; in the very wonderful quick time of two hours and 28½ minutes:—The average speed of ringing this peal was thirty-five changes each minute, and towards the close of the peal, thirty-six changes a minute, being the best and quickest ringing ever performed in this kingdom.

The College Youths of Ashton-underline, being highly pleased with their excursion to, and treatment at the romantic village of Hilly Mottram, in Longdendale, Cheshire, they paid a second visit on Sunday morning, June the 19th, and highly delighted the natives in that part of the country with another remarkably fine-rung peal of Mr. John Holt's grandsire tripples, in ten courses, containing 5,040 harmonious changes, which they completely and most nobly again brought round in the astonishing quick time of two hours and 29½ minutes.—Weight of the Mottram tenor, 19 cwt. net bell metal.

THE ARTISTS WERE AS UNDER:—

Ashton College Youths.

Treble.—Mr. Jonathan Wild
2. Mr. Thomas Dewsnap
3. Mr. Samuel Moss
4. Mr. Thomas Hammond
5. Mr. Aaron Walker
6. Mr. Joseph Burgess
7. Mr. James Moss
Tenor.—Mr. Charles Greaves
Conductor.—Mr. Jonathan Wild.

Weight of the Ashton tenor, 12 cwt. net bell metal.

Oldham Youths.

Treble.—Mr. James Taylor
2. Mr. Robert Coope
3. Mr. Henry Hindle
4. Mr. Joseph Newton

5. Mr. William Rigby
6. Mr. Joshua Kershaw
7. Mr. John Whitehead
Tenor.—Mr. James Gartside
Conductor.—Mr. Joseph Newton.
Weight of Oldham tenor, 13 cwt. net bell metal.

The above eight peals being rung for practice, we must now approach towards the day of decision.—Both companies of ringers met on the ground at Flixton, on Thursday, June the 23d, 1808, and each alternately ascended the Gothic tower of St. Michael's Church, and rung practice peals, according to their articles of ringing, during the day.

On Friday, June the 24th, early in the morning, both societies met and cast lots, which company was to ring first.—The Oldham Youth, had the first inning, and they ascended St. Michael's Gothic towers at this village, and completely brought round a fine and true-rung peal of Mr. John Holt's grandsire tripples, in ten courses, containing 5,040 changes, which they performed according to the articles of agreement, and in the quick time of 2 hours, 32 minutes, and 50 seconds.

The College Youths of Ashton-underline, ascended St. Michael's Gothic tower, and rung a superlatively fine half peal, (say 2,520 changes) made the single in fine stile, and rang most nobly fine to the 21st treble lead of the sixth course, when the conductor of the peal called a bob two treble leads too soon, which threw the bells out of course, and then they were obliged to call bobs irregularly afterwards for some time.—The two last courses were rung true, after all the miscalling; the single at last completely made; and round at the change of 5,012, being the two

A a   treble

treble leads short of the whole peal, (or 28 changes) which intitled the Oldham Youths to the wager of 40 guineas, and was paid to them by the decision of the four censurers and umpire, who were as follow :—

Ashton-underline Censurers.

Mr. Thomas Ogden, of Ashton-underline.

Mr. John Moss, of Ashton-underline.

Oldham Censurers.

Mr. Daniel Bamford, of Middleton.

Mr. John Amellows, of Oldham.

Ashton Treble Lead taker down.

Mr. Joseph Tebbs, from Leeds.

Oldham Treble Lead taker down.

Mr. Jonathan Hague, of Manchester.

The Grand Umpire for both parties, and sworn to do justice, was Mr. Joseph Grayson, silver plater, of Birmingham, but formerly of Sheffield, Yorkshire.

The Ringing Artists for this Wager, at Flixton, were as follow :

Ashton College Youths.

Treble.—Mr. Jonathan Wild

2. Mr. Thomas Dewsnap
3. Mr. Samuel Moss
4. Mr. Thomas Hammond
5. Mr. Aaron Walker
6. Mr. Joseph Burgess
7. Mr. James Moss

Tenor.—Mr. Charles Greaves

Conductor.—Mr. Jonathan Wild.

Oldham Youths.

Treble.—Mr. James Taylor

2. Mr. Robert Coope
3. Mr. Henry Hindle
4. Mr. Joseph Newton
5. Mr. William Rigby
6. Mr. Joshua Kershaw
7. Mr. John Whitehead

Tenor.—Mr. James Gartside

Conductor.—Mr. Joseph Newton.

Weight of the tenor, 14cwt. 2qrs. 24lb. net bell metal.

Time of Ashton ringing, 2 hours, 34 minutes, and 2 seconds.

The Society of College Youths of Ashton-underline received the following flattering testimonial from Ralph Wright, Esq. Justice of Peace, at the village of Flixton, on this ringing occasion.

" Mr. Wright has the honour to present his best compliments to Major Lees, and to request that he will take the trouble to divide *ten guineas* among the Ashton-underline ringers, as a small compliment due to their merit, on this day, in delighting the village of Flixton with their most excellent peal of Holt's grandsire tripples.

" *Flixton, Midsummer-Day,* 1808."

N. B. The inhabitants of Ashton-underline, and the change-ringers, conjecture that the conducting of the peal of Mr. John Holt's 5,040 changes, was wilfully lost at Flixton on the above day, and the Ashton College Youths purpose challenging the Oldham Youths to ring them again, the same peal, for *one hundred guineas,* on their own peal of eight bells, at Oldham, off hand, with another conductor.

DIALOGUE ON A DOG,

BETWEEN A LADY AND A LAWYER.

Lady F—.I Was walking, Sir, this morning, in the Mall, when a certain extraordinary Lady, whose actions are always of a very extraordinary nature, was pleased in a most peculiar manner to steal my lap-dog from me.

Counsellor

Counsellor G—. Steal your lap-
dog, Madam! I protest a very extraordinary action indeed! and
pray, Madam, what could induce
her to be guilty of such misbeha-
viour?

Lady F—. Induce her!— She
wants no inducement to be guilty
of any thing that is audacious and
impudent. But, Sir, I desire you
will immediately commence a suit
against her in Chancery, and push
the affair on with all possible rapidity, for I am resolved to recover
the dog if it costs me ten thousand
pounds.

Counsellor G—. Madam, undoubtedly your ladyship does right
to assert your property, for we
should all soon be reduced to a state
of nature, if there were no courts
of law, and therefore your ladyship is highly to be applauded.—
But there is something very peculiar in the nature of dogs. There
is no question, Madam, but they
are to be considered under the de-
nomination of property, and not to
be deemed things of no value, as
ignorant people foolishly imagine;
yet, I say, Madam, there is something very peculiar in their nature,
Madam. Their prodigious attachment to man inclines them to follow any body that calls them, and
that makes it so difficult to fix a
theft. Now if a man calls a sheep,
or calls a cow, or calls a horse,
why he may call long enough before they would come, because
they are not creatures of a *following nature;* and therefore our pe-
nal laws have made it felony with
respect to these animals; but dogs,
Madam, have a strange and undis-
tinguishing proneness to run after
people's heels.

Lady F—. Lord bless me, Sir,
what do you mean by following
people's heels? I do protest that

she took him up in her arms, and
carried him away in defiance of
me, and the whole Mall was witness of the theft.

Counsellor G—. Very well, Madam, very well; I was only stating
the case fully on the defendant's
side, that you might have a com-
prehensive view of the whole affair, before we came to unravel it
again, and shew the advantages on
the side of the plaintiff.—Now,
though a dog be of a *following
nature,* as I observed, and may
sometimes be tempted, and seduced, and inveigled, in such a
manner as makes it difficult—do
you observe me—makes it difficult
—I say, Madam, to fix a theft on
the person seducing, tempting, and
inveigling; yet, whenever property is discovered and claimed, if
the possessor refuses to restore it,
on demand, to the proper lawful
owner, there an action lies, and
under this predicament we shall
recover our lap-dog. If, therefore,
Madam, this lady, whoever she is,
A. or B. or any other name that
suits our purpose—if, I say, this
extraordinary lady, as your ladyship just now described her, took
your dog before witnesses, and refused to restore it, on demand, why
then we have a lawful action and
shall recover damages. Pray, Madam, can you swear to the identity
of the dog, if he should be produced in a court of justice?

Lady F—. Yes, Sir, I can
swear to him against a million, for
there never was so remarkable a
dear creature!

Counsellor G—. And pray, Madam, what is the colour of your
dog?

Lady F—. Black and white,
Sir.

Counsellor G—. A male or female, Madam?

A a 2　　　　*Lady*

Lady F—. I cannot positively tell, Sir.

Counsellor G—. Well, Madam, I will search my books for a precedent, and wait on you in a few days to receive your final determination.—I will certainly use my utmost endeavours to reinstate you in the possession of your lap-dog.—*(Aside)* What a b—!

EXTRAORDINARY DUEL.

A Very novel species of duel has lately taken place at Paris.—M. de Granpree and M. Le Pique having quarrelled about Mademoiselle Tirevet, a celebrated opera dancer, who was kept by the former, but had been discovered in an intrigue with the latter, a challenge ensued. Being both men of *elevated* mind, they agreed to fight in *balloons*, and in order to give time for their preparation, it was determined that the duel should take place on that day month. Accordingly, on the 3d of May, the parties met in a field adjoining the Thuilleries, where their respective balloons were ready to receive them. Each, attended by a second, ascended his car, loaded with blunderbusses, as pistols could not be expected to be efficient in their probable situations. A great multitude attended, hearing of the balloons, but little dreaming of their purpose; the Parisians merely looked for the novelty of a balloon race. At nine o'clock the cords were cut, and the balloons ascended majestically, amidst the shouts of the spectators. The wind was moderate, blowing from the N. N. W. and they kept, as far as could be judged, within about 80 yards of each other. When they had mounted to about the height of 900 yards, M. Le Pique fired his piece ineffectually; almost immediately after, the fire was returned by M. Granpree, and penetrated his adversary's balloon; the consequence of which was its rapid descent, and M. Le Pique and his second were both dashed to pieces on a house-top, over which the balloon fell. The victorious Granpree then mounted aloft in the grandest stile, and descended safe with his second, about seven leagues from the spot of ascension.

FEMALE PUGILISM.

Copy of an Advertisement in a Diurnal Print, in June, 1722.

CHALLENGE.

I Elizabeth Wilkinson, of Clerkenwell, having had some words with Hannah Hyfield, and requiring satisfaction, do invite her to meet me on the stage, and box me for *three guineas*; each woman holding *half-a-crown* in each hand, and the first woman that drops the money to lose the battle.

ANSWER.

I, Hannah Hyfield, of Newgate-Market, hearing of the resoluteness of Elizabeth Wilkinson, will not fail, *God willing*, to give her more blows than words—desiring home blows, and from her no favour; she may expect a good thumping.

FEAST

FEAST OF WIT.

THE Judges who do not attend in the Court of Session in Scotland, or give a proper excuse for their absence, are, by law, liable to a fine. This law, however, is never enforced, but it is common, on the first day of the Session, for the absentee to send an excuse to the Lord President. Lord Stonefield having sent such an excuse, on the President mentioning it, the late Lord Justice Clerk said, in his broad dialect, " What excuse can a stout fallow like that hae ?" —". My Lord," said the President, " he has lost his wife." The Justice replied, " Has he ? that is a gude excuse indeed ; I wish we had a' the same."

In Ireland, *flying the kite* is used as a cant phrase for raising money on accommodation bills. Lord Redesdale, when Irish Chancellor, enquiring, in the course of a trial, the meaning of the phrase, was informed by Mr. Plunket, that in England the wind raises kites, but in Ireland, *kites raise the wind.*

An Irish paper observes, that the best mode to *prevent* school-boys from being drowned, is to take care that they be not suffered to go *into the water.*

A FELLOW being recently condemned to be publicly whipped, addressed the Judge thus :—" My Lord, I'll submit to the punishment if you insist upon it, but I don't like it ; I might have been a good scholar now, if I had been fond of that *amusement* at school."

EXTRAORDINARY APOLOGY. — In a Welch paper, a country butcher asks pardon of a gentleman, for having sold to him, in Swansea market, a loin of veal, under the kidney fat of which he had stuffed a quantity of rags and paper so artfully, that the joint was dressed before the trick was discovered.

A STAGE-COACH master at Oxford, infected with the classical enthusiasm which pervades that celebrated seat of the muses, has affixed to his vehicles a recommendation from Martial — " *Ride si sapis.*"

ROYAL CHASTITY.—M. Segrais, in his Memoirs, relates that a certain preacher, making a panegyric on Louis XIII. and praising his chastity, gave the following example :—" This Prince, playing one day at shuttlecock with one of the ladies of the Court, and the shuttlecock having fallen into her bosom, she desired that his Majesty would take it out himself. But what did this chaste Prince? To avoid the snare, he took the tongs from the chimney corner, and by means of that instrument prevented the danger to which he might have otherwise been exposed from such a temptation."

ANECDOTE of Lord Shaftesbury. The history of this nobleman, in the Biographia Britannica, is a kind
of

of panegyric on him; but a *bon-mot* of himself conveys the truest idea of his character. Charles the Second said to him one day—" Shaftesbury, I believe thou art the wickedest fellow in my dominions."—He bowed, and replied, " Of a *subject*, Sir, I believe I am."

———

A YOUNG Lieutenant, meeting his Captain in the street, enquired where he meant to dine? " I shall step into the first coffee-house," said he. — " How does the *stuff* hold out (said the Lieutenant); have you enough for two?" —" Why, 'faith, the stuff runs rather low."—" Come, (said the other) I will take you to a *chupe* bit of a shop of my own, where you will be *well used*." He accordingly took him into a house, and ordered two plates of beef. The Captain, not at all satisfied, told his companion, that he had not used him well, in taking him to a cook's shop; " and especially (continued he) as I visit in this part of the town, and frequently dine with my Lord *Such-a-one*, in the next square. Suppose one of my Lord's servants should come in, and see me here?" Be *asy*, (returned the other) and *ate* your *bafe*. Do you think any of my Lord *Such-a-one's* servants would set a foot in such a *blackguard* place as this?"

———

A GENTLEMAN, who was going to a masquerade in Dublin, in the character of a piper, was stopped by the populace near Carlisle-bridge, to whom he very politely exhibited himself, and, in the spirit of his character, played them a tune on his bagpipes, which they were so well pleased with, that a party of coal-porters and flour-por-

ters insisted on taking him into a house on Aston's Quay, where they made him play for them until four o'clock in the morning, when falling out among themselves, and having got drunk, they broke his bagpipes and his piper's mask, and he retired to rest without the enjoyment of a ball or supper, for which he had purchased his ticket of admission.

———

A PUNSTER being told that a friend of his, a *clumsy fellow*, had distinguished himself in the management of a *convivial* company, replied, " No wonder; he was intended by *Nature* to be a *Chairman*."

———

ON A LATE PUBLICATION.

AH! Brewer W—B—D, are you one of those
That broach dull politics in duller prose?
Freely I'll spend my sixpence for your beer;
But sixpence for your nonsense is too dear.

———

RIGID ECONOMY.—The lady of a celebrated banker in town, who is no less desirous of accumulating wealth than her lord and master, engaged a maid-servant on trial for a month. The lady wishing to inform the woman on what principles the house was conducted, told her that the most rigid economy was observed therein— as for instance, the ashes are never to be carried away till they are thoroughly *riddled*, and in order to save your clothes from being soiled in the operation, your master has appropriated an old great coat, for the purpose of wrapping yourself in, and a large wig for covering your head.—" Alack-a-day!" observed the girl, " should I agree to this, I am afraid the next step of his economy would be, to search the

the great coat, and the wig too, for the remains of his cinders."

A NEW Mode of pounding Pigs. —The following is given as a specimen of a pig-fancier: — A small grunter, the property of a publican in Manchester, on one of the late race-days at that place, strayed near one of the sacred edifices, a church; the sexton, no doubt with the purest intention, though without warrant or mittimus, lodged the profane trespasser a prisoner in the church steeple, till a more convenient opportunity, when he might remove him by *habeas corpus*. As the *swinish multitude*, (according to Mr. Burke) are a little tenacious of their liberty, so it happened in this instance: the poor prisoner not only made a lusty outcry, but thrust his anti-mosaic carcase through one of the orifices of the belfry, and, like thousands of the world, fell a sacrifice to his struggles for freedom, fatally tumbling upon some iron spikes beneath.

THE following curious and laconic letter was sent, some years since, to Mr. Herbert, manager of an itinerant company of players, by Mr. Collins, better known by the name of Brush Collins, lately deceased:—

" Sir — Fortunately for your company, I am disengaged. I am up to Melpomene, down upon Thalia, twig Farce, and smoke Pantomime. They say I am a very good figure, and I never saw a looking-glass that contradicted that report. To have me now is your time or never.—Your's, &c."

A GENTLEMAN being told that the poor Curate's horse was dead, and having purchased a black pad of the name of Beelzebub, said, " Send *Beelzebub* to the Curate, and tell him to work him as long as he lives."

PETITION of the Tutelary Genius of Hyde-park, to the Surveyors of Woods and Forests—*Humbly sheweth*—That the domain, commonly called Hyde-park, including Rotten-row, the Serpentine, and thence extending to Kensington-gardens, and thence round to Oxford-road and eastward by Park-lane, has, from time immemorial, been deemed a free open park, with liberty of ingress and egress to all his Majesty's well-dressed and well-mounted liege subjects, male and female, of all ages and sexes, without discrimination, and that one-half of the good citizens of London have no idea of woods, or forests, or lakes, or rivers, but what they receive from their Sunday visits to said Park.

That it has been the favourite haunt of lovers, accustomed in all ages to unfold their passion, unheeded and unobserved by every eye but that of the sparrow that chirrups on the branches of the spreading oak, or the snow-white swan who glides majestic upon the bosom of the river.

That it has been long the seat where wounded honour has sought reparation, exhibiting deeds of courage worthy of the greatest heroes.

That the betrayed damsel, the dishonoured husband, the broken merchant, and the despairing lover, have been accustomed to seek in Hyde-Park a *quietus* for all their cares, by suspension from a tree, or a plunge in the Serpentine.

That the *Belles* and *Beaux* of the metropolis here mix in sweet confusion; the city fair catching the *airs* of the West end of the town;

town; while consumption, care, and loss of appetite, vanish before the breezes that play without restraint or limit over its verdant surface.

"Your Suppliant further sheweth, that a rumour prevails of an intention to erect a line of large houses round the said Park, by means whereof it will become a mere inclosure, differing only in extent from Leicester-fields or Golden-square, and that the benefits and advantages above stated, with many others, will thus cease and determine.

That a lady or gentleman can, in such event, no longer make love in Hyde Park, without being exposed to the malice of all the old maids in the row.

That the desperate and unfortunate cannot drown themselves but in sight of the public.

That the man of honour cannot be shot, or shoot his antagonist, in private; and Chalk Farm must possess a monopoly of duellists.

That the air, now fresh as the breeze from the mountain, must lose its purity, and become mixed with the steam from the luxurious kitchens and fœtid offices of the surrounding edifices.

That Hyde Park, long a scene of health and recreation, will thus lose all its attractions, and with its attractions all its visitors and admirers.

Your Suppliant, therefore, humbly hopes, that said plan of Brick and Mortar may not be adopted; And your Suppliant will ever pray.

A PUBLICAN's Reasons for not permitting Card-playing in his House.—" You amused yourselves all last night upon *All-Fours*, but I am determined not to *Put* up with such behaviour any longer.

What is worse than all the rest, you even *Brag* that you have not been in bed all night. Gentlemen, I like to *Laugh* and *lay down* as well as any of you, but I can see no reason why I am to sit up all the night, and not have a *single deal* in *Matrimony*. You are all *knaves*, from the *highest* to the *lowest* of you, and you must not think to make *game* of me in this manner. By such *tricks* as these you will forfeit all your *honours*, and dig your graves with your own *spades*. If your pockets were full of *diamonds*, you are within an *ace* of ruining yourselves. In short, you deserve to be well *clubbed*, for having the *heart* to treat me in this manner, and the *curse of Scotland* attend you; for the *Deuce* take me if I will bear it any longer, but will *Drive the Knaves out of Doors*."

———

A SOLDIER, the first time he was at a battle, said, " Of all the sports of the field, *man-shooting* he liked the least."

———

STRONG BEER, AN EPIGRAM.

NO wonder, cries Ned, we're poison'd by beer,
If you look to the process of hops thro' the year:
'Tis blubber and horse-dung that rear up the plant,
Which is brought to perfection by brimstone, you'll grant.
But the Brewer, not finding these nauseous enough,
Has *Cocculus Indicus, Quassia,* and *Snuff.*

———

DR. Browne courted a lady unsuccessfully for many years, during which time he every day drank her health; but, being observed at last to omit the custom, a gentleman said, " Come, Doctor, your old toast." " Excuse me," said he; " as I cannot make her *Brown*, I'll *toast* her no longer."

WIN-

WINNERS OF ROYAL PLATES, AT YORK,

FROM 1710 TO 1807.

To the EDITOR of the SPORTING MAGAZINE.

SIR,

THE following is a complete List of the Horses, &c. that won the Royal Plates at York,* from their first commencement, in the year 1710, to 1807, inclusive; the insertion of which in your next Number, will oblige Your old Correspondent,

W. P.

York, July 20, 1808.

1710 Sir Matthew Peirson's Bay Bolton,† by Grey Hautboy
1711 Mr Hall's Sampson, }
1712 Mr Watson's Farmer, } Sires unknown
1713 Mr Græme's Champion, by the Harpun Arabian
1714 Mr Childers's Duchess, Mr Peirson's Foxhunter, Mr Young's Shy, and Mr Moore's Dragon, with two others that were distanced, started; when the former two ran four heats, and the latter two ran three heats each; after which the Plate was disputed, in consequence of the riders of Duchess and Foxhunter, Robert Hesletine, and Stephen Jefferson, shewing foul play, and fighting on horseback:—A law-suit ensued, and all bets were agreed to be withdrawn:—It was afterwards agreed by the Court (before which the cause was heard) that the Plate should be divided, when the owners of the above horses, &c. sold their shares for 25gs each; two of whom were purchased by the Duke of Rutland, one by the Earl of Carlisle, and the other by Sir William Lowther, Bart. who agreed that the same should be run for over again in the year 1719, by horses, &c. of their own breed.

---

* The first commencement of the Races at York, took place in the year 1709, and the Course was over Clifton and Rawcliffe Ings, about a mile and a half North of the City.—In the year 1710, the first Gold Cup given by her Majesty Queen Anne was of 60gs value; and afterwards of 100gs value, and run for by six-year old horses, &c. carrying 12st each, the best of three four-mile heats. In 1721, his Majesty, George I. gave 100gs in specie, in lieu of the Gold Cups.

† Bay Bolton was only five years old, and beat eight six-year old horses, a case at that time very rare, especially in a county then renowned above all others in the kingdom, for producing high-bred horses, and the greatest number of them.—He was sold to the Duke of Bolton, who sent him to Newmarket, where he won a match against the Duke of Somerset's Wyndham; one against Sir M. Peirson's Merlin; and two against Mr. Frampton's Dragon.—He was afterwards a famous Stallion.

1715 Duke of Rutland's Brocklesby, by Mr Curwen's Bay Barb
1716 Mr Honywood's True-Blue, by his White Turk, *out of Mr*
   Bowes's Byerly Turk Mare.
1717 Duke of Ancaster's Great-Head.—Sire unknown
1718 Duke of Rutland's Coneyskins, by Mr Lister's Turk
1719 In July, Lord Carlisle's Buckhunter, by the Bald Galloway.—This
   was the Gold Cup alluded to above.
1719 In August, Lord Carlisle's Buckhunter*
1720 Mr George Witty's Merryman, (afterwards called the Witty Gelding)—Sire unknown
1721 Mr Raikes Fulthorpe's Woodcock, by Merlin
1722 Mr Duncombe's Hazard, *alias* Dart, by the Bald Galloway,
1723 Lord Tankerville's Sophonisba, by Mr Dyer's Dimple
1724 Mr Honywood's Young True-Blue, by his White Turk
1725 Mr Williams's Squirrel, by Snake
1726 Sir Michael Newton's Bald Jack, } Sires unknown
1727 Mr Rickaby's Kiss-in-a-Corner, }
1728 Mr. Alcock's Spot, by his Arabian, (sire of Old Crab)
1729 Mr Bathurst's Robinson Crusoe, by Jigg, (sire of Partner)
1730 Mr Humberson's Stump, by Mr Darley's Manica
1731† Lord Lonsdale's Monkey, by his Lordship's Bay Arabian
1732 Mr Bathurst's Diamond, by Jew Trump
1733 Duke of Bolton's Syphax, by Bay Bolton
1734 Captain Appleyard's Conqueror, by Lord Portmore's Fox

---

* Buckhunter, *alias* the Carlisle Gelding, also won the King's Plates
at Lincoln, at Newmarket in October, and at Newmarket in April following :—After which, he won several Plates and Matches there, and
supported the severity of running trials at Newmarket for many years;
and when sold from thence, though *fourteen* years old, he won *eighteen*
Plates and Prizes; and when running for a Plate at Salterley-Common,
near Stilton, he broke a leg, (after winning the first heat) which deprived him of his life in the year 1731.—Though Buckhunter was in a
very high form, yet there were horses of his time that would beat him;
but he had rarely an equal, and hardly ever a superior, with relation to
those principal points of being capable of running with all degrees of
weight, of supporting repeated heats, of travelling and running often,
and continuing the whole for so great a number of years, and to the age
that he did,—The excessive spirits of his youth rendered him almost
ungovernable, and caused him to be castrated, which lost to breeders a
promising English Stallion. Buckhunter was rode for the above King's
Plates by Mr. Match'em Timms, who was greatly esteemed as a Jockey,
and afterwards for training.—*Pick's Turf Register.*

† At York, in August, 1730, in consequence of heavy rains, the
River Ouse was so much swelled as to overflow great part of the Course
on Clifton and Rawcliffe Ings, which made it necessary to postpone the
racing for Wednesday's Plate until Saturday:—After which, it was
agreed, that the Races, should, in future, be run for over Knavesmire, a
short distance South from York; where a Course was planned by Mr.
Alderman Telford, and very much approved of.

1735 Lord

1785 Lord Portmore's Croke, by Mr Darley's Skipjack
1736 Duke of Bolton's Goliah,* by Lord Portmore's Fox
1737 Mr Panton's Cato, by Mr Croft's Partner
1738 Lord Weymouth's Scrutineer, by Mr Darley's Aleppo
1739 Mr Proctor's Smallhopes,† by Mr Bartlett's Childers
1740 Mr Marley's Ragman, by Young Greyhound
1741 Mr Constable's Cottingham, by Mr Hartley's Blind Horse
1742 Mr Croft's Forester, by Mr Hartley's Blind Horse
1743 Mr Hutton's Phantom, by Hobgoblin
1744 Miss Betty Routh's Othello, by Hawksworth's Oroonoko
1745 Mr Vavasour's Champion, by the Duke of Bolton's Goliah
1746 Sir Marmaduke Wyvill's Primate, by Young Belgrade
1747 Sir W Middleton's Squirrell, by a Son of Bay Bolton
1748 Lord Portmore's Highlander, by Victorious
1749 Mr Jenison's Joseph Andrews, by Roundhead
1750 Mr Routh's Looby, by the Duke of Bolton's Looby
1751 Sir William Middleton's Thwackum,‡ by a Son of Bay Bolton
1752 Sir Marmaduke Wyvill's Antelope, by Young Belgrade
1753 Lord Rockingham's Scampstone-Cade, by Cade
1754 Mr Fenwick's Duchess, by Lord Portmore's Whitenose
1755 Sir William Middleton's Whistlejacket, by the Duke of Bolton's Mogul.
1756 Mr Williams's Forester, by Mr Croft's Forester
1757 Duke of Kingston's Prince T'Quassaw, by Snip
1758 Duke of Devonshire's Atlas, by Babram
1759 Mr William Preston's (of York) Hero, by Cade
1760 Mr Swinburn's Belford, by Cade
1761 Mr J. B. Warren's Fearnought, by Regulus
1762 Duke of Kingston's Manby, by Blank
1763 Mr Sotherton's Elephant, by Regulus
1764 Hon. Francis Charteris's Favourite, by Tartar
1765 Hon. Francis Charteris's Blank, by Blank
1766 Mr Egerton's Aurelianus, by Attilus, (a Son of Regulus)
1767 Mr Beatson's Alexander, by Lot, (a Son of Young Sweepstakes)
1768 Mr Osbaldeston's Ragman, by Matchless
1769 Mr Bland's Diana, by Regulus.

* It was a remarkable circumstance, that in the year 1736, there were only *ten* Royal Plates in England, for six-year old horses, &c. 12st, the first of which was won by Mr. Hartley's Whitefoot, at Newmarket, in April, and the remaining *nine* by the Duke of Bolton's Goliah and Merry-Andrew.

† Smallhopes beat Lord Portmore's Spectre, (&c.) who was backed at 20 to 1.—During the time of running, there were thirty coaches, with six horses to each, upon the Course, besides a great number of others with four horses, &c.

‡ Thwackum was the first horse, and the only one in this list, that walked over for the King's Plate at York, until 1770.

To be concluded in our next.

YOUNG

YOUNG DUCKS ALARMED.

AN ENGRAVING.

THIS pretty plate, as may be observed by the writing, is from a painting by Mr. Northcote, and engraved by H. R. Cook. It is a fanciful production, and as the subject explains itself, illustration is unnecessary.

ECCENTRIC CHARACTER.

MR. Gordon, founder of the hospital that goes by his name in the city of Aberdeen, was, perhaps, one of the greatest misers that ever appeared in any country, and, from his extreme attachment to riches, is still spoken of by the name of *Sillerton.*

This eccentric being was a well-informed man, and fond of reading, but would on no account be at the expence of a candle:—As good luck would have it, a cobler lived immediately below the miser's garret ; Sillerton bored through his floor, and thus availing himself of Crispin's lamp, enjoyed his favourite amusement. The use of a fire he never indulged himself in, even during the extreme rigours of winter. As a substitute for this necessary element, he kept in his garret a hamper, or creel, full of stones, [which he carried about the room on his back, until he felt himself sufficiently warm. A pennyworth of *butter-milk,* in summer, generally served to dilute all his victuals for eight days. One Monday, whilst Sillerton was from home, a half-starved rat got at the precious bowl, and made a greedy repast (such a delicious banquet seldom fell to his lot in this mise-

rable abode of famine) but having over-ate itself, it tumbled into the bowl, and, like Gray's immortal tabby, met its destined fate! Sillerton returned immediately after the melancholy accident happened, ran to his bowl, found it half empty, and the expiring robber drenched in the costly liquid. The enraged miser seized the rat by the head with one hand, whilst with the other he squeezed the milk into the bowl from the shoulders to its tail, saying, " D—n ye, ye sha'nt get off with that !" And then making the ill-fated animal disgorge what it had drank, thus preserved a scanty supply for his porridge during the remainder of the week ! !

This wretched character at last died of a surfeit, after *dining at the house of a friend.*

RURAL SPORTS.

AT Thrale Fair, Somersetshire, on the Monday, there was an unusual display of gymnastic talent, to as numerous a field of amateurs as ever was witnessed on any similar occasion. At six o'clock in the morning the pastimes commenced, with a damsel-race for *chemises ;* then several matches of single-stick playing took place for various prizes, the greater part of which were won by Male and Robson, scientific players. A pitched battle was fought at noon, betwixt Robinson, a yeoman from the west, and Harrold, a coachman, for 20 guineas a side. This match was diverting to the lovers of the sport, as it lasted two hours without intermission. The combatants were fresh young men of promise, who had never before been pitted, and they proved themselves

selves to possess no inconsiderable knowledge at *giving* and *taking*. Each alternately had the best of the contest, and their powers did not forsake them until the combat had lasted one hour and a half. The contest was continued half an hour longer, when Robinson was declared the victor.

At Boughton-Green Fair, the building of Saunders's Booth for the exhibition of his company of Equestrians, in consequence of being too much crowded with company, gave way, and many persons were precipitated in the space below. The wife of a Quarter-Master had a foot completely severed from the leg at the ancle joint; a man had his thigh broken, and his wife her leg so dreadfully crushed, that it was obliged to be amputated; three other persons had limbs broken, and many were shockingly bruised.

ATTACHMENT IN DOGS.

INNUMERABLE instances of this animal's sagacity have been produced in every age, but a stronger instance than the following, has, perhaps, never yet been heard of.

A few months ago, the Rev. Duncan Ferguson, who was Missionary in the Island of Bonbicula, South Uist, Scotland, on Queen Ann's Royal Bounty, being taken very ill, and not entertaining any hopes of recovery, he signified his wish that his body should not be interred among the Roman Catholics in that Island, but that it should be carried to Carnish, and interred in the magnificent but ruined cathedral of that place. After his death, his corpse was accordingly laid in the ancient consecrated ground, which was distant five miles from the place where he died, and was separated therefrom by an arm of the sea, fordable indeed at low water, but at high water sufficient to navigate a vessel of 400 tons burthen. The only faithful companion that Mr. Ferguson found in that island was a large Newfoundland dog, which did eat of his own meat, drank of his own cup, and lay in his bosom, and was unto him as a child. This grateful animal followed his lamented master's body to the grave, where he remained howling a day and a night. —A neighbour, more kind than others, pitying the attached, but starving animal, forcibly dragged him away, and carried him to his own home, from whence, after refusing to take any nourishment, taking the first opportunity of flying to the speechless tomb, he swam across the sound, and, on the fourth day after his master's interment, he was found also dead, and lying across the grave.

A singular instance of the sagacity of a Newfoundland dog occurred a few days since on the River:—As Mr. Cook, who keeps a tavern, in Cleveland-street, and a party of friends, were returning from Richmond, where they had been spending the day, the boat upset a little below Kew Bridge, in consequence of Mr. C. (who is a very corpulent man) shifting from his side too suddenly. Having a Newfoundland dog on board, the faithful animal immediately laid hold of his master, and took him on shore, and returned again with an astonishing speed to the boat, and continued to go backwards and forwards until he had rescued six men from their perilous situations in less than a quarter of an hour, to the admiration of a multitude of spectators. *SPORT-*

SPORTING INTELLIGENCE.

THE mowers have, this summer, been dreadful enemies to the incubation of partridges. In many places, these birds have suffered their heads to be cut off with the scythe, rather than be driven from their eggs, some of which were afterwards taken from the nests, and have been hatched under hens.

THE Duke of Queensberry, so long known on the town and on the turf, where, during more than sixty years, he has held a distinguished place, is much declined in his health. His faculties continue, however, at near eighty-four, to be as vigorous as ever.

LORD Middleton has taken the moors belonging to the late Mr. Darley, of Aldby Park, which are held to be amongst the best in England. His Lordship having sold his stag-hounds, has established a pack of fox-hounds in the country formerly hunted by Lord Vernon.

IRVINE Races, Scotland, were attended by a very numerous and gay assemblage of nobility and gentry. A large subscription is raised for next year's sport; and the Stewards are, Lord Elphinstone, Sir John Maxwell, Colonel Brisbane of Brisbane, and Robert Wallace, Esq. of Kelly.

STAMFORD.—The Races were most numerously and fashionably attended; the horses, &c. were in high condition, and the heats extremely well contested. The Macaroni Stakes (rode by gentlemen)

afforded great amusement; and the noted Jeffery Gambolla, rode by Dr. John Willis, won, it was supposed, entirely by jockeyship, as the race was most arduously contested at the distance-post; and the odds were very high on Mr. S. S. Prime, who rode Longitude, a beaten horse, in a very superior style. Mr. Prime and Dr. John set off immediately after the race, to ride at Bibury.

AN unfortunate accident happened at the above Races. Shortly previous to the appointed time of the horses starting on Monday, the barouche belonging to Arthur Annesley, Esq. was overturned, and several ladies in it were thrown out with violence. Miss Fanny O'Brien, we are concerned to say, was much hurt by the fall.

AT Kelso Races, the two 50l. Plates were won by Mr. Collinson's ch. h. Streamer, by Star, 5 yrs old, beating several others.—*A more particular account will be given in our next.*

THERE was much company at Lamberton Races; and we are informed that next year there will be four 50l. Plates run for, and a Hunters' Stakes, to which there are already ten subscribers.

THERE will be no Races at Musselburgh this year, as the Course will not be completed in due time.

ROMNEY Races afforded but little sport, there being only two well-contested heats. The only accident of any consequence observed

served on the ground, was the up-setting of a respectable country banker's gig, which was actually dashed to pieces. He had en-trusted the reins to a military friend, generally supposed a good whip, but as it was after dinner, we imagine the Son of Mars had sacrificed too freely to the God of Wine. We are happy to add, nei-ther of the gentlemen was mate-rially hurt.

A writer for the London news-papers at Brighton, thus announces the coming races at that place:— "The Pavilion Stakes at Brighton Races will be one of the most spor-tive of the season. Some of the first horses in the kingdom will start for these Stakes, among which are, the Duke of Grafton's Van-dyke; the beaten favourite for the Derby Stakes at Epsom, and Pan, the winner of those Stakes. The interest is excited betwixt these horses, both of which are entered for the Pavilion Stakes. The sporting men at Epsom backed Vandyke against the field, and the betting was 20 to 1 against Pan, which horse is said to have won in the following manner :—Vandyke was making play during the last half mile, and, amongst the multi-plicity of horses, none were sup-posed to have any chance except one, which Vandyke's rider had got the whip hand of; and, to make a tolerable race, he held Vandyke back, whilst the other horse was trying every effort to win. During this contention, Pan's jockey, a cunning Yorkshireman, rode on the right side of the other two horses, and when within a few yards of the coming-in post, let loose and won the heat, without Vandyke's jockey being aware that Pan was near him, his attention

being stedfastly fixed on the horse before described.—Some thousands are depending on the next race, and the odds are betted freely on Vandyke.

WEDNESDAY, the 6th inst. was Huntington Feast—a pleasant and salubrious village near this city.— On the occasion, Mr. Knapton, of the Star Inn, well known to most gentlemen of the turf, gave a most liberal entertainment to many of his friends at his farm there ; and who were much gratified by a view of some of his blood stock by Delpini and Paynator ; two colts by the latter are the most promising we have for a long time seen, espe-cially the brown colt, out of a Be-ningbrough mare ; grandam, sister to Old Tatt. During the course of the afternoon, many loyal and sporting toasts were drank ; and his friends from York and the neighbourhood returned to their homes, highly gratified with the entertainment of the day.—*York Herald.*

AT the Beverley Midsummer Fair, the show of horses was pretty good for the time of the year, and all the good ones of sufficient size and bone for barouche-horses were greedily purchased at high prices : these are now a never-failing ar-ticle.

DRIVING.—This rage is increas-ing daily. The gentlemen now all affect the dress of *coachmen*; and friends who attend them imitate the appearance of the *mail-guard*, with a strap and a horn.—The style for the carriage is to be a re-semblance of the mail, in colour and furniture, and the box to have a *sack-cloth* for a seat, and the pole to have *chains* to it, which is called—" the music of the bars."

Os

On Wednesday, the 29th ult. thirteen Members of the Whip Club assembled in Audley-square, with their carriages and four.—They started about two o'clock from thence for Bedfont, to dine at the Black Dog Inn. Sir Henry Peyton led the way with his four handsome greys.

A new Club is just established in town, in opposition to the Barouche Driving Club, called " The Four-in-hand." They are violent opponents of each other in the articles of reins, whips, and harness, but it is difficult to say which Club " kicks up the greatest dust."

On Monday, the 27th ult. a well-contested foot-race was run on Leicester course, between Jas. Shipley, of Nottingham, and the Brighton Shepherd. The distance was seven score yards, for 120 guineas a side. The odds were, previous to the day of the race, 5 to 4 against Shipley, but on the day of starting, the odds turned in favour of him. It was won by Shipley only by two yards.—Shipley beat the Brighton Shepherd once before, on Lord's Ground.

Some time ago, a singular wager was laid by a Mr. Kerr, of Greek-street, Soho, that he would start from Storey's Gate, and walk once round the railings of St. James's Park, three times over Westminster-bridge, three times over Blackfriars-bridge, three times round St. Paul's, three times over London Bridge, and row a wherry through the three bridges, within two hours. He started on Saturday morning, the 2d instant, at six o'clock, and arrived at Storey's Gate twenty minutes within the time. A number of bets depended.

On Monday, the 4th instant, a trotting match against time took place on the Hampton-court Road, a mare, the property of Mr. Nooks, of Holborn, having been backed to perform four miles in fifteen minutes, for 50gs. The match was a very close one, and lost only by a few seconds. Before starting, bettings were in favour of the performance.

A foot race, for ten guineas, distance forty rods, took place on Thursday the 14th instant, in the Dean John Field, Canterbury, between Mr. John Chapman, and Mr. Allen Engeham, which was won with ease by the latter; although Chapman was to give his antagonist one rod and a half at coming in.

The foot race between Benjamin Coleman, of Canterbury, and —— Milgate, of Maidstone, was decided on Saturday evening, the 9th instant, in favour of Coleman, who beat his antagonist very easily.

During the present month, a young man from Hampshire, undertook, for a wager of ten guineas, to go from London to the eight-mile stone on Shooter's Hill, and back again, in one hour and three quarters; when he started at fifteen minutes past five o'clock, arrived at Shooter's Hill eight minutes after six; and after resting a few minutes started afresh, and arrived at the starting-post five minutes before seven.

Fatal Bet.—On Friday evening, the 8th instant, about seven o'clock, a gentleman undertook, for a trifling wager, to over-leap the railing of St. James's Park, opposite the Guard House, Buckingham Gate—the gentleman took a smart race, but unfortunately not clearing the rails, one of his legs was completely broke, and he was besides much hurt.

hunt. He was immediately carried in a state of insensibility to the Westminster Hospital.

A RACE of one mile against time was performed on the 27th instant, in the Park, by Mr. Torrens, of St. James's, who undertook for a stake of 20 guineas, to do the mile in five minutes, at two starts, and to win half a minute. He did the first half mile in two seconds less than half the time, and he did the first mile in four minutes and forty-five seconds. Bets were against the performance.

ON Monday, the 27th ult. a wager for 20 guineas, was decided, by setting off three pigeons, belonging to a young man named Wilson, in the Borough, who undertook, for the above sum, that they would fly 35 miles in one hour. They were accordingly set off the same evening, at five o'clock, five miles beyond Tunbridge Wells, and arrived again at the residence of their owner in the short space of 53 minutes, being seven minutes within the time allowed.

A PIGEON match took place at Hareford, Middlesex, on Friday, the 1st instant, for a wager of one hundred guineas, between Messrs. Joseph and Adams, known shots, at 21 birds each. It was an extremely well-contested match, as the last bird was required to be killed to give Mr. Adams the stake. Joseph killed 14 successive birds, and missed three others. His adversary killed 10, he having missed only the second and tenth birds.

PUGILISM.—On Monday morning the 11th instant, a pitched battle was fought at Roemash, Berks, for 50 guineas, between a Worcestershire professor, of six feet in height, of the name of Gee, against Rhodes,

a West-countryman. The match was made on the 16th ult. between Captain Stunt, on the part of Gee, and a gentleman of the name of Glede, on the part of Rhodes, who is no more than five feet six inches in height. The exhibition was of very short duration, Gee having been beat in a manner not often witnessed, in a few minutes. Rhodes, who is a teacher of this elegant pastime, planted his hits, and got away with such dexterity, that his adversary, who proved a game novice, was vanquished in twelve minutes, and carried away in a state which will not induce him again to enter into a similar combat.

ON Monday afternoon, the 27th ult. a desperate battle was fought near Pennyfields, Poplar, between two journeymen carpenters, of the names of Smith and White. Smith received a violent blow on the head, and was killed on the spot. White has surrendered himself.

ON Monday the 18th instant, a pitched battle, for 40l. was fought on Kirsted Green, Norwich, between William Underwood, a jobber, of Seething, and John Chase, a horse-breaker, of Brooke; the cause of their fighting was some words and a few blows on the Castle Ditches, the Saturday preceding. Hall was second to Underwood, and Warton to Chase. The battle commenced at fifteen minutes past five o'clock in the afternoon.—They fought eighty-five rounds; and it lasted two hours and two minutes. During the first sixty rounds, Chase was so much the favourite, that the bets were two to one in his favour; in the ten succeeding rounds he however received several severe blows in the face, and his right eye was completely closed.

C 2

closed. Underwood was considerably beaten about the body, had been much punished, in the cant phrase, by a blow under the left ear, and both of them appeared so weak as to be scarcely able to stand; the contest was, nevertheless, continued during fifteen more rounds, when Chase gave in, being completely exhausted. Upwards of 1000 amateurs were present.

MONDAY morning, July 25, a well-contested battle was fought in a field near Bermondsey, for ten pounds, between Wallis, a journeyman tanner, and Simmonds, a retail coal dealer, both residing near the scene of action. These two combatants, who are allowed to possess some scientific knowledge in the bruising art, met in consequence of a quarrel that happened on Saturday night, at a public-house in the neighbourhood, about a 5l. note, which the latter was accused of secreting, after it had been paid to him by the former in a mistake, when they agreed to decide the dispute by fighting for double the sum which had caused the altercation. At the commencement, odds were greatly in favour of Simmonds, till the sixth round, when he received a violent blow in his neck, which left him for several seconds unable to move: he, however, stood up again with great resolution, and after a few more severe rounds was, with seeming reluctance, obliged to yield to the superior skill of his antagonist.

A few days since, at a public house in Brighton, a man ate, in 7 minutes and a half, raw, with their whites, 101 hens' eggs, which were provided at the expence of a person in company, and severally broken into a cup for that purpose. After having swallowed 61, he voluntarily agreed to pay double the price of the other 40, if he failed in eating them; and having accomplished his task, offered a bet that he would eat 40 more.

A SMITH, in the employ of Messrs. Tomlins, London, on Friday se'nnight, undertook for a wager of one guinea (and the loser to pay for the beer) to drink a Butt of porter, of 108 gallons, in six days, being at the rate of eighteen gallons per day, and, extraordinary to say, he performed the disgusting feat with apparent ease.

A JOURNEYMAN carpenter, at Glasgow, lately, for a trifling wager, drank seven gills and a half of whiskey, and died in consequence a few hours after.

CRICKET.—The grand match at Lord's Ground, for one thousand guineas aside, on Thursday the 30th ult. and two following days, between nine of the Homerton Club, with T. Mellish, Esq. Lambert, Hammond, and T. Walker, against eight of the county of Essex, with Lord F. Beauclerc, B. Aislabie, Esq. G. Burrell, Esq. Beldam, and Pontifax, was decided in favour of the latter by forty-three runs.

ANOTHER grand match was played in the above ground, on Monday the 4th instant, and two following days, between eleven of the county of Surrey against eleven of all England, for one thousand guineas aside, which was decided in favour of the former, by sixty runs.

On Thursday the 7th instant, a grand match of cricket was played at Mr. Aram's Ground, Montpelier, for 300 guineas aside, between eleven gentlemen of the Friday's Mary-le-bone Club, and eleven gentlemen

gentlemen of the Tuesday's Montpelier Club, which was won by the latter by ninety runs.

Rowing Match.—On Tuesday, the 12th instant, at five o'clock in the afternoon, four four-oared cutters started from Blackfriars-bridge, to contend for a silver cup, given by the proprietor of a public-house at Milbank. The competitors, who were young aquatic amateurs, exhibited much strength and skill in their favourite amusement, having pulled to the King's Arms, on the Bank, in four heats, during which the Hope was the winning cutter. The three winning boats were to have decided the match by another heat, but it was considered too dark that night, and the parties agreed to defer the final trial till another day.—The River was covered with boats, and the Bank crowded by spectators.

A REMARKABLE instance of the fatal effects of the introduction of virulent animal matter into the human system, lately happened in the case of James Grey, a shepherd, in the service of Mr. Archbold, of Hetton; who, in the act of skinning a sheep which had died of disease (the rhotter ill), and was at the time in a state of putrescence, accidentally cut one of his fingers with the knife. The effect of the poisonous matter was truly astonishing; for on his going home in the evening he complained to his wife, "that he had inoculated himself, and already began to feel the bad consequences of it over all that side of his body on which the finger was cut." At five the next morning, medical assistance was sent for, but no kind of relief could be given, and with such rapidity did the mortific matter attack his system, that he became a corpse, in

the highest degree of putridity, by eleven o'clock that day, being less than twenty-four hours from the introduction of the matter.

A MELANCHOLY instance of the effects of canine madness has lately occurred in the neighbourhood of Ledbury.—A girl, about nine years old, whose parents live near the above place, was bit in the mouth, on the 15th of May, by a pointer bitch, which immediately afterwards ran off towards Ledbury, and in passing through the town, bit several dogs: the bitch was shot at and wounded, but made her escape; and it being apprehended she was mad, the girl was taken to the sea, and the usual methods of cure resorted to; a little time after her return home, symptoms were observed which rendered it more than probable that the remedies used had failed: she refused to eat her food, but snapped at it: during the forenoon on Wednesday she foamed at the mouth, and in the afternoon of the same day expired in convulsive agonies.

THAT symptoms arising from the bite of mad animals do not take place at certain periods, is demonstrated by the following occurrence:—On the 23d of March, a cow, the property of Mr. William Chalk, at Milton Chapel, was bit by a mad dog, which Mr. C. succeeded in killing at the time; from that period the cow has never shewn the least symptom of derangement, till the early part of the present week, when, from its wild conduct and appearance, with a spumous saliva running from its mouth, there remained no doubt but it was attacked with the hydrophobia; and it was consequently put into a place of confinement,

where

where it now remains in a state of raving madness.

HEDGEHOGS. — The following fact will prove, that these quadrupeds are not so innoxious as several of our historians declare them to be; and that charges alledged against their race, by gamekeepers, warreners, and others, may have been well founded. A short time since, a servant of Mr. Ellis, of Cooksbridge, Sussex, hearing a noise among some chickens, of a size nearly fit for the poulterer, got up to discover the cause, when he found a large female hedgehog, in the act of killing one of the fowls, and with the body of another which she had killed lying bleeding by her. Mr. Ellis had previously lost upwards of thirty young ducks, which he has now no doubt fell martyrs to the same depredator, or to some of her family. 'Tis unnecessary to add, that the man executed immediate vengeance on the prickly thief.

To the Curious in Natural History.—Lately were found, at Charlton, near Somerton, in a quarry belonging to Mr. John Cary, the vertebræ and part of the ribs of a large fish, enclosed in a fragment of a blue rock. This singular phenomenon is now in the museum of Lieutenant-Colonel Woodforde, at Galhampton, who supposes, from the magnitude of the spondyles, and the ribs, that the fish, when entire, must have measured nine or ten feet in length, and weighed two or three hundred pounds.

Court of Exchequer, July 13.—George Harrop was accused of shooting a hare, without a game certificate. No defence being made, he was convicted, and ordered to pay 20l. being the penalty appointed by Act of Parliament.—James Vade, and several others, were prosecuted for similar offences, found guilty, and ordered to pay their respective penalties.

SINGULAR OCCURRENCE.—A singular occurrence took place with the Edinburgh mail-coach, this month. A gentleman having a gun-case, had persuaded the servants of the coach to place it behind the coachman's seat, to prevent its rubbing. They had not proceeded far from Newark, where the passengers dine, when one of the outsides, who sat upon the roof, smoking his pipe, the embers fell on the gun-case, which was wrapped in a mat, containing under it three pounds of gunpowder, in separate parcels, one of which exploded, and blew the man from off the roof, and the driver and another on the box, precipitately into the road. The guard, with praiseworthy exertion, stopped the horses, and proceeded to cut away the gun-case, being told by the passengers that there was more powder; when another pound blew up, and on getting it off to the ground, the third exploded; fortunately no other injury was sustained than the coachman spraining his ancle, and the guard burning his hand. The rule with mail-coaches is, not to suffer any luggage on the outside; little can be said to a simple gun-case, though, in this instance, it might have proved serious; but the servants of public carriages are very reprehensible in suffering passengers to smoke on the journey.—A lamentable circumstance lately occurred, in the like manner, to a baggage-waggon in Hampshire.

POETRY.

POETRY.

THE HIGH COURT OF DIANA.

GROUSE SHOOTING.

From a Poem lately published, entitled
" Fowling."—(Vide p. 175.)

THE pleasing labours of the sylvan
   war
Wag'd by the fowler on the feather'd race,
Through the revolving seasons, summer's
   heat,
And winter's cold, I sing. Assist my
   song
Nature, great goddess! and if still thy
   pow'r
From the first dawn of reason my rapt
   soul
Has duly own'd, if ever to thy name,
Midst woods and wilds and streams, has
   offer'd up
With sacred rapture vows and incense
   meet,
On altars never rear'd by human hands,
Breathe thy blest influence on my rising
   strain!
Lovers of Nature, and the cheerful sports
Her wide domain affords! whether the
   chace
Fill your whole souls, or the swift silent
   folk
That dwell beneath the wildly wand'ring
   streams,
Oft mixing with the main, call forth your
   skill;
Attend my lay; let no ungen'rous pride,
No narrow prejudice, forbid your hearts
To sympathise with mine, for I your sports
Admire and love. Oft at the dawn of day,
Rous'd by the cheerful horn, my bounding
   steed
Receives me eager through the doubling
   chace
O'er hills and vales and far extended plains
Or deep entangled depth of woods remote,
With joyous heart to press the flying prey.
Nor less when genial spring revives the
   world,

And rising in a robe of fleecy clouds,
Spun by the dewy fingers of the south,
The sun begins his course, with silent step
Along the river's misty banks I stray
By many a pebbly ford, or rushing fall,
Or still deep pool by crowding alders
   screen'd,
And from his chrystal bed the spotted
   trout
Solicit, or the salmon silver bright.

But chief ye brother sportsmen to my
   song
Give ear; ye, who the far resounding gun
And faithful dog attending, love,—who
   chase
Nor o'er the earth, nor through the wat'ry
   plains
Your game, but through the spacious realms
   of air
Pursue it, and when vainly deem'd secure
On wind-swift pinions borne, with steady
   aim
Unerring hurl it to the ground, attend!
Whilst by experience led, the Muse un-
   folds
Your ever-varying sport; nor that alone,
But ev'ry rural charm shall she pourtray:
Now pausing on some mountain's brow
   sublime,
Now in some silent glen, or at the source
Of some clear nameless stream, the while
   she marks
Around her rise ten thousand sights and
   sounds
Unseen, unheard, unheeded, and un-
   known;
For she has witness'd oft the earliest dawn,
And latest close of day, with ev'ry change,
Through ev'ry season, beautiful and new,
Of vale or upland, field or forest wide.

Gen'rous and bold as varied is your
   sport,
Ye fowlers! manly strength your toils re-
   quire;
Defiance of the summer's burning sun
   And

And winter's keenest blast, of hail or
    storm,
Of ice, or driving snow; nor must the
    marsh
That quivers to your step deter you, nor
    the brake
That seems impervious, in whose thorny
    depth
You struggle long, and lose the cheerful
    day,
Till bursting through, again the sylvan
    scene,
Tranquil and smooth, re-opens to your
    view.
Well are those toils repaid, when by your
    side,
Or underneath your crouching spaniel's
    feet,
That strongly manifests his eager joy
With gestures eloquent, you view your
    prey
With rapt'ious eye,—or, when at day's
    decline,
Your bag well fill'd, with step sedate and
    slow
Along the beaten village path you pass,
As the light lingers in the western sky,
And see far off your dusky home arise.

Be silent Prejudice, nor call our sport
By any term severe ;—Bigot forbear ;
Nor dare arraign us at your angry bar!
Has the Creator made, himself, the grant
Of ev'ry living thing, fish, fowl or beast,
To lordly man, and shall your vain decree
Annul the grant? And ye, who proudly
    boast
Of feelings delicate, and most refin'd,
Ye male or female SENSIBILITISTS,
Who shrink and shudder at the fowler's
    sport,
Yet from your doors unpitied, unreliev'd
Turn the poor vet'ran, whose best blood
    has stream'd
For your security so ill deserv'd,
Blush and be silent:—blush again with
    shame
When you reflect upon the cruel cates
Your tables often yield, with which the
    Muse
Will not pollute her strain. One only
    hint
She gives ; sportsmen, be merciful in
    death,
Nor ever let your prey breathe out its life
In ling'ring agonies. Of this no more!
My eager muse invites you to the field:
What though beneath the lion's sultry
    sign
The fervid sun scorch the parch'd earth,
    abroad

Freely along the wide extended moors,
And on the heath-clad mountain uncon-
    fin'd
Refreshing breezes blow : thither the
    grouse
My untir'd footsteps leads, and ere the
    dews
Collected by the fost'ring night have fled,
I may remit my toil. O let the morn,
Ye sportsmen, let the fresh and whole-
    some morn,
Whether in Summer's frolic robe array'd
Or Winter's soberer garb, still call you
    forth !
And if the forespent night have witness'd
    nought
But healthful fare, and modest temp'rate
    cups,
Lib'ral, yet chasten'd, full without ex-
    cess,
No bell, nor loud alarum shall you need,
To rouse you from your sleep, refresh'd
    and clear,
And ready for the field. Observe the
    heavens ;
Nor yet disdain the aid of the small tube,
Whose metal sensitive inclos'd foretells
The weather's changes. Should the
    low'ring skies
And hollow winds proclaim approaching
    rain,
Midway the mountains hunt : if wilder
    still
Tempestuous gales and driving mists pre-
    vail,
Still lower—but, when all serene and fair,
The face of Nature nought but smiles
    displays,
Then to the mountain's summits bend
    your way.
As up the rugged path I press, how wide
The prospect opens ! but not here be-
    deck'd
From Summer's varied and fantastic
    loom,
But clad in mantle coarse of sober brown,
And dusky purple mix'd : one homely
    hue
Stretches unvaried round.
             No tow'ring trees
In these rude solitudes diffuse a shade :
Their loss not felt, whilst my observant
    eye
Follows my ranging setters. How they
    wind
Along the bending heath ! and now they
    climb
The rocky ridge, where, mid the broken
    crags,
The whortle's purple berries peep.—
    "Take heed,"
                    The

The pack is near at hand ; the wary dogs
Draw slowly on. They stand immove-
   able,
Backing the leader. Now my pulse beat
   quick
With expectation, but, by practice train'd,
At once subside, that coolness may assist
My steady aim. Meantime, my well-
   taught dogs
Enjoy their sett : I hie them in : the birds
On sounding pinions rise, and with af-
   fright,
Swift as the winds, make off ; yet not so
   swift
But that the whistling shot o'ertake their
   flight.
One, flutt'ring, beats the ground with
   broken wing
And breast distain'd with blood ; the rest
   far off,
Urg'd on by fear, skim o'er the distant
   moors,
Till, by the haze obscur'd, my eye no
   more
Discerns their flight. Vain is their hope
   of peace,
Their hope of safety vain, tho' by no eye
Observ'd, save the high tow'ring hawks,
   or larks,
Their fellows of the air, they drop at
   once,
Then cow'ring run to where the bushy
   ling
Offers a shelter, or the deep black rut
A safer seeming hold ;—each for himself
Seeks a retreat, where, still and close, he
   lies,
The thund'ring gun yet sounding in his
   ears.
Short is your respite ! with sagacious nose
My dogs far off shall wind you, 'till at
   length,
Upon your foot advancing, they denote
With steady sett your hiding place.—
   Again,
Upstarting from the ground, where close
   they lie
Till the re-loaded gun shall give them
   leave,
They bound along, and spreading o'er the
   heath,
With circling footsteps, ply their busy
   work.
Light is my heart, with joyful hope elate
As I pursue their course ; no careful
   thoughts
Have room to enter : the cerulean sky,
Th' unclouded sun, diffuse a livelier joy ;
The very passing breeze, with breath as
   soft
As youthful virgins breathing purest love,

Whispers delight : nature, and health,
   and sport,
Life's chiefest goods, are mine—What
   need I more?
There, where yon rising hillocks mark
   the spot,
I saw the pack with wings that seem'd
   declin'd
And intermitted speed ; not far from
   thence
Perchance they lie ; ah, no! the rising
   ground
Must have deceiv'd my eye. Push on
   my dogs ;
Their flight was further still. But Pero
   stands
With head erect ; his fellows strait pro-
   claim
The glad intelligence, distinctly borne
Upon the bosom of the adverse gale.
With steady pace how they draw on, and
   see
How short that dog has turn'd ; with
   body curv'd
Amost a semicircle, there he stands.
Up springs the game, resounds the well-
   aim'd gun,
And the swift death seals up his swim-
   ming eyes.

THE ANGLER'S SONG.

*From a very old Copy of Hawkins's Com-
plete Angler.*

AN inward love breeds outward talk :
   The hound some praise, and some
    the hawk :
Some, better pleas'd with private sport,
Use tennis—some a mistress court ;
But these delights I neither wish,
Nor envy, while I freely fish.

Who hunts, doth oft in danger ride ;
Who hawks, lures off both far and wide,
Who uses games shall often prove
A loser ; but who falls in love
Is fetter'd in fond Cupid's snare :—
My angle breeds me no such care.

Of recreation, there is none
So free as fishing is alone ;
All other pastimes do no less
Than mind and body both possess ;
My hand alone my work can do,
So I can fish and study too.

                I care

I care not, I, to fish in seas,
Fresh rivers best my mind do please,
Whose sweet calm course I contemplate,
And seek the like to imitate:
In civil bounds I fain would keep,
And for my past offences weep.

And when the timorous trout I wait
To take, and he devours my bait,
How poor a thing, sometimes, I find,
Will captivate a greedy mind:
And when none bite, I praise the wise,
Whom vain allurements ne'er surprise.

But yet, though while I fish I fast,
I make good fortune my repast,
And thereunto my friend invite,
In whom I more than that delight;
Who is more welcome to my dish
Than to my angle was my fish.

As well content no prize to take,
As use of taken prize to make:
For so our Lord was pleased when
He fishers made fishers of men;
Where, which is in no other game,
A man may fish and praise his name.

The first men whom our Saviour dear,
Did choose to wait upon him here,
Blest fishers were, and fish the last
Food was, that he on earth did taste;
I therefore strive to follow those,
Whom he to follow him hath chose.

LINES

On the Chancellor of the Exchequer making Woodcocks and Snipes Game.

THE woodcocks and snipes t'other eve
    met together,
To talk o'er the news of the day,
When the president, shaking indignant
    each feather,
    Cry'd, " List, friends, to what I've to
        say :—

" By the Chiefs of this land we've been
    deem'd a rich prize.
    " We have flown far to pamper their
        wills ;
" And, year after year, when they want-
    ed supplies,
    " We were all on the wing with some
        BILLS.

" Nay, so much were we lik'd, at the
    feasts of the great,
    " Tho' I never before of it boasted,
" That Princes and Lords of our merits
    would prate,
    " And even our TRAILS have they
        TOASTED.

" But now they may cry up a crow or
    woodpecker,
    " Their owls and their pies, great and
        small,
" For the Chancellor vile, of the British
    Exchequer,
    " Has fairly MADE GAME of us all."

By this story depress'd, they all slowly
    took wing,
    For to fly fast they seem'd quite un-
        able,
And each took this oath—" BY rill
    SWEET WATER-SPRING,
    " I'LL BE SHOT, if I e'er grace his
        table."

THE GREENLAND HUNTER.

A MASQUERADE SONG.

COLD are the breezes on Greenland's
    coast,
    Where breakers of ice meet the billow ;
But love is the Greenland hunter's host,
    His pole star, his pilot, his pillow.
    Joyous he welcomes the solar ray,
    Dancing the twilight all away.

When the sun o'er his hazy horizon
    rides,
    In his radiant course thus surround-
        ing ;
In his fur-clad sledge, through the val-
    lies he slides,
    Where the bear and the beaver are
        bounding.
    How jovial the sport of a Greenland
        day,
    Hunting the six months' sun away.

Pale is the light of the polar star,
    From the chase that directs him so
        weary ;
When the sun in the ocean sinks his star,
    And consigns him to darkness so
        dreary ;
    Then how sweet in the arms of his
        love to lay,
    Slumbering the six months' night
        away.

THE
SPORTING MAGAZINE;
OR,
MONTHLY CALENDAR
OF THE
TRANSACTIONS
OF
THE TURF, THE CHASE,
And every other Diversion interesting to
THE MAN OF PLEASURE, ENTERPRISE, AND SPIRIT.

AUGUST, 1808.

CONTAINING

Pedigree of Mr. Cave Browne's celebrated Dog Rocket .... *Page* 208

Disputes between Gentlemen, on
Points of Honour, &c. &c. 203

Sir Arthur Paget and Lady Boringdon................................203

Lord Sackville and Mrs. Poulett ..205

C. Hodge, Esq. and Mrs. Guard..206

Trial of Major Campbell for shooting Captain Boyd 206

Summary of the Sport at Egham Races............................207

Cruel Bet 208

Humorous Dissertation on Pedestrianism 209

Singular Account of a Game Cock,
Instinct in Pigeons, &c........211

Incongruous Adoption 212

Encouraging Instances of Humanity
to Beasts of Burden 212

Kingly Diversions 213

Singular Account of an Eagle's Nest 214

Sir John Sinclair, on Punch 215

The Perplexities of a Man of Letters 216

Shooting in Preserves 220

Campanology 222

The Trap; or, German Method of
catching the Fox 224

Liberality 225

Pedigree and Performances of Regulus 226

The Africans; or, War, Love, and
Duty ....*Page* 227

Unnecessary Speed 229

Instinct of a Dog................230

Dancing Women of Mysore........231

FEAST OF WIT 232

Baron Munchausen 232

Munchausen Reproved 234

Winners of Royal Plates at York, from
1710 to 1807 235

Delpini 237

Action for a Breach of the Game
Laws 238

The Aswamedha Jug, or Horse Sacrifice......................238

The Siller Gun..................239

Remarkable Instance of Courage....240

Mexican Tennis 240

SPORTING INTELLIGENCE.........241

Remarkable Shot 243

Wrestling and Single-stick 243

Extraordinary Fox-chase 244

POETRY.

Song, sung by Mr. Fawcett, in The
Africans 245

The Siller Gun—a Poem.........245

Partridge Shooting 247

Pugilism 248

RACING CALENDAR 57

Embellished with—I, A beautiful Engraving of Rocket, the Property of Mr. C. Browne;
II. The Trap, an Etching.

LONDON:
PRINTED FOR THE PROPRIETORS,
By J. Pittman, Warwick Square;
AND SOLD BY J. WHEBLE, 18, WARWICK-SQUARE; C. CHAPPLE, 66, PALL-MALL;
J. BOOTH, DUKE-STREET, PORTLAND-PLACE; JOHN HILTON, NEWMARKET;
MAYNARD, PANTON STREET, HAYMARKET; AND ALL OTHER
BOOKSELLERS IN THE UNITED KINGDOM.

TO CORRESPONDENTS.

THE Gentleman who sent us two Letters from the North with the postage unpaid, should have recollected that this is not a general custom, and that in this case the reception of such communications might have been refused, or returned.—The request of the same correspondent for reprinting what he calls a favourite Shooting Song, beginning " Every Mortal some favourite Pastime pursues," is very singular, this song being to be had at all the ballad stalls in town.—The other Song, " A Southerly Wind and a Cloudy Sky," may be really scarce, and we shall be glad to obtain a copy of it.

The curious old Songs sent us by another correspondent, "The Original Jolly Anglers," &c. are not forgotten.

We are sorry to find ourselves under the necessity of declining any further correspondence on the subject of " Harmonious Change Ringing," as we cannot think of becoming a party in a difference uninteresting to the generality of our readers ; and besides, most of these articles previously appear in the public papers.

" A WELL-WISHER" should give us credit for not suffering ourselves to become the dupes of his *raillery* ; 'tis a pity that good language should be so unprofitably thrown away.

ERRATUM.—In our last Magazine, page 162, line 17, of the 2d column, for *" sweet lilies,"* read *" sweet lilacs."*

Gentlemen disposed to favour the Publisher of this Magazine with Original Paintings of Sporting Subjects, are assured that the utmost care shall be taken of them, and of their being safely returned. The Engravings thus taken, will be executed by the most approved Artists, and in the first style of excellence.

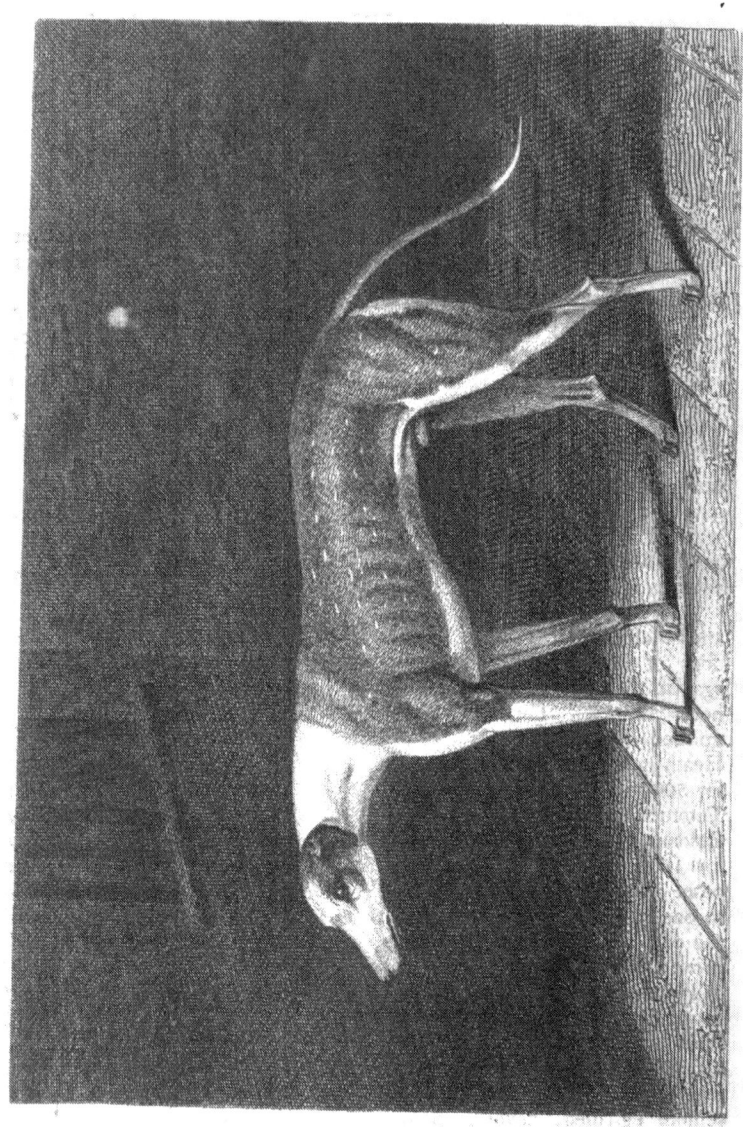

ROCKET, the property of CAVE BROWNE Esqr.

THE

SPORTING MAGAZINE;

FOR AUGUST, 1808.

PEDIGREE
OF
MR. C. BROWNE'S CELEBRATED DOG ROCKET.

With an Engraving of his Portraiture.

ROCKET was got by Spartacus, out of White Fly ; Spartacus was got by Mr. Swinfin's Spartacus, out of Dun Swallow ; White Fly was got by the late Lord Effing-ham's Balloon, out of Fairy, own sister to Firetail.

Rocket, though challenged by, and challenging, all the superior dogs of his day, and contending against them in all counties, was never beaten. He first distinguished himself over Newmarket Heath in the year 1805, in a match for 500gs. p. p. against the famous Tetotum, which was purchased by Colonel Graham, of Mr. Tyson, for 100gs. expressly for that purpose. The bets were two and three to one in favour of the bitch, but the dog, after an arduous struggle, proved gallantly victorious.

He afterwards ran against a famous Berkshire bitch at Ashdown Park, where victory was again his lot. This match was for 100gs. and the severity of the course was seldom equalled, never surpassed. The hare was found four miles from covert, and it was allowed by all the Berkshire and Essex sportsmen that Rocket won in a canter ; the owner of the bitch also candidly admitting, that after the first mile his adversary never served him a turn.

He has run at various coursing meetings, and with decided success, whenever the goodness of the ground, and the stoutness of the hare, allowed a trial for his superior powers ; indeed he is allowed by the most experienced sportsmen to be the stoutest and best greyhound that has been exhibited for many years.

DISPUTES
BETWEEN GENTLEMEN,

On Points of Honour, &c. &c. &c.

SIR A. PAGET AND LADY BORINGDON.

OUR readers will find, by recurring to our last Number, that in this notorious case, the guilty actors in this matrimonial tragedy very discreetly suffered judgment to go by default. By this tacit admission of their criminality, the progress of the lady's *seduction* was held aloof from human observation, nor were the public disgusted with a circumstantial detail of events, which contaminate in their exhibition, and merely afford matter to some depraved journalists, to insult the feelings of a suffering husband, by endeavouring to make the injured ridiculous, at the expence of a nation's morals !

There are some features of interest in this event, which excite an unusual degree of concern and reprobation. We find a young lady of rank and fortune, with a mind highly embellished, and the immediate member of an illustrious family; she is married to a nobleman of dignified manners, whose mind was untainted with those systems of frivolity, which too generally form the prominent characteristic of our young men of fashion. From such an union it might reasonably be supposed, that an example would be firmly established to which Hymen would refer with triumph, when the force and purity of his dominion was questioned either by Vice or Folly.

This seemingly happy pair were blessed with children, and their felicity became undoubted, as the lady wrote letters to her Lord, of which Cornelia need not have been ashamed, comprehensively expressive of the utmost tenderness of affection. In accordance with her noble husband, she received the sacramental test at the altar of her God! What further confirmation would dissolute scepticism itself require of a spotless mind? Her Lord attended his duty in Parliament, as a Peer of the realm, anxious for his country's good; and, while deliberating upon the fearful crisis of his native land, a martial *Lothario* knocks at his door, trips deliberately up stairs to his beloved wife, and stylishly arranges the meretricious *denouement* for the ensuing day; when he repeats his illicit visit, and, in the full meridian, unvizored and undisguised, he takes the lady from her supplicating infants and her household gods, under *his* protection, walks with *sang froid* towards Oxford-street, calls a hackney coach, and drives to an obscure house at Walham Green, where they remained during seve-

ral weeks, in defiance of the law, the Gospel, and an inquisitive and offended world!—May we not exclaim with the ghost in Hamlet, on this occasion,

" Oh! what a falling off was there!"

—If it were possible, it would be essentially momentous to enquire and ascertain, by what secret means the judgment can be thus suddenly twisted from its moral bias.—Though we have a propensity to original sin, certainly we have the ability to counteract that inclining; otherwise the satirical poet would be fully warranted when he asserts, that

" When weak women go astray,
" Their stars are more in fault than they."

Or is it, that there is an innate repugnance to control, of any species, so mingled in our anatomy and affections, that we would rather be erroneously free than virtuously coerced?

The evil effects of this barefaced deed of infidelity are not lessened by the consideration, that the gallant has had the honour of being the representative of his Majesty, on a diplomatic mission of the first order. We are aware that it is the growing fashion of the times to laugh all reproof out of countenance that may be directed against offences of this cast, and that even the monitor is not exempt from danger; but as they militate, in a heavy manner, against the required importance of the softer sex, and leave all the advantages to man, we are persuaded that the thinking part of society will not deem a violation of duty less odious, because the perpetrator can brave mankind, and claim an unqualified exemption from shame, in the profligacy of modern manners.

It was said of the Richlieu family, in France, that they were licentious by descent ; but this apology
for contaminated blood will not apply either to the hero or the he-
roine of this modish pantomime ;
at least by the maternal sources.—
The grandfather and grandmother
of the lady were an honest, plod-
ding, moral couple, who scrupu-
lously obeyed the injunctions of
the Sabbath, and became rich upon
the solid basis of character ! The
grandfather of the gallant was a
dignitary of the church in Ireland,
who had a large but amiable family, and of whom it has been
said, that all his sons were brave,
and all his daughters virtuous.—
The writer of this knew him well,
and once inscribed under his portrait,

Magnum et venerabile nomen.

He was not one of those Mus-
cadins of the church, who encourage the establishment of sectaries
by a carelessness of agency, which,
in an ecclesiastic, is most fatal to
orthodoxy ; but one who solemnly
applied the ethics of the New Tes-
tament for the amelioration of human misery, and was so singularly
exemplary as to make his life an
illustration of his text.

We shall conclude these remarks
on connubial irregularities, by a
quotation from a courtly but ca-
nonical author, who wrote on the
same theme in the latter part of
the reign of Louis the Fourteenth,
when the ladies of Paris were reported to have been more addicted
to gallantry than grace.

" Les desordres que l'on voit
dans les mariages ne viennent-ils
point de la mauvaise education,
que l'on donne aux jeunes filles ?
on n'a jamais tant vu de demandes
en separation ni de divorces. Toutes
les filles souhaitent avec empresse-
ment d'etres mariées ; toutes les
femmes voudroient etre veuves.—
A peine ont-elles la patience d'at-
tendre qu'une mort naturelle les
delivre de leurs epoux, qu'elles re-
gardent comme leurs tyrans, ou
leurs plus grands ennemis. On ne
croioit pas, si on ne le voyoit de
ses yeux, au quels remedes elles
ont recours, & dans quel abime de
malheurs elles se plongent pour
s'affranchir de cette tyrannie ima-
ginaire !"   W.

Under this head, of disputes
among gentlemen, on points of
honour, &c. we shall briefly state,
in a few paragraphs, such occurrences as have application to this
article of our Miscellany, and are
therefore placed here for future
comment.

Lord Viscount Sackville, by appointment, met Mrs. Poulett, wife
of Colonel Poulett, of Southampton (a lady who has children by
her husband) at the White Hart,
Winchester, on the 10th of June,
and with very little precaution or
secrecy on either side, contrived to
get together in a bedchamber up
stairs, in the day-time, and in
which a criminal intercourse took
place between them. The mistress of the inn, who witnessed
enough to prove the fact, disclosed
the transaction, and her husband
acquainted Colonel Poulett with it.
An action was brought by the Colonel against his Lordship, and
tried at the present Summer Assizes at Winchester : the damages
were laid at 10,000l. the Jury gave
3000l.

Two or three similar instances of
dishonourable baseness and depra-
vity have since taken place between
                                 parties

parties of inferior note. There is, however, one that claims mention, being of some importance. At the last Assizes for the county of Devon, an action for Crim. Con. was tried, brought by Lieutenant-Colonel Guard, of the 45th regiment of foot, against Charles Hodge, Esq. of Ottery St. Mary, and the damages were laid at 10,000l.

By the evidence, it appeared that the plaintiff, in the year 1800, had married Miss Coxon, of Kinsale, in the kingdom of Ireland, and that three children were the fruit of this union; that they lived together on terms of the greatest possible affection. That in November, 1806, the regiment being ordered to Buenos Ayres, the plaintiff was obliged to accompany it; his wife could scarcely be prevailed on to remain at home, and nothing but the positive orders of the Commander in Chief hindered her from sharing, with her husband, the dangers of the campaign. Lieutenant-Colonel Guard having embarked at Plymouth, his disconsolate wife came to reside during his absence at Ottery St. Mary, near the friends of her husband: here her acquaintance with the defendant first commenced. The lady was about twenty-six years of age; Mr. Hodge twenty-three. It came out in evidence, that Mrs. Guard was a fine handsome woman, of a volatile disposition, possessing a levity of manners, and fond of admiration. Mr. Hodge was a handsome gay young man, particularly attached to the fair sex. The consequence of this intimacy was a mutual attachment: and in the March following the criminal connexion appeared to have taken place, which continued, in the most open and unguarded manner, till the return of the husband.

We shall forbear detailing any of the circumstances which came out in the course of the trial, contenting ourselves with stating, that a child was the consequence of this amour. On Lieutenant-Colonel Guard's return from abroad, a correspondence took place between him and his wife, in which she acknowledged her guilt, upbraided herself for the levity of her conduct, which had brought her into this state of disgrace, and sent to her injured husband all the letters of her paramour. These being the principal points which came out on the prosecution, Mr. Jekyll, on the part of the defendant, made as good a speech as a bad cause would admit, in mitigation of damages; described the defendant's age and situation, the temptation placed before him, as well as the inability of his client to pay large damages if they were awarded. The Jury returned a verdict for 3000l.

———

DUELLING in Ireland has received a check by the trial and conviction of Brevet-Major Thomas Campbell, a Captain in the 21st regiment of foot, for the murder of Captain Alexander Boyd, of the same regiment: he was tried at the Armagh Assizes. Campbell and Boyd had a dispute about some orders given out by General Ker, at an inspection, and some irritating language passed; this was in the evening. Shortly after, Major Campbell sent a message by a mess-room waiter to Captain Boyd, and they met unattended: they fired in a room at each other, at seven paces, and Boyd was mortally wounded. The case rested much on the evidence of Lieutenant Macpherson, of the same regiment, and which was as follows:—John Mac-

Macpherson stated, that he is a Lieutenant in said regiment; knew Major Campbell and Captain Boyd; recollects the day of the duel; on the evening of that day, going up stairs about nine o'clock, he heard, as he thought, Major Campbell say—"On the words of a dying man, is every thing fair?" He got up before Captain Boyd replied; he said "Campbell, you have hurried me—you're a bad man." Witness was in coloured clothes, and Major C; did not know him, but said again—" Boyd, before this stranger, and Lieutenant Hall, was every thing fair?" Captain B. replied —" O no, Campbell! you know I wanted you to wait and have friends." Major C. then said— "Good God, will you mention before these gentlemen, was not every thing fair; did not you say you were ready?" Captain B. answered " Yes;" but in a moment after said—" Campbell, you're a bad man." Captain B. was helped into the next room, and Major C. followed, much agitated, and repeatedly said to Captain B. that he (Boyd) was the happier man of the two—" I am (says Major C.) an unfortunate man, but I hope not a bad one." Major C. asked Captain B. if he forgave him; he stretched out his hand, and said—" I forgive you—I feel for you, and am sure you do for me." Major C. then left the room.

Much collateral evidence was adduced, but nothing more occurred as to any thing said by Captain Boyd in his last moments, except his asking the Quarter-Master of the Regiment for Major Campbell, and adding, " Poor man, I am sorry for him."

The Jury, after half an hour's consultation, brought in a verdict Guilty of Murder, but recommend-ed him to mercy on the score of character only. He was sentenced to be executed on the Monday following the trial, but was afterwards respited. Petitions were sent off immediately to the Lord Lieutenant for mercy. The Grand and Petty Juries signed petitions in his favour. Mrs. Campbell, wife of Major Campbell, instantly proceeded to Dublin, where, on finding the packet had sailed, she hired an armed boat, and a couple of undaunted Irish watermen, after a tedious and dangerous voyage, safely landed her at Holyhead, from whence she proceeded in all haste to Windsor, to implore the royal mercy. She has, on her knees, solicited in the most pathetic terms the intercession not only of her Majesty, but of all the Princesses, and the Prince of Wales; but it is understood that no hopes have been given that her application would be attended with success.

SUMMARY OF THE SPORT
AT THE
EGHAM RACES.

(The Details in our next Month's Racing Calendar.)

TUESDAY, (first day) the Noblemen and Gentlemen's Plate, of Fifty Pounds, for all ages, was won by Lord Barrymore's Pavilion, beating Mr. Jeffrey's gr. f. Miss Slender, and Mr. Heath's b. h. Rumbo.

A Subscription of Forty Guineas each, the owner of the second horse to receive back his Stake, for all ages, was won by Lord Egremont's Canopus, beating the Duke of York's b. c. Fuscus, and three others.

The

The first year of the Surrey Stakes, of 50gs. each, h. ft. for colts and fillies, then two years old, foals in the county of Surrey, the last half the new mile, was won by Mr. Durand's br. c. by Teddy, out of Ramschoondra, beating Sir Joseph Mawbey's br. c. Botley's, and Mr. Page's b. f. Cinderella, by Teddy.

Wednesday, the Magna Charta Stakes, of 50gs. each, h. ft. for three-year olds', the new mile, were won by Lord Egremont's b. c. brother to Trafalgar, beating Mr. Ladbroke's b. c. by Teddy, dam by Precipitate.

The Ladies' Plate of 50l. for three and four-year olds, the best of three two-mile heats, was won by Lord Stawell's b. f. Brighton Lass, beating Mr. Fermor's br. c. Stripling, Mr. Ladbroke's b. c. by Gohanna, and Lord Egremont's b. f. by Gohanna.

Lord Egremont's Lazy filly bolted during the first heat, and was distanced.—Before starting, 6 to 4 on the field against the favourite, the Lazy filly; 4 and 5 to 1 against Brighton Lass, and 3 to 1 against Lord Egremont. Both heats won easy.

Mr. Trevanion's Lewes, beat Mr. F. Craven's Bantam, for 50gs; two miles.—A good race.

Thursday, (the last day) the Sweepstakes of 30gs each, 20 ft. for two-year olds', the last half of the new mile, was won by Lord Egremont's ch. f. by Gohanna, beating Sir C. Bunbury's b. f. by Sorcerer, Mr. Ladbroke's b. c. Trinculo, the Duke of Clarence's Cinderella, the Duke of York's ch. h. Silvermere, and Mr. Fermor's b. f. Jocasta.

Egham and Stanes Handicap Plate of 50l. for all ages; the best of three heats, two miles and a quarter to each heat, was won by Mr. Heath's b. h. Rumbo, beating Lord Barrymore's br. b. Pavillion, Mr. Trevanion's b. h. Lewes, Mr. Cumming's br. h. Jump-off, and Ld Stawell's b. f. Brighton Lass.—Before starting, 5 to 4 agst Brighton Lass, 2 to 1 agst Pavilion, 3 to 1 against Lewes, and 5 to 1 against Rumbo and Jump-off.—The heat cast a gloom over the countenances of the betting men. Brighton Lass was a great favourite, and at the turn into the strait mile, the whole of the horses run on the wrong side the post. The favourite and Jump-off run in, and Brighton Lass won the heat; but, on the arrival of the other horses at the stand, it turned out that they had returned and gone round the post, and that the two which were afterwards declared to be distanced, had not. The Dukes of York and Clarence (Stewards) were consulted, who declared the heat in favour of Rumbo. The three horses started for the second heat, and bettings were 2 to 1 against Rumbo, 6 to 4 against Pavilion, and 5 to 2 against Lewes.

CRUEL BET.

ON Saturday evening, the 27th instant, a number of persons assembled at Hyde Park Corner, to witness the setting out of a pony, which was matched for a bet of 500 guineas, to start with the Exeter mail and to be in Exeter first, with or without a rider. The man who led the pony is at liberty to take a fresh post-horse as often as he pleases. It was with the mail, on Sunday morning, at Basingstoke; odds were then in favour of the pony.—The distance is near 180 miles, and is generally performed by the mail in about 28 hours.

HUMOUR-

HUMOROUS DISSERTATION ON PEDESTRIANISM.

MR. EDITOR,

IN this age of pedestrianism, perhaps it may not be unamusing to some of your very numerous readers, to see a few strictures on the different modes of walking.

An eminent divine (Barrow) remarks, that "by an usual and apposite manner of speaking, our tenor of life is called a *way*, our conversation *walking*, our actions *steps*, our observing good laws *uprightness*, our transgressing of them *tripping, faultering, falling*. The metaphor of *walking*, indeed, as applied to conduct in general, occurs so frequently in that book, which, above all others, abounds in beautiful imagery, that it would be superfluous to point out instances.

A variety of *gaits* may be observed in this metropolis, and which arise from the freedom of our political constitution. Every man, whatever other restraints he may be under, is permitted to walk as he pleases, provided he does not jostle his neighbour. This is not the case in despotic countries, nor among a frivolous people; the one is confined by power, and the other by fashion, to a certain stated and uniform way of walking. I think it would be no superfluous part of education to learn to *walk consistently*, and *in character*, and I shall therefore suggest a few hints on the different modes of *walking*, which, I hope, will be found not altogether unprofitable.

Of all others, the *upright walk* is best in itself, and at the same time most becoming in appearance. Even a dancing-master will agree with me in this, although he and I may differ as to the means by

which it is to be acquired. My instructions would be entirely directed to such means of walking uprightly as would leave the scholar at perfect freedom, and yet inspire him with an uniform disposition to hold up his head in any way through which he has to pass, or in any society or company in which he is required to display his motions. For this purpose, it is merely necessary that he preserve the exact perpendicular, by carefully avoiding those inclinations which are deviations from it.— Among these may be mentioned, the looking too much on one side, bending too much forward, and the filling the breeches pocket too frequently, and with that eager squeeze and pressing down, which seldom fail to make a man stoop lower than becomes his character.

Another direction, not less profitable, may be, to walk in a straight-forward direction. The moment a man begins to turn, sometimes to the right and sometimes to the wrong, down crooked alleys and oblique passages, he no longer crosses the horison at right angles; he loses his balance; and if he escapes a fatal fall, yet he stumbles so frequently and so awkwardly, that even his friends are ashamed of him, and the world at large, without any great breach of charity, doubts whether he be the *good walker* he pretends to be.

When we see another taking pains to get on in the road, not by bold strides, by spirited efforts of uncommon daring, but by little and pitiful steps, we may conclude he has contracted an incurable *hobble in his gait*.

On the other side, there are men who have such a natural aversion to the foundation of all *good walking*, as not to know, or, if they

E e 　　 know,

know, to despise the first principles thereof, who are to-day of one opinion and to-morrow of another, sometimes influenced by flattery, sometimes by passion, and sometimes by drink ; such *walkers* we may at once see are addicted to *halting.*

Some again there are who, without being absolutely ignorant of them, yet despise all rules of *upright walking,* who study laws only to evade them, acquire some knowledge of religion only to sneer at it, and form acquaintances only to deceive them. Their motions and actions are bounded by no prospect but that of a gibbet, and while they can act on this side of that object, they think themselves safe. With the affectation of simplicity, they are perfect masters of all the arts of cunning, and with many of the excuses of poverty, study nothing but the accumulation of wealth. These may be known by their *gambling gait,* and are therefore denominated *shufflers.*

There is a very considerable class of *walkers,* who are regardless of the way, and seem to have very confused notions of time and distance. They are to be seen sometimes *walking* slower than is necessary, sometimes *running* faster than their health will permit, and sometimes *leaping* or *hopping* as the frolic seizes them. They are supposed to have some defect in their sight, as they cannot see far before them, and run headlong upon every thing hurtful in their way. They are therefore easily misled, and unfortunately, in great towns especially, there are some persons who take a great delight in misleading them. They have likewise this peculiarity in the affair of walking, that their feet have a

sort of habitual tendency to carry them into any house rather than their own. They may be seen constantly stepping into taverns and bagnios, where they trip and fall upon one mischievous object or another, without the least foresight or apprehension. Such men, who are generally of the younger sort, cannot with much propriety be said to *walk,* as their motion, more closely observed, resembles *reeling.*

There is another class, not wholly unconnected with the former, whose only object is quickness of motion, and to reach their journey's end by rapid strides. They care little about the forms of walking, or the uprightness of motion, suggested above. All their desire is, to go over a certain *course* in the shortest time possible. In order to perform this, they disencumber themselves of every thing that can add to their weight, as common sense, reflection, the relative duties, and particularly the metals of gold and silver, which are reckoned the heaviest, and they derive the most enlivening encouragement from moving in great numbers, cheering one another with noise, and not only starting fair, but moving in as equal a pace as if by the aid of music. Such is the rapidity of their career, that if any drop by the way they are left there, the remainder having neither time nor inclination to attend to them ; and often indeed are disposed to laugh at the fallen for their presumption, in endeavouring to keep pace with them. The names of many of these expeditious persons, who do not contend who shall walk uprightly, but who shall walk most swiftly, may be frequently seen in a publication, entitled, *The London Gazette.*

I shall mention another class of walkers,

walkers, viz. that of men who walk so straight, and carry their heads so high, as to pass for upright, although they have in fact a wonderful tendency to move in another direction, and would have moved in another direction, if by some incident they had not got a twist upwards. From some circumstance in their history, and particularly from a toss or jerking motion of their heads, they have been called *upstarts*, and the reason of their holding up so firmly as rather to incline backwards than forwards, is said to be, that they originally held their heads as low as they could, consistently with life, and having been, as already hinted, enabled to rise, they rose with such an elastic bounce, or spring, as to give their shape a direction towards the other extreme. Their gait is not, however, very graceful, as they soon swell so immoderately as to impede free breathing, and, in fact, it has been found, they cannot breathe where and in what manner they formerly did. From their peculiar motions, their distance of aspect, their carrying their head so high as not to be able to see their nearest relations or oldest acquaintances, they may be considered as *walking upon stilts*.

In a Dissertation on Walking, the interests of the fair sex must not be overlooked. Perhaps some of them may be virtually included in one or other of the classes abovementioned; but in whatever way they think proper to walk, it behoves them to consider that *circumspection* is of more importance to them than to the other sex, particularly as

" One false step entirely damns their fame."

Your's, &c.
PETER PERIPATETIC.

SINGULAR ACCOUNT OF A GAME COCK;

INSTINCT IN PIGEONS, &c.

IN Captain Careleton's Memoirs, lately published, he relates the circumstance of a game cock being on board Lord Rodney's ship on the famous 12th of April. This noble fellow being by accident loose, took his station on a coil of ropes on the quarter-deck, near to the Admiral, and on the firing of every broadside, he crowed with all his might and main; as if he fully comprehended that this was an effort against an enemy, in which he concurred with all his heart. This champion is immortalised by being painted in Gainsborough's picture of Admiral Lord Rodney, by whom the cock was highly valued.

The Captain states further:—
" We had on board the London, (where he was a volunteer), a great number of pigeons, of which our commander was very fond; these, on the first firing of our cannon, dispersed and flew away, and were seen no more near us during the fight, (viz. the 12th of April.) The next day it blew a brisk gale, and drove our fleet some leagues to the southward of the place where they had forsaken our ship, yet the day after they all returned safe aboard—not in one flock, but in small parties of four or five at a time. Some persons at that time a-board the ship, were told by Sir Edward Spragge, that he brought those pigeons with him from the Streights; and that when, pursuant to his order, he left the Revenge man of war, to go a-board the London, all those pigeons, of their own accord, and without the trouble of carrying, left the Revenge

E e 2　　　　likewise,

likewise, and removed with the sailors on board the London, where I saw them, all which many of the sailors confirmed to me.—What sort of instinct this could proceed from, I leave to the curious."—*Memoirs of Captain Careleton, p.* 11.

INCONGRUOUS ADOPTION.

TO THE EDITOR,

SIR,

LATELY reading in one of your former volumes an anecdote of a leveret nurtured by a cat, it called to my remembrance an incident nearly similar to it, which happened some years since at the house of a gentleman of my acquaintance.— A fox had been dug out of its earth, and was brought one evening to the house, to be kept till the next morning, when it was to be turned out before a pack of hounds. A female rabbit, with two sucking ones, were procured for his refreshment, and the fox accordingly ate up one for his supper; but in the night he found means of effecting his escape. A cat, who had lately kittened in the house, found suck for the young rabbits, and taking compassion on the poor orphans, nourished them as she would have done were they her own offspring, and seemed even to pay them uncommon attention; for she frequently carried them in her mouth to different parts of the house, even into garrets, for greater security from any enemies, whom she apprehended might injure them, and more particularly from a young terrier, who was also kept in the house. One of these rabbits died in two or three days, but the other lived till it was able to run

about the house after its nurse, who continued to treat it with the utmost tenderness and affection, but whose cares were unavailing to preserve her adopted from the enemy she most suspected, the terrier, who finally demolished the poor rabbit, to the great grief of its foster-mother.

M. C.

July 23d.

ENCOURAGING INSTANCES
OF
Humanity to Beasts of Burden.

MR. EDITOR,

HAVING lived in a neighbourhood, where a man in a very humble walk of laborious life used daily to serve some of the neighbours with vegetables, whose good humour with his beast, and the playfulness of the latter, as well as appearance, were a " a credit to his keeper" if such a thing of an ass may be spoken, give me leave to relate another anecdote of a third person, who rejoices in every trait characteristic of humanity even to brutes. Reflecting, says he, upon the blessings arising from social intercourse and domestic happiness, as an old woman was leading a female ass, followed by her foal, the latter was rather playful, and she was stopping till it came up; I demanded of her the price of the young one. " 'Tis not to be sold," she replied; " my husband means to keep it to do the work of this poor old creature," patting the ass upon the back : " she has been the best creature in the world; when she first became the property of my husband, she had been used

most

most cruelly, her back was hurt, she was all over sores and bruises, and could scarcely walk, but we nursed her up, and by good treatment soon got her about. She has amply rewarded us for our pains, for in Midsummer time we make a good deal by her milk, and she serves well for my husband to bring fruit and other things out of the country; in winter, too, she does all that is required of her; but, poor thing, her feet now begin to fail, and she must soon give up working, but a better tempered quieter creature never lived; and, as for that little fellow, though he can be playful occasionally, he means no harm; he is so gentle, you may do any thing with him, and see how well he looks.' This, (said she, in a tone of affection and pleasure) is all from good treatment; and shame on those, for many there are, who behave with cruelty to poor dumb animals."

KINGLY DIVERSIONS.

A Striking instance of the rude and unpolished manners in ancient times, occurs in a very curious and authentic manuscript, a copy of which is in possession of Thomas Astle, Esq. containing, amongst other things, the private expences of King Edward the Second, who was born in the Eagle Tower of Carnarvon Castle, wherein it appears, that *cross and pile*, or tossing up *heads or tails*, (as it is now called) was a royal diversion; that the King travelled in a returned barge, which had conveyed faggots to his court, and was not only highly delighted with the coarse humours of a buffoon dancing on a

table, and another falling several times from his horse, but also deemed them worthy of a reward. The record is written in Welch, of which the following is a translation:—

Item, paid to the King himself, to play at cross and pile, by the hands of Richard de Morworth, the receiver of the treasury, 13d.

Item, paid there to Henry, the King's barber, for money which he lent to the King to play at cross and pile, 5s.

Item, paid there to Peres Barnard, Usher of the King's Chamber, money which he lent to the King, and which he lost at cross and pile, to Monsieur Wattewylle, 8d.

Item, paid to the King himself to play at cross and pile, by Peres Barnard, 2s. and which the said Peres won of him.

Item, paid to Sir William de Kyngeston, for cabbage to make pottage in the boat.

Tuesday, the 17th day of October, at Walton, paid at Shene, to James Hoggesworth, Henry de Anstran, Robert Sealour, Henry May, Robyn Stronball, John Warwyn, and Henry Smallsponne, for the wages of the seven bargemen, working in the barge or boat, and Thomas Atte Lese, each taking 3d. per day, from Tuesday the 13th day of October, to Friday the 18th day of the same month, reckoning four days, and bringing from Byflete and Shene 1540 faggots, in a boat, for my Lady Despencer, residing at the said Shene, by water, in the said boat or barge, to Cyppenham, 7d.

The 11th of March. —Item, paid to James de St. Albans, the King's painter, who danced before the King upon a table, and made him laugh heartily, being a gift from the King's own hands, in aid
to

to him, his wife, and children, 1l. 1s.

Item, paid at the lodge at Wolmer, when the King was stag-hunting there, to Morrice Ken, of the kitchen, because he rode there before the king, and often fell from his horse, at which the King laughed exceedingly; a gift by command, 20s.

SINGULAR ACCOUNT

OF AN

EAGLE's NEST.

From Hall's Travels in Scotland, by an Unusual Route.

NOT many miles from Castle Grant, I found a gentleman who was not displeased that a couple of eagles, whose nest I went to see regularly every summer, build one on a rock in the hill, not far from his house. There was a stone within a few yards of it, about six feet long, and nearly as broad, and upon this stone, almost continually, but always when they, the eagles, had young, the gentleman and his servants found a number of muir fowl, partridges, hares, rabbits, ducks, snipes, ptarmacans, rats, mice, &c. and sometimes kids, fawns, and lambs. When the young eagles were able to hop the length of this stone, to which there was a narrow road, hanging over a dreadful precipice, as a cat brings live mice to her kittens, and teaches them to kill them, so the eagles, I learned, often brought hares and rabbits alive, and placing them before their young, taught them to kill and tear them to pieces. Sometimes, it seems, hares, rabbits, rats,

&c. not being sufficiently tamed, got off from the young ones while they were amusing themselves with them; and one day, a rabbit got into a hole, where the old eagle could not find it. The eagle, one day, brought to her young ones the cub of a fox, which, after it had bitten some of them desperately, attempted to escape up the hill, and would, in all probability, have accomplished it, had not the shepherd, who was watching the motion of the eagles, with a view to shoot them, (which they do with bullets, swan-shot not being able to penetrate their feathers) prevented it. As the eagles kept what might be called an excellent larder, when any visitors surprised the gentleman, he was in the habit of sending his servants to see what the eagles had to spare, and who scarcely ever returned without something good for the table.— Game of all kinds, it is well known, is the better for being kept a considerable time.

When the gentleman or his servants carried off things from the eagle's shelf or table, near the nest, (for it was next to impossible to approach the nest itself) the eagles were active in replenishing it; but when they did not take them away, the old ones loitered about inactive, amusing themselves with their young, till the stock was nearly exhausted.

When the hen eagle was hatching, the table or shelf of the rock was generally kept well furnished for her use. While the eagles were very young, her mate generally tore a wing from the fowls for her, and a leg from the beasts he frequently brought. Those eagles, as is generally the case with animals that are not gregarious, were faithful to one another, but would not permit

permit any of their young to build a nest, or live near them, always driving them to a considerable distance. The eagles of this country are uncommonly large and voracious, and their claws are so long and strong, that they are used by young people as a horn, with a stopper, for holding snuff, and carried regularly in the pocket for that purpose.

SIR JOHN SINCLAIR, ON PUNCH.

NO species of liquor has been more condemned*, or more loudly celebrated, than Punch.—This drink consists of spirits diluted with water, and a certain proportion of acid and sugar, making a mixture of substances very opposite in their nature, being strong and weak, sweet and sour. Some contend, that half a pint of old strong beer, in a moderate bowl of punch, will mellow the fire of the spirit considerably, or that half a pint of green tea is a useful additional ingredient. Where the acid does not disagree with the stomach, punch is certainly wholesomer than grog, or spirits and water, or toddy, which is grog with the addition of sugar,† When punch is made in perfection, the water should be thoroughly boiled; the sugar, water, and fruit, should be well mixed before the spirits are put in, and the fruit used should be ripe and generous.

As punch was some years ago the principal liquor drank, after dinner and supper, in Glasgow, I thought it right to enquire into the effects of that practice on the general health of those who took it, and whether it had any particular effect in producing or preventing the gout or gravel. The answers to those enquiries differ so much from each other, that it is impossible to draw any positive conclusion from them, though, on the whole, the evidence seems to be rather favourable to the article in question. It appears from these answers, that the most opulent merchants in that great commercial city do not drink so much punch as formerly, wine having become a more fashionable drink; or, instead of one overflowing social bowl, in the preparing

* Cheyne in his Essay on Health, p. 55, says, " That next to drams, no liquor deserves to be more stigmatised, and banished the repast of the tender valetudinary and studious, than punch. It is a composition of such parts, as not one of them is salutary or kindly to such constitutions, except the pure element in it."

† It is remarked, that the drinkers of toddy get sooner intoxicated than those who drink punch.

Punch, says Dr. Falk (Guard of Health, p. 449), is an extemporary kind of wine, and, if judiciously made, there is no doubt of its being the finest drink in the universe to the palate, but there is not a more pernicious liquid to the constitution, if abused.

Dr. Adair observes (Essay on Diet and Regimen, p. 47), that punch, which is a species of wine, is the safest manner of diluting ardent spirits; both the acid and the sugar counteracting the stimulus of the spirit. It is therefore a safer drink than grog or toddy. A very strong man, who drank grog instead of punch, found that his hand shook. He returned to his weak punch, and his hand became steady.

of which more attention was paid to the cookery, every guest now makes his own punch in a separate glass or tumbler.

The punch that was the ordinary drink of the people of Glasgow some years ago, was in general made weak, with more or less acid, according to taste. Great care was taken to use none but the best old Jamaica rum. This kind of liquor might be drank in large quantities with safety; it passed freely off, and seldom occasioned a head-ache. Many persons, I am informed, used this drink for a great number of years, without feeling any bad effects from it, and arrived at a good old age, in health of body and vigour of mind : " and I believe (adds one of my informants), that punch is the safest of all drinks."

With some persons, the acid in punch is found not to agree, occasioning heartburn, and unpleasant acidity in the stomach ; but this effect can be easily corrected by a little magnesia. Persons who have injured the tone of their stomachs by dram-drinking, or high-seasoned dishes, are those with whom the acid is most apt to disagree. The stone is a disease very little known in Glasgow, and the gout, hitherto, has been seldom heard of. The punch formerly used had little tendency to produce either of those diseases, unless where there existed a strong hereditary disposition to it. They are now more frequent than formerly, and will increase as the luxury of the table, and the use of wine and strong ale, increases.

From another respectable quarter I am informed, that in the best society of Glasgow, neither wine nor punch is drank to such excess as formerly: that in cold weather some drink hot punch, in warm weather all drink it cold ; and some, who value themselves on the superior flavour of their rum and fruit, drink it cold, at all times. There are many suppositions regarding the peculiarities of Glasgow, in respect to living and diseases ; but it is generally believed that gout and gravel are less prevalent there than in other great towns ; an enquiry into the causes thereof would lead to much discussion. Besides drinking more punch than wine, the merchant of Glasgow spends the forenoon in healthful exercises, by which he avoids many diseases incident to those who are daily cooped up in crowded courts, or in small apartments among musty papers.

Whatever are the effects of punch taken in moderation, yet when taken in great quantities, it must weaken the stomach ; and has a tendency, when conjoined with other causes, to bring on the gout, the gravel, and other disorders of a similar nature.

THE PERPLEXITIES

OF

A MAN OF LETTERS.

From the German—In Letters from Goodwin to his Friend.

DEAR ***

MY attachment to my old friend Thompson, at Henningstone, and my extreme partiality to the plain, but the heartfelt enjoyments his house affords, are well known to you.

Yesterday morning, the duke's private secretary came with a message from his highness to my friend, and, as soon as his business was over, Thompson brought him into

into the parlour, where his wife and I were sitting, and introduced me to him. As soon as the stranger heard my name and place of abode mentioned, he enquired if he had the honour of speaking with the author of several moral treatises, and a book of devotion, which he named? and, on my replying in the affirmative, he politely commended my works, said the Duke had read them; and that they met with his entire approbation.

The conversation then became general, till he went away, and when he took leave, he assured me, with great volubility, that he esteemed himself very fortunate in having made such a valuable acquaintance that morning; and that, if it were ever in his power to be any ways useful to me, he begged I would command his services without reserve. I regarded his profession of friendship as words of course, and forgot both them and him as soon as he was out of sight:

But, to my no small surprise, a note from my new friend was brought to me, whilst I was at dinner, in which he informed me that he told the Duke of my being at Mr. Thompson's, and that his Highness wished to see me; he, therefore, desired me to come to him at four o'clock, that he might present me to him, and added, that the porter would shew me to his room. I had above an hour's time to dress and prepare myself for the part I was going to act. As a man of learning; and one who was entirely independent, I determined to deliver my sentiments with modest freedom, assume an air of graceful dignity, preserve the equanimity of my mind, and not suffer myself to be dazzled by the glare of royalty.

I intended to avoid contradicting the Duke as much as was in my

power, and equally resolved to assert my opinion, with the same ease and frankness as if I was speaking to an equal. That he would mention my literary productions was certain; that subject would afford me a desirable opportunity of making several learned and interesting observations, which I carefully recorded in my mind; and they would insensibly lead to a train of instructive and amusing ideas, with which I determined to entertain the Duke, and in a manner repay him for his kind attentions to me. I had finished my dress before I had settled my plan of operations, although the care with which I curled and powdered my hair, brushed my clothes, and adjusted every part of my dress, had required a considerable time. Thus adorned, I began my peregrination with such hasty strides, that my friend's eldest son, a rosy-cheeked boy, who had offered to shew me the way to the palace, could hardly keep pace with me.

My curiosity to know what would happen in a sphere that was entirely new to me, and, to own the truth, some movements of vanity, that the hope of appearing to advantage in it excited, were not powerful enough to suppress a certain uncomfortable and confused idea of my mind's not being quite at ease; although I would not own to myself that that was the case; but it certainly was, and my whole being was as much out of its place as the hat that I held in my hand, that it might not disorder my hair, was.

I unfortunately fancied that there was an awkwardness in my gait, as well as in the manner of carrying my hat; and my attention to myself, and endeavours to assume an easier air, gave me an appearance of pedantry and affectation, that, I believe, is not natural to me. I looked like a lad who is strutting about in a new suit of clothes: and even my little guide discovered (probably by my answers to his questions being shorter than usual) that I was not quite the same person who had walked out with him in the morning.

He told me, as we went along, that the boys at school were obliged to make orations twice a-year, to accustom them to speak in public, and that the last time he had rehearsed a fable. The reason of his telling it to me did not strike me at the time, but it occurred to me afterwards, that I probably appeared to him as fine, as stiff, and as anxious to gain applause, as he felt when he was going to mount the rostrum.

In this manner we arrived at the palace gate. You must go in there, said the friendly lad, pointing to it, and running back. The enquiries of the sentry who I was, and what I wanted? before he would allow me to enter, and the porter's interrogations before I had time to desire him to conduct me to my new friend, confused me a good deal; for immaterial as the questions they asked were, and easily answered, yet they flurried my spirits, and made me feel the uncomfortable sensation of being out of my own element, in which I could come and go unquestioned, as every one knew who I was. I, therefore, when shewn into the secretary's room, found myself less composed, and less eloquent, than I was an hour before.

The man was buried in papers, and informed me that some unexpected business, that he was obliged to dispatch immediately, prevented his having the pleasure of enter-

taining me till the Duke could send me, but that he would conduct me to two noblemen, whose names he mentioned, that wished to be acquainted with me, and that he had no doubt of my spending my time very agreeably with them, till the Duke sent for me, which he believed would be in about an hour. He desired me to follow him, without giving me time to recover from the surprise his unexpected reception had thrown me into, or even to answer him; ran down stairs, opened a room door, mentioned my name in a hasty manner, and immediately disappeared.

The magnificence of the apartment, the beauty of the hangings and ceiling, the number of ornaments, and the richness of the furniture, confused me, as I had not time to regard them distinctly; and my perplexity was increased by the extreme civility of the two strange gentlemen (one was old and the other young) and their frequently saying the politest things at the same time, to which I could only reply with a humble, and, I believe, a clumsy bow. Another vexatious circumstance was, that I had entirely forgotten their names and long titles; and the fear of their thinking me familiar or impertinent, if I only said Sir, greatly increased my ridiculous distress.

Oh! that those who are placed in the higher ranks of life possessed humanity and perspicuity enough not to judge too harshly of their inferiors, who happen to be thrown among them sometimes for an hour or two, because they appear a little awkward, unpolished, and unentertaining; or, if the custom seem as strange to them, as the etiquette which is observed at the Emperor of China's court, would appear to the most polished courtier,

courtier, if he was suddenly transplanted from a German Prince's to that of Pekin! Something of this kind darted confusedly through my head, whilst the gentlemen were surveying me with curious eyes; but that reflection was far from tranquillising me, for I, perhaps unjustly, fancied that their want of feeling would not suffer them to think as I did. Their frigidity formed such a contrast to my warmth, and their composure to my uneasiness, that my disgust increased every moment, and with it, my taciturnity and reserve. I endeavoured to collect myself once or twice, but failed in every attempt; for, whatever I said, even when I was convinced of its propriety, seemed to me, as I pronounced it with hesitation, either affected or rude, pedantic or frivolous, that made me dissatisfied with myself, and when we are so, we are utterly incapable of pleasing others.

"You are probably an admirer of fine prospects!" said the young gentleman. He opened the window as he spoke, made a motion with his hand for me to approach it, and stepped back, to make way for me, with a look of indifference.

Had I been left alone a quarter of an hour, or, what would have been still more desirable, in your company that space of time, I should have recovered myself, and thought and acted in my usual manner. The view was enchantingly beautiful, and thawed, although but for a moment, my frozen mind: an extensive prospect, that inclosed some towns, and several villages, in their domains, majestic mountains, covered with dark groves on one side, and on the other fields and meadows, decked in the gay and variegated attire of summer, and striped with different hues of pleasing colours; just under the window the Duke's elegant garden, in which nature was so happily assisted by art, that the improving hand of the latter was hardly perceptible; and the *tout ensemble* formed the most picturesque scene that can be well imagined.

The river gently flowed along one side of the garden, then meandred through a grove, and at last formed an extensive angle that encompassed part of the town; and the busy bustle that was visible in the town, amused my mind, which, at the same time, was lulled into a pleasing melancholy by the various lights the whole prospect appeared in; for one side of it glittered in sunshine, whilst the other was covered with an awful gloom, that was caused by the dark clouds that were gathering in the west, and between both long streaks of light and shade were to be seen.

I turned round in the room with a head full of confused ideas. The two gentlemen were standing near the fire-place, and looking at some figures in bass-relief that were over it. It did not strike me at the moment that persons to whom the prospect was familiar could not admire its beauty with the rapture I did; but my warmth, and, perhaps, the secret wish to prove to them that I was not devoid of sensibility, made me express myself in terms that I felt the impropriety of the moment I had uttered them:—"Good God!" exclaimed I, is it possible for any heart to be cold and unfeeling enough to view such a prospect as this with indifference! those who can, are, in my opinion, objects of pity."

The

The eldest of my companions looked at me with contracted eyebrows, as if he was curious to know if any still greater absurdity would follow; the other smiled, and I stood as much out of countenance, as a child that has just broke a glass. That was foolish, very foolish indeed, thought I, and I felt as if I ought to make an apology for my seeming rudeness. I stammered something, that was intended to circumscribe my former unlimited assertion, which, as well as I am able to recollect, was not much wiser than what I said before; and I felt so depressed, and so much out of humour with myself, that I was not able to turn my eyes towards the window, nor to look at the prospect, the fatal cause of my present confusion, again, which must have made the gentlemen fancy my former violent admiration either affected, or very transient. They, however, did all in their power to keep up the conversation, and asked me a number of questions about the village I lived in, and my house, garden, and family—subjects that were totally indifferent to them; nor would they probably have made any enquiries of the kind, if they had not seen, and wished to relieve, my distress.

My replies were frequently incoherent and foreign to the purpose; and I once so entirely forgot myself, that I talked about my neighbour, John Morris, with a prolixity as if the man had been their cousin. I then recollected that I was tedious, and, to avoid that fault, ran into the contrary extreme; for my answers were so short and unconnected, that I am certain I must have been utterly unintelligible to them. In short, I every moment committed some

fresh blunder, and my endeavours to repair my fault never failed in leading me into new ones. My thoughts continually wandered from the society of strangers I was in, to that of my old acquaintance, and from the Duke's palace to my own village; it was, therefore, an impossibility for me to be entertained, or entertaining.

This company does not suit me!—was a thought that frequently started into my mind; but I now perceive how much I was in the wrong, and that the noblemen were quite in the right if they said, as soon as my back was turned,—" this man does not suit us!" for it was I alone who was in fault.

To be continued.

SHOOTING IN PRESERVES.

AT the Essex Assizes, held in Chelmsford, an action of trespass was tried before Lord Chief Baron Macdonald, and a Special Jury, wherein Lord Braybrooke, the Lord Lieutenant of that county, was plaintiff, and John King Eagle, Esq. was defendant.

Mr. Pooley, for the plaintiff, shortly opened the pleadings.—Mr. Serjeant Shepherd, on the same side, stated, that the plaintiff was well known to many of the Gentlemen of the Jury; that his Lordship lived at Audley End, in the county, and near his mansion-house had preserves for the protection of game. That the defendant, Mr. Eagle, in the month of October last, was sporting in one of these preserves, called the Warren Ring, or Hare Warren, with his gun and a brace of pointers; that the dogs put up a cock pheasant, close to the

the pales of the menagerie, which the defendant, Mr. Eagle, fired at and killed. The report of th un brought one of the keepers, Robert Plum, (whom he should afterwards call before them as a witness) to the spot, and going up to the defendant, he asked him if he had Lord Braybrooke's authority to shoot there, but the defendant made no answer. Plum then told him that the place where he was shooting was a preserve, and that Lord Braybrooke never shot there himself, or permitted any of his friends, and requested the defendant to go away, which he refused, and continued hunting his dogs through the plantation. As soon as he came out, Plum asked him his name, and desired him to produce his certificate; but the defendant gave him no answer, and proceeded across the lawn in front of the house, towards the turnpike road. Plum again applied to him for his name and certificate, which he still declined giving. The defendant then went up the turnpike road, and seeing one of the dogs pointing, near the hedge adjoining to a small plantation, called the Oaks, was going to get over, when Plum told him, he hoped that he would not go into that plantation, as it was another preserve of Lord Braybrooke's, where his Lordship never shot himself; notwithstanding this, the defendant persisted, and went over into the Oaks, and a cock pheasant rising, he attempted to fire at it, but the gun flashed in the pan. The defendant said it was a pity the gun had missed fire, or he should have had another pheasant in his bag. Some conversation then passed between the keeper and the defendant, who at length told him that his name was Eagle, and produced his certificate;

he lamented that it was a wet day, and said he should come again. There were other persons of the party, who were not included in this prosecution; one of them of the name of Baker, who assisted in beating the plantations, and two others, who waited in the turnpike road with a curricle and gig.

The learned Serjeant stated, that Lord Braybrooke had great reluctance in bringing this action, but the continued depredations committed upon his manors, owing to the vicinity of Audley End to the University of Cambridge, compelled him so to do; that he had shewn great indulgence to many persons who had been found sporting upon his manors without leave; and the learned Serjeant pointed out an instance of a young friend of his own having been found trespassing, and had been treated by his Lordship with the greatest lenity. The practice, however, had got to such a pitch, that it was absolutely necessary to make an example: and he hoped the Jury would, under the circumstances of the present case, not only find a verdict for the plaintiff, but mark the defendant's conduct, by giving such damages as they might think reasonable.

The keeper, Robert Plum, was then called, who fully corroborated the statement of the learned Serjeant. Upon being asked the distance of the Warren Ring (where the defendant killed the pheasant) from Lord Braybrooke's house, he stated it to be three furlongs, and that the plantation called the Oaks adjoined his Lordship's garden wall.

There was another witness called, of the name of Elliott, but he was not examined.

Mr. Garrow made an eloquent speech for the defendant, but did not call any witness. The Jury, after

after a few minutes consultation, and a severe animadversion from the learned Judge on so unjustifiable an outrage, gave a verdict for the plaintiff, damages, 20l.

CAMPANOLOGY.

THE word *bell* is derived from *pelvis*, a bason; for before the invention of bells, sounding brass and basons were used instead of them. The soundness of earthen or china vases is still tried by ringing them with a finger. Bells must have been first used as signals to convene the people to their public devotions. Durand, who lived about the end of the twelfth century, says, " When any one is dying, bells must be tolled, that the people may put up their prayers. Let this be done twice for a woman, and thrice for a man; if for a clergyman, as many times as he had orders, and at the conclusion, a peal on all the bells, to distinguish the quality of the person. A bell, too, must be rung while we are conducting the corpse to the church, and during the bringing it out of the church to the grave."

Ray says, in his Collection of old English Proverbs,

" When thou dost hear a toll or knell,
" Then think upon thy passing-bell."

The Romans had small bells, which they called *tintinabula*; they were summoned by these to their hot-baths, and business of public places. The large kind of bells now in use is, by Pollydore Virgil and others, ascribed to Paulinus, Bishop of Nola, a city in Campania, about the year 400, and to have been generally used in churches about the 600th year of

the Christian æra. In the time of Clothair, king of France, and the year 610, the army of the king was frightened from the siege of the city of Sens, by ringing of the bells of St. Stephen's church. In the time of Popery, bells were baptised and anointed Oleo Chrismatis; they were exorcised and blessed by the Bishop, from a belief that when these ceremonies were performed, they had power to drive the devil out of the air, to calm tempests, to extinguish fires, and even to recreate the dead. There are two Monkish Latin lines preserved, in which all the ancient offices of bells seem to be included, and are thus translated:—

We praise the true God, call the people,
        convene the clergy,
Lament the dead, dispel pestilence, and
        grace festivals.

The ritual for these ceremonies is contained in the Roman Pontifical; and it was usual in their baptism to give each bell the name of some Saint. The first consecrated bell was a very large new-cast one, by Pope John XIII. A. D. 968; it was called John.

In the little sanctuary, at Westminster, Edward III. erected a clochier, and placed therein three bells for the use of St. Stephen's chapel; about the largest of them were cast in the metal these words:

King Edward made me three thousand
        weight and three;
Take me down and try me, and more
        you shall find me.

But these bells being to be taken down in the reign of King Henry the VIIIth, one writes underneath with a coal,

But Henry the Eight,
Will bait me of my weight.

Sir Miles Partridge once staked 100l. against four bells, erected near

near St. Paul's School, the greatest in all England, and won them of Henry VIII. at a cast of dice.

In Fuller's History of Waltham Abbey, 1542, 34th Henry VIII. relative to the wages of bell-ringers, it is preserved from the churchwarden's account, " Item, paid for ringing at the Prince his coming, a penny."

It is said that the foundation of the fortunes of the Corsini family, in Italy, was laid by an ancestor, who, at the dissolution of the religious houses, purchased the bells of abbeys and other churches, and by the sale of them in other countries acquired a vast estate.

In the steeple of the great church at Rouen, in Normandy, is a bell with this inscription :

I am George of Amboïs,
Thirty-five thousand in pois ;
But he that shall weigh me,
Thirty-six thousand shall find me.

It is a common tradition, that the bells of King's College Chapel, in the University of Cambridge, were taken by Henry V. from some church in France, after the battle of Agincourt ; they were sold a few years ago to Phelps, a bell-founder, in Whitechapel, who melted them down.

At Moscow, in Russia, the great bell weighs 432,000lbs. and which exceeds in dimensions every bell in the known world; it is nineteen feet high, twenty-one yards eleven inches in circumference at the bottom, and twenty-three inches its greatest thickness. At Pekin, in China, there are seven bells, each of which weighs 120,000lbs.

The following is the weight of some of the largest bells in England. The Great Tom of Lincoln weighs 9,894lb. when gauged, it will hold 4,024 gallons; its compass is seven yards and a half and

two inches. The bell Dunstan, of Canterbury cathedral, weighs 70 cwt. The great bell of Exeter cathedral weighs 12,500lb. ; the tenor bell of St. Mary-le-Bow, London, weighs 53 cwt. ; that in York Minster, 53 cwt.; St. Peter's Norwich, 41 cwt.; St. Giles's, in Cripplegate, London, 36 cwt. ; St. Chad's, Shrewsbury. 34½ cwt. ; St. Margaret's, at Lynn, in Norfolk, 30 cwt.

In the year 1500, a flash of lightning struck the church of St. Alkmond's, in Shrewsbury, which is stated in their own Doomsday-book, that, " the Devil had got his claw upon the clapper of the great bell ; and from his claw there issued a flame of fire, which did melt every bell in the church, threw the spire upon the ground, and melted much of the brass-work candlesticks—because an holy and righteous monk had, in a sermon, spoken tauntingly of his power and authority upon earth."

Some time ago, the large bell of the Cathedral of Glasgow was broke, and afterwards sent to London to be re-founded ; it has lately been returned, bearing the following inscription :—

" In the year of grace 1594, Marcus Knox, a merchant, zealous for the interests of the reformed religion, caused me to be fabricated in Holland, for the use of his fellow-citizens of Glasgow, and placed with solemnity in the tower of their Cathedral.—My function was announced by the impress on my bosom, " Me audito doctrinam sanctam ut discas," and I was taught to proclaim the hours of unheeded time. CXC.V. years had I sounded these awful warnings, when I was broken by the hands of inconsiderate and unskilful men.

In

In the year M.DCC.XC. I was cast into the furnace, re-founded at London, and returned to my sacred vocation.

—Reader—

THOU, ALSO, SHALT KNOW A RE-
SURRECTION.

May it be unto Life Eternal !"

The practice of ringing bells in change is said to be peculiar to this country; but the antiquity of it is not easily ascertained. There are in London several societies of ringers, particularly one called the College Youths. of this, it is said, Sir Matthew Hale, Lord Chief Justice of the Court of King's Bench, was, in his youth, a member. Some of the most celebrated peals now known were composed about fifty years ago by one Patrick.

In 1684, Abraham Rudhall, of Gloucester, brought the art of bell-founding to great perfection; his descendants have followed the same business; and by a list published by them in 1774, the family, in peals and odd bells, had cast to the amount of 3,594.

We still retain a vestige of the old Norman curfew, at eight in the evening. William the Conqueror, in the first year of his reign, commanded that in every town and village a bell should be rung every night at eight o'clock, and that all people should then put out their fire and candle, and go to bed.— The ringing of this bell was called in French, Curfew; viz. cover fire.

The method of convening religious assemblies in monasteries, before the invention of bells, was going by turns to every one's cell, and with the knock of a hammer calling the monks to church. The instrument was called the night-signal and the wakening mallet.—

In many of the Colleges at Oxford, the Bible-clerk knocks at every room door with a key, to waken the students in the morning before he begins to ring the chapel-bell; a vestige, it should seem, of this ancient monastic custom.

THE TRAP.

An Etching, by Mr. W. Nicholls, from the Works of Ridenger.

THE cap that distinguishes the German hunter, is made up *à-la-mode* of the skin of the wild fox : and so much in esteem is this part of the sportsman's habiliment; that he is known to give to the amount of twenty rix-dollars to procure it, a sum almost equal to five pounds British; but if the pelt be torn, or any way damaged, it becomes of less value; and is no way respected by gentlemen who delight in the sports of the forest : for this reason, the woodmen who supply the furriers in Germany are particularly careful to furnish the skin unimpaired. To accomplish this end, they set a trap in a way unknown in our country, although it has some small affinity in the operation to that set by our mole-catchers.

They first ascertain the fox being within his earth, and then form the sides of the trap so close to the entrance, that there is no other way for him to come forth, but through the wire prepared for him, at the end of a beam of elastic wood. It may be some time before he quits his station; at length, however, he is compelled by hunger, and rushing to the wood makes every thing loose, up springs the beam, and he is suspended beyond the possibility of

THE TRAP.

Ridinger pinx.

Etched by W. Nicholson.

of escape; and, to the great satisfaction of the woodman, without a
flaw in the skin, for'the noose giving way to his struggles, presently
deprives him of life, and the pelt
is thus secured.

The annexed etching, by our
ingenious artist, will convey a more
perfect representation of the manner of making the trap, and of
course be most desirable to our
sporting readers.

T. N.

LIBERALITY.

THE present is, without doubt,
the *age of liberality*, Every
day is pregnant with instances of
the most splendid acts of munifi-
cence ; and it is truly said that he,
she, or they, who in any deviation
from the strict rules of decorum,
or in any embarrassment of fortune, address themselves to the
liberal feelings of the public, are
sure of *indulgence* and *protection*.
Thus, when an actor gets too much
in spirits, or an actress makes a
faux pas, they have only to throw
themselves on the *liberality* of the
audience. And thus when a capital singer made the *amende honor-
able* for a foolish advertisement, by
a letter in which she concluded with
a *liberal* declaration, that she desired permission from the managers
of the Opera, only to sing for *two
public charities*—the world rung
with her praises—it was an act so
very magnificent !—In two days
after we were informed, by a regular notice from a *music master*, that
he had *engaged* her to sing at *four
public concerts*, and that *four* ladies
of fashion had been so *liberal* as to
give him up their houses for the
performance. Here are instances

of *liberality* worthy of commemo-
ration. First, the manager of the
Opera is so *liberal* as to permit
Madame Catalani to do what she
did not require of him, to sing for
a private, instead of a public charity, and the gentleman, we suppose, gives her a *liberal* douceur
for her trouble.

But the condescension of the ladies of fashion, who generally permit their mansions to be converted
into *spectacles*, and who open their
doors to all the *miscellany* of a foreigner's subscription, illustrates the
liberal character of the age. This
is a point of refinement in liberality to which the sullen dignity of
our ancestors made no pretension.
And it is a mode of setting at defiance the *prudery* of the Theatre
in Argyll-street, " that is to be totally dedicated to the class which
ought to be kept separate and distinct from any other,"—as well as
the *nice arrangement* at the Opera,
from which " the persons whom
it is easier to understand than to
describe" are to be excluded.—
At the elegant *public rooms* of the
Marchioness of *this*—or the Marchioness of *that*—or the Marchioness of *t'other*—or of any Marchioness, let me ask, who will question the *right of admission* to any
one whom the *fiddler* has put down
in the books of his *dear* and *liberal*
Duchess of A. the Countess of B.
or the Lady C. ?—It is a most
happy expedient to secure *freedom*
under the mask of *restraint*, and
to enjoy the most perfect relief
from *censure*, by having one' house
too *crowded* for *observation* !—We
must also admire the *œconomy* of
this new fashion. Of old, when a
noble Lady gave a splendid concert
at her mansion, the noble Lord's
oaks or his *elms* paid for the *piping*.
She was obliged to *engage* the *fa-

Gg   vourite*

vourite voices and instruments of the year.—Now she is herself engaged, and receives a number of tickets in proportion to the capacity of her rooms, and the extent of her attraction.—In this way the palace of a Duchess may let for more than that of a Countess—And the hotel of a Baroness for double that of a 'Squire's Lady.— It would be an edifying caricature, worthy of Gilray's pencil, to contrast the anxious features of a lady of high fashion, standing in an attitude of suspence, while an Italian musician was pacing her suite of rooms to ascertain their length and breadth, and to fix the number of tickets he would give for the accommodation!

People talk of the waste and extravagance of the present age.— Does this look like waste!—To what an exquisite degree of domestic management we have attained, when we can thus convert even the extremity of ostentation into a source of revenue!—Opening one's own house has other advantages—It is obviously commode. —It affords facilities which are incompatible with the conspicuous character of a public place, every avenue to which is necessarily open : but here publicity is united with retirement—and the péle-méle with the select.—For while in the state room the crowd are astonished by the mellifluous starts and compass of Catalani—delighted by the executive science of Billington —or captivated by the graceful attitude of Grassini — while the Misses are all thrilling enamoured over the dulcet cadenzas of Le Kaneu—and the Dowagers are enraptured with the full organic volume of Dragonetti—my Lord and my Lady may now have their partie choisee in the parlour; or each may have a partie fine in the library and boudoir, for the age is too liberal for any malevolent constructions —We are all too polished to harbour the vulgarity of scandal.— And it is manifest, that the ladies of fashion give up their houses to their music masters and fiddlers— only because their music masters and fiddlers are the very best people in the world, and because the present is the age of liberality.

PEDIGREE AND PERFORMANCES OF REGULUS.

To the Editor of the Sporting Magazine.

SIR,

IN your last Magazine, page 156, under the head, " The Godolphin Arabian," where it is stated, " He was sire of Lath, Cade, Blank, Babraham, and Regulus, who were all afterwards stallions of repute, and the latter (who won, in one year, seven King's Plates, and was never beat) proved, &c."—To correct a mistake in the number of the Royal Plates said to be won by Regulus, I have taken the liberty of sending you the Pedigree and Performances of that once favourite Racer and approved good Stallion, whose blood is now, and ever will be, esteemed and valued by every breeder who is a judge of Pedigree. Your's, &c.
W. P.

August 15, 1808.

REGULUS was bred by Lord Chedworth, at whose death he was sold to Mr. Martindale, of St. James's-street, London.

Regulus was got by Lord Godolphin's Arabian; his dam, Grey Robinson,

Robinson, by the Bald Galloway; grandam, (own sister to Country-Wench) by Snake; great grandam, Grey Wilkes, (own sister to Clumsy) by Mr. Wilkes's Hautboy, out of Miss D'Arcy's Pet Mare, a daughter of a Sedbury Royal Mare.—*Grey Robinson* and her dam (the *Snake Mare)* were both bred by Mr. Robinson, of Easby, near Richmond, Yorkshire; the former he sold to Mr. Howe, and the latter, after she bred Shock, (1729) to Mr. Metcalfe, which mare was distinguished by the name of " Mr. Metcalfe's Old Snake Mare." The *Snake Mare* was also the dam of Mr. Howe's Foxhunter, by the Bald Galloway; and Shock, by Jigg; of Lord Portmore's Squirt, by Mr. Bartlett's Childers; Mr. Metcalfe's Gay, by Mr. Bethell's Arabian; Brown Russett, by Lord Lonsdale's Bay Arabian; Lady Caroline, by Flying Childers; Lady Betty, by the Duke of Devonshire's Blacklegs, &c. &c. *Squirt* was sire of Marsk, Syphon, and Mr. Pratt's favourite Old Mare, that was the grandam of Rockingham, Walnut, &c.—*Marsk* was sire of Eclipse, &c. and *Syphon* was sire of Tandem, &c.

In 1745, *Regulus* (in the name of *Sweetlips)* won 50l. carrying 12st. at Epsom, beating Poppet, Brisk, and Chance. He was then named *Regulus*, and in the same year won the King's Plate at Winchester, beating Mr. Grisewood's Teazer; walked over for the King's Plate at Salisbury; won the King's Plate at Nottingham, beating Mr. Hutton's Wormwood, Mr. Vavasour's Champion, and distanced two others; the King's Plate at Canterbury, beating Mr. Grisewood's Teazer; the King's Plate at Lewes, beating Mr.

Smith's Grey Lincoln; the King's Plate at Lincoln, beating Mr. Vavasour's Champion; and the King's Plate at Newmarket, in October, beating Lord Portmore's Grey Lincoln, and Mr. Everett's Lowther:—Regulus won the first heat so very easy, that Lord Portmore and Mr. Everett withdrew their horses. At Newmarket, in April, 1746, he won the King's Plate, beating easy, Mr. Grisewood's Teazer, who was drawn after the first heat.

Regulus, at six years old, won *eight* Royal Plates, and a 50l. Plate, 12st each.—He was *never beat*, and was much superior to any other horse of his time.

Regulus then became a favourite and very valuable Stallion in the North of Yorkshire, and was sire of an uncommon number of racers, stallions, and brood-mares; notwithstanding, it has been asserted that Mr. Martindale cleared by him, as a stallion, little more than one thousand guineas.

He died at Low-Gaterley, near Catterick, Yorkshire, in 1765, aged 26.—He covered at 10gs. and 5s.

THE AFRICANS;
OR,
WAR, LOVE, AND DUTY.

HAYMARKET THEATRE.

THIS new Drama, imputed to the pen of Mr. Colman, has produced houses tolerably crowded for several evenings past.—It is called *The Africans*, because the scene is laid in Africa, and the characters are principally of the sable cast. The second title of the Play is *War, Love, and Duty.*—Of

these

these; the war consists of an attack on the Mandingos, and on the Foulhas, whose town of Tatticonda they destroy, &c. This happens just as Selico (Mr. Young), is to be joined in wedlock with his love, Berissa, (Mrs. Gibbs) daughter of an aged priest. Some time after, amidst the horrors of war, Selico thinks he finds the headless and mangled bodies of Berissa and her father; on which, of course, he makes a very pathetic speech.— Well, now comes the duty. Amidst the distress of the place, Dariha, the mother of Selico, Madiboo, (Fawcett), and Torribal, (Farley), is absolutely starving, and her dutiful sons consult on the means of preserving her. This in itself is a curious circumstance, that although we hear of much distress, she appears to be the only individual in a state of wretchedness. The most natural remedy, we think, would have been, that as the three brothers must have some food themselves, each of them might contribute his share, after the common observation, that what is enough for three will do for four. But this simple means would not suit the tragic story of the poet. No, Selico insists that his brothers shall sell him as a slave to some English merchants then arrived, to which they reluctantly agree, but on coming to the market he finds that he will fetch so small a sum, as to be inadequate to relieving his mother. Fortunately, at this moment, a very large reward is offered for the apprehension of some unknown person, who had, on the preceding night, procured access to the favourite captive of the King; he determines that his brother shall give him up as the delinquent. This is done, and Madiboo obtains the reward. He is for this alledged crime sentenced to be burned with the female prisoner he is supposed to have visited. The culprits are led to stakes opposite each other, and in his fellow-sufferer he discovers his Berissa. Her father now rushes in, and proves to have been her clandestine visitor. Dariha also appears with Torribal and Madiboo; and the King, touched with the constancy and filial affection of the lovers, pardons, and gives them to each other.—Such is the tragic part of the piece, to enliven which Madiboo, amidst the serious scenes around him, is always cracking his jokes, besides singing à-la-Fawcett, a song about a blind priest of Kajaaga and his wife's romp. But the principal comic personage is Henry Augustus Mug, of Snow-Hill, turner, (Liston), who has come to Africa to purchase ivory, and is there made a slave; but in the course of the play, in consequence of the revolution, occasioned by the war aforesaid, becomes Prime Minister to the Mandingo King. This gentleman takes great delight in repeating his own name, and in clapping together the most abominable collection of vile puns that we had ever the misfortune to hear, and of disgusting political clap-traps.

There is much fine writing in the piece, rather too much indeed to put into the mouths of savage Africans. 'Tis a great pity, that *The Africans* was not reserved for a Christmas vacation, as our young masters would doubtless have been greatly delighted with a rising st , brilliant scenery, a burning city, tawdry dresses, grotesque dancing, and horrid yelling; although even they would have asked why Madiboo, when he proposes to reconnoitre the enemy, stops to join Mug and Sutta in a trio; why Mr.
                                        Mug

Mog is continually repeating his name and his business; why he is made a Secretary of State; and why Madiboo, when he has obtained provisions for his famishing mother, stops to pronounce a Philippic against Napoleon, to make and listen to several beautiful puns, and to panegyrise the English, who are purchasing and enslaving his countrymen. These are questions it would not be difficult to answer; for the young gentlemen might be told, that the first is in imitation of an Italian Opera, where Mentor holds Telemachus on the brink of a rock, from which he is about to throw him into the sea, while he sings a bravura. That the second is in compliance with the elegant and classic modern fashion of having something, which the author fancies *funny*, well imprinted on the memories of his audience, as " *Peter Trot, of the Minories, in the tatoe line*;"—that the third is on the model of Mr. Cherry's Irishman in China; and that the fourth is caused by a consciousness that the play cannot rest on its own merits for support, but must depend on the good humour of the audience, whom it is therefore necessary to inform, that Bonaparte is a ferocious murderer, that the French are slaves, and that John Bull alone is witty, brave, benevolent, and full of virtue.

We shall only now remark one egregious impropriety. While all the Mandingos are completely black, and the Foulhas copper-coloured, yet Berissa, a Foulah lady, and daughter of a copper-coloured priest, appears with as fair a skin, both face and arms, as was ever displayed by the handsome Mrs. Gibbs. If this lady is above colouring herself on the occasion, Mr. Colman should have somehow

accounted for his fair friend retaining her native hue.

The piece has undergone several improvements. The song we have inserted in our poetical department, from this piece, will serve as a specimen of the poetry.

UNNECESSARY SPEED.

INNKEEPERS and others, who keep horses to run this very hot season of the year, ought to provide the following medicine, that every coachman or post-boy may have it in readiness to give to those horses taken sick upon the road:

Recipe.—Take tincture balsamic, and compound spirits of ammoniac, each one ounce; prepared kail, two drachms; one cordial ball, or, in its stead, one ounce of ginger root, fresh powdered; to be given in a pint and a half, or a quart, of cold water. This will greatly refresh the animal, and in general prevent those ill consequences, which daily occur through heat and over-driving. If the beating or palpitation of the heart be severe, add two drachms of tincture of opium to the above, which may be repeated every two hours, if required.

Upon the above subject a sensible correspondent observes:—

" It rarely occurs that any individual can be so imperiously situated as to be under the necessity of depriving these very useful creatures of existence, or of reducing them to that wretched state of suffering in which they are so often seen; nine times out of ten, the only object of this speed is to shorten the traveller's drive through a pleasant country, in order to take possession three minutes sooner

sooner of a dirty parlour in a still dirtier inn, from the window of which he may view the miseries which his impatience has produced.

" When I observe advertisements which state the short time in which certain coaches run certain distances, I cannot help reflecting on the daily sufferings of the poor horses. Are such noble animals to be wantonly abused, contributing as they do, in such a variety of ways, to our uses and comforts ? and is it not a disgrace to humanity, and to a civilised country, to hear and read of the numbers which have of late fallen victims to over fatigue ?

" In circumstances where the interference of the Legislature would be next to impossible, the discretion of the driver ought to counteract the want of humanity in the traveller.

" That these observations may tend to awaken some sparks of pity in the breasts of my countrymen, for the sufferings of a noble, useful, and beautiful race of animals, who, though they have not the gift of speech, can feel as keenly as ourselves, is the sincere wish of   " VIATOR."

INSTINCT OF A DOG.

To the Editor.

SIR,

IF you think the following instance of sagacity in a dog worth recording, I beg you will insert it in your Magazine.

I shall detail the facts, leaving to your better judgment the manner in which they ought to be given to the public.

On Wednesday last, my groom went to Windsor on horseback, accompanied by three dogs, two pointers, and a terrier ; on his return, within about half a mile of home, the horse on which he rode took fright, threw him, and ran home, attended by two of the dogs; the terrier and one pointer : the appearance of the horse at home without the man, naturally excited in the hearts of the other servants an apprehension that some accident had befallen him, and two of them, a man and woman, went in quest of him ; after searching in vain about two hours in the lane, which is in the direct road from hence to Windsor, they were induced to look into the cross road, whither they went through a field ; whilst in the field, the man called the groom's name aloud, which was answered by the barking of a dog. The woman observing, that she thought it the voice of the dog which had not come home, they directed their course to the spot whence the voice proceeded. As soon as they got into the lane, they descried a dog at a distance making towards them, which proved to be the very dog. Upon coming up to them, he discovered alternate symptoms of joy and uneasiness, and ran before them, as if desirous of shewing them the cause. They followed, when lo! he conducted them to the spot where lay the man in a ditch by the road side, apparently lifeless ! They dragged him along home, and laid him in a bed, the dog staying with him the whole time, and, by a whining noise, discovering his anxiety. The persons who were in the room made several attempts to turn the dog out, but without success ; they were at length so won upon by the creature's manners, that they allowed him

him to remain, when he at length placed himself on the man's bed, and watched him with the most painful anxiety, and as he groaned, so did the dog mourn, proportioning the height and duration of his voice to that of the man; nor did he quit the bed until twelve o'clock of the following day, when the man seemed restored to his senses! What is more remarkable is, that from the time he was laid upon the bed, the man was alternately affected with a stupor or total insensibility, and a most ungovernable frenzy, and in the latter state directed his violence to the poor animal, treating him most unmercifully, but the dog would not leave him. The man, I am glad to say, is recovering fast, and the dog is in my possession, his value not a little increased by the circumstances I have related.—I have the honour to be, Sir, your most obedient servant, JAMES DOVE.

Wexham House, Stoke Green,
July 31, 1809.

DANCING WOMEN OF MYSORE.

From Buchanan's Journey in that
Country.

A Certain number of dancing women are attached to every temple of any consequence. The allowances which the musicians receive for their public duty is very small, yet morning and evening they are bound to attend at the temple, to perform before the image. They must also receive every person travelling on account of the government, meet him at some distance from the town, and conduct him to his quarters with music and dancing. All the handsome girls are instructed to dance

and sing, and are all prostitutes, at least to the Brahmins. In ordinary sets they are quite common; but, under the Company's government, those attached to temples of extraordinary sanctity, are reserved entirely for the use of the native officers, who are all Brahmins, and who would turn out from the set any girl that profaned herself by communication with persons of low cast, or of no cast at all, such as Christians or Musselmen. Indeed, almost every one of these girls that is tolerable sightly, is taken by some officer of revenue for his own special use, and is seldom permitted to go to the temple, except in his presence. Most of these officers have more than one wife, and the women of the Brahmins are very beautiful; but the insipidity of their conduct, from a total want of education or accomplishment, makes the dancing women sought after by all natives with great avidity. When a dancing girl becomes old, she is turned out from the temple without any provision, and is very destitute, unless she has a handsome daughter to succeed her; but if she has, the daughters are in general extremely attentive and kind to their aged parents. To my taste nothing can be more silly and unanimated than the dancing of the women, nor more harsh and barbarous than their music. Some Europeans, however, from long habit I suppose, have taken a liking to it, and have even been captivated by the women. Most of them that I have had an opportunity of seeing, have been very ordinary in their looks, very inelegant in their dress, and very dirty in their persons; a large proportion of them have the itch, and a still larger proportion are more severely diseased.

FEAST

FEAST OF WIT.

A Gentleman having written the word *terror* in a letter he was sending to a friend, an acquaintance standing by, told him it would have been an *error*, if the *t* had been left out.

A PERSON who had been dining on board a ship of war at Spithead, observed to a friend, the day following, "that naval officers drank a vast quantity of wine."—To which his friend immediately replied, "Ah! but you should make some allowance, for they do not drink in that sort of way when they are *out of port* !"

A MAN at a fair was asked, as he passed along, if he would have a chance at one of the *E. O. Tables* ? happening to be very hungry, he cried, "No, no, but shew me the place where I can find some *E.-A.-Tables* and depend on it, *they* will stand no *chance* at all."

A STORY-TELLER.—A great teller of stories was in the midst of one of the best at his evening club, when notice was brought him, that a ship, in which he was going to the West Indies, was on the point of sailing; he was therefore obliged to leave off abruptly. On his return from Jamaica some years afterwards, he repaired to the club, and taking possession of his old seat by the fire-side, resumed his tale: —" Gentlemen, as I was saying——"

BARON Munchausen.—The Captain of a West Indiaman, who could shoot a long bow, told this story—" Gentlemen, last year, coming over the banks of Newfoundland, we hooked an immense shark, and there appeared a difficulty of getting him on board. I went down to my cabin for my pistols, which I always kept loaded, and just as I was going to fire one of them at the monster, it slipped out of my hand, and fell into the sea. Soon after the shark broke the line, and made his escape.—Well, Gentlemen, coming home this voyage, nearly about the same latitude, we again hooked a shark, and with some difficulty he was hooked on deck. As the people were cutting him up, I was surprised to hear a report something like a pistol-shot; and, Gentlemen, would you believe it ? this was the identical shark that had swallowed my pistol, which now went off in consequence of a stroke of the knife with which they were ripping up his belly. You may, perhaps, think I have used a licence too often indulged in by travellers, and fabricated this story; but my mate, and all my ship's company, if they were here, would tell you the same."

MUNCHAUSEN Reproved—The same West India Captain, talking of the tenacity of life in turtles, affirmed that he had seen the head of one which had been cut off three weeks, and was in a complete state of putrefaction, open its jaws. The company seemed by their looks rather to doubt the veracity of the story, but did not choose to give the gentleman the lie. One of them, however, observed, that

it

It was indeed very strange; adding, "Pray, Captain, could you have believed such a thing if you had not seen it?"—"Indeed," answered he, "I could not."—"Then," rejoined the other, "I hope you'll excuse me, if I don't believe it."—It is almost unnecessary to add, that the laugh was completely against the Captain.

LATELY, a poor woman applied to the overseers of a parish in the city for relief, and among other particulars stated, that she had had seventeen children.—"What was your husband, good woman?"—"He was a labouring man, Sir!"

A DESERTER being conducted to his regiment, assured his comrades, who had volunteered for Spain, that he came by forced marches to assist in the glorious struggle.

THICK ANCLES.

"HARRY, I cannot think," says Dick,
"What makes my ancles grow so thick."
"You do not recollect," says Harry,
"How great a CALF they have to carry."

THE insolvency of a late attorney was accounted for by one of his friends very logically. "He lived without causes, and died without effects!"

A WOMAN of indifferent character, being lately examined by a certain Barrister with his usual boldness, she observed, "Impudence, which has been the making of you, has caused my ruin."

A THEATRICAL report, in the modern style, forms a very curious combination. Sometimes a piece is received with thunders of applause—then the appearance of a favourite performer is hailed with

rapture! A comedian is praised for his fire—a tragedian reproved for being cold as ice—and a singer applauded for his excellence in a particular air! Mix these ingredients properly together, and the result will truly be the elements of criticism.

A PERSON has been tried at the country assizes for stealing a silver spoon, which he pretended to have carried off in a joke. The Jury, however, happened to be too dull to understand such jokes, and the wit was sentenced to be transported!

KING JOE AND JO-KING.

QUOTH NAP to his Brother, "What
makes you so sad?
"If thus wildly you look, folks will think
you're turn'd mad!"
Poor JOSEPH deep sigh'd,
And dolorously cried—
His visage most ruefully stroking—
"Tis all over, you know,
"With wretched King JOE,
"And therefore 'tis no time for Jo-
king!"

A SUITOR having applied at Serjeant Cockle's Chambers, was told, Mr. Cockle was going out of town, "I thought so," said the enquirer, a Feversham dredger, "for oysters are coming in."

CURIOUS PUN.—A wise man (observes a Scots punster,) is like a blind man, because he is apt to feel less of eyes (philosophize).

ANOTHER. — Mr. Whitbread's porter store is like Dukes' Place, because it is where Hebrews (he brews) drink in.

WHEN any of the Jew prigs are pulled up, viz. apprehended, they invariably produce a number of Israelitish witnesses, to swear they are very industrious people.

A FEW

A FEW days ago an *attorney's clerk*, of the name of *M'Rarey*, and a *journeyman taylor*, of the name of *Macintosh*, were prevented from fighting a duel at Chalk-farm, by the interposition, of the police. The following is a literal copy of the challenge :—

" Mr. Mac Rarey—You are to come to cholk farm to morrowe morning at halfe past six o'clock and you are to harm yourself with whatever you please acept sword.

" William Macintosh.
" 103, *Warder-strette*."

AN advertiser of *fire-arms* very strongly recommends to the notice of the public his *duelling pistols*. We suppose they are calculated to make a *noise* in the world, without *killing* the combatants.

THE *bailiffs* are particularly displeased with the rage for *running races*, that exists among young men at present, as few of the former have the *agility* to accomplish an arrest.

AT a recent dinner in the city, the chairman proposed a health, but neglected to pass the bottle ; upon which a facetious citizen exclaimed—" Mr. President, I will thank you for some wine, for a *dry toast* always gives me the *heart-burn*."

AT the assizes on the Northern Circuit, a bumpkin was tried for the rural amusement of *breaking a head*. The Counsel for the prosecution observed, " that the offence was of a most serious nature, as it affected the security of the *Crown !*"

Poor Delpini—We have to announce, died the 23d ult. in a sta-

ble, a few miles from York. He is much regretted by those who were acquainted with his qualifications ;—as a public character, he was perfectly *well-bred*, and was accustomed to strain every nerve in the service of his employer. He was too frequently *spurred on* from the hopes of gain ; and, like other objects of general animadversion, he often endured the *lush*. From circumstances unnecessary to mention, he was, in the course of his life, *saddled* with heavy incumbrances ; and, on several occasions, he was reduced to the necessity of *biting the bridle*. He was free from any material *blemish* ; and such was the estimation he enjoyed, that in most instances he has distanced his competitors. The greatest shade in his character was, a propensity to *indiscriminate amours* ; for though never married, he has left behind him a *numerous progeny*, many of whom he lived to see take good *courses* ; and yet such was his general abstinence, that, during a long existence, he drank nothing but water.—To prevent mistakes, it may be necessary to mention that the deceased was not the facetious *clown*—but a celebrated *race horse*.

FRIENDSHIP.

FRIENDSHIP is like a cobler's tie,
That joins two *soles* in unity,
But love is like the cobler's awl,
That pierces through the *sole* and all.

A GENTLEMAN was heard to say, that he would at all times be his own *lawyer* if he had occasion for one ; a wag replied, " then you will very frequently have *a fool* for your *client*."

LEARNED dogs and pigs have formerly given much amusement to the public ; and in all probability we we shall soon hear of learned *cats*, as there were lately sent to the master of an academy, in Monmouthshire, a hamper, containing *twenty-three* living cats, the *music* of which was so inharmonious to the passengers, that the coachman was obliged to take them from the roof, and leave them to be brought on by the next stage, to the great mortification of their owner, who anxiously expected their arrival.

THE lady of a new-made Knight being asked to drink a glass of wine, refused, because her physician had put her upon a *regimen*, which was to drink water; "Then, Madam," said Mr. Alderman Birch, " I presume you belong to the *Cold-stream*."

As a *dashing female*, habited in the fashionable costume of the whip, was exercising her skill in driving, the charioteer was complimented by an *Hibernian inamorato*, " That she looked for all the world like a *male* couchman."

THE Earl of Ormond (whose family name is Butler) and the Hon. Mr. Cooke encountered a chimney-sweeper one morning in the streets of Dublin. His Lordship, in a vein of humour, said, " Well, Sooterkins, what news from Hell?" " Nothing, (replied the gentleman in black) but that the Devil stands in need of a *Cook* and a *Butler*."

AT a late festive meeting of volunteers, the following toast was given, " *A plum pudding*, in the heart of France;" which was thus explained—" The flour of England, and the fruit of Spain."

THE *cubs of fashion*, who have not cash to go to any of the watering places, are now called *Bond-street owls*, as they never stir out of doors before *midnight*, lest they should be discovered to be so *horribly ungenteel* as to *remain in town*.

The following *jeu d'esprit* was occasioned by the circumstance of a son of Vulcan having fallen in love with the niece of a Norfolk Baronet :—

A CAUTION TO ALL ASPIRING YOUNG MEN.—Whereas I, (a son of Vulcan) having been misled by the glances and encouraging smiles of a fair damsel (exalted far above my humble situation), dared avow to her the flame which she kindled, bright as the brightest that ever supplied my forge, strong as the bout-hammer, and steady as the hand that wields it; it required no fuel but what her eyes supplied, and her lips acting like bellows, blew it to such a pitch, that as the sparks rise from my chimney, so it escaped the confines of prudence, and issued forth in the language of love;—fond and fervent was the strain—long and anxious the interval that succeeded—again the quill was active—still all was silent as the grave—despair seized on my heart—wan is my cheek—lost is the lustre of my eyes—the music in the village has ceased—my song in the church is no more—I returned to the house of prayer, silent and dejected I sat—I wandered forth to meet no smiles but those of scorn, no words but of derision.— My sun of hope is set. Ye youths, beware of the syren smiles of beauty, the *seeming* looks of kindness that beguile our easy hearts, and like the Will o' the Wisp, lead but to destruction.

WINNERS OF ROYAL PLATES AT YORK.

Continued from our last Magazine, Page 187.

1770 MR. O'Kelly's Eclipse,* by Marsk—*walked over*
1771 Mr. Wentworth's Melpomene, by Alcides
1772 Hon. J. S. Barry's Raggamuffin, by Northumberland.
1773 Mr. Wentworth's Achilles, (late Presumption) by Jalap
1774 Mr. G. Hartley's Towzer† (alias Counsellor) by Alcides
1775 Mr. Isaac Cape's Teucer, by Northumberland
1776 Mr. Ayrton's Cashkeeper, by Doge
1777 Sir James Lowther's Ajax, by Carnatic
1778 Mr. Ellis's Diana, (late Zingara) by Shakspeare
1779 Mr. Bethell's Magnumbonum, by Match'em
1780 Mr. Coates's Orpheus, by Le Sang
1781 Mr. Freeman's Standby, by Prophet
1782 Sir John Lade's Nottingham, by Tantrum
1783 Mr. Vernor's Drone, by King Herod—*walked over*
1784 Sir J. L. Kaye's Recovery, by Hyder Ally.—*(Young Eclipse dislocated a fetlock-joint in running)*
1785 Lord Surrey's Cumberland, by Phlegon
1786 Lord Archibald Hamilton's Alexander, by Mungo (late Leviathan)
1787 Mr. Bullock's Rockingham, by Highflyer
1788 Duke of Norfolk's Merrylass, by Young Marsk
1789 Mr. Wetherell's Windlestone, by Magnet
1790 Mr. Baker's Cavendish, by Young Morwick
1791 Lord Lauderdale's Scorpion, by Il'mio
1792 Mr. Wastell's Tickle Toby, by Alfred—*walked over*
1793 Mr. Welburne's Comet,‡ by Phœnomenon
1794 Mr. Cornforth's Antæus, by Phlegon, 5 years old—*Beatles broke down*
1795 Lord Darlington's St. George, by Highflyer
1796 Mr. Baker's Screveton, by Highflyer
1797 Mr. Wentworth's Trimbush, by Young Morwick

* *Eclipse* won *eleven* King's Plates, (the weights for *ten* of which were 12st. each) which was one more than was ever won by any horse in England.—He was never beat, and was allowed by all ranks of sportsmen to be the fleetest horse that ever ran in England, since the time of *Childers.*—He was afterwards a very valuable stallion, and died at Cannons, Middlesex, on Saturday the 28th of February, 1789, aged 25.

† Previous to the races, the Duke of Ancaster, Master of the Horse, gave notice in the London Gazette, that it was his Majesty's command, that the one hundred guineas usually run for at York, should, in future, be determined by *one four-mile heat only*, subject in all other respects to the usual rules.

‡ *Comet* was only five years old, and the only horse in that year who had won the Royal Plate at York since 1710, (the first commencement) which was won by Bay Bolton.

1798 MR.

1798 Mr. Cookson's Diamond, (brother to Screveton) by Highflyer
1799 Sir Frank Standish's Stamford,* by Sir Peter Teazle, 5 yrs old
1800 Mr. Johnson's Sir Solomon, by Sir Peter Teazle, 4 years old
1801 Lord Darlington's Agonistes, by Sir Peter Teazle, 4 years old
1802 Mr Dawson's Quiz, by Buzzard, 4 yrs old
1803 Lord Darlington's Agonistes, by Sir Peter Teazle, 6 yrs old
1804 Sir H. Williamson's Honest Starling, by Sir Peter Teazle, four
     years old
1805 Mr Garforth's Evander, by Delpini, 4 years old
1806 Lord Fitzwilliam's Sir Paul, by Sir Peter Teazle, 4 years old
1807 Mr Mellish's Luck's-All, by Stamford, 4 years old.

DELPINI.

ON Saturday, July 23, at four o'clock in the afternoon, died, aged 27, at Mr. Thomas Kirby's Stables, without Walmgate - Bar, York, that once celebrated racer and favourite stallion, DELPINI.— He was bred by the Duke of Bolton, and sold, at three years old, to Sir Frank Standish, Bart. He was got by Highflyer, out of Countess, by Blank :—Countess was the dam of Cobscar, Vizard, Greybeard, Achilles, and Horatia, the dam of Stamford, Archduke, Paris, &c.

On Monday, at York August Meeting, 1786, he won the 25gs. stakes for all ages, four miles, beating Verjuice, Grey Highflyer, and Optimus. On Wednesday, he won the Subscription Purse for five-year olds, four miles, beating Pitch, Leveret, and Posthumous ; and on Thursday, he won (giving his year) the Subscription Purse for six-year old and aged horses, four miles, beating Faith and Glancer. He

also won several stakes and matches at Newmarket, and was the best runner of his year, Rockingham excepted.

Delpini was sire of the following winners; viz.

Mr. Wharton's Kilton.
Mr. Goodricke's Prior, Cardinal, St. Anne, Rigadoon, and Agnes, afterwards Mr. Whaley's (of Ireland) Duchess of York.
Mr. Wetherell's Skelton.
Mr. Cradock's Tiptoe.
Mr. Lumley's Miss Ann.
Mr. Cholmondeley's Abraham Wood, Nixon, and Knutsford.
Mr. H Sitwell's Clymene.
Mr. Artley's Dido and Duchess.
Sir T. Gascoigne's Golden-Locks, Flutter, Opposition, Timothy, Symmetry, Maid of the Mill, Slapbang, Flutter, Theophania, Lenox, Confederate alias Drum-Major, &c.
Mr Fenton's Allegro and Dapple.

---

* March, 1799, The Earl of Westmoreland, Master of the Horse, gave notice, that it was his Majesty's command, that the one hundred guineas usually run for at York, by six-year old horses, were not to be limited to such in future, but to extend to the following ages, viz. four-year olds, carrying 10st 4lb ; five-year olds, 11st 6lb ; six-year olds, 12st ; and aged, 12st 2lb. but subject in all other respects to the usual rules.

Mr.

Mr J. Hutchinson's Little Scot.
Colonel Maxwell's Miss Beverley.
Sir J. Leicester's Blue-Beard.
Mr. Fletcher's Camperdown.
Mr. Clough's Hopwell.
Mr. Trapps's L'Abbé.
Mr. Tatton's Laborie.
Mr. Singleton's Patch.
Mr. Fenton's Stourton.
Mr. Alderson's Baron Nile.
Mr. Coventry's St. Ives.
Hon. R. L. Savile's Sabella.
Mr. Smith's Confessor.
Hon. G. Watson's Striver.
Sir H. T. Vane's Capricio.
Mr. Wastell's Scotia.
Mr. G. Hutton's Saxoni.
Mr. Garforth's Evander, Vesta, and
  Helen.
Lord Stamford's Gayman.
Mr. N. B. Hodgson's Priscilla.
Mr. Topham's Young Lucy.
Colonel King's Hessle.
Colonel Harbord's Master Betty.
Sir M. M. Sykes's Sir Launcelot.
Mr. Mason's Trafalgar.
Mr. Mellish's Bradbury.
  And several others.

ACTION FOR A BREACH OF THE GAME LAWS.

TRIED AT THE SUSSEX ASSIZES.

Hebden v. Luff.

THIS was an action to recover a
penalty for a breach of the
Game Laws. The action was
founded on the Statute of the 9th
of Anne, cap. 25, sect. 2, which
gives a penalty against any unqualified person having game in his
possession, and makes the mere
having of it evidence of an exposure to sale. Mr. Courthorpe
having stated the law, next produced evidence of the fact, which
was proved by two gamekeepers, as

follows :—That being on the watch
early in the morning, they heard
the screams of a hare, upon which
they looked about, and discovered
a hare in a trap, not far from the
cottage of the defendant ; they lay
in wait, expecting that the person
who set the trap would come to
see what it produced : they saw
the defendant come to the trap,
and take the hare out : upon this
they came out of their concealment, but the defendant seeing
them, threw the hare away, and
denied that he had had any ; they,
however, found the hare at a little
distance from him.

Mr. Serjeant Best submitted to
the Court, that this was not such a
possession as the Act meant when
it made possession an exposure to
sale.

The Learned Judge, on referring
to the Act, declared he did not
wish to extend the Game Laws,
but the words were so very positive,
that he did not know how to get
over them. It in express terms
made all possession of game by an
unqualified person an exposure to
sale.

The Jury found the defendant
Guilty.

THE ASWAMEDHA JUG;
OR,
HORSE SACRIFICE.

*From the Rev. Mr. Maurice's Indian An-
tiquities.*

THIS ceremony, the Indians,
doubtless, derived from the
Persians, among whom, according
to the whole stream of classic antiquity, the *horse* was in a peculiar
manner sacred to the sun. In their
pompous sacrifices to that deity, a
radiant

radiant car, glittering with gold and diamonds, and drawn by *white horses*, in imitation of those æthereal coursers which, they imagined, rapidly conveyed the orb of day in its progress through the expanse of heaven, constantly formed a part of the procession. It was preceded by a train of led horses, sumptuously arrayed, and of uncommon beauty and magnitude, who were the destined victims of that splendid superstition. The Massagetæ, too, that warlike race, who, according to Strabo, opposed the arms of the great Cyrus, adored the sun, and sacrificed horses to that deity. Horses, however, were not only sacrificed to the sun in the ancient æras of the Persian empire; for the Persians paid likewise a religious homage to water: and Herodotus says, that on the arrival of the army at the Strymon, the Magi sacrificed nine *white horses* to that river, into which they threw them with a quantity of rich aromatics.

In a Hindoo commentary upon the Vedas, the Aswamedha-Jug, we are told, does not merely consist in bringing a horse and sacrificing him, but the rite is also taken in a mystic signification.— " The horse so sacrificed is in the place of the sacrificer, and bears his sins with him to the wilderness into which he is turned adrift."— From this particular instance, it seems that the sacrificing knife was not always employed.

Mr. Halhed, in the preface to the Code of Gentoo Laws, observes, that this ceremony reminds us of the scape-goat of the children of Israel, and, indeed, it is not the only one in which a particular coincidence between the Hindoo and Mosaic systems of theology may be traced.

The Ayeen Akberry says, the Aswamhedha Jug is performed only by great monarchs previous to their entering upon a war ; that he then carries victory wherever he goes ; and that whosoever has performed this ceremony a hundred times, will become a monarch in the upper regions. The annotator upon the Hectopades differs from this account ; for he says that the sacrifice of the horse, in ancient times, was performed by a king at the conclusion of a great war, in which he had been victorious.

We shall take another opportunity of selecting from the Indian Antiquities an account of the Gomedha Jug, or Sacrifice of the Bull.

THE SILLER GUN.

A Poem, in Four Cantos; with Notes, and a Glossary. By John Mayne, Author of the Poem of Glasgow, &c.

THIS new poem, though written in a great measure in the Scottish dialect, is uncommonly perspicuous, and by no means deficient in vivacity. It is founded on an ancient custom in Dumfries, called " *Shooting for the Siller Gun.*"

The gun is a small silver tube, like the barrel of a pistol, but derives great importance from its being the gift of James VI, that Monarch having ordained it as a prize to the best marksman among the Corporations of Dumfries. The contest was at first intended to take place every year, but now, whenever the festival is appointed, the birth-day of the reigning sovereign is invariably chosen for that purpose. The institution itself may be regarded as a memorial of the Waponshaw—the shooting at butts and bow-marks, and other military sports,

sports, intended to keep alive the martial ardour and heroic spirit of the people.

We further learn, from the author's preface, that it was the contest for this gun, in June, 1777, that gave rise to the composition of the first verses, entitled, " *The Siller Gun*." They were afterwards published by Mr. Ruddiman, in the Edinburgh Weekly Magazine, and thence copied, and printed in various forms, by different persons.

These verses, in some respect, constitute the ground-work of the present poem ; but the additions and alterations are so numerous, that scarcely an original stanza remains. The author has also ventured to introduce a circumstance which occurred at a festival posterior to that period. He trusts, however, that the illustrious names which irresistibly dictated this little anachronism, will, with every candid and patriotic reader, plead its excuse.

In our poetical department will be found a specimen of the author's versification.

A REMARKABLE INSTANCE OF COURAGE.

A Young French Nobleman, not quite twenty years old, (the Count de B. Lieutenant of cavalry) was attacked by a wolf of an extraordinary size. The furious animal first seized the horse, and tore off such large pieces of his flesh, that M. de B. was soon dismounted.— Then the wolf flew at him, and would certainly have torn him in pieces, had he not had great presence of mind. With one hand he seized the wolf's foaming tongue, and with the other hand one of his paws. — After struggling awhile with the terrible creature, the tongue slipped from him, and his right thumb was bitten off; upon which he leaped upon the wolf's back, clapped his knees fast to his flanks, and called out for help to some armed peasants who were passing by, but none dared to advance. " Well, then," said he, " fire ; if you kill me, I forgive you." One of them fired, and three bullets went through the brave officer's coat, but neither he nor the beast were wounded. Another, bolder than his comrades, seeing the Cavalier was intrepid, and kept firm upon the wolf, came very near, and fired at him ; the animal was mortally wounded, and after a few more furious motions expired. In this dreadful conflict, besides the losing of his thumb, the young Count's left hand was torn, and he got several bites in his legs and thighs.

MEXICAN TENNIS.

THE people of Mexico have a singular law in their play with the tennis-ball.—In the walls of the court where they played, certain stones, like mill-stones, were fixed, with a hole in the middle, just large enough to let the ball pass through, and whoever drove it through, which required a great deal of skill, and was, of course, but rarely effected, won the cloaks of such as were standing by to witness the game. They, therefore, took to their heels, to save their cloaks, and others pursued to catch them, which was a new source of amusement.

SPORT-

SPORTING INTELLIGENCE.

THE disputed race, last year, at Lewes, between Orville and Cerberus, has been settled by the stewards, to whom the case was returned by the Jockey Club, as depending upon a point of fact which the latter had no means of ascertaining.—The stewards have decided, that as the evidence was equally strong on both sides, the prize be equally divided between the parties.

Mr. Thomas Gascoygne has accepted a challenge given by a Hampshire courser, Mr. Villebois, to produce a *North Country greyhound* to run against a Norfolk dog. The match is for 100 guineas, and is to be run at the next Swaffham Meeting.

His R. H. the Prince of Wales, it is reported, having entertained an opinion that Rubens was lame, and would not be able to run at Lewes, offered him to Lord Darlington for 1000 guineas, to which his Lordship assented, with a proviso that Sam. Chifney, the jockey, should give him a gallop, and he would be determined by his judgment.—This was accordingly done; and the *knowing one* warranting Rubens sound, Lord Darlington concluded the bargain, by means of which he saved forfeiting two matches in which he was engaged against him, and won about 12,000l. besides. Chifney, who rode Rubens in a capital style, also *netted* considerably. His Lordship has been since offered 3000l. for his purchase.

The Duke of Grafton's Vandyke has completely disgraced his breeding, by not having won the Derby Stakes, at Epsom, or the Pavilion Stakes at Brighton; for the latter he was a considerable favourite; and for the Derby, a celebrated sporting man, who about six months previous to the race had taken 1,300l. to 100l. that he did not win, was so confident of his winning, that he would not embrace the opportunity of hedging, which the change of the odds afterwards afforded, but stood it all, and was consequently minus 100l.

At Brighton races, on the Wednesday, the practice of running across the course, when cleared for the jockies, had nearly caused the complicated destruction of three *stupid animals* in female garb, who, in the act of crossing after the bell had rung for the starting of the horses, precipitated themselves violently against Lord Egremont's Canopus, by which two of them were thrown under his feet. The rider manifested a skill in their preservation almost unparalleled, and deservedly received the commendations of hundreds who witnessed the accident, for though almost at speed, he so directed the animal as to pass over them, and a man who fell at the same instant, without the slightest injury, except the shock of the fall.

On Tuesday the 2d instant, a match against time, for twenty guineas, was decided on Northampton race-course, by a four-year old mare,

mare, belonging to Mr. William Dunkley, of that town. The mare was to run ten miles within half an hour, which was performed with great ease in twenty-nine minutes; keeping an uniform pace the whole distance, without the application of whip or spur to increase her speed.

On Tuesday, the 2d instant, three excellent races were run over the North Sands of Ardrossan, Scotland, for subscription purses. The first and third afforded good sport. The second was very keenly contested. The whole was conducted in such a manner as to do great credit to the stewards.—The fineness of the day greatly contributed to the other sports, which were attended by many thousands of spectators, who, after regaling themselves in the inns and booths fitted up for the purpose, retired, much pleased with the sports of the day. The stewards, after electing their successors, dined at the ordinary at Campbell's.

The officers of a regiment of light dragoons, stationed at Deal, lately made up a subscription purse of 100 guineas, to be run for on the Downs by ten officers' horses, each gentleman being his own rider. The gentleman who was foremost at starting, continued to increase his advantage until he was about two horses lengths a-head of the second horse. The horse then stumbled, and the gentleman was thrown. Notwithstanding the nine following horses passed over him, he did not receive the slightest injury from any of them. There were several bye-matches, which afforded a great deal of sport; and the evening concluded with a ball, given by the military gentlemen to the principal inhabitants of Deal, and its vicinity.

The Caledonian Hunt is fixed this year to be held at Stirling, and continues a fortnight; it begins early in October.—The Fife Hunt is held at Cupar, and continues a week.—Cupar races are also during the week. The Hunt commences on the 19th of October.

A very excellent and well-contested race took place on Wednesday the 10th, on Epsom Downs, between a bay horse belonging to Captain Birch, of the 1st regiment of dragoon guards, and Captain Oliver's brown mare Humming Bird. Captain Birch's groom rode the horse, and Captain Oliver the other. It was one heat only, over a two-mile course. At starting, the mare took the lead; she was afterwards distanced, but soon recovering the ground again got a-head, and came in at the winning post by a length at least. The mare won easily. The race was for 100 guineas.—Although the intended sport was but little known, there were on the Downs many elegant equipages; among the pedestrian spectators were many amateurs of note.

Coach Race.—On Sunday the 7th of August, a coach called the Patriot, belonging to the Master of the Bell, Leicester, drawn by four horses, started against another coach called the Defiance, from Leicester to Nottingham, a distance of twenty-six miles, both coaches changing horses at Loughborough.—Thousands of people from all parts assembled to witness the event, and bets to a considerable amount were depending. Both coaches started exactly at eight o'clock; and after the severest contest ever remembered, the Patriot arrived at Nottingham

tingham first by two minutes only, performing the distance of twenty-six miles in two hours and ten minutes, carrying twelve passengers.

The 4th instant, a master shoemaker, of no small stature, in the Borough, undertook, for a wager of five guineas, to pick up an hundred stones, placed at the distance of a yard from each other, in the space of an hour and twenty minutes. The spot fixed on for honest Crispin's pedestrian feat was in a field near Walworth. At the commencement, odds were greatly in favour, but after having gathered up fifty in less than twenty minutes, he became so exhausted by his exertion, that he was actually compelled to lie down; and from the violent state of perspiration which he was then in, was incapable of renewing his labour with any chance of success.

On Tuesday the 9th instant, a foot race was run in a field near Shooter's-hill, between a soldier in the artillery at Woolwich, and a carpenter, at the same place. The wager was for five guineas; the former to run one hundred yards whilst his opponent went fifty, carrying a heavy man on his back; several bets were depending. The wager was decided in favour of the latter.

Thursday the 13th instant, Mr. J. Bateman, wheelwright, of Spilsby, after pitching four heavy loads of hay, engaged to walk six measured miles within the hour, on the turnpike-road leading from Spilsby to Boston, which he performed with ease, having a minute and half to spare. The last mile he walked in eight minutes. During the given time he stopped twice to drink.

A man of the name of Mitchell, a labourer of Shearn, in the New Forest, was produced by Mr. Mitchell, a country gentleman, in pursuance of a bet, in the early part of this month, to go sixty miles a day for eight successive days. It was generally supposed on the sixth day he would accomplish the undertaking. He however was taken feverish on going to rest on the sixth day, and was unable to proceed further than a public-house near Romsey, Hants, at which place he slept. The pedestrian did sixty miles in fourteen hours on the first day.

A singular shooting-match took place on the 30th ult. at Little Chart, near Canterbury, between Mr. Davis, of Pleukley, and Mr. Hatch, of Westwell, for five guineas, to shoot at twenty-five potatoes, thrown up in the air, which were all hit by the sportsmen, and the wager consequently was not decided.

Remarkable Shot. — As the park-keeper, (Frost) belonging to Lord Grenville, at Boconnoc, in Cornwall, was lately in pursuit of a strayed buck, an old vixen was roused in a wood, by the dogs, and shot by him with a single ball, which entered the centre of her forehead, and passed through the neck into the ground, as she approached him full speed on the common, at a distance of upwards of fifty paces, to the astonishment of the spectators who accompanied him.

Wrestling, Single-stick, and a Fight. — The olympic games of single-stick, wrestling, &c. at White-horse-hill, near Uffington, Berks, Friday and Saturday the 5th and 6th instant, were numerously and respectably attended, and afforded a high treat to the amateurs. The prize at single-stick, after much excellent play, was won by Flowers, from Somersetshire.—And on the Monday following a most determined and sanguinary pitched battle was fought, adjoining Rottinden-common, between George Marsh, a hostler, and Samuel Beven, a champion from the west.—The match was for one hundred guineas, and the exhibition took place in the presence of a numerous field of country sportsmen. Marsh was two stone heavier than Beven, who was something under eleven stone, but to balance the match, he was a better fighter than Marsh, who, however, with the same bottom, ultimately won the battle, by weight and strength. The conflict was obstinately maintained for full two hours, and even at the conclusion, both were so hit, that it was even betting that neither would be brought to set-to again; Marsh did so, however, with the assistance of his second and bottle-holder, and his adversary was carried off the ground.

THE match of single-stick in Salisbury race-week, for want of previous proper arrangement by persons skilled in the game, did not at all answer public expectation. The Wiltshire men uniformly play with the arm naked; the Somersetshire men generally play with the arm padded; hence each kept a different guard, and either can conquer in their own mode of play. It had been advertised that the play should be on Wednesday with the arms naked; the Wiltshire men contended that they were of course to play as usual for two bloods, by which they hoped not only to gain the prize of the

day, but to have time and opportunity so to disable their adversaries, playing out of their usual mode, as to have an equal chance of victory on the following day.—The Somersetshire men insisted on playing the first day one blood, that they might the less expose their unpadded arms. On this point the day was wrangled away with very little play, and without any contest between the crack men of the two counties.—The Somersetshire men thus reserved their arms, and in consequence, on Thursday, they gained every head of the Wiltshire men, and played off the ties for the prizes in a friendly way among themselves.

MONDAY the 22d instant, as some boys were gathering mushrooms in St. James's Park, they started a fox on the north side of the bason. Reynard ran with great velocity towards the Horse-Guards; but by the time he got to the end of the canal, the cry of " fox! fox!" had been echoed from one end of the Park to the other, so that a great number of people were collected there to impede his progress. Reynard was, however, too cunning to encounter a host of soldiers, and immediately took the water, and swam a considerable distance up the canal, bidding defiance to his pursuers. In the mean time, two recruits, expert swimmers, stripped and went after him, but they were soon distanced. Reynard, however, got tired of his aquatic excursion, and approached the shore, when he was at last caught by Serjeant Lovie, of the 3d foot-guards, who carried him in triumph to the guard-house.—The fox was afterwards discovered to be the property of Major Stanhope, of the guards.

POETRY.

POETRY.

THE HIGH COURT OF DIANA.

SONG.

Sung by Mr. Fawcett, in the new Play called " The Africans."

A Priest of Kajaaga, as blind as a stone,
  When he took to his bosom a wife,
Cry'd " Deary, I never shall see you, I
    own,
" But you'll be the delight of my life."
Then his arm o'er her shoulder he lov-
    ingly pass'd,
And says he, " My love, what is this
    lump?"
She faultered a little—but told him at last,
" Please your Holiness, only my hump."

Says the Priest, " then we cannot coha-
    bit, d'ye see,
" Though I tenderly love you indeed!
" For I've taken an oath, that my chil-
    dren shan't be
" Of the camel and buffalo breed."
So he married another he fancied would
    fit—
Coming home in sweet conjugal talk,
She stopp'd the blind Priest, saying " sit
    " down a bit,
" For my legs are too bandy to walk."

" Bandy legs," said the Priest, " can't
    " be counted for sins,
" So sit there, as still as a mouse ;
" For Mahomet curse me if ever your
    " shins
" Shall waddle you into my house."
Then he turn'd up his eyes, like the white
    of boil'd eggs,
And pray'd thus, to Mahomet, smack ;
" Good Prophet, afford me a wife with
    good legs,
" And with never a hump on her
    back."

Then the voice of the Prophet in thun-
    der was heard,
And rumbled thus over his head ;

" A handsome young woman that can't
    speak a word,
" Shall bless your blind Rev'rence's
    bed."
The Priest he bow'd low, crying, " Ma-
    homet's kind ;
" Of happiness this is the sum !
" For a handsome young wife likes her
    old husband blind,
" And most men like a wife that is
    dumb."

THE SILLER GUN.

A POEM.

(Vide Page 239 of this Number.)

AFF to the Craigs, the hale forenoon,
  By a' the bye-gates round and round,
Crouds after crouds were flocking down,
    In nines and tens,
Deserting, fast, the bonniest town
    That Scotia kens.

O! happy they wha, up twa story,
Saw the procession in its glory !
Alang the roads it left out o'er ye
    Sic clouds o' stour,
Ye cou'dna see your thoomb before ye
    For ha'f an hour !

They wha had corns, or broken wind,
Begood to pegh and limp behind :
Laith to sit down, and still inclin'd
    To try their pith,
" I hope we'll dance yet, ere we've din'd,"
    Cries Geordy Smith.

To cheer them wha began to fag,
The Minstrels lows'd Apollo's bag,
And lilted up, tho' still they lag,
    " The Reel o' Boggie,"
And " Willy was a wanton wag,"
    Wi' " Kath'rine Oggie."

But

But " Robert's March to Bannockburn,"
To leave his banes in Freedom's urn,
Or, glorious and triumphant, spurn
    Intended thraldom,
Sae rais'd their hearts at ilka turn,
    That nought cou'd bald them.

" O! blessings on his warlike name!
" On Wallace, and Sir John the Græme!
" While Freedom dare assert her claim,
    " Or virtue blossom,
" Wallace and Bruce shall aye inflame
    " The patriot bosom!"

A' this, and mair, they seem'd to say,
And rent the air wi' thrice huzzay!
" Out owr the hills and far away,"
    The pipers play'd;
And soon they reach'd, fu' blithe and
      gay,
    Their grand parade—

Where louder grew the busy hum
O' friends rejoicing as they come :
Wi' double vir the drummer's drum,
    The pint-stowps clatter,
And bowls o' negus, milk and rum,
    Flow round like water.

" Tak a gude waught— I'm sure ye're
      weary,"
Quoth Anny Kaillie to her deary :
John, fain to see his wife sae cheary,
    Indulg'd the fun,
Got fou, and danner'd lang and eerie,
    And tint his gun—

And miss'd, mairowr, the endearing
    charms
(The very thought ilk bosom warms!)
Of auld acquaintances in swarms,
    Meeting like brithers,
And wie-things giggling i' the arms
    O' their fond mithers!

And bonny lasses, tight and clean,
Buskit to please their ain lad's ein,
Lasses, whose faces, as the scene
    Its tints discloses,
In glowing sweetness intervene,
    Like living roses!

Conveener Tamson's troop, the while,
Prepare for action in great style;
The lave their various firelocks pile,
    By three and three,
And, 'tween ilk corps, for ha'f a mile,
    Their banners flee.

The drums and fifes a flourish made;
Three loud buzzas the menyie gaed,

And clear'd the stance, that ilka blade
    The mark might view,
Far glist'ning, like a white cockade
    Wi' spraings o' blue !

Then there were tents, where, frank and
      free,
On divet-seats, sae cozielie,
Auld birkies, innocently slee,
    Wi' cap and stowp,
Were e'en as blithe as blithe could be,—
    A' fit to lowp !

Pleas'd, they recount, wi' meikle joy,
How aft they've been at sic a ploy;
Descrive past scenes ; re-act the boy,
    And a' his wheems :
Sweet days of youth, without alloy,
    Like fairy dreams!

Meantime, the younkers on the green,
In merry rounds are dancing keen :
Wi' rapture sparkling i' their ein,
    They mind fu' weel
The sappy kiss, and squeeze, between
    Ilk blithesome reel.

And, as the Highland flings begin,
Their heels grow lighter wi' the din ;
They smack their hands, and chin to chin,
    They cut and caper;
Ev'n the by-standers figure in,
    And flounce and vapour !

But a' this while, wi' mony a dunner,
Auld guns were brattling aff like thun-
      ner,
Three parts o'whilk, in ilka hunner,
    Did sae recoil,
Fowk thought their liths and limbs asun-
      ner,
    In this turmoil.

Wide o' the mark, as if to scar us,
The bullets ripp'd the swaird like har-
      rows ;
And, fright'ning a' the craws and spar-
      rows
    About the place,
Ramrods were fleeing thick as arrows
    At Chevy Chace!

Yet still, as thro' the tents we steer,
Unmov'd the festive groups appear !
Lads oxter lasses without fear,
    Or dance like wud ;
Blithe, when the guns gaed aff so queer,
    To hear the thud !

Steeking his ein, big John M'Maff
Held out his musquet like a staff ;
Turn'd tho' the chield was ha'f-and-ha'f,
        His

His head away,
And, panting, cry'd, " Sirs! is she aff?"
In wild dismay.

Poor gowk! ne'er us'd to wars' alarms,
And but ae holiday in arms,
His fears foresaw a thousand harms—
But here the Muse
Proponcs, in Verity's sweet charms,
A short excuse :

Peace and gude-will had been sae lang
The burthen o' the people's sang,
Their arms like useless lumber hang,
Till France, amain,
Decreed, wi' fell invasion's fang,
Our soil to stain !

Then, ere our King cou'd gi' command,
Up raise the genius o' the land !
Dumfries, in mony a chosen band,
Enarm'd appears,
Fit, in ae phalanx, to withstand
A host o' spears !

O ! in his King and Country's cause,
How blest is he wha nobly fa's !
Bright Fame her gowden trumpet blaws,
And deathless story
Devotes his name, wi' loud huzzas,
To endless glory !

Amid the scenes, depainted here,
Of inexperience, doubt, and fear,
Auld sportsmen fir'd correct and clear;
And Samuel Clark,
Mild as the spring when flow'rs appear,
Just miss'd the mark !

When his gun snappit, James M'Kee,
Charge after charge, charg'd to the eie:
At length she bounc'd out-owr a tree,
In mony a flinner—
" For God's sake, bairns, keep back !" ·
cries he,
" There's sax shot in her !"

Wull Shanklin brought his firelock hither,
And cock'd it in an unco swither :
Ae drunken Souter jeer'd anither
To come and learn—
Fuff play'd the priming—heels owr ither,
They fell in shairn !

Just i' the moment o' disgrace,
Conveener Tamson saw their case :
O ! how he hid his manly face,
And fleech'd thae fallows,
To think upo' the glorious race
O' godlike Wallace !

William M'Nish, a taylor slee,
Rouz'd at the thought, charg'd his
fuzee ;
Took but ae vizzy wi' his eie—
The bullet flies
Clean thro' the target to a tee,
And wons the prize !

His winsome wife, wha long had miss'd
him,
Press'd thro' the croud, caress'd and kiss'd
him :
Less furthy dames, (wha' cou'd resist
them ?)
Th' example take ;
And some held up his bairns, and bless'd
them,
For daddy's sake !

In William's hat, wi' ribbons bound,
The GUNNY was wi' laurel crown'd ;
And while triumphant owr the ground,
They bore him tenty,
His health in streams o' punch gaed
round,
" Lang life and plenty !"

Wi' loud applause frae man and woman,
His frame spread like a spate wide foam-
ing :
Warse deeds hae gi'en to mony a Ro-
man
Eternal fame ;
But prodigies are grown sae common,
They've tint the name !

PARTRIDGE SHOOTING.

From a Poem lately published, entitled
" FOWLING."

SEPTEMBER comes to cheer the fowl-
er's heart,
And raise his anxious hopes ; day after
day
He marks the fruitful country change
around
With eager eye. First from the fertile
meads,
Divested of their widely-waving load,
The fragrant hay-rick rises. Gentle
swains,
If chance should lead you to the chosen
spot,
Where the shy partridge forms her simple
nest,
The embryo offspring spare ; and, when
your scythe
Levels

Levels the grassy vallies, should your foot
Approach the helpless brood, step back
   with care,
Nor our fond hopes destroy: the trusty
   cur
That nightly guards your house, or in the
   fields.
Protects your vestments and your frugal
   fare,
Whilst far from home you ply your mid-
   day work,
Permit not to approach ;—so may success
And plenty wait upon your rustic toils,
And crown the circling year with joyful
   gains.

As nearer now the sportive season comes,
The fowler marks the corn-fields change
   around,
From green to yellow ; 'till the potent
   sun
Embrowns the nodding ear: When ev'n-
   ing comes,
He walks around, and carefully surveys
The promis'd grounds, and ev'ry well-
   known haunt
Of the coy game recalls ; whilst warm
   Desire,
By Fancy fir'd, Time's narrow limits
   bursts,
Or the dull interval, impatient, chides.
Should he some spot between thick shel-
   t'ring woods
Espy, where, in long range, the clus-
   t'ring shocks
O'erspread the ground, a livelier joy in-
   vades
His beating heart, and, with no niggard
   praise,
He loads the skilful farmer's early care.
But when the jolly harvest o'er the plains
Diffusive reigns at large, his joy is full,
And mingles with the mirth that cheers
   the scene.
Welcome to him the busy sickle's sound
Among the rustling fields, or sweeping
   scythe ;
Welcome the laugh, the shout, and noise
   confus'd,
That from the early dawn to day's de-
   cline,
Load ev'ry swelling gale. He joins the
   throng,
Partakes their pleasures, and foretells his
   own;
Then not alone he walks; beside him
   wait,
Attentive to his voice, of aspect grave,
His trusty pointers, soon to be indulg'd
In the full freedom of their fav'rite sport.
At length arrives the glad important eve ;

To-morrow from the strict, but just re-
   straint,
Let loose, th' unshackled fowler shall re-
   joice.
What joyous hurry and what pleasing cares
Through Britain's coasts prevail ! from
   east to west,
From north to south, continuous they
   extend ;
What region, or what district so unblest,
Where the prolific partridge is unknown,
Or eager fowlers doom them not to death?
For me, before the welcome hour arrives,
What wild emotions agitate my breast!
Sleep oft forsakes my couch, or should
   its dews
My heavy eye-lids bathe, in dreams I
   view
Th' expected covies, and the happy morn
Rises with all its joys before my eyes.
Come, long anticipated hour, oh come !
Depart, ye envious shades of Night; and
   thou,
Fair Dawn arise, and o'er the humid
   world,
With rosy fingers lead the cheerful Day !

PUGILISM.

OH! for a muse, to whom the Nine
   must yield,
To sing the glories of the Sebright field,
Where Gregson like a huge volcano
   stood,
And pour'd irruptions fierce of boiling
   blood ;
His less'ning eyes a mourning hue disclose,
While crimson torrents issue from his
   nose ;
Now gapes his face in many a gory ridge,
And now his nose has lost her stately
   bridge;
Loud, and yet louder, rings the pond'rous
   pound,
While savage shouts re-echo to the sound;
And now the batter'd wretch essays to
   trace
The ragged remnants of his mangled face,
Less horrid !only than Grimaldi's smile,
When the baboon attempts some humo-
   rous wile ;
Or, like the visage grim, that frowns before
The knocker huge, of Newgate's massy
   door ;
Or, as the softness of an Irish bog
Reveals the countless nails in Paddy's
   brogue,
So, Gregson, did thy varied face declare,
How often Gully's fist was planted there.

THE

SPORTING MAGAZINE;

OR,

MONTHLY CALENDAR

OF THE

TRANSACTIONS

OF

THE TURF, THE CHASE,

And every other Diversion interesting to

THE MAN OF PLEASURE, ENTERPRISE, AND SPIRIT.

SEPTEMBER, 1808.

CONTAINING

Description of the Frontispiece to the Volume................Page 251
Summary of the Sport at Chesterfield Races....................251
    Boroughbridge..........,251
    Warwick.............252
    Morpeth..............252
    Ayr..................252
    Doncaster............252
Races appointed in October, 1808 ..253
Notice of a new Work, the History of the Horse..................253
Disputes between Gentlemen, on Points of Honour, &c. &c. 253
Cocking at Oxford................256
His Majesty's cream-coloured Charger.........................256
The Philosophical Sportsman, Number VIII......................257
The Fool and the Falcon..........261
Canine Anecdotes 262
Satirical Hints to Criminals........262
American Duelling 264
American Cock-fighting...........266
Actions for alledged Violations of the Game Laws—Currie v. Petty ..266
    Fox v. Hodgson .267
Charge of the Judge on the Trial of Major Campbell 268
Winners of the Royal Plates at Hambleton, from 1715 to 1808 271

Trial of a Cause between Colonel Thornton and Mr. Flint..Page 274
Sentence of a Court-Martial on Captain Hallilay, of the 10th Regt. 276
Race between the Poney and Mail-Coach 278
Sporting Cause tried at the York Assizes, Beaumont v. Shaw......279
FEAST OF WIT.........,....282
    Comical Idea....282
    Spanish Grandees 282
SPORTING INTELLIGENCE........283
    Hints to Sportsmen on the Law relating to Gamekeepers 284

POETRY.

Hunting Song—A Southerly Wind and a cloudy Sky 289
The Cockney's Adieu to Brighton.. 289
Inscription, by Mr. Pratt, on the Tomb of Mrs. Robinson 290
Woodcock Shooting, (from the Poem entitled ' Fowling') 290
Ancient Hunting Song...........292
Drinking Song, by W. R. Spence, Esq........................292
The Whist Table 292

RACING CALENDAR 73

Embellished with—I, An Engraved Frontispiece, the Subject, Milo.—II, Vignette Title-Page to the Thirty-Second Volume.

III. An Engraving of his Majesty's Cream-coloured Charger.

LONDON:

PRINTED FOR THE PROPRIETORS,

By J. Pittman, Warwick Square;

AND SOLD BY J. WHEBLE, 18, WARWICK-SQUARE; C. CHAPPLE, 66, PALL-MALL; L. BOOTH, DUKE-STREET, PORTLAND-PLACE; JOHN HILTON, NEWMARKET; MAYNARD, PANTON STREET, HAYMARKET; AND ALL OTHER BOOKSELLERS IN THE UNITED KINGDOM.

TO THE PUBLIC.

THE Thirty-second Volume of the SPORTING MAGAZINE being now completed, we have again to address our numerous Readers and Correspondents, for the distinguished preference with which they are still disposed to countenance our humble attempts and exertions, among so great a number of monthly competitors, whose object, like our own, is to please, instruct, or amuse.—Our task, though arduous, we shall never feel difficult, while we can command the approving voice of a large majority.—While we are thankful for the hints of our friends, to us the objections of our *enemies* will not be disagreeable : the latter we shall probably always be able to turn to account ; these are thorns which may keep us on the alert, when otherwise we might be apt to slumber on the down of panegyric.—In our latter Volumes we have paid particular attention to Disputes between Gentlemen on Points of Honour.—Here, while we profess ourselves the advocates for true religion and genuine morality, it will be seen that we have kept clear of the precision of the Puritan, or the moroseness of the Methodist.—We would be mirthful without being mischievous, and presume that men may be occasionally delighted without being driven to despair.

Gentlemen disposed to favour the Publisher of this Magazine with Original Paintings of Sporting Subjects, are assured that the utmost care shall be taken of them, and of their being safely returned. The Engravings thus taken, will be executed by the most approved Artists, and in the first style of excellence.

THE
SPORTING MAGAZINE;
FOR SEPTEMBER, 1808.

MILO.

THE subject of the Frontispiece given in this Number, to the Thirty-second Volume of our work, is that of Milo destroying the Bullock, and of which the books on Mythology furnish the following account:—

"Milo was a celebrated athlete of Crotona, in Italy. His father's name was Diotimus. He early accustomed himself to carry the greatest burdens, and by degrees became a monster in strength. It is said that he carried on his shoulders a young bullock four years old, for above forty yards, and afterwards killed it with one blow of his fist, and ate it up in one day. He was seven times crowned at the Pythian games, and six at Olympia. He presented himself a seventh time, but no one had the courage or boldness to enter the lists against him. He was one of the disciples of Pythagoras; and to his uncommon strength the learned preceptor and his pupils owed their lives.— The pillar which supported the roof of the school suddenly gave way, but Milo supported the whole weight of the building, and gave the philosopher and his auditors time to escape. In his old age, Milo attempted to pull up a tree by the roots, and break it. He partly effected it, but his strength being gradually exhausted, the tree, when half cleft, re-united, and his hands remained pinched in the body of the tree. He was then alone, and being unable to disentangle himself, he was eaten up by the wild beasts of the place."

SUMMARY OF SPORT,
AT THE
CHESTERFIELD, WARWICK, AND OTHER RACES;

The Details of which will appear in our next Month's Racing Calendar.

CHESTERFIELD.

WEDNESDAY, August 31.— The Sweepstakes was won by Mr. Sitwell's Gooseander, beating Miss Blanchard, &c.—The Maiden Plate was won by Mr. Harrison's Bonny Hodge, beating Green Peas, &c.

Thursday, the 50l. Plate was won by Mr. Clifton's Josephine, beating Sir Andrew;—and the Handicap Plate by Mr. Smith's Miss Blanchard, beating Bonny Hodge, and five others.

BOROUGHBRIDGE.

Thursday, Sept. 1.—The 50l. for three and four-year olds, was won by the Duke of Leeds's Mowbray, by Pandolpho, beating three others. The two 50l. Plates advertised for Wednesday and Friday were not run for—not from a want of horses, but a want of money; notwithstanding, since the year 1799, there have been seven 50l. Plates not run for at that place, for want of horses.

WARWICK.

Tuesday, Sept. 6.—The King's Plate was won by Mr. Daly's Bob Booty, by Chanticleer, beating General Benningsen, Thorn, and Viper.—The Stakes of 10gs. each, with 20gs. added, was won by Mr. Richardson's Castanos.—The 50l. Plate was won by Mr. Butler's Miss Coiner.

Wednesday, the Stakes of 10gs. each, with 20gs. added, was won by Sir T. Standley's Viper, beating Miss Coiner and General Benningsen.—And the 50l. Plate was won by Mr. Richardson's Castanos, beating Romeo, &c.

MORPETH.

Tuesday, Sept. 6.——The 50l. Plate was won by Sir H. T. Vane's b. m. by Sir Peter, beating Silvio and Cramlington.

Wednesday.—No race.

Thursday, the 50l. Plate was won by Sir H. T. Vane's b. m. by Sir Peter, beating Cramlington and Silvio.

AYR.

Tuesday, Sept. 6.—The Stakes of 20gs. each was won by Lord Montgomorie's b. f. by Beningbrough, beating four others.—The Gold Cup was won by the same filly, beating five others.—The 50l. Plate was won by Sir John Johnstone's Fortuna, beating Petera.

Wednesday.—The 50l. Purse was won by Lord Montgomerie's Irvine, beating Petera, Streamer, and Merry Tricks.

Thursday.—The 50l. Purse was won by Sir J. Johnstone's Fortuna, beating two others.

DONCASTER.

Monday, Sept. 26.—The Fitzwilliam Stakes of 10gs. each, with 20gs. added, was won by Mr. Shaftoe's b. c. by Agonistes, beating Pumpkin, Stamford, Fair Candidate, and Scud; 2 to 1 and 7 to 4 on the winner.

His Majesty's Plate of 100gs. was won by Lord Monson's b. f. by Hambletonian, beating Ranger, and 5 others. Six to 4 on the winner.

The St. Leger Stakes of 25gs. each, was won by the Duke of Hamilton's b. c. Petronius, by Sir Peter, beating Mr. Sitwell's Clinker, Lord Milton's Easton, Mr. Garforth's b. c. by Hambletonian, Sir M. M. Sykes's Theresa, and seven others. Two to 1 against Theresa, and 100 to 6 against the winner.

Match between Colonel Horton's b. c. by Bustard, and Mr. E. L. Hodgson's gr. f. by Shuttle, 100gs. Mr. Hodgson paid 40gs. compromise.

Lord Monson's Scud beat Lord Fitzwilliam's Paulina, 200gs. h. ft.

The Two-year old Stakes of 20 gs. each, was won by Lord Fitzwilliam's Cervantes, beating Sir T. Gascoigne's b. f. by Sir Solomon, and four others.

Mr. Hewett's Scud rec. ft. from Mr. Mellish's Harry Longlegs, 200 gs. b. ft.

Tuesday, the Prince's Stakes of 25gs. each, was won by Lord Fitzwilliam's Paulina, beating Lord Darlington's b. c. Brother to Expectation. Two to 1 and 5 to 2 agst Paulina.

The

The Corporation Plate of 50l. was won by the Duke of Hamilton's Grazier, beating Mr. Nalton's b. c. Ranger, Mr. Cooke's ch.c. by Beningbrough, Ld. Milton's Pumpkin, and Sir T. Gascoigne's ch. f. by Hambletonian.

RACES APPOINTED IN 1808.

NEWMARKET First October Meeting........... *Oct.* 8
Stockton, Yorkshire............ 3
Wrexham, Denbeighshire 4
Northallerton, Yorkshire...... 6
Stafford 11
Penrith, Cumberland 13
Newmarket Second Oct. Meeting 17
Holywell-Hunt Meeting, Flintshire.................... 17
Newmarket Houghton Meeting 31

HISTORY OF THE HORSE.

WE have seen the prospectus of an intended publication, to be comprised in a quarto volume, entitled, a History of the Horse, containing directions in breeding, rearing, training, &c. the racehorse, the hunter, the hackney, the carriage and the cart-horse, for the different purposes of the turf, the field, and the road; interspersed with anecdotes appertaining to each class.

By the proposals, the work is to be embellished with not less than twenty engravings, executed in a very superior manner, from pictures by masters most celebrated for their painting of animals.

It is to be what booksellers call "a GENTLEMAN's BOOK," the price being named at five guineas

to subscribers and six guineas to non-subscribers.

Those who are concerned in the protection, or gratified with the labours, of that generous creature, the horse, are informed, that the work will also comprise an account of the most approved methods of treating those disorders the animal is by nature liable to, as well as those originating from too indulgent or too careless management.

Our readers will form their own idea of what is to be expected from this production when we state, that it will be by the Author of RURAL SPORTS, under whose inspection, we understand, the Plates will be engraved.

DISPUTES
BETWEEN GENTLEMEN,

On Points of Honour, &c. &c. &c.

COLONEL PAULETT, *versus* LORD SACKVILLE.

HAVING furnished the substance of this trial in our last, we now, in pursuance of our engagement, offer some remarks on the subject; and it is a duty more imposing than ordinary, from some very extraordinary consequences which have attended the principal witness, and which must not be suffered to pass away without a serious comment.

Mrs. Bell, who kept the White Hart Inn, at Winchester, and who is a truly respectable woman, and the mother of daughters, had reason to believe, from the deposition of her servant, that a vicious correspondence was taking place between a strange gentleman and the lady of her husband's benefactor; in consequence of which information,

formation, she took such methods as might lead to an actual confirmation of the guilt of the parties, or to a rejection of the suspicion altogether.—As the evidence of facts were conclusive, she was so *ridiculously moral* as to think her house disgraced; and, in despite of large offers to suppress her evidence, and that of her servants, was resolved not to stifle her opposition to the growing infidelities towards the marriage bed!—How contemptibly antideluvian and old-fashioned all this must appear among an assemblage of modern beaux and belles!

When the trial took place, and the *misfortunes* of the lady and gentleman were fully established, (misfortune is the fashionable term for adultery, according to the new Dictionary) an unprecedented murmur of disapprobation was manifested towards Mrs. Bell; and this murmur was pursued, almost generally, in every circle of males and females in the city of Winchester and its vicinity. The bucks cursed her in anathemas, and the demoiselles called her an *officious* hussey! —We will now venture to examine this point slightly.

Mrs. Bell is both a wife and a mother, and such characters are of the very first importance in life, and derive all their dignity from the pure execution of their required functions. Was Mrs. Bell, because she kept an inn for public accommodation, expected to keep a brothel for the furtherance of human infamy? Her house was dependent upon a license annually granted by the County Magistrates, and that license was wholly dependent upon the admitted morals of the hostess; now was it expected that she should forfeit that license in compliment to the irregular desires of Lord Sackville?—Mrs. Bell has daughters; now was it expected that she should criminally tolerate examples of high impurity under her own roof, and thereby furnish examples of personal destruction to her own children? Certainly not; at least so will say all men and women who have any trace of religion in their system.

But whatever might have been the expectations of Mrs. Bell's enemies, we are clear in one melancholy result, and that is, that she was obliged to quit the White Hart and Winchester together, and to take refuge at the Hotel at Alresford; where, we are informed, the vengeance of the *Haut Ton* still pursues her; as many of them would rather fatigue their cattle, than take post-horses from *her* precise establishment.

Now, what sort of deduction are we to draw from this species of oppression?—Do they wish to hoist the flag of terror against all future evidence? Or have they resolved that the sin of adultery may have an understanding, but that it shall have no tongue?—In either way, the subject deserves the deep consideration of the pulpit and the legislature, as the immorality is becoming too formidable for the light drops of ridicule to assail with effect.

To what cause are we to attribute the non-marriage of such an innumerable mass of our young ladies of distinction, as they are phrased?—In every *gala*, whether metropolitan or provincial, they are to be found in a vast and distressing disproportion to those who are married! This is not as it should be; we have Dukes, Marquisses, Earls, Barons, and Baronets, besides an endless train of gentry, who

who have large families of lovely daughters, among whom the marriage of one in a month is pompously emblazoned in the newspapers; while the rest, which are hourly encreasing, are compelled to *sigh* in secret, and perhaps accusing men with *insensibility,* who are only actuated by *fear !*—It should never be forgotten by the ladies, that whatever tends to obliterate the weight and obligations of matrimony, is a death-wound to female dignity and happiness.—Flippancy, as applied to trifles, may be rendered agreeable by manners; but flippancy in morals, like the grinning of a wretch in torment, is only significant of misery; we must not be permitted to disport with ignominy, or abolish the injunctions of shame; if we are, the sooner we burn the connubial compact the better, and make nature independent of reason.

We will now turn from the surreptitious claims of the *privileged orders,* to that humble *order of nature,* whose privileges seem yearly to be narrowed by intolerant prescription.

It is curious, but afflictive, to behold the opposite directions which are taken in this wonderful epocha, by the extreme classes of society in this nation.—While the *high vulgar* are indulging in licentiousness, and affecting to be elevated above the administrations of censure, and whisperings of conscience, the *low vulgar* are plunging in the gloomy abysses of fanaticism, and affecting to seek salvation by *grace,* independent of *charity* in principle, or *morality* in action ! though in good old times, they were both considered as the real buttresses of Christianity : while the well-born consort of the Patrician scatters her bank-bills among *Castrati* and *Oltromontani* minstrels, to enliven the *beau-*

monde of Westminster with a song and a concert on the eve of the Sabbath, the puritanic Magistrate of the suburbs is fulminating pains and penalties upon the harmless fiddlers of an annual fair, because dancing creates sin, as the Devil was the inventor of country dances; and absolutely prohibiting the exposure of the little God of Love, unless dressed in pantaloons, to hide his infantine nudities from the female eye.

Now, to which of these absurd innovations upon social order should reason most seriously direct her scorn ? To that rantipole dame of distinction who would destroy those checks and balances which religion and law have established to tranquillise misery, and uphold decorum ; or, to those repulsive hypocrites, who would bottle up the passions of the multitude, and put the hermetic seal of stupefaction upon the noblest energies of our nature ?

Whether a philosopher shall laugh or weep, at such exceeding instances of mortal folly, let those determine who are wiser than ourselves.   **W.**

UNDER this head we must have reference to an article in the present month's Magazine, *page 200,* containing the Judge's charge to the Jury on the trial of Major Campbell, and some particulars of the wayward fate and execution of that unfortunate gentleman. The Judge's charge is an admirable composition, and contains the best observations on the laws of duelling we ever read.

There is likewise another subject to which a like reference must be had :—Namely, the proceedings of a Court Martial, on Captain

tain Hallilay, *page* 276; we shall offer no observations on the circumstances of the case at present, but merely give place to a communication which has recently appeared in the public papers:—

To the Editor.

" Sir — Under circumstances with which the public has become publicly acquainted, through the medium of a report in the newspapers, of some proceedings of a Court-Martial held at Weeley Barracks, Essex, on Captain John Hallilay, of the 10th regiment, I feel it incumbent on me to make an appeal to the public in vindication of my character, which, though not likely to suffer in the estimation of any *military* gentleman to whom I have the honour of being known, must necessarily be subject to misconstruction in the minds of persons not having the advantage of *professional* knowledge of the subject.

" My intention, Sir, is, to relieve my wounded feelings, by a publication of the minutes of the Court Martial, with explanations.

" I am, Sir,
" Your obedient servant,
" JOHN NEWMAN."

Baker-street North, Sept. 24.

. THE proceedings of another Court Martial has lately been given out in General Orders, and which shall appear in our next Magazine. It commenced at Canterbury on the 25th of May, on Captain George Hewitson, of the 2d battalion of the 9th Regiment, on a variety of charges, for having, at sundry times, while Quarter-Master of the Regiment, made unwarrantable charges, and committed various acts of disgraceful peculation, and for which he is sentenced to be *dismissed the service.*

COCKING.

IN the race-week, at Oxford, a Main of Cocks was fought between the Gentlemen of the county of Oxford, (Eaton, feeder) and the gentlemen of the county of Berks, (Fisher, feeder) for five guineas a battle, and two hundred guineas the main, which was a drawn one, each party having won eight battles; they also each won the same number of byes.

HIS MAJESTY'S
CREAM-COLOURED CHARGER.

THE Hanoverian horse of which we here give an engraving, is one of his Majesty's stud, and was originally intended as a coach-horse, but not being found sufficiently strong for that purpose, and being remarkably handsome, he was broke in for a charger, and his Majesty, till lately, always rode him at the reviews, but he is now turned off, with the rest of the cream-coloured stud; which his Majesty discontinued the use of, when he was informed that Bonaparte had possessed himself of part of his stud at Hanover, and ordered his carriage to be drawn by them, that his equipage may be like that of the King of England.

The picture from which the engraving is taken, is by Mr. H. B. Chalon, and though it is not one of his late productions, the execution of the painting, and the great spirit in the drawing of the horse, evince that it comes from the hand of a master.

THE

Cream Coloured Charger.

THE
PHILOSOPHICAL SPORTSMAN.

NO. VIII.

MRS. SENDAWAY'S TALE OF POOR
JACK.

*" He will tell thee that the wealth of
worlds*
Should ne'er seduce his bosom to forego
Those sacred hours, when, stealing from
the noise
Of care and envy, sweet remembrance
soothes,
With virtue's kindest looks, his aching
breast,
And turns his tears to rapture."
*Akenside's Pleasures of
Imagination.*

"OH! poor Jack!" said Mrs.
Sendaway, " he is my child;
my unsettled rambling son, the
kindest, the mildest, the sweetest
tempered, and the best disposed
man on earth. Poor Jack was the
first fruit of his fond father's love,
the flower of our flock, the pride
of our lives, and the darling of our
hearts ; the picture of health, all
gaiety, and manly spirit ; yet discretion, truth, and gentleness,
guided all his words and actions :
but, oh ! Sir, what a change ! how
have I lived to see my poor Jack
fallen !—"

All the tender affections and
concern of the mother appeared
on the countenance of the venerable orator, in their genuine traits,
and put a stop to her utterance.—
" The beginning of an affecting
relation, Mrs. Sendaway," said I,
" is like the meeting of an old
and long absent friend ; the mind,
in such situations, rushes at once
on a multitude of circumstances,
and remembrance arouses a tumult
of various sensations ; it is therefore nothing strange that we are

overcome on such occasions ; we
should, however, remember, that
man must submit to every change
of circumstances and fortune, whether adverse or prosperous, and
should endeavour to do it becom-
ingly, with calmness and firmness
of spirit. But man is born to feel
for others, and that we are so, does
not, perhaps, deserve to be called a
weakness in our nature :—the miserable are entitled to compassion,
the wretched to our pity, the ne-
cessitous and helpless to our assistance. The paternal feelings and
affections of a mother will excite
emotion—but poor Jack, your son,
appears to be happy ; his looks are
chearful, void of care and life-
consuming passions, and his words
and looks lean toward mirth and
pleasantry. But you have seen him
in a more desirable situation and
disposition of mind ; the remembrance of what he has been, and
the knowledge of what he is, raise
in your breast mingled sensations, a
kind of melancholy pleasure and
sorrow."

" Very true," said Mrs. Sendaway, " and although that remembrance raises a melancholy
pleasure, yet I would not forget
it for the wealth of nations ; it
soothes my mind to think on the
sprightly willing dutifulness of my
dear boy, his ready wit and quickness of observation, and his readiness at learning any thing—what
he was taught he remembered,
what he heard and saw accidentally
was his own, yet never was boy
fonder of play. He worked hard
and cheerfully with his father, but
his daily task over, his mind was
bent on some diversion, and none
pleased, or seemed to suit his genius so well, as that of hunting.—
Poor Jack soon after became clever in the dressing and managing

of horses, very fond of and kind to dogs, and he was taken notice of and received into gentlemen's families. When but a young man, he was made whipper-in to a great man, where he behaved so well, that on the huntsman getting old, and meeting some hurt, my poor Jack was promoted to his place, and was allowed to be the best huntsman in the county; so civil and obliging to all the sporting gentlemen, careful of offending or doing injury to any one in the chase, so well acquainted with the country round, so kind to the dogs, and clever in hunting and managing them, that every body praised and admired, and every body loved my dear Jack. The greatest and richest men in the land, even lords and knights, would ride beside my poor child, ask him questions, and follow his advice, and he was growing rich and great, as well as loved and respected. Still he was dutiful to his fond poor parents, and when he was only a whipper-in gave us many a half-crown, bought his dear father a breeding sow, and me some geese, and we had soon pigs in the stye, and a flock of geese grazing on the green : but when our poor boy was raised to be huntsman, he bought us two cows, which crowned all our wishes ; we smiled on each other, then looked on our unexpected property, and we said, now we shall live on the fat of the land. Every thing went well with us, all prospered under our care ; the sow farrowed thrice in the year, the goslings covered the green in the summer, and our cows gave the richest milk in abundance, and we had such charming health and spirits to enjoy those blessings, as created envy in the breast of some of our neighbours, who said, that it could not only rain, but it must pour, on old Jack and his wife.

" What a holiday we used to have at Whitsuntide!—that was the season in which our dear Jack came yearly thirty miles to see us, and to bless our eyes with his presence for two or three days ; it was a time of mirth and glee, of joy and gladness, to all around—a day of diversion to the whole neighbourhood, to which every one looked with impatience, though some, I fear, were unable to enjoy it when it arrived, through envy.— Then the farmers, their sons, tradesmen, and some lively servants, met on the green to play a game at cricket; our Jack was foreman among them, the best player ; how neatly and forcibly he struck the ball, how swiftly and gracefully did he run the innings. The banks were lined with spectators, and every one extolling the play of our poor Jack, which our ears heard with unutterable delight, and we saw him with that pleasure no tongue can describe ; all cares were then forgotten ; though in years, we felt ourselves young again, and were as happy and blithesome as in the days of our courtship.

" The match ended, we repaired to this our little cottage, and our barrel of ale, which my husband yearly prepared for the occasion, was set a running, and my girls handed round the cake and ale to the happy welcome company. In that corner before me sat the kindest, the best of husbands, and the most indulgent of fathers ; at the farther end our children, and on each side sat our rich neighbours, who would on that evening honour our poor dwelling with their company : nay, the good curate of the

parish

parish, God bless him, condescend-
ed one evening to give us his company, unasked, and he was as merry and easy in our cottage as I
ever saw a man any where in my
life. The song and witty jest went
round, and every face about us was
covered with cheerfulness and satisfaction. But when our dear
Jack tuned his voice, then we were
all silent; attentive to his delightful
songs of the chase; some praised
his voice, others his manner of
singing, which was free and full,
without hesitation or constraint."—
' I hear Mr. Huntsman with pleasure,' said the good curate; ' but
I commend his piety towards his
worthy parents here before us—
that is a commendable virtue indeed; it manifests a good understanding as well as a good disposition; to remember one's parents is
the next degree of virtue to that of
remembering one's Creator. Amiable manners and abilities always
please wherever seen and found,
whilst piety commands our esteem.
Our peaceable industrious parish-
ioners here, are peculiarly blessed
in their offspring; I liken them
with the spreading venerable elms
at the end of our green; they are
shaded and sheltered by their own
branches.'—These were hours of
happiness in which our hearts delighted; we ever loved a day of
social innocent amusement and
cheerfulness, which has, as I think,
preserved us in health, lightened
the cares and labours of bringing up
a large family, and carried us plea-
santly through them. We delighted in the country dance, taught
each of our children to figure in
them upon occasion; it promoted
their growth, gave something of
gracefulness to their motions, dif-
fused a cheerful gaiety and spright-
liness of manners to all their words

and actions. So, after the song
and pleasant discourse had gone
round, our friends and children
stood up for a dance, made up six
couple, and most gaily did they
trip it about. Old Jack, my dear
master, and I, sat looking on with
hearts void of every care. The
harmony of their voices all in uni-
son, tuning the lively notes; their
graceful motions and nimble steps
were a feast to our eyes; we looked at them, we looked at each
other, till we forgot our age, and the
untractableness of our limbs, long
used to hard labour; we sprung
from our seats at the conclusion of
the dance, and set ' The Flowers
of Edinburgh;' how swimmingly
I tripped it after my manly partner,
and he after me, and the dance became doubly alive; every one was
pleased and happy to see their hosts
so enjoy themselves, and to join,
with one consent, in unexpectedly
partaking of their amusements;
but poor Jack, our dear boy, was
in raptures, at beholding his fond
father and mother leading down
the dance; he took my hand with
the tender fondness of a lover;
when I tripped and must have fallen, he caught me with the
quickness of lightning, and prevented it. Happy days! now
past; I remember them with a melancholy pleasure, though I can
never more see their return—our
fairest goodliest branch is blighted;
the praise of every tongue, the admiration of every eye, now roves
about like a feather in the wind;
our dear child, who rode the finest
horse, and governed the chase,
now runs every where after it
on foot, consuming his life and
strength in severe exercise, and at
night sleeping on a lock of straw,
covered with a horse-cloth, known
wherever he is by the name of

Shanny-headed Jack.—Poor dear child! thou art dearer to this heart than in thy days of sprightly blooming health and prosperity."

The feelings of a mother were again working too forcibly to admit of utterance.—In the pause, I took occasion to observe, that poor Jack might, and probably often did, sleep sounder and sweeter on his lock of straw than many do on beds of down; his exercise, though it wears him out fast, yet it is his pleasure, and constitutes, perhaps, all the enjoyment of his days, and will probably preserve him active and healthy till they are very near their end. Look to the bright side —this house is well furnished for a common cottage, the garden before neat and flourishing; those geese and cows I saw on the green perhaps belong to the owners of these premises; and did I not hear poor Jack singing these lines just now ?

" Bid care and sorrow keep away ;
The tender heart should still be gay ;
Serenely o'er it time shall roll,
When no remorse can wound the soul."

" You might," replied Mrs. Sendaway ; " poor Jack sung them at the gate ; they are his own composing, and he sings them at parting to cheer up my spirits ; for if there is any thing gives serious concern to his unsettled mind, it is to see me sorrowful or low in spirits, I therefore do my endeavours to appear calm and cheerfully contented ; but a mother must feel."
—" Very true," said I ; " not to feel for the misfortunes of others, particularly those who are near, and ought to be dear to us, is a sure indication of insensibility or ostentatious arrogance : and not to notice and think of those blessings left for our comfort and enjoyment,

as forcibly indicates our want of reflection and gratitude."

" I thank you, for the gentle reproof," returned she ; " I still am blessed with the enjoyment of many blessings ; my cows are well and prosper, my geese numerous, and my garden flourishing ; my health good, my spirits not bad, and, to crown every other blessing, my husband lives, the best of men lives in health, contentment, and manly cheerfulness ; he is the support of my life and spirits ; at his approach my heart revives within me ; cheerfulness returns, and fortitude springs up to animate my breast. If you can have patience to hear the conclusion of my tale, my husband may come in to take his dinner, and then you will see a man wise without learning, healthy without physic, good without zeal, humane and kind without ostentation, and a man who would be faithful and honest were there no laws in the world. For his dear sake I would be always cheerful, always in health to wait upon him to the last moment ; and then,"—
" Aye, Mrs. Sendaway," said I, interrupting her, " and then you would say, let me follow him to the peaceful mansions of the dead ; but then, perhaps, you would feel the general weakness of human nature, which is so great and prevalent in us, that when the friendly stroke is about to dismiss us after those whom we loved, and whose existence constituted our prime happiness and enjoyment in life, we shrink from it, and petition to live on, though deprived of those friends, and have nearly out-lived those senses and faculties which alone can render life tolerable and a blessing. But that fervent expression of your's, declares the love
and

and esteem you bear towards your husband, and which must have gained you the esteem of many, as well as it has mine. Long may you live together in health, and peaceably enjoy that prosperity which has hitherto contented you; and may you feel at the same time the approaches of that period which arrives to every man, and meet it together in joyful hope and comfortable expectation.

M.

To be continued.

THE FOOL AND THE FALCON,

AN ANECDOTE.

THE immortal Shakspeare says well,

" This fellow is wise enough to play the fool;
And, to do that well, it craves a kind of wit:
He must observe their mood on whom he jests,
The quality of the persons and the time.
                  This is a practice
As full of labour as the wise man's art."

An instance may vindicate our poet's assertion, and convince, were they capable of conviction, our dashing witlings, that they have not sufficient sense to play the fool; moreover, wise fools have been of use on sundry occasions; but of what use have their foolish wisdom been?

Kel Anayet was the jester of Abbas the Great of Persia. His fame is still fresh in that country for his sprightly wit, his burlesque drollery, his uncouth attitudes, and his uncontroulable command over the laughing powers of all who saw or heard him. The Shah, by punning on his name, called him *Ketchel Anayet,* " Scald Pate," and suffered him to joke without danger on occasions which would have cost others dearly.

Abbas was excessively fond of a white hawk, which had been sent him as a present from Mount Caucasus. Being out one day on a hawking excursion, the Shah discovered that this bird was sick. In great vexation he called his grand falconer, named *Hossein-bec,* and charged him most solemnly to take care of this hawk; adding, " whoever pronounces him dead, shall lose his head, depend upon it." Nevertheless, the bird died in a few days. *Hossein-bec,* in utter despondency, saw *Kel Anayet* walking before the Mews, in his way to the Court. To him he told the disaster, conjuring him, with many tears, to save his life. " Agreed," said the droll; " if the Shah takes off any body's head to-day, it shall be his own." Pursuing his intention, he found the Shah in the greatest good humour, just after dinner. " *Scald Pate,* where do you come from?" said Abbas. *Anayet,* assuming the most jocose air imaginable, answered, " From your Majesty's falconry, and pray listen with your utmost attention, for I am going to tell you the most marvellous!—most wonderful!—most astonishing sight that was ever seen in the world. There I saw *Hossein-bec,* with his broom in hand, sweeping a little square place, just before the gilded aviary, then he besprinkled it over with rose-water, then he spread over it a little silken carpet, very curiously enriched with artificial flowers, then he went and fetched your white hawk, and would you believe it? shedding scalding tears over it, he laid it very gently

gently on its back. There lay the hawk, without motion, his wings fallen, his bill uppermost, his claws clasped, his eyes shut—" What, then!" says Abbas surprised,—" my bird is dead."—" Heaven preserve your Majesty's head," replied *Anayet*, " for surely it is safe to-day, notwithstanding your threat !—You have announced the tidings to yourself."

CANINE ANECDOTES.

THERE is a chapter in one of our metaphysical writers, shewing how dogs make syllogisms. The illustration is decisive. A dog loses sight of his master, and follows him by scent till the road branches into three ; he smells at the first, and at the second, and then without smelling farther, gallops along the third. That animals should be found to possess every faculty which is necessary for their well-being, is nothing wonderful ; the wonder would be, if they did not ; but they sometimes display a reach of intellect beyond this.

For instance :—dogs have a sense of time, so as to count the days of the week. My grandfather had one, who trudged two miles every Saturday to market, to cater for himself in the shambles.—I know another more extraordinary and well-authenticated example : a dog which had belonged to an Irishman, and was sold by him in England, would never touch a morsel of food on a Friday ; the Irishman had made him as good a catholic as he was himself. This dog never forsook the sick bed of his last master, and, when he was dead, refused to eat, and died also.

A dog of my acquaintance found a bitch in the streets, who had lost her master, and was ready to whelp; he brought her home, put her in possession of his kennel, and regularly carried his food to her, which it may be supposed he was not suffered to want during her confinement. For his gallantry his name deserves to be mentioned —it was Pincher ; some of his other acquaintance may remember him. Whenever Pincher saw a trunk packing up in the house, he absconded for the next four-and-twenty hours. He was of opinion that home was the best place.

J. AIKIN, M.D.

August 27, 1808.

SATIRICAL HINTS TO CRIMINALS.

MR. EDITOR,

IN the celebrated novel of " *Tom Jones*," Fielding remarks, with his accustomed humour, that if every man were to be believed on his own testimony, we should not be shocked with the frequency of executions ; but as I fear this implicit credulity will not obtain the sanction of the sages of the law, I shall endeavour, as the sessions approach, to attain the same desirable end, by addressing a few *memoranda* to such ladies and gentlemen whose virtue is about to undergo the superfluous ceremony of a trial.

You must take special care to plead " *Not Guilty*," in order to acquire some physical chances in your favour ; for among the extraordinary occurrences of this world, it is not impossible that there should be a flaw in the indictment ; the

principal

principal evidence against you die suddenly before examination ; all the Judges and senior counsel sympathetically expire at the same moment of an apoplexy ; or the jury be carried off by a surfeit. Besides, there is an after chance of softening the adamantine breast of the turnkey ; of Newgate being destroyed by a new set of rioters ; of *mysteriously* escaping like a late celebrated *smuggler ;* or, lastly, as you may read, or get read to you, in the chaste and fashionable romance of the " *Monk,*" a certain sable gentleman may whip you off as expeditiously and suddenly as he did the amorous *Ambrosio.*

Should you have a *friendly* counsel from whom you may expect *gratuitous* service, be sure *not* to depend on him ; for, in that profession, give the greatest stranger a *guinea,* and he will exert himself more than your brother would for twenty shillings. Remember also the sage observation of *Gibbet,* in the " *Beaux Stratagem,*"—' I must reserve a sufficient sum to get me off, in case of the worst.'

You must carefully avoid bringing on your trial late in the evening, so great is the danger of being in the hands of a jury when they are hungry ; in this case business is always *dispatched.* To persons of your information I need scarcely hint that this subject is finely touched upon by our poets—

" The lank-jaw'd hungry Judge will hang the guiltless,
" Rather than eat his mutton cold."

Again—

" And wretches hang that jurymen may dine."

If your indictment be for a rape, you would do well, on being arraigned, to challenge any man on the jury who is old enough to have a grown daughter.—*Mem.* Wives and sisters are not half so dangerous.

If you are charged with a highway robbery, you must ask your prosecutor some questions about the reward given in such cases on conviction. Taxes are now very heavy, and juries will of course be cautious how they increase county rates.

Should it be a case of perjury, let your counsel be particularly keen-scented in hunting after a flaw ; indeed, he cannot do better than study attentively the following quotation from Foote's farce of " *The Devil upon Two Sticks* :"— " Up starts little Beelzebub in the form of an able practitioner, and humbly conceived that his client could not be convicted upon that indictment ; forasmuch as therein he was charged with forswearing himself *now,* whereas it clearly appeared by the evidence that he had only forsworn himself *then.* If, indeed, he had been indicted generally for committing perjury, *now and then,* proofs might be produced of *any* perjury he may have committed ; whereas, by limiting the point of time to the *now,* no proof could be admitted as to the *then !* so that, with submission, he humbly conceived his client was clearly absolved, and his character as fair and as spotless as a babe's that is just born, and immaculate as a sheet of white paper."

If your crime be a burglary, the best defence you can make is, to shew that you belonged to the revenue or excise, and in that case you will have a licence for it.

If you have occasion to call witnesses to your character, it would be prudent to procure one friend blind, and another deaf ! The first may

may safely swear that he never *saw* any harm of you; and the second can affirm, with equal truth, that he never *heard* any thing to your prejudice.

If you are a woman, and any thing handsome, you must try to make some impression on the Judge, or even on the jury; for should your offence be capital, the latter may commend you to mercy; or if they think it too much trouble, his Lordship may do it himself. It would also be wise to appear

> " As women wish to be who love their Lords !"

If you are guilty of a robbery, and escape by the lenity of your prosecutor, you can do no less in duty to yourself than rob him as soon as possible again, knowing his principles to be safe.

If you are unfortunate in the formation of your countenance, you have a better right to the assistance of art and painting than the greatest lady at St. James's.— At the present crisis it would not be amiss if you were to give your face the appearance of a *Spaniard;* but take particular care to avoid the most distant resemblance of a *French phiz,* for in that case you must expect no mercy !

When you come on your defence, you need not be too minute in the relating of circumstances, lest some of them should unfortunately contradict each other: afterwards, if you should chance to be acquitted, you may put out your tongue and laugh at the jury.— This may induce some people to think you an impudent dog, but it may as well proceed from the triumph of innocence over unmerited persecution.

AMERICAN DUELLING.

IN an American newspaper, called *The Columbian Centinel,* of the 6th of July, nearly two columns are occupied with a statement of a boarding-house *fracas,* between Mr. Sylvester Thompson, and Mr. Charles Ward Apthorp Morton. The latter appears to have acted in a hasty, imprudent manner, and, being tired of his life, according to his own confession, he wished to get rid of it in an *honourable* way. The following paragraphs of a letter from Mr. T.'s second, we extract for the amusement of our readers. It appears that the style frightened his antagonist, as nothing further has appeared on the subject. It is a real curiosity; and, in all similar cases it may serve as a copy for the friends of the humane and fashionable practice of duelling. The arrangements for burying the bodies are rather an innovation, as public funeral honours are invariably decreed to the ' victims' of honour. After mentioning terms, the gentleman proceeds thus :—

" These terms are by no means humiliating; the proudest Potentate in Europe, in acceding, would have no cause to blush. Now, Sir, permit me to ask, what can be more truly noble in these gentlemen than to subdue the unworthy and immoral suggestions of false pride and false honour, and thus bring those resentments into mutual acknowledgements, which otherwise must end in the death of one or both ! This being done, both parties will have cause to congratulate themselves on the propriety of their conduct; they will be reinstated in the good opinion of their particular friends; and will
obtain

obtain a respectable estimation in the public mind. Let me entreat you, Sir, with ardent and honest sincerity, to co-operate with me, in saving the lives of those gentlemen, and securing to ourselves the honour of being the founders of a new and rational mode of settling the differences which occur among young men, and which so frequently terminate in their own destruction, and the ruin of their families. If you will not accede to those conditions, we must throw ourselves into the hands of fate, and await her decision. You are aware, Sir, that as Mr. Morton is the challenger, the right of choosing the time, place, distance, and weapons, remains in our choice. We propose to agree verbally on the place and day ; the hour to be at half past six o'clock, P. M. pistols shall be the weapons, and four paces the distance. The parties shall stand face to face, with their coats and braces off. We can have no *eclaircissement* on the ground. The parties will answer "Yes," to the question, "Are you ready ?" and then discharge their pistols after the command "Fire," has been distinctly and finally uttered. The right of giving the word "fire," you and myself will determine by some mode of chance. It will be necessary for us to be accompanied by a surgeon. They are seldom willing to be engaged in such affairs, and if we cannot get one, we must be provided with two tourniquets, bandages, &c. with such instruments as are requisite to extract balls. We will make verbal arrangements for burying one or both of the bodies of our principals. Should only one be wounded, and the wound is not mortal, the victim shall not be entitled to another shot; but the

wounded party may take another, on equal terms, provided the wound does not disable the pistol arm.— The parties may exchange their weapons, or each may use his own.

"My duty is nearly done : it only remains now for me to suggest to you, Sir, that if you cannot persuade Mr. Morton to accede to our honourable and amicable terms, and you do accompany him in the quality of a second, you take on yourself a weight of responsibility, which good principles cannot sustain ; and you may fall under the imputation of being accessary to the perpetration of murder in form.

"Should Mr. Morton persist in forcing this unhappy affair to a final crisis, and have the great misfortune of surviving, he must, from the moment of the catastrophe which his rashness may occasion, be the most miserable being in creation : not all the mercy of heaven can absolve his crime ; the united tears and prayers of all the angels of forgiveness can procure no expiation. If Heaven has but a little grace and kindness for your friend, she has already issued her decree, commanding him to hasten to the bar of everlasting retribution ; for though his desire of revenge may now act as an opiate to his conscience, yet when that revenge is obtained, either by the death or mangling of my friend, this opiate will lose its efficacy, and leave the infatuated subject of its operation awake to years of guilt and misery.

"I am, Sir, with much respect,
"Your obedient servant,
"* * * * * * *"

"I have no more to say ; let the world be judges between Mr. Morton and myself—he and they

M m   have

have all that could be required from an injured man, who was willing to meet his disappointed, forlorn, and ambitious enemy, either in *honourable* combat, or to end our disagreement in mutual reconciliation.

" SILVESTER THOMPSON."

AMERICAN COCK-FIGHTING.

Raleigh, North Carolina,
June 15, 1808.

THE main of seventeen pair of cocks, fought at Hillsborough, last week, Mr. J. J. Alston, of Chatham, against Mr. Henry Adkinson, of Caswell, terminated, after the warmest-contested battles ever witnessed in this state; each party exhibiting uncommon skill in keeping, gafting, pitting, &c.—At the close of the first day, Alston had won seven out of nine fights; but, on the second day, six out of seven were decreed to Adkinson. Thus, each party were equal gamesters, each having won eight battles. The 17th fight was to terminate the main, to decide bets to the amount of eighteen hundred dollars. This was an interesting battle indeed—the little animals appeared as if sensible of the importance with which they were viewed by the punters—each contending for his life, and the cocking reputation of his master—each on his guard not to put himself in the power of the other.—Neither appeared to have the advantage, until they were both cut down, and, for a time, neither exhibited signs of recovering life.

This was an awful moment.—None, but one of the talents of Hogarth, could give a true representation of this interesting scene.

Just before, at every peck of either cock, Huzza for Alston! Huzza for Adkinson! Give it to him red! Stick to him grey! That's he, my chicken! resounded from the throats of hundreds; consisting of white and black, rich and poor, those dishonest, and those not over-honest—all were at this moment struck dumb. At length it was discovered that Adkinson gave last signs of fight, and the judges were proceeding to count out his antagonist, but before they had finished the count, Alston, in the agonies of death, raising his head, gave a peck at (for he could not reach) his opponent, won the fight and the main, and completely turned the misery and mortification of defeat upon his opponent. Thus one thousand eight hundred dollars were won and lost upon a single peck or motion of the head, resembling fight! And thus ended this rational, humane, and reputable amusement!

ACTIONS

FOR

ALLEDGED VIOLATIONS OF THE GAME LAWS.

YORK SUMMER ASSIZES.

CURRER, ESQ. v. PETTY.

THIS was an action to recover the penalty of 5l. under the game laws.

Mr. Serjeant Cockell stated, that the defendant was unqualified, and incurred the penalty; he was found sporting in the manor of Brimham, on the 16th of December last; he hoped it would be a warning to him, and that he would not be suffered to travel
about

about the country with a dog and gun; he was seen to take a shot, and, as poachers are generally good marksmen, down came the bird.— The defendant pretended to be a game-keeper; if so, he is not to the plaintiff; perhaps he may attempt to prove some other qualification.

Henry Dawson Roundell, Esq. brother to the plaintiff, proved the defendant, on the 16th of December last, was seen in Cow-close, in the parish of Kirby Malzeard, with a gun and dog, beating for game; the close belongs to the plaintiff, and is occupied by Christopher Reynolds.

Being cross-examined, witness said he was not very well acquainted with Cow-close; supposed it to be in the manor of Hartwith cum Brimham.—Witness understood defendant had a deputation from Sir John Ingilby, for the manor of Dacre, which he afterwards produced to the witness.

Wm. Grange was present when the defendant was sporting in Cow-close with a dog and gun; he understood defendant was game-keeper to Sir John. Cow-close is in the manor of Brimham, which belongs to Lord Grantley, or the Aislaby family.

On being cross-examined, defendant said, he came there by order of Sir John. Witness never knew Sir John Ingilby was owner of the manor.

Mr. Park, on behalf of the defendant, said, it was true the defendant sported in the close with his dog and gun; he was a game-keeper over the manor in which the close is situated; he supposed this trial was brought for the purpose of fishing out the title to this manor; perhaps some inclosure there is in agitation; but his Lord-

ship would not suffer them to try the title on a *qui tam* action; he produced Court Rolls as far back as 1627, and gamekeepers' deputations as far back as 1734, from the Ingilby family, for the manor of Dacre cum Hartwith, and, by parole evidence, for twenty-five years back, proved the close to be within Sir John's manor.

Under his Lordship's directions, the plaintiff was non-suited.

—————————

FOX, ESQ. *v.* HODGSON.

THIS was an action of trespass against the defendant, for shooting game within the plaintiff's manor.

Mr. Park, on behalf of the plaintiff, stated, that Mr. Fox was Lord of the manor of Bingley; when this trespass was committed; the Defendant had notice, but still persisted in going there. The Plaintiff was desirous of preserving his game for the accommodation of his friends: his gamekeeper gave notice in writing to the defendant, in August, 1807; the defendant was then shooting moor-game, and behaved in a very outrageous manner; he erected a tent on the moor for the accommodation of himself and the party he had taken with him, so that the plaintiff was greatly annoyed in the exercise of his own sport. The defendant had a notice in writing, besides a verbal notice at another time, so that he was a wilful trespasser. The defence understood to be set up is, that the notice in writing being dated the 12th of August, 1806, and delivered the 12th of August, 1807, is not sufficient; but I contend a verbal notice in this case is sufficient—it will hardly be disputed that Mr. Fox is Lord of the manor.

Mr.

Mr. Delafare, attorney, holds the courts for the plaintiff's manor of Bingley, knows Bingley Moor, and proved it part of that manor.

Samuel Pickard, the plaintiff's gamekeeper for that manor, proved that he had orders from the plaintiff to discharge all persons trespassing thereon; and that on the 12th of August, 1807, witness saw the defendant sporting on Bingley Moor. Mr. Penney, a clergyman, who had leave from the plaintiff to sport there, filled up the notice, which the witness delivered to the defendant upon the moor; the notice was signed by the plaintiff in August, 1806. Witness gave the defendant notice verbally several times; he saw the defendant on the 18th and 19th of August last shoot at grouse on the moor; he had a gun and an English spaniel with him.

Cross-examined by Mr. Topping.

Witness said the name of the defendant was inserted in the notice by Mr. Penney, upon the moor, in 1807.

It was here agreed that the plaintiff should take a verdict for 1s. damages, and each party pay his own costs.

MAJOR CAMPBELL.

IN our Magazine of last month, *page* 200, we gave an account of the trial and conviction of Major Campbell, since which his trial has been published, and the following is the CHARGE OF THE JUDGE.

" IT has been very properly stated to you by the counsel for the prosecution, that the illegal killing a man, by the law of England,

must fall within one of the three species—homicide, manslaughter, or murder; and that with homicide you had nothing to do, as the case before you was clearly neither chance-medley, self-defence, nor any kind of justifiable homicide. The case, then, must either be manslaughter or murder. Manslaughter is the illegal killing a man under the strong impulse of natural passion. Three qualities are necessary to constitute it. In the first place, the passion must be natural; that is to say, such as is natural to human infirmity, under the provocation given:—secondly, the act must be such as the passion naturally, and according to the ordinary course of human actions, would impel—and thirdly, and indeed mainly, the criminal act must be committed in the actual moment of the passion, *flagrante animo*, as it is termed, and before the mind has time to cool. The act of killing, under such circumstances, is manslaughter. But if any of these circumstances are wanting; if the passion be beyond the provocation—beyond what the provocation should naturally and ordinarily produce; if the act be beyond the passion—beyond what the passion would naturally and ordinarily impel, or if it be not committed in the very moment of the passion, and before the passion either has or should have passed away;—in all such cases the act of criminal killing is not manslaughter, but murder.

" Now to apply this to the present case.—The provocation, as stated by the evidence, consisted in the words, " Do you say I am wrong?"—" Yes, I do;" and the manner in which those words were said. It remains for you, therefore, gentlemen, to consider whether such a provocation were sufficient

cient to constitute that passion, which, under the interpretation of the law, would render the prisoner at the bar guilty of manslaughter only; or whether the consequent passion was not above the provocation, and therefore that the prisoner is guilty of murder. You will consider this coolly in your own judgments, and will remember upon this point the evidence that has been given; that the words were certainly offensively spoken, but that it was in the heat of argument, and that, by a candid explanation, as the evidence expressed it, the affair might not have occurred.

" You will next have to consider, whether the criminal act was committed in the moment, the actual moment of the passion—or whether the prisoner had time to cool, and to return to the use of his reason. Upon this point, you must keep your attention more particularly fixed on that part of the evidence which goes to state, that Major Campbell returned home, took his tea, and executed some domestic arrangements, after the words, and before the meeting. If you are of opinion, either that the provocation, which I have mentioned to you, and which you collect from the evidence, was too slight to excite that violence of passion which the law requires for manslaughter; or that, be the passion and the provocation what it might, still that the prisoner had time to cool, and return to his reason—in either of these cases, you are bound upon your oaths to find the prisoner guilty of murder.

" There is still another point for your serious consideration. It has been correctly stated to you by the counsel, that there is such a thing which is called the point of honour—a principle totally false in itself, and unrecognised both by law and morality; but which, from its practical importance, and the mischief attending any disregard of it to the individual concerned, and particularly to a military individual, has usually been taken into consideration by juries, and admitted as a kind of extenuation. But in all such cases, gentlemen of the jury, there have been, and there must be, certain grounds for such indulgent consideration—such departure from the letter and spirit of the law. In the first place, the provocation must be great; in the second place there must be a perfect fair-dealing—the contract to oppose life to life must be perfect on both sides—the consent of both must be full, neither of them must be forced into the field:—and thirdly, there must be something of a necessity, a compulsion, to give and take the meeting; the consequence of refusing it being the loss of reputation, and there being no means of honourable reconciliation left.

" Let me not be mistaken on this serious point. I am not justifying duelling; I am only stating those circumstances of extenuation which are the only grounds that can justify a jury in dispensing with the letter of the law.—You have to consider, therefore, gentlemen of the jury, whether this case has these circumstances of extenuation. You must here recall to your minds the words of the deceased Captain Boyd—' You have hurried me—I wanted you to wait and have friends —Campbell, you are a bad man.' These words are very important, and if you deem them sufficiently proved, they certainly do away all extenuation. If you think them proved, the prisoner is most clearly guilty

guilty of murder; the deceased will then have been hurried into the field; the contract of opposing life to life could not have been perfect."

EXECUTION.

Our readers are already in possession of the circumstances of the trial and conviction of this unfortunate gentleman, and the recommendatory memorials which were addressed to the Lord Lieutenant in his behalf.—On this occasion his Grace declined deciding, but sent the entire documents, with the Judge's notes. to the King, and on the 16th sent a special messenger, with a further respite till the 24th. —Major Campbell passed the painful interval, as may be imagined, in a state of extreme anxiety, agitated between contending hopes and fears; but receiving all the consolation which affectionate friendship and commiseration could bestow.

On the 23d of August, about four o'clock in the evening, a second messenger arrived at Armagh, with the fatal tidings, that the King's pleasure was unfavourable; that his Grace could interfere no longer; and that the awful sentence must take place next day. Early on Wednesday morning another messenger arrived from the castle, with an order to remit that part of the sentence with respect to the anatomising and dissecting his body.

The Sheriff sent a message, to fix his own hour; and he chose between eleven and twelve o'clock in the day.

The Rev. Mr. Ball, the curate of Armagh church, remained with him the whole of the night; and we are informed, that too much cannot be said for this gentleman's humane concern for him, during his unhappy state. The Major was attentive to his religious duties, and was well prepared to meet his fate with the greatest firmness of mind; and the night before his execution, he settled all his money accounts with the gaoler with the greatest composure.

Shortly before his execution, when the sheriff's attendants waited on him to confine his arms, he observed to them, that "it was very proper; it would prevent him from struggling;" adding, "that he thought he should have died a more honourable death; but, since this was his fate, he would submit himself to the laws." He then walked firmly up stairs to the execution-room, took off his cravat, put it in his breast, and opened his neck, stooping his head to the executioner to receive the halter, which he complained was too thick, and that a smaller one would have been more effectual.

He prayed most fervently to Heaven for himself, and that his poor wife and children might be protected. He then bade farewell to the people in the room, and with the most becoming fortitude, he stepped out on the fatal drop, and saluted the people on every side of him. He spoke a few words in the Erse language to the soldiers, which were understood to be desiring them to pray for him. He asked a few moments longer: he was told to take his own time. He again repeated a fervent prayer for his wife and family—drew down the cap over his face—clenched his hands firm in each other—and then was removed from this world to eternity. He struggled a short time; and after hanging thirty-
five

five minutes, was cut down, and his body given to his friends.— They put it into a coffin, which was enclosed in a deal box, and im- mediately sent off in a car for Do- naghadee, to be interred at Ayr, in Scotland.

WINNERS OF THE ROYAL PLATES AT HAMBLETON, &c.

FROM 1715 TO 1808.

To the Editor of the Sporting Magazine.

SIR,

AS you have given the Winners of the Royal Plates at York, I have taken the liberty of sending you a complete List of the Mares who have won the Royal Plates at Black Hambleton,* Yorkshire, beginning with the year 1715, which is as far back as I can trace with accuracy :— The insertion thereof in your next number, will oblige,

Your's, &c.

York, September 10, 1808.   W. P.

1715 Mr Gage's Who-would-have-thought-it, (sire unknown) beating fourteen others
1716 Mr Pelham's Brocklesby Betty, by Mr Curwen's Bay Barb—beating ten others
1717 Mr Wrigglesworth's Creeping Kate—beating twenty others
1718 Mr Atkinson's bay mare—beating eighteen others
1719 Duke of Rutland's Bonny Black, by Black Hearty, 4 years old— beating thirty others :—Five were drawn, so that thirty-six entered, which was the largest number ever known.
1720 Duke of Rutland's Bonny Black, by Black Hearty—beating nineteen others
1721 Mr G. Witty's grey mare—beating nineteen others
1722 Lord Halifax's Sophonisba, by Mr Dyer's Dimple—beating twenty-one others
1723 Mr Græme's Whitelips—beating eighteen others
1724 Mr Panton's grey mare—beating twenty-five others
1725 Mr Match'em Timms's Bald Peg, by Snake—beating several others.—This Plate was run for over Richmond Course

* The Royal Cup run for at Hambleton, at its first commencement, was free for either horse, mare, or gelding, provided they were no more than five years old, carrying 10st. each, four miles.—Queen Anne altered it to be run for by five-year old mares, the same weight and distance.— The first Cup (ever run for at that place) was won by Sir William Strickland's *Syphax*, who was sire to the famous *Hambleton Mare*, who also won the Royal Plate at Hambleton.—She was the dam of Mr. Elstobb's Shadow, (afterwards Sir Edward O'Brien's Dairymaid) by Mr. Darley's Almanzor.

1726 Mr

1726 Mr Taylor's Ladylegs, (afterwards called Bald Charlotte) by Captain Appleyard's Old Royal—beating twenty-three others

1727 Captain Appleyard's black mare, by Mr Darley's Manica—beating twenty-four others

1728 Mr Newstead's Miss Pert, by the Thoulouse Barb—beating thirteen others

1729 Mr Egerton's Nanny, by the Pigott Turk—beating twelve others

1730 Mr Jackson's Favourite, by Lord Widdrington's grey horse, out of Mother Neesbam's dam—beating fourteen others

1731 Duke of Bolton's Mary Grey, by Mr Darley's Almanzor—beating twenty-three others

1732 Mr Read's grey mare—beating fourteen others

1733 Mr Durham's Favourite, by a son of the Bald Galloway—beating nineteen others

1734 Miss Dolly Routh's Jenny-come-tye-me, by Mr. Bartlett's Childers—beating fourteen others

1735 Mr Hendrey's Miss Hendrey, by Mr Smith's Son of Snake—beating Mr Crofts's Legacy, by Old Greyhound, and eleven others

1736 Hon. Mr Vane's Little Partner, by Mr Crofts's Partner—beating six others

1737 Mr Hutton's Aquilina, by Mr Bartlett's Childers—beating Mr Hudson's Peggy-grieves-me, by Hipp ; Mr Darley's Miss Patty, by Skipjack ; Mr Read's Lucy, by Smiling Tom ; and twelve others

1738 Mr Simpson's Mopping Jenny, by a Son of Almanzor—beating Mr Pearson's Selima, by Mr Bethell's Arabian, and eleven others —This race was so near run between Mopping Jenny and Selima, that it was supposed to have been a dead heat ; but being submitted to arbitration, it was given to Mopping Jenny.—*Selima* was the dam of Scampston-Cade, Cypron, &c.—*Cypron* was the dam of King Herod, &c.

1739 Mr Metcalfe's Shepherdess, by a Grey Barb, at Hampton-Court— beating Mr Crofts's Miss Cloudy, by Bloody-Buttocks, and fourteen others

1740 Mr Widdrington's Spinster (alias Mr Panton's Widdrington Mare) by Mr Croft's Partner—beating Mr Wilkie's Miss Barforth, by Partner, and thirteen others

1741 Mr Selby's Coughing Polly, by Mr Bartlett's Childers—beating Mr Holme's Miss Meynell, and eight others

1742 Lord Gower's Vixen, by Fox-Cub—beating Mr Thornborough's Daphne ; Mr Hartley's Countess ; Sir Arthur Hasleridge's Miss Patch ; Mr Holmes's Miss Makeless ; and seven others

1743 Mr Simpson's Mopsey, by Captain Appleyard's Cuddy—beating ten others

1744 Lord Portmore's Lady Caroline, by Flying Childers—beating nine others

1745 Mr Garthside's Pamela, by Fearnought (son of Doctor), dam by Manica—beating Mr Langley's Gipsy ; Mr Metcalfe's Lady Betty, (fell) and seven others.

1746 Duke

1746 Duke of Ancaster's Dizzy, by his Grace's Driver—beating Mr Mylott's Northern-Lass, by Syphax; Mr Trout's Patch, by Goliah; and eight others

1747 Mr Hutton's Mab, by Hobgoblin—beating Mr Keck's Brown Betty, by Lath, and four others.—This Plate was run for at Malton

1748 Mr Leedes's Spinster, by Mr Panton's Crab, out of the Widdrington Mare—beating Mr Fletcher's Cumberland Lass by his Arabian; Mr Martindale's Shepherdess; and three others

1749 Mr H. Vernon's Lady Caroline, by Mr Panton's Crab—beating Mr Shafto's Pamela, by Orion, and nine others

1750 Mr Duncombe's Duchess, by the Duke of Devonshire's Black-legs—beating Mr Hale's Miss Doe, by Sedbury; Mr Clarke's Lass of the Mill, by Traveller; and six others

1751 Sir Robert Eden's Miss Western*, by Sedbury—beating Sir W. Middleton's Camilla, by a Son of Bay Bolton; Mr Tilly's Milkmaid, by Spot; and seven others

1752 Mr Shuttleworth's Miss Wilkinson, by Regulus—beating Mr Parker's Ladythigh, by Regulus; Mr Routh's Brown Betty, by Regulus; and five others

1753 Mr Fenwick's Duchess, by Whitenose—beating Mr Vernon's Amelia, by the Godolphin Arabian, and three others

1754 Sir Charles Sedley's Cadena, by Cade—beating Mr Croft's Sally, by Forester; Mr Hutton's Sister to Stately; and three others

1755 Mr Hutton's Stately, by the Bolton Mogul—beating Mr Robinson's Music, by Forester, and five others

1756 Mr Robinson's Mary Tartar, by Tartar—beating Mary Scott, Mary Gray, Mary Regulus, and Mary Andrew

1757 Lord Rockingham's Lisetta, by Regulus—beating Mr Swinburn's Smallbones, by Traveller, and five others

1758 Countess of Northumberland's Irené, by Cade—beating Mr Mann's Belinda, by Tartar; Sir J. Lowther's Sophia, by Blank; Mr Shafto's Miss Belsea, by Regulus, and two others

1759 Lord Downe's Ferdinandinia, by Cade—beating Mr A. Smith's Gipsy, by Young Cade, and six others

1760 Mr Wentworth's Maria†, by Second; dam, Spinster, by Crab, out of the Widdrington Mare—beating Mr Lister's Patient Grizzle, by Regulus, and eleven others

1761 Mr Duncombe's Ceres, by Cade—beating Mr A. Pearson's Flashing Molly, by Oroonoke, and five others

1762 Lord Grosvenor's Alipes, by Regulus—beating the Duke of Cleveland's Miss Lincoln, by Second

1763 Mr Stanhope's Blackeyes, (afterwards Miss Cape) by Regulus—beating Mr Hutton's Portia, by Regulus; Mr Pigott's Shropshire Lady, by Blank; and two others

* Miss Western was rode in her exercise by the late Mr John Hutchinson.—She was the first that he attended on.

† Maria's dam and grandam also won Hambleton Guineas.—See the years 1740 and 1748.

1764 Mr Stapleton's Carleton, by Regulus—beating Mr Elliott's Imo-
 inda, by Sampson, and three others
1765 Lord A. Hamilton's Charlotte, by Blank—beating Lord Northumberland's Fair Rachel, by Mr Wilson's Arabian, and seven
 others
1766 Mr Fenwick's Nannette, by Match'em—beating Lord Farnham's
 Shadow, by Blank ; and seven others
1767 Lord George Sutton's Fortune, by Blank—beating Mr Shafto's
 Hyæna, by Snap ; Lord Grosvenor's Stately, by Bandy, and seven others
1768 Mr Bethell's Laura, by Lofty—beating Mr Vernon's Hermione,
 by Blank ; Mr Sotheron's Queen Elizabeth, by Regulus ; Mr
 Coates's Calliope, by Slouch ; Mr Bland's Diana, by Regulus ;
 and Mr Law's Camilla, by Slouch
1769 Mr Atkinson's Dulcinea, by Whistlejacket—beating Mr Ellerker's
 Lass of Patagonia, by Regulus ; Mr Fortescue's Laycock, by
 South ; and two others
1770 Sir Joseph Pennington's Creeping Kate, by Babram-Blank—beating Mr Pratt's Riddle, by Match'em, and two others
1771 Mr Cornforth's Shepherdess, by Mr Shepherd's Crab—beating
 Sir L. Dundas's Fair Helen, by Babram-Blank ; Mr Patterson's
 Silvertail, by Careless ; and Lord Strathmore's Maria, by Northumberland—Maria broke down
1772 Mr Radcliffe's Shepherdess, by Mr Shepherd's Crab, beating Mr
 Cornforth's Jocasta, by Forester, and seven others

(To be concluded in our next.)

✱✱✱ For the Pedigrees and Performances of the above Mares, we refer our Readers to
 Pick's Turf Register.

COLONEL THORNTON AND MR. FLINT.

THE cause so long depending between the above parties, in
which the Colonel was the plaintiff,
and Flint the defendant, was at last
brought to a hearing at the Guild-
hall, York, before Sir George
Wood, on Saturday, the 6th instant.

The counsel for the plaintiff
stated, that this being an undefended
cause, he would not go at length
into the history of the transactions
which led to it,—and the more especially, because there were some
circumstances belonging to it,

which, from delicacy to persons,
not parties on the record, ought
not, but through necessity only, to
be stated. He was extremely sorry
he should then be occupying his
Lordship's and their time, because
the cause never ought to have
come there. It had twice been
referred to gentlemen of the profession to which he had the honour to belong, and whose judgment would long before, had it
not been for the perverse obstinacy
of the defendant, have set the matter at rights ; and he observed,
that indeed he was by no means
certain they would ever have heard
of the cause, (for whatever damages

mages he might recover at their hands, the plaintiff never expected to get a single shilling from the defendant, who was at that moment in prison for debt) had it not been for the idle boasting of the defendant, that the plaintiff was indebted to him in considerable sums of money; their verdict would tell the world whether that was true or false. However, he would not make use of any harsh language towards the defendant, because he was ever disinclined so to do, and still more so in a case where the defendant was not represented by counsel; nor did he believe it to be the wish of his client, otherwise than from an anxious honourable desire to have his whole conduct, in a case so unparalleled as the present, publicly sifted and examined; indeed he knew the defendant was already sufficiently fallen and degraded. He then observed, that he ought to state, before he proceeded to detail to them the particulars of the demand, that the declaration in the cause was so extremely defective, through the inattention of the London attorney, who being now no more, " *de mortuis nil nisi bonum*," that he should be under the necessity of abandoning several of the items, to a large amount, contained in the bill of particulars of the demand, with such observations on them as he thought necessary for explanation to the jury.

After a full investigation, the learned Judge directed the jury to find a verdict for plaintiff—Five Hundred Guineas.

The delays to bring this matter to trial had not lessened, but excited considerable desire to hear the business elucidated. At Mr. Flint's particular request, and a solemn assurance on the part of his attorney, that he had fulfilled *one sacred* promise with Colonel Thornton, he permitted it to go to the reference of three able counsel; by Mr. Flint's conduct (though the Colonel's witnesses were examined) the arbitration was not closed, and the Colonel obliged to fly to the only redress—a court of justice, which court had now done him *ample* justice.

The pretension or excuse Mr. Flint gave for his unparalleled conduct towards Colonel Thornton, and the dignity of the company, at the Grand Stand, was a demand for money due; this the Colonel had repeatedly denied, and Mr. Flint's assertions were found to be completely erroneous, as in the above instance only, he has been sentenced to pay Colonel Thornton 525l. and interest. Other claims equally *well* founded, as stated by the counsel, could not be tried on this occasion; but the Judge gave him to understand, that these claims might still be entered into at the next assizes; they are of moment, and some of them most extraordinary; for horses, and particularly for Brown Thornville, or Black Strap; (it may be remembered that this horse was the one that beat Vinagrillio over York;) a match the Spring Meeting before for 100gs. for which Colonel Thornton's mare walked over, Mr. Flint's being lame; also for other horses—but the most extraordinary item is a demand upon Mr. Flint, which the arbitrators would have entered to, for having, under *vague pretences*, occupied Colonel Thornton's house; in spite of all the representations of Colonel Thornton by letters, read to him by his steward, and he remained until he heard Colonel Thornton was on his way down to his house.

COURT MARTIAL ON CAPTAIN HALLILAY.

AT a General Court Martial held at Weeley, on the 8th July, 1808, and continued by adjournments to the 3d of August following, Captain George John Hallilay, of the tenth regiment of foot, was arraigned upon the following charges; viz.

First Charge.—" For unofficer-like conduct in preferring charges against Lieutenant and Adjutant Spike, and Lieutenant and Acting Quarter-Master Simpson, of the said tenth regiment of foot, to Lieutenant-Colonel Newman, then being Commanding Officer of the same regiment, on or about the 18th of June, 1808, which charges were malicious, vexatious, and groundless."

Second Charge.—" For conduct highly unbecoming the character of an officer in preferring complaints against Lieutenant-Colonel Newman, his Commanding Officer, to Lieut.-Gen. Lord Charles Fitzroy, in the month of June, 1808, without allowing the same to be forwarded through the regular channel, although Lieutenant-Colonel Newman had offered to forward any complaints Captain Hallilay might have to make against him, or any other officers of the regiment, being highly prejudicial to good order and military discipline."

Third Charge.—" For personal disrespect to Lieutenant-Colonel Newman, his Commanding Officer, on the parade at Weeley barracks, on Saturday, July 2, 1808, in presuming to interfere with the duties of Lieutenant-Colonel Newman, then Commanding Officer of the regiment, and for making use of very ungentlemanly and insolent expressions to Lieutenant-Colonel Newman, and also applicable to him and Lieutenant Simpson, of the tenth regiment, on having been informed that Lieutenant Simpson was then acting in obedience to the orders which he had received from Lieutenant-Colonel Newman, he, Captain Hallilay, having made use of the following expressions in answer to an observation of Lieutenant-Colonel Newman—" It is of no consequence, birds of a feather flock together."

Fourth Charge.—For disgraceful conduct, unbecoming the character of an officer and a gentleman, in making use of disrespectful language against the officers of the regiment, in front of the mess-room, on or about the 15th or 16th of May, 1808, by saying, ' that he would be damned if ever he was concerned with such a rascally set in his life,' meaning the officers of the said tenth regiment."

Fifth Charge.—" For quitting the parade on the morning of the 13th of June, 1808, without leave, and refusing to return, when ordered so to do by Major Short, the then Commanding Officer of the parade, and disgracefully sending a direct falsehood by the serjeant-major of the regiment, in desiring him to tell Major Short, that he, Captain Hallilay, was gone away, when in point of fact he was not."

Upon which charges the Court came to the following decision :—

The Court having well and maturely considered the evidence adduced in support of the charges against the prisoner, as well as the observations and statement made by him, by way of defence, is of opinion, that the prisoner, Captain Hallilay, is *not guilty* of the offence contained in the first charge ; but that he is *guilty* of having preferred charges against Lieutenant and

and Adjutant Spike, and Lieutenant and Acting Quarter-Master Simpson, to Lieutenant-Colonel Newman, the prosecutor, *unbecoming an Officer to prefer*, although the court feels itself bound to say, that it does not appear to it that the motives which induced the prisoner to prefer such charges, were *either malicious or vexatious*.

The court is of opinion that the prisoner is *guilty* of the second charge.

That he is *not guilty* of the first part of the third charge, but that he is *guilty* of having behaved with personal disrespect to Lieutenant-Colonel Newman, the prosecutor, his Commanding Officer, in having made use of improper expressions *before him*, although it does not appear to the court, that such expressions were intended by the prisoner to apply to him, Lieutenant-Colonel Newman.

The court is further of opinion, that the prisoner is *not guilty* of the fourth charge, and the court doth therefore acquit him thereof.

With respect to the fifth charge, it appears to the court, that the prisoner has already been severely punished, by having been put into, and kept in arrest, for the offence stated and alledged against him in that charge, and by having been severely reprimanded in orders, and afterwards released from arrest, and therefore the court considers that the charge ought not to have been preferred by Lieutenant-Colonel Newman, the prosecutor, against the prisoner, and it has therefore declined to proceed upon the investigation of it.

For the offences of which the court hath so found the prisoner to be guilty, it doth adjudge, that he, the prisoner, *shall be suspended from rank and pay for the space of three months.*

Having thus performed a very unpleasant part of its duty, with respect to the prisoner, the court considers itself compelled to turn its attention to the conduct of those officers of the second battalion of the 10th regiment, who composed the mess of that battalion at the time the sentence of the late court martial on the prisoner was officially communicated to him, and who refused to re-admit the prisoner as a member of their mess, after it had come to their knowledge that his Majesty had been graciously pleased to extend his forgiveness to the prisoner, and to reinstate him in his rank, as a Captain in the 10th regiment. The court has felt great concern at the inattention of those Officers to the merciful consideration, which his Majesty was pleased to shew towards the prisoner, not having been by any means satisfied with the reason which was attempted to be given for the resolution to which those Officers came ; for the court considers that it was the duty of those Officers, if they had any charges against the prisoner for ungentlemanlike conduct, whilst he was so under arrest and awaiting the publication of the sentence of the late court martial, to have submitted them to the Commanding Officer of the battalion, for the purpose of their being laid before the General Officer commanding the District, as soon as the offences, on which such charges could be founded, came to their knowledge.

The court is concerned to be obliged to notice the conduct of Lieutenant-Colonel Newman, the prosecutor, in having confirmed an improper

proper arrest of Lieutenants Spike and Simpson, and at the same time continued to associate with those Officers, and to permit them to dine at the mess whilst so under arrest; and also in having, on the present occasion, preferred the fifth charge against the prisoner, when he, Lieutenant-Colonel Newman, must have been conscious, that he had before punished the prisoner for the offence in such charge alledged against him, by a public censure and admonition inserted in the orders of the battalion.

His Majesty has been pleased to approve and confirm the finding and sentence of the court; but from various circumstances in the conduct of the prosecutor, Lieutenant-Colonel Newman, as they appear upon the proceedings, and as they have been noticed by the court, his Majesty has commanded, that it should be intimated to the Lieutenant-Colonel that he does not consider him a fit person to have the command of the second battalion of the 10th regiment, and that he will be immediately removed from it; and, as it appears upon the proceedings, and which has been fully noticed in the opinion of the court, that the Officers of the second battalion of the 10th regiment, who composed the mess of that battalion at the time the sentence of the court martial on Captain Hallilay was officially communicated to him, did not give that attention to the merciful consideration which his Majesty was graciously pleased to extend towards the prisoner, by reinstating him as a member of the mess, which, after such pardon from his Majesty, it was their duty to have done, and by their neglect of such duty they not only did not manifest a due sense of respect to-

wards his Majesty's clemency shewn to the prisoner, but they appeared to cherish, by such conduct, a disposition detrimental to the prisoner's professional reputation, and tending to subvert that harmony which it ought to have been their object to have preserved; his Majesty was therefore pleased to command, that it should be intimated to those Officers, that their promotion should for the present be suspended.

His Majesty has been further pleased to command, that it may be intimated to Captain Hallilay, that his having been twice tried by a general court martial, by the first of which he was sentenced to be cashiered, and by the second to be suspended from rank and pay for three months, his Majesty does not consider him a fit person to remain any longer in the 10th regiment, and that he will be immediately removed from it.

His Royal Highness the Commander in Chief is pleased to direct that the foregoing charges, together with the opinion and sentence of the court, and his Majesty's pleasure thereon, shall be read at the head of every regiment, and entered in the regimental orderly books.

By order of his Royal Highness the Commander in Chief.

(Signed) HARRY CALVERT, Adj. Gen. of the Forces.

Dated Horse-Guards, September 14, 1808.

THE PONEY AND MAIL COACH.

WE briefly noticed in our last Magazine, *page* 208, that on Saturday evening, August 27, a poney started from Hyde-Park corner,

ner, which was matched, for a bet of five hundred guineas, to start with the Exeter mail, and to be in Exeter first, with or without a rider. The man who led the poney was to be at liberty to take a fresh post-horse as often as he pleased.

We have now to state, that the poney won the wager, having arrived there quite fresh forty-five minutes before the mail The odds were all the way in its favour. He arrived at Salisbury at the same time as the mail-coach, and kept the lead from thence to Exeter.— From London to Exeter is about 174 miles ; so that from eight on Saturday evening until eleven on Sunday night, a duration of twenty-seven hours, it must have travelled, including the time of refreshment, at the constant rate of about six miles and a half an hour. Several sporting gentlemen, who went as far as Salisbury, where the coach and the poney were even, have been seriously touched ; they considered, that as the poney had to go the whole of the journey, and the mail coach would have relays of horses, he must be worn out before the others reached the journey's end. But they did not take into their calculation the fact of the ground from London to Salisbury being nearly all level, whilst the remainder of the road is such a continued hilly country, that a set of horses, with a weight to drag, must inevitably be circumstanced materially to their disadvantage, when opposed to another carrying only his own weight. Several thousands were depending on this singular exploit. The poney drank ale during its journey, as it is accustomed to do : it has also frequently drank a pint of port.

On the subject of bets of this description, the *York Herald* of the 17th instant has the following remark :—" We are glad to find, that the practice of exposing horses to the most barbarous trials of their strength, by wagers against time, is held in general detestation.— The last experiment upon the poney, which was engaged in a contest with the mail coach, seems to have particularly excited the censure of all persons who have expressed their sentiments on the subject."

ANOTHER SPORTING CAUSE,

TRIED AT THE YORK ASSIZES.

Beaumont v. Shaw.

MR. Topping, on behalf of the plaintiff, stated this to be an action under the game laws, to recover of the defendant several penalties of 5l. each, for using his dogs and gun in pursuit of game, not having a legal qualification.

The plaintiff, Richard Henry Beaumont, Esq. of Whitley Hall, in this county, is lord of the manor of South Crosland, in the West-Riding of this county, in which manor the defendant was seen sporting. The learned Counsel said, he should call a witness to prove the fact, which would entitle him to a verdict. He did not understand the defendant could make any defence, unless he meant to attempt to prove a qualification : if so, he should be obliged to trouble them again.

David Harrison was called ; he saw defendant on the 12th of October last, in the plaintiff's manor of South Crosland, in the parish of Almondbury ; he had three dogs in a field—the defendant was outside

side the fence; the dogs were spaniels or setting dogs; defendant was carrying a gun. Witness was upon the high road, which defendant crossed and went into the waste; he did not see him do any thing but hunt for game.

Being cross-examined by Mr. Serjeant Cockell, he said they were light-coloured setting-dogs, or spaniels, but could not identify what kind. He said he told Mr. Beaumont the defendant was endeavouring to shoot.

Mr. Serjeant Cockell rose on behalf of the defendant, and, addressing himself to the witness, said he was a meddling fellow, and was the sole cause of this trial.—The defendant is a qualified man, residing near Huddersfield, and through this meddling fellow was brought here, to his great inconvenience, to prove his qualification. He had no intention whatever to shoot on the plaintiff's land; he was going to the Moors, and his dogs strayed; he disliked the *manor* as well as the *manners* of the plaintiff. He trusted he should prove him properly qualified, which would put an end to this petty action.

Joshua Crosland proved a conveyance of the 28th of July, 1806, to the defendant, of an undivided moiety of a piece of ground at Wakefield, near the river Calder, and a building or warehouse, &c. there, in consideration of 1436l. which conveyance was executed on the day it is dated.

Two respectable witnesses were then examined, as to the annual value of the warehouse, who said they would willingly give 300l. a year for it; whilst three builders, on the part of the plaintiff, considered 150l. to be its full value.

Mr. Serjeant Cockell rose again, and commented on the evidence for the plaintiff, which, he said, was of the most trumpery kind. Here were three builders, men that valued according to brick and timber only; they just squared the timber, and saw what it was worth; none but merchants could value these warehouses. The money laid out by the defendant would have qualified him. His witnesses were acknowledged to be respectable; and he contended, *that what a thing will fetch is its value.*— What could be made of it? The defendant had a *bonâ fide* qualification above 100l. a year.

Mr. Topping, in reply, contended there was nothing which the witnesses had sworn could be pretended to be perjury. Nothing appeared against the plaintiff, Mr. Beaumont; he was owner of very large property, and wished to prevent trespassers coming upon his estates, insulting his tenants.— There was no doubt of the fact. It was equally true that a clear freehold estate of 100l. a year, or 150l. of leasehold for ninety-nine years, was a sufficient qualification.

Mr. Justice Chambre observed to the Jury, the fact of the defendant carrying a gun was made out; that of the setting-dogs not. With respect to the law, 100l. a year is a qualification. The builders merely valued the building itself, and calculated by a per centage. If, from all the evidence which had come before them, they were of opinion the value was above 100l. they would find for the defendant; if of less value, for the plaintiff— one penalty.

The Jury returned a verdict for the defendant.

FEAST

FEAST OF WIT.

A Certain Baronet, celebrated for his breed of pigs, rising once in the House of Commons to re-probate the coalition between Lord North and Mr. Fox, expressed his astonishment, that two men, who had for so many years been in the habit of opposing and reviling each other, should have the confidence to appear in that house as friends—" but such friends, so very dear are they to each other," added he, pointing to a stick which Lord North held in his hand, " that his Lordship will not walk without a stick with a *Fox's head* carved on it."—On this Lord North instantly rose,—" I am sorry, very sorry," said he, " to find, that the worthy Baronet, who has just sat down, should have spent his life, and employed his *great* talents, in the study of a subject which it seems he does not yet understand—that he should have passed so many years in the *education of pigs*, and yet should not know a *fox's* head from a *hog's*." His Lordship then hand-ed round his cane, on which a pig's head was carved, and the Senate was convulsed with laughter.

Dr. Robertson having observed, that Johnson's jokes were the re-bukes of the righteous, which are like excellent oil—" O!" exclaim-ed Burke, who was present, " *Oil of Vitriol!*"

A *languishing Widow*, in the last stage of the *tender passion*, has engaged a residence in the vicinity of *Si-on!*

At the grand entertainment given to the Spanish Deputies, it was observed, that the Citizens bore a strong resemblance to *Parson Supple*, in " Tom Jones ;" for they were remarkably *taciturn* du-ring dinner, though *their mouths were never shut* the whole time !

Lloyd, the poet, was, like other poets, subject to occasional fami-liarities from the *shoulder-tapping* fraternity. On being introduced into his apartment in a spunging-house, he enquired, with affected simplicity, what the huge bars at the window were intended for ? " Why to keep you in, to be sure," replied Cerberus. " Strange ! (re-joined the poet) that you should take such pains to keep me *in*, who could never keep myself *out.*"

Mr. Curran, the Irish Master of the Rolls, was in company with an Honourable Baronet, in the course of a late Session, who distinguished himself, upon one or two occasions, by speeches, whose excellence was not in proportion to their *length*. It was observed, that continued speaking made the voice husky and the mouth parched. " That may be," observed the Baronet ; " but for my part, I have spoken three hours together without getting at all thirsty." " But are you quite sure, Sir Thomas," demanded the wit, " that you did not get *dry* ?"

An old Jack Tar, just returned from sea, met his old messmate, *Bet Blowsy* ; he was so overjoyed, that he determined to commit ma-
O o   trimony ;

trimony; but at the altar the Parson demurred, as there was not cash enough between them to pay the fees; on which Jack, thrusting a few shillings into the sleeve of his cassock, exclaimed, "Damn it, brother, never mind! marry us *as far as it will go!*"

KEMBLE was once playing Hamlet; a countryman, a novice, who acted Guildenstern, but who was a tolerable musician, on being repeatedly beseeched by Hamlet to "play upon the pipe," at length said, "*Well, if your Lordship insists on it, I shall do as well as I can;*" and, to the great confusion of Kemble, and the no small amusement of the audience, he played *God save the King.*

A CAUSE was lately tried at the Cornwall Assizes, respecting some leather *small-clothes*, which induced one of the Judges to say, that it was the first time he had heard of *cutting a suit* from a *pair of breeches!*

A COMICAL IDEA. — Amongst other complaints against Sir Henry Mildmay, for cutting down an avenue of trees on his estate by the road side, at Hartley-row, one is, that if a cottager wishes to correct a termagant wife, he is obliged to trudge at least three miles before he can *find a stick!*

THE Duke of Clarence, being one of the Stewards at the late Egham Races, reproached a constable for not keeping the course clear opposite the Judges' Stand; the fellow (whether he knew the Duke or not) answered with as much spirit as he had been assailed, and said, he had done his duty. "You have not," said the Duke. "I have," said the man. "Well," said the Duke, "they lie pretty well in Middlesex, but by G— you beat them hollow in Surrey!"

ABOUT the time when Murphy so successfully attacked the *stage-struck heroes*, in the pleasant farce of "*The Apprentice*," an eminent poulterer went to a spouting club in search of his servant, who, he understood, was that evening to make his *debût* in *Lear*, and entered the room at the moment Dick was exclaiming, "I am the King —you cannot touch me for coming!" "No, you dog!" cried the enraged master, catching the mad monarch by the collar, "but I can for *not picking the ducks!*"

A COUNTRYMAN, after attending a debate in Parliament, being asked his opinion respecting the *orators*, replied — "Why, they talked a great deal about *eyes* and *nose*, but had'nt any thing to do with the *head!*"

SPANISH GRANDEES.—A Knight of Spain, as high in birth as a King, as catholic as the Pope, and equal to Job in poverty, arriving one night at an inn in France, knocked a long time at the gate, till he had alarmed the landlord.— "Who is there?" said the host, looking out of the window.—The Spaniard replied, "*Don Juan Pedro Hernandes Rodriquez de Villa Nova, Count of Malafra, Knight of Santiago and Alcantara.*"— "I am very sorry," replied the landlord, shutting the window, "but I have not room enough in my house for all those gentlemen you have mentioned."

SPORTING INTELLIGENCE.

LORD Monson refused 2500gs. for Stud, by Beningbrough, out of Eliza, by Highflyer, before he won the Produce Stakes of 1300gs. in the York August Meeting.

MR. F. Buckle purchased for H. Howorth, Esq. Lord Strathmore's Cassio, by Sir Peter Teazle, out of Queen Mab, by Eclipse, for 600gs. after being beat by Rosette and Julius Cæsar, in the York August Meeting.

MR. Cave Browne purchased Mr. Garforth's Hylas, by Beningbrough, out of Caroline, by Phenomenon, in the York August Meeting.

LORD Monson lately purchased the Duke of Hamilton's Easy, by Hambletonian, out of Bay Javelin, for 1000gs.

THE following singular circumstance took place at Knutsford Races, in 1786, 1787, and 1788: the Sweepstakes of 10gs. each. and the 60l. Plate in each year, were won by Mr. Clifton's Josephina, by Sir Peter Teazle, out of Fanny, by Diomed.—She is own sister to Sir Oliver, Fyldener, Poulton, Fadladinida, &c.

IN 1793, Mr. Goodricke's Drowsy ran four two-mile heats against Mr. Clifton's Chariot, &c, for a 50l. Plate, at Preston:—She won the first heat, and was three times second.—And at Boroughbridge, she won 50l. at five twomile heats, beating Mr. Donner's Meanwell, and five others.—At Preston, in 1794, she won 50l. at five four-mile heats, beating Telescope, Citizen, Mulespinner, and Young Traveller:—The first heat was deemed a dead one between Drowsy and Mulespinner; and she won the fourth and fifth heats from Telescope and Citizen.—And at Boroughbridge, she won 50l. at five three-mile heats, beating Chariot, Heiress, and Treecreeper. Drowsy was got by Drone, out of Mr. Goodricke's Old England Mare.—She is a brood mare in Lord F. G. Osborne's Stud, and is the dam of Dotterel, Susan, &c.

AT Stockton, September 12, 1793, Mr. Donner's Meanwell ran four two-mile heats, against Colonel Radcliffe's Villager, beating eight others.—At Boroughbridge, October 3, he ran five two-mile heats against Drowsy, beating Byrom, Young Posthumous, and three others:—The third heat was a dead one between Meanwell and Byrom.—And at Malton, October 16, he ran five two-mile heats, beating Young Posthumous, Brother to Swordsman, &c.—The fourth heat was a dead one between Meanwell and Young Posthumous.

LORD Egremont's horse Scorpion is matched against Mr. Shakespear's Mungo, at the Second October Newmarket Meeting, for 200gs.

At the Houghton Meeting, Sir C. Turner's Mister Gundy is matched against Mr. Howorth's Cassio, for 200gs. h. ft. as is General Grosvenor's Rifleman against Sir C. Turner's Cousin Abraham, for 150gs.

THE Scottish moors, especially those of the Duke of Gordon, have been been very plentifully supplied with game—as being removed from all quick conveyance of it. Those of Northumberland have afforded but very indifferent sport to their visitors; the game being scarce, leave to shoot there was very liberal. The moor-fowl, on the English moors, have been in abundance on the preserved parts, and the broods, in general, very great.

ON the 26th ult. William Jamieson, in Craghead, of Auchinleck, in his eighty-sixth year, went to the head of Aird's Moss, Scotland, to take a day's sport at the pouting; and, although the day was unfavourable, and the game shy, he returned, in high spirits, with two brace and half of birds.

JOHN Lacy, Esq. of Wimborne Minster, shot over the Manor of Verwood, in the county of Dorset, on the third day's shooting, this season, thirty brace of partridges, ten brace of hares, and twelve couple of rabbits; he commenced his day's sport with the rising sun, and closed it at four o'clock. Six servants, with four brace of pointers, attended him.—What makes this day's sport the more extraordinary is, that the whole manor is not more than 2,500 acres.

MR. Adam French, wine-merchant, Leith, being shooting upon the lands of Colonel Colbrooke, in the parish of Crawfordjohn, and county of Lanark, his pointer dog having stopped short, and making a remarkable noise, attracted his attention, and going up to the spot, he was astonished to see a lage ad-

der in the act of swallowing a lark; being half erected in the air, he fired at it, and, after blowing its head entirely off, it measured no less than thirty-five inches in length.

A CONSIDERABLE wager was decided on Laucresse Common, Guernsey, on the 5th instant, where the 2d battalion of the 24th infantry were then encamped :— Captain Andrews's bay blood galloway, 24th infantry, carrying ten stone, and rode by an officer, running twice round a course, a distance of two miles, while Surgeon Wylde ran one mile, and once round the course. Great odds in favour of the horse before starting, but he was beat easily.

GAME LAWS.—Hints to Sportsmen.—By the 22d and 23d of Charles II. chap. 25, sec. 2, All Lords of Manors or other Royalties, *not under the degree of an Esquire,* may authorise one or more gamekeeper or gamekeepers, within their respective manors or royalties. Upon this statute, it has been held, that the Lord of a Manor is *not an Esquire by virtue of his manor or royalty,* and that no Lord of a Manor *under that rank,* can appoint a gamekeeper, *whatever his estate may be.* All unqualified persons acting as gamekeepers under deputations from persons, *under the rank and degree of an Esquire,* are subject and liable to all the penalties of the game laws, to which any person is subject, who is not qualified to kill game, notwithstanding such deputations. By a subsequent statute, no Lord or Lady of a Manor, can appoint more than one gamekeeper *for any one manor,* consequently, where two gamekeepers kill game, *in one and the same manor,* the act

...of one is illegal, and he is liable to the same penalties as any other unqualified person. These hints are given, that qualified sportsmen may know how to chastise game-keepers, acting contrary to the above statutes, who are guilty of any impertinence, or assume any unlawful authority.

DURING this month, a poney, twelve hands high, started from the Plough, Cheltenham, to carry a gentleman, weighing thirteen stone, to the Bell, Gloucester, nine miles and a half, in thirty minutes, for 100gs. and notwithstanding the badness of the road, performed it in forty seconds within the time.

AMONG the *whimsicalities* at Leicester Races, was that of a gentleman's carriage in the *trim of the mail*. *Jehu* sported the *blue rag*, appeared an excellent *crack*, and *pulled up in style*: a one-horned Buck, habited in his Majesty's livery, personated *the guard*, and lost nothing of the *manners* of the original.—The *coup d'œil* of the whole was ludicrous enough, and had all the effect intended—it " *astonished the natives !*"

THE following unfortunate and shocking accident, in the vicinity of Bishop's Lydeard, Somerset, happened in the course of the present month, to George Knight, game-keeper to John Winter, Esq. As Knight was attending his master in the diversion of partridge-shooting, a covey of birds being sprung, and marked in an adjoining field, Knight went with his pointer, and found them, and on shooting at one of the birds, his gun burst, whereby his left hand, fingers, and thumb, were literally blown to atoms. His mas-

ter being at some distance, came up, and conducted him to an adjoining farm-house, and with laudable zeal, the farmer conveyed him home. An eminent surgeon being immediately called to his assistance, pronounced the wound dangerous, and very much lascerated, inasmuch that he was under the unavoidable necessity of amputating the limb a few inches above the hand-wrist. He bore the operation with manly fortitude, and hopes are entertained of his recovery.

DURING the present month, a running match took place between twelve gentlemen of Feversham, and the like number from Canterbury, on the Barham Course. It was won by the latter, seven to one.

A RESPECTABLE farmer, on the banks of the Eden, in Cumberland, has, we hear, challenged any father and son in that county, or in the whole kingdom, to try their pedestrian powers with him and his son, under like circumstances. The wager is to be at the pleasure of the opponent. The father is forty years of age, the son only eleven months ! and they together weigh near $2\frac{1}{2}$ cwt.

A MAN who sells fish about Chelsea and Fulham lately undertook, for a wager of five guineas, to run from Hyde-park Corner, to the seven-mile stone at Brentford, in one hour, with 54lbs. weight on his head, which he performed in 45 minutes, with ease.

ON Monday the 5th instant, a young man, named Blewet, from Crewkerne, Somersetshire, for a wager of ten guineas, undertook to

go

go on foot from Shoreditch Church to Theobalds, in Hertfordshire, and back again, within three hours, the distance being twenty-four miles. He started at five o'clock, stopped at Edmonton to rest four or five minutes, set off running a regular pace till he arrived at Theobalds, which was at twenty minutes past six, where he drank a tumbler of brandy and water, and ate a biscuit; after stopping ten minutes, he started afresh on his return, stopped again at Edmonton, and arrived at the starting-post at fifty-two minutes after seven, so that he won the wager by eight minutes, with seeming ease.

One of the best foot-races ever known, took place on Monday, the 19th instant, between a gentleman of the name of Williams, and Cooke, the soldier, for fifty guineas a side. Lord's Cricket Ground was the scene of action. At three o'clock, there was a numerous assemblage of amateurs upon the ground. Bets were at that time 6 to 4 in favour of Cooke. At half past three the judges appeared: the ground was measured, 200 yards, and inclosed on each side with a rope line. At four o'clock, the two swift-footed heroes came, dressed only in white pantaloons, and without shoes. The line on each side was two deep; bets now became even. The signal for starting was given by the firing of a pistol. It took place at a quarter past four. They both started at the same instant, and kept elbow to elbow for the first hundred yards, when Cooke took the lead until the first 150 yards. Mr. Williams then came up with him, and got again elbow to elbow, until the 190 yards, when Cooke again took the lead, and kept it to the winning post.—

Mr. Williams appeared much tired, but shewed blood. Cooke was quite fresh, and won by a yard and a half. Mr. Williams appeared so eager, that at the last five yards he stumbled, and nearly fainted away within the last yard and a half.— The race was run in twenty seconds and a half.—Mr. Williams has challenged to run Cooke again, 150 yards for 100 guineas. The challenge has been accepted.

Ormskirk, Sept. 17.— On Sunday evening last arrived in this town a host of *knowing-ones,* bringing with them two persons, for the avowed purpose of running a race on Aughton Common, on the following day. Enquiry was eagerly made by numbers after the names, &c. of the pedestrians. It was soon learnt, that one was Unsworth, the celebrated ball-shooter, but the name of the other could not be ascertained. The distance was seven score yards; the prize, according to some accounts, 100, but, according to others, 200 guineas.— Expectation was on tiptoe all the morning of Monday, and an hour prior to the starting, the roads leading to the race-course were crowded with people. At two o'clock the competitors arrived on the ground; and after the distance was measured, and other matters adjusted, they stripped for the sport. At twenty minutes past two o'clock they started—the distance was run in fourteen seconds and a half. Unsworth was beaten, apparently with ease. The hitherto unknown now proved to be no other than Curly, the Brighton shepherd! The *black-legs* were anxious to bet, and much money, no doubt, was won by them. It seems Unsworth, who resides at Ashton, in this county, fancied himself the swiftest foot-

man

man in England, and had been fre-quently heard to express a wish for an opportunity to display his ability as a racer. Curly happening to be at Manchester, and hearing of this circumstance, a match was quickly made, and decided, as above related. Curly, a few hours afterwards, was matched with a poney to run the same distance as before, for the trifling sum of five guineas. The poney passed Curly at about half the way, and consequently beat him with ease.

An obstinate pugilistic contest for a purse of twenty guineas, took place on Saturday, the 27th ult. at Hillesdon, in Bucks, between a carpenter of the name of Joseph, and George Groves, a sawyer. The combatants were both professors from Somersetshire, and had each won several battles. The carpenter was the favourite; but after fighting in earnest fifty minutes, he received a cross buttock, which so disabled him, that Groves won the purse without further trouble.

Friday, September 9, a pugilistic contest ensued between two hackney coachmen in Parliament-street, which afforded much amusement to many spectators. One of the champions, named Bob Sutton, had driven the pole of his coach into the pannel of his antagonist's coach, and, after a few compliments had passed, they agreed to decide who was the best man. A ring was formed close to the statue of King Charles, and they set to in regular style. During seven hard rounds, Bob Sutton had the worst of it, and at the ninth round he resigned the contest. The parties then shook hands, and finally drowned all animosity at the Ship public house.

On the morning of the 16th in-stant, a pitched battle was fought in a field near Bayswater, for ten guineas, between a soldier in the Guards, named Richardson, and one Gerrard, a coal-heaver. At the commencement, odds were greatly in favour of the latter, owing to his known scientific skill as a pugilist, and the inferior strength of his antagonist. During this contest, the battle was desperate on both sides, and after an obstinate resistance of nearly forty minutes, Gerrard became so extremely weak, that he was not able to face his opponent, and in consequence thereof was, with seeming reluctance to many of his fraternity, obliged to give it up, on which the soldier was then carried off the ground by his comrades, in triumph, to a public house nearly adjoining.

On Saturday, the 17th, a battle was fought in the Long Fields, near the New Road, between a bricklayer and a carpenter, for one guinea, which lasted thirty-five minutes. The contest was severe, and the victory for some time appeared doubtful, but in the 18th round, the latter received a violent blow on the stomach, which put an end to the conflict.

A very severe battle was fought during the present month, between two countrymen, in the parish of Clayton, Sussex, the one named Buff, a sawyer, and the other Smoker, a carter, which, after a stubborn contest of nearly two hours, was won by the former.

Besides the grand match which will take place on the 10th of October, between Gregson and Crib, the following have also been made: Jem Belcher is matched against Elias Sprey, the coppersmith, who fought the Chicken, and Richman the

the black is about to contend with a Kentish man.

The Duchess of York is particularly fond of dogs, and keeps a great number at Oatlands; sometimes her Royal Highness has had near one hundred and fifty. Her favourite breeds are pugs, spaniels, and terriers: among them are several very large ones. If she is not fond of any of them, and they follow her about, she gives them away. Her Royal Highness makes presents of her favourite breeds of pug and spaniels to her female friends. An establishment is kept up for them, and a fixed place and hours for them to be fed, when her Royal Highness frequently goes among them. There are stated hours for them to be put to bed. When any of them are ill, Dr. Blaine attends them. A piece of land is set out for their burial place, and tomb-stones are placed over them, with their names, and time when they died, &c. inscribed upon them.

The following account, however improbable it may appear, we are assured is a fact:—In the afternoon of the 21st inst. as one of the late Duke of Bridgewater's boatmen was amusing himself by fishing in the canal, near Stockton-quay, he saw a hawk flying over his head, and instantly drawing his line out of the water, and throwing it upwards, caught the bird by the wing, and now keeps him as a living proof of his dexterity.—*Chester Chron.*

At Bedford Races, on the Thursday, the company were surprised by the appearance of a hare, which crossed the course. Immediately the gentlemen on horseback, as well as those on foot, pursued poor puss, who took refuge in a bush, which was soon surrounded; she made an attempt to bolt out, but finding herself blocked up on all sides, she was unable to clear the ring, and in her leap was caught by a gentleman in his arms.

A few days since died, at Hothfield, aged 94, Mr. Thomas West, sen. paper-maker; well known on the turf, he being one of the oldest, (perhaps the oldest) jockey in the kingdom.

During the present month, as some gentlemen, near Ivy Bridge, Devon, were coursing a hare with a brace of greyhounds, after a long chase it was killed; and, as they were carrying her home, a palpitation was observed in the stomach. Curiosity led them to paunch her, and they took out of her paunch three hares, one dead and two alive. The two latter were brought home to Mr. Williams's, at Ivy Bridge, where a cat, which had been just deprived of her kittens, suckled them very readily, and they are now alive, and likely to do well.

The second grand cricket-match between T. Wybergh, H. Plumer, and T. Lawson, Esqrs. with nine of the Wetherby Club, against R. Yorke, T. Duncombe, and W. Fox, Esqrs. with nine from Harewood, was decided on Monday the 19th instant, at Clifford Moor, in favour of Wetherby, by 31 runs. The first match, between the same parties, played in Lord Harewood's Park, was decided by 24 runs, in favour of Harewood. Lord Harewood, Mr. Lascelles, and a numerous assemblage of ladies and gentlemen, were present on both occasions.

POETRY.

POETRY.

THE HIGH COURT OF DIANA.

HUNTING SONG.

A Southerly wind and a cloudy sky
Proclaim a hunting morning ;
Before the sun rises we nimbly fly,
Dull sleep on a down-bed scorning.
To horse, to horse, my boys away,
The chase admits of no delay ;
  On horseback we're got,
  Together we'll trot :
Leave off your chat, see the cover appear,
The hound that strikes first, cheer him
    without fear.
Drag on him, yoicks ! wind him !
Drag on him, yoicks ! wind him !
    The cover resounds.

How complete the cover and furze they
    draw !
Ne'er talk of *Barry* or *Meinell* ;
Young Lasher, he flashes now thro' the
    shaw,
And Saucebox, rous'd out of his kennel.
Away we fly as quick as thought,
The new-sown ground soon makes them
    fault.
  Cast round the sheep's train,
  Cast round, cast round ;
  Try back the deep lane,
  Try back—try back.
Hark ! I hear some hounds challenge, in
    yonder spring sedge,
Comfort bitch hits him off in that old
    thickset hedge ;
  Hark forward—Hark forward—
  Zounds ! don't make a noise.

A stormy sky, o'er charg'd with rain,
Both hound and huntsman opposes,
In vain on your metal, you try boys in
    vain,
But down you must with your noses ;
Each moment now the sky grows worse,
Enough to make a parson curse.
  Pick thro' the plough'd ground,
  Pick thro', pick thro',
  Well hunted, good hounds,
  Well hunted, well hunted.

If we can but get on we'll soon make
    them quake ;
Hark ! I hear some hounds challenge in
    midst of yon brake.
  Tally-ho ! Tally-ho !
  Then across the green plain,
  Tally-ho ! Tally-ho !
  There have at him again.

Thus we ride, whip, and spur, for a three-
    hours chase,
Our horses go panting and foaming,
Young Madcap and Riot begin now to
    race—
Ride on, Sir, and give them some mob-
    bing ;
But hold, alas ! you'll spoil all sport,
For thro' the hounds, you'll head him
    short.
  Clap round him, dear Jack,
  Clap round, clap round,
  Hark, Drummer, hark back,
  Hark back, hark back.
He's jumping and dodging at every bush,
Little Riot has fasten'd her teeth in his
    brush.
  Who-whoop !—Who-whoop !
  He's fairly run down,
  Who-whoop !—Who-whoop !
  Give Jack half-a-crown.

THE COCKNEY's ADIEU TO BRIGHTON.

  " *Farewell, a long farewell to all my
    greatness.*"

ADIEU, adieu to Brighton races !
  Adieu to all the pretty faces !
Adieu to every lady's graces !
  So late in beauty seen ;
Adieu to all the rides and walks,
To all the promenades and talks ;—
My landlord shews a list of chalks,
  And I must quit *the Steyne.*

     P p   Adieu

Adieu to all the lovely lasses,
With whom the time so gaily passes;
Adieu as well to all their asses
  Which bore them safe along ;
And I besides must bid adieu
To all the sweets of one-card loo,
If Pam on ev'ry night I drew :—
  How sorrowful my song !

No more !—I cannot bear the theme,
It wakes my mind to mis'ry's dream;
I cannot find hopes golden gleam,
  Nor yet a golden guinea !
I have a one-pound note, 'tis true,
And that must pay my landlord's due :
To Brighton then a long adieu!
  I feel myself a ninny!!!

                   J. M. L.

Brighton, August 6, 1808.

INSCRIPTION ON THE TOMB OF MRS. ROBINSON.

A Correspondent has favoured us with the following lines, which are inscribed on the tomb of the celebrated Mrs. Robinson, in the church-yard of Old Windsor, in which parish her residence on Englefield Green was situated. —Our Correspondent says they have never before appeared in print, that he has been able to learn.

MRS. MARY ROBINSON,

Author of Poems and other literary Works,
Died on the 26th December, 1800, at Englefield Cottage, Surry.

On one side of the Tomb.

OF Beauty's Isle, her daughters must
  declare,
She who sleeps here was fairest of the
  fair ;
But ah ! while Nature on her favourite
  smil'd,
And Genius claim'd his share in beauty's
  child,
Ev'n as they wove a garland for her
  brow,
Sorrow prepar'd a willowy wreath of
  woe ;
Mix'd lurid night-shade with the buds
  of May,
And twin'd her darkest cypress with the
  bay ;

In mildew tears steep'd every opening
  flower,
Prey'd on the sweets, and gave the canker
  power.
Yet, Oh! may pity's angel, from the
  grave,
The early victim of misfortune save ;
And as she springs to everlasting morn,
May glory's fadeless crown her brow
  adorn.

               J. J. PRATT.

On the Flat Stone on the Top.

OH! thou, whose cold and senseless
  heart
Ne'er knew affection's struggling sigh,
Pass on ! nor vaunt the Stoic's art,
Nor mock this grave with tearless eye.

For oft when evening's purple glow
Shall slowly fade from yonder steep,
Fast o'er the sod the tear shall flow,
From eyes that only wake to weep.

No wealth had she, nor power to sway,
Yet rich in genius' proudest ore,
She wept her summer hours away ;
She hears the winter storm no more.

Yet o'er this low and silent spot,
Full many a bud of spring shall wave,
While she by all, save one forgot,
Shall snatch a wreath beyond the grave.

WOODCOCK SHOOTING.

(From " Fowling," a Poem.)

WHEN first he comes
From his long journey o'er th' unfriendly
  main,
With weary wing the woodcock throws
  him down,
Impatient for repose, on the bare cliffs ;
Thence with short flight the nearest co-
  ver seeks,
Low copse or straggling furze; till the
  deep woods
Invite him to take up his fixt abode.
Oft on the shelter'd side of some high
  hill,
If cruel frost bind not th' ungrateful soil,
Content he wanders, or beneath the
  shade
Of scatter'd hollies, turns with curious
  bill

The fallen leaves, to find his hidden food.
When the thick shelter of the spreading
    woods
His wand'ring eye with friendly aspect
    tempts,
At morn and eve he seeks the limpid
    streams,
And springing thence, his stated flight
    he takes
By the dim light, through op'ning glades :
    there oft
The treach'rous net his rapid course cuts
    short,
And his fast flutt'ring pinions beat in
    vain.
But if with steep ascent he top the snare,
Or side-long 'scape it, through the wi-
    ther'd ferns
He picks his silent way, or dozing lies
In the o'er-shadowing bush, till with
    keen nose
The ranging spaniel winds his close re-
    treat,
And drives him forth to meet the fowler's
    aim.
    Where breaking into clumps, the scat-
      ter'd wood
First opens to the sun, and winding
    down
Between opposing hills, receives a stream
Whose bubbling .fountain yields not to
    the force
Of keen invading frost, let us commence
Our earnest sport. Though silently we
    beat
At other seasons, let our joyful cheers,
In concert with the op'ning dogs, resound
" Hie in."—At that glad word away they
    dart,
And winding various ways, with careful
    speed
Explore the cover. Hark that quest
    proclaims
The woodcock's haunt. Again! now
    joining all,
They shake the echoing wood with tune-
    ful notes.
I heard the sounding wing—but down
    the wood
He took his flight. I meet him there
    anon.
As fast I press to gain the wish'd-for
    spot,
On either side my busy spaniels try,
At once they wheel—at once they open
    loud,
And the next instant, flush th' expected
    bird.
Right up he darts amongst the mingling
    boughs ;

But bare of leaves, they hide not from
    my view
His fated form, and ere he can attain
Th' attempted height, with rapid flight
    to cleave
The yielding air, arrested by the shot,
With shatter'd wing revers'd and plumage
    fair
Wide scatt'ring in the wind, headlong he
    falls.
The pliant branches to his weight give
    way,
And the hard frozen ground his fall re-
    turns.
See how the joyful dogs exulting, press
Around the prostrate victim, nor pre-
    sume
With lawless mouths to tear his tender
    skin.
Obedient to my voice, one lightly brings
The lifeless bird, and lays it at my feet.
Thus oft, when skimming o'er some
    thorny brake,
Struck by the shot, the wounded bird has
    dropt
Full in its centre, through the tangl'd
    briars .
The trusty dog his painful passage works,
Nor leaves, till from the dark abyss he
    drags
The flutt'ring prey, and yields it to my
    hand.
" Forward again." Long is our beat to-
    day,
And unremitting. Merrily we trace
The winding vales, and through the fo-
    rest brush ;
Upon the bord'ring plain emerging oft,
We swiftly glide along, then plunge
    again
Into the woody labyrinth profound ;
Whilst Echo, starting from her hollow
    seat,
With babbling voice reverberates our
    course.
Sport o'er our jovial toils presides, and
    fans
The ardent flame that in our bosom
    glows.
Now granting, now denying to our
    hope
The threaten'd bird, enhancing thus the
    prize,
Till with increas'd delight the feather'd
    spoil
Fills high our breast; and rocks, and
    woods and streams,
Steep hill, or precipice abrupt, appear
As smooth and easy as the new-mown
    mead.

AN ANCIENT HUNTING SONG.

From " Queen Hoo Hall."

WAKEN Lords and Ladies gay,
  On the mountain dawns the day ;
All the jolly chase is here.
With hawk, and horse, and hunting
    spear,
Hounds are in their couples yelling,
Hawks are whistling, horns are knelling ;
Merrily, merrily, mingle they,
" Waken Lords and Ladies gay."

Waken Lords and Ladies gay,
The mist has left the mountain grey ;
Springlets in the dawn are streaming,
Diamonds in the brake are gleaming,
And foresters have busy been,
To trace the buck in thicket green ;
Now we come to chaunt our lay,
" Waken Lords and Ladies gay."

Waken Lords and Ladies gay,
To the green-wood haste away ;
We can shew you where he lies,
Fleet of foot, and tall of size.
We can shew the marks he made
When 'gainst the oak his antlers fray'd ;
You shall see him brought to bay,
" Waken Lords and Ladies gay."

Louder, louder chaunt the lay,
Waken Lords and Ladies gay!
Tell them youth, with mirth and glee,
Run a course as well as we ;
Time, stern huntsman ! who can baulk,
Staunch as hound, and fleet as hawk ?
Think of this, and rise with day,
" Gentle Lords and Ladies gay."

A DRINKING SONG.

BY W. R. SPENCE, ESQ.

IF the stock of our bliss is in stranger
    hands vested,
The fund, ill-secur'd, oft in bankruptcy
    ends,
But the heart issues bills which are never
    protested,
When drawn on the firm of Wife, Chil-
    dren, and friends.

Though valour still grows in his life's
    waning embers,
The death-wounded tar who his colours
    defends,

Drops a tear of regret, as he dying re-
    members
How blest was his home with Wife,
    Children, and Friends.

The soldier, whose deeds live immortal
    in story,
Whom duty to far distant latitudes sends,
With transport would barter whole ages
    of glory,
For one happy hour with Wife, Children,
    and friends.

Though spice-breathing gales o'er his ca-
    ravan hover,
And round him Arabia's whole fragrance
    descends,
The merchant still thinks on the wood-
    bines that cover
The bow'r where he sat with Wife, Chil-
    dren, and Friends.

The day-spring of youth, if unclouded
    by sorrow,
Alone on itself for enjoyment depends ;
But drear is the twilight of age, if it
    borrow
No charms from the smile of Wife, Chil-
    dren, and Friends.

Let the breath of the muse ever freshen
    and nourish
The laurel which o'er her dead favourite
    bends ;
O'er me wave the willow, which only
    can flourish,
When dew'd with the tears of Wife,
    Children, and Friends.

THE WHIST TABLE.

AT a table in Margate was plac'd Mis-
    tress Grist,
  Her partner a butcher by trade ;
She brandish'd the cards in her brawny
    red fist ;
She enforc'd with her voice all the man-
    dates of whist,
  Tho' she scarce knew a club from a
    spade.

The corpulent lady, when nine was the
    score,
  Won the trick by a fortunate trump ;
" What are *Stakes?*" she exclaim'd, with
    a masculine roar—
The sly *butcher* replied, as he view'd her
    all o'er,
  " Nice and fat, Ma'am, *if cut from
    the rump !"*

INDEX.

A.

ADVERTISEMENT, a singular, 91.

Adoption, incongruous, 212.

Africans, or, War, Love, and Duty, a new Drama, 227.

Amusements of Paris described, 29, 61, 109.

Ascot-Heath, Newton, and Newcastle Races, summary of the sport at, 105.

Attorney, the Qui-tam, 8.

Apology Extraordinary, 181.

Anecdotes of the late Col. J. Mordaunt, 13, 67.

Anecdote of Lord Shaftesbury, 181.

Anglers, the, a Song, 199.

Ass, the, his qualities and perfections, 110.

American Duelling, 264.

———— Cockfighting, 266.

Aviary, a Parisian, described, 62.

B.

Bashful man, metamorphose of a, 140.

Bet, a cruel, 208.

Bettings, for the Derby and Oaks' Stakes, 4.

———— at Tattersall's, for the St. Leger Stakes, 144.

Barley-corn, an old ballad, 151.

Blindness in a mare, successful treatment of, 24.

Beasts of Burden, humanity encouraged to, 212.

Bride, the Mysterious, a new play, 121.

Brutes, attachment in, 141,

Bonifacio and Bridgetina, a Melodramatic Satire, 10.

Boxing, between Dockarty and Peatikin, 137.

Boxing, between Dutch Sam and William Cropley, Tom Belcher and Dogherty, 33, 45, 72.

———— Gregson and Gulley, 75.

———— Dutch Sam and Cropley, 78.

———— Crib and Horton, ibid. 96.

———— On Willsden Green, 89, 97, 144, 145, 193, 194, 248.

Bull-baiting, 52.

Bully, John, Epitaph on, 21.

C.

Campbell, Major, trial of, 206, 268, 270.

Campanology, 222.

Caractacus, a new Melo-drame, 43.

Caricatures, Parisian, 110.

Canine Madness, method of discovering, 50.

Canine Sagacity, 50, 189, 262.

Cats, Wild, caution to farmers, 82.

Change-ringing, Harmonious, 176.

Chastity, Royal, 181.

Character, Eccentric, 188.

Content, stanzas on, 152.

Coursing, northern, 6.

Court-Martial, on Richard Corrall, Esq. 79.

— On Assistant-Surgeon Thomas Talbot, 92.

— At Portsmouth, 105, 108.

— Upon Captain Hallilay, 276.

Courage, remarkable instance of, 240.

Cock, account of a singular game, 211.

Cocking, at the Royal Cockpit, Manchester, and Newton, 143.

— At Nantwich, Preston, Newcastle, and Stamford, 159.

— At Oxford, 252.

Cream-coloured Charger, 256.

Cricket

Cricket Matches, 141.
Criminals, Satiric Hints to, 262.

D.

Dash, my Spaniel, lines to the memory of, 99.
Dancing Women of Mysore, 231.
Delpini, death of, 237.
Derby, Earl of, his Stud, 118.
Derby and Oaks' Stakes, winners of, 27, 60.
Delpini, account of, 237.
Disputes between Gentlemen, on Points of Honour, 7. The King v. Watson, 57. Thoughts on, 107. Sir Arthur Paget and Lady Boringdon, 203. Lord Sackville and Mrs. Poulett—Hodge and Mrs. Guard, 157, 205, 206.
Ditto, pedigree and performances of, 37.
Duel, between the Barons Duben and Wrede, 21.
— Between two Fleas, 30.
— Upon Epping Forest, 108.
— Extraordinary, 180.
Diversions, kingly, 213.
Divertissement, grand, and Spectacle, at Lisle, 164.
Driving Club, their cavalcade, 147.
Driving, Rage for, 191.
Dogs, Newfoundland, sagacity of, 189.
Dog, Instinct of, 230.
— Dialogue on a, between a Lady and a Lawyer, 178.

E.

Egham Races, sport at, 207.
Eleanor, some account of this celebrated mare, 43. Pedigree and performances of, 71.
Elephant drawn by a Flea, 30.
Eagle's Nest, singular account of, 214.

F.

Faden, the King versus, 7.

Feathered Race, friendship in the, 123.
Foxes, German method of catching, 224.
Fox-chase, the Kilruddery, a hunting Song, 149.
— Extraordinary, 160, 244.
Fool and Falcon, 261.
Footmen, running, curious particulars of, 168.
Fowling, a Poem, 175, 197.

G.

Game, buyers of, and poachers, lesson to, 46.
— Act, new, 146.
— Licenses, alterations in issuing, 3.
Game Laws, copy of the Bill lately passed, 127.
— Breach of the, 136. Actions upon, 266. Hints upon, 284.
Gaming Action, Mazzinghi v. Stephenson, 26.
Gaming-table, fashionable, 87.
Gamesters, the Philosophical, 37.
— Fortunate, apology for, 117.
Gamblers at Paris, account of, 63.
German Winter Amusement, 26.
Grosvenor, account of the late Earl of, 3.
Grouse-shooting, 197.
Gun, the Siller, 239, 245.

H.

Hall's Travels, Anecdotes from, 173.
Hedge-hogs, 196.
Horse, action to recover the value of a, 172.
Horse Sacrifice, or Aswamedha Jug, 238.
Horses, cruelty to, punished, 97.
Hunter, the Greenland, a Masquerade Song, 200.
Hunting Season concluded, 5.
Hunting Song, 289.
——————— Ancient, 292.
Hyde Park, petition of the tutelary genius of, 183.

Inscrip-

I.

Inscription, remarkable, 28.
———— upon Mr. Samuel Burder, 93.
Irruption extraordinary, in America, 128.

L.

Letters, man of, perplexities of, 216.
Liberality of the present age described, 225.

M.

May, in London, 86.
Mary, lines to, 153.
Murder in a duel, 17.
Munchausen, and Munchausen reproved, 232.
Mountebank, the Italian, at Paris, 65.
Mordaunt, Colonel, Sporting Anecdotes of, 13, 65.

N.

Ninepins, new game at, 112.

P.

Paragon Prologue, a *jeu d'esprit*, 150.
Pedestrian, an epistle from a, 122.
Pedestrianism, *vide* Walking, 145.
———— Humourous Dissertation on, 209.
Philosophers, eclipsed by sportsmen, 168.
Performer, popular, Anecdotes of, 170.
Pigeons, instinct in, 211.
Pigeon shooting, 45.
———— stealing, 46.
Poney and mail coach, 278.
Preserves, shooting in, 220.
Printing Office, on a, 172.
Pugilism, *vide* Boxing.
———— Female, 180.
Punch, Sir John Sinclair on, 215.

R.

Races appointed in 1808, 57, 59, 252.
Ringing, harmonious changes, 81.
Rocket, Mr. Cave Browne's celebrated dog, pedigree of, 203.
Robinson, Mrs.' inscription upon her tomb, 290.

S.

Sailor, his journey in a stage coach, 88.
———— turned pedlar, 115.
Shot, remarkable, 243.
Song, a drinking, 292.
Spaniard, incombustible, or fireeater, 112.
Spanish pride, 130.
Spaniard's letters from England, anecdote from, 182.
Sparring exhibition, 144.
Speed unnecessary, censured, 229.
Sport, summary of, at the Chesterfield, Boroughbridge, Warwick, Morpeth, Ayr, and Doncaster Races, 251.
Sporting subjects in the Royal Academy, 33.
———— Cause at York, 279.
———— Intelligence, 44, 94, 142, 192, 241, 283.
Sportsman, Philosophical, 65, 161, 257.
———— Old, death of, 49.
Sports, rural, account of, 188.
———— at Plowden Fair, 98.
Stamford, pedigree and performances of, 138.
Stallions to cover, alphabetical list of, 22, 85.
Stallions to cover in Ireland, 125.
Stubbs, G. Esq. Memoirs of, 55.

T.

Tennis, Mexican, 240.
Thornton, Colonel, and his attornies, 84.
———— and Mr. Flint, 274.
Trespass

Trespass causes at the Horsham Assizes, remarks upon, 13.
Trotting Match in Harness, on the late, &c. 104.
———— against time, 93, 144.
———— Cruel abuse of Horses in, a 114, 144.
Tumblers and Jugglers, the Parisian described, 61.

V.

Vivaldi, Brother to, his pedigree and performances, 124.
Viper, Mr. Ward's terrier, account of, 140.

W.

Walking extraordinary, vide Pedestrianism, 47, 48, 98.

Wit, Feast of, 43, 91, 129, 181, 232, 281.
Woman, the Strong, 112.
World the, a new Comedy, account of, 14.
———— Epilogue to, 51.
Whip Club, account of, 147.
Whist Table, the, 292.
Who Wins; or, the Widow's Choice; Quintetto, from the Farce of, 100.
Walking Sticks and Umbrellas, hints to the bearers of, 133.
Wrestling at Falmouth, 143.
———— and single-stick, 243.
Woodcock Shooting, 290.

Y.

York Spring Meeting, 50.
——— Winners of Royal Plates at, 185, 236.
Yew-tree, remarkable, 137.

DIRECTIONS TO THE BINDER.

FRONTISPIECE, to face the.................... Title Page.
Richard, late Earl of Grosvenor .... Page 3
Portrait of Eleanor............................ 43
The Horse and Lion 55
The Shepherd's Dog 93
Brother to Vivaldi 124
The Viper, an Etching.......................... 140
The Lion and Horse 155
Young Ducks Alarmed 188
Mr. Cave Browne's Rocket 203
The Trap 324
His Majesty's Cream-coloured Charger 256

THE
RACING CALENDAR,

MALTON CRAVEN MEETING, 1808.

TUESDAY, April 5.——The Craven Stakes of 10gs each, for all ages; two-year olds, 6st, and three-year olds, 8st. The last Mile and half.—Eleven Subscribers.

Mr Wentworth's b f Margaret, by Beningbrough, 3 yrs old (G. Humble) 1
Mr Nalton's b c Ranger, by Hyacinthus, 3 yrs old............ 2
Sir M. M. Sykes's b f Harriet, 3 yrs old...................... 3
Mr Thompson's b c Hornby-Lad, 3 yrs old 4
Mr Gorwood's b c, by Hyacinthus, out of Dairy-Maid, 2 yrs old ... 5
Mr Marris's b c, by Stamford, dam by Phenomenon, 2 yrs old...... 6
Lord Scarbrough's br c, by Sir Solomon, dam by Jupiter, 2 yrs old.. 7

Five to 4 on Margaret.—Won in a canter.

Sweepstakes of 20gs each; colts, 8st 3lb, fillies, 8st.—The last Mile and half.—Eight Subscribers.

Mr Garforth's ch c, by Hyacinthus, out of Flora (G. Humble) 1
Mr Shepperd's b c, by Ormond, dam by Young Morwick 2
Lord Milton's b c Easton, by Stamford 3
Mr Garforth's b c, by Hambletonian, out of Caroline 4
Lord Monson's b c, by Expectation 5
Sir M. M. Sykes's b c, by Hyacinthus 6
Mr Nalton's b c, by Delpini 7

Even betting on the winner.—A good race.

Sweepstakes of 20gs each, for fillies, 8st.—The last Mile.

Mr Watt's bay, by Delpini, dam by Trumpator (W. Peirse)........ 1
Sir M. M. Sykes's bay, Lady Rachel, by Stamford 2
Lord Scarbrough's brown, by Sir Solomon, dam by Magnet........ 3
Mr Robinson's bay, by Stamford, out of Fanny 4
Lord Hawke's chesnut, Mother Goose, by Stamford 5

Five to 4 agst Mr Watt's filly.—A very good race.

Produce Stakes of 50gs each, h. ft. colts, 8st, fillies, 7st 12lb.—Two Miles.—Nine Subscribers.

Sir M. M. Sykes's ch f, by Stamford, out of Stella (J. Garbutt) 1
Sir T. Gascoigne's b c Bumtrap, by Agonistes 2
Lord Fitzwilliam's bl f Charcoal, by Sir Peter 3
Mr Pickering's b f, by Sir Solomon 4

Bumtrap the favourite.—Very little betting.—Won rather easy.

WEDNESDAY, April 6.——Sweepstakes of 20gs each, for colts rising four years old, 8st 4lb, fillies, 8st.—Three Miles.—Four Subscribers.

Mr Garforth's b c, by Beningbrough, out of Caroline (W. Peirse) .. 1
Sir M. M. Sykes's b c Ranger, by Hyacinthus (J. Jackson) 2
       Two to 1 on the winner.—Won by half a neck.

Sweepstakes of 5gs each, for horses, &c. not thorough bred, 12st.—Gentlemen riders.—Two-mile heats.—Eleven Subscribers.

Sir M. M. Sykes's ch g, by St. George (rode by Mr Dowker)..	1	1
Mr Knowsley's bay gelding	2	2
Mr Frankland's b g Brilliant............................	3	3
Mr Watt's br h, by Screveton	4	4

   Five to 4 on Mr Watt's horse; after the heat, 2 to 1 on the winner.
                   Won easy.

    Fifty Pounds for all ages.—Heats, one Mile and a half.

Mr Acred's br colt Wansford, by Stamford, 3 yrs old, 8st 4lb (J. Garbutt)..	1	1
Mr Walker's ch c, by Hyacinthus, 3 yrs old, 8st 4lb.........	6	2
Mr Garforth's b c, by Hambletonian, 4 yrs old, 8st 10lb......	2	3
Mr Pickering's b g, by Sir Solomon, 2 yrs old, 6st 11lb.......	6	4
Mr Thompson's br c Hornby-Lad, 3 yrs old, 8st 4lb	3	5
Mr Bell's br c, by Stamford, 2 yrs old, 7st..................	4	dr
Mr Hobson's b c Grenadier, 4 yrs old, 8st 10lb	7	dr
Mr Hotham's br f Olivia, 4 yrs old, 8st 7lb	8	dr

      Six and 7 to 4 against Wansford.—Won easy.

THURSDAY, April 7.—Fifty Pounds for all ages.—Two-mile heats.

Mr T. Kirby's b c Whitenose, by Hyacinthus, 3 yrs old, 8st 3lb (J. Shepherd).......................................	1	1
Mr Nalton's bay colt Ranger, by Hyacinthus, 3 yrs old, 8st 3lb (J. Jackson)..	2	2
Mr Walker's ch c, by Hyacinthus, out of Dairy-Maid, 3 yrs old, 8st 3lb (J. Garbutt)	3	3

   Six to 4 on Ranger; after the heat, 2 to 1 on Whitenose.—A very good
                   race.

The Farmers' Stakes of 90l. 6s. for half-bred hunters, 14st.—Rode by
            Farmers.—Two-mile heats.

Mr L. Dale's ch g Patch, by St. George, 6 yrs old	1	1
Mr Dale's chesnut horse	4	2
Mr Dawson's br h Weathergall, by Rainbow, 6 yrs old	9	3
Mr Sawdon's ch h Nevison, by Windleston, 5 yrs old	7	4
Mr Frost's gr h Achilles, by Dapple, 6 yrs old...............	8	5
Mr Wright's ch h Harlequin, 5 yrs old	4	6
Mr Grove's ch h Tanner, by Heigh-ho, 5 yrs old	2	7
Mr Seaton's br m, by Screveton, 6 yrs old	3	dr
Mr Marshall's b h Sportsman, 5 yrs old...................	6	dr

        Even betting on Patch.—Won very easy.

   The Course was extremely deep on account of the rain; the horses in many places were literally up to their knees in mud.

                          BURTON.

BURTON-HUNT MEETING (Lincoln Course).

TUESDAY, April 5.——Sweepstakes of 5gs each, for hunters, bonâ fide the property of Subscribers one month before running, having hunted with the Burton hounds, 11st each.—Two Miles.—Seventeen Subscribers.

Mr Grant's ch h Felix, by Precipitate, 5 yrs old (Mr Skipworth) 1
Mr Wallace's b g Southton, by Pegasus, 5 yrs old (Mr Douglas) 2
Mr F. Chaplin's ch g Navigator, aged, 7lb extra (Mr Uppleby) 3
Mr Kent's b g Mechanic, 6 yrs old (Mr T. Johnson).............. 4
Navigator the favourite.—Won easy.

The Gold Cup given by Lord Monson, for horses, &c. belonging to Far-mers.—Two Miles.

Mr S. Codd's ch m Miss Heath, 6 yrs old (the Owner)........... 1
Mr W. Danby's b m Rosebud, 6 yrs old (the Owner) 2
Mr G. B. Child's ch m Susan, 6 yrs old (the Owner) 3
Mr Brett's ch h, by Turk, dam by Weasel, 5 yrs old............. 4
Mr J. Greetham's b h Ploughboy, 6 yrs old (Mr Wing) 5
Rosebud took the lead until near the distance-post; the race was then very smartly contested, and won by half a neck.

WEDNESDAY.—Sweepstakes of 5gs each, for horses, &c.—Two Miles.—Fifteen Subscribers.

Mr C. Mainwaring's bay gelding, 5 yrs old (Mr Brett)........... 1
Mr Grant's ch h Felix, 5 yrs old (Mr Skipworth)............... 2
Mr C. E. Kent's b g Mechanic, 6 yrs old (Mr Johnson) 3
Mr F. Chaplin's ch g Navigator, aged (Mr Uppleby)............. 4
Mr R. Denham's ch c Orion, 4 yrs old (Mr Douglas)........... 5
Lord Pollington's bl g, 6 yrs old (Mr T. Rose) 6

Handicap Stakes of 3gs each.—One Mile.—Eight Subscribers.

Mr Brown's bay gelding (Mr Cholmley) 1
Lord Monson's br h Ptarmigan (Mr Douglas) 2
Mr W. Danby's b m Rosebud (Mr Hawke) 3
Mr Terrewest's ch h, by Achilles (Mr Uppleby) 4
Mr Wallace's br h Quack (Mr Handley) 5

The Cup, value 50gs, given by the Gentlemen of the Hunt, for horses, &c.—Two Miles.

Lord Monson's br h Cleveland, by Overton, 5 yrs old, (Mr Douglas).. 1
Mr C. White's b g Southton, by Pegasus, 5 yrs old (Mr Hawke).... 2
Mr F. Chaplin's ch g Navigator, by Admiral, aged (Mr Uppleby).. 3
Two to 1 on Cleveland.

NEWMARKET CRAVEN MEETING.

MONDAY, April 18.—The Craven Stakes of 10gs each, for all ages.
—Across the Flat.—Fifteen Subscribers.

Lord Stawell's b c Deceiver, by Buzzard, 4 yrs old, 8st 9lb (W. Ar-nold) 1

A 2   Lord

Lord Foley's b f, by Worthy, out of Miss Furry, 3 yrs old, 5st 10lb.. 2
Major Wilson's ch c Juniper, by Whiskey, 2 yrs old, 5st 10lb....... 3
          The following also started, but were not placed:
Lord Grosvenor's b c Osiris, by Sir Peter, out of Ibis, 3 yrs old, 8st.. 0
Duke of Grafton's b f Vanity, 4 yrs old, 8st 9lb................ 0
Mr Goulburn's ch c Romeo, by Vernator, 3 yrs old, 8st.......... 0
Sir J. Honywood's b c Hawk, 3 yrs old, 8st 0
Lord Lowther's ch h Brainworm, 6 yrs old, 9st 5lb............ 0
Mr Wilson's br h Pavilion, 6 yrs old, 9st 5lb 0
Mr Fermor's br m Pelisse, 6 yrs old, 9st 5lb 0
Mr Wyndham's b c, by Schedoni, 4 yrs old, 8st 9lb............ 0
Mr Abbey's b f Clorinda, by Hercules, 2 yrs old, 5st 10lb....... 0
Lord Jersey's ch c, by Buzzard, 4 yrs old, 8st 9lb............. 0
Seven to 2 against Pavilion, 7 to 2 against Brainworm, 4 to 1 against
      Deceiver, and 12 to 1 against Juniper.—Won cleverly.

Produce Stakes of 100gs each, h. ft. colts, 8st 4lb, fillies, 8st.—Across
          the Flat.—Eight Subscribers.
Sir F. Standish's b f, by Sir Peter, out of Eagle's dam (W. Arnold).. 1
Mr Wilson's b c, by Hambletonian, out of Pavilion's dam......... 2
    Seven to 4 and 2 to 1 on Sir F. Standish's filly.—Won very easy.

Sweepstakes of 200gs each, h. ft. colts, 8st 4lb.—Abingdon Mile.
Mr Ladbroke's b c Tristram, by Teddy the Grinder, dam by Precipi-
      tate (W. Arnold).................................... 1
Lord G. H. Cavendish's b c, by Coriander, dam by Sir Peter....... 2
Mr Wyndham's b c, by Whiskey, out of Minion 3
          Seven to 4 on Tristram.—Won quite easy.

Sweepstakes of 100gs each, h. ft. colts and fillies rising three years old.
          Ditch Mile.—Eight Subscribers.
Lord Grosvenor's b c Chester, by Sir Peter, dam by Woodpecker,
      8st 4lb (F. Buckle) 1
Duke of Grafton's filly, by Sorcerer, out of Hornby-Lass, 7st 13lb.. 2
Mr Mellish's b c Weaver, by Shuttle, out of Strap's dam, 8st 7lb.... 3
Mr Lake's b c Noyeau, brother to Rumbo, by Whiskey, 8st 7lb.... 4
Sir F. Standish's b c, by Mr Teazle, dam by Volunteer, out of Sto-
      race, 8st 4lb.. 5
Two to 1 against Chester, 3 to 1 against the Duke of Grafton's filly, 3
    to 1 against Weaver, and 10 to 5 against Sir F. Standish's colt.—Won
    very easy.

Sweepstakes of 100gs each, h. ft. 8st 3lb each.—Two-year Olds' Course.
Mr Goddard's b c Crim. Con. by Gohanna, out of a Sister to Horns
      (W. Clift) 1
Lord G. H. Cavendish's br c, by Trumpator, dam by Coriander (broke
      down)... 2
General Grosvenor's gr c Welch Fusileer, by Dapple, dam by Shark pd
          Seven to 4 on Crim. Con.

          Match for 500gs.—Beacon Course.
Lord Lowther's b c Trafalgar, by Gohanna, 8st 7lb (S. Chifney).... 1
Lord Foley's br c Paris, by Sir Peter, 8st 7lb (broke down)........ 2
          Seven to 4 and 2 to 1 on Trafalgar.

                                                  Match

Match for 300gs.—Ditch-in.

Lord Darlington's b c Giles Scroggins, by Sir Solomon, 8st. (S. Chifney).. 1
Lord Grosvenor's br c Eaton, by Sir Peter, 8st 3lb................ 2
    Thirteen to 8 on Eaton.—A good race, and won by a neck.

The first Class of the Oatlands' Stakes of 50gs each, h. ft.—Ditch-in.—
Eleven Subscribers.

Mr Lake's br f Nymphina, by Gouty, 3 yrs old, 6st 12lb.......... 1
Sir J. Honywood's b c Hawk, 3 yrs old, 6st 12lb................. 2
Mr Fermor's ch h Cerberus, 5 yrs old, 9st 1lb................... 3
Mr Lloyd's b h Cardinal Beaufort, 5 yrs old, 8st 5lb............ 4
Lord Foley's ch h Captain Absolute, aged, 8st.................. 5
Lord Grosvenor's br f Olive-Branch, 3 yrs old, 7st 1lb.......... 6
Mr Kellerman's b f Streatlam-Lass, 4 yrs old, 8st 2lb.......... 7
Two to 1 against Cerberus, 5 to 1 against Cardinal Beaufort, 6 to 1 against
    Captain Absolute, 7 to 1 against Olive-Branch, 10 to 1 against Hawk,
    11 to 1 against Streatlam-Lass, and no odds taken against Nymphina.
    —Won easy.

Match for 100gs.—Clermont Course.

Mr Harbord's b f, by Saxe Cobourg, 7st 13lb (W. Arnold)........ 1
General Grosvenor's ch g Roast-Beef, by Old England, 8st 7lb.... 2
    Seven to 4 on Mr Harbord's filly.—Won easy.

Sweepstakes of 100gs each, h. ft, colts, 8st 5lb, fillies, 8st 2lb.—Ab. M.
Lord Grosvenor's b f Isis, by Sir Peter, out of Ibis, received forfeit from
Lord F. G. Osborne's colt, by Hambletonian, out of Eustatia.
Lord F. G. Osborne's br f, by Sorcerer, out of Drowsy.
Lord Grosvenor's b f Leopardess, by Alexander, out of Nimble.

Mr Sitwell's Clinker, by Sir Peter, 8st 5lb, received forfeit from Mr
Mellish's Anna, 8st.—Across the Flat, 200gs, h. ft.
Mr Sitwell's Renishaw, by Coriander, 8st 3lb, received forfeit from
Mr Mellish's Hit-or-Miss, (dead) 8st.—Two-year Olds' Course, 200gs,
h. ft.
Mr Sitwell's Gooseander, by Hambletonian, received forfeit from Mr
Mellish's Experiment, 8st 3lb each.—Two-year Olds' Course, 200gs,
h. ft.
Mr Vansittart's Currycomb, by Buzzard, 8st 7lb, received 40gs compromise from Mr Wilson's Smuggler, 8st.—Two-year Olds' Course,
200gs, h. ft.
Mr Batson's Gladiator, by Buzzard, 8st 7lb, received 10gs compromise
from Mr Scrope's The Monk, 7st 8lb.—Across the Flat, 50gs.

TUESDAY, April 19.—(A very snowy day.)—Match for 50gs.—
Bunbury Mile.
Mr Kellermann's ch c Jamaica, by Buzzard, 4 yrs old, 6st........ 1
Lord F. Bentinck's br h Bagatelle, 6 yrs old, 7st 7lb........... 2
    Seven to 4 on Bagatelle.—A fine race.
Match for 300gs.—Two-year Olds' Course.
Mr Payne's b c Tudor, by John Bull, 8st 2lb (F. Buckle)......... 1

                  Mr

Mr Shakespear's ch f Wretch, 8st 2lb 1
Five and 6 to 4 on Wretch.—A good race.

The second Class of the Oatlands' Stakes of 50gs each, h. ft.—Ditch-in.
Eleven Subscribers.

Lord Grosvenor's b m Violante, by John Bull, 5 yrs old, 9st 9lb (F.
    Buckle) 1
Duke of Grafton's b m Parasol, aged, 8st 12lb 2
Sir J. Honywood's br c Delville, 4 yrs old, 7st 12lb 3
Sir C. Turner's b c Thorn, 4 yrs old, 8st 1lb.................... 4
Mr Delmé Radcliffe's bl c Mungo, 3 yrs old, 7st 5
Mr Kellermann's b f L'Huile de Venus, 3 yrs old, 7st 6lb......... 6
Mr Hallett's ch f Jewess, 4 yrs old, 7st 4lb 7
Six to 4 against Violante, 4 to 1 against L'Huile de Venus, 5 to 1 against
    Parasol, 6 to 1 against Thorn, and 8 to 1 against Delville.—Won quite
    easy.

Sweepstakes of 100gs each.—Across the Flat.

Mr Shakespear's ch h Zodiac, by St. George, 9st.
Lord Jersey's b h Langton, 7st 7lb—paid 10gs.
Lord Foley's ch h Captain Absolute, 7st 3lb—paid 10gs.

Mr Payne's Ferdinand, by John Bull, 7st 9lb, received 50gs compromise from Mr Lake's Coriolanus, 8st 7lb.—Across the Flat, 200gs, h. ft.

Duke of Grafton's Musician, by Worthy, 6st 12lb, received 40gs compromise from Mr Lloyd's Cardinal Beaufort, 8st 10lb.—Ab. M. 100gs, h. ft.

Mr Vansittart's Momentilla, by a brother to Repeater, 8st 9lb, received 80gs compromise from Lord Jersey's Roko, 7st 3lb.—Two-year Old Course, 100gs.

WEDNESDAY, April 20.—Match for 100gs.—Abingdon Mile.

Mr Barmon's ch horse, Cerberus, by Gohanna, 8st 3lb (H. Buckle) 1
Mr Shakespear's br h Wormwood, 8st 3lb 2
Six to 5 on Wormwood.—Won cleverly.

The Subscription Plate of 50l. for two-year olds, 7st; three-year olds,
    8st 7lb; and four-year olds, 9st.—Two-year Olds' Course.
Lord Stawell's b c Deceiver, by Buzzard, 4 yrs old (W. Arnold) 1
Sir C. Turner's ch c Mr Gundy, 3 yrs old 2
Sir J. Shelley's br c Clasher, 4 yrs old 3
The following also started; but were not placed:
Lord Grosvenor's br c Bullrush, 3 yrs old 0
Mr Wilson's b f, by Stamford, out of Miss Judy, 2 yrs 0
Sir C. Bunbury's ch c Snug, 4 yrs old.......................... 0
Sir F. Standish's ch c, by Mr Teazle, 2 yrs old................ 0
Lord G. H. Cavendish's b f Pagoda, 4 yrs old 0
Mr Abbey's b f Clorinda, 2 yrs old 0
Seven to 4 against Deceiver, 7 to 2 against Mr Gundy, 4 to 1 against Bullrush, 9 to 2 against Clasher, and 6 to 1 against Snug.—Won easy.

Match for 100gs.—Two-year Olds' Course.
Mr Shakespear's bay colt Discount, by Teddy, the Grinder, dam by
    Highflyer, 8st 2lb (W. Arnold) 1
M2

Mr Panton's colt, by Buzzard, out of Mandane, 8st 2lb 2

Seven to 4 and 2 to 1 on Mr Panton's colt.

The third Class of the Oatlands' Stakes of 50gs each, h. ft.—Ditch-in.—
Ten Subscribers.

Mr Batson's ch c Charmer, by Whiskey, 4 yrs old, 6st 13lb (a Boy).. 1
Lord Grosvenor's Meteora, 5 yrs old, 8st 9lb 2
Sir J. Honywood's Bacchanal, 3 yrs old, 7st 3
Mr Lake's Gaiety, 5 yrs old, 8st 4

The following also started, but were not placed:

Mr Wyndham's b c, by Schedoni, 4 yrs old, 7st 12lb.............. 0
Sir C. Turner's Thomasina, 3 yrs old, 7st 9lb 0
Mr Fermor's Brighton, 3 yrs old, 7st 2lb....................... 0
Mr C. Browne's Miltonia, 3 yrs old, 6st 6lb 0
Eleven to 5 against Brighton, 3 to 1 against Bacchanal, 4 to 1 against
Meteora, 5 to 1 against Thomasina, and 20 to 1 against Charmer.—
Won rather easy.

The following having declared forfeit by the time prescribed, paid only
10gs each, which was divided between the Owners of the second
horses, &c. in the three Classes, viz. Hawk, Parasol, and Meteora.

	st. lb.
Mr Elwes's Pavilion, 6 yrs old	8 14
Mr Fermor's Pelisse, 6 yrs old	8 10
Mr Delmé Radcliffe's Trafalgar, 4 yrs old....................	8 7
Mr Forth's Watery, 6 yrs old	8 5
Lord Jersey's Langton, 5 yrs old	8 3
Lord Foley's Jasper, 5 yrs old	8 3
Mr Sitwell's Taurus, 4 yrs old	8 1
Sir J. Hawkins's Clermont, 4 yrs old	8 0
Mr Goddard's Bronze, 4 yrs old	7 7
Mr Cave Browne's Brother to Maidstone, 4 yrs old............	7 1
Mr Fermor's Bantum, 3 yrs old...............................	6 11

Lord Grosvenor's br c Chester, by Sir Peter Teazle, 8st 3lb, received
forfeit from Lord F. G. Osborne's bl f Scar, (dead) by Trumpator, out
of a sister to Royalist, 8st.—Ab. M. 200gs, h. ft.

Lord Lowther's Brainworm, by Buzzard, 8st 8lb, received forfeit from
Mr Fermor's Stripling, 7st.—Across the Flat, 100gs, h. ft.

Major Wilson's b c, by Sir Peter Teazle, out of Brown Charlotte,
8st 2lb, received forfeit from Mr Cave Browne's Brother to Maidstone,
8st 8lb.—Ditch-in, 50gs, 30 ft.

THURSDAY, April 21.—Sweepstakes of 100gs each, h. ft. 8st each.
—Across the Flat.

Mr Sitwell's br c Clinker, by Sir Peter, out of Hyale, (R. Goodison) 1
General Gower's ch c John-o'-Gaunt, by Buzzard 2
Mr Briggs's colt, by Kill-Devil, out of Portia .... pd

Five to 2 on Clinker.—Won in a canter.

Match

Match for 50gs.—Two-year Olds' Course.

Mr Batson's ch c Charmer, by Whiskey, 4 yrs old, 8st. (F. Buckle).. 1
Duke of St. Alban's b h Prodigal, 5 yrs old, 8st 4lb 2

Even betting.—Won easy.

Match for 100gs.—Abingdon Mile.

Mr F. Craven's br f, by Trumpator, out of Beda, 8st 1lb (F. Buckle) 1
Mr S. Prime's ch c, by Ambrosio, 8st 2lb 2

Three to 1 on Mr Craven's filly.—Won easy.

Match for 200gs.—Two-year Olds' Course.

Mr Craven's br c Beau Nash, by Trumpator, 2 yrs old, 6st 4lb (C.
Goodisson) 1
Duke of Grafton's b c Musician, 3 yrs old, 8st 9lb............. 2

Six to 5 against Beau Nash.—Won very easy.

Match for 200gs.—Two-year Olds' Course.

Mr Shakespear's ch h Selim, by Buzzard, 8st 7lb (W. Arnold)...... 1
Mr Andrew's b m Lydia, 7st 7lb 2

Three to 1 on Selim.—Won quite easy.

Match for 100gs.—Rowley Mile.

Sir C. Bunbury's b c Rambler, by Whiskey, 8st (F. Buckle)...... 1
Mr Vansittart's ch f Momentilla, 8st 4lb 2

Six to 5 on Rambler.

Match for 200gs.—Across the Flat.

Mr Mellish's b c Weaver, by Shuttle, 8st 1lb (F. Buckle)........ 1
Sir C. Turner's b c Bramble, by Hambletonian, 8st 1lb........... 2

Five to 2 and 3 to 1 on Weaver.—Won easy.

The Subscription-Plate of 50l. for two-year olds, 6st 7lb, three-year olds,
8st 5lb, four-year olds, 8st 13lb, and five-year olds, 9st 4lb.—Ditch
Mile.—The winner was to be sold for 200gs. if demanded, &c.

Mr Goddard's ch c Achilles, by Young Woodpecker, 4 yrs old, (S.
Chifney) 1
Sir C. Bunbury's ch c Snug, 4 yrs old........................ 2
Mr Lake's br h Gaiety, 5 yrs old............................. 3
Lord Stawell's ch c, brother to Bustard, 2 yrs old 4

The following also started, but were not placed :—

Mr Goodisson's b c Foxberry, 3 yrs old 0
Mr Hallett's ch f Jewess, 4 yrs old.......................... 0
Mr Goulburn's ch c Romeo, 3 yrs old 0
Mr Boyce's b f, by Stamford, 2 yrs old....................... 0
Mr Emden's b f Highland-Lass, 2 yrs old 0
Mr Mellish's br c, by Hambletonian, 2 yrs old................. 0
Mr Golding's ch f, by Boaster, 2 yrs old 0
Lord G. H. Cavendish's b c, by Trumpator, 2 yrs old........... 0
Mr Panton's ch c Fun, by Worthy, 2 yrs old................... 0

Five to 2 against Snug, 4 to 1 against Gaiety, and 4 to 1 against Achilles.
Won very easy.

Match for 200gs.—The last three Miles of B. C.

Sir J. Honywood's br colt Delville, by Beningbrough, 8st 6lb (F.
Buckle) 1
Mr

Mr Sitwell's br c Taurus, 8st 4lb 2
       Five to 2 on Taurus.—Won easy.

Lord Foley's Paris, by Sir Peter, received 50gs compromise from Mr Shakespear's Canopus, 8st 2lb each.—B. C. 500gs.

CATTERICK-BRIDGE MEETING.

WEDNESDAY, April 20.——The Produce Stakes of 25gs each, for colts and fillies, rising three years old.—Two Miles.—Five Subscribers.

Sir W. Gerard's ch colt, by Hambletonian, out of Mary-Ann, 8st 3lb (W. Peirse) 1
Mr S. Coulson's ch colt, by Expectation, out of Bonny Kate, 8st 3lb 2
Mr Baillie's br c, by Delpini, dam by Beningbrough, 8st 3lb 3
      Two to 1 on Sir W. Gerard's colt.—Won easy.

     The 50l. for all ages.—Two-mile heats.

Mr W. Hutchinson's bay colt Silvio, by St. George, 3 yrs old, 8st 2lb (F. Jordon) 4 1 1
Mr Acred's br c Wansford, 3 yrs old, 8st 2lb 1 3 4
Lord Strathmore's br. f, by Hambletonian, 3 yrs old, 7st 9lb (R. Johnson) 3 2 2
Mr Lonsdale's gr c Sultan, 3 yrs old, 8st 2lb 2 4 3
Mr Dunn's b f Miss Decoy, 4 yrs old, 8st 9lb .... 5 dr
Mr Collinson's b c, by L'Orient, 2 yrs old, 6st 11lb .... dis
Two to 1 against Wansford, 3 and 4 to 1 against Lord Strathmore's filly, and 4 to 1 against Silvio; after the first heat, 6 to 4 on Wansford.— Won easy.

Sweepstakes of 5gs each, for hunters not thorough bred, 12st.—Gentlemen riders.—Three Miles.—Ten Subscribers.
Mr T. Milner's br g, by Screveton (Mr T. Sykes)................. 1
Mr Trotter's br g Gunpowder, by Traveller 2
Mr W. Hutchinson's gr h, by St. George 3
     Two to 1 on Mr Milner's gelding.—Won easy.

THURSDAY, April 21.—Sweepstakes of 10gs each, for colts rising three years old, 8st 3lb, fillies, 8st.—Two Miles.—Six Subscribers.

Mr Shafto's b c, by Agonistes, dam by Jupiter.................... 1
Duke of Leeds's ch c, by Pandolpho, out of Mother Redcap........ 2
Mr Plew's b c Temple, by L'Orient 3
Mr Gascoigne's b c Bumtrap, by Agonistea 4
Sir J. Lawson's b c, by Expectation, dam by Dart 5
    Two to 1 against either Mr Shafto's colt, or Bumtrap.—Won easy.

Sweepstakes of 20gs each, for fillies rising three years old, 8st.—One Mile and a half.—Four Subscribers.

Mr W. Fletcher's bay, Miss Staveley, by Shuttle (W. Peirse) 1
Sir H. Williamson's bay, by Hambletonian, dam by Coriander...... 2

Mr Baillie's bay, by Delpini, dam by Highflyer.................. **8**
     Two to 1 on Miss Staveley.—Won very easy.

Sweepstakes of 10gs each, for all ages.—Two Miles.—Ten Subscribers.
Mr Wentworth's bay filly Margaret, by Beningbrough, 3 yrs old, 7st
     11lb (G. Humble) 1
Mr Walker's b f, by Stamford, out of Belle-Fille, 3 yrs old, 7st 11lb   2
Mr Cradock's b f, by St. George, dam by Pontac, 3 yrs old, 7st 11lb. .   3
Mr. Danby's b c Presentation, 3 yrs old, 8st 4
Mr W. Fletcher's b f Easter, 3 yrs old, 7st 11lb 5
     Two to 1 on Margaret.—Won in a canter.

RACING INTELLIGENCE EXTRA.

NEWMARKET SECOND SPRING MEETING, 1808.

MONDAY, May 10.——Sweepstakes of 100gs each, h. ft. for four-
year old colts, 8st 7lb, fillies, 8st 2lb.—Last three Miles of B. C.
Lord Grosvenor's b c Eaton, by Sir Peter Teazle
Lord Grosvenor's b f Pearl, by Sir Peter Teazle
Lord Foley's b c Chaise-and-One, by Whiskey
Mr Blachford's b c Tony Lumpkin, by Ambrosio
Mr Craven's ch f Frances, by Ambrosio
Lord F. G. Osborne's b c, by Trumpator, out of Beda
Duke of Grafton's b c Barbarian, by Worthy
Mr Delmé Radcliffe's b c; by Sir Peter Teazle, dam by Walnut, bought
     of Mr Ellerker
Mr Fermor's b c Hawk, by Buzzard.

     Sweepstakes of 100gs each, h. ft.—Across the Flat.
Lord C. Somerset's b c Ethelfred, brother to White-Rose, by Beningbro',
     8st 7lb
Duke of Grafton's filly, by Coriander, out of Peppermint, 8st 7lb
Sir J. Shelley's filly, by Buzzard, bought of Mr Panton, 8st 7lb
General Grosvenor's gr c Welch Fusileer, by Dapple, dam by Shark,
     8st.

     Lord Stawell's ch c, by Sorcerer, out of Sir David's dam, against Lord
Grosvenor's br colt Chester, by Sir Peter Teazle, 8st 2lb each.—R. M.
100gs, h. ft.

     Duke of Grafton's Brother to Forester, by Grouse, agst Mr Shake-
spear's Discount, by Teddy the Grinder, 8st 2lb each.—Two-year Olds'
Course, 100gs, h. ft.

     General Grosvenor's filly, (sealed up) 4 yrs old, 8st 12lb, against Lord
C. Somerset's b c Ethelfred, 3 yrs old, 8st.—Two-year Olds' Course,
200gs, h. ft.

                                     Mr

Mr Delmé Radcliffe's Selim, 11st, against Mr Lake's Tim, a feather.—Abingdon Mile, 200gs.

Mr Shakespear's Brainworm, against Mr Fermor's Hippomenes, 8st 2lb each.—Across the Flat, 100gs, h. ft.

Mr F. Craven's br filly, by Trumpator, out of Beda, 8st 5lb, against Mr Hallett's br c, by Kill-Devil, 8st 3lb.—Rowley Mile, 50gs.

Handicap Stakes of 100gs each, h. ft.—Beacon Course.

	st.	lb.
Mr Wilson's b h Pavilion, by Waxy	8	2
Lord Grosvenor's b m Meteora, by Meteor	8	0
Mr Lloyd's b h Cardinal Beaufort, by Gohanna	7	5
Lord Foley's ch h Captain Absolute, by John Bull	7	4

WEDNESDAY, May 18.—Handicap Stakes of 100gs each, h. ft.—Across the Flat.

	st.	lb.
Mr Kellermann's b f L'Huile de Venus, by Whiskey	8	3
Mr Fermor's br c Brighton, by Gohanna	7	11
Duke of Grafton's b c Musician, by Worthy	7	10
Sir C. Bunbury's br c Rambler, by Whiskey	7	2

THURSDAY, May 19.—Mr Sitwell's Clinker, 8st 3lb, against Mr Shakespear's Discount, 8st.—Abingdon Mile, 100gs.

Mr Shakespear's Discount agst Mr Wyndham's Susan, 8st 1lb each.—Two-year Olds' Course, 100gs.

Mr Shakespear's Zodiac, 8st 5lb, against Lord Grosvenor's Violantè, 8st.—Across the Flat, 300gs, h. ft.

PONTEFRACT RACES, 1808.

SECOND Day.—Macaroni Stakes of 10gs each, for horses that never won before April the 1st, 1808.—Four-yr olds, 10st 11lb, 5-yr olds, 11st 8lb, 6-yr olds and aged, 12st, mares and geldings allowed 3lb.—Gentlemen riders.—Three Miles.

Ld Pollington's ches filly, by Hyacinthus, dam by Carbuncle, 4 yrs old
Mr Milnes' b colt Aper, by a son of Lurcher, dam by Phlegon, 4 yrs old
Mr F. Sotheron's ches colt Darrington Cade, by Hyacinthus, 4 yrs old
Mr G. Neville's b colt, by Hambletonian, 4 yrs old
Mr Sykes's b h, by Idris, dam by Highflyer, 5 yrs old
Mr Gascoigne's b m, by Hambletonian, out of Golden-Locks, 5 yrs old
Mr Cole's b m, Mrs Downce, by Oberon, dam by Stride, 6 yrs old
Mr T. Duncombe did not name.

THIRD DAY.—Mr Lee's ches colt, by Shuttle, dam by Pot8o's, out of Winnifred, against Mr Clark's bay colt, by Cockfeeder, 8st. each.—Last Mile, 100gs, h. ft.

A Hunter's

A Hunter's Stakes of 5gs each, for horses not thorough bred; 4 yrs old, 11st 4lb, 5 yrs old, 11st 10lb, 6 yrs old, 12st 4lb; and aged, 12st 7lb, mares and geldings allowed 3lb.—A winner once, to carry 5lb, twice, 7lb extra.—Gentlemen riders.—Two-mile heats.

Mr Cole's bay gelding, by Noble, 4 yrs old
Mr Townroe's b f, by Sextus Pompeius, 4 yrs old
Mr Alderson's b f, by Stamford, 4 yrs old
Mr F. Hartley's gr g Aukward Customer, by St. George, 5 yrs old
Mr G. Neville's b g, by Young Espersykes, 5 yrs old
Mr Milnes' b horse, by Stamford, 5 yrs old
Mr W. Blythe's b h Rose-Bell, by Grog, 5 yrs old
Mr Milner's br h, by Screveton, 6 yrs old
Mr F. Sotheron's b m, by Patch, aged
Mr Earnshaw's b m, by Grog, aged.
Ld Pollington did not name.

PRESTON MEETING, 1808.

FIRST Day.—The Produce Stakes of 50gs each, for three-year old colts, 8st 4lb, fillies, 8st.—Two Miles.
Sir W. Gerard's ch c, by Hambletonian, out of Mary-Ann
Mr Tarleton's br f, by Mr Teazle, out of Jack Tar's dam
Mr E. L. Hodgson's gr f, by Shuttle, dam by Sir Peter Teazle
Mr Clifton's b c Poulton, (late Alexander the First) brother to Fyldener, by Sir Peter Teazle.

SECOND DAY.—The Gold Cup, given by the Gentlemen of Preston, added to a Sweepstakes of 10gs each, for three-year olds, 6st 6lb, four-year olds, 8st, five-year olds, 8st 10lb, six-year olds and aged, 8st 12lb.—Mares to be allowed 2lb.—The Gold Cup Course, about four miles.

Duke of Hamilton's b c Petronius, by Sir Peter Teazle, 3 yrs old
Duke of Hamilton's b c Peter Little, by Sir Peter Teazle, 3 yrs old
Lord Derby's br f Margaret, 4 yrs old
Lord Milton's br h Sir Paul, 6 years old
Lord Stanley's br c Jacobus, by Sir Peter Teazle, 3 yrs old
Sir W. Gerard's br h Julius Cæsar, 5 yrs old
Mr Horrock's ch c Constellation, by Star, 4 yrs old
Mr J. L. Blackburn's br f, by Hambletonian, 4 yrs old
Mr Aspinall's b m Crazy, 5 yrs old
Mr Rookwood's gr f, by Shuttle, dam by Sir Peter Teazle, 3 yrs old
Mr Clifton's b h Fyldener, 5 yrs old
Mr Benson's b c, by Pegasus, dam by Rockingham, 4 yrs old
Mr Lomax's b m Josephina, aged
Mr C. Smith's b c Phlebotomist, 4 yrs old.

SKIPTON MEETING.

WEDNESDAY, April 27.——Sweepstakes of 10gs each, colts, 8st 3lb, fillies, 8st.—Twice round the Course.—Five Subscribers.

Duke of Hamilton's b c Petronius, by Sir Peter, out of Louisa, by Javelin (B. Smith) 1
Mr Cunliffe's b f Clotilda, by Hambletonian, dam by Young Marsk 2
Mr B. Livesey's br f, by Expectation, dam by Star 3
Six to 4 on Petronius.—Won easy.

Sweepstakes of 10gs each, for horses not thorough bred.—(Ages as in May.)—Heats, twice round.—Six Subscribers.

Lord Ribblesdale's br g Neighbour, by Noble, 5 yrs old, 11st 9lb (Mr Simpson) 2 1 1
Mr W. Hutchinson's gr g, by St. George, 5 yrs old, 11st 9st.. 1 3 dr
Mr Hutchinson's gelding the favourite ; after the first heat, 2 to 1 he won. Neighbour's bridle broke the first heat, but for the second heat he took the lead, was never headed, and won cleverly.

Sweepstakes of 20gs each, for hunters, 10st.—Four Miles.—Four Subscribers.

Mr Tempest's ch g Marquis, by Prophet .... walked over.

THURSDAY, April 27.——The Macaroni Stakes of 10gs each, for maiden horses, &c.—(Ages as in May.)—Gentlemen riders.—Heats, twice round the Course.—Six Subscribers.

Mr Gascoigne's b m, by Hambletonian, out of Golden-Locks, 5 yrs old, 11st 6lb (Mr Tatton Sykes) 2 1 1
Mr J. Fieldes' b g, by Young Diomed, 5 yrs old, 11st 9lb (Mr Sandiford) 1 2 3
Mr T. Chamberlain's br c Aper, 4 yrs old, 10st 11lb (Mr C. Simpson) 3 2 2
Even betting on Mr Gascoigne's mare ; after the first heat, the same ; after the second heat, 2 and 3 to 1 she won.—Won easy.

The Maiden Plate of 50l. for all ages.—Heats, twice round the Course.

Lord Strathmore's br f, by Hambletonian, out of Beatrice, 3 yrs old, 7st 5lb (R. Johnson) 1 1
Mr Harrison's Bonny Hodge, by Moorcock.................. 2 2
Mr Lonsdale's b f Clotilda, 2 yrs old, 5st 11lb........... 3 fell
Six to 4 on Lord Strathmore's filly, and 2 to 1 against Clotilda ; after the heat, 2 to 1 on Lord Strathmore's filly.—A fine race.

————

DURHAM MEETING.

WEDNESDAY, April 27.——Sweepstakes of 10gs each, with 20gs added, for colts, 8st 3lb.—Two Miles.—Five Subscribers.

Mr D. Shafto's b c, by Agonistes, dam by Jupiter 1
Colonel Horton's b c, by Bustard, dam by Sir Peter Teazle........ 2
Sir H. T. Vane's b c, by Shuttle, dam by Phenomenon 3
Mr Shafto's colt the favourite.—Won by half a length.

Seventy Pounds for all ages.—Three-mile heats.

Mr W. Hutchinson's b c Silvio, by St. George, 3 yrs old, 8st 5lb
  (F. Jordon) 6 1 1
Sir H. T. Vane's b f, by Sir Peter Teazle, out of Katherine, 4 yrs
  old, 8st 9lb 1 2 2
Mr Kirby's b c Whitenose, 3 yrs old, 8st 5lb................ 3 4 3
Mr Cradock's b f, by St. George, dam by Pontac, 3 yrs old,
  8st 2lb 4 6 4
Mr Storey's b c Cramlington, 4 yrs old, 8st 10lb............ 2 5 5
Mr Bates's b c Honest Harry, 4 yrs old, 8st 10lb........... 5 3 6
Whitenose the favourite ; after the first heat, 2 and 3 to 1 against
  Whitenose ; after the second heat, 2 to 1 on Silvio.—A good race.

THURSDAY, April 28.——The Lambton-Hunt Stakes of 5gs each,
for hunters, 12st.—Two-mile heats.—Eleven Subscribers.

Sir H. T. Vane's br m Buckram, by Oberon..,............... 2 1 1
Mr Witham's b g Cliffe, by Hutton........................... 1 2 2
Mr Allan's br m Plaything, by Oberon 3 3 3
Mr T. Shafto's ch g Rufus, by Horatio 4 4 4
Mr Leaton's ch h Sir Hugh, by Jupiter...................... 5 dis
        Sir Hugh the favourite.—A good race.

FRIDAY, April 29.—Sweepstakes of 10gs each, for hunters, that
never won before the day of naming.—Gentlemen riders.—Four Miles.
—Six Subscribers.

Mr T. Shafto's b m, by Oberon, dam by Stride, 5 yrs old, 11st 9lb
  (Mr Wright) 1
Mr Wilner's br h, by Screveton, 6 yrs old, 12st (Mr T. Sykes).... 2
Mr Mason's ch h Honest Charles, by Hermes, 6 yrs old, 12st (Capt.
  Browne) 3
Mr D. Shafto's b f, by St. George, dam by Pontac, 4 yrs old, 11st
  (Mr Surtees) 4
        Five to 4 against Honest Charles.

The Maiden Plate of 70l. for three-year old colts, 8st 4lb.—Two-mile
                        heats.

Colonel Horton's bay colt, by Bustard, dam by Sir Peter Teazle.. 1 1
Lord Darlington's b c, by St. George 4 2
Mr Thompson's b c Liberty, by L'Orient 3 3
Mr Coulson's ch c Aimwell, by Expectation................. 2 4
        Even betting on Colonel Horton's colt.—A good race.

SATURDAY, April 30.—Handicap Stakes of 10gs each, for hunters.—Gentlemen riders. —Once round and a Distance.—Six Subscribers.

Mr Allan's b h Curricle, aged, 11st 7lb (the Owner) 1
Colonel Seddons's b h Cliffe, by Hutton, 5 yrs old, 11st 10lb (Cap-
  tain Browne) 2
Mr Witham's br m Columbine, aged, 10st 7lb (Mr Robinson)...... 3
Mr Surtees's b m Tipsy, by Ticket, 5 yrs old, 10st (Mr R. Dormer) 4
Mr Lyon's ch m Hetton-Lass, aged, 10st 7lb (the Owner) 5
        3 and 4 to 1 on Cliffe.—A good race.

                                                Match

Match for 100gs.—Two Miles.

Mr Witham's br m Columbine, by Harlequin Junior, 11st 7lb (Mr Tatton Sykes) 1

Colonel Seddons's gr m Betsy, 10st 7lb (Captain Browne) 2

Columbine the favourite.

Match for 50gs.—Two Miles.

Colonel Seddons's b g Cliffe, by Hutton, 11st 7lb (Mr Tatton Sykes) 1

Mr J. Maling's bay hunter, 12st (the Owner) 2

Cliffe the favourite.

NEWMARKET FIRST SPRING MEETING.

(Ages as if the Meeting had taken place in April.)

MONDAY, May 2.—Match for One Hundred Guineas, Ditch-in.
Lord C. Somerset's b c White-Rose, by Beningbrough, 3 yrs old, 9st 2lb (T. Goodisson) 1

General Grosvenor's ch g Roast-Beef, 4 yrs old, 8st............. 2

Two to 1 on White-Rose.—Won very easy.

Sweepstakes of 100gs each, h. ft.—Rowley Mile.

Mr Craven's br c Beau Nash, by Trumpator, 8st 5lb (W. Arnold).. 1

Mr Hallett's br c, by Kill-Devil, dam by Trumpator, 8st 2lb...... 2

Mr Scrope's b c The Monk, 8st 2lb (dead)......................pd

Seven to 4 and 2 to 1 on Beau Nash.—Won easy.

Produce Stakes of 100gs each, h. ft. colts, 8st 4lb, fillies, 8st.—Across the Flat.—Seven Subscribers.

Duke of Grafton's br c Vandyke, by Sir Peter Teazle, out of Dabchick, by Pot8o's (W. Clift) 1

Mr Lake's b f Oberea, by Sorcerer, out of Deceit................ 2

Lord Grosvenor's b f Isis, by Sir Peter........................ 3

Sir F. Standish's ch c, by Mr Teazle, out of Parisot 4

Sir C. Bunbury's b f Agnes, by Sorcerer, out of Amelia.......... 5

Six and 7 to 4 on Isis, 2 to 1 against Sir F. Standish's colt, 2 to 1 agst Agnes, and 8 to 1 against Vandyke.—Won in a common canter.

The Prince's Stakes of 100gs each, h. ft. colts, 8st 7lb, fillies, 8st 4lb, Across the Flat.—Six Subscribers.

Mr Mellish's b c Bradbury, by Delpini, dam by Young Marsk (F. Buckle) 1

Duke of Grafton's filly, by Coriander, out of Peppermint, by Highflyer... 2

Two to 1 on Bradbury.—Won very easy.

Sweepstakes of 100gs each, h. ft. colts, 8st 5lb, fillies, 8st 2lb.—Across the Flat.—Seven Subscribers.

Duke of Grafton's br c Vandyke, by Sir Peter Teazle (W. Clift).... 1

Mr Howorth's b c Weaver, by Shuttle 2

Lord Grosvenor's b c Chester, by Sir Peter.................... 3

Lord Foley's b f, by Worthy, out of Miss Fury................. 4

Five and 6 to 4 against Chester, 5 to 2 against Vandyke, and 7 to 2 agst Weaver.—Won in a canter.

C 2   Match

Match for 100gs.—Across the Flat.

General Grosvenor's b c Rifleman, by Asparagus, dam by Justice, 2 yrs old, 6st 3lb 1

Mr Vansittart's ch f Momentilla, 3 yrs old, 8st 10lb............. 2

Three and 4 to 1 on Momentilla.—Won very easy.

Match for 50gs.—Abingdon Mile.

Lord Stawell's Brother to Bustard, by Buzzard, 8st 3lb (W. Arnold) 1

General Grosvenor's ch c John O'Gaunt, 8st.................... 2

Seven to 4 on the Brother to Bustard.—A very near race.

Match for 200gs.—Abingdon Mile.

Lord Lowther's b c Trafalgar, by Gohanna, 8st 8lb (W. Arnold).... 1

Lord Foley's br f Pipylina, 8st................................ 2

Seven to 4 and 2 to 1 on Trafalgar.—Won easy.

Match for 100gs.—Abingdon Mile.

Sir O. Turner's ch c Mr Gundy, by Star, 8st 11b (F. Collinson)...... 1

Sir J. Hawkins's br c Clermont, 8st 7lb........................ 2

Six and 7 to 4 on Mr Gundy.—Won by half a neck.

Match for 100gs.—Abingdon Mile.

Lord Sackville's b h Bustard, by Buzzard, 8st 4lb (W. Wheatley).. 1

Mr Wilson's br h Pavilion, 8st 4lb............................ 2

Seven to 4 on Bustard.—Won easy.

Match for 100gs.——Abingdon Mile.

Lord Stawell's b c Deceiver, by Buzzard, 8st (W. Arnold) 1

Mr Payne's b c Ferdinand, 6st 10lb 2

Five to 2 and 3 to 1 on Deceiver.—A good race.

Match for 100gs.—Two-year Olds' Course.

Mr Shakespear's b c Discount, by Teddy the Grinder, 8st 4lb (W. Arnold) 1

Mr Wyndham's b c, by Whiskey, out of Minion, 8st 4lb.......... 2

Six and 7 to 4 on Discount.—Won tolerably easy.

Match for 100gs.—Two-year Olds' Course.

Mr Watson's Brother to Fathom, by Trumpator, 6st 3lb (a Boy).... 1

Mr Payne's b c Tudor, 8st 9lb 2

Eleven to 8 alternately.—A very good race.

Match for 200gs.—Ditch-in.

Sir John Honywood's br c Bacchanal, by St. George, 7st 4lb (C. Goodisson) 1

Duke of Grafton's b m Parasol, 8st 9lb 2

Two to 1 on Parasol.—Won easy.

Mr Shakespear's ch h Brainworm, by Buzzard, 8st 6lb, received 10gs compromise from Mr Fermor's b h Hippomenes, 8st.—Ab. M. 100gs.

Mr Wilson's b c Smuggler, by Hambletonian, received 60gs compromise from Lord Foley's br c Paris, 8st 5lb each.—Ditch-in, 200gs, h. ft.

Lord Foley's br f Pipylina, by Sir Peter Teazle, 7st, received 20gs compromise from Mr Shakespear's br h Wormwood, 8st 7lb.—Ab. M. 200gs, h. ft,

Lord

Lord Foley's ch h Captain Absolute, by John Bull, 9st 12lb, received 25gs compromise from General Grosvenor's ch c John-o'-Gaunt, 8st.—Across the Flat, 100gs, h. ft.

TUESDAY, May 3.—Match for 50gs.—Two-year Olds' Course.

Mr Sitwell's b f Gooseander, by Hambletonian, out of Rally, 8st (J. Goodisson.) 1
Mr F. Craven's br f Fly-by-Night, 8st........................ 2
Five to 1 on Gooseander.—Won easy.

Match for 200gs.—Across the Flat.
Lord Lowther's ch h Brainworm, by Buzzard, 9st (S. Chifney).... 1
Mr Fermor's br c Stripling, 7st.............................. 2
Seven to 4 and 2 to 1 on Stripling.—A fine race.

Match for 100gs.—Across the Flat.
Sir C. Bunbury's br colt Rambler, by Whiskey, 8st 7lb (F. Buckle).. 1
Sir C. Turner's ch f Thomasina, 8st 7lb..................... 2
Thirteen to 8 on Thomasina.—A fine race.

Match for 300gs.—Across the Flat.
Mr Shakespear's ch h Zodiac, by St. George, 8st 5lb (W. Arnold).. 1
Lord Grosvenor's b m Violante, 8st.......................... 2
Eleven to 5 on Violante.—Won very easy.

Sweepstakes of 100gs each, h. ft. colts, 8st 7lb, fillies, 8st 3lb.—Abingdon Mile.—Twelve Subscribers.

Lord Grosvenor's bay colt Chester, by Sir Peter Teazle (F. Buckle).. 1
Lord Grosvenor's b c, by Meteor, out of Hind................. 2
Sir F. Standish's b f, by Sir Peter Teazle, out of Eagle's dam...... 3
Mr Wilson's b c, by Agonistes, out of Bennington's Sister.......... 4
Sir J. Shelley's filly, by Buzzard, bought of Mr Panton.......... 5
Mr Lake's br c Noyeau, Brother to Rumbo.................... 6
Six and 7 to 4 against Chester.—Won very easy.

The Claret Stakes of 200gs each, h. ft. colts, 8st 7lb.—Ditch-in.—The second withdrew the Stake.—Eight Subscribers.

D. of Grafton's b c Musician, by Worthy (W. Clift)............ 1
Lord Darlington's b c Giles Scroggins, by Sir Solomon............ 2
Lord Grosvenor's b c Eaton, by Sir Peter.................... 3
Mr Mellish's b c Comrade, by Beningbrough.................... 4
Sir F. Standish's b c, by Sir Peter, dam by Volunteer............ 5
Six to 5 against Giles Scroggins, 11 to 5 against Eaton, and 6 to 1 against Musician.—Won very easy.

Fifty Pounds for four-year olds and upwards.—The last three miles of B. C.

Lord Egremont's bay colt Canopus, by Gohanna, 4 years old, 7st 9lb (S. Barnard) 1
Lord Sackville's ch h Prospero, 6 years, 8st 7lb............... 2
Major Wilson's b h Vivaldi, aged, 8st 7lb................... 3
Four to 1 on Canopus.—Won easy.

The

The King's Plate of 100gs, for mares, all ages.—The last three Miles of B. C.

Lord Grosvenor's bay, Violantè, by John Bull, 5 years old, 9st 10lb, (F. Buckle)... 1
Lord G. H. Cavendish's bay, Pagoda, 4 years, 9st 4lb.............. 2
       Twenty to 1 on Violantè.—Won very easy.

WEDNESDAY, May 4.—Match for 100gs.—Two middle Miles of B. C.
Mr Sitwell's br c Taurus, by Sir Peter Teazle, 8st 8lb (W. Wilkinson) 1
Mr Hallett's ch f Jewess, 8st.................................... 2
       Four and 5 to 1 on Taurus.

Match for 100gs.—Two-year Olds' Course.
Lord Foley's b f, by Worthy, out of Miss Fury, 7st 12lb (a Boy, allowed to be a good rider)..................................... 1
Mr Craven's br c Beau Nash, 7st 12lb............................. 2
       Four to 1 on Beau Nash.—Won easy.

The Newmarket Stakes of 50gs each, h. ft. colts, 8st 7lb, fillies, 8st 2lb.—Ditch Mile.—Sixteen Subscribers.

Duke of Grafton's ch f Morel, by Sorcerer, out of Hornby Lass, (W. Clift) 1
Lord Grosvenor's b c Chester, by Sir Peter Teazle............... 2
Lord Grosvenor's b c, by Meteor, out of Hind................... 3
Mr D. Radcliffe's br c Tekeli, by Waxy......................... 4
Lord G. Osborne's br f, by Sorcerer, out of Drowsy............. 5
Five to 4 against Chester, 2 to 1 against Morel, and 8 to 1 against Tekeli.—Won very easy.

Fifty Pounds for three, four, and five-year Olds.—B. C.
Lord Egremont's bay colt Canopus, by Gohanna, 4 years old, 8st 11lb (S. Barnard)... 1
Mr Goulburn's ch c Romeo 3 years old, 7st 5lb.................. 2
       Twenty to 1 on Canopus.

Sweepstakes of 100gs each, h. ft. for four-year Olds.—Ditch-in.—Five Subscribers.
Sir C. Turner's bay colt Thorn, by Beningbrough, 8st 11lb. (W. Arnold).. 1
Sir J. Hawkins's br c Clermont, 7st 6lb......................... 2
Mr Wyndham's b c, by Schedoni, 7st 7lb......................... 3
Even betting, and 6 to 5 on Clermont, 7 to 4 and 2 to 1 against Thorn, and 6 to 1 against Mr. Wyndham's colt.—Won quite easy.

THURSDAY, May 5.—Match for 100gs.—Beacon Course.
Duke of Grafton's b m Parasol, by Pot8o's, 8st (W. Clift)........ 1
Mr Sitwell's br c Taurus, 7st 2lb............................... 2
       Two to 1 and 5 to 2 on Parasol.

Lord Lowther's Brainworm, 8st 8lb, and Mr Fermor's Cerberus, 8st. Ab. M. 100gs.—Ran a dead heat.—This was one of the finest races ever run.

                                    Sweepstakes

Sweepstakes of 50gs each, h. ft. for three-year Olds.—Two-year Olds' Course.—Eight Subscribers.

Lord Darlington's b c Giles Scroggins, by Sir Solomon, 8st 9lb (S. Chifney) 1
Mr Ladbroke's b c Corsican, 7st 6lb........................ 2
Lord Grosvenor's br c Bullrush, 7st 7lb..................... 3
Lord Stawell's b f Pantina, 7st 13lb........................ 4
Mr Fermor's ch c Bantum, 7st 7lb........................... 5
Mr Howorth's b f Lauretta, 7st 8lb......................... 6
Mr Lake's br f Nymphina, 7st 6lb........................... 7

Five to 2 against Giles Scroggins, 3 to 1 against Corsican, 3 to 1 against Pantina, 5 to 1 against Nymphina, 7 to 1 against Bantum, 8 to 1 against Lauretta, and 10 to 1 against Bullrush.—A fine race.

Match for 100gs.—Two-year Olds' Course.
Sir G. Turner's ch c Mr Gundy, by Star, 8st (W. Arnold)........ 1
Sir C. Bunbury's ch c Bull-Calf, 7st 5lb...................... 2
Six to 4 on Mr. Gundy.—Won cleverly.

Match for 100gs.—Two-year Olds' Course.
Mr Shakespear's ch h Zodiac, by St. George, 8st 7lb (W. Arnold).. 1
Mr Andrew's b m Lydia, 7st 10lb............................ 2
Six to 1 on Zodiac.

The King's Plate of 100gs, for four-year olds and upwards.—The last three miles of B. C.
Mr Sitwell's br c Taurus, by Sir Peter Teazle, 4 years old, 11st.................................... walked over.
Trafalgar, Violante, Canopus, Thorn, Pavilion, Parasol, and Clermont, were also entered, but withdrawn.

Match for 50gs.—Ditch-in.
Major Wilson's br c Brown Stout, by Sir Peter Teazle, 9st (rode by the Groom)... 1
Mr Emden's b f Miss Prince, 7st 8lb......................... 2
Five to 2 on Miss Prince.

Mr Vausittart's b h Currycomb, by Buzzard, 8st 10lb, received 50gs compromise from the Duke of Grafton's b c Musician, 7st 2lb.—Ab. M. 200gs, h. ft.

Sir J. Honywood's br c Bacchanal, by St. George, 8st, received forfeit from Mr Fermor's br c Brighton, 8st 3lb.—Ab. M. 200gs, h. ft.

Sir J. Shelley's br c Clasher, by Sir Peter Teazle, 8st 11lb, received forfeit from Mr Lake's br f Nymphina, 8st.—Ab. M. 200gs, h. ft.

FRIDAY, May 6.—Sweepstakes of 25gs each.—Two-year Olds' Course.
Mr Sitwell's b f Gooseander, by Hambletonian, out of Pipylina's dam, 8st 6lb... 1
Mr Watson's b c Hymen, Brother to Fathom, 7st 12lb........... 2
Colonel Childers's ch c, Brother to Baron, by Stamford, 7st 11lb.... 3
Mr Elwes's b c, by Agonistes, out of a Sister to Bennington, 8st.... 4
Five to 4 on Hymen, and 7 to 4 against Gooseander.—Won very easy.
Sweepstakes

Sweepstakes of 25gs each.—Two-year Olds' Course.

Mr Batson's ch c Charmer, by Whiskey, 4 years old, 8st 7lb
   (F. Buckle).. 1
Mr Cave Brown's b f Miltonia, by Patriot, 3 years old, 6st 9lb...... 2
Lord Grosvenor's b f Isis, by Sir Peter, 2 years old, 6st 9lb........ 3
Lord G. H. Cavendish's Buff, by Trumpator, 2 years old, 6st 4
Mr Goddard's ch h Achilles, 4 years old, 9st.................... 5
Seven to 4 against Isis, 5 to 2 against Achilles, and 3 to 1 against
            Charmer.—Won very easy.

Match for 200gs·—Yearling Course.

Lord Foley's b f Blowing, by Buzzard, 8st 7lb (F. Buckle)........ 1
Lord Lowther's b c Trafalgar, 8st 7lb (S. Chifney).............. 2
     Five to 4 on Trafalgar.—Won by a head.

The Subscription Handicap Plate of 50l. for horses, &c. all ages.—
             Ditch Mile.

Mr Girdler's b c, by Worthy, 4 years old, 8st 1lb (J. Wheatley).... 1
Mr Batson's ch c Charmer, 4 years old, 8st 8lb.................. 2
Duke of Grafton's b f Vanity, 4 years old, 8st 10lb............. 3
   The following also started, but were not placed :
Mr Shakespear's br h Wormwood, 5 years old, 9st 10lb............. 0
Lord Lowther's br h Sot, 5 years old, 9st 10lb.................. 0
Mr Wilson's b h Pavilion, 6 years old, 9st 0
Sir C. Bunbury's ch c Snug, 4 years old, 8st 10lb 0
Lord Jersey's b h Langton, 5 years old, 8st 8lb................. 0
Mr Kellermann's ch c Jamaica, 4 years old, 8st 8lb............. 0
Lord Foley's b f Pipylina, 4 years old, 8st 8lb.................. 0
Sir C. Turner's ch f Thomasina, 3 years old, 8st 7lb........... 0
Mr Hallett's ch f Jewess, 4 years old, 8st 5lb.................. 0
Lord Grosvenor's b c Osiris, 3 years old, 8st 4lb 0
Mr Wyndham's b c, by Whiskey, 2 years old, 8st 9lb............ 0
Mr Panton's b c Ernest, by Buzzard, 2 years old, 5st 9lb......... 0
  Curryeomb, White-Rose, Lydia, Comrade, Stripling, Achilles, Gaiety,
Miltonia, and two others, were also entered, but withdrawn.—Three to
1 against Charmer, and 20 to 1 against Mr Girdler's colt.—A good race.

Match for 100gs.—Two-year Olds' Course.

Lord G. H. Cavendish's b f, by Gouty, 7st (a Boy).............. 1
Duke of St. Alban's b h Prodigal, 8st 12lb..................... 2
     Seven to 4 on the filly.—Won very easy.

Lord Lowther's br h 'Tot, by Trumpator, 8st 12lb, received forfeit
from Mr Fermor's ch c Bantum, 8st.—Two-yr Olds' Course, 100gs, h.ft.

Mr. Lake's b f Oberea, by Sorcerer, received 100gs compromise from
Sir J. Shelley's filly, by Buzzard, bought of Mr Panton, 8st 4lb each,
Ab. M. 200gs.

CHESTER MEETING.

MONDAY, May 2.—Sweepstakes of 25gs each, for three-yr old fillies,
   8st.—Once round the Course and a Distance.—Ten Subscribers.
Mr J. Richardson's bay, by Stamford, out of Coriolanus's dam, by Pegasus (J. Jackson).. 1
                                     Mr

Mr. R. Benson's bay Overproof, by Shuttle...................... 2
Sir W. W. Wynne's bay Deva, by Meteor...................... 3
Lord Stamford's brown Petronilla, by St. George............... 4
Lord Wilton's bay, Sister to Bucephalus....................... 5
Sir T. Stanley's bay, by Alexander, dam by Anvil............... 6
Mr. E. L. Hodgson's grey, by Shuttle....................... 7
General Grosvenor's bay, by King Bladud..................... 8
Six and 7 to 4 against Petronilla, 5 to 2 against Overproof, 3 to 1
   against Deva, and 8 to 1 against Mr Richardson's filly.—Overproof
   made play ; a fine race, but won easy at the end.

The Maiden Plate of 50l. for all ages ; 3-year olds, a feather ; 4-year
   old colts, 8st 6lb, fillies, 8st 3lb.—Four-mile heats.—The second re-
   ceived 10l.
Sir W. W. Wynne's bay filly, Mademoiselle Prisle, 4 years old.. 1 2 1
Mr Harris's b g Viper, by Serpent, 4 years old................ 5 1 2
Sir T. Mostyn's br c, by Mr. Teazle, 3 years old............... 2 3 3
Lord Derby's br f Margaret, 4 years old..................... 3 4 dr
Mr Bettinson's b f, by Beningbrough, 3 years old............ 4 5 dr
Five and 6 to 4 against Margaret, 2 and 3 to 1 against Mademoiselle
   Prisle, and 6 to 1 against Mr Harris's colt; after the first heat,
   5 and 6 to 4 on Mademoiselle Prisle; after the second heat, even
   betting on the field.—Won by half a neck.—Sir Thomas Mos-
   tyn's colt swerved twice in running for the third heat; but he re-
   covered his ground, and made play during the remainder of the race.
   Mr. Tarleton's br filly, Pussy-Cat, by Mr Teazle, received forfeit from
Mr Egerton's br colt, by John Bull, out of Cordelia, 8st each.—Two
Miles, 100gs, h. ft.

TUESDAY, May 3.—Sweepstakes of 15gs each, for maiden horses,
&c.—Two Miles.—Ten Subscribers.
Mr Clifton's br colt, by Sir Solomon, dam by Pot8o's, 4 years old, 8st
   (T. Carr)... 1.
Mr Egerton's b c, by Gohanna, 3 years old, 6st 12lb........... 2
Lord Scarbrough's br c, by Sir Solomon, 4 years old, 8st.......... 3
                  The following also started, but were not placed :
Mr E. Hodgson's gr f, by Shuttle, 3 years old, 6st 9lb........... 0
Mr Grosvenor's b f, by King Bladud, 3 years old, 6st 9lb......... 0
Mr R. Benson's br f Dimple, 3 years old, 6st 9lb................ 0
Mr Hanmer's b g, by Stickler, 4 years old, 8st................. 0
Mr Acker's ch c Apollo, 3 years old, 6st 12lb................ bolted
Six to 4 against Apollo, 5 to 2 against Mr Egerton's colt, 3 to 1
   against Mr Clifton's colt, and high odds against any other,—Won by
   half a length.

The Earl of Chester's Plate of 100gs, for horses, &c.—Thrice round
                  the Course.
Sir W. W. Wynne's b h General Benningsen, 5 years old, 9st. 6lb.. 1
Mr. Clifton's br colt, by Sir Solomon, 4 years old,
   8st 2lb... 2
Duke of Hamilton's br h Banker, 5 years old, 9st............... 3

Lord Scarbrough's br c Hospodar, 4 years old, 8st 2lb............ 4
Mr Smith's b g, by Sir Peter, aged, 9st........................ 5
Mr Benson's b c, by Pegasus, 4 years old, 8st 9lb............bolted
Six and 7 to 4 against Hospodar, and 7 to 4 against General Benningsen.
  Mr Clifton's colt and Banker made play, and it was as fine a race as
  ever was run, but won cleverly at the end.

Sixty Guineas (clear) the gift of Thomas Grosvenor, and John Egerton,
  Esqrs. for three and four-year old colts and fillies.—Two-mile beats.
Mr Richardson's b f, by Stamford, out of Coriolanus's dam, 3 years
  old, 6st 6lb....................................... 1 1
Mr Goodall's b f Miss Whitley, 4 years old, 8st 1lb............ 4 2
Mr Bettison's br f, by Sir Peter, 3 years old, 6st 6lb............. 3 3
Lord Grosvenor's b f Pearl, 4 years old, 8st 1lb.......... 2 dr
Mr Hodgson's ch f Shuttle, 3 years old, 6st 6lb.............. bolted
Two to 1 on Mr Richardson's filly; and in running the second heat,
          5 to 1 she won.—Won very easy.

WEDNESDAY, May 4.—Sweepstakes of 20gs each, for 3-year old
colts, 8st 7lb, fillies, 8st 3lb.—Once round the Course and a Distance;
starting at the Distance-Chair.—Five Subscribers.
Mr Egerton's br c, by Gohanna......................... 1
Sir W. W. Wynne's b f Deva, by Meteor,.................. 2
Mr Benson's b f Overproof, by Shuttle.................. 3
Mr Acker's ch c Apollo, by Hyacinthus.................. 4
Mr F. R. Price's gr c Pretender, by Delpini.................. 5
  Two to 1 against Apollo, 3 to 1 against Mr Egerton's colt, and 9 to
          2 against Deva.—Won cleverly.

The Annual City Plate of 60gs, (clear) given by the Corporation, free
          for any horse, &c.—Four-mile heats.
Sir W. W. Wynne's b h General Benningsen, by Meteor, 4 years
  old, 8st 4lb.. 1 1
Lord Grey's ch h St Domingo, 5 years old, 8st 4lb............. 2 2
Even betting before and after the heat.—A better contested race was
  never witnessed, and won with great difficulty, by not more than half
  a length each heat.

          Match for 100gs.—Four Miles.
Mr H. Trafford's Slapbang.................................. 1
Sir Thomas Stanley's Stiffrump............................ 2
          Six to 4 on Slapbang.—Won easy.

THURSDAY, May 5.—The Cup, value 60gs, the gift of Earl Grosvenor, free for any horse, &c.—Four-mile heats.
Sir W. W. Wynne's b h General Benningsen, by Meteor, 5 years
  old, 8st 2lb.. 1 1
Gen. Grosvenor's b f, by King Bladud, 3 years old, a feather...... 3 2
Mr Clifton's b m Josephina, aged, 8st 12lb.................. 2 dr
Six to four on General Benningsen, 7 to 4 against Josephina, and 6 to 1
  against the King Bladud filly; after the heat, and in running, 6 and
  10 to 1 on General Benningsen.—Won easy.

                                        Sweepstakes

Sweepstakes of 20gs each for all ages.—Two Miles.—Seven Subscribers.

Lord Grey's b colt, Gustavus, by Beningbrough, 4 years old, 7st 12lb 1
Mr Clifton's b m Josephina, aged, 9st 2lb. 2
Duke of Hamilton's b h Grazier, 5 years old, 8st 10lb............ 3
Mr Ackers's br h Luck's-All, 5 years old, 8st 10lb................ 4
Sir W. W. Wynne's Mad: Prisle, 4 years old, 7st 9lb....,....... 5
Lord Scarbrough's br c Hospodar, 4 years old, 7st 12lb....:....... 6
Two to 1 against Gustavus, 2 to 1 against Josephina, 3 to 1 against
Luck's-All, 7 to 2 against Hospodar, and 4 to 1 against Mademoiselle
Prisle.—Won easy.

FRIDAY, May 6.—A Handicap Stakes of 10gs each, with 20gs added
by the Stewards, for Horses, &c. all ages.—Two Miles.—Four Subscribers:
Sir W. W. Wynne's br f Mademoiselle Prisle, by Sir Peter Teazle,
4 years old!.... 1
Mr C. Smith's b g, by Sir Peter Teazle, aged................... 2
Lord Grosvenor's b f Pearl, 5 years old...................... 3
Six to 4 against Mademoiselle Prisle, 2 to 1 against Pearl, and 7 to 2
against Mr Smith's gelding.—Won easy.

The Ladies' Purse of 50l. for all ages.—Four-mile heats.
Mr Goodall's b f Miss Whitley, by Old Tatt, 4 years old, 7st 5lb 1 2 1
Mr Brooke's b h Banker, 5 years old, 8st 5lb (received 10l.).... 3 1 2
Mr Harris's b g Viper, 4 years old, 7st 5lb................. 2 3 dr
Five to four on the field ; after the first heat, 6 to 4 on Miss Whitley ;
after the second heat, even betting.—A good race.
Sir W. W. Wynne's b f Deva, by Meteor, received forfeit from Mr
E. L. Hodgson's ch f by Shuttle, out of Miss Muston, 8st each.—
Two Miles, 100gs. h. ft.

NEWMARKET SECOND SPRING MEETING.

MONDAY, May 16.—Match for 50gs.—Two-year Olds' Course.—
Mr Cave Browne's b f Miltonia, by Patriot, 8st 2lb (S. Chifney) 1
Mr F. Craven's br f Fly-by-Night, 8st 2lb...................... 2
Seven to 2 on Miltonia.—Won easy.

Match for 50gs.—Rowley Mile.
General Grosvenor's b c Rifleman, by Asparagus, 7st (a Boy)...... 1
Lord Lowther's ch m, by Master Bagot, 8st 10lb................ 2
Seven to 2 on Rifleman.—Won easy.

Match for 100gs.—Abingdon Mile.
Mr Payne's b c Ferdinand, by John Bull, 8st 4lb (F. Buckle)...... 1
Mr Vansittart's ch f Momentilla, 8st 4lb...................... 2
Eleven to 8 on Ferdinand.

Match for 200gs.—Abingdon Mile.
Mr Lake's gr h Tiny, by Whiskey, 5 years old, a feather (Young Day) 1
Mr

Mr D. Radcliffe's ch h Selim, 6 years old, 11st............... 2
Eleven to 8 on Tim.—Won very easy.
Match for 100gs.—Abingdon Mile.

Lord G. H. Cavendish's b h Dreadnought, by Buzzard, aged, 7st 6lb
  (W. Wheatley) 1
Sir J. Shelley's br h Clasher, 5 years old, 7st 11lb............. 2
Six to 5 on Dreadnought.—A fine race.
Match for 200gs.—Abingdon Mile.

Lord Sackville's br h Bustard, by Buzzard, aged, 8st 3lb (W.
  Wheatley) 1
Lord Lowther's ch h Brainworm, aged, 9st.................. 2
Eleven to 8 on Bustard.—Won very easy.
Match for 100gs.—Abingdon Mile.

Mr Fermor's br c Stripling, by Totteridge, 8st (F. Buckle)....... 1
Sir J. Honywood's br c Bacchanal, 8st...................... 2
Eleven to 5 on Bacchanal.—Won easy.
Match for 200gs.—First half of Abingdon Mile.

Mr Wyndham's b f Mouse, by Gohanna, 8st (S. Barnard)....... 1
Sir C. Turner's ch c Mr Gundy, 8st...................... 2
Six and 7 to 4 on Mouse.—A good race, and won by a head.
Match for 100gs.—Two-year Olds' Course.

Mr Shakespear's b c Discount, by Teddy the Grinder, 8st 2lb (W.
  Arnold) 1
Duke of Grafton's Brother to Forester, by Grouse, 8st 2lb........ 2
Six to 4 on Discount.
Sweepstakes of 100gs each, h. ft.—Across the Flat.

Sir J. Shelley's filly, by Buzzard, bought of Mr Panton, 8st 7lb .. 0 1
Duke of Grafton's filly, by Coriander, out of Peppermint, 8st 7lb
  (W. Clift) 0 2
Lord C. Somerset's b c Ethelfred, by Beningbrough, 8st 7lb...... 3
General Grosvenor's gr c Welch-Fusileer, by Dapple, 8st........ 4
Seven to 4 against the Duke of Grafton's filly, and 11 to 5 against Sir
  J. Shelley's filly.—S. Chifney rode the Buzzard filly for the dead heat ;
  and F. Buckle for the second, when she won easy.   —

Match for 100gs.—Ditch-in.

Sir C. Turner's b h Thorn, by Beningbrough, 5 years old, 8st 4lb (W.
  Arnold) 1
Lord Darlington's b c Master Goodall, (late Giles Scroggins) 4 years
  old, 8st 7lb.. 2
Seven to 4 and 2 to 1 on Master Goodall.—A fine race.
Sweepstakes of 100gs each, h. ft.—Beacon Course.

Mr Lloyd's b h Cardinal Beaufort, by Gohanna, 6 years old, 7st 5lb
  (Charles Goodisson)................................. 1
Lord Grosvenor's b m Meteora, 6 years old, 8st.............. 2
Lord Foley's ch h Captain Absolute, aged, 7st 4lb............. 3
Mr Wilson's br h Pavilion, aged, 8st 2lb.................. pd
Five and 6 to 4 on Meteora, 5 to 2 against Cardinal Beaufort, and
4 to 1 agst Captain Absolute.—A good race.

Sweepstakes

Sweepstakes of 100gs each, h. ft. for 4-year old colts, 8st 7lb, fillies, 8st 2lb.—The last three Miles of B. C.—Nine Subscribers.

Lord Grosvenor's b c Eaton, by Sir Peter Teazle (F. Buckle) 1
Duke of Grafton's b c Barbarian, by Worthy 2
Mr Fermor's b c Hawk, by Buzzard 3

Two to 1 on Eaton.—Won very easy.

Lord Lowther's Brainworm, by Buzzard, received 10gs compromise from Mr Fermor's Hippomenes, 8st 2lb each. — Across the Flat, 100gs, h. ft.

Mr F. Craven's Fly-by-Night, by Trumpator, 8st 5lb, received 15gs compromise from Mr Hallett's br c, by Kill-Devil, dam by Trumpator, 8st 3lb.—R. M. 50gs.

Duke of Grafton's Parasol, by Pot8o's, 8st 12lb, received 100gs compromise from Sir C. Turner's Thorn, 8st.—B. C. 200gs.

TUESDAY, May 17.—Match for 100gs.—Two-year Olds' Course.
Mr Goddard's ch h Achilles, by Young Woodpecker, 5 years old, 7st 2lb (C. Goodisson) 1
Mr Andrew's b m Lydia, 6 years old, 8st 7lb 2

Five to 4 on Lydia.

Fifty Pounds for three year old colts, 8st 4lb, fillies, 8st.—Rowley Mile.
Major Wilson's ch c Juniper, by Whiskey, out of Jenny Spinner, (W. Clift) 1
Lord Grosvenor's b c Sun-Beam, by Meteor 2
Mr Watson's b c Hymen, by Trumpator 3

The following also started, but were not placed :

Lord Rous's b c Wood-Demon, by Lop 0
General Grosvenor's b f, by Stickler 0
Mr Abbey's b f Clorinda, by Hercules 0
Mr Panton's b c Ernest, by Buzzard 0
Sir F. Standish's ch c, by Mr Teazle 0

Even betting, Juniper and Sun-Beam against the field; 5 to 2 against Sun-Beam, 3 to 1 against Juniper, and 4 to 1 against Hymen.—Won very easy.

Handicap Plate of 50l. by Subscription, (being the third of the three 50l. Plates) for three-year olds' and upwards.—Across the Flat.
Sir C. Bunbury's ch h Snug, by Whiskey, 5 years old, 8st 10lb (a Boy) 1
Mr Cave Browne's br h Pavilion, aged, 9st 2lb 2
Mr Smith's br h Gaiety, 6 years old, 8st 8lb 3
Mr Girdler's b h by Worthy, 5 years old, 8st 11lb 4
Sir F. Standish's br c, by Sir Peter Teazle, dam by Volunteer, 4 years old, 8st 5lb 5
General Grosvenor's ch c John-o'-Gaunt, 3 years old, 6st 6lb 6

Even betting, Pavilion and Mr Girdler's horse against the field; 5 to 2 against Pavilion, 3 to 1 against Mr Girdler's horse, and 10 to 1 against Snug.—Won easy.

Match

Match for 50gs.—From the Turn of the Lands in.

Lord C. Somerset's b c White-Rose, by Beningbrough, 4 years old, 9st 5lb (T. Goodisson) 1

General Grosvenor's ch colt John-o'Gaunt, by Buzzard, 3 years old, 8st (F. Buckle) 2

Five to 2 on White-Rose.—A fine race.

Lord Lowther's Tot, by Trumpator, 9st, received 5gs compromise from Lord C. Somerset's White-Rose, 7st.—Across the Flat, 50gs.

Mr Payne's Tudor, by John Bull, 8st 4lb, received forfeit from Sir J. Shelley's Clasher, 8st 2lb.—Y. C. 200gs, 50gs ft.

Lord Foley's Cecilia, by Worthy, 8st 10lb, received 50gs compromise from Lord Lowther's Trafalgar, 8st 9lb.—Two-year Olds' Course, 200gs, h. ft.

Mr Craven's Beau Nash, by Trumpator, received 25gs compromise from General Grosvenor's Welch-Fusileer, 8st 2lb each.—Two-year Olds' Course, 100gs, h. ft.

WEDNESDAY, May 18.—The Jockey-Club Plate of 50gs, for 4-year olds' and upwards.—Beacon Course.

Mr Lake's b f Nymphina, by Gouty, 4 years old, 7st 2lb (a Boy) 1

General Gower's br m Pelisse, aged, 8st 11lb...................... 2

Lord Sackville's ch h Prospero, aged, 8st 11lb.................... 3

Lord Lowther's br h Tot, 6 years old, 8st 9lb.................... 4

Lord Foley's ch h Captain Absolute, aged, 8st 11lb.............. 5

Six and 7 to 4 against Prospero, 3 and 4 to 1 against Nymphina, 4 to 1 against Pelisse, 7 to 1 against Tot, and 8 to 1 against Captain Absolute.—A fine race.

Sweepstakes of 100gs each, h. ft. for four-year olds.—Across the Flat.

Mr Fermor's br c Brighton, by Gohanna, out of Cyprus's dam, 7st 2lb (F. Buckle) 1

Duke of Grafton's b c Musician, 7st 10lb 2

Mr Kellerman's b f L'Huile de Venus, 8st 3lb 3

Sir C. Bunbury's b o Rambler, 7st 2lb 4

Six to 4 against Musician, 6 and 7 to 4 against Brighton, 4 to 1 against Rambler, and 7 to 1 against L'Huile de Venus.—A capital race.

Match for 200gs.—Two-year Olds' Course.

Mr Craven's br c Beau Nash, by Trumpator, 3 years old, 7st (J. Goodisson) 1

Mr Payne's b c Tudor, 4 years old, 9st.................... 2

Seven to 4 on Beau Nash.—Won easy.

Match for 100gs.—Two-year Olds' Course.

Duke of Grafton's b c Barbarian, by Worthy, 5 years old, 8st 9lb (W. Clift).. 1

Lord Foley's b f Cecilia, by Worthy, 3 years old, 7st........... 2

Seven to 4 and 2 to 1 on Cecilia.—Won easy.

Match for 50gs.—First half of Ab. Mile.

Mr Craven's br c Beau Nash, by Trumpator, 3 years old, 7st (J. Goodisson) 1

Sir

Sir J. Shelley's br h Clasher, 5 years old, 8st 8lb................ 2
Six to 5 on Clasher.—Won easy.

Match for 50gs.—Two-year Olds' Course.
Lord G. H. Cavendish's b m Pagoda, by Sir Peter Teazle, 5 years
old, 8st 1lb (W. Wheatley)................................. 1
Duke of Grafton's b c Barbarian, 4 years old, 8st 1lb.............. 2
Six to 5 on Pagoda.—Won easy.

General Grosvenor's b c Woodcutter, by Lop, 8st, received 40gs compromise from Mr Howorth's b f Lauretta, 8st 7lb.—Ditch-in, 200gs.

THURSDAY, May 19.—Match for 100gs.—Beacon Course.
Mr Andrew's b c Thorn, by Beningbrough, 5 years old, 8st 8lb
(W. Clift)... 1
Mr Cave Browne's br h Pavilion, aged, 8st 1lb.................... 2
Six to 4 on Pavilion.—Won very easy.

Match for 100gs.—Abingdon Mile.
Mr Sitwell's br c Clinker, by Sir Peter Teazle, 8st 3lb (T. Goodisson) 1
Mr Shakespear's h c Discount, 8st............................. 2
Four and 5 to 1 on Clinker.—Won in a canter.

Match for 200gs.—Abingdon Mile.
Mr Vansittart's ch f Momentilla, by a Brother to Repeator, 8st 2lb
(S. Chifney)... 1
Lord Grosvenor's br c Bullrush, 8st 2lb........................ 2
Seven to 4 and 2 to 1 on Bullrush.—Won very easy.

Match for 300gs.—Two year Olds' Course.
Lord Darlington's b c Master Goodall, by Sir Solomon, 8st 8lb (S.
Chifney).. 1
Sir C. Turner's ch c Mr Gundy, 7st 13lb........................ 2
Six and 7 to 4 on Master Goodall.—Won cleverly.

Match for 50gs.—Abingdon Mile.
Lord Grosvenor's br c Bullrush, by John Bull, 4 years old, 7st 12lb
(F. Buckle)... 1
Lord G. H. Cavendish's b h Dreadnought, aged, 8st 4lb........... 2
Eleven to 5 on Dreadnought.—Won easy.

Fifty Pounds for all ages.—Two middle Miles of B. C.
Lord Rous's b c Wood-Demon, by Lop, 3 years old, 6st 2lb. (a Boy).. 1
Mr Goulburn's ch c Romeo, 4 years old, 8st..................... 2
Mr Goddard's ch h Achilles, 5 years old, 8st 7lb............... 3
General Grosvenor's John-o'Gaunt, 3 years, 6st 2lb............. 4

The following also started, but were not placed.:

Mr Prince's Brother to Woodman, 3 years old, 6st 2lb............ 0
Mr Goodisson's b c Foxberry, 4 years old, 8st.................. 0
Mr Panton's b c Ernest, 3 years old, 6st 2lb................... 0
Lord G. H. Cavendish's b c Buff, 3 years old, 6st 2lb.......... 0
Eleven to 5 against Achilles, and 10 to 1 against Wood-Demon.—A
good race.

Match

Match for 200gs.—Two-year Olds' Course.

Duke of Grafton's bay colt Musician, by Worthy, 4 years old, 7st 6lb
(B. Moss). 1
Mr Shakespear's br h Wormwood, 6 years old, 8st 13lb.......... 2
Six to 4 on Musician.—Won very easy.—Benjamin Moss rode Musician
in a very fine style.

Match for 100gs.—Abingdon Mile.

Lord Grosvenor's b c Eaton, by Sir Peter Teazle, 4 years old, 8st
(F. Buckle).. 1
Lord Lowther's b h Trafalgar, 5 years old, 8st 9½lb............. 2
Six to 4 on Trafalgar.—Won quite easy.

Match for 100gs.—Across the Flat.

Duke of Grafton's bay colt Musican, by Worthy, 4 years old, 7st 6lb
(B. Moss).. 1
Lord Sackville's br h Bustard, aged, 8st 10lb................... 2
Six to 5 on Musician.—Won in a canter.

Lord Darlington's b c Master Goodall, by Sir Solomon, 8st 7lb, received 70gs compromise, from Sir C. Turner's ch c Mr Gundy, 8st.—
Two-year Olds' Course, 200gs, h ft.

FRIDAY, May 20.—Match for 50gs.—Two-year Olds' Course.

Lord G. H. Cavendish's b h Dreadnought, by Buzzard, aged, 7st 9lb
(W. Wheatley)... 1
Lord Foley's br m Pipylina, 5 years old, 8st 4lb................ 2
Three to 1 on Dreadnought.—Won easy.

Match for 200gs.—Across the Flat.

Sir J. Honywood's br c Bacchanal, by St. George, 4 years old, 7st 12lb
(J. Croft).. 1
Mr Fermor's ch h Cerberus, 6 years old, 9st 2lb................ 2
Twenty to 12 on Cerberus.

Match for 100gs.—Abingdon Mile.

Mr Watson's b c Hymen, by Trumpator, 3 years old, 8st ½lb (W.
Wheatley) 1
Lord Grosvenor's b c Sunbeam, 3 years old, 8st 5½lb............ 2
Ten to 6 on Sunbeam.

Match for 100gs.—Rowley Mile.

Mr Vansittart's ch h Burleigh, by Stamford, 5 years old, 8st 3lb (S.
Chifney)... 1
Mr Panton's b f Ralphina, by Buzzard, 4 years old, 8st 9lb 2
Seven to 4 on Burleigh.

Sweepstakes of 25gs each for all ages.—Two middle Miles of B. C.

General Grosvenor's b c Osiris, by Sir Peter Teazle, 4 years old, 8st
(F. Buckle) 1
Lord Lowther's br h Tot, 6 years old, 8st 12lb................. 2
Mr C. Browne's br h Pavilion, aged, 8st 12lb.................. 3
Mr Fermor's br c Stripling, 4 years old, 8st................... paid
Even betting on Osiris.

Match

Match for 100gs.—Two-year Olds' Course.

Sir J. Shelley's filly, by Buzzard, (bought of Mr Panton) 8st 1lb
    (F. Buckle).. 1
Lord G. H. Cavendish's b f, by Gouty, 8st 2lb................. 2
    Seven to 4 on Lord G. H. Cavendish's filly.—Won easy.

Match for 25gs.—First half of Ab. M.

Mr Wyndham's b c, by Schedoni, five years old, 7st 9lb (S. Barnard).. 1
Lord Lowther's br h Wormwood, six years old, 8st 8lb............. 2
    Six to 4 on Wormwood.—A fine race.

Match for 50gs.—Rowley Mile.

Duke of Grafton's b m Vanity, by Buzzard, five years old, 8st 9lb
    (W. Clift) 1
Lord Foley's b c Comrade, 4 years old, 7st 11lb............... 2
    Seven to 4 on Comrade.—Won easy.

Match for 200gs.—Ditch-in.

Lord Grosvenor's b m Meteora, by Meteor, six years old, 8st 10lb
    (F. Buckle).. 0
Mr Fermor's ch c Brighton, by Gohanna, 4 years old, 7st 8lb (C.
    Goodisson) 0
    Seven to 4 on Brighton.—Ran a dead heat.

=======

YORK SPRING MEETING.

MONDAY, May 23.—Sweepstakes of 20gs each, for all ages.—Two
    Miles.—Seven Subscribers.

Mr Duncombe's bt f Ceres, by Hambletonian, out of Miss Gunpow-
    der, 3 years old, 6st 10lb (Matthew Ward)................. 1
Lord Strathmore's br h Cassio, by Sir Peter Teazle, 5 years old, 9st
    (F. Buckle).. 2
Mr Wentworth's bay filly Margaret, by Beningbrough, 4 years old,
    8st 5lb.. 3
Even betting between Cassio and Margaret, and 8 to 1 against Ceres.
    —A good race, and won by a neck.—Run in 4 minutes and 2 se-
    conds.

Match for 500gs, h. ft.—Four Miles.

Mr Goulburn's gr h Grimaldi, by Delpini, 6 years old, 12st (the
    Owner) 1
Mr Benson's gr h Atlas, by Sir Peter Teazle, 5 years old, 11st 7lb
    (the Owner).. 2
Five and 6 to 4 on Grimaldi.—Won easy.—Run in 9 minutes and 20 se-
    conds.

Match for 200gs, h. ft.—Four Miles.

Mr Brandling's br h Smasher, by Star, 7st 12lb (J. Shepherd)...... 1
Mr Wentworth's bay horse Centurion, by Beningbrough, 8st 4lb (G.
    Humble) 2
Six and 7 to 4 on Smasher.—Smasher made severe play, was never
    headed, and won very easy.—Run in 8 minutes and 54 seconds.

TUESDAY, May 24.—Sweepstakes of 20gs each, for three-year old colts, 8st 3lb, fillies, 8st.—Last Mile and three quarters—Ten Subscribers.

Mr Garforth's ch c, by Hyacinthus, out of Flora (B. Smith) 1

Mr Garforth's bay colt, by Hambletonian, out of Caroline (W. Peirse) 2

Duke of Leeds's ch c, by Pandolpho, out of Mother Redcap (J. Garbutt) 3

Mr Hewett's b c M'George, by St. George, dam by Buzzard (J. Jackson) 4

Mr Hewett's bay colt Stilton, by Stamford, out of Scud's dam (F. Collinson) 5

Sir E. Smith's gr c, by St. George, out of Quid's dam (G. Humble) . . 6

Sir T. Gascoigne's ch c, by Hambletonian, out of Golden-Locks (J. Shepherd) 7

Lord Strathmore's b c, by Hambletonian, out of Beatrice (F. Buckle) 8

Twenty-two to 10 against the Hyacinthus colt, 5 to 2 against M'George, 3 to 1 against Stilton, and 6 to 1 against Mr Garforth's Hambletonian colt.—Won very easy.—Run in 3 minutes and 35 seconds.

Sweepstakes of 20gs each, for three-year old fillies, 8st 3lb.—The last Mile and a half.

Mr W. Fletcher's bay, Miss Staveley, by Shuttle, dam by Drone (R. Franks) 1

Mr W. Sawdon's brown, by Warter, out of Isabel, by Woodpecker (J. Garbutt) 2

Mr F. Watt's bay, by Stamford, dam by Boudrow (W. Peirse) 3

Mr Duncombe's chesnut, Laurel Leaf, by Stamford, out of a sister to Druid . . . . pd

Seven to 4 on Miss Staveley.—Won very easy.—Run in 3 minutes and 7 seconds.

Sweepstakes of 30gs each, 10gs ft. for two-year old colts, 8st 2lb, fillies, 8st.—Two-year Olds' Course.—Six Subscribers.

Duke of Hamilton's ch c Middlethorpe, by Shuttle, dam by Pipator (B. Smith) 1

Mr Dinsdale's b f Fair Candidate, by Delpini, dam by Weasel (J. Shepherd) 2

Mr Garforth's bay colt, by Hambletonian, out of Caroline (W. Peirse) 3

Colonel Childers's ch c, by Waxy, out of Remnant (F. Collinson) . . 4

Six to 4 on Colonel Childers's colt, and 2 to 1 against Middlethorpe.—Won very easy.—Run in 1 minute and 20 seconds.

The Oatlands' Stakes, of 30gs each, h. ft. for horses, &c.—The last Mile and half.—Eight Subscribers.

Lord Darlington's b c, by Archduke, out of Beningbrough's sister, four years old, 7st 11lb (W. Peirse) 1

Sir M. M. Sykes's b f Harriet, by Precipitate, 4 years old, 6st (W. Waller) 2

Lord Scarbrough's br colt Hospodar, by Sir Solomon, 4 years old, 5st 12lb (M. Ward) 3

Lord

Lord Scarbrough's br colt, by Sir Solomon, dam by Jupiter, 4 years old, 5st 10lb (W. Rainer)................................. 4
Lord Darlington's br colt, brother to Expectation, 4 years old, 7st 2lb (R. Johnson) 5
Mr Wentworth's gr f Irené, 4 years old, 5st 12lb (E. Bateman) 6
Sir J. Lawson's bay colt Presentation, by Star, 4 years old, 7st 9lb (J. Jackson) 7
Six to 4 that either the Archduke colt, or the Brother to Expectation, won.—Won cleverly.—Run in 3 minutes and 1 second.

WEDNESDAY, May 25.—The Stand Plate of 50l. free for any horse, &c. of all ages.—Four Miles.
Lord Strathmore's br horse Cassio, by Sir Peter Teazle, 5 years old, 8st 4lb (F. Buckle)............................. 1
Mr Goulburn's gr h Grimaldi, by Delpini, 6 years old, 8st 10lb (G. Boast) 2
Five to 2 and 3 to 1 on Cassio.—A good race.—Run in 3 minutes and 5 seconds.

GOODWOOD MEETING, SUSSEX.

TUESDAY, May 10.—Fifty Pounds for hunters, 12st each.—Three Miles.
Mr Gage's br g Pic Nic, by Ramsden, out of Skysweeper, aged.... 1
Mr Best's Tickle Toby, aged.............................. 2
Six and 7 to 4 on Pic Nic.—Won easy.

WEDNESDAY, May 11.—The Silver Cup, by Subscription of 10gs each, for horses, &c. the property of Subscribers.—Gentlemen riders.—Three-mile heats.—Thirteen Subscribers.

Mr Trevanion's b h Bucephalus, by Alexander, 6 years old, 12st (Mr Germaine)	4	1	1
Captain Haffenden's b h Sir Launcelot, 6 years old, 12st (Mr Douglas)	6	2	2
Sir H. Lippincott's b g Ploughboy, 5 years old, 11st 11lb	2	4	4
Mr Rush's ch h Timekeeper, 6 years old, 12st	5	5	3
Mr David's b g Prodigal, (late Watery) aged, 12st	1	3	dr
Duke of Richmond's br h Tetuan, 5 years old, 12st	3	dr	

Sir Launcelot the favourite.—A good race.

Fifty Pounds for hunters.—Two-mile heats.

Mr Gage's br g Pic Nic, by Ramsden, aged, 11st 3lb	1	1
Captain Bridgewater's b m Little Polly, 11st	2	dr

Six and 7 to 4 on Pic Nic.

The Ladies' Plate of 60gs, for all ages.—Two-mile heats.

Lord Egremont's ch c Election, by Gohanna, 4 years old, 10st 4lb	1	1
Mr Butler's br c Epsom, 4 years old, 10st 4lb	2	2
Captain Haffenden's ch c Tom Pipes, aged, 12st 2lb (the rider mistook the Course)	dis	

High odds on Election.—A good race.

E 2   HEX

HEXHAM MEETING, NORTHUMBERLAND.

(Over the New Course, on Stagshaw Bank.)

WEDNESDAY, May 25.—The Hunters' Stakes of 5gs each, for horses, &c. not thorough-bred.—Heats, twice round the Course.— Ten Subscribers.

Mr Wetherburn's br m Archduchess, by Archduke, 5 years old, 8st 11lb	1	1
Mr Leighton's bay mare	4	2
Mr Wilson's Goldspink	3	3
Mr Thompson's Highland-Lassie	2	4
Mr Maddison's Simon	5	dis
Mr Liddle's ches. colt	dis	

THURSDAY, Fifty Pounds for all ages.—Four-mile heats.

Mr Bates's br h Honest Harry, by Star, 5 years old, 8st 7lb	1	1
Mr Wray's b f, by Merry-Andrew, 4 years old, 7st 4lb	2	dr
Mr Heslop's ch f, by Stride, 3 years old, a feather	3	dr

BEVERLEY MEETING, YORKSHIRE.

TUESDAY, May 31.—Sweepstakes of 20gs each, for three-year old colts, 8st 3lb, fillies, 8st.—One Mile and a half.—Six Subscribers.

Mr Gascoigne's b c Bumtrap, by Agonistes, out of Kilton's sister (J. Shepherd)	1
Sir M. M. Sykes's ch f Anna-Maria, by Stamford, out of Stella (J. Garbutt)	2
Mr F. Watt's bay filly, by Stamford, dam by Boudrow (W. Peirse)	3
Mr Nalton's bay colt, by Delpini, dam by Slope (J. Jackson)	4

Six to 4 on Anna-Maria.—Won easy.

Sweepstakes of 10gs each, for hunters of all ages.—Four Miles.—Five Subscribers.

Mr W. Jordon's br gelding, by Ruler, 5 years old, 11st 8lb (Mr Acklom)	1
Mr T. Shafto's b h, by Zachariah, dam by Tandem, 5 years old, 11st 8lb (Mr W. Harrison)	2
Mr T. Sykes's b h, by Idris, dam by Highflyer, 5 years old, 11st 8lb (the Owner)	3

Mr Jordon's gelding the favourite.—A very fine race, and won by only half a neck.—It was also a very nice point to determine which was second.

The Holderness Stakes of 20gs each ; colts, 8st, fillies, 7st 10lb.—Two Miles.—Five Subscribers.

Mr Mosey's b c Tar, by Pitch (B. Smith)	1
Mr Foster's b c, by Trumpator (R. Johnson)	2
Mr Tanton's b f Fair Star, by Ormond (F. Jordon)	3

Six to 4 on Tar.—Won easy.

WED-

WEDNESDAY, June 1.——The Gold Cup, by Subscription of 10gs each, for all ages.—Four Miles.—Seventeen Subscribers.

Mr S. Duncombe's b m Hipswell-Lass, by Sir Peter Teazle, 5 yrs old, 8st 5lb (J. Jackson) 1

Sir M. M. Sykes's b f Harriet, by Precipitate, 4 yrs old, 7st 9lb (J. Garbutt) 2

Mr Gascoigne's b m Dowager, by Hambletonian, 5 yrs old, 8st 5lb (J. Shepherd) 3

Mr Watt's b f, by Delpini, dam by Trumpator, 3 yrs old, 6st (Ward Taylor) 4

Mr Stephenson's b c Jack-o'-the-Green, by Stamford, 4 yrs old, 7st 12lb (J. Cade) 5

Six to 4 against Hipswell-Lass, and 4 to 1 agst Jack-o'-the-Green.—A good race, and won by a neck.

The Maiden Plate of 50l. for all ages.—Two-mile heats.

Mr S. Duncombe's b c Rossington, by Star, 4 yrs old, 7st 7lb (J. Garbutt) 3 1 1

Mr Key's b c Sir John Barleycorn, by Ormond, 3 yrs old, 6st 4lb (J. Shepherd) 1 3 2

Mr Skelton's ch g, by Hyacinthus, 4 yrs old, 7st 7lb (R. Johnson) ....2 2 dr

Five to 4 against the Hyacinthus gelding; after the second heat, even betting between Rossington and Sir John Barleycorn.—A very good race.

THURSDAY, June 2.——Sweepstakes of 20gs each, for all ages,—Four Miles.—Six Subscribers.

Mr S. Duncombe's b m Hipswell-Lass, by Sir Peter Teazle, 5 yrs old, 8st 4lb (J. Jackson) 1

Mr Gascoigne's b c Bumtrap, by Agonistes, 3 yrs old, 5st 12lb (D. Masterman).. 2

Six to 4 on Bumtrap.—A good race.

Fifty Pounds for three and four year olds.—Two-mile heats.

Mr Mosey's bay colt Tar, by Pitch, 3 yrs old, 7st 13lb (B. Smith) 4 1 1

Mr F. Watt's b f, by Stamford, 3 yrs old, 7st 7lb (J. Sherwood) 2 4 2

Mr Seymour's b c Cliffe, 4 yrs old, 8st 12lb (F. Jordon) 5 2 3

Mr S. Duncombe's b c Rossington, 4 yrs old, 9st 1lb (J. Garbutt) 1 3 dr

Mr Stephenson's b c Jack-o'-the-Green, 4 yrs old, 8st 12lb (G. Humble) ....3 5 dr

Six to 4 Tar against Cliffe; after the first heat, the field the favourite; after the second heat, 2 and 3 to 1 on Tar. A good race, and won with difficulty.

FRIDAY, June 3.——The Macaroni Stakes of 20gs each, for horses, &c.—Four Miles.—Five Subscribers.

Mr Gascoigne's bay mare Dowager, by Hambletonian, 5 yrs old (Mr Treacher)... 1

Mr Johnston's br horse Sir Andrew, by Hambletonian, 6 yrs old (Mr T. Sykes) 2

Mr Brandling's br h Smasher, by Star, 5 yrs old (Mr H. Boynton).. 3

Five to 4 on Sir Andrew.—Won easy.

Fifty

Fifty Pounds for all ages.—Three-mile heats.

Sir M. M. Sykes's b f Harriet, by Precipitate, 4 yrs old, 7st 7lb
   (J. Garbutt)...................................... 1 2 0 1
Mr Johnston's br h Sir Andrew, 6 yrs old, 8st 10lb (G. Humble) 2 1 0 2
Six and 7 to 4 on Harriet; after the first heat, 8 and 10 to 1 on Harriet;
   after the second heat, 8 to 1 on Sir Andrew; after the dead heat, 5
   and 6 to 4 on Sir Andrew.—A very capital race.

EPSOM MEETING—SURREY.

WEDNESDAY, June 1.——The Epsom Stakes of 7gs each, with
   20gs added, for all ages.—Two Miles.
Mr Goodisson's bay colt Foxberry, by Screveton, 4 yrs old, 7st 10lb
   (C. Goodisson) 1
Mr Ladbroke's bl m Honeysuckle, 5 yrs old, 8st 4lb.............. 2
Mr Hyde's b g Canterbury, 5 yrs old, 8st 4lb 3
Mr Butler's ch f Bonnylass, 3 yrs old, 6st 4lb......:.......... 4
Two to 1 against Foxberry, 2 to 1 against Honeysuckle, and 3 to 1 agst.
               Canterbury.—A good race.

        Fifty Pounds for all ages.—Two-mile heats.
Lord Foley's b c Comrade, by Stamford, 4 yrs old, 7st 8lb (B.
   Moss) 3 2 1 1
Mr T. Butler's b m Miss Coiner, aged, 8st 10lb 1 3 3 2
Lord Egremont's ch f, by Young Woodpecker, 4 yrs old, 7st 2lb 2 1 2 3
Even betting on Lord Egremont's filly, 3 to 1 against Comrade, and 4 to
   1 1 against Miss Coiner; after the first heat, 6 to 4 against Miss Coiner; after the second heat, even betting on Lord Egremont's filly, 7 to
   4 against Comrade, and 4 to 1 against Miss Coiner; after the third
   heat, 3 to 1 on Comrade. For the first heat, Lord Egremont's filly
   made play, and headed the others by several lengths, until the last
   mile, when Miss Coiner contested for the heat, and won it tolerably
   easy; the second heat was won easy; as also were the third and
   fourth heats.

THURSDAY, June 2.——The Derby Stakes of 50gs each, h. ft. for
three-year old colts, 8st 7lb, fillies, 8st 2lb.—The last Mile and half.
—Thirty-eight Subscribers.—The owner of the second received 100gs
out of the Stake.
Sir H. Williamson's ch c Pan, by St. George, out of Walton and
   Ditto's dam (F. Collinson) 1
Duke of Grafton's br c Vandyke, by Sir Peter Teazle, out of Dabchick
   (W. Clift) 2
Lord Grosvenor's b c Chester, by Sir Peter Teazle (F. Buckle) 3
His R. H. the Prince of Wales's ch c Rubens, by Buzzard (S. Chif-
   ney)... 4
        The following also started, but were not placed :—
Mr Sitwell's br c Clinker, by Sir Peter Teazle, out of Hyale (T. Good-
   isson) 0
                                                   Mr

Mr Mellish's b c Bradbury, by Delpini, dam by Young Marsk (J. Arnold) 0
Lord Stawell's ch c, by Sorcerer, out of Sir David's dam (S. Arnold) 0
Lord Egremont's b c, brother to Trafalgar, by Gohanna (W. Wheatley) 0
Lord Egremont's b f, by Gohanna, dam by Sir Peter Teazle, out of Nimble (S. Barnard) 0
Mr Ladbroke's b c Tristram, by Teddy the Grinder, dam by Precipitate (W. Arnold) 0

Even betting Vandyke and Rubens agst the field; 5 to 2, Vandyke, Rubens, and Clinker, agst the field ; 2 to 1 agst Vandyke, 7 to 2 agst Rubens, 5 to 1 agst Clinker, 6 to 1 agst the Brother to Trafalgar, 7 to 1 agst Lord Stawell's colt, 20 to 1 agst Pan, 20 to 1 agst Chester, 25 to 1 agst Lord Egremont's filly, 100 to 4 agst Tristram, and 100 to 2 agst Bradbury.—A very great betting race. Lord Egremont's filly took the lead, and kept it until they came round Tottenham Corner; then Clinker and Vandyke came up, and had a severe run ; after which, Rubens took the lead for a short space by the Distance-post; Pan then came up, and won by half a length. It was allowed to be one of the finest races ever run for the above Stakes, and Collinson rode in a masterly Yorkshire style.

Fifty Pounds for Horses, &c.—Two-mile heats.

Lord Foley's b c Comrade, by Stamford, 4 yrs old, 7st 4lb (B. Moss)..4 1 1
Mr Butler's b c Epsom, 4 yrs old, 7st 4lb.....................1 2 3
Mr Goodisson's b c Foxberry, 4 yrs old, 7st 4lb.............5 4 2
Mr Fenwick's ch g Tom Pipes, aged, 8st 11lb ....2 3 dr
Mr Emden's gr g Speculation, 5 yrs old, 8st 3lb.............3 dr
Even betting on Comrade.—Won easy.

FRIDAY, June 3.——The Oaks' Stakes of 50gs each, h. ft. for three-year old fillies, 8st 4lb.—The last Mile and half.—The owner of the second received 100gs out of the Stakes.—Thirty-one Subscribers.
Duke of Grafton's chesnut, Morel, by Sorcerer, out of Hornby Lass (W. Clift) 1
Mr Sitwell's bay, Gooseander, by Hambletonian, out of Pipylin's dam (T. Goodisson) 2
Lord Barrymore's brown, Miranda, by Sorcerer, dam by Tandem, Eclipse (F. Collinson)....................................... 3
Mr Lake's black, Oberea, by Sorcerer, out of Deceit (W. Wheatley) 4
The following also started, but were not placed:—
Mr Ladbroke's filly, by Teddy the Grinder, out of Princess (W. Arnold) 0
Lord Egremont's bay, Sister to Mouse, by Gohanna, out of Humming Bird (S. Barnard).. 0
Lord Egremont's bay, by Gohanna, dam by Sir Peter Teazle, out of Nimble (T. Butler)... 0
Mr Howorth's bay, Dilemma, Sister to Elizabeth, by Waxy (W. Wheatley) 0

Sir

Sir F. Standish's bay, by Sir Peter Teazle, out of Eagle's dam (B. Moss) 0

Mr Mellish's bay, Agnes, by Shuttle (F. Buckle).............. 0

Fifty-five to 20 agst Morel, 5 to 1 agst Miranda, 5 to 1 agst Gooseander, 6 to 1 agst Oberea, 7 to 1 agst Lord Egremont's Nimble filly, 100 to 7 agst the Sister to Mouse, 100 to 8 agst Agnes, 100 to 8 agst Sir F. Standish's filly, 25 to 1 agst Mr Ladbroke's filly, and 100 to 4 agst Dilemma.—The Nimble filly took the lead and kept it to Tottenham Corner, and then Morel took the lead, and won by a length and a half.—A great betting race.——*Double betting*—9 to 1 agst Vandyke and Morel both winning.

Fifty Pounds for three and four year olds.—Two-mile beats.

Lord Foley's b c Comrade, by Stamford, 4 yrs old, 8st 12lb (B. Moss) 3 1 1

Mr Ladbroke's br c Corsican, 4 yrs old, 8st 4lb (W. Arnold).... 1 2 2

Mr Fermor's ch c Bantum, 4 yrs old, 8st 8lb................2 dr

Six to 4 against Comrade, 7 to 4 agst Corsican, and 5 to 1 agst Bantum ; after the first beat, 7 to 4 agst Comrade ; after the second heat, 10 to 1 on Comrade.

Match for 100gs.—Last three quarters of a Mile.

Mr Ladbroke's br c, by Teddy the Grinder, out of Princess, 8st 5lb (W. Arnold) 1

Mr Lake's filly, by Gouty, dam by Volunteer, 7st 9lb 2

Two to 1 on Mr Ladbroke's colt.

The Woodcot Stakes of 30gs each, h. ft. for two-year old colts, 8st 5lb, fillies, 8st 2lb.—The last half Mile.—Six Subscribers.

Mr Emden's b f Miss Seedling, by Totteridge, out of Seedling (W. Clift) 1

Mr. Fermor's b f, by Gohanna, dam by Mercury 2

Mr Ladbroke's b f, Sister to Election.......................... 3

Mr Lake's ch c Silvermere, by Gouty........................... 4

Mr Durand's b f, by Teddy the Grinder, out of Kitty Bean 5

Two to 1 against Mr Fermor's filly, 2 to 1 against Mr Durand's filly, and 3 to 1 agst Miss Seedling.—Won easy.

SATURDAY, June 4.——The Hedley Stakes of 30gs each, 10gs ft. for three-yr old colts, 8st 7lb, fillies, 8st 4lb.—The last Mile.—Nine Subscribers.

Mr Lake's br e Fuscus, brother to Forester, by Grouse (W. Wheatley) 1

Lord Egremont's ch f Quail, by Gohanna..................... 2

Seven to 4 and 2 to 1 on Quail.

MANCHESTER MEETING.

WEDNESDAY, June 8.—Sweepstakes of 10gs each, with 20l. added, for three-year old colts, 8st 3lb, fillies, 8st.—One Mile.—Ten Subscribers.

Mr. E. Hanson's b f Overproof, by Shuttle, out of Ambo's dam 1

Lord

Lord Stamford's br f Petronilla, by St. George.................. 2
Mr Ackers's ch c Apollo, by Hyacinthus..................... 3
Petronilla the favourite.

Fifty Pounds for three and four-year olds.—Two-mile heats.
Mr R. Benson's br f Cecilia, by Beningbrough, 4 yrs old, 8st.... 1 1
Mr J. Bettison's b f, by Sir Peter Teazle, dam by Alfred, 3 yrs
   old, 6st 8lb..2 2
Sir T. Stanley's b f Cowslip, by Alexander, 3 yrs old, 6st 8lb ..3 3
Five to 4, and after the heat 3 to 1, on Cecilia.

THURSDAY, June 9.—The Manchester Stakes of 10gs each, with
50l. added, for all ages.—Four Miles.—Eleven Subscribers.
Colonel Childers's b c Baron, by Stamford, 4 yrs old, 7st 12lb...... 1
Lord Grey's b f Belinda, 4 yrs old, 7st 9lb..................... 2
Mr Astley's ch g Newton, 5 yrs old, 8st 7lb.................. 3
Six and 7 to 4 on Baron.

Sweepstakes of 10gs each, for hunters, 12st.—Four Miles.
Mr R. Benson's br h, by Sir Peter Teazle, dam by Snap,
   5 yrs old .... walked over.
The Maiden Plate of 60l. for all ages, four-mile heats.
Mr Harris's br g Viper, by Serpent, 4 yrs old, 7st 11lb..........1 1
Sir T. Stanley's b f Cowslip, 3 yrs old, 6st....................2 2
Mr J. Bettison's br f, by Sir Peter Teazle, out of a sister to Tickle
   Toby, 4 yrs old, 7st 8lb 3 3
Six to 4 on Viper.

FRIDAY, June 10.——Sweepstakes of 10gs each, for hunters, 13st.
—Gentlemen riders.—Four Miles.—Eleven Subscribers.
Mr Benson's br h, by Sir Peter Teazle, dam by Snap,
   5 yrs old .... walked over.
Eighty Pounds for all ages.—Four-mile heats.—Post Entry.
Mr Harris's br g Viper, by Serpent, 4 yrs old, 7st 12lb 3 1 1
Sir T. Stanley's b f Cowslip, 3 yrs old, 6st 11b 1 2 2
Mr Thompson's b m Creeper ....2 3 dr

MADDINGTON MEETING.

(Over Stockbridge Course.)

WEDNESDAY, June 8.——Match for One Hundred Guineas.—
Two Miles.
Mr Goddard's b h Mountaineer, by Magic, 6 yrs old, 9st 12lb (Mr
   Germain).. 1
Mr Dundas's b h Rubens, 5 yrs old, 9st 9lb 2
Sweepstakes of 10gs each, with 25gs added, for horses, &c.—Two Miles.
Four Subscribers.
Mr Trevanion's b h Bucephalus, by Alexander, 6 yrs old, 12st (Mr
   Germain) 1
Mr Craven's br m Bronze, 5 yrs old, 11st 3lb (Mr Lindow)........ 2
Even betting.—A good race.

The Maddington Stakes of 25gs each, 15 ft. and only 5gs if declared, &c.—Four Miles.

Mr Goddard's b h Mountaineer, by Magic, 6 yrs old, 11st 6lb (Mr Germain)... 1
Mr Dundas's bay colt Cambrian, by Sir Solomon, 4 yrs old, 9st 9lb— 2
The following also started, but were not placed :—
Mr Trevanion's b h Bucephalus, 6 yrs old, 11st 10lb............. 0
Lord C. Somerset's br h Delville, 6 yrs old, 11st 7lb............ 0
Sir H. Lippincott's br c Chaise-and-One, 4 yrs old, 10st 5lb........ 0
Four Subscribers paid 15gs each, and six who declared forfeit within the time prescribed, 5gs each.—Won by a head.

Match for Fifty Guineas.—One Mile and a half.

Sir H. Lippincott's b g Ploughboy, by Volunteer, 5 yrs old, 9st 7lb (Mr Worrall) 1
Mr Best's ch f Augusta, by Buzzard, 4 yrs old, 9st 7lb (Mr Douglas) 2
Won easy.

THURSDAY, June 9.—Sweepstakes of 5gs each, with 50gs added, for horses, &c.—Three Miles.—Sixteen Subscribers.

Mr Trevanion's bay colt Gammon, by Beningbrough, 4 yrs old, 10st 3lb (Mr Douglas) 1
Mr Biggs's br colt Rosario, by Ambrosio, 4 yrs old, 10st 7lb (Mr Germain)... 2
Sir H. Lippincott's b g Ploughboy, 5 yrs old, 11st 3lb (Mr Worrall).. 3
Five to 4 on Rosario, and 5 to 2 against Gammon.—A good race.

Sweepstakes of 50gs each.—Red-Post Home.

Sir H. Lippincott's br f Sorceress, by Sorcerer, out of Quiz, 9st 6lb (Mr Douglas) 1
Mr Worrall's b f, by Kill-Devil, out of Peggy Rose, 9st 6lb (the Owner)... 2
Mr Goddard's Crim. Con. by Gohanna, 9st 12lb ....pd
Six to 4 on Sorceress.—Won easy.

Fifty Pounds for horses, &c. of all ages.—Heats, about two Miles and a quarter.

Sir J. Hawkins's br h Clermont, by Trumpator, 5 yrs old, 11st (Mr Germain) 3 1 1
Sir H. Lippincott's b c, by Trumpator, out of Beda, 4 yrs old, 10st (Mr Worrall) 1 3 3
Mr Fellowes's br colt Mandarine, 4 yrs old, 9st 10lb (Mr Douglas) 4 2 2
Mr Goddard's b m Old Maid, 6 yrs old, 11st 3lb (Mr Lindow) 2 dr
The third heat was won by half a neck.

FRIDAY, June 10.—Match for 50gs.—Red-Post Home.

Mr Dundas's b c Cambrian, by Sir Solomon, 4 yrs old, 9st 10lb (Mr Worrall) 1
Mr Biggs's br colt Rosario, 4 yrs old, 10st 2lb (Mr Germain)...... 2
Won very easy.

Match

Match for 50gs.—Red-Post Home.
Sir H. Lippincott's br f Sorceress, 3 yrs old, 9st 3lb (Mr Worrall) .. 1
Mr Goddard's b h Mountaineer, 6 yrs old, 11st 4lb (Mr Douglas) .. 2
Five to 4 on Mountaineer.

Match for 50gs. —Two Miles.
Mr Dundas's b h Rubens, by Pencil, 5 yrs old, 11st (Mr Worrall) .. 1
Mr Best's ch f Augusta, 4 yrs old, 9st 7lb 2

Handicap Plate of 50l. for all ages.—Heats, the last Mile.
Mr Biggs's br colt Rosario, by Ambrosio, 4 yrs old, 10st 5lb
    (Mr Douglas) 1 4 1
Mr Dundas's b c Cambrian, by Sir Solomon, 4 yrs old, 10st 7lb
    (Mr Lindow) 4 1 2
Sir H. Lippincott's br c Chaise-and-One, 4 yrs old, 10st 7lb (Mr
    Worrall) 3 3 3
Mr Goddard's b m Old Maid, 6 yrs old, 9st 11lb (Mr Germain) 5 2 4
Mr Best's ch f Augusta, 4 yrs old, 10st 2½lb .... 2 dr
Six to 4 agst Cambrian, 3 to 1 against Rosario, and 3 to 1 agst Chaise-
and-One.

RACING INTELLIGENCE EXTRA.

NEWMARKET JULY MEETING, 1808.

MONDAY, July 11.—Mr Panton's Ralphina, 8st 7lb, against the
Duke of Grafton's filly, by Coriander, out of Peppermint, 8st.—
The first half of Ab. M. 50gs.

Lord Jersey's colt, by the Wellesley Arabian, out of Blowing's dam,
against Lord G. H. Cavendish's colt, by Coriander, out of Mrs. Candour, 8st 3lb each.—Ab. M. 100gs, h. ft.

General Grosvenor's John O'Gaunt, 8st 7lb, against Mr Lake's Fuscus,
8st 3lb.—Ab. M. 50gs.

Lord Stawell's Deceiver, 8st 7lb, against the Duke of Grafton's Vanity, 8st.—Two-year Olds' Course, 50gs.

TUESDAY.—Mr Shakespear's Tot against Mr Vansittart's Currycomb, 8st 7lb each.—Two-year Olds' Course, 200gs, h. ft.

General Grosvenor's John O'Gaunt, 8st 3lb, against the Duke of
Rutland's Ned, by Teddy, dam by Precipitate, 8st.—Across the Flat,
100gs, h. ft.

WEDNESDAY.—Mr Panton's Ralphina, 8st 1lb, against General
Grosvenor's John O'Gaunt, 7st 3lb.—Two-year Olds' Course, 50gs.

Lord Foley's Cecilia, 8st 6lb, against Mr Wilson's Shuttle filly, 6st
4lb.—Two-year Olds' Course, 100gs, h. ft.

THURSDAY.—Mr Shakespear's Tot, 8st 12lb, against Lord Grosvenor's Bullrush, 8st.—Two-year Olds' Course, 50gs.

NEWMARKET FIRST OCTOBER MEETING, 1808.

MONDAY.—Duke of Grafton's Musician, 8st 4lb, against Mr Vansittart's Momentilla, 8st 1½lb.—Ditch-in, 100gs, h. ft.

Lord Foley's Cecilia, 8st 4lb, against General Grosvenor's Rifleman, 7st 10lb.—R. M. 100gs, h. ft.

Sir C. Turner's Mr Gundy, 9st, against the Duke of Grafton's Morel, 8st.—Two-year Olds' Course, 100gs, h. ft.

Sir C. Turner's Jock, by Hyacinthus, out of Flora, 8st 7lb, against Mr Shakespear's Discount, 8st 3lb.—Two-year Olds' Course, 200gs.

TUESDAY.—Mr Shakespear's Harpocrates, (late Trafalgar) 8st 3lb, against Lord Grosvenor's Eaton, 8st.—Across the Flat, 200gs, h. ft.

Lord Grosvenor's Violante, 8st 7lb, against Mr Shakespear's Selim, 8st 2lb.—B. C. 200gs, h. ft.

WEDNESDAY.—Duke of Grafton's Vandyke, 8st 7lb, against Mr Shakespear's Discount, 8st.—D. I. 200gs.

Mr Craven's Beau Nash, 8st 2lb, against General Grosvenor's Rifleman, 8st.—B. M. 200gs, h. ft.

THURSDAY.— Mr Shakespear's Harpocrates, 9st 6lb, against Sir C. Turner's Jock, 8st.—Across the Flat, 200gs.

Lord Sackville's Bustard, 8st 13lb, against Sir C. Turner's Mr Gundy, 9st. Ab. M.—Lord Sackville stakes 800gs to 600gs, h. ft.

Mr Shakespear's Zodiac, 8st 6lb, against Mr Fermor's Brighton, 8st.— B. C. 200gs, h. ft.

General Grosvenor's Rifleman, 8st, against Mr Lloyd's Fun, 7st.—R. M. 100gs, h. ft.

FRIDAY.—Sir J. Shelley's Fanny, 8st 6lb, against Sir C. Turner's Bramble, 8st.—Across the Flat, 200gs, h. ft.

Sweepstakes of 50gs each, 8st 3lb.—Two-year Olds' Course.
Lord G. H. Cavendish's Diavolina, by Kill-Devil
General Grosvenor's filly, by Asparagus, out of Lady Jane
Mr Panton's b f Chloris, by Waxy, out of Ralphina's dam.

NEWMARKET HOUGHTON MEETING, 1808.

MONDAY.——Sir C. Turner's Cousin Abraham, by Hambletonian, out of Rosalind, agst Mr Shakespear's Discount, 8st 3lb each.— Ab. M. 200gs, h. ft.

LAST DAY.—Sir C. Turner's Peter Plimley, by Hambletonian, out of Caroline, against Mr Shakespear's Discount, 8st 7lb each; 200gs, h. ft.

MONDAY after the Meeting.—Mr Shakespear's Harpocrates, 8st 10lb, against Mr Vansittart's Currycomb, 8st.—Ab. M. 200gs, h. ft.

BIBURY MEETING, 1808.

SWEEPSTAKES of 100gs each.—Two Miles.——Clermont, 10st 9lb; Rubens, by Pencil, 10st 7lb; Rosario, 9st 5lb.

GUILDFORD MEETING—SURREY.

TUESDAY, June 7.——The King's Plate of 100gs, for four-year olds and upwards.—Four-mile heats.

Mr Ladbroke's ch c Master Jackey, by Johnny, 4 yrs old, 10st 4lb (W. Arnold) 1 1
Mr Dilly's br h Gnat-ho! 5 yrs old, 11st 6lb ....2 dr
Mr Braham's b h Oxford, aged, 12st 2lb ....dis

Ten to 1 on Master Jackey.

WEDNESDAY, June 8.—The Town Plate of 50l. for three and four year olds, two-mile heats.—The winner was to have been sold for 200gs, if demanded, &c.

Mr Goodisson's b c Foxberry, by Screveton, 4 yrs old, 8st 10lb 3 1 1
Mr Goulburn's ch c Romeo, 4 yrs old, 8st 7lb............1 2 dis
Mr Jeffrey's gr f Miss Slender, 3 yrs old, 7st 1lb ....2 3 dr

Romeo the favourite; he was thrown down the third heat by a man riding across the course, and the boy who rode was very much hurt.

THURSDAY, June 9.——The Members' Plate of 50l. for four-year olds and upwards, four-mile heats.—The winner was to have been sold for 300gs, if demanded, &c.

Mr Goodisson's b c Foxberry, by Screveton, 4 yrs old, 7st 12lb....1 1
Mr Handley's b h Skipjack, 6 yrs old, 9st 1lb 2 2

Five to 1 on Foxberry.

IRVINE MEETING—AYRSHIRE.

(Over Bogside Race-Course.)

TUESDAY, June 7.——Sweepstakes of 10gs each, for all ages.—Three Miles.—Eight Subscribers.

Mr Boswell's gr f, by Delpini, out of Knee-Buckle's dam, 3 yrs old, 6st 10lb 1
Lord Montgomerie's b f, by Beningbrough, out of Daffodil, 3 yrs old, 6st 10lb 2

Lord Montgomerie's filly ran on the wrong side of a post.

Fifty Pounds given by the Town of Irvine, for all ages.—Three-mile heats.

Mr Bates's br h Honest Harry, by Star, 5 yrs old, 8st 13lb 5 1 1
Lord Montgomerie's gr c Irvine, by Sir Charles, 4 yrs old, 8st 4lb 1 2 2
Mr Henderson's gr f Peteria, 4 yrs old, 8st 1lb 4 3 3
Mr W. Collinson's b m Miss Decoy, 5 yrs old, 8st 10lb........2 dr
Mr Boswell's b f, by Pensioneer, dam by Young Marsk, 3 yrs old, 6st 9lb ....3 dr

Honest Harry fell the first heat, when leading, within the distance-post.
A good race.

WEDNESDAY, June 8.—Fifty Pounds, given by Lord Eglintoun and Lord Montgomerie, for all ages.—Two-mile heats.

Mr Bates's br h Honest Harry, by Star, 5 yrs old, 8st 11lb......1 1
Mr W. Collinson's b m Miss Decoy, 5 yrs old, 8st 8lb.........2 2
Lord Montgomerie's b f, by Beningbrough, 3 yrs old, 6st 9lb....3 3
Mr Henderson's gr f Peteria, 4 yrs old, 7st 13lb 4 4

Honest Harry the favourite.

NEWTON MEETING—LANCASHIRE.

WEDNESDAY, June 15 ——The Gold Cup, value 100gs, with 10gs in specie, a Subscription of 10gs each, by eleven Subscribers, for all ages.—Four Miles.

Sir W. Gerard's br h Julius Cæsar, by Alexander, 5 yrs old, 8st 5lb
(W. Peirse).. 1
Colonel Childers's b c Baron, 4 yrs old, 7st 13lb (J. Garbutt)...... 2
Lord Grey's b f Belinda, 4 yrs old, 7st 7lb 3
Mr C. Smith's b c Phlebotomist, 4 yrs old, 7st 10lb............. 4
Mr Astley's ch g Newton, 5 yrs old, 8st 2lb................... 5

Five to 2 and 3 to 1 on Julius Cæsar.—A good race.

The Maiden Plate of 70l. for all ages.—Three-mile heats.

Lord Wilton's b f, sister to Bucephalus, by Alexander, 3 yrs old,
6st (a Boy) 1 1
Sir T. Stanley's bl c, by Sir Harry, 4 yrs old, 7st 12lb (recd 10gs) 4 2
Mr T. Richardson's b f Cleopatra, 3 yrs old, 6st 2 8
Mr Ackers's ch c Apollo, 3 yrs old, 6st 2lb 6 4
Mr Bagshaw's b c Telemachus, 3 yrs old, 6st 2lb.............5 5
Mr Harris's bay filly, 3 yrs old, 6st (bolted) ....3 dis

Lord Wilton's filly, and Sir Thomas Stanley's colt, against the field;
4 to 1 against any other.—Won very easy.

THURSDAY, June 16.——Seventy Pounds, given by Major-General Heron, for all ages.—Two-mile heats.

Sir W. W. Wynne's b f Mademoiselle Presle, by Sir Peter Teazle,
4 yrs old, 8st 4lb...............................1 5 1
Mr Heywood's b c Honest Bob, 4 yrs old, 8st 5lb..........4 1 4
Mr Clifton's br c, by Sir Solomon, 4 yrs old, 8st 5lb.........2 2 3
Mr Goodall's b f Miss Whitley, 4 yrs old, 8st 5lb............5 4 2
Mr Peacock's b c, by Expectation, 3 yrs old, 6st 10lb.......3 3 dr

Mademoiselle Presle won very easy.

Sweepstakes of 15gs each, for three-year old colts, 8st 3lb, fillies, 8st.—
Two Miles.—Four Subscribers.

Mr Benson's b f Dimple, by Sir Peter Teazle, dam by Rockingham 1
Lord Wilton's b f, sister to Bucephalus.............................2

Dimple the favourite.

FRIDAY, June 17.—Sweepstakes of 10gs each, with 20gs added, for all ages.—Four Miles.—Six Subscribers.

Colonel Childers's b c Baron, by Stamford, 4 yrs old, 7st 7lb (J. Garbutt) 1
Mr

Mr Walker's ch h Baronet, 5 yrs old, 8st 4lb 2
Mr Clifton's b m Josephina, aged, 8st 12lb 3
Six to 4 on Baron.—Won very easy.

Seventy Pounds for all ages.—Four-mile heats.
(Seven entered, but no race.)—Sir W. W. Wynne's b h General Ben-
ningsen, by Meteor, 5 yrs old, 8st 11lb, received the appointed
Premium.

NEWCASTLE MEETING—NORTHUMBERLAND.

MONDAY, June 20.——The Produce Stakes of 50gs each, h. ft. for
three-year old colts, 8st 4lb, fillies, 8st.—Two Miles.—Eleven
Subscribers.

Sir W. Gerard's ch colt, by Hambletonian, out of Mary-Ann (W.
Peirse) 1
Mr Riddell's b f, by Expectation, dam by Spadille (R. Franks) 2
Mr W. Hutchinson's bay colt Dorimond, by St. George (F. Jordon) 3
Three to 1 on Sir W. Gerard's colt.—Won easy.

Sweepstakes of 20gs each, for three-year old colts, 8st 4lb, fillies, 8st.
Two Miles.—Five Subscribers.
Colonel Horton's b c Howroyde, by Bustard, dam by Sir Peter Teazle
(J. Jackson)................................... 1
Mr Baillie's gr colt Marc Antony, by Delpini, dam by Beningbrough 2
Mr Hammond's b c, by L'Orient, dam by Paymaster 3
Mr Ilderton's ch colt, by Stride, dam by Tickle-Toby............ 4
Two to 1 on Howroyde.—Won easy.

Sweepstakes of 20gs each, for four-year old colts, 8st 4lb.—Four Miles.
Five Subscribers.
Mr G. Hutton's br c Cardinal York, by Sir Peter Teazle (J. Shepherd) 1
Sir J. Lawson's ch c Oran, by Expectation (R. Franks).......... 2
Mr W. Hutchinson's b c Silvio (F. Jordon) 3
Seven to 4 on Cardinal York.—Won very easy.

TUESDAY, June 21.——The King's Plate of 100gs, for horses, &c.
—Four Miles.
Mr G. Hutton's br colt Cardinal York, by Sir Peter Teazle, 10st 4lb
(J. Shepherd) 1
Mr Nalton's b c Ranger, by Hyacinthus, 4 yrs old, 10st 4lb (F.
Collinson) 2
Three and 4 to 1 on Cardinal York.—Won very easy.

The Gentlemen's Purse of 50l. for maiden horses, &c.—Three-mile
heats.
Mr Riddell's b f, by Expectation, dam by Spadille, 3 yrs old, 6st
7lb (J. Jones) 1 1
Mr Hammond's bay colt, 3 yrs old, 6st 10lb 3 2
Mr Stevenson's bay colt, 3 yrs old, 6st 10lb 2 3

Sir H. Williamson's b f, by St. George, 3 yrs old, 6st 7lb. . . . . . . 4 — 4

Two to 1 agst Mr Riddell's filly; after the heat, 2 to 1 she won.—A good race.

WEDNESDAY, June 22.—The Silver Cup, value 60gs, added to a Subscription of 5gs each, for horses, &c.—The owner of the second to receive 20gs out of the Stakes.—Heats, two Miles and a quarter each.—Fourteen Subscribers.

Mr Hutchinson's b c Silvio, by St. George, 4 yrs old, 8st 5lb (F. Jordon) 1   1

Mr Nalton's b c Ranger, 5 yrs old, 8st 3lb. 2   2

Six to four on Silvio; after the heat, ten to one on Silvio.—Won cleverly.

The Members' Purse of 50l. for horses, &c.—Four Miles.

Mr Storey's b h Cramlington, by Pipator, 5 yrs old, 8st (G. Sowerby) 1

Mr Cradock's bay filly, by St. George, 4 yrs old, 6st 11lb (J. Jones) 2

Mr Lonsdale's gr c Posthumous, 4 yrs old, 7st 3

Mr Collinson's ch h Streamer, 5 yrs old, 8st. 4

Five to 4 on Streamer, 2 to 1 against Mr Cradock's filly, 6 to 1 against Posthumous, and 10 to 1 against Cramlington.—Won easy.

THURSDAY, June 23.——The Gold Cup, value 100gs, the surplus was paid to the winner in specie, by subscription of 10gs each, for all ages.—Four Miles.—Fourteen Subscribers.

Mr G. Hutton's br c Cardinal York, by Sir Peter Teazle, 4 yrs old, 7st 12lb (J. Shepherd) 1

Mr W. Hutchinson's b h Harmless, 5 yrs old, 8st 7lb (F. Jordon). . 2

Mr Storey's b h Cramlington, 5 yrs old, 8st 7lb 3

Mr Brandling's br h Smasher, 5 yrs old, 8st 7lb 4

Mr Ord's b c, by Delpini, dam by Slope, 3 yrs old, 6st 6lb 5

Mr Storey's ch c Lysander, by Stride, dam by an Arabian, 3 yrs old, 6st 6lb 6

Two and 3 to 1 on Cardinal York.—Won easy.

The Subscription Purse of 50l. for horses, &c. of all ages.—Heats, two Miles and a quarter each.

Mr Collinson's b m Fortuna, by Beningbrough, 5 yrs old, 8st 6lb. 2 2 1 1

Mr Cradock's b f, by St. George, 4 yrs old, 7st 11lb (J. Jones) 3 1 2 2

Mr Riddell's b f, by Expectation, 3 yrs old, 6st 6lb (W. Raper) 1 3 3 3

Two to 1 on Fortuna; after the first heat, 5 to 4 on Mr Riddell's filly; after the second heat, 2 to 1 on Mr Cradock's filly; after the third heat, 6 to 4 on Fortuna, who was beat for the first and second heats, much against her will; after which they changed her rider to J. Jackson, when she won the third and fourth heats in a canter, which clearly proved the superiority of horsemanship.

FRIDAY, June 24.—The Northumberland Stakes of 10gs each, (with 20gs added, to be paid to the owner of the second) for horses, &c. not thorough-bred.—Heats, two Miles and a quarter each.

Mr Ridley's b f Spitfire, by Archduke, 4 years old, 10st 11lb . . 4 1 1

Colonel

Colonel Seddons's b h Cliffe, by Hutton, 6 years old, 12st. ... 1 2 3
Mr Johnson's ch mare Cammis, by Archduke, 5 years old,
   11st 9lb 2 4 3
Mr Watson's bay mare Bess, by Cardinal, aged, 12st. 5 5 4
Mr Weatherley's ch h Sir Hugh, by Jupiter, aged, 12st. 6 6 5
Mr Loftus's br h Young Archduke, by Archduke, 5 years old,
   11st 9lb 7 5 6
Mr Ilderton's br h Hector, by Archduke, 5 years old, 11st 9lb.. 5 7 dr
Mr Davidson's ches filly Lovely-Lass, by Stride, 3 years old,
   9st 4lb .... 3 dr

Six to 4 on Cliffe; after the first heat 6 and 7 to 4 on Cliffe; after the
second heat, even betting.

ASCOT HEATH MEETING—BERKS.

TUESDAY, June 21.—The King's Plate of 100gs for horses, &c.
   which had been regularly hunted with his Majesty's Stag-Hounds.
   —Four-mile heats.
Mr. Shackle's b g Felton, by Beningbrough, aged, 12st (S.
   Chifney) 1 1
Mr. Deane's b h Le Maitre, by Jupiter, aged, 12st. 3 2
Mr Villiers's ch h Strideaway, 6 years old, 11st 12lb 2 3
Mr Howlett's b h Zebukeo, 5 years old, 11st 9lb .... dis.
       Five to 2 on Felton.—Won in a canter.

Sweepstakes of 100gs each, h. ft. for three-year old colts, 8st 7lb;
   fillies, 8st 3lb.—The Old Mile.—Five Subscribers.
Sir C. Bunbury's b f Agnes, by Sorcerer, out of Amelia (F. Buckle) 1
Mr B. Craven's b c Beau Nash, by Trumpator................... 2
Lord G. H. Cavendish's b c, Brother to Ducat, by Coriander....... 3
Mr Lake's b c, by Trumpator, dam by Wallnut (fell) 4
Even betting on Beau Nash, 3 to 1 against Agnes, and 3 to 1 against
       Mr Lake's colt.

The first year of a Sweepstakes of 10gs each, for all ages.—Once
   round, about two Miles and a half.—The winner was to have been
   sold for 300gs, if demanded.—Eleven Subscribers.
Mr Ladbroke's br c Corsican, by Guildford, 4 years old, 7st 9lb (S.
   Arnold) 1
Captain Haffenden's b h Sir Launcelot, 6 years old, 8st 11lb......... 2
Mr Batson's ch h Charmer, 5 years old, 8st 5lb................. 3
Mr Butler's b m Miss Colner, aged, 8st 11lb.................... 4
His R. H. the Duke of York's b f Nymphina, 4 years old, 7st 6lb .. 5

The following also started, but were not placed.
Mr White's bl c Mungo, 4 years old, 7st 9lb.................... 0
Mr. Lake's b h Gaiety, 6 years old, 8st 11lb................... 0
Two to 1 against Corsican, 2 to 1 against Charmer, and 2 to 1 against
       Nymphina.

Match

Match for 100gs.—The last Mile.

Lord Jersey's b c, by the Wellesley Arabian, out of Blowing's dam, 8st 7lb (F. Buckle).. 1

Mr Freemantle's ch c Englefield, by the Wellesley Arabian, dam by Prospect, 8st 7lb... 2

Even betting.—A good race.

Match for 25gs.—The last half Mile.

Lord Jersey's b c Poke, by Waxy, 3 years old, 9st (F. Buckle).... 1

Mr Lake's ch c Silvermere, 2 years old, 7st......................... 2

Two to 1 on Poke.

Lord Egremont's b f, by Gohanna, out of Humming-Bird, 8st 5lb, received forfeit from Lord Foley's filly, by Vermin, dam by Highflyer, 8st 2lb.—The last Mile, 100gs, h. ft.

WEDNESDAY, June 22.—His R. H. the Duke of York's Purse of 50l. for all ages.—Once round and a distance.—The winner was to have been sold for 350gs, if demanded, &c.

Sir J. Honywood's b c Hawk, by Buzzard, 4 years old, 8st 2lb (F. Buckle) 1

Mr Fenwick's b h Sir Launcelot, 6 years old, 9st................. 2

Mr Lake's b h Gaiety, 6 years old, 9st............................ 3

Mr Goodisson's Foxberry, 4 years old, 8st 2lb.................... 4

Mr Halstead's b f Dilemma, 3 years old, 6st 7lb................. 5

Seven to 4 against Hawk, and 5 to 2 against Sir Launcelot.

The Swinley Stakes of 25gs each, 15gs ft. for three and four-year olds.—The last Mile and a half.—Six Subscribers.

Lord Egremont's ch c Election, by Gohanna, 4 years old, 8st 10lb (S. Barnard) 1

Mr Fermor's br c Stripling, 4 years old, 8st 10lb................ 2

Five to 2 and 3 to 1 on Election.—A fine race.

Sweepstakes of 15gs each, for horses, &c. all ages.—About two Miles and 124 Rods.—Nine Subscribers.

Mr Fermor's ch c Bantum, by Gohanna, 4 years old, 7st 12lb (C. Goodisson) 1

Sir J. Honywood's br h Delville, 5 years old, 8st 7lb............. 2

Lord C. H. Somerset's b c White-Rose, 4 years old, 7st 12lb....... 3

Lord Egremont's b c, Brother to Hedley, 4 years old, 7st 12lb 4

The following also started, but were not placed:

Sir J. Mawbey's ch f Grasshopper, 3 years old, 6st 4lb........... 0

Mr G. Villiers's ch c, by Pegasus, out of Friskey, 3 years old, 6st 7lb 0

Mr. Abbey's b f Clorinda, 3 years old, 6st 4lb (broke down)........ 0

Six to 4 against Delville, 4 to 1 against Grasshopper, and 10 to 1 against Bantum, who took the lead, and was never headed.—He was rode in great style.

THURSDAY, June 23.—The first year of a Sweepstakes of 10gs each, for three-year old colts, 8st 7lb, fillies, 8st 2lb.—The New Mile.—Twelve Subscribers.

Mr

Mr Ladbroke's br f Trimbush, by Teddy the Grinder (W. Arnold) .. 1
Lord Egremont's b f, by Gohanna, out of Lazy.................. 2
Mr Witherden's br f, by Teddy the Grinder, out of Kitty Bean.... 3
His R. H. the Duke of York's b c Tumbler, by Trumpator........ 4
Lord Jersey's b c Poke, by Waxy.............................. 5
Six to 4 on Tumbler, 5 to 2 against Lord Egremont's filly, and 3 to 1
    against Trimbush.—Won easy.

The Gold Cup, value 100gs, the surplus in specie ; a Subscription of
    20gs each, for horses, &c. of all ages.—Two Miles and a half.—Se-
    ven Subscribers.
Mr Fermor's br c Brighton, by Gohanna, 4 years old, 8st 2lb (F.
    Buckle)... 0 1
Mr Butler's b c Epsom, 4 years old, 8st 2lb.................. 0 2
Mr Best's ch f Augusta, 4 years old, 7st 13lb................ 3
Mr Trevanion's b c Lewes, 4 years old, 8st 2lb............... 4
Mr Freemantle's ch c Englefield, 3 years old, 6st 12lb........ 5
    Two to 1 on Brighton ; after the dead heat, 6 to 4 on Epsom.

Match for 100gs.—The last half Mile.
Lord G. H. Cavendish's b m Pagoda, by Sir Peter Teazle, 5 years old,
    8st 8lb (W. Wheatley) 1
Mr B. Craven's b c Beau Nash, 3 years old, 7st 7lb (C. Goodisson).. 2
    Six to 4 on Beau Nash.—A fine race.

Match for 100gs.—The last Mile.
Lord Jersey's b c, by the Wellesley Arabian, out of Blowing's dam,
    8st 2lb (F. Buckle)...................................... 1
Lord Foley's filly, by Vermin, 8st 7lb 2
    Six to 4 on Lord Jersey's colt.

Fifty Pounds for horses, &c. the property of Yeomen Prickers, &c. 12st.
                    . Four-mile heats.
Mr Starling's b g Blenheim, by Coriander, aged, received the 10gs pre-
                    mium.
    Lord Egremont's b f, by Gohanna, out of Lazy, 8st 5lb, received
forfeit from Lord Foley's Miss Prince, 8st 2lb.—The last Mile, 100gs.
half forfeit.

FRIDAY, June 24.—Sweepstakes of 20gs each, for four-year olds
and upwards.—Three Miles.—Five Subscribers.
Lord Egremont's b h Canopus, by Gohanna, 5 years old,
    8st 4lb .... walked over.

Sweepstakes of 30gs each, 20gs ft. for two-year old colts, 8st 5lb ; fil-
    lies, 8st 2lb.—Half a Mile.
His R. H. the Duke of York's ch c Silvermere, Brother to Humility,
    by Gouty (W. Wheatley).............................. 1
Mr Fermor's b f, Sister to Bantum, by Gohanna 2
Mr Emden's b f Miss Seedling, by Totteridge (3lb extra)........ 3
Mr Ladbroke's b f, Sister to Election, by Gohanna............. 4
    Two to 1 on Miss Seedling, and 10 to 1 against Silvermere.
                                                Sweepstakes

Sweepstakes of 20gs each.—Two Miles.

Mr Batson's ch c Gladiator, by Buzzard, 6st 7lb (F. Buckle) 1
Mr Turner's b c Drake, by Grouse, 8st 5lb 2
Mr Taighe's b c Wrynose, by Worthy, 8st 5lb. p4

Handicap Plate of 50l.—Heats, about two Miles and 124 Rods.

Mr Batson's ch c Gladiator, by Buzzard, 4 years old, 7st 12lb (S.
  Arnold) 1 1
Mr Goodisson's b c Foxberry, 4 years old, 7st 12lb. 8 8
Captain Haffenden's ch g Tom Pipes, aged, 8st 13lb. 5 3
Lord Jersey's b c Poke, 3 years old, 6st 4lb. .... 2 dr
Mr F. Craven's ch c Bantum, 4 years old, 8st 8lb .... 3 dr
Sir H. Lippincott's b g Ploughboy, 5 years old, 8st 6lb. ...... 4 dr
Mr Sutton's ch f Hasty, by Gouty, 4 years old, 7st 12lb. ...... 6 dr
Mr Hyde's b c Teddy, 3 years old, 5st 12lb. .... 7 dr
Mr Braham's b g Oxford, aged, 8st 11lb. .... dis

Five to 1 against Gladiator, the same against Bantum, and the same
  against Foxberry; after the heat, 6 to 4 against Gladiator, whose rider
  broke a stirrup just after starting for the second heat; notwithstanding, he won easy.

TENBURY MEETING—WORCESTERSHIRE.

WEDNESDAY, June 22.——The Maiden Plate of 50l. for all ages.
  —Three-mile heats.

Mr Turner's b f Maid of Dunham, by Chaunter, 3 yrs old, 5st
  11lb. 3 1 1
Mr Wakeman's ch m Goldfinch, 5 years old, 8st 3lb. 1 2 2
Mr Denham's ch c, by Kite, 4 years old, 7st 7lb. .... 2 3 dr
Mr Benson's b f Dairymaid, 3 years old, 5st 11lb. .... 5 fell
Mr Webber's ch m Peppercorn, aged, 8st 11lb. .... 4 dr
Mr Saunders's b c, by Moorcock, 4 years old, 7st 7lb (ran out
  of the Course). .... dis
Dairymaid the favourite.

THURSDAY, June 23.—The Noblemen and Gentlemen's Purse of
50l. for all ages.—Four-mile heats.

Mr Benson's gr h Atlas, by Sir Peter Teazle, 5 years old, 8st 6lb.. 1 1
Mr Tinkler's b c, by Hambletonian, 3 years old, 6st 4lb........ 2 2
Mr Webber's ch m Peppercorn, aged, 8st 13lb. .... 3 dr
Five to 1 on Atlas.—Won easy.

STAMFORD MEETING.—LINCOLNSHIRE.

TUESDAY, June 28.—Sweepstakes of 20gs each, for three-year old
  colts and fillies.—Once round and a distance.—Seven Subscribers.
Mr Sitwell's b f Gooseander, by Hambletonian, 8st 7lb. 1
Lord Grosvenor's b f Isis, by Sir Peter Teazle, 8st 3lb. 2
Lord Fitzwilliam's ch c Pumpkin, by Stamford, 8st 2lb 3

Mr

Mr O'Brien's ch f Jalietta, by Young Drone, 8st 3lb 4

Even betting on Gooseander, and 7 to 4 against Isis.

The Town Plate of 50l. for all ages.—Heats, twice round the Course.

Mr C. Browne's b f Miltonia, by Patriot, 4 yrs old, 8st 4lb (S.
   Chifney) 0 1 1
Mr Andrew's ch h Achilles, 5 yrs, 9st 7lb.................... 0 2 3
Mr Inchley's b h Buzzard, 5 yrs, 9st 3lb 3 3 2

Six to 4 against Buzzard, 2 to 1 agst Achilles, and 3 to 1 agst Miltonia.

WEDNESDAY, June 29.——The Gold Cup, value 100gs, the surplus to be paid the winner in specie, a Subscription of 10gs each, for all ages.—Four Miles.—Twelve Subscribers.

Lord Grosvenor's bay mare Meteora, by Meteor, 6 yrs old, 8st 10lb
   (F. Buckle) 1
Mr Andrew's b m Lydia, 6 yrs old, 8st 10lb.................. 2
Mr Sitwell's br c Clinker, 3 yrs old, 6st................... 3
Mr C. Browne's b c Wildair, 4 yrs old, 7st 7lb 4

Five to 4 agst Meteora, 5 to 4 against Clinker, and 10 to 1 agst Lydia.

The Maiden Plate of 50l. for three-year old colts, 8st 2lb, fillies, 8st.—
         Heats, once round the Course.

Lord Fitzwilliam's ch c Pumpkin, by Stamford, out of Matron (W.
   Clift) 1 1
Mr Girdler's br c Worthy the Second......................... 2 2
Mr C. Browne's b f Anna, by Coriander...................... 3 3
Mr Fisher's b f, by Sir Solomon............................ 4 4

Two to 1 against Worthy the Second; after the heat, 2 to 1 on Pumpkin.

THURSDAY, June 30.——Fifty Pounds, given by the Trustees of the Marquis of Exeter, for all ages.—Heats, thrice round the Course.

Mr Addy's b h Buzzard, by Buzzard, 5 yrs old, 8st 10lb 1 1
Mr C. Browne's b f Anna, 3 yrs old, 6st 3lb................... 2 2
Major Wilson's b c Wildair, 4 yrs old, 8st................... 3 3

Mr Andrew received 10gs to withdraw Thorn.

Five and 6 to 4 on Buzzard.

Sweepstakes of 5gs each, for hunters.—Heats, twice round the Course.
       Gentlemen riders.—Thirteen Subscribers.

Mr Watson's bay horse Monarch, by a Son of Young Marsk, 12st
   (Mr Tatton Sykes) 1 1
Mr. W. Noel's b m Maid of the Oaks, by Traveller, 11st 11lb
   (Mr Calcraft) 2 2
Mr Clementson's ch g Burgundy, by Bourdeaux, 11st 11lb (Mr
   Bolton) 3 3

Even betting, and 5 to 4 on Monarch.

The Macaroni Stakes of 5gs each, for horses, &c. 12st.—Gentlemen
      riders.—One-mile heats.—Twelve Subscribers.

Mr O'Brien's Jeffery Gambolla (Dr. J. Willis)................ 1 1
Mr Phelps's Longitude (Mr S. S. Prime)...................... 2 dr
Mr Johnson's gr g Young Alfred .... 3 dr

Ten to 1 on Longitude.—An uncommonly fine race.

CARDIFF MEETING—GLAMORGANSHIRE.

WEDNESDAY, June 29.——The Maiden Plate of 50l. for all ages. Two-mile heats.

Mr Lord's ch c, by George, 4 yrs old, 8st 6lb 1   1
Mr Lewis's ch c, by Caustic, 3 yrs old, 7st 2   2
Mr Webber's ch m Peppercorn, aged, 9st 4lb 3   3
Captain Richards's b f Win-if-she-can, 4 yrs old, 8st 3lb 4   dr

Sweepstakes of 10gs each, for all ages.—Two-mile heats.—Six Subscribers.

Mr Hurst's ch g Wild-Oats, by Buzzard, 6 yrs old, 9st 4lb, walked over.

THURSDAY, June 30.—Fifty Pounds for three and four-year olds. Two-mile heats.

Mr Lord's ch c, by George, 4 yrs old, 8st 12lb 1   1
Mr Lewis's ch c Buckler, 4 yrs old, 8st 12lb 2   2
Mr Hurst's b c Red-Rose, by Beningbrough, 3 yrs old, 7st 5lb . . 3   dr

Sweepstakes of 5gs each, for horses, &c. 10st.—Two-mile heats.—Ten Subscribers.

Mr Wood's b m Elvira 1   1
Mr Wrixon's br g Singlepeeper 2   2

FRIDAY, July 1.—Fifty Pounds for horses, &c. all ages.—Four-mile heats.

Mr Hurst's ch g Wild-Oats, by Buzzard, 6 yrs old, 9st 4lb 1   1
Mr Lord's b c, by Stickler, 4 yrs old, 8st 6lb 2   2
Mr Lewis's ch c Buckler, 4 yrs old, 8st 6lb 3   3

BIBURY MEETING—OXFORDSHIRE.

MONDAY, July 4.——The Sherborne Stakes of 50gs each, 30gs ft. and only 10gs ft. if declared, &c. for horses, &c.—Four Miles.

Mr Goulburn's gr h Grimaldi, by Delpini, 6 yrs old, 11st 3lb (Mr Draper) 1
Lord C. H. Somerset's b c White-Rose, 4 yrs old, 9st 8lb (Mr Germaine) 2
Sir H. Lippincott's br c Chaise-and-One, 4 yrs old, 9st 8lb (Mr Worrall) 3
Mr B. Price's ch g Malmsbury, 6 yrs old, 8st 13lb (Mr Douglas) . . 4
Mr Goddard's br m Bronze, 5 yrs old, 10st 10lb (Mr Lindow) 5
Six to 4 against White-Rose, 6 to 4 against Chaise-and-One, 3 to 1 against Grimaldi, and 6 to 1 against Malmsbury.—A good race.

The following having declared forfeit within the time prescribed, paid only 10gs each.

Mr Vansittart named Mountaineer, 6 yrs old, 11st 10lb.
Sir J. Hawkins's Clermont, 5 yrs old, 11st 6lb.
Major Harvey named Knee-Buckle, 5 yrs old, 10st 11lb.
Lord Monson named Docter, 5 yrs old, 10st 10lb.

Sir H. Peyton named Timekeeper, 6 yrs old, 10st 9lb.
Mr Whitmore named Laura, aged, 10st 13lb.

Sweepstakes of 100gs each, h. ft.—Two Miles.

Sir J. Hawkins's br h Clermont, by Trumpator, 10st 9lb (Mr Worrall) 1
Mr Biggs's br c Rosario, 9st 5lb (Mr Douglas) 2
Mr Dundas's Rubens, 10st 7lb (Mr Germaine) 3

Five to 4 against Clermont, and the same against Rosario. A good race, and won by a neck.

Handicap Stakes of 10gs each, with 25gs added, for horses, &c.—Two Miles.—Five Subscribers.

Mr Hallett's ch m Jewess, by Ambrosio, 5 yrs old, 10st 6lb (Mr. Germaine) 1
Mr Rush's ch h Timekeeper, 6 yrs old, 10st 10lb (Mr Lindow) 2
Mr B. Price's bay horse Knee-Buckle, 5 yrs old, 11st 1lb (Mr Douglas) 3
Sir H. Lippincott's b g Ploughboy, 5 years old, 10st 10lb (Mr Worrall) 4

Five to 2 against Jewess.—Won rather easy.

TUESDAY, July 5.—Sweepstakes of 25gs each, 15gs ft, with 100gs added, for horses, &c.—Four Miles.—Three Subscribers.

Lord Egremont's b h Canopus, by Gohanna, 5 yrs old, 11st 7lb .... walked over.

Sweepstakes of 5gs each, with 100gs added, for horses, &c.—Three Miles.—Twenty Subscribers.

Sir J. Hawkins's br h Clermont, by Trumpator, 5 yrs old, 11st 5lb (Mr Douglas) 1
Lord Egremont's b c, Brother to Hedley, 4 yrs old, 10st 4lb (Mr Germaine) 2
Mr R. Canning's ch g Sweeper, aged, 12st (Mr Tatton Sykes) 3
Mr Goulburn's ch c Romeo, 4 yrs old, 10st 4lb (Mr Draper) 4
Colonel Kingscote's b h Doctor, 5 yrs old, 11st 2lb (Mr Worrall).. 5
Mr C. Dundas's b h Rubens, 5 yrs old, 11st 5lb (Mr Lindow).... 6

Even betting on Clermont, and 7 to 4 against Rubens.—A good race.

Handicap Plate of 50l. for horses, &c.—Two-mile heats.

Sir H. Lippincott's b c, by Trumpator, out of Beda, 4 yrs old, 9st 9lb (Mr Worrall) 1 1
Mr B. Price's ch g Malmsbury, 6 yrs old, 9st 5lb (Mr Douglas)..2 2

Five to 2 on Malmsbury.

WEDNESDAY, July 6.——Match for 50gs.—Two Miles.

Mr Biggs's br c Rosario, by Ambrosio, 4 years old, 10st (Mr Douglas) 1
Mr Goulburn's grey horse Grimaldi, 6 yrs old, 11st 7lb (Mr Germaine) 2

Two to 1 on Grimaldi.
H 2   Sweep-

Sweepstakes of 10gs each, with 50gs added, for horses, &c.—Two Miles and a half.—Four Subscribers.

Sir H. Lippincott's b g Ploughboy, by Volunteer, 5 yrs old, 11st 3lb (Mr Worrall) 1
Mr Price's ch g Maltmsbury, 6 yrs old, a feather (Mr Draper)....... 2
Mr Goddard's br mare Bronze, 5 yrs old, 11st (Mr Germaine) 3

Even betting between Ploughboy and Bronze.—A good race.

The 100gs Plate for horses, &c.—Three Miles.
Lord Egremont's b h, Canopus, by Gohanna, 5 yrs old, 11st 4lb (Mr Douglas) 1
Mr Goulburn's gr h Grimaldi, 6 yrs old, 11st 3lb (Mr Germaine).. 2

Five to 1 on Canopus.—Won easy.

THURSDAY, July 7.—Match for 50gs.—Two Miles.
Lord C. H. Somerset's b c White-Rose, by Beningbrough, 10st (Mr Germaine) 1
Lord Egremont's bay colt, Brother to Hedley, 9st 11lb (Mr. Douglas) 2

Even betting.—Won by a head.

Match for 50gs.— Three Miles.
Mr Hallett's ch m Jewess, by Ambrosio, 5 yrs old, 10st (Mr Germaine) 1
Mr Rush's ch h Timekeeper, 6 yrs old, 10st (Mr Worrall)........ 2

Won by a neck.

Match for 25gs.—The New Mile.
Lord C. H. Somerset's b c White-Rose, by Beningbrough, 4 yrs old, 9st 12lb (Mr Germaine).................................... 1
Mr B. Price's bay horse Knee-Buckle, 5 yrs old, 10st 7lb (Mr Worrall) 2

Won very easy.

Handicap Plate of 50l.—Heats, the New Mile.
Mr Biggs's br c Rosario, by Ambrosio, 4 yrs old, 10st 10lb (Mr Lindow) 1 1
Lord Egremont's bay colt, Brother to Hedley, 4 yrs old, 10st 6lb (Mr Douglas) 3 2
Sir H. Lippincott's b c Chaise-and-One, 4 yrs old, 10st (Mr Worrall) 2 3
Mr Cope's b g Nettle, aged, 9st 3lb .... dis

Rosario the favourite.—Won by a head.

NANTWICH MEETING—CHESHIRE.

WEDNESDAY, July 6.—The Maiden Plate of 50l. for horses, &c. of all ages.—Three-mile heats.
Mr C. Smith's b c Phlebotomist, by Beningbrough, 4 yrs old, 8st 1 1
General Grosvenor's b f, by King Bladud, 3 yrs old, 5st 12lb.... 2 2

Two to 1 on Phlebotomist.

THURSDAY, July 7.——Sweepstakes of 10gs each, for horses, &c. of all ages.—Three-mile heats.—Five Subscribers.
Mr Leigh's b g Plunder, by Moorcock, 5 yrs old, 8st 7lb 1 1

Mr

Mr Downes's gr f Twig'em, by Dapple, out of Fairy, 8 years old,
    6st 5lb 2 2
    Five to 4 on Plunder ; after the heat, 2 to 1 he won.

FRIDAY, July 7.—Fifty Pounds for all ages.—Four-mile heats.
Mr Smith's b c Phlebotomist, by Beningbrough, 4 years old,
    7st 6lb.. 3 1 1
General Grosvenor's b f, by King Bladud, 3 years old, (re-
    ceived 10l.) a feather............................... 2 2 2
Lord Wilson's b f, Sister to Bucephalus, 3 years old, a feather.. 1 dis
The Sister to Bucephalus the favourite, who ran out of the course the
       second heat.

———————

NEWMARKET JULY MEETING.

MONDAY, July 11.——Match for Fifty Guineas.——Abingdon
    Mile.
General Grosvenor's ch c John O'Gaunt, by Buzzard, 8st 7lb (F.
    Buckle) 1
Mr Lake's b c Fuscus, Brother to Forester, by Grouse, 8st 3lb...... 2
    Five and 6 to 4 on Fuscus.—Won easy.

    Match for 100gs.—Two-year Olds' Course.
Lord Grosvenor's b c Sunbeam, by Meteor, 8st 6lb (F. Buckle).... 1
Lord G. H. Cavendish's b f Podagra, 8st 1lb 2
    Six to 4 on Sunbeam.—Won very easy.

The July Stakes of 50gs each, 30gs ft. for two-year old colts, 8st 6lb ;
    fillies, 8st 4lb.—Two-year Olds' Course.—Seventeen Subscribers.
Mr Wilson's bay filly Spindle, by Shuttle, out of Dimple, by High-
    flyer (W. Clift) 1
Lord Jersey's gr c Nicholas, (late Favourite) by Don Quixote, out of
    Darling's dam (Buckle) 2
Mr Payne's ch f, by Don Quixote, out of Lady Cow, by John Bull.. 3
Mr Emden's b f Miss Seedling, by Totteridge.................. 4

    The following also started, but were not placed :

Mr Blachford's b f Medina, by Worthy........................ 0
Lord F. G. Osborne's b f, by Sorcerer or Whiskey, out of Canary, by
    Coriander 0
Sir C. Bunbury's b f, by Sorcerer, out of Amelia.............. 0
Mr Harbord's ch f, by Young Woodpecker, out of a Sister to Pet-
    worth, by Precipitate 0
Lord Barrymore's br c, Brother to Luck's-All 0
Mr Elwes's b f, by Waxy, out of a sister to Peter Pindar, by Javelin 0
Duke of Grafton's f, by Waxy, out of Penelope................ 0
Mr Panton's b f Chloris, by Waxy, out of Ralphina's dam, by Dun-
    gannon.. 0
Lord Foley's b c, by Don Quixote, out of Adelina 0
                          Forty-

Forty-five to 20 against Mr Payne's filly, 5 to 1 against Spindle, 7 to 1 against Nicholas, 7 to 1 against Lord Foley's colt, and 8 to 1 against Miss Seedling.—Won by half a length, and very easy.

Match for 100gs.—Abingdon Mile.

Lord Jersey's b c, by the Wellesley Arabian, out of Blowing's dam, 8st 3lb (F. Buckle)... 1

Lord G. H. Cavendish's b c, by Coriander, out of Mrs Candour, 8st 3lb... 2

Eleven to 8 on Lord Jersey's colt.—Won very easy.

Match for 100gs.—Ditch Mile.

Mr Payne's br c Bullrush, by Sir Peter Teazle, 4 years old, 8st 2lb (F. Buckle)... 1

Lord G. H. Cavendish's b h Dreadnought, aged, 8st 3½lb........... 2

Six to 5 on Dreadnought.

Match for 50gs.—Two-year Olds' Course.

Duke of Grafton's b m Vanity, by Buzzard, 8st (W. Clift)........ 1

Lord Sackville's b h Deceiver, 8st 7lb.......................... 2

Even betting.—A fine race.

Match for 100gs.—Two-year Olds' Course.

Mr Wyndham's b h Empingham, by Schedoni, 5 years old, 8st 6lb (S. Barnard).. 1

Duke of Rutland's br c Rambler, 4 years old, 8st (F. Buckle)...... 2

Eleven to 8 on Empingham.—Rambler bolted on the wrong side of the Ending-Post when first.

Match for 200gs.—Two-year Olds' Course.

Mr Vansittart's b h Currycomb, by Buzzard, 6 years old, 8st 7lb (S. Chifney)... 1

Lord Lowther's b h Tot, aged, 8st 7lb........................... 2

Five to 4 on Currycomb.—A fine race, but won cleverly at the end.

TUESDAY, July 12.—Match for 100gs.—Across the Flat.

General Grosvenor's ches. colt, John O'Gaunt, by Buzzard, 8st 3lb (F. Buckle).. 1

Duke of Rutland's bay colt Ned, by Teddy the Grinder, dam by Precipitate, 8st... 2

Five to 4 on Ned.—Won easy.

The July Stakes of 100gs each, h. ft. for three-year old colts, 8st 7lb; fillies, 8st 3lb.—The winner of the Derby or Oaks' Stakes, carrying 5lb extra.—Across the Flat.—Seven Subscribers.

Duke of Grafton's b f Morel, by Sorcerer, out of Hornby-Lass, won the Oaks' (W. Clift)... 1

Mr Ladbroke's b c Chester, by Sir Peter Teazle.................. 2

Five to 4 on Morel.—Won quite easy.—Mr. Ladbroke gave Lord Grosvenor 1200gs for Chester, with his engagements, after running for the Derby Stakes.

The first year of a renewal of a Sweepstakes of 10gs each, for all ages. Two middle Miles of B. C.—Ten Subscribers.

Sir C. Bunbury's ch h Snug, by Whiskey, 5 yrs old, 8st 10lb (a boy) 1

Mr

Mr Watson's bay colt, by Coriander, out of Mrs Candour, 3 years old 6st 9lb.. 2
Mr Lake's br c Fuscus, 3 years old, 6st 9lb 3
General Grosvenor's br colt Woodcutter, 4 years old, 8st 1lb........ 4
Mr Wyndham's b c, by Whiskey, out of Minion, 3 years old, 6st 9lb 5
Lord F. G. Osborne's b f, by Stickler, 3 years old, 6st 9lb 6
Lord Jersey's br f, by Stamford, out of Alexina, 3 years old, 6st 9lb.. 7
Mr Wilson named Empingham, 5 years old, 8st 10lb................. 8
Three to 1 against Snug.—Won in a canter.

WEDNESDAY, July 13.—Match for 100gs.—Abingdon Mile.
Duke of Grafton's b f Morel, by Sorcerer, 8st (W. Clift).......... 1
Lord Stawell's ches. colt, by Sorcerer, out of Sir David's dam, 8st 4lb 2
Five to 2, and 3 to 1 on Morel.—Won in a canter.

Match for 25gs.—Two-year Olds' Course.
Duke of Grafton's b f Pennyroyal, by Coriander, out of Peppermint,
3 years old, 7st 8lb (B. Moss)................................. 1
Lord Stawell's b f Pantina, 4 years old, 8st 8lb.................. 2
Two to 1 on Pantina.—Won easy.

Match for 50gs.—Two-year Olds' Course.
General Grosvenor's ches. colt, John O'Gaunt, by Buzzard, 3 years
old, 7st 3lb (B. Moss)... 1
Mr Panton's b f Ralphina, 4 years old, 8st 1lb................... 2
Six to 4 on Ralphina.—Won by half a neck.

Match for 50gs.—Two-year Olds' Course.
Duke of Grafton's filly, by Waxy, out of Penelope, 8st 3lb (W.
Clift) 1
Mr Panton's b c Satyr, by Waxy, 8st 3lb 2
Seven to 4, and 2 to 1 on Satyr.—A fine race.

Match for 50gs.—Across the Flat.
Lord Jersey's b h Langton, by Precipitate, 6 years old, 9st (F. Buckle) 1
Duke of Rutland's b c Ned, 3 years old, 7st 6lb................. 2
Four to 1 on Langton.—Won easy.

Match for 50gs.—Abingdon Mile.
Lord Sackville's ch h Prospero, by Whiskey, aged, 8st 1lb (W.
Wheatley) 1
Mr Shakespear's Wormwood, 6 years old, 8st 7lb 2
Seven to 4 and 2 to 1 on Prospero.—Won easy.

Fifty Pounds for all ages.—Ditch-in.
Duke of Grafton's b m Vanity, by Buzzard, 5 years old, 8st 8lb (W.
Clift) 1
General Grosvenor's Woodcutter, 4 years old, 8st.............. 2
Ten and 15 to 1 on Vanity.—Won in a canter.

THURSDAY, July 14.—The Town Plate of 50l. for three-year old
colts, 8st 4lb; fillies, 8st.—Last Mile and a Distance.
Lord Grosvenor's b c Sunbeam, by Meteor, out of Hind (F. Buckle) 1
Major Wilson's ch c Juniper, by Whiskey..................... 2

Lord

Lord Stawell's ch c, by Sorcerer............................1/3

Seven to 4 on Juniper, and 2 to 1 against Sunbeam.—Won very easy.

Sweepstakes of 25gs each.—Yearling Course.

Lord Foley's b c, by Don Quixote, out of Adelina, by Highflyer, 7st 11lb (B. Moss)............................1
Lord Jersey's gr c Nicholas, 8st 7lb (F. Buckle)............2
Sir C. Bunbury's b f, Sister to Agnes, 7st 13lb............3

Five to 4 on Nicholas, 6 to 4 against the Sister to Agnes, and 10 to 1 agst Lord Foley's colt.—A fine race.

Match for 200gs.—First half of Ab. M.

Mr Payne's ch f, by Don Quixote, out of Lady Cow, 8st (W. Clift) 1
Sir J. Shelly's c, by Waxy, out of Julia, 8st 4lb............2

Three to 1 and 7 to 2 on Mr Payne's filly.—Won easy.

Match for 50gs.—Ditch Mile.

Mr Payne's br c Barbarian, by Worthy, 4 years old, 8st 12lb (W. Clift)............1
General Grosvenor's ch c John O'Gaunt, 3 years old, 7st 6lb (B. Moss)............2

Five to 4 on Barbarian.—A fine race, and won by a neck.

PRESTON MEETING.

TUESDAY, July 12.—The Produce Stakes of 50gs each, for three-year old colts, 8st 4lb; fillies, 8st.—Two Miles.—Four Subscribers.

Mr Clifton's b c Poulton, Brother to Fyldener, by Sir Peter Teazle, (J. Shepherd)............1
Mr Tarleton's br f Pussy Cat, by Mr Teazle............2
Mr E. L. Hodgson's gr f, by Shuttle............3

Five and 6 to 1 on Poulton.—Won easy.

The Maiden Plate of 50l. for all ages.—Two-mile heats.

Mr Clifton's br c Dusronnal, by Sir Solomon, 4 years old, 8st (J. Shepherd)............1 1
Lord Derby's br c Jacobus, by Sir Peter Teazle, 3 years old, 6st 10lb (received 10l.)............2 2
Mr Morley's b f, by Hambletonian, 3 years old, 6st 7lb............4 3
Mr Gillibrand's b g, by Telescope, 5 years old, 8st 7lb............6 4
Mr Jordon's br g, 6 years old, 8st 10lb............5 5

Six to 4 against Dusronnal.—Won easy.

WEDNESDAY, July 13.—The Union Cup, value 100gs, added to a Subscription of 10gs each, for all ages.—Near Four Miles.—Nineteen Subscribers.

Sir W. Gerard's br h Julius Cæsar, by Alexander, 5 years old, 8st 10lb (W. Peirse)............1
Mr Clifton's b m Josephina, aged, 8st 10lb............2
Duke of Hamilton's b c Petronius, 3 years old, 6st 6lb............3

1 Mr Wentworth's b f Margaret, 4 yrs old, 7st 12lb 4
Mr Pearse's b c Bedalian, 4 yrs old, 8st 5
      Six to 4 against Julius Cæsar.—Won easy.
   Fifty Pounds for three and four year olds.—Two-mile heats.
Mr Harris's br g Viper, by Serpent, 4 yrs old, 8st 5lb 1 11
Mr Morley's b f, by Hambletonian, 3 years old, 6st 12lb (re-
  ceived 10l.) 2 12
      Three and 4 to 1 on Viper.—Won easy.

THURSDAY, July 14.—Fifty Pounds for all ages.—Two-mile heats.
Mr Harris's br g Viper, by Serpent, 4 yrs old, 8st 11lb 1 1
Mr W. Hutchinson's ch h Harmless, 5 years old, 8st 11lb (re-
  ceived 10l.) 2 2
    Three and 4 to 1 on Harmless.—Won very easy.

IPSWICH MEETING—SUFFOLK.

TUESDAY, July 5.—The King's Plate of 100gs for three and four-
  year olds.—Two-mile heats.
Major Wilson's ch c Juniper, by Whiskey, 3 yrs old, 7st 11lb 1 1
General Grosvenor's gr c Woodcutter, 4 yrs old, 9st 5lb 3 2
Mr Goodisson's b c Foxberry, 4 yrs old, 9st 5lb 4 3
Mr Williams's ch f, 3 yrs old, 7st 1lb .... 2 dr
    Juniper the favourite.—After the heat, 2 to 1 on Juniper.

WEDNESDAY, July 6.—Fifty Pounds for horses, &c.—Heats,
about two Miles and a quarter.
Mr Goodisson's br c Foxberry, by Screveton, 4 yrs old, 8st 11lb .. 3 1 1
Mr N. Bacon's b c Patriot, 3 yrs old, 7st 7lb 1 4 2
Colonel Harbord's b m, by Saxe Cobourg, 5 yrs old, —st 1lb .. 3 3 4
Major Wilson's br c Brown Stout, 4 yrs old, 8st 11lb 4 5 3
Sir C. Bunbury's ch h Snug, 5 yrs old, 9st 4lb .... 2 2 dr
      Snug the favourite.

THURSDAY, July 7.—Fifty Pounds for horses, &c.—Two-mile heats.
Mr Goodisson's b c Foxberry, by Screveton, 4 yrs old, 8st 11lb 1 1
Mr N. Bacon's b c Patriot, 3 yrs old, 7st 3 2
Major Wilson's br c Brown Stout, 4 yrs old, 8st 8lb 2 3
      Foxberry the favourite.

NEWMARKET.

MONDAY, July 18, (after the Meeting.)—Match for 200gs.—
  Abingdon Mile.
Mr. Payne's ch f, by Don Quixote, out of Lady Cow, 8st 4lb (F.
  Buckle) 1
Sir J. Shelly's filly Pea-Blossom, by Don Quixote, dam by Pipator,
  grandam by Slope, 7st 4lb 2
      Two to 1 on Mr Payne's filly.

STOCKBRIDGE MEETING.—HAMPSHIRE.

THURSDAY, July 14.—Sweepstakes of 5gs each, for horses, &c.—Heats, two Miles and a quarter.—Fifteen Subscribers.

Sir J. Hawkins's br c Rosario, by Ambrosio, 4 years old, 10st 2lb 3 1 1
Mr Seckham's br c, by Trumpator, out of Beda, 4 yrs old, 10st 2lb 1 5 4
Lord Egremont's b c, Brother to Hedley, 4 years old, 9st 13lb .. 4 2 2
Mr Fellowes's b c Mandarine, 4 yrs old, 9st 13lb 5 4 3
Mr Butler's br c Epsom, 4 yrs old, 9st 13lb .... 4 3 dr

Fifty Pounds for three and four-year olds.—Two-mile heats.

Sir H. Lippincott's br c Choise-and-One, by Sir Peter Teazle, 4 yrs
old, 8st 12lb 1 1
Mr Barrett's br c, by Skyrocket, 3 yrs old, 7st 5lb 4 2
Mr Bacon's Coquetilla, 3 yrs old, 7st 3lb 5 3
Lord De Dunstanville's br f Fawn, 4 yrs old, 8st 10lb .... 2 dr
Mr Butler's ch f Bona-Lass, 3 yrs old, 7st 3lb .... 3 dr

FRIDAY, July 15.—Sweepstakes of 15gs each, for three and four-year olds.—The last Mile and a half.—Four Subscribers.

Sir J. Hawkins's br c Rosario, by Ambrosio, 4 yrs old, 8st 12lb 1
Sir H. Lippincott's br f Sorceress, 3 yrs old, 7st 8lb 2
Six to 4 on Sorceress.—Won easy.

The Maiden Plate of 50l. for all ages.—Four-mile heats.

Mr Rush's ch h Timekeeper, by Hambletonian, 6 years old,
9st 5lb 3 3 1 1
Lord Egremont's b c, Brother to Hedley, 4 years old, 8st 3lb.. 0 1 3 2
Mr Goddard's br m Bronze, 5 yrs old, 8st 10lb............ 0 2 2 3
Hedley the favourite.

BRIDGENORTH MEETING—SHROPSHIRE.

THURSDAY, July 14.—Fifty Pounds for three and four-year olds.—Two-mile heats.

Mr Benson's b f Cecilia, by Beningbrough, 4 years old, 8st 10lb.. 1 1
Mr Goulbourn's b c Whitenose, 4 years old, 8st 12lb.........,.. 2 2
Sir T. Mostyn's b c, by Mr Teazle, 3 yrs old, 7st 7lb......... 3 dr
Lord Stamford's b c Gustavus, by Beningbrough, received 10l. to
withdraw.

FRIDAY, July 15.—Sweepstakes of 10gs each, for all ages.—Four Miles.—Five Subscribers.

Lord Stamford's ch h St. Domingo, by Hambletonian,
5 years old .... walked over

Fifty Pounds for all ages.—Four-mile heats.

Lord Stamford's St. Domingo received 10gs .... ●

WINCHESTER MEETING—HANTS.

TUESDAY, July 19.—Match for Fifty Guineas.—Last Mile and half.

Mr Batson's ch h Charmer, by Whiskey, 5 years old, 7st 9lb........ 1
Mr

Mr Goddard's b h Mountaineer, 6 years old, 8st 9lb................ 2
Mountaineer the favourite.

Match for 50gs.—Two Miles.
Mr F. Craven's ch c Bantum, by Gohanna, 7st 12lb 1
Mr Trevanion's b c Lewes, 7st 12lb........................... 2
Five to 4 on Bantum.

The King's Plate of 100gs, for four-year olds and upwards.—Four-mile heats.
Mr Trevanion's b h Bucephalus, by Alexander, 6 years old, 12st
(S. Chifney) 3 1 1
Mr Blachford's b h Shittlecock, 5 yrs old, 11st 6lb.......... 1 2 dr
Mr Dundas's b c Cambrian, 4 yrs old, 10st 4lb.............. 2 3 dr
Cambrian the favourite, and 5 to 4 against Bucephalus.—Won by a
length.

WEDNESDAY, July 20.—Fifty Pounds for all ages.—Four-mile heats.
Mr Dilly's br b Gnat-ho! by Sir Peter Teazle, 5 yrs old, 8st 4lb
(M. Dilly) 1 1
Mr Rush's ch h Timekeeper, 6 yrs old, 8st 12lb 3 2
Mr Martin's br h Witchcraft, aged, 9st..................... 2 3
Even betting on Gnat-ho! after the heat, 2 to 1 he won.

Fifty Pounds for three and four-year olds.—Two-mile heats.
Sir J. Hawkins's br c Rosario, by Ambrosio, 4 years old, 8st 11lb
(S. Chifney) 1 1
Mr Trevanion's b c Lewes, 4 yrs old, 8st 8lb 2 2
Two to 1 and 5 to 2 on Rosario.

The Hunter's Plate of 50l. for Maiden Horses, &c. 11st.—Two-mile
heats.
Mr Barrett's br c, by Skyrocket, 3 yrs old (T. Goodisson) 2 1 1
Mr Todd's Scrip, 6 yrs old (M. Dilly)..................... 1 2 2
Even betting; after the second heat, 2 to 1 on Mr. Barrett's colt.

THURSDAY, July 21.—The Gold Cup, value 100gs, with 50gs in
specie, by 15 Subscribers of 10gs each, for all ages.—Four Miles.
Mr Goddard's b h Mountainer, by Magic, 6 yrs old, 8st 12lb (W.
Chifney) 1
Mr Dilly's br h Gnat-ho! 5 yrs old, 8st 6lb................ 2
Mr Butler's b m Miss Coiner, aged, 8st 12lb................ 3
Mr Dundas's b h Rubens, 5 yrs old, 8st 6lb................. 4
Even betting on Mountaineer, 2 to 1 against Gnat-ho! and 4 to 1 agst
Rubens.—Won by a length.

The Ladies' Plate of 50l. for Maiden Horses, &c.—Four-mile heats.
Lord Egremont's b c, Brother to Hedley, by Gohanna, 4 yrs old,
7st 12lb (C. Goodisson)................................... 1 1
Mr Trevanion's b c Crab, 3 yrs old, 6st................... 2 2
Mr Worrall's b f, by Kill-Devil, 3 yrs old, 6st........... 3 3
Six and 7 to 4 on the Brother to Hedley.

CANTER-

CANTERBURY MEETING—KENT.

TUESDAY, July 19.——Sweepstakes of 10gs each, for all ages.——Two Miles.—Eight Subscribers.

Sir J. Honywood's bay colt Hawk, by Buzzard, 4 yrs old, 8st 4lb..	1
Mr Watson's b c Hymen, 3 yrs old, 7st	2
Mr Best's b c, by St. George, 3 yrs old, 7st	3
Mr Baldock's ch f Miss Hawk, 3 yrs old, 6st 12lb.., ...	4

Five to 4 on Hawk.

Sweepstakes of 20gs each, for all ages.—Four Miles.—Ten Subscribers.

Mr W. Fenwick's b h, Sir Launcelot, by Delpini, 6 yrs old, 9st.. ..	1
Mr Ladbroke's ch c Master Jackey, 4 yrs old, 7st 7lb.;	2
Sir J. Honywood's br h Delville, 5 yrs old, 8st 7lb...............	3
Mr Baldock's b h Resolution, 5 yrs old, 8st 7lb..............	4

Six to 4 on Master Jackey.

The Kentish Hunters' Stakes of 5gs each, for horses, &c, 12st.—Four Miles.—Twenty-five Subscribers.

Mr Watson's b h Monarch.............................	1
Sir E. Knatchbull's Clifton.............................	2

Sweepstakes of 10gs each, for all ages.—Two Miles.

Mr Ladbroke's ch c Master Jackey, by Johnny, 4 yrs old, 8st 4lb..	1
Mr Hyde's ch f Augusta, 4 yrs old, 8st 1lb	2
Mr Watson's b c Hymen, 3 yrs old, 7st 7lb....................	3
Mr Witherden's colt, by Gobanna, 4 yrs old, 8st 4lb	4

Two to 1 on Master Jackey.

WEDNESDAY, July 20.—The King's Plate of 100gs, for four-yr, olds and upwards.—Four-mile heats.

Mr Ladbroke's b c Corsican, by Guildford, 4 yrs old, 10st 4lb....	1	1
Mr Fenwick's b h Sir Launcelot, 6 yrs old, 12st.............	2	dr
Sir J. Honywood's b c Hawk, 4 yrs old, 10st 4lb.............	3	dr

Seven to 4 and 2 to 1 on Corsican.

The Maiden Plate of 50l. for all ages.—Four-mile heats.

Mr Best's b c, by St. George, out of Petruchio's dam, 3 yrs old, 6st 1	1	
Mr Cramp's b h Driver, aged, 9st........................	3	2
Mr G. Witherden's b f Miss Kitty, 3 yrs old, 6st (bolted)......	2	dis

Five and 6 to 4 on Mr Best's colt.

THURSDAY, July 21.—Fifty Pounds for three and four-year olds. Two-mile heats.

Mr Ladbroke's b c Corsican, by Guildford, 4 yrs old, 8st 9lb....	1	1
Mr Witherden's b f Miss Kitty, 3 yrs old, 6st 12lb.........	2	dr
Sir J. Honywood's b c Hawk, 4 yrs old, 8st 9lb.............	3	dr

Two and 3 to 1 on Corsican.

FRIDAY, July 22.—Fifty Pounds for all ages.—Four-mile heats.

Mr. Fenwick's b h Sir Launcelot, by Delpini, 6 yrs old, 9st 6lb....	1	1
Mr Hyde's ch f Augusta, 4 yrs old, 7st 5lb	2	2

Five to 1 on Sir Launcelot.

Handicap

Handicap Stakes of 10gs each.—One-mile heats.—Five Subscribers.

Sir J. Honywood's br h Delville, by Beningbrough, 5 yrs old, 9st 1 . 1

Mr Trevillon's Hotspur, 8st 10lb 2 2

Mr Fowle's Mignionette, 6st 10lb 3 3

Two and 3 to 1 on Delville.

TOTNESS MEETING—DEVONSHIRE.

TUESDAY, July 19.— Fifty Pounds, for horses, &c.—Three-mile
 heats.

Mr Webb's b g Vidette, 5 yrs old, 8st 3lb..................1 2 1

Mr Weir's ch g Woodcot, aged, 8st 11lb 2 1 2

Mr Coward's b g Canterbury, aged, 8st 11lb..............3 3 3

Mr Kempson's br g Andrew, aged, 8st 11lb...............4 dr

WEDNESDAY, July 20.—Handicap Stakes of 5gs each, for hunters.—Two mile heats.—— Subscribers.

Captain Harding's ch g Sir Hugh, aged, 10st 4lb.............1 1

Captain Weir's b g Canterbury, aged, 10st 6lb..............2 2

Mr Kempson's br g Andrew, aged, 10st 6lb.................3 dr

ORMSKIRK MEETING—LANCASHIRE.

WEDNESDAY, July 20.—Sweepstakes of 10gs each, for three-year
 old colts, 8st 5lb, fillies, 8st 2lb.—Two Miles.—Five Subscribers.

Mr Benson's br f Dimple, by Sir Peter Teazle, dam by Rockingham
 (W. Peirse) 1

Mr Ackers's ch c Apollo, by Hyacinthus 2

 Three and 4 to 1 on Dimple.—A good race.

The Maiden Plate of 50l. for all ages.—Heats, twice round the Course.

Sir T. Stanley's bl c, by Sir Harry, dam by Pot8o's, 4 yrs old, 8st
 (T. Carr) 4 1 1

Mr Hammond's bay colt, 3 yrs old, 6st 10lb (received 10l.)....1 2 3

Mr Benson's b c, by Pegasus, 4 yrs old, 8st...............2 3 2

Mr Harris's bay filly, 3 yrs old, 6st 8lb....................3 3 4

Even betting on Mr Hammond's colt, 3 and 4 to 1 against Mr Benson's
 colt.

 Mr R. Rawlinson's br c Pepper, 4 yrs old, beat Mr W. Smith's d m
Camilla, 5 yrs old, a feather each.—Two Miles, 50gs.

THURSDAY, July 21.—The Loyalty Gold Cup; added to a Subscription of 20gs each, for all ages.—Four Miles.—Five Subscribers.

D. of Hamilton's b c Peter Little, by Sir Peter Teazle, dam by Walnut, 3 yrs old, 6st 6lb (R. Johnson) 1

Sir W. Gerard's br h Julius Cæsar, 5 years old, 9st 4lb 2

Five to 1 on Julius Cæsar, who was thrown out at the turn, and ran in
 the ditch for about a hundred yards, before his rider, W. Peirse, could
 bring

bring him into the Course : he was then pulled up, owing to his antagonist having cleared so much ground.

Fifty Pounds for three and four-year olds.—Two-mile heats.

Mr Harris's br g Viper, by Serpent, out of Rosaletta, by Walnut,
    4 yrs old, 8st 6lb 1 1
Mr Knapton's b f Amity, by Expectation, 3 yrs old, 7st 3lb (received 10l.) 3 2
Mr Clifton's br c Dusronnal, 4 yrs old, 8st 8lb............... 2 dr

Two and 3 to 1 on Viper.—Won easy.

FRIDAY, July 22.—Sweepstakes of 10gs each, with 20gs added, for all ages.—Four Miles.—Six Subscribers.

Mr W. Walker's ch h Baronet, by Stride, 5 yrs old, 8st 11lb....... 1
Mr Benson's br f Dimple, 3 yrs old, 6st 8lb.................... 2

Two and 3 to 1 on Dimple.—Won by a neck.

Fifty Pounds for all ages.—Heats, twice round.

Mr Harris's br g Viper, by Serpent, 4 yrs old, 8st 1lb..., ,..... 1 1
Mr W. Hutchinson's ch h Harmless, 5 yrs old, 8st 7lb (recd 10l.) 4 2
Mr Walker's ch h Baronet, 5 yrs old, 8st 7lb .... 2 dr
Mr Benson's gr h Atlas, 5 yrs old, 8st 7lb................... 3 dr

Two to 1 on Viper.—Won easy.

LUDLOW MEETING—SHROPSHIRE,

THURSDAY, July 21.—The Maiden Plate of 50l. for all ages.—Three-mile heats.

Mr Goulborn's ch c Romeo, by Vernator, 4 yrs old, 7st 6lb ,....3 1 1
Mr Stevens's ch g, 4 yrs old, 7st 3lb......................... 1 3 2
Mr Benson's b f Dairymaid, 3 yrs old, 5st 11lb....,.......... 2 2 3
Mr Greaves's b c Ivy, 4 yrs old, 7st 6lb .... 4 4 dr

Dairymaid the favourite.

Sweepstakes of 10gs each, for all ages.—Four Miles.—Seven Subscribers.
Lord Stamford's ch h St. Domingo, 5 yrs old,........... walked over.

FRIDAY, July 22.—Sweepstakes of 10gs each, for hunters.—Four Miles.—Six Subscribers.

Mr Benson's b h Fisherman, by Glaucus, 6 yrs old, 9st ...,....... 1
Mr Adams's black gelding, 5 yrs old, 8st 10lb................. 2

Six to 4 on Fisherman.

Handicap Plate of 50l.—Course not mentioned.

Mr Benson's b f Cecilia, by Beningbrough, 4 yrs old, 8st 2lb....2 1 1
Mr Goulburn's b c Whitenose, 4 yrs old, 8st................1 2 2

Whitenose the favourite.

EDINBURGH MEETING.

MONDAY, July 25.—The City Plate of 50l. for hunters, 11st, four-mile heats.

Mr Nicholson's b h Bampton, by Star, out of Green-Dragon's dam,
    5 yrs old (Jackson) 1 1
                                      Lord

Lord Montgomerie's br m, by Sir Charles, dam by Disguise, 5 yrs old (F. Collinson) 4   2
Mr Henderson's br m Country-Lass 2   dr
Mr Hendry's br g, by Pensioner, 5 yrs old................. 3   dr
Mr T. King's b m Whitelegs.............................. dis

Won easy.—No betting.

TUESDAY, July 26.—The King's Plate of 100gs, for four-year olds and upwards.—Four-mile heats.
Mr W. Collinson's b m Fortuna, by Beningbrough, 5 yrs old, 8st 2lb (J. Jackson) 1   1
Mr F. Collinson's b c Sting, by Stickler, out of Gnat, 4 yrs old, 7st 4lb 3   2
Mr Henderson's gr f Peteria, 4 yrs, 7st 4lb.................. 2   3

Won very easy.

WEDNESDAY, July 27.—Fifty Guineas for all ages.—Four-mile heats.
Mr W. Collinson's h Streamer, by Star, 5 yrs old, 8st 2lb (J. Jackson) 1   1
Mr Henderson's br m Country-Lass, by Bangtail.............. 2   dr
Lord Montgomerie's gr c Irvine, 4 yrs old, 7st 4lb (bolted) ...... dis

THURSDAY, July 28.— Fifty Guineas, for hunters, 11st.—Four-mile heats.
Mr Baillie's b h, by Zachariah, dam by Tandem (R. Walker).... 1   1
Mr Brown's br m, by Sir Charles 5   2
Mr Hendry's br g, by Pensioner............................. 2   3
Mr Reid's br g Toby, by Tickle Toby 4   4
Lord Montgomerie's ch m, by Nobleman 3   dr
Mr Smith's br g, by Bangtail............................... 6   dr
Mr King's b m Whitelegs 7   dr

The second heat was well contested, and won by a length.

FRIDAY, July 29.—Fifty Guineas for all ages.—Four-mile heats.
Mr W. Collinson's h Streamer, by Star, 5 yrs old, 8st 2lb (J. Jackson) 2   1   1
Mr Henderson's Peteria, 4 yrs old, 7st 4lb.................. 1   2   2

A very capital race, and won with difficulty.

KNUTSFORD MEETING.

TUESDAY, July 26.—The Maiden Plate of 50l. for all ages.—Three-mile heats.
Mr Smith's b f Miss Blanchard, by Hambletonian, 4 yrs old, 7st 10lb 1   1
Mr T. Carr's h g, by Sir Peter, 4 yrs old, 7st 10lb (received 10l.)..3   2
Mr Thompson's b m Creeper, aged, 8st 8lb 2   3

Five to 2 on Miss Blanchard.—Won easy.

WEDNESDAY, July 27.—Sweepstakes of 10gs each, for all ages. —Three times round the Course.—Seven Subscribers.
Mr Clifton's b m Josephina, by Sir Peter Teazle, 8st 10lb........ 1
Lord

Lord Stamford's b f Belinda, 4 yrs old, 7st 12lb, ... 2
        Six to 4 on Josephina.—A good race.

Fifty Guineas for three and four-year olds.—Two-mile heats.
Lord Wilton's b f Berenice, sister to Bucephalus, by Alexander,
    3 yrs old, 7st 5lb.. 2 1 1
Mr Egerton's b c Cestrian, 3 yrs old, 7st 7lb 1 2 2
        Five to 2 on Cestrian.—Won easy.

THURSDAY, July 28.—Sixty Pounds for all ages.—Four-mile heats.
Mr Clifton's b m Josephina, by Sir Peter Teazle, aged, 9st 1lb. 2 1 1
Mr Hutchinson's ch h Harmless, 5 yrs old, 8st 9lb (received 10l) 1 3 3
Sir T. Stanley's bl c, by Sir Harry, 4 yrs old, 8st 8lb. 3 2 4
Mr Smith's b f Miss Blanchard, 4 yrs old, 8st 3lb............. 4 4 2
Josephina the favourite ; after the first heat 6 to 4 on Harmless ; after the
    second heat, 6 to 4 on Josephina.—Won cleverly.

SALISBURY MEETING—WILTS.

TUESDAY, July 26.—The King's Plate of 100gs for four-year olds'
  and upwards.—Four-mile heats.
Mr Goddard's b h Mountaineer, by Magic, 6 years old, 12st (S.
    Chifney)... 1 1
Lord Egremont's b c, Brother to Hedley, 4 yrs old, 10st 4lb 2 2
Mr Dilly's b c Buckler, 4 yrs old, 10st 4lb .... 3 dr
        Two and 3 to 1 on Mountaineer.
Sweepstakes of 10gs each, for all ages.—Gentlemen riders.—Two-
    mile heats.—Eight Subscribers.
Mr Trevanion's b h Bucephalus, by Alexander, 6 yrs old, 12st 5lb 1 1
Sir J. Hawkins's br c Rosario, 4 years old, 11st.............. 2 dr
      Five to 2 and 3 to 1 on Bucephalus.

WEDNESDAY, July 27.—The City Silver Bowl, free for any
horse, &c. 10st.—Four-mile heats.
Mr Rush's ch h Timekeeper, by Hambletonian, 6 yrs old........ 1 1
Mr Dilly's b h Felton, aged .... 2 dr
    Even betting, and 5 to 4 on Timekeeper.
    The Members' Plate of 50l. was not run for.

THURSDAY, July 28.—The Maiden Plate of 50l. for all ages.—
Four-mile heats.
Mr Trevanion's b c Crabs, by Coriander, 3 yrs old, a feather..... 1 1
Mr C. Day's ch c Barrows' Brook, 3 yrs old, a feather......... 2 2
Mr Radclyffe's ch h Laucaster, 5 yrs old, 8st................. 3 dr
Mr Scott's b m Ten Bones, 6 yrs old, 8st 10lb................ dis
Mr Smith's b m Little Mary, 4 yrs old, 7st 4lb .... dis
Mr Turner's b g Drake, 4 yrs old, 7st 4lb................... dis
    Crabs the favourite ; after the heat, 2 to 1 he won.

    Handicap Plate of 50l.—Course not mentioned.
Mr Trevanion's b h Bucephalus, by Alexander, 6 yrs old, 11st 9lb 1 1
Mr Dilly's b g Felton, aged, 9st 5lb........................ 2 2
                               Lord

Lord Egremont's b c, Brother to Hedley, 4 yrs old, 9st 10lb 3 3
Mr C. Day's ch c New Buckler, 4 yrs old, 9st 4 4
Six to 4 on Bucephalus.

KNIGHTON MEETING—RADNORSHIRE.

TUESDAY, July 26.—Sweepstakes of 5gs each, for Hunters bred in the Counties of Radnor, Hereford, and Salop, carrying 12st each.—Four-mile beats.—— Subscribers.
Mr Brown's b g, by Transit, 5 yrs old .... walked over

WEDNESDAY, July 27.—Sweepstakes of 10gs each, for horses, &c.—Heats, twice round the Course.—Six Subscribers.
Mr Goulburn's ch c Romeo, by Vernator, 4 yrs old, 10st 4lb, walked over

Fifty Pounds for all ages.—Four-mile beats.
Mr Goulburn's ch c Romeo, by Vernator, 4 yrs old, 7st 3lb.... 1 1
Mr Canning's ch g Sweeper, aged, 8st 6lb 2 2

BRIGHTON MEETING—SUSSEX.

TUESDAY, August 2.—Sweepstakes of 200gs each, h. ft.—Four Miles.—Four Subscribers.
Mr Fermor's ch h Cerberus, by Gohanna, 6 years old, 8st 11lb (F. Buckle). 1
Mr Wyndham's b c, by Ambrosio, 4 yrs old, 6st 10lb 2
Six and 7 to 4 on Cerberus.—Won easy.

The third year of the Pavilion Stakes of 100gs each, h. ft. for three-year old colts, 9st; fillies, 8st 9lb.—The last Mile.—Seventeen Subscribers.
Lord Darlington's ch c Rubens, by Buzzard (S. Chifney) 1
Duke of Grafton's br c Vandyke, by Sir Peter (W. Clift)........ 2
Lord Egremont's b c, Brother to Trafalgar, by Gohanna 3
Mr Kellermann's ch c, by Sorcerer, out of Louisa............... 4
Five to 4 on Vandyke, 7 to 2 against Rubens, 6 to 1 against the Brother to Trafalgar, and 7 to 1 against the Sorcerer colt.—A very fine race, and won by a neck.—A great betting race.

The Silver Cup value 50gs, a Subscription of 5gs each, the surplus in specie, for horses, &c.—The New Course.—Nineteen Subscribers.
Mr Bowes Daly's ch h Sasenagh, by Waxy, 6 yrs old, 9st 1lb (W. Arnold) 1
Lord Egremont's b f, by Gohanna, out of Lazy, 3 yrs old, 7st..... 2
His R. H. the Duke of York's gr h Tim, 5 yrs old, 8st 10lb........ 3
Mr Wyndham's b c, by Ambrosio, 4 yrs old, 8st 3lb 4
Mr Slarke's b m Wren, by Waxy, 6 yrs old, 9st 1lb............... 5
Six and 7 to 4 against Tim, 5 to 2 against Lord Egremont's filly, and 5 to 1 against Sasenagh.—Won easy.

General-Gower's Cardinal Beaufort, by Gohanna, 8st 7lb, received 100gs compromise from Mr B. Daly's Sasenagh, 7st 9lb.—The Last Mile, 300gs, h. ft.

WEDNESDAY, August 3.—The Petworth Stakes of 10gs each, for horses, &c.—Four Miles.—Eleven Subscribers.

His R. H. the Duke of York's gr h Tim, by Whiskey, 5 years old, 8st 7lb (W. Wheatley) 1
Mr Daly's ch h Sasenagh, 6 yrs old, 9st 2
Mr Cave Browne's br h Delville, 5 yrs old, 8st 7lb 3
Mr Wyndham's b c, by Ambrosio, 4 yrs old, 7st 7lb 4

Two to 1 against Tim, 2 to 1 against Delville, 5 to 2 against Sasenagh, and 5 to 1 against Mr Wyndham's colt.—Won easy.

The Somerset Stakes of 50gs each, h. ft. for Horses, &c.—Four Miles.
—Horses bred in Ireland allowed 7lb.—Ten Subscribers.
Lord Grosvenor's b m Meteora, by Meteor, 6 years old, 8st 7lb (F. Buckle) 1
Mr Daly's ch c Bob Booty, (bred in Ireland) by Chanticleer, 4 yrs old, 7st (B. Moss) 2
Lord Egremont's b h Canopus, 5 yrs old, 8st 5lb 3

Six to 5 against Canopus, 7 to 4 against Meteora, and 4 to 1 against Bob Booty.—Before starting, Canopus ran over two women, and was thought to be lamed.—This was a great betting race.

The Hippocampus Stakes of 50gs each, h. ft. for three-year old colts, 8st 5lb, fillies, 8st.—The New Course.—Eight Subscribers.
Lord Egremont's b f, by Gohanna, dam by Highflyer, out of Nimble .... walked over

Fifty Pounds for three, four, and five-year olds.—Heats, the New Course.—No race.

THURSDAY, August 4.—Lord Darlington's ch c Rubens, by Buzzard, received forfeit from Mr Mellish's Bradbury, 8st 3lb each.— The Last Mile, 200gs, h. ft.
Handicap Plate of 50l.—No race.

FRIDAY, August 5.—The Gold Cup given by his R.H. the Prince of Wales, added to a Subscription of 10gs each, for all ages.—Four Miles.—Twenty-seven Subscribers.—Horses bred in Ireland allowed 7lb.
Ld Grosvenor's b m Meteora, by Meteor, 6 yrs old, 8st 9lb (F. Buckle) 1
Mr Daly's ch c Bob Booty, 4 yrs old, 7st 1lb 2
Duke of York's gr h Tim, 5 years old, 8st 6lb...................... 3
Mr Fermor's ch h Cerberus, 6 yrs old, 8st 12lb..................... 4
Mr Shakespear's bl e Mungo, 4 yrs old, 7st 6lb.................... 5

Five to 4 against Meteora, 6 to 4 against Cerberus, 8 to 1 against Bob Booty, 10 to 1 against Tim, and 100 to 8 against Mungo.—A fine race, but won by half a length.

The Darlington Stakes of 200gs each, h. ft. for three-year old colts, 8st 7lb, fillies, 8st 3lb.—The Last Mile.—Sixteen Subscribers.
Lord Grosvenor's b f Plover, by Sir Peter Teazle, out of Popinjay's dam (F. Buckle)... 1

Mr

Mr Ladbroke's b c, by Gohanna, out of Catherine........................ 2
Lord Foley's b f Agnes, by Shuttle................................ 3
Sir C. Bunbury's b f Agnes, by Sorcerer 4
Lord Egremont's b f, by Driver, out of Fractious................ 5
Six to 5 against Plover, 3 to 1 against Sir C. Bunbury's Agnes, 7 to 1 against Lord Foley's Agnes, 8 to 1 against Mr Ladbroke's colt, and 10 to 1 against Lord Egremont's filly.—Won easy.

Sweepstakes of 10gs each, for three-yr old colts, 8st 7lb, fillies, 8st 4lb. —The last Mile.—Eight Subscribers.

Lord Egremont's b f, by Gohanna, out of Lazy, by Driver (S. Barnard) 1
Mr Ladbroke's b c, out of Catherine........................ 2
Duke of York's b c, by Gouty, out of a sister to Oatlands, by Dungannon 3

Five to 4 agst Lord Egremont's filly.

Fifty Pounds for horses, &c.—No race.

NEWBERY MEETING—BERKS.

TUESDAY, August 2.—Sweepstakes of 10gs each, with 25gs added, for three-year old colts, 8st 3lb, fillies, 8st 2lb.—Two Miles.—Nine Subscribers.

Mr Bacon's ch f Coquetilla, by Skyscraper, out of the dam of Horns (C. Goodisson) 1
Mr Butler's ch f Bona Lass, by Bonaparte...................... 2
Mr C. Dundas's br c Yeoman, by St. George 3
Yeoman the favourite.—A good race.—Yeoman had not recovered from the Strangles, otherwise, it was thought, he would have won easy.

Fifty Pounds for all ages.—Two-mile heats.

Mr Batson's ch h Charmer, by Whiskey, 5 years old, 8st 10lb (C. Goodisson) 1 1
Mr Butler's b m Miss Coiner, aged, 8st 13lb 2 2

WEDNESDAY, August 3.—Sweepstakes of 5gs each, with 25gs added, for horses, &c.—Four Miles.—Seven Subscribers.

Mr C. Dundas's b c Cambrian, by Sir Solomon, 4 years old, 8st .... walked over

Handicap Plate of 50l.—Two-mile heats.

Mr Butler's b m Miss Coiner, by Don Quixote, aged, 9st 3lb (T. Goodisson)... 1 1
Mr Heath's br h Rumbo, aged, 9st 4lb 2 2
Mr Bacon's ch f Coquetilla, 3 yrs old, 7st 4lb 3 3

Match for 50gs.—Once round the Course.

Mr C. Dundas's br h Capias, by Overton, 6 yrs old, 8st 12lb (T. Goodisson) 1
Mr Montagne's white horse Sultan, by an Arabian, 8st 12lb (C. Goodisson) 2

Won in a canter.

K 3   Match

Match for 50gs.—Once round the Course.

Mr F. Craven's gr g Curricle, by Aimator, 6 yrs old, 10st (T. Goodison) 1

Mr Montagne's gr g Coachman, by an Arabian, 10st (C. Goodison) .. 2

Won easy.

YORK AUGUST MEETING, 1808.

SATURDAY, August 20.—Match for One Thousand Guineas, h. ft.— Two Miles.

Lord Foley's (late Mr. Mellish's) b f Agnes, by Shuttle, 8st (F. Buckle) 1

Mr Hewett's b c Teazle Evitch, by Sir Peter Teazle, 8st 4lb (J. Jackson) 2

Two and 3 to 1 against Agnes.—Won easy.

Agnes ran for the Darlington Stakes at Brighton, on Friday, August 5, and soon after the race, she was sent off for York, travelled 23 miles that day, and arrived at Dringhouses on Sunday morning, August 14, a little after nine o'clock. The road she travelled is computed to be 255 miles.

Match for 500gs.—Two Miles.

Sir W. Gerard's ch c, by Hambletonian, out of Mary Ann, 8st 2lb (W. Peirse) 1

Mr Howorth's (late Mr Mellish's) b c Weaver, 8st 2lb (F. Buckle) .. 2

Six to 5 on the winner.—Won very easy.

Match for 200gs, h. ft.—Two Miles.

Mr J. Acred's b c Wansford, by Stamford, dam by Sir Peter, 8st (J. Shepherd) 1

Mr W. Hutchinson's b c Silvio, by St. George, out of Mary, 8st (F. Jordon) 2

Five to 4 on Silvio.—Silvio swerved near the ending-post.

Match for 200gs, h. ft.—One Mile and Half.

Mr Boulton's b c Cliffe, by St. George, 8st (F. Jordon) 1

Mr Nalton's b c Ranger, 8st (F. Buckle) 2

Six to 5 on Ranger.—Won easy.

Match for 500gs, h. ft.—Two Miles.

Mr Clifton's b c Poulton, Brother to Fyldener, by Sir Peter Teazle, 8st 3lb, received forfeit from Mr Mellish's b c Experiment, 8st.

MONDAY, August 22.—The first year of a Subscription of 25gs each, for four-year old fillies, 7st 5lb, colts, 7st 9lb, five-year olds, 8st 5lb, six-year olds and aged, 8st 10lb.—Four Miles.—Seventeen Subscribers.

Lord Darlington's b c, by Archduke, out of Beningbrough's sister, 4 yrs old (W. Peirse) 1

Lord Strathmore's b h Cassio, by Sir Peter, 5 yrs old (F. Buckle) ... 2

Mr Garforth's b c Hylas, by Beningbrough, out of Caroline, 4 yrs old (J. Garbutt) 3

Lord

Lord Milton's b b Sir Paul, 6 yrs old (W. Clift) 4

Six to 4 against Cassio, 5 to 2 against Sir Paul, 5 to 1 against Archduke, and 6 to 1 against Hylas.—Run in 7 minutes and 40 seconds.

At starting, the Archduke colt lost the bridle bits out of his mouth, and the reins came across his nose to the right side, he then went off at score, and ran first for about a mile and a half; after which he ran alternately second and third, until they came opposite to the Grand Stand, when he crossed the Course, and ran close to the rails and the Judge's Chair, and won by rather better than the head.—Several people who were upon the course, (contrary to the Stewards' order) were thrown down, but none dangerously hurt.

The Produce Stakes of 100gs each, h. ft. for four-year old colts and fillies.—Four Miles.—Twenty-three Subscribers.

Lord Monson's b c Scud, by Beningbrough, out of Eliza, 8st 4lb (F. Buckle) 1

Duke of Hamilton's b f Easy, by Hambletonian, dam by Javelin, 8st 1lb (B. Smith) 2

Mr Hodgson's b f Miltonia, by Patriot, out of Miss Muston, 8st 1lb (J. Shepherd) 3

Five to 2 on Scud, 4 to 1 against Easy, and 10 to 1 against Miltonia.—A fine race, and won by near a length.—Run in seven minutes and fifty-two seconds.

The King's Plate of 100gs for four-year olds, 10st 4lb; five-year olds, 11st 6lb; six-year olds, 12st; and aged, 12st 2lb.—Four Miles.

Mr Nalton's b c Ranger, by Hyacinthus, 4 yrs old, (F. Buckle) 1

Mr Gorwood's ches geld. by Hyacinthus, out of Dairy Maid, (J. Shepherd) 2

Mr Walker's ch h Baronet, by Stride, 5 yrs old (R. Franks) 3

Mr Hutchinson's b c Silvio, 4 yrs old (F. Jordon) 4

Mr S. Duncombe's b c Rossington, by Star, 4 yrs old (J. Jackson) 5

Five to 2 against Silvio, 4 to 1 against Ranger, 4 to 1 against Baronet, and 5 to 1 against Rossington.—A good race.—Run in eleven minutes and nine seconds.

Mr E. L. Hodgson's b f, by Hambletonian, out of Eustatia, received forfeit from Mr T. Duncombe's ch f, by Chance, out of a sister to Maid of All-Work.—One Mile and a Half, 100gs, h. ft.

TUESDAY, August 23.—Sweepstakes of 20gs each, for two-year old colts, 8st 5lb; fillies, 8st 2lb.—Two-year Olds' Course.

Lord Fitzwilliam's b c Cervantes, by Don Quixote, out of Evelina (W. Clift) 1

Mr Dinsdale's b f Fair Candidate, by Delpini, dam by Weasel (F. Buckle) 2

Mr Thompson's b f, by Shuttle (J. Garbutt) 3

Sir T. Gascoigne's ch c, by Delpini, out of Wryneck (J. Shepherd) 4

Sir W. Gerard's ch c, by Coriander, dam by Antæus .... pd

Eleven to 9 on Cervantes, 4 to 1 agst Mr Thompson's filly, and 50 to 6 against Fair Candidate.—Won easy.

Fifty

Fifty Pounds, for three-year olds, 5st 4lb, four-year-olds, 7st 7lb, five-year olds, 8st 5lb, six-year olds and aged, 8st 12lb ; mares allowed 3lb, and maiden horses, &c. 4lb.—Four-mile heats.

Mr Acred's b c Wansford, by Stamford, 4 yrs old (R. Johnson)..4 1 1
Sir H. T. Vane's b m, by Sir Peter, 5 yrs old (B. Smith)........1 3 0
Mr Nalton's b c Ranger, by Hyacinthus, 4 yrs old (B. Moss)....2 2 dr
Sir M. M. Sykes's b f Harriet, by Precipitate, 4 yrs old (J.Garbutt) 3 dr
Six to 4 against Sir H. T. Vane's mare, 4 to 1 against Wansford, and 4 to 1 against Ranger ; after the first heat, 7 to 4 on the mare ; after the second heat, 2 to 1 on Wansford. The first heat was won by half a head ; the second by half a length ; and the third by rather more than half a length. The first heat was run in 8 minutes and 14 seconds ; the second heat, in 8 minutes and 51 seconds ; and the third heat, in 8 minutes and 33 seconds.

WEDNESDAY, August 24.—Sweepstakes of 50gs each, h. ft. for three-year old colts, 8st 2lb, fillies, 7st 13lb.—Two Miles.—Four Subscribers.
Sir T. Gascoigne's ch c, by Hambletonian, out of Golden Locks
   (J. Shepherd) .... walked over.

Sweepstakes of 100gs each, h. ft. for four-year old colts, 8st 4lb, fillies, 8st.—Three Miles.—Eight Subscribers.
Sir T. Gascoigne's ch f, by Hambletonian, out of Golden-Locks (J.
   Shepherd) 1
Lord Darlington's b c, brother to Expectation, by Sir Peter (W. Peirse) 2
Seven to 4 on the Brother to Expectation.—A good race ; run in 5 minutes and 30 seconds.

Fifty Pounds, given by the City of York, added to one-third of a Subscription Purse, by 26 Subscribers of 25gs each, for five-year olds, 8st 7lb each.—Four Miles.
Mr Peirse's b m Rosette, by Beningbrough (J. Shepherd).......... 1
Sir W. Gerard's br h Julius Cæsar (W. Peirse).................. 2
Lord Strathmore's b h Cassio (F. Buckle)...................... 3
Six to 4 on Rosette, 3 to 1 against Julius Cæsar, and 7 to 2 against Cassio.—Won easy.—Run in 8 minutes and 5 seconds.

Mr Howorth's b c Weaver, by Shuttle, received forfeit from Mr Watt's b c, brother to Gratitude, by Shuttle, 8st 3lb each.—Two Miles, 500gs, h. ft.

THURSDAY, August 25.—The Produce Stakes of 100gs each, h. ft. for three-year old colts and fillies.—Two Miles.—Sixteen Subscribers.
Sir M. M. Sykes's b f Theresa, by Hambletonian, 8st (J. Garbutt).. 1
Mr Clifton's b c Poulton, by Sir Peter, 8st 2lb (J. Shepherd)..... 2
Mr Peirse's b c, by Expectation, 7st 13lb (F. Collinson) 3
Mr Peirse's b f, by Pipator, dam by Delpini, 7st 11lb (B. Smith). . 4
Sir T. Gascoigne's b f, by Hambletonian, out of Violet, 8st (F. Buckle) 5
Lord Fitzwilliam's bl f Charcoal, by Sir Peter, 8st (W. Clift)...... 6
Six to 4 on Poulton, 4 to 1 against Theresa, 6 to 1 against either of Mr Peirse's, 10 to 1 against Charcoal, and the same against Sir T. Gascoigne's

coigne's filly.—A good race, and won by half a length.—Run in 5 minutes and 58 seconds.

Fifty Pounds, given by the City of York, added to one-third of a Subscription Purse, by 26 Subscribers of 25gs each, for six-year olds, 8st 10lb, and aged, 9st.—Four Miles.

Mr Peirse's b m Rosette, by Beningbrough, 5 yrs old (J. Shepherd) .. 1
Duke of Hamilton's b h Grazier, 5 yrs old (B. Smith)............ 2
Mr N. B. Hodgson's gr m Priscilla, by Delpini, aged (F. Collinson).. 3
L. rd Strathmore's b m Desdemona, by Sir Peter, 5 yrs (F. Buckle).. 4

Two to 1 against Rosette, 4 to 1 against Desdemona, and 8 to 1 against Priscilla.—After running two miles, Rosette took the lead, was never headed, and won easy.—Run in 8 minutes and 20 seconds.

FRIDAY, August 26.—Sweepstakes of 50gs each, 10gs ft. for three-year old fillies, 8st.—Last Mile and three quarters.—Seven Subscribers.

Mr Duncombe's chesnut, Laurel-Leaf, by Stamford (B. Smith).... 1
Mr Fletcher's Miss Staveley, Sister to Staveley, by Shuttle (J. Jackson) 2
Seven to 4 on Miss Staveley.—Won easy.

Fifty Pounds, given by the City of York, added to one-third of a Subscription Purse, by 26 Subscribers of 25gs each, for four-year old colts, 8st 7lb, fillies, 8st 4lb.—Four Miles.

Lord Darlington's b c, by Archduke, out of Beningbrough's sister (W. Peirse)..................................... 1
Duke of Hamilton's b f Easy, by Hambletonian, dam by Javelin (B. Smith).. 2
Mr Garforth's b c Hylas, by Beningbrough (W. Clift)........... 3
Sir T. Gascoigne's ch f, by Hambletonian, out of Golden-Locks (F. Buckle) 4
Mr Peirse's b c Bedalian, by Beningbrough (F. Collinson) 5
Lord Scarborough's b c, by Sir Solomon, dam by Jupiter (J. Shepherd) 6

Two to 1 and 5 to 2 on the Archduke colt, and high odds against all the others.—Won very easy.

Match for 100gs.—From Middlethorp Corner in.

Mr Howorth's b c Weaver, by Shuttle, 8st 7lb (F. Buckle)......... 1
Sir C. Turner's b c Skylight, Brother to Bumper, by St. George, 8st 7lb (S. Chifney)................................. 2
Five to 2 on Weaver.—Won very easy.

SATURDAY, August 27.—Sweepstakes of 30gs each, 10gs ft. for three-year old colts, 8st 2lb, and fillies, 7st 12lb.—Last Mile and three quarters.—Ten Subscribers.

Mr Hewett's b c Stilton, by Stamford (Jackson) 1
Sir C. Turner's (late Mr Garforth's) ch c Cousin Abraham, by Hambletonian (Chifney) 2
Mr Shepherd's b c, by Ormond, dam by Morwick (J. Shepherd).... 3
Sir T. Gascoigne's ch c, by Hambletonian, out of Golden-Locks (F. Buckle) 4

Five to 4 against Stilton.—Won by half a length.

The King's Plate of 100gs, for five-year old mares, 10st.—Four Miles.

Lord Strathmore's bay, Desdemona, by Sir Peter (W. Anderson) .. 1

Mr

Mr S. Duncombe's bay, Hipswell-Lass, by Sir Peter (J. Jackson) **3**

Sir T. Gascoigne's chesnut, Dowager, by Hambletonian (F. Buckle). . **3**

Six and 7 to 4 on Hipswell-Lass, 4 to 1 against Desdemona, and the same against Dowager.—Won very easy.

The Ladies' Plate for Horses, &c.—Two Miles.

Mr Howorth's b c Weaver, 3 yrs old, 7st (W. Walter) **1**

Mr Boulton's b c Cliffe, 4 yrs old, 8st 1lb (F. Jordan) **2**

Mr N. B Hodgson's gr m Priscilla, aged, 9st (F. Collinson). **3**

Sir T. Gascoigne's b f Thwat, by Hambletonian, 3 yrs old, 6st 7lb (D. Masterman) **4**

Mr Peirse's b c Bedalian, 4 yrs old, 8st (J. Shepherd). **5**

The following also started, but were not placed :

Mr Walker's ch h Baronet, 6 yrs old, 8st 8lb (R. Franks). **0**

Sir C. Turner's b c Skylight, 3 yrs old, 6st 11lb (R. Chapman). **0**

Mr E. L. Hodgson's b f, by Shuttle, out of Miss Muston, 3 yrs old, 6st 11lb (J. Thompson) **0**

Mr S. Duncombe's Rossington, 4 yrs old, 7st 12lb (J. Jackson). . . . **0**

Five to 2 against Weaver, 3 to 1 against Cliffe, and the same against Priscilla.—A fine race.

Sir T. Gascoigne's b c Bumtrap, by Agonistes, 8st 7lb, against Sir C. Turner's b c Skylight, Brother to Bumper, 8st 7lb.—From Middlethorpe Corner in, 100gs.—Off by consent.

Lord Monson's (late Mr Hewett's) b c Scud, by Beningbrough, 8st 4lb, recd. ft. from Mr Mellish's gr c Bedale, by Star, 8st 4lb.—Four Miles, 200gs, h, ft.

RACING INTELLIGENCE EXTRA.

KINGSCOTE MEETING.

TUESDAY, September 20.—The following horses, &c. were nomi-nated on the last day of Bibury Meeting, for the Kingscote Stakes of 25gs each, 15 ft. and only 5gs if declared within the time to be set-tled by the Handicappers.—The Kingscote Club will add 50gs to the Stakes.—Gentlemen riders.—Three Miles.

Sir H. Lippincott's Sorceress, by Sorcerer, 3 years old

Lord C. H. Somerset's White-Rose, by Beningbrough, 4 yrs old

Mr Biggs's Rosario, by Ambrosio, 4 yrs old

Lord Egremont's Brother to Hedley, by Gohanna, 4 yrs old

Sir H. Lippincott's Chaise-and-One, by Sir Peter, 4 yrs old

Mr Wheatley's Hawk, by Buzzard, 4 yrs old

Mr C. Dundas's b h Rubens, by Pencil, 5 yrs old

Lord C. H. Somerset's Osiris, by Sir Peter, 5 yrs old

Mr Goddard's Bronze, by Buzzard, 5 yrs old

Sir J. Hawkins's Clermont, by Trumpator, 5 yrs old

Colonel Kingscote's Doctor, by Precipitate, 5 yrs old

Sir H. Lippincott's Ploughboy, by Volunteer, 5 yrs old

Mr Haffenden's Sir Launcelot, by Delpini, 6 yrs old

Mr Trevanion's Bucephalus, by Alexander, 6 yrs old

Mr Rush's Humility, by Gouty, 6 yrs old

Mr Douglas's Delville, by Beningbrough, 6 yrs old.

CHELMSFORD MEETING—ESSEX.

TUESDAY, July 19.——The King's Plate of 100gs, for three and four-year old fillies.—Two-mile heats.

Lord Grosvenor's b f Isis, by Sir Peter Teazle, 7st 7lb.......... 1 1
Mr Williams's ch f, by Boaster, 3 yrs old, 7st 7lb............... 2 dr
Four and 5 to 1 on Isis.

Sweepstakes of 5gs each, with 50l. added, for hunters, 12st.—Gentlemen riders.—Two-mile heats.—Five Subscribers.

Mr Hearn's b g, by Coriander, aged....................... 1 1
Mr Emden's gr h Speculation, 5 yrs old...................... 2 2
Mr L. Kortright's br m Flirtilla, 6 yrs old.................. 3 3

WEDNESDAY, July 20.—The Maiden Plate of 50l. for three and four-year olds.—Two-mile heats.

Mr Williams's ch f Gift, by Boaster, 3 yrs old, 6st 11lb........ 1 2 1
Mr Emden's b f Highland-Lass, 3 yrs old, 6st 11lb............ 3 1 2
Sir F. Standish's ch c, by Mr Teazle, 3 yrs old, 7st............ 2 dr

The Hunter's Plate of 50gs, with 5gs entrance added, (the whole to the winner) 12st each.—Gentlemen riders.—Two-mile heats.

Mr C. Parker's filly 1 2 1
Mr J. Wright's mare... 2 1 2
Mr Harding's mare .... 3 dr

THURSDAY, July 21.—The Steward's Plate of 50l. for all ages.—Heats, two Miles and a half.

Mr Williams's ch f, by Boaster, 3 yrs old, 6st 10lb........... 1 1
Mr Hearn's b g, by Coriander, aged, 8st 13lb................. 3 2
Mr Emden's b f Highland-Lass, 3 yrs old, 6st 7lb.............. 4 3
Mr Golding's b m Merrymaid, 5 yrs old, 8st 10lb.............. 2 dis

Before starting for the above Plate, an objection was made that the Boaster filly and Merrymaid were both the property of one person.—Merrymaid crossed Highland-Lass the second heat, and was in consequence deemed distanced though she came in second. The Stewards agreed that the Plate should be divided between Mr Williams and Mr Hearn.

TAUNTON MEETING—SOMERSETSHIRE.

TUESDAY, August 2.——The Maiden Plate of 50l. for horses, &c.—Four-mile heats.

Mr Fellowes's b c Mandarine, by Patriot, 4 yrs old, 8st 2lb..... 1 1
Mr Radclyffe's ch h Lancaster, 5 yrs old, 8st 12lb............. 3 2
Mr Jones's ch h Laburnam, 5 yrs old, 8st 12lb................ 2 dr

Sweepstakes of 5gs each, for horses, &c. bred in the County.—Heats, twice round the Course.—Eleven Subscribers.

Mr Jones's ch h Laburnam, 5 yrs old, 11st 6lb................ 1 1
Mr Weatherburn's br c, by St. George, 4 yrs old, 10st 10lb...... 2 2

WEDNESDAY, August 6.—The County Members' Plate of 50l. for all ages.—Four-mile heats.

Mr Martin's br h Witchcraft, by Sir Peter Teazle, aged, 9st 3lb. . r 2
Mr Day's gr f Kitty, by Lop, 3 yrs old, 7st 2 2
Mr Fellowes's b c Mandarine, 4 yrs old, 7st 12lb . . . . 3 dr

The Members' Plate of 50l. for horses, &c.—Four-mile heats.

Mr Martin's br h Witchcraft, aged, 9st 6lb 1   1
Mr Webb's b g Vidette, 5 yrs old, 8st 7lb 2 2
Mr Jones's ch h Laburnam, 5 yrs old, 8st 7lb . . . . 3 dr

WORCESTER MEETING.

TUESDAY, August 2.——— Sweepstakes of 10gs each, for all ages.—— Two-mile heats.—Ten Subscribers.

Lord Stamford's ch h St. Domingo, by Hambletonian, five yrs old. . . . . walked over.

The City Members' Plate of 50l. for all ages, three-mile heats, was not run for, only two being entered; viz. Lord Stamford's St. Domingo and Lord Oxford's Tudor, who received 10gs each.

WEDNESDAY.———Match for 100gs.—Two Miles.

Mr Goulburn's b c Whitenose, by Hyacinthus, 4 yrs old, 8st 10lb.. 1
Mr Canning's b m Daphne, aged, 8st. 2

The Ladies' Plate of 50l. for all ages.—Two-mile heats.

Lord Oxford's b h Tudor, by John Bull, 5 yrs old, 8st 2lb 2 1 1
Lord Stamford's ch h St. Domingo, 5 yrs old, 9st 9lb. 1 2 2
Mr Goulburn's b c Whitenose, 4 yrs old, 8st . . . . 3 3 dr
Five to 1 on St. Domingo.

The County Members' Plate of 50l. added to a Subscription of 5gs each, for hunters, the property of Freeholders, and bred in the County.— Four-mile heats.

Mr Prattenton's ch c Acton, by Alfred, 4 yrs old, 10st 4lb. . . . . , 1   1
Mr Hope's br mare, by General, 6 yrs old, 11st 11lb (recd 10gs) . . 2 2
Mr Crane's b g Pumpkin, aged, 11st 13lb 3 3

THURSDAY.—Match for 100gs.—Two Miles.

Mr Prattenton's ch c Acton, by Alfred, 4 yrs old, 8st. 1
Mr Goulburn's b m Daphne, aged, 9st 2

Handicap Stakes of 10gs each, h. ft. with 30gs added.—Three-mile heats.

Lord Oxford's b f, by Hambletonian, out of Beatrice, 4 yrs old, 8st 12lb 1   1
Mr Goulburn's b c Whitenose, 4 yrs old, 8st 5lb 2 2
Mr Canning's b g Sweeper, aged, 8st. 3 3

The County and City Subscription Purse of 50l. for horses, &c.—Four-mile heats.

No race, only two being entered; viz. Lord Stamford's Domingo, and Lord Oxford's Tudor, who received 10gs each.

THE

TRE-MADOCK MEETING—CARNARVONSHIRE.

THURSDAY, August 4.——The Tan-yr-Allt Stakes of 5gs each, for all ages.—Two-mile heats.—Nineteen Subscribers.

Sir W. W. Wynne's b f Mademoiselle Prisle, by Sir Peter Teazle,
    4 yrs old, 7st 4lb................................1 1
Mr Boycott's b m, by Meteor, dam by Sir Peter, 5 yrs old, 8st 4lb 2 2
    Six and 7 to 4 on Mademoiselle Prisle.

The Gentleman's Purse of 50l. for three and four-yr olds.—Two-mile heats.
Mr Boycott's b f Pussy Cat, by Mr Teazle, 3 yrs old, a feather..1 1
Sir W. W. Wynne's b f Mademoiselle Prisle, 4 yrs old, 7st 10lb..2 dr
Mr W. A. Madock's b c Sylvester Daggerwood, 3 yrs old, a feather 3 dr
    Five and 6 to 4 on Mademoiselle Prisle.

The Snowden Welter Stakes of 5gs each, for horses, &c. 13st.—Two-mile heats.—Twelve Subscribers.—The winner was to have been sold for 150gs, if demanded, &c.
Mr Lloyd's br h Artichoke, by Don Quixote, 6 yrs old.........1. 1
Sir T. Mostyn's ch h Mousetrap, 6 yrs old 2 2
Mr Ackers's br h Sir Sampson, 5 yrs old......................3 3
    Sir Sampson the favourite.

FRIDAY, August 5.—The Traeth-Mawr Stakes of 10gs each, for all ages.—Four-mile heats.—Nine Subscribers.
Mr Jones Parry's b f Little Harlot, 3 yrs old, a feather..,.....2 1 1
Sir T. Mostyn's b c Master Teazle, 3 yrs old, a feather..........1 2 2
Sir W. W. Wynne's ch h, by Glaucus, 5 yrs old, 8st 5lb ......3 dis
    Even betting; after the second heat, 6 to 4 on Little Harlot.

The Cup, value 50l. given by W. A. Madock, Esq. for all ages.—Two-mile heats.
Mr Boycott's b f Pussy-Cat, by Mr Teazle, 3 yrs old, a feather..1 1
Sir W. W. Wynne's b f Mademoiselle Prisle, 4 yrs old, 7st 10lb..2 dr
Sir T. Mostyn's ch h Mousetrap, 6 yrs old....................3 dr
    Pussy Cat the favourite.

Fifty Pounds given by Sir T. Mostyn and Sir W. W. Wynne, Barts.—Two-mile heats.
Mr Ackers's br h Sir Sampson, by Stamford,...............4 2 1 1
Mr Lloyd's br h Artichoke, 6 yrs old 2 1 2 2
Mr Boycott's b m, by Meteor, 5 yrs old ....1 3 dr
Mr W. A. Madock's b c Sylvester Daggerwood, 3 yrs old ....3 dr
    Artichoke the favourite.

SATURDAY, August 6.—The Ladies' Purse of 50l. for all ages.—Two-mile heats.
Mr W. A. Madock's b c Sylvester Daggerwood, by Worthy,
    3 yrs old. 7st ....walked over.

The Vron-Iw Stakes of 5gs each, for horses, &c. 9st.—Once round the Course.—Eleven Subscribers.
Sir T. Mostyn's ch h Mousetrap, 6 yrs old 1
Mr Lloyd's br h Artichoke, 6 yrs old...........................2
    Two to 1 on Artichoke.

BLANDFORD MEETING—DORSETSHIRE.

TUESDAY, August 9.——The Dorsetshire Gold-Cup, a Subscription of 10gs each, for all ages.—Four Miles.—Thirteen Subscribers.

Lord C. H. Somerset's b c White-Rose, by Beningbrough, 4 yrs old,
   7st 10lb (T. Goodisson) 1
Mr Worrall's ch f, by Ambrosio, dam by Don Quixote, 3 yrs old,
   5st 11lb 2
Sir J. Hawkins's br c Rosario, 4 yrs old, 7st 10lb................ 3
Mr Trevanion's b c Gammon, 4 yrs old, 7st 10lb (fell lame)...... 4
         Six to 4 against White-Rose.

Fifty Pounds for horses, &c.—Four-mile heats.
Mr Scott's b m Ten-Bones, by Flying Gib, 6 yrs old, 9st 3lb ...: 1   1
Mr Radclyffe's ch h Lancaster, 5 yrs old, 9st.................. 2   2
Mr C. Day's ch c Barrows'-Brook, 3 yrs old.................. 3   dr

WEDNESDAY, August 10.——Handicap Stakes of 5gs each, for horses, &c. heats, two Miles and a quarter.—Ten Subscribers.
Mr Trevanion's b h Bucephalus, by Alexander, 6 yrs old, 9st 12lb 1   1
Sir H. Lippincott's b g Ploughboy, 5 yrs old, 9st.............. 2   2
Lord Ilchester named Gloucester, 3 yrs old, 6st 4lb........... 4   3
Mr Scott's b m Ten-Bones, 6 yrs old, 6st 3   dr
       Five and 6 to 4 on Bucephalus.

Fifty Pounds for three and four-year olds.—Two-mile heats.
Sir H. Lippincott's br c Chaise-and-One, by Whiskey, 4 yrs old,
   8st 3lb......................................:........... 1   1
Mr Worrall's ch f, by Ambrosio, 3 yrs old, 6st 9lb............3   2
Mr Trevanion's b c Crabs, 3 yrs old, 7st 1lb................2   3
      Chaise-and-One the favourite.

Fifty Pounds, for horses, &c.—Four-mile heats.
Mr Day's ch c Buckler, by Hyacinthus, 4 yrs old, 7st 12lb 1   1
Mr Scott's b m Ten-Bones, 6 yrs old, 9st 3lb................2   2
   Mr Trevanion's Bucephalus received 20l. to withdraw.

HUNTINGDON MEETING.

TUESDAY, August 9.—Sweepstakes of 10gs each, for all ages.—Two Miles.—Thirteen Subscribers.

General Grosvenor's gr c Woodcutter, by Lop, 4 yrs old, 8st 1lb (F.
   Buckle) 1
Mr Elwes's ch h Achilles, 5 yrs old, 8st 10lb................. 2
   The following also started, but were not placed:——
Mr J. Fletcher's b g Cockspinner, aged, 9st 2lb 0
Mr Cave Browne's b f Anna, 3 yrs old, 6st 9lb..... 0
Mr Goodisson's b c Foxberry, 4 yrs old, 8st 1lb 0
Mr Annesley's b h Buzzard, 5 yrs old, 8st 10lb................. 0
Mr Williams's ch f Gift, 3 yrs old, 6st 9lb 0
                                  Fifty

Fifty Pounds for three and four-year olds.—Two-mile heats.

Mr Golding's br f Mary Brown, by Guildford, 3 yrs old, 6st 11lb
  (Williams) 1 1
General Grosvenor's gr c Woodcutter, 4 yrs old, 8st 12lb 2 2
Mr Cave Browne's b f Anna, 3 yrs old, 6st 11lb .... 3 dr

Match for 50gs.—Four Miles.

Mr Fletcher's b g Cockspinner, by Moorcock, aged (rode by Mr
  Storey) 1
Mr Annesley's b h Buzzard, 5 yrs old (the Owner) 2

WEDNESDAY, August 10.—Fifty Pounds for four-year olds.—Two-mile heats.

Mr Golding's b m Merrymaid, by Buzzard, 5 yrs old, 8st 2lb,
  (Williams) 1 1
Mr Panton's b f Ralphina, 4 yrs old, 7st 2lb 2 2

THURSDAY, August 11.—Fifty Pounds, for all ages.—Two-mile heats.

Mr Williams's ch f Gift, by Boaster, 3 yrs old, 6st 6lb 1 1
Mr Goodisson's b c Foxberry, 4 yrs old, 8st 4 2
Mr Annesley's b h Buzzard, 5 yrs old, 8st 10lb 3 3
Mr Cave Browne's b g Bright Phœbus, aged, 9st .... 2 dis

---

LEWES MEETING.—SUSSEX.

TUESDAY, August 9.—Sweepstakes of 10gs each, for three-year old colts, 8st 3lb; fillies, 8st.—The last Mile and half.—Ten Subscribers.

Lord Egremont's b f Anderida, by Gohanna, out of Lazy (S. Barnard) 1
Lord G. H. Cavendish's b c, by Coriander 2
Lord Chichester's br c Ferdinand, by Waxy 3
    Two and 3 to 1 on Anderida.—Won easy.

The King's Plate of 100gs, for horses, &c.—Four-mile heats.

Lord Egremont's ch c Election, by Gohanna, 4 yrs old, 10st 4lb
  (S. Barnard) 1 1
Mr B. Daly's ch c Bob Booty, 4 yrs old, 10st 4lb 2 2
    Three and 4 to 1 on Election.—Won in a canter.

Lord Darlington's Rubens, by Buzzard, 8st 3lb, received forfeit from Mr Fermor's b c, by Gohanna, bought of Mr Bird, 8st 6lb.—The last Mile, 200gs.

WEDNESDAY, August 10.—The County Plate of 50l. for all ages. Heats, two Miles and a half.

Mr B. Daly's ch h Sasenagh, by Waxy, 6 yrs old, 8st 8lb 1 1
Lord Egremont's b f Anderida, 3 yrs old, 6st 2lb .... dis
Mr Hyde's ch f Augusta, 4 yrs old, 7st 6lb .... dis
Two to 1 on Anderida; who, with Augusta, ran on the wrong side of
    a post.

The

The Town Plate of 50l. for all ages.—Heats, two Miles and a half.—
The winner was to be sold for 250gs, if demanded, &c.

Mr B. Daly's ch h Sasenagh, by Waxy, 6 yrs old, 8st 7lb	1	1
Mr Wyndham's b c, by Ambrosio, 4 yrs old, 7st 11lb	3	2
Mr Rush's b h Humility, 5 yrs old, 8st 3lb	4	3
Mr T. Brown's b f Lydia Languish, 4 yrs old, 7st 8lb (bolted)	2	dis

Two to 1, and 5 to 2 on Sasenagh, who was claimed.

THURSDAY, August 11.—Match for 100gs.—One Mile.

Mr J. Croft's b c Hawk, by Buzzard, 4 yrs old, 8st 10lb	1
Mr Witherden's b f Miss Kitty, 3 yrs old, 7st 6lb	2

Two and 3 to 1 on Hawk.—Won easy.

The Ladies' Plate of 60gs, for all ages.—Four Miles.

Lord Egremont's ch c Election, by Gohanna, 4 yrs old, 7st 7lb (S. Barnard)	1
Mr B. Daly's ch c Bob Booty, 4 yrs old, 7st 7lb	2

Ten to 1 on Election.—In running, they both ran on the wrong side of a post, and completed the four miles before it was known to the jockies, who, not having dismounted, started again, when Election won by a neck.

Handicap Plate of 50l.—Heats, two Miles and a half.

Mr J. Croft's b c Hawk, by Buzzard, 4 yrs old, 8st 10lb	1	1
Mr Hyde's ch f Augusta, 4 yrs old, 8st	2	2
Mr Rush's b h Humility, 5 yrs old, 9st 3lb	3	3

Two and 3 to 1 on Hawk; after the heat, 10 to 1 he won.

NOTTINGHAM MEETING.

TUESDAY, August 9.—The King's Plate of 100gs, for horses, &c.—Four-mile heats.

Mr Andrew's b h Thorn, by Beningbrough, 5 yrs old, 11st 6lb (W. Clift)	1	1
Mr Johnson's br h Sir Andrew, 6 yrs old, 12st	2	2
Major Morris's b c Wildair, 4 yrs old, 10st 4lb	3	dr
Mr Cooke's ch c Chance, 4 yrs old, 10st 4lb	dis	

Six and 7 to 4 on Thorn.—Won easy.

The County Members' Purse of 50l. with the Entrance of 5gs each, (two entered) for three-year old colts, 8st 2lb; fillies, 8st.—One-mile heats.

Mr J. Richardson's b f Tutelina, by Stamford . . . . walked over.

WEDNESDAY, August 10.—The Gold Cup, value 100gs, and 30gs in specie, a Subscription of 10gs each, for all ages.—Two Miles.—Thirteen Subscribers.

Lord Grey's b c Gustavus, by Beningbrough, 4 yrs old, 7st 7lb	1
General Grosvenor's b f Briseis, 4 yrs old, 7st 5lb	2
Mr Sitwell's b f Gooseander, 3 yrs old, 5st 12lb	3

Mr

Mr Andrew's b m Lydia, 6 yrs old, 8st 12lb..................... 4
Mr Ilderton's b h Roseden, 5 yrs old, 8st 7lb..................... 5
Mr Bettinson's br f, by Sir Peter Teazle, dam by Alfred, 4 yrs old,
 7st 5lb.. 6
Six to 4 against Gooseander, 7 to 4 against Gustavus, 6 to 1 against Bri-
 seis.—Won cleverly.

Sweepstakes of 10gs each, for hunters.—Four Miles.—Eight Subscribers.
General Grosvenor's ch h Superstition, by Buzzard, 5 yrs old, 12st
 (F. Buckle)... 1
Mr Benson's br h, by Sir Peter Teazle, dam by Snap, 5 yrs old, 12st 2
Mr Harnew's b g Little Chance, by Spartacus, 11st 11lb 3
 Superstition the favourite.

 Fifty Pounds for three and four-year olds.—Two-mile heats.
Mr J. Richardson's b f Tutelina, by Stamford, 3 yrs old, 6st 13lb 1 1
Major Morris's b c Wildair, 4 yrs old, 8st 3lb 2 2
Mr Cooke's ch c Chance, 4 yrs old, 8st 3lb .... 3 dr
 Ten to 1 on Tutelina.—Won in a canter.

THURSDAY, August 11.—Sweepstakes of 5gs each, for hunters.—
Four Miles.—Twenty-six Subscribers.
Mr Keen's b g, by Moorcock, dam by Pot8o's, 6 yrs old, 12st...... 1
Mr Denham's gr g Hassop, by Sir Solomon, dam by Coriander, 4 yrs
 old, 10st 4lb.. 2
Mr Dyott's gr c Lichfield, by Gouty, 4 yrs old, 10st 4lb 3
Duke of St. Albans's b h Tristram Fickle, by Weathercock, aged,
 12st 2lb 4
Mr T. B. Johnson's b m Kitty Fisher, by Cavendish, aged, 12st 2lb.. 5
Mr Towle's b h, by Gayman, aged, 12st 2lb 6

 The Maiden Plate of 50l. for all ages.—Four-mile heats.
Mr Cooke's ch c Chance, by Beningbrough, 4 yrs old, 7st 12lb.. 2 1 1
Mr Bettinson's b f, by Sir Peter Teazle, dam by Alfred, 3 yrs old,
 6st 5lb.. 1 2 2
Mr Fisher's b f, by Sir Solomon, 3 yrs old, 6st 5lb .... 3 dr
Mr Bettinson's filly the favourite; after the first heat, 4 to 1 she won;
 after the second heat, 6 to 4 on Chance.—For the first heat, Mr Bettinson's filly ran with an intention to distance the other two, which
 she was not able to accomplish, and through that she lost the Plate.

OXFORD MEETING.

TUESDAY, August 9.—The Gold Cup, value 100gs, with 80gs in
 specie, a Subscription of 10gs each, for all ages.—Four Miles.—
Eighteen Subscribers.
Mr Ladbroke's ch c Master Jackey, by Johnny, 4 yrs old, 7st 7lb.... 1
Mr Sitwell's br h Taurus, 5 yrs old, 6st 7lb..................... 2
Mr F. Craven's ch c Bantum, 4 yrs old, 7st 7lb................. 3
Mr Dundas's b c Cambrian, 4 yrs old, 7st 7lb.................. 4
 Six to 4 against Master Jackey.

The

The Town Plate of 30l. for horses, &c.—Four-mile heats.
Mr Butler's b m Miss Coiner, by Don Quixote, aged, 9st 5lb 1 1
Mr F. Craven's ch c Bantum, 4 yrs old, 7st 7lb 2 2
Even betting, and 5 to 4 on Miss Coiner.

The Produce Stakes of 25gs each, for three-year olds.—Two Miles.—
Four Subscribers.
Mr Lucas's b f, by Guildford 1
Mr Beechey's b g, by Tom Tring 2

WEDNESDAY, August 10.—Fifty Pounds for three and four-year
olds.—Two-mile heats.
Mr Lucas's b f, by Guildford, 3 yrs old, 6st 11lb 1 1
Mr Beechey's b g, by Tom Tring, 3 yrs old, 7st 3 2
Mr Butler's ch f Bona-Lass, 3 yrs old, 6st 11lb 2 3

Sweepstakes of 10gs each, for hunters.—Gentlemen riders.—Four Miles.
—Eight Subscribers.
Mr Pryse's ch m, by Waxy........................ walked over.

THURSDAY, August 11.—Fifty Pounds given by his Grace the
Duke of Marlborough, for horses, &c.—Two-mile heats.
Mr Sadler's br h Rumbo, by Whiskey, aged, 9st 3 1 1
Mr Faulkener's b g Doubtful, aged, 9st 1 3 3
Mr Butler's b m Miss Coiner, aged, 9st 5lb 2 2 2
Ten to 1 on Miss Coiner ; after the first heat, 6 and 7 to 1 she won ;
after the second heat, 5 to 4 on Miss Coiner.—A very good race.

SWANSEA MEETING.—GLAMORGANSHIRE.

TUESDAY, August 9.—Fifty Guineas given by the Stewards, for
horses, &c.—Two-mile heats.
Mr Munsey's b g, by Pastor, dam by Highflyer, 4 yrs old, 8st 6lb 1 1
Mr Jenner's b m Elvira, 5 yrs old, 9st..................... 2 2
Mr Hurst's b c Master Ben, 4 yrs old, 8st 6lb............. dis
Mr R. Jenkins's ch f Fair Rachel .... dis

WEDNESDAY, August 10.—Fifty Pounds for all ages.—Two-mile
heats.
Mr Hurst's b c Red-Rose, by Beningbrough, 3 yrs old, 6st 4lb .. 2 1 1
Mr Munsey's b g, by Pastor, 4 yrs old, 8st 1lb 1 2 2
Mr Benson's gr h Atlas, 5 yrs old, 8st 11lb .... 3 3 dis
Mr Jones's ch c Governor Aris, 4 yrs old, 8st 3lb .... dis

Fifty Pounds for horses, &c.—Two-mile heats.
Mr Hurst's b c Humbug, by Hambletonian, out of Jack Tar's
dam, 4 yrs old, 7st 10lb....................... 1 1
Mr R. Jones's ch c Governor Aris, 4 yrs old, 8st 3lb 2 2

THURSDAY, August 11.—Fifty Pounds for horses, &c.—Four-
mile heats.
Mr Hurst's b c Red-Rose, by Beningbrough, 3 yrs old, a feather 1 1
Mr

Mr Lord's b c, by Stickler, 4 yrs old, 7st 9lb 2 2
Mr Jenner's b m Elvira, 5 yrs old, 8st 7lb.................... 3 3

A Free Handicap Stakes of 10gs each, with 25gs added from the Racing
Fund.—Two Miles.—Four Subscribers.
Mr Hurst's b c Humbug, by Hambletonian, 4 yrs old, 7st 8lb 1
Mr Lord's b c, by Stickler, 4 yrs old, 8st...................... 2

NEWCASTLE MEETING—STAFFORDSHIRE.

WEDNESDAY, August 10.—Sweepstakes of 10gs each, for all ages.
—Four Miles.—Five Subscribers.
Lord Gower's ch g Newton, by Mr Richardson's Marsk, 5 yrs old,
8st 6lb 1
Mr Macdonald's b m Snowdrift, by Grouse, 5 yrs old, 8st 6lb 2
Mr Smith's gr f, by Dapple, out of Fairy, 3 yrs old, 6st 8lb 3
Mr Tollett's ch m, by Hickwall, out of Paroquet, 5 yrs old, 8st 6lb .. 4
Five to 4 against Newton.

The Maiden Plate of 50l. for all ages.—Four-mile heats.
Mr Birch's b c Telemachus, by Orange-Flower, 3 yrs old, 6st 4lb 4 1 1
Mr Eyre's b f, by King Bladud, 3 yrs old, 6st 2lb 1 2 2
Mr Tollett's b f Linnet, by Hickwall, out of Paroquet, 4 yrs old,
7st 2lb 3 4 3
Mr Harris's b f, 3 yrs old, 6st 2lb.......................... 2 3 dr
Mr Carr's b c Ned Bentley, 4 yrs old, 7st 2lb............... 5 dr
Three to 1 against Telemachus.

THURSDAY, August 11.—The Members' Purse of 50l. for horses,
&c.—Four-mile heats.
Mr C. Smith's br f Miss Blanchard, by Hambletonian, 4 yrs old,
7st 8lb 1 1
Mr Richardson's b c Honest Bob, 4 yrs old, 7st 7lb............. 3 2
Mr Booker's b h Plunder, 5 yrs old, 8st 6lb 2 3
Two to 1 on Miss Blanchard.

FRIDAY, August 12.—The Publicans' Plate, of 50l. for all ages.—
Four-mile heats.
Sir T. Stanley's bl c, by Sir Harry, dam by Pot8o's, 4 years old,
8st 3lb.. 1 1
Mr J. Richardson's b c Honest Bob, 4 yrs old, 8st.............. 2 2
Mr J. Turner's b f Maid of Dunham, 2 yrs old, 8st 6lb........ 3 3

READING MEETING—BERKS.

TUESDAY, August 16.—The Gold Cup, value 80gs, with 10gs in
specie, (the Owner of the second entitled to his Stake) for all ages.—
Four Miles.—Twelve Subscribers.
Mr M. Dilly's b h Gnat-ho! by Sir Peter Teazle, 5 yrs old, 8st 6lb .. 1

Mr Goddard's b h Mountaineer; 6 yrs old, 8st 12lb................. 3
Lord Barrymore's b h Pavilion, aged, 9st...................... 3
   Five to 4 on Mountaineer, and 5 to 2 against Gnat-ho!

Fifty Pounds for three and four-year olds.—Two-mile heats.
Lord Barrymore's b f Miranda, by Sorcerer, 3 yrs old, 7st 2lb.... 1 1
Captain Haffenden's br c Corsican, 4 yrs old, 8st 7lb (broke down) 2 dr
      Two to 1 and 5 to 2 on Corsican.

WEDNESDAY, August 17.—Sweepstakes of 5gs each, with 25gs
added by the Stewards, for three-year old colts, 8st 4lb, fillies, 8st.—
Two Miles.—Ten Subscribers.
Lord Barrymore's br f Miranda, by Sorcerer .... walked over.

     Fifty Pounds for all ages.—Four-mile heats.
Mr Dilly's br h Gnat-ho! by Sir Peter Teazle, 5 yrs old, 8st 6lb.. 1 1
Captain Haffenden's b h Sir Launcelot, 6 yrs old, 8st 12lb 2 2
  Six to 5 on Sir Launcelot; after the heat, 6 and 7 to 4 on Gnat-ho!

THURSDAY, August 18 —Handicap Plate of 50l.—Two-mile heats.
Lord Barrymore's br h Pavilion, by Waxy, aged, 8st 5lb 1 1
Mr Teighe's ch g Strideaway, 7st 3 2
Mr Dilly's b g Felton, aged, 7st 10lb...................... 2 3
     Five to 2 and 3 to 1 on Pavilion.

EXETER MEETING—DEVONSHIRE.

TUESDAY, August 16.—Sweepstakes of 5gs each, free for all horses,
  &c.—Four Miles.—Eighteen Subscribers.
Lord C. H. Somerset's b c White-Rose, by Beningbrough, 4 yrs old,
  10st 4lb (T. Goodison) 1
Mr Martin's b h Witchcraft, aged, 12st 2lb (Mr Douglas) 2
Mr C. Day's ch c Buckler, 4 yrs old, 10st 4lb (C. Day) 3
    White-Rose the favourite.—Won by half a length.

    Match for 200gs.—Once round the Course.
Sir J. Hawkins's br h Clermont, by Trumpator, 8st 13lb (P. Ryan).. 1
Mr Fellowes's ch h Salamander, by Dragon, 8st 6lb (T. Goodisson) .. 2
    Five to 4 on Salamander.—Won easy.

The Maiden Plate of 50l. given by the Members of the County, for
     horses, &c.—One-mile heats.
Mr Worrall's ch f, by Ambrosio, dam by Don Quixote, 3 yrs
  old, a feather 1 4 0 1
Mr J. Day's gr f Miss Kitty, by Lop, 3 yrs old, a feather 4 1 0 2
Mr Major's b g Highflyer, aged, 9st 2 2 4
Captain Ilbert's b h Phœnix, aged, 9st.,.................. 3 3 3

Sweepstakes of 5gs each, for horses, &c. not thorough bred.—Two-mile
     heats.—Thirteen Subscribers.
Captain M'Allister's br g Sir Robert, aged, 8st 11lb 4 1 1
Captain Johnson's br g Vidette, 5 yrs old, 8st 5lb............... 1 2 2
                  Captain

Captain Harding's ch g Sir Hugh, aged, 8st 11lb 3 4 3
Mr Cock's Laburnum, 5 yrs old, 8st 8lb................... 2 3 dr

WEDNESDAY, August 17.—The Gold Cup, value 100gs, given by
Lord Viscount Courtenay; for all ages.—Four Miles.
Mr Martin's br h Witchcraft, by Sir Peter Teazle, aged, 9st 4lb (Mr
    Douglas) 1
Mr Fellowes's Salamander, 5 yrs old, 8st 10lb (T. Goodisson)...... 2
Mr Worrall's ch f, by Ambrosio, 3 yrs old, 6st 7lb............... 3
Lord C. H. Somerset's b f Osiris, 4 yrs old, 8st (broke down)...... 4
Mr Trevanion's b c, by Crabbs, 3 yrs old, 6st 7lb 5
Captain M'Allister's br g Sir Robert, aged, 9st 4lb.............. 6
    Osiris the favourite, and 6 to 4 against Witchcraft.

    Fifty Pounds for all ages.—Two-mile heats.
Lord C. H. Somerset's b c White-Rose, by Beningbrough, 4 yrs
    old, 10st 4lb (T. Goodisson) 1 1
Mr Fellowes's br c Mandarine, 4 yrs old, 10st 4lb (Mr Douglas) 2 2
    Even betting.—Won by half a length.

Fifty Pounds for horses, &c. regularly used in the Yeomanry Cavalry or
   Volunteer Infantry, before the 25th of April, 1808.—One-mile heats.
   —Five horses, &c. not being entered, there was no race.
Handicap Stakes of 5gs each, for the beaten horses, &c.—One-mile
    heats.—Ten Subscribers.
Mr Fellowes's ch h Salamander, by Dragon, 5 yrs old, 9st 8lb (Mr
    Douglas) 1 1
Mr Fellowes's br c Mandarine, 4 yrs old, 8st 9lb (T. Goodisson) 4 2
Mr Day's ch c Buckler, 4 yrs old, 7st 11lb.................... 3 3
Mr Trevanion's b c Crabbs, 3 yrs old, 6st 10lb................ 2 dr

---

DERBY MEETING.

TUESDAY, August 16.—Fifty Pounds given by his Grace the Duke
    of Devonshire, for maiden horses, &c. of all ages.—Two-mile heats.
Mr Stevens's ch g, by No-Pretender, 4 yrs old, 8st 2lb........ 5 1 1
Mr Dyott's gr c Litchfield, 4 yrs old, 8st 5lb................. 1 3 3
Mr Carr's b g Bryan, 4 yrs old, 8st 2lb 4 2 2
Mr J. Hayes's gr f Maid of the Mill, 3 yrs old, 6st 13lb........ 3 5 4
Mr Boultbee's b c, by Waxy, 3 yrs old, 7st 2lb............... 6 6 5
Mr T. Richardson's ch f Cleopatra, 3 yrs old, 6st 13lb........ 2 4 dr

Sweepstakes of 10gs each, for all ages.—Two Miles.—Eight Subscribers.
Lord Grey's b c Gustavus, by Beningbrough, 4 yrs old, 8st 2lb...... 1
Mr Sitwell's b f Gooseander, 3 yrs old, 6st 11lb 2

WEDNESDAY, August 17.—Fifty Pounds for all ages.—Four-mile
heats.
Mr Andrews's b h Thorn, by Beningbrough, 5 yrs old, 8st 13lb 1 1
Mr Johnson's br h Sir Andrew, 6 yrs old, 8st 9lb.............. 2 2
Mr J. Birch's b c Telemachus, 2 yrs old, 6st 3lb.............. 3 3
    Six and 7 to 4 on Thorn; after the heat, 2 and 3 to 1 he won.

TAVISTOCK MEETING—DEVONSHIRE.

TUESDAY, August 23.—Fifty Pounds for all ages.—Three-mile heats.

Mr J. Day's gr f Miss Kitty, by Lop, 3 yrs old, 6st 4lb	1	1
Mr Douglas's br c Mandarine, 4 yrs old, 7st 10lb	2	2
Captain Weir's ch g Woodcote, aged, 8st 11lb................	3	dr
Mr Fellowes's ch h Salamander, 5 yrs old, 8st 10lb	4	dr

WEDNESDAY, August 24.—Sweepstakes of 5gs each, for horses, &c. that had been regularly hunted, carrying 12st.—Those bred in Cornwall or Devon allowed 7lb, and for having been hunted in the said counties, 4lb more.—Four-mile heats.—Ten Subscribers.

Captain Weir's ch g Woodcote, by Guildford, aged............	1	1
Mr Johnson's br g Vidette, 5 yrs old.........................	2	2
Captain Ilbert's b g Phœnix, aged...........................	3	3

EGHAM MEETING.

TUESDAY, August 23.—The Gold Cup, value 100gs, the surplus was paid to the winner in specie, for all ages.—Four Miles.—Fourteen Subscribers.

Lord Egremont's b h Canopus, by Gohanna, 5 yrs old, 8st 6lb......	1
Duke of York's b c Fuscus, 3 yrs old, 6st 3lb...................	2
Mr Ladbroke's Master Jackey, 4 yrs old, 7st 10lb...............	3
Mr Fermor's br c Stripling, 4 yrs old, 7st 10lb	4
Sir J. Honeywood's Hawk, 4 yrs old, 7st 10lb	5

Six and 7 to 4 on Canopus, 7 to 2 against Stripling, and 7 to 2 against Master Jackey.—A fine race.

The Surrey Stakes of 50gs each, h. ft. for two-year old colts, 8st 4lb; fillies, 8st.—The last half of the New Mile.—Four Subscribers.

Mr Ladbroke's br c Trinculo, by Teddy, out of Ramschoondra, by Sir Peter	1
Sir J. Mawbey's br c Botleys, by Teddy......................	2
Mr Page's b f Grinderella, by Teddy	3

Trinculo the favourite.—Won easy.

Fifty Pounds for all ages.—Two-mile and half heats.

Lord Barrymore's br h Pavilion, by Waxy, aged, 9st 4lb........	1	1
Mr Heath's br h Rumbo, aged, 9st 4lb.......................	2	2
Mr Jeffrey's gr f Miss Slender, 3 yrs old, 6st 5lb.............	3	3

Two to 1 on Pavilion.—Won in a canter.

WEDNESDAY, August 25.—The Magna Charta Stakes of 50gs each, h. ft. for three-year old colts, 8st 5lb; fillies, 8st 2lb.—The New Mile.—Five Subscribers.

Lord Egremont's b c Scorpion, brother to Trafalgar, by Gohanna....	1
Mr Ladbroke's b c Tristram, by Teddy	2

Three and 4 to 1 on Scorpion.

Match for 50gs.—Two Miles.

Mr Trevanion's b c Lewes, by Gohanna, 8st 2lb................	1

Mr

Mr F. Craven's ch c Bantum, 8st 2lb 2

Five to 4 on Lewes.

The Ladies' Plate of 50l. for three and four-year olds.—Two-mile heats·
Lord Stawell's b f Brighton-Lass, by Gohanna, out of Goth's Sis-
    ter, 3 yrs old, 7st 4lb................................... 1 1
Mr Ladbroke's b c, brother to Hedley, by Gohanna, 3 years old,
    7st 3lb 2 2
Mr Fermor's Strapling, 4 yrs old, 8st 7lb.,................... 3 3
Lord Egremont's b f Anderida, by Gohanna, out of Lazy, 3 yrs
    old, 7st 6lb.. dis

Anderida the favourite, who ran out of the course.

THURSDAY, August 25.—Sweepstakes of 30gs each, 20gs ft. for
two-year old colts, 8st 5lb; fillies, 8st 2lb.—The last half of the New
Mile.—Nine Subscribers.
Lord Egremont's ch f Castanea, by Gohanna, out of Nitre's dam.... 1
Sir C. Bunbury's b f Hannah, Sister to Agnes, by Sorcerer, out of
    Amelia... 2
Mr Trevanion's b f Jocasta, by Gohanna 3
Mr C. Day's f Snow-drop, by Highland-Fling 4
Mr Ladbroke's b c Trinculo (4lb extra) 5
Mr Villiers's ch c Silvermere (4lb extra) 6

Castanea the favourite.

Handicap Plate of 50l. for all ages.—Heats, two Miles and a quarter
each.

Mr Heath's br h Whiskey, by Rumbo, aged, 8st 4lb 1 1
Lord Barrymore's br h Pavilion, aged, 9st....,.............. 2 2
Mr Trevanion's b c Lewes, 4 yrs old, 7st 12lb 3 3
Lord Stawell's Brighton-Lass, 3 yrs old, 6st 13lb .... dis
Mr Cumming's br h Jump-off, aged, 7st 12lb................ dis -
Five to 4 on Brighton-Lass, 2 to 1 against Pavilion, and 5 to 1 against
 Rumbo; after the heat, 2 to 1 on Rumbo.—Won easy.—All the
 horses took the wrong side of a post at the turn into the strait mile,
 when Brighton-Lass and Jump-off ran in; but the others returned,
 and went round the post; the two former were declared distanced.—
 The bets have been paid, subject to a future investigation; but Lord
 Stawell and Mr. Cumming assert, that the post being down, the
 first heat, under all circumstances, ought to have been run over
 again,

HEREFORD MEETING.

WEDNESDAY, August 24.—— Fifty Pounds for all ages.—Four-
 mile heats.
Mr Goulburn's gr h Grimaldi, by Delpini, 6 yrs old, 8st 9lb 1 1
Lord Oxford's b h Tudor, 5 yrs old, 8st 10lb...,........... 2 dr

THURSDAY, August 25.—Sweepstakes of 10gs each, for all ages.—
Four Miles.—Eight Subscribers.
Mr Goulburn's gr h Grimaldi, 6 yrs old, 9st 1

Lord

The Macaroni Stakes of 10gs each, for horses, &c. that have been regularly hunted.—Gentlemen riders.—Three Miles.—Eight Subscribers.

Mr Tatton Sykes's b h, by Idris, dam by Highflyer, 6 yrs old, 12st (Mr T. Sykes)... 1

Mr Sotheron's ch c Darrington-Cade, by Hyacinthus, 4 yrs old, 10st 11lb (Mr Lindow)... 2

Mr Gascoigne's b m Dowager, by Hambletonian, out of Golden-Locks, 5 yrs old, 11st 5lb (Mr Treacher).................... 3

Dowager the favourite.—A remarkably fine race, and admirably rode by the Gentlemen.

THURSDAY, Sept. 15.—Sweepstakes of 20gs each, with 20gs added, for three-yr old fillies, 8st.—A winner of a Plate, Sweepstakes, or Subscription, this year, carrying 3lb, and of two, 4lb extra.—The last Mile and three quarters.—Eight Subscribers.

Mr T. Duncombe's chesnut, Laurel-Leaf, by Stamford, out of Pet's dam, 8st 3lb (B. Smith)............................... 1

Mr Sitwell's bay, Gooseander, by Hambletonian, out of Rally, 6st 4lb (W. Clift)..................................... 2

Lord Hawke's ches. Mother Goose, by Stamford, out of Duchess, 8st 3

Mr E. L. Hodgson's chesnut, by Shuttle, out of Miss Muston, 8st .. 4

Even betting on Laurel-Leaf.—A good race, and won with difficulty. Mother Goose made play.

Sweepstakes of 20gs each, for two-year old colts, 8st 3lb, fillies, 8st.—The last Mile.—Eight Subscribers.

Lord Fitzwilliam's b c Cervantes, by Don Quixote, out of Evelina, by Highflyer (W. Clift).................................... 1

Mr Dinsdale's b f Fair Candidate, by Delpini, dam by Weasel (W. Peirse)... 2

Mr Thompson's b f, by Shuttle, dam by Pegasus.............. 3

Four to 1 on Cervantes.—Won very easy.

One Hundred Pounds for all ages.—Three-mile heats.

Duke of Leeds's ch c Mowbray, by Pandolpho, out of Mother Redcap, 3 yrs old, 6st 9lb (J. Jones)................... 1 1

Mr Sotheron's ch c Darrington-Cade, by Hyacinthus, 4 yrs old, 7st 6lb (R. Johnson)....................................... 3 2

Duke of Hamilton's b h Grazier, by Sir Peter Teazle, 5 yrs old, 8st 7lb (B. Smith)....................................... 2 3

Six to 4 against Mowbray ; after the heat, 10 to 1 on Mowbray. The first heat was won easy, and the second with some difficulty.

Sweepstakes of 5gs each, for hunters, not thorough-bred ; four-year olds, 11st 4lb, five-yr. olds, 11st 10lb, six-year olds, 12st 4lb, and aged, 12st 7lb ; mares and geldings allowed 3lb. A winner of a Stake, Match, or Plate, to carry 5lb, and of two, 7lb extra. Gentlemen riders.—Heats, two Miles and a half each.—Eleven Subscribers.

Mr Milner's b g, by Screveton, aged, 12st 4lb (Mr T. Sykes).... 1 1

Mr G. Neville's b g, by Young Espersykes, 5 yrs old, 11st 7lb (Mr Harrison)....................................... 2 2

Six to 4 on Mr Milner's gelding.—Won easy.

Lightning Source UK Ltd.
Milton Keynes UK
UKHW041034111219
355146UK00008B/182/P